Conflicts and Crises

Conflicts and Crises

The Life and Times of James K. McGuire

DR. DANIEL F. SCHULTZ

LitPrime Solutions
21250 Hawthorne Blvd
Suite 500, Torrance, CA 90503
www.litprime.com
Phone: 1-800-981-9893

© 2021 Dr. Daniel F. Schultz. All rights reserved.

No part of this book may be reproduced, stored in a retrieval system, or transmitted by any means without the written permission of the author.

Published by LitPrime Solutions   11/22/2021

ISBN: 978-1-954886-09-4(sc)
ISBN: 978-1-954886-47-6(hc)
ISBN: 978-1-954886-10-0(e)

Any people depicted in stock imagery provided by iStock are models, and such images are being used for illustrative purposes only.

Certain stock imagery © iStock.

Because of the dynamic nature of the Internet, any web addresses or links contained in this book may have changed since publication and may no longer be valid. The views expressed in this work are solely those of the author and do not necessarily reflect the views of the publisher, and the publisher hereby disclaims any responsibility for them.

CONTENTS

Prologue ix
Preface xiii

CHAPTER I – A
    Syracuse, 1890: The Context of the Man and His City . . . 1

CHAPTER I – B
    The Boy Mayor's "Wide Open Town":
    Sports, Slots, Sluts, Tramps, Thieves, Trusts, Trash 13

CHAPTER I – C
    The Boy Mayor, 1895-1901: Patronage, Graft,
    Deficiency, Defeat. 49

CHAPTER I – D
    The Dream Denied: Failure to Win State-Wide Office . . 77

CHAPTER II – A
    "The Asphalt Jungle": Post-Mayoralty Meddling and
    a Marriage of Convenience 121

CHAPTER II – B
The "Asphalt Jungle": Barber Asphalt, Bribery and
The Brothers McGuire 147

CHAPTER II – C
"Asphalt Jungle": "Boss" Murphy, the Brothers
McGuire – Mistakes and Miscalculations, 1912- 13" . . . 163

CHAPTER II – D
Asphalt Jungle: Subpoenas, Sullivan and Santo
Domingo. 191

CHAPTER II – E
"Asphalt Jungle": The Investigations Conclude-
Bosses, Bagmen, Bribery, Buncombe 213

CHAPTER III – A
Shamrocks, Subversion, Sabotage and Sedition:
Anglophobia and The Celtic Renaissance in America . . 241

CHAPTER III – B
Shamrocks, Subversion, Sabotage, Sedition:
McGuire's Irish Nationalist Pedigree 263

CHAPTER III – C
Shamrocks, Subversion, Sabotage, Sedition: The
Hyphenates Alliance, 1907-1917. 291

CHAPTER III – D
The Teutonic Embrace- Espionage, Sedition,
Subversion and Sabotage on Three Continents,
1890-1918 321

CHAPTER III – E
   Shamrocks, Subversion, Sedition, and Sabotage–The Piratical Cruise of the Good Ship Gladstone, or; Raiders of the Lost Shark 419

CHAPTER III – F
   They Voted Their Illusions: The Contested Election of 1916 441

CHAPTER III – G
   Accommodation to Intervention: Protests, Surveillance, Pragmatic Patriotism 461

CHAPTER IV – A
   Post-War Irish Nationalist Politics 1918-1923 511

CHAPTER IV – B
   Epilogue, 1923: "Such a Marvelous and Phenomenal Boy" 559

Works Cited 575
Index 599

PROLOGUE

Who is James K. McGuire? His name is little-known even to specialists in Irish-American studies, yet he was intimately involved in the cause of Irish freedom for over thirty years. It is ironic that his life ended shortly before Ireland won its independence.

As the title suggest, James K. McGuire had multiple careers, each overlapping the other. In each, McGuire came into contact – and conflict – with major players in each arena. He was indicted three times-as mayor, twice as asphalt lobbyist and investigated by the federal government concerning his Irish Nationalist activities. His humble origins and ultimate business success hearken to the Horatio Alger stories of his generation. He authored five books, numerous articles and editorials, wrote and delivered countless speeches – an impressive record of achievement, especially given his limited formal education. As Mayor of Syracuse, New York, his most cherished contribution to his adopted city was the financial gift he obtained from Andrew Carnegie to establish a public library. He often found himself at odds with such colorful Republican politicians, such as James Belden, Frank Hiscock, James Hancock, Francis Hendricks and even with members of his own party, such as Alderman Frank Matty, Eugene Hughes, Sim Dunfee and others.

At the state level he was on familiar terms with Tammany politicians David B. Hill, "Big Bill" Devery, Richard Croker, "Fingy" Conners and Charles Murphy. His ties to the Asphalt Trust brought him into contact with Governor William Sulzer, investigator John A. Hennessy, crusading District Attorney and later Governor Charles S. Whitman and diplomat James M. Sullivan. An Irish nationalist, McGuire worked with and was active in numerous organizations such as the Clan na Gael, The Friends of Irish Freedom, The American Association For The Recognition of The Irish Republic and others. As a ranking member of them, McGuire met and worked with John Devoy, Daniel Cohalan, James Addis Emmett, Harry Boland, Eamon deValera and James Larkin. Their intrigues led him to work for the propaganda arm of the Imperial German government, the German Information Service. In that capacity, McGuire mingled with diplomats and spies, such as Franz Rintelen, Count Johann von

Bernstorff, Dr. Heinrich Albert and George Sanders. He authored two books sympathetic to the German cause. He engaged in activities that compromised the neutrality of the United States during the Wilson administration, earning the president's enmity in the process.

After World War I, progress for Ireland was stalled as a result of a split into rival factions each aiming for the loyalty and support of the Irish in America. James K. McGuire was torn between the two groups, ultimately siding with the De Valera and John McGarrity much to the chagrin of John Devoy and Daniel Cohalan. Despite his efforts he did not live to see Ireland achieve independence as a Republic. This multi-dimensional figure is dimly understood and nearly forgotten. In all his endeavors he was largely successful – businessman, three-term mayor of Syracuse, lobbyist for the Asphalt Trust. His efforts on behalf of the cause of Irish freedom won him notoriety during his lifetime and limited acclaim at his death. There were times when McGuire turned a blind eye to ethical considerations in all these endeavors, yet he was a man of his times. His was a world of transition. McGuire used his personal ambition with his cultural capital and combined them with the opportunities and connections of the moment to advance his career.

This study is the outgrowth of years of research and a number of papers and publications on Irish and Irish-American history.

The importance of this study is that for the first time it brings to public attention the roles of the important yet lesser players in both New York State politics and the cause of Irish nationalism. It provides an in-depth case study of a man involved in many facets of American life during the Progressive period in America – Tammany politics, reform movements, trusts, political corruption and international intrigue.

PREFACE

I was introduced to James K. McGuire several years ago while teaching an honors seminar on "imperialism". Ireland was a case study and it obviously included information on Irish-American support for its independence.

McGuire left few letters and thus is known largely through the writings of others. Until recently, his story was elusive, mentioned often in passing by scholars, and then usually in the context of his Irish Nationalism and/or pro-German collaboration.[1] This suggests he worked mostly behind the scenes, often using his position (mayor, lobbyist, nationalist) for his advantage. A recent biography of McGuire[2] has much to recommend it, especially the details of his early life in Syracuse and later as an object of interest by federal agents. But there are several gaps in this story and there is need for a more complete picture of the man and his multiple careers. There are times when the author treads lightly when there is controversy, and there are places where incidents are overlooked which would provide a richer portrait of the man and his times, particularly the scandals associated with his multiple terms as mayor, his controversial role as lobbyist for the Asphalt Trust and his links to the corrupt Democratic political machine, Tammany Hall. Some significant omissions are those dealing with his fight for Irish independence. Unmentioned is his direct employment as a propagandist for the German Information Service, his connections to subversion and sabotage via ties to fellow Nationalists James Larkin, James Mark Sullivan and others, his participation in the Gladstone Incident and his role in the controversial Brogan affair for which he was condemned by fellow Clan member, John Devoy. His participation in the East Side gun-running episode during the War of Independence is dismissed in a single sentence.

McGuire was a complex personality and not easy to characterize. He deserves an in-depth treatment which more accurately portrays the man and his times.

The evidence of his story is scattered in government archives, newspaper articles and occasional letters requiring a diligent effort to unearth them. The purpose of this volume is to tell the story of an Irish-immigrant who used a variety of means to achieve the "American Dream" until money and power corrupted him. It is also designed to paint a more accurate composite of a man whose presence is largely forgotten, yet in his time was an important figure.

I would like to acknowledge the assistance and support of Sharon Farrar and other members of the Library and Technical Support staff at Cayuga Community College who accessed numerous materials for me and who showed extreme patience at my insatiable demands. I am grateful to the staff of Onondaga County Library and the Local History section of the Onondaga County Historical Society who kindly supplied me with documents necessary for completion of the manuscript.

I am grateful to my wife and children who tolerated an absentee parent throughout the writing process. I could not have done it without their encouragement and support.

1 Cronin, Sean. The McGarrity Papers Reflections of the Irish revolutionary Movement in Ireland and America, 1900-1940. New York: Anvil Books, 1999.

Devoy, John. Recollections of an Irish Rebel. Dublin: Irish University press, 1969;

Dorries, Reinhard. Imperial Challenge: Ambassador Bernstorff and German-American Relations, 1908-1917. Chapel Hill: University of North Carolina Press, 1989;

Fitzpatrick, David. Harry Boland's Irish Revolution. Ireland: Cork University Press 2013;

Golway, Terry. Irish Rebel: John Devoy and America's Fight For Irish Freedom. New York: St. Martin's Press, 1999;

Larkin, Emmet. James Larkin (1876-1947). Irish Labor Leader. London: Routledge and Kegan Paul, 1965;

Landau, Henry. <u>The Enemy Within: The Inside Story of German Sabotage in America</u>. New York: Putnam, 1937;

Leslie, Shane. <u>The Irish Issue In Its American Aspect</u>. New York: Scribners and Sons, 1917;

Peterson, H.C. <u>Propaganda For War: The Campaign Against American Neutrality, 1914-1917</u>. Norman: University of Oklahoma Press.

<u>2</u> Fahey, Joseph E. <u>James K. McGuire: Boy Mayor and Irish Nationalist</u>. Syracuse: Syracuse University Press, 2014.

Chapter 1 - A
Syracuse, 1890:
The Context of the Man and His City

By the time James K. McGuire became mayor, Syracuse had become industrial, multiethnic city. It had grown from a village of 3200 in 1832 to a city of about 130,000 by the turn of the century.[1] It had electric street cars, the competing companies of which merged in 1896.[2] Industrial growth was encouraged by the completion of the Erie Canal and the local salt mines and the drainage of the local swamp nearly seven decades earlier. His city's name changed seven times until 1820, when John Wilkinson changed the name of growing community from Gossits Corners to Syracuse, having read an article describing a community in Sicily where salt and fresh water mingled. Syracuse was a well-established railroad hub through which such notables as W. L. Marcy, Winfield Scott, Henry Clay, John C. Fremont, Ulysses Grant, Charles Dickens and Jenny Lind had passed.[3] Just as cotton was king in the ante-bellum south, salt dominated Syracuse industry until the time McGuire was making his bid for public office.

When its salt monopoly was destroyed in the post Civil War era, an ancillary industry, the making of soda ash by combining salt and limestone, took its place. It is used in manufacturing glass, chemicals, textiles, paper, metallic alloys, soaps, adhesives, and ceramic wares. The business was incorporated as Solvay Process in 1881, and employed 1500 workers.[4]

The Charles Lipe Company invented machinery for removing hulls from rice and coffee beans, and manufactured automobile transmissions, later becoming a division of General Motors Corporation. The Smith-Corona Typewriter had its origins in Syracuse at this time. Syracuse China was a well-established industry in ante-bellum Syracuse. The Pass-Seymour Company by 1890 manufactured knobs, tubes, spark plugs and electric switches. By the turn of the century, the Crouse-Hinds Company was manufacturing switches, head-lamps and searchlights.[5] Sutherland notes the existence of the Moyer Wagon Works employing 350 workers, building buggies and wagons, exporting them throughout the United States.[6] Another lighting business – candles – was established as early as 1855. Two companies consolidated in 1896 to form the Will and

Baumer Company.⁷ Syracuse was home to a dozen breweries, the names of many no longer in production – Haberle's, Greenway, Bartels, Thomas Ryan, Moore and Quinn, Zetts and Carneys. The breweries brought prosperity to farmers harvesting crops of barley and hops.⁸ The prominence of agriculture spurred the manufacturing of machinery and tools for farmers, furniture and hardware. For example, the C.C. Bradley Company employed over 300 workers manufacturing harvesters, mowers, reapers, carts and carriages. The Syracuse Chilled Plow Company began in 1876 had 225 employees and was bought out by John Deere in 1911.⁹ In addition, there was a steel manufacturing plant operated by Henry Sweet employing over 500 men. Whitman and Barnes employed 275 men, making knives and machine parts. Fifty mechanics of the Syracuse Twist Drill Company turned out drill bits for wood-workers. Other industries employing between 100 – 500 men were the Phoenix Foundry Company, The Steam Gauge and Lantern Company, the Butler Manufacturing Company, makers of fine furniture, E. C. Stearns and Company, manufacturers of tools and hardware, The Syracuse Malleable Iron Works, and Frazer and Jones, dealers in hardware and iron castings. In addition, there was the O.H. Short Company, manufacturers of brick-boards, the Marsellus Casket Company making undertakers' supplies and numerous smaller companies.¹⁰ Syracuse even had an automobile manufacturing plant. The brainchild of engineer John Wilkinson and financier Herbert Franklin was an air-cooled engine automobile. The Franklin Motor Car Company was for three decades the largest employer in the area.¹¹

Syracuse was a microcosm of industrializing America in other ways as well. There was labor strife and exploitation which facilitated the growth of labor unions, an issue that would reveal itself during the time James K. McGuire was mayor. In 1890, stonecutters struck to increase daily wages from $3.10 to $3.50, delaying construction of the new city hall which was completed the following year. That same year state labor inspector Margaret Gibson reported that Syracuse contained numerous sweatshops, employing women and children, many of whom were eastern European Jews and African-Americans working under "dingy" conditions. One of the worst offenders was J.P. Hier, a cigar manufacturer. By 1899 there were nearly 10,000 men and women in 76 unions.[12]

None of these industries could have prospered without the various immigrant stocks – the Irish and Germans during the early 1880's who joined the Dutch and English who arrived earlier. They were the predominant groups providing labor to the growing industries until the arrival of the Italians, Poles, and Ukrainians in the 1880's. Many groups had their own ethnic press. The arrival of Jews was first noted in 1839. Blacks had been recorded as slaves in the area as early as 1800, and the first AME Zion Church was formed in 1841. By mid-century, Syracuse was a center of abolitionism. Nonetheless, the black population increased significantly only after 1890 when Southern blacks were imported for use as domestics and because many returned from Canada where they had sought refuge as a result of the Fugitive Slave Law of 1850.[13] Of the city's 134,835 people in 1900, 22 percent were foreign-born with Germans the most numerous (8900), Irish (6625), Italians (5465), English (2700), Canadians (2700), Poles (1500), Russians (1000), and a sprinkling of Norwegians, Scots, French, Swiss, Austrians, Danes, Hungarians, Chinese, and 2500 French Canadians. Each group brought its cultural baggage, including religion. Presbyterians established the first Protestant church in 1822, followed by the Baptists in 1824 and Episcopalians two years later. In response to the growing numbers of Irish and German Catholics, ethnic parish churches were erected between 1829 and 1843.[14] Jews established their first society in 1839, with a house of worship following in 1851. German Lutherans founded a church in 1848. In 1891, Christian Scientists established a place of worship.[15] The Salvation Army had a difficult time establishing itself in Syracuse in the 1880's. Its street corner meetings were broken up by ruffians. Local ordinances forbade street meetings without a license. None could be obtained and the preachers were arrested and jailed. A form of passive resistance occurred, filling jails with Salvation Army troops. Supreme Court Judge Samuel Kennedy declared the arrests illegal and the Salvation Army was allowed to function in 1884.[16]

In addition to manufacturing, other commercial successes of the late 19th century included retailers, such as Deys, Edwards, Witherill's, and Chappel's.[17] The need for a sound national currency during the Civil War encouraged the growth of banking in Syracuse and within a half century there were 13 banks in the growing city.[18]

Syracuse was also home to several hospitals starting with St. Joseph's (Catholic) in 1869, the House of Good Shepherd (Episcopal) in 1872, (later Upstate Medical Center), followed by the Women's and Children's Hospital and Training School for Nurses in 1887. In 1912, it became Crouse-Irving. The city established a university in 1870, transferring operations of a small Methodist College from Lima, New York to Syracuse. Starting with 41 students by 1892 it had grown to 649 reaching 1613 by the turn of the century. Similar growth attended the public schools with a total student population of 11,425 in 28 buildings staffed by 281 teachers.[19] By the time McGuire began his public career, Syracuse had three newspapers – The Journal, The Herald and The Post. The Post and Standard merged in 1899. It became the Republican party house organ. As Mayor, McGuire had a long-running feud with it dating from the onset of his administration. In fact, Mayor McGuire lambasted the paper in his acceptance speech. The Post responded: "To have merited the Mayor's approval would be deemed by this paper a calamity; to have incurred his wrath and earned it, too, is as though the best citizenship of Syracuse were saying, "Well done, good and faithful servant." The Evening Telegram, a Democratic party paper was begun in 1898 but failed soon after.[20] By 1886, the electric light companies consolidated, revolutionizing all aspects of urban life. Electricity-powered streetcars replaced the horse-drawn variety, power being generated from the Fulton Street plant beginning in 1893. McGuire would have his issues with these public utilities as well. Syracuse also boasted several "professional" athletic teams. Its minor league baseball team from 1876-1929, The Syracuse Stars, featured African-Americans as prominent players until their removal by International League fiat in 1889.[21] It would be more than a half century before baseball was integrated again. Sports would become a moral and a political issue during McGuire's tenure as mayor.

Some Syracusans pursued other leisure-time activities which encouraged the growth of a "criminal element." Connors recalls the Earl Gang, the "Chain Gang" and a red light district along East Washington Street near Townsend better known as "the line." Much of the activity consisted of gambling on horse races, boxing matches, baseball games and numbers. The toughest sections of town were "Robbers Row" on James Street and Orange Alley. It would only be on the eve of World War I that the vice districts were cleaned up.[22] The allegations of widespread vice and corruption surfaced during McGuire's tenure as mayor. Accused of running a "wide open town", it may have contributed to his electoral defeat in 1901. The jail was in the basement of city hall, a county penitentiary being built in 1901. Emblazoned in electric lights over its door, were the words, "Syracuse Welcomes You". In light of McGuire's subsequent political and private sector careers, it may have proven to be an ill omen.[23] To protect its citizens, Syracuse organized a police force in 1838 and its fire department some forty years later.[24] The city hosted the first State Fair in 1841. Although Elmira, Buffalo, Albany and Rochester also sponsored it, Syracuse became its permanent home by the time James K. McGuire left public office.[25] Despite these developments, Sutherland reported there was "no sweetness and light" in Syracuse, no museums, no libraries, no art galleries, no handsome monuments, fountains and public works, no parks, no public baths, good pavements or a good water supply.[26] McGuire would attempt to deal with these issues, but each would generate it political conflict. The water problem was resolved with fresh water pumped in from Skaneateles Lake 20 miles away in 1894 during the time of James K. McGuire's predecessor as Mayor, Jacob Amos.[27]

This was the city that James K. McGuire's family made its home beginning in 1880. It became the source of his early business success, it launched his political career and inaugurated him into the rough and tumble world of urban political machines. These early experiences would move McGuire into other venues, each having an impact on the man and his multiple careers.

James K. McGuire's family was part of the larger Irish diaspora to the United States which occurred from the mid 19th century on. Many Irish chose Central New York because of job opportunities, such as the Erie Canal and the Salt Works forming the base of the 6625 Irish residents of Syracuse by 1900.[28]

McGuire's parents migrated from Northern Ireland in 1858. James Kennedy McGuire was born in New York City. Ten years later, William Marcy Tweed, the ruling "Boss" of the Democratic machine, had made himself a millionaire, and Tammany Hall into a political dynamo with state-wide influence. Tweed perfected fraud and bribery. He was virtual czar of New York City politics until undone by malcontents and the editorial cartoons of Thomas Nast. Tweed, in the popular mind, is usually associated with New York City, but he also conducted business upstate in Albany. While in Central New York, he made the Vanderbilt Hotel in Syracuse a center of Tammany Hall politics, dispensing drinks to the faithful at a cost of $1500 per day.[29]

James was the second of seven McGuire children, their first son dying in infancy. Another brother Frank, drowned in the Oswego Canal.[30] There were four surviving brothers, James, Edward, George, Charles, and a sister Mary.[31] It is not clear why the McGuires moved to Syracuse in 1880. Possibly there were job opportunities in its growing industries, but they arrived too late to be recorded among the McGuires as "pioneer Irish in Onondaga County.[32] However, a letter by Richard Wright, dated 19 August 1981 in the James K. McGuire files at the Onondaga County Historical Association states McGuire's father was a shoemaker on what is now North Salina Street.[33]

James K. McGuire began his formal education on Butternut Street in the basement of a German language school. This linguistic ability assisted him in political campaigns on Syracuse's North Side, the German section. Later it helped him obtain an endorsement for his books supporting Germany's role in the fight for Irish freedom.

It was probably no small factor in his obtaining employment as propagandist for the German Imperial government during the early years of World War I as well.³⁴ Like many in that era, his formal education was brief. He left school at age 12, to attend to a variety of jobs. One source credits him with several jobs-newsboy, candy factory worker, printer, baker, machine operator, and clerk in a law office.³⁵ McGuire would later exploit the poor newsboy image in his attempt to win the Democratic gubernatorial nomination in 1898. That same year an article in <u>The New York World</u>, "Poor Newsboys Who Have Been Elected The High Political Office" features McGuire as one of two urban mayors who overcame many obstacles to achieve success. It was strictly Horatio Alger: how he sold papers during the day, went to school at night, he was an orphan, living in a lodging house and through hard work was able to achieve material and political success.³⁶ McGuire's father, unable to work, made James the family breadwinner at age 16. But McGuire did nothing to correct the rags-to-riches persona given him by journalistic license, for political advantage. At the time, the lack of formal education was no barrier to success in business or politics. According to a contemporary journalist Arthur Judson Brewster:

When I surveyed the city I found that aside from professional men, very few of those who controlled the affairs of Syracuse had attended college. The mayor, James K. McGuire was a young businessman who had little schooling. Onondaga's representative in Congress was not a college man nor were the political leaders of both parties. Practically all of the city's industries were owned by non-collegians. Prominent in the national picture at that time were John D. Rockefeller, Andrew Carnegie and many others who never darkened the halls of learning in their youth.³⁷

McGuire was essentially a Populist at the time. Early in his career he was Secretary of the Farmers Industrial Union, but he later resigned when it moved into third party politics. A chapter of the Farmers' Alliance had formed in New York in 1875. Two farmer groups merged in 1888 as the Farmers Alliance and Industrial Union which by 1890 had about three million members nation-wide, one branch of which included African-Americans. In addition, McGuire was an early champion of ballot reforms, advocating its adoption in cities throughout the Northeast and Midwest.[38] McGuire delivered speeches to farmers and workers in Syracuse, his efforts attracting enough attention to win Democratic Party support for the State Assembly. He had to decline the offer because of his youth. He later delivered speeches on various subjects at major cities in New York, Ohio, Pennsylvania and Illinois. His topics included, "American History," "Irish Ballad Music," "German Poetry," and "The Irish Soldier on American Battlefields." His eloquence earned him the nickname, "The Silver-Tongued Orator of Onondaga." He began writing professionally for the Syracuse Courier,[39] a short-lived Democratic newspaper. His speaking tours on behalf of Grover Cleveland won him a chance at a position in consular service which he declined.[40]

McGuire began to move more actively into politics in the 1890's. He became a delegate to the Democratic State Convention at Saratoga in 1893[41] serving on the arrangements committee for the convention in Syracuse the following year. In that capacity he worked with future political rivals, Henry J. Mowry, W.B. Kirk and Thomas Ryan.[42] The latter three were supporters of David B. Hill, a major power in New York State politics at the time.[43] Mowry, in his role as Chairman of the Convention, complimented Hill for his "sturdy efforts on behalf of the Democracy." McGuire was then the recognized leader of the anti-Hill faction beating Kirk in winning the party nomination for Mayor, obtaining 75 of 90 delegates. Kirk, Chairman of the City Convention failed to see McGuire as a formidable challenge until it was too late. McGuire's allies, John Cummins, James E. Newell and Melvin Z. Haven, worked the convention for him.[44] Thus began the first of the political lives of James K. McGuire. During those politically formative years, the most dominant force in upstate Democratic politics was David B. Hill, a man whom he first opposed, but later admired and used as his mentor.

In looking at his political record, we see in McGuire a kind of political ambivalence necessitated by politics. He exacted concessions from recalcitrant businessmen and politicians when he could, made inter- and intra-party alliances as necessity demanded and ultimately may have been ensnared by the corruption of those who surrounded him. Three such persons were Democrats David B. Hill, Frank Matty and Republican James J. Belden.

Notes

1 Roseboom, William and Schramm, Harry. They Built A City: Stories and Legends of Syracuse and Onondaga County (Fayetteville, NY, Manlius Publishing Company, 1976), 126.
2 Ibid., 50.
3 Ibid., 43; "Local History". Post-Standard. 25 February 2018, A-2.
4 Sutherland; The City of Syracuse and its Resources. (Syracuse, NY; Syracuse News Publishing H. J Company, 1893),3; Roseboom and Schramm, They Built A City, 59.
5 Sutherland, 4; Connors, Dennis J. Crossroads In Time: An Illustrated History of Syracuse; (Syracuse: Onondaga County Historical Association 2006)78, Roseboom and Schramm, They Built A City, 61; 66.
6 Sutherland, The City of Syracuse, 3.
7 Roseboom and Schramm, They Built A City, 69.
8 Ibid., 70.
9 Connors, 76.
10 Sutherland, The City of Syracuse, 4.
11 Brewster, Arthur Judson. Life Was Never Dull: Memories of Clinton Square and Other Tales of Syracuse (Syracuse: Syracuse University Press, 1953), 162; Roseboom and Schramm: They Built A City, 62-3; Conners, Dennis Crossroads In Time, 76.
12 Connors, Crossroads In Time, 74; 80.
13 Roseboom and Schramm, They Built A City, 122-126; Connors, 67-68.
14 Roseboom and Schramm, 129-131; Connors, 68-69.
15 Roseboom and Schramm, 129-30.
16 Schramm, Harry and Roseboom, Henry. Syracuse From Salt to Satellite (Syracuse Chamber of Commerce, 1979), 69.
17 Ibid, 47-49.
18 Ibid, 42-43
19 Ibid, 73; Roseboom and Schramm, 132-33.
20 Schramm and Roseboom, 75-76;127-8.
21 Connors, Crossroads In Time, 65; Roseboom and Schramm, 144-45.
22 Schramm and Roseboom, 52; Connors, 57.
23 Brewster, Arthur Judson. Life Was Never Dull (Syracuse: Syracuse University Press, 1953), 42.
24 Connors, Crossroads In Time, 58.
25 Roseboom and Schramm, They Built A City, 158-9.
26 Sutherland, The City of Syracuse, 3.
27 Schramm and Roseboom, Syracuse: From Salt..., 59-61; Connors, 55.
28 Roseboom, William and Schramm, Harry. They Built A City: Stories and

Legends of Syracuse and Onondaga County, (Fayetteville, NY: Manlius Publishing Company, 1976), 127.
29 Ibid., 44.
30 "Body of James K. McGuire On Train Arriving Today: City will Bow In Tribute", July 1923 n.p. James K. McGuire File, Onondaga County Historical Association.
31 "James K. McGuire" – June 30, 1923". Article fragment, in Obituaries and Biographical Clippings of Residents of Syracuse, Onondaga County, 1860-1926, vol. 15 Ma-Mc. Compiled by Local History Department, Syracuse Public Library, 1915-26.
32 Bannon, Theresa, Pioneer Irish In Onondaga County, 1776-1847. (New York: G.P. Putnam and Sons, 1911).
33 Richard Wright, letter dated 19 August 1981, JKM File, Onondaga County Historical Association.
34 "Body of James K. McGuire…" James K. McGuire File, Onondaga County Historical Association; "Mayor Rivals Were Neighbors", Herald 29 April 1947.
35 "James K. McGuire". In Dwight, Bruce H. The Empire State In Three Centuries New York: Century History Company, 1908, 264-6.
36 "Poor Newsboys Who Have Been Elected to High Political Office" James K. McGuire File, Onondaga County Historical Association.
37 Arthur Judson Brewster. Life Was Never Dull (Syracuse: Syracuse University Press, 1953) 129.
38 "James K. McGuire". Empire State In Three Centuries, 164-6.
39 "James K. McGuire." Cyclopedia of American Biography, (New York: James T. White and Company, 1897:) 19; "James K. McGuire. History of The Democratic Party In New York State (New York: American History Book Publishing, vol. II, 1905), 445.
40 "James K. McGuire". Cyclopedia, 19; "Conciliate The Minorities". New York Times 5 August 1895; "James K. McGuire, Former Mayor, Dies At Capital". James K. McGuire File, Onondaga County Historical Association. Kingsley, M.J., Knauber, J.K., Neville, J.J., Buckenberger, A.C. The Political Blue Book of Syracuse, New York (E.M. Grover, 1902), 203.
41 "Solid Delegation For Kirk". New York Times 30 September 1893.2.
42 "Mr. Hill Opens The Campaign". New York Times 10 December 1894:3.
43 "Syracuse City Caucuses". New York Times 17 September 1895:3.
44 "Deaths of the Day: James K. McGuire" 30 June 1923. James K. McGuire File, Onondaga County Historical Association.

CHAPTER I - B

The Boy Mayor's "Wide Open Town": Sports, Slots, Sluts, Tramps, Thieves, Trusts, Trash

During McGuire's tenure as mayor, there were constant allegations that he ran a "wide open town".[1] Most of the charges revolved around issues of street crime, vice, gambling, illegal distribution of alcohol and Sunday sports. Most critics were members of the clergy who believed such behaviors as a passport to perdition. The reformers were not unique to Syracuse, but all were shocked by the modernization of cities and its resultant social problems – crime, poverty, disease. The religious doctrines of a better fate in the next world held little relevance to huddled urban masses and hence church attendance dropped off among the poor. Abandoning the emphasis that faith alone would help the poor transcend the material miseries of their daily lives, a number of clergy began to focus on improving living conditions through social reform. The result, they believed, would be the moral regeneration of the entire community. In America, the movement had numerous advocates and organizations among various denominations.

In New York State, one of the more famous was Rev. Charles H. Parkhurst.[2] Coming from a rural, agricultural background in New England, he became pastor of a Presbyterian Church in New York City in 1880 and soon found himself interested in urban affairs. By the early 1890's, Parkhurst had noticed the interconnections between politics, graft, crime and police. When his observations as to the extent of vice and crime in the city were challenged Parkhurst and two others went in disguise to provide evidence of widespread vice and corruption. His efforts aroused indignation which resulted in the Lexow investigation of 1894 and a series of municipal reforms. McGuire in his first term as mayor, found himself the butt of criticism from a variety of reform-minded clergy, both Catholic and Protestant. And while the issues seem almost prosaic now, they unleashed a storm of controversy giving credence to his critics that McGuire ran a "wide open town".

By the time McGuire was mayor, baseball had been called "the national pastime" for at least a generation. Transformed from a genteel past-time of the upper classes, it had become a professional sport in the post-bellum era with the formation of leagues, rules, umpires and equipment transforming it into a big business. With increased interest, especially among working classes, rowdy behavior became commonplace. Local team owners were often proprietors of local breweries and brawls among drunken fans were commonplace. Low admission prices and access to spirits encouraged their attendance.[3] McGuire enjoyed baseball and often threw out the first ball to inaugurate the season.[4] Two years after McGuire was elected mayor, two baseball pitchers were arrested after playing a game on Sunday. Two clergymen, Rev. H. N. Kinney and Monsignor Kunitzch sought to test the legality of the city's blue laws which prohibited "shooting, fishing, hunting, playing, horse racing, gambling, exercises or shows and all noise disturbing the peace".[5] The players pleaded guilty as charged. This was only the beginning of the campaign by concerned clergy to outlaw Sunday baseball. The issue went to the courts but until it was resolved there was a flurry of publicity by those for and against. The Journal quoted Robert G. Ingersoll, noted agnostic, lawyer and lecturer[6] as saying the common people should be able to enjoy themselves. "Preachers", he lamented, "want to take one-seventh of our time. We should be able to relax and play. Why think about Hell? Give pitchers and preachers an equal chance. One kiss gives more joy than a thousand sermons".[7] Two local religious leaders entered the fray, Frederic Dan Huntington, Episcopal Bishop of the Diocese of Syracuse and Rev. Patrick Ludden, Roman Catholic Bishop of Syracuse.[8] Both saw the issue of Sunday baseball as undermining faith and morals, alienating youth from church and worship, and injurious to the interests of the working classes. The Syracuse Sunday baseball controversy made the national edition of Sporting Life magazine. Mayor James K. McGuire was the focus on an interview on the question. The mayor was described as an ardent supporter of the idea of Sunday baseball as a worthy use of leisure time for the young men of the city who after attending church services, have no other outlet for activity on a Sunday afternoon. Without such activities, McGuire said, they form vicious habits, indulging in drinking bouts and worse things behind closed doors…"Idleness", he piously intoned "is the mother of crime". Casting his critical net further, McGuire condemned the Raines Law as conducive to an atmosphere of vice "allowing men and women to promiscuously congregate… creating wayward children who frequent these resorts". Under such circumstances, the Mayor observed, it was the city's duty to encourage Sunday sports.[9] The two clergy who were original plaintiffs were also quoted, one saying he was "a friend of the game" but playing it on Sunday was illegal. The other, possibly more insightful than his colleague, said the purpose of Sunday baseball was not recreation for the laboring classes, but simply to make money.[10]

In the case of the two pitchers, McGuire met with the judge and the concerned clergy. The magistrate had dismissed the charges against the two players, believing the "laboring classes" favored Sunday sports. The clergy objected to the noise of the game, especially during Sunday services. McGuire stated he was in favor of Sunday baseball, but would do all he could to ensure the games were conducted in an orderly manner.[11] The clergy responded by calling for massive protests against the practice.[12] McGuire, running for a second term, was forced to defend his position, claiming that baseball was morally and legally correct. Times had changed since the archaic blue laws were written. Reformist clergy should focus their attentions on more serious issues, such as abuses by jobbers and contractors. Little was heard of the controversy until a year later when one of the original plaintiffs complained of the use of nickel slot machines at games, forcing aldermen to threaten to terminate Sunday baseball unless the use of machines was discontinued.[13]

The issue of Sunday baseball seemed to ebb and flow during municipal elections. The problem was resuscitated by would-be reformers during the mayoralty campaign of 1901. Having failed by moral suasion, Rev. Guy B. Galligher took the issue to the courts, demanding McGuire's Director of Public Safety, Duncan Peck, enforce the statute banning Sunday baseball. Peck regarded it as "harmless amusement", that neither he nor the Mayor were against it, but should a "few, narrow-minded people ask him, he supposed he would have to enforce it". Rev. Galligher served papers on Peck requiring him to do so. Players were arrested, tried and found innocent after the jury deliberated less than three minutes. The same judge who had found the two players innocent in 1897 ruled that Syracuse wants Sunday baseball. Since the one played was not between professional teams, and the law preventing such activity was enforced only once the last decade, if the participants were ignorant of the law, or did not intentionally violate it as per prior Court of Appeals decisions had ruled, they were innocent. An outraged Rev. Galligher promised to take the issue to the Supreme Court.[14] The Herald, to its credit, believed the majority of the public did not support a ban on Sunday sports, claiming it was "innocent recreation" for men who labor six days a week, with playing fields far removed from populated areas. The editorial concluded that if there was no Sunday baseball, the working men would go to "worse places", adding the law was unenforceable. Most juries acquitted those arrested, suggesting there was limited support for enforcement.[15]

The clergy struck back. In an interview with reporter Edith Cornwall, the Rev. Guy B. Galligher, responding to the issue that other corporations do business on Sunday, said it was the laws job to protect the sanctity of the Sabbath. The good reverend declared he was fond of baseball, but its games were "scenes of debauchery, revelry and uproarious mirth with gambling on the outcome of the game for money". This, would lead to worse abuses – "faro, roulette, cigars and drink". Sunday, said Rev. Galligher, "should be spent with family and friends, engaged in works of mercy, studying the grandeur of the Heavens and the Earth beneath". He further stated his belief that Sunday newspapers, excursions, bicycles, baseball and other sport were largely responsible for the vacant pews during Sunday services.[16] During the initial controversy over baseball in 1897 a petition signed by over 1200 people was circulated in Syracuse. It is doubtful the petition had any effect. Sunday reform bills had been introduced in Albany every year since 1897, but upstate Republicans controlled both Chambers and the Democrats rarely got their bills out of committee.[17] So, the underlying issue then, was not Sunday baseball, but the alleged moral decay of the city under McGuire's administration.

While the baseball issue may not have been a substantive one, there were others, the cumulative effect of which would lead to defeat in his bid to become mayor of Syracuse for a fourth consecutive term.

Along with Sunday sports, municipal reformers in Syracuse condemned the other vices associated with it, believing they contributed to the moral decline of Salt City. Many reforms begin with the best of intentions, but are often sidelined in application by businessmen who exploit loopholes in the laws, rules or regulations in order to continue operating. Such was the impact of the Raines Law, passed by the State Legislature in March 1896, in the first three months of McGuire's first term as mayor. It was sponsored by Republican State Senator John Raines of Canandaigua who fought against the prominence of liquor interests in state affairs. The bill put the retail trade in liquor under high license fees and, with limited exceptions, prohibited sales on Sundays. It exempted inns and hotels, focusing primarily on saloons. However, state law defined a hotel as such if it served liquor with meals, had a kitchen and had at least ten rooms.[18] Enterprising tavern-keepers simply installed bedrooms above their saloons and served sandwiches. Since the work week for the laboring man was six days, Sunday was the only day left for a full day of drinking.

One result of the Raines Law, was that hundreds of saloons, the majority of them decent and orderly places, were turned into "hotels"… To cover the costs of the bedrooms, the proprietors were obliged to obtain some revenue from these rooms. In almost all cases, there was no actual demand for such hotel accommodations; the result was that the great majority of these hotels became houses of assignation or prostitution. These [were] the so-called "Raines Law Hotels.[19]

Anyone who properly filled out the application was granted a license which was revoked if a violation was found and could also result in criminal prosecution.[20] The law came under fire almost immediately by the clergy and the Anti-Saloon League resulting in some changes, but violations continued. In Syracuse, the most notorious of those showing indifference to the law was Alderman Frank Matty. Matty had a prior history of violations of the Raines

Law. As early as May 1896, there were accusations of bribery in connection with 53 violations of the law. A Grand Jury refused to bring an indictment, claiming the evidence was all hearsay.[21] The conflict between Matty and McGuire over patronage jobs in the Board of Health had its roots in a clergyman's lament that "city government was run from Matty's saloon".[22] The pastor insisted the existence of Matty was a sign the devil was at work; and condemned him for his current indictments for violating the Raines Law. He complained Matty's saloon was a "gambling den" and that city police "wink at the social evil of disorderly women", demanding "the municipal stench" of the City Hall Ring be eradicated. All this did was exasperate tensions between McGuire and Matty and prevent city jobs from being filled. Matty ultimately had his license revoked, but obtained a new one simply by paying the court costs.[23]

The Rev. W. H. Main of the Central Baptist Church also criticized McGuire's administration. Reiterating comments of others, he complained that saloons, gambling dens and brothels abound, are open on the Lords Day and he condemned Sunday sports. He demanded McGuire enforce the laws, especially those operating as notorious "Raines Law hotels". Failure to do so, said Main, was cause to remove him from office.[24] Despite the pressure, Matty continued to do business. In August 1898, the courts ordered him to remove his name from the saloon and cease his liquor sales. In December, Matty barricaded the doors to his saloon from the attorney for the State Excise Committee, who unsuccessfully sought an injunction to ban Matty from doing business.[25] Perhaps the delays had something to do with the fact that Matty and McGuire had become political allies, dating back to Fall 1897 during the mayor's bid for re-election. The alliance was harshly critiqued by Methodist clergyman and Syracuse University Chancellor, James R. Day.[26] Initially praising McGuire for his reformist stance, Day now condemned him:

McGuire is now aligned with the old combine, ...He now runs with them to win re-election; he is a helpless figurehead in bed with a pirate crew; Matty and his franchise gang have captured the mayor.[27]

Catholics too, condemned McGuire's "wide-open town". Fr. John

Grimes joined the chorus against immorality following a police raid which netted 14 girls aged 14-22 having been involved in "orgies". The good Reverend reiterated his message in a sermon referring to saloons a "slaughterhouses for our young" where young girls have now to confront evils unknown to their mothers.[28]

One vehicle whereby the youth of the city were to be removed from temptation was by imposing a curfew. The Rev. J.B. Kenyan proposed all youth under 16 be off the streets after 8 pm., a proposal which earned the scorn of Frank Matty.[29]

Evangelist A. S. Orne claimed Syracuse was the state's second "wickedest city". He had stated he visited numerous cities during his ministry, but had only been propositioned by a prostitute in Syracuse. Echoing the comments of Rev. J. B. Kenyon, he insisted on a curfew, and condemned the fact that blacks and whites congregated together at the Oriental Hotel. He further demanded the use of slot machines be suppressed. Both Police Commissioner Duncan Peck and Mayor James K. McGuire denied the allegations - partly. Peck said the only slot machines in existence were for cigars, not money. Both said blacks and whites were separated insofar as possible and tacitly admitted the existence of prostitution by stating that "certain resorts were necessary to protect decent women". If they were eliminated, vice would taint the entire city.[30]

Another reformer, Rev. A.P. Burgess, charged there was widespread gambling in the city, demanding its suppression. Many Alderman, including Frank Matty, were indignant that such claims were made, stating piously they had no interest in gambling. Would-be Republican rival to McGuire, District Attorney Jay Kline would summon a Grand Jury to investigate the allegations.[31]

The Rev. Guy B. Galligher, an avowed enemy of Sunday baseball, believed Sunday saloons were even worse, demanding police close offending taverns. He condemned the streetcars which delivered customers to "vile resorts" along the lake, "where the scarlet woman and lascivious man linked arm and arm flaunt their shamelessness with remorseless indifference". Galligher saw a progressive moral decline, starting with baseball fraught with scenes of debauchery, mirth, revelry and gambling to faro, roulette, cigars and drink, people becoming victims of a fatal passion for gambling.[32] Teaming up with Rev. Burgess, Galligher supplied a list of 45 gaming houses to Duncan Peck, demanding their closure. The hapless Mayor and his Commissioner of Police claimed ignorance as to the existence such places, but promised to investigate. Because of his alleged tolerance of such violations, Galligher and the Anti-Saloon League were pursuing the possibility of legal charges against Commissioner Peck.[33] The Herald also condemned the use of slot machines as dishonest and harmful because they appealed to those who could least afford to lose and because it formed bad habits which encouraged gambling. A subsequent article in the Herald noted their existence was commonplace, especially in saloons, cigar stores, hotel lobbies, railway stations and pharmacies. They had moved from being a toy to a gambling instrument[34]

The police responded to the pressure, notifying the saloons and cigar stores to remove the offensive machines. If the police knew where the machines were located, didn't that beg the question as to the truthfulness of the professions of ignorance of their existence by Peck and McGuire? The Herald ridiculed them both in a cartoon, "Their Sunday School Lesson" portraying the Police Commissioner and several judges sitting on a bench with Rev. Galligher reading from a book, entitled; "The Law As It Is". The cartoon's subtitle: "Now Will They Be Good"?[35]

The Herald was correct in this instance as demonstrated in the case of gambler Peter O'Neill. He claimed his business was destroyed and he was jailed because he refused to pay protection money to Frank Matty and Sim Dunfee. Mayor McGuire urged him to close down his operations voluntarily until the Grand Jury investigating his administration was over. O'Neill refused on the grounds that no other gaming establishments had shut down. An editorial in the Herald indicated the existence of two faro rooms, five poker rooms, one horse pool, one crap game and two policy rooms in Syracuse.[36] Obviously, the mayor knew what was going on.

Coming as it did during the campaign for a fourth consecutive term as mayor, the accusation of Fr. Grimes that under McGuire Syracuse was a "wide open town" may have had some credibility. For example, a cartoon in the Herald showed McGuire playing to a crowd, asking, "When In The History of The City Have You Had A More Liberal Mayor Than I?" Sitting in the audience were items labeled "salaries", "slot machines" "baseball", and "beer mugs".[37]

The timing of the "Christian Endeavors" Convention in Syracuse in late October 1901 was not helpful to McGuire's re-election campaign. Begun in 1881 by Francise E. Clark, a Congregational minister, the organization focused on training young people to encourage their "spiritual efficiency and practical service." It grew to an interdenominational organization of over 70,000 societies with an international membership of over 3.5 million.[38] It's presence in Syracuse at this time focused attention on the city administration at a time when McGuire was scrambling to obtain popular support. The convention's theme was "The Power of The Saloon In Politics". Its main speaker, Rev. Howard H. Russell, was founder of the Anti-Saloon League. His address, "Old Battles Yet To Be Won" raised the spectre of moral decay claiming the "saloon was where the assassin of McKinley was raised and received his training and we fear anew the terrors emanating from the saloon". Assisting the local reformers crusade, he also proclaimed the Sabbath be observed as Christ envisioned it.[39]

In addition to the taint of immorality, the designation of "radicalism" may also have hampered McGuire's electoral efforts. He had been labeled an anarchist, a radical and proponent of class war since his first term, especially after endorsing and working for Bryan in the campaigns of 1896 and 1900. In addition, the Mayor's efforts alleviating the plight of the poor and unemployed also created ammunition for his critics. They saw them instead as dangerous Populist politics. This too, may have been a factor in the demise of McGuire's public service career. The issue of "tramps", stereotyped as criminals, indigents and labor rabble-rousers contributed to McGuire's problems as mayor.

The Depression of 1893 had its roots in the failure of several major railroad companies. The ripple effect closed banks, businesses and precipitated a decline in agricultural prices. Unemployment rates spiked to 25 percent in some cities. Workers responded to their misery and suffering in three ways; by organizing and violence, by passive acceptance of the status quo, and by becoming itinerant workers, seeking employment in other locations. These were the tramps referred to above.

Government response at the state and federal level was swift and sure repression best seen in Coure d'Alene miners' strike, the Homestead Steel Strike and the Pullman Strike. Other workers panhandled to survive, slept in parks or municipal lodging houses. Vagrancy laws provided some homeless workers with shelter in local jails. Newspapers warned of the public menace and pointed to growing crime rates blamed on the dangerous classes.[40] Thousands of others "rode the rails" or "went on the tramp" looking for work. Often legitimate strikes called by laborers were muddled in the public mind with tramps, seen as unemployed criminals and troublemakers. In the mind of government officials, it justified stern repression as was done by Democratic Governor Roswell Flower of New York in the switchmen's strike of 1892-94.[41]

The term tramp received much approbation during the 1890's in large measure because of Jacob Coxey's army's "March on Washington." Coxey, a self-made businessman from Ohio believed he could save the country by having Congress enact legislation to create large amounts of legal currency to be spent on public works, thus creating jobs for the unemployed during the Depression of 1893. While his "army" of 500 was disbanded by club-wielding police following his arrest at the capital, other armies, much larger than his paltry band, began mobilizing. They, often became disorderly mobs. Railroads refusing to provide free transit had their trains stolen. In some instances, local authorities were unable to restrain them. The federal government issued injunctions and often used troops to dispense the "soldiers'. A handful made it to the capital, but were provided carfare back home by the government of District of Columbia. While unsuccessful, it demonstrated widespread labor discontent at the economic distress and government antipathy towards workers in the wake of economic downturn.

The Depression lingered on until the turn of the century. In Syracuse, during McGuire's first administration. The Journal noted the streets filled with idle men, clamoring for relief.[42] Six months later, in January, trained machinists claimed the only work they could find was shoveling dirt for 80 cents an hour to avoid starvation.[43] Later that month, the paper noted how worse the destitution was than three years previous, the men suffering in silence, selling their furniture simply to stay alive. Some relief was provided by City Hall providing jobs to 30 men shoveling snow. By Summer, 1897 Mayor McGuire estimated the unemployed at about 10,000. He expressed hope the Dingley tariff[44] would alleviate the problem. He expressed a concern that skilled artisan who used to disdain such work were now willing to clean streets with Italians and Hungarians. He called on Syracuse's wealthy residents to assist those in need.[45] Critics assailed the mayor's efforts to ease the plight of the unemployed by giving them paving jobs and painting City Hall as vote getting ploys for the upcoming election. It was alleged that "drunks and bums" wore McGuire election buttons to police court in the hope of not being punished.[46]

The word "tramp" took on even more sinister implications during McGuire's unsuccessful attempt to win a fourth successive term as mayor. Critics condemned abuses in the Poor budget of Commissioner Sehl. In response to Kline and Driscoll referring to the Municipal Lodging House as a "tramp mecca", McGuire defended it, claiming its budget was minimal, yet it fed hundreds.[47] Kline reissued the challenge late in the campaign, claiming McGuire "colonized" Syracuse with "tramps" to obtain their votes, a claim the Herald insisted he support with evidence.[48] McGuire's campaign retaliated in kind. His campaign claimed Kline was "endeavoring to enlist the support of the criminal classes.. rape fiends, burglars, thugs, thieves and scurvy lawbreakers, all under indictment who Kline released on bail. They are dragging the dives and gutters for votes".[49] It was this kind of vitriol which led McGuire to claim his was a campaign of "decency vs. deviltry".⁵⁰ Kline responded by reiterating the charge the mayor had been colonizing Syracuse with tramps from surrounding towns for months and registered them for the upcoming election.⁵¹ And while there were some expose's alleging electoral manipulation, they were far less than what Kline and the Republicans had claimed. For example, the <u>Herald</u> found an increase of 325 employees in the two months preceding the election, mostly in the Water Department. Eight men from a workingman's hotel were arrested for illegal voter registration on the eve of the election.⁵²

Despite the acrimony then, the Republican margin of victory was such that, even if the charges leveled against McGuire were true, they could not overcome the rancor of the Republican machine which was united on one purpose-the overthrow of McGuire by any and all means.

There were other issues McGuire had to confront during his administrations, especially the awarding of contracts for city projects. It inaugurated a series of intra-and inter-party disputes which also contributed to his undoing.

Another of Rev. Parkhurst's targets for reform was the graft, crime, corruption rampant in Gotham City. Similar efforts to weed out these urban evils were made by social reformer in Syracuse during McGuire's successive terms of office. Allegations of corruption began to surface almost immediately. For example, within his first six months of office, he had to open the city's books to pre-empt charges of corruption. McGuire used this opportunity to call for the creation of a City Controller and push for an inventory of all municipal property.⁵³ The issue of municipal finance would come back to haunt him during the final years as mayor.

Rev. John Grimes
(1852-1922)
Syracuse Priest, later Bishop
(Source: Notable Men of Central New York
of XIX and XX Centuries, 1903)
Public Domain

Patrick Anthony Ludden
(1836-1912)
First Catholic Bishop of Syracuse, New York
(Source: Notable Men of Central New York
of XIX and XX Centuries, 1903)
Public Domain

Frederic Dan Huntington
(1819-1904)
Minister, Reformer
(Source: Notable Men of Central New York
of XIX and XX Centuries, 1903)
Public Domain

Robert G. Ingersoll
(1833-1899)
Lawyer, Agnostic
Library of Congress, LC-BH-832-31136, Public Domain

By far the most contentious issues were the letting of contracts for city public works projects and the granting of franchises. McGuire was adamant-and consistent-in demanding no franchises be granted unless the city derived revenue from their operations. McGuire was not reluctant to bring suit against public transportation companies who reneged on payments to the city, promising he would "force the arrogant monopoly to submission."[54] McGuire, having his veto of "franchise grabbers" over-ridden by the Common Council, encouraged out-raged citizens to attend its meetings. The aldermen, when faced with a hostile crowd, would adjourn within a few minutes, further worsening relations between the mayor and Frank Matty.[55] McGuire was particularly incensed about railway franchises. As noted, McGuire portrayed himself as a Populist. His constituents were upset that in tearing up brick streets to lay railway lines the railroads were lowering property values. Often, critics of the "franchise-grabbers" alleged bribery was used to win their approval of the Common Council.[56] For example, in the granting of a franchise for the Suburban Railway Company, it was rumored the alderman were being bought for $300-$400 each.[57] The problem of abuse in the distribution of railway franchise predated McGuire's administration when the West Shore Railroad obtained concession to run its trains through the center of the city.[58] In his first inaugural address, the mayor promised to have the railroad companies pay their proper obligations to city coffers.[59] His efforts at controlling the "franchise grabbers' brought him into direct conflict with Eugene Hughes and Frank Matty and later rival in the asphalt scandals of his post-mayoralty career, Patrick Quinlan.

Initially the company to come into question was The Lake Side Railway. It promised to remit two percent of its revenues to Syracuse. Immediately after obtaining the franchise, Matty was involved in Grand Jury proceedings alleging he received a $7000 bribe for granting it, but the charges "vanished into thin air". The Grand Jury refused to return an indictment, alleging the evidence was all "hearsay".[60] McGuire ultimately signed the Lake Side franchise. A pliant Common Council granted the company an extension by a one vote majority to meet its commitments.[61]

The franchise grabbing continued. Despite McGuires' liberal use of the veto, it was often over-ridden by the Common Council. The scramble for lucrative awards became especially intense in the Fall 1899, before the White Charter became operational. It's provisions limited the parameters under which franchises operated and allowed no partial franchises. In Syracuse, six railroad companies were vying for bids, with McGuire once again threatening to use his veto power.[62]

A second railway franchise which caused McGuire even greater consternation concerned the Rapid Transit Company. It culminated in the mayor's active involvement in a street riot to force the company to submit. Throughout the country, urban transportation was undergoing significant changes. Horse-drawn trolleys were being replaced by electric streetcars. They were cheaper, cleaner and quieter. They eliminated tons of manure, but also created congestion and safety hazards.[63] Trolley lines also radiated out from the city center, bringing in commuters, shoppers, encouraging the economic development of downtowns, expanding the over –all size of cities. On the down side, it lead to increasing outward migration to the suburbs, segregating the poor in ghettos.[64] It also brought pleasure-seekers to "unwholesome" resorts, a focus of concern for clerical critics and social reformers.

In Syracuse, the dispute began initially over the company's refusal to pay $140,000 in back taxes. Since legal documents were silent on the issue, a compromise was sought but neither side could agree. The city initiated a lawsuit to obtain the back taxes, and the issue widened the breech between the mayor and Frank Matty, who supported the Transit Company. McGuire was upset not only because of the intransigence of the company to pay its back taxes, but it was moving its trains at speeds in excess of city ordinances, police at one point being positioned to pull unwary pedestrians from the path of oncoming trains. McGuire assumed the Common Council would support him in his struggle with The Rapid Transit Company in his attempt to have it pay its back taxes. McGuire applied pressure by trying to annul the franchise. Matty complained he should sue the company instead.[65]

Matty showed his control over the Common Council by granting the company permission to string an electric wire in the disputed area, over-riding the mayor's veto. In response, McGuire organized a "Citizens Committee" to support his polices. By the end of March, the Common Council agreed to accept Rapid Transits' offer of almost $77,000 to resolve the issue. In addition, it would pay the city a minimal fee into the City treasury based on each passenger.[66]

Problems with Rapid Transit resurfaced in August 1898 when its workers went out on strike, the company having discharged several motormen and conductors. Rapid Transit refused to arbitrate the matter but eventually backed down for two reason: there was widespread public support for the workers, and there was pressure from State mediation officials.[67] Tempers were short as a result of the company's refusal to negotiate. It precipitated a riot between railway workers and Italian laborers. A second visit from State mediators forced concessions from the company.[68] But a month later, Rapid Transit had not complied with the arbitrators' award, discharging several employees, explaining their work was deficient. A planned walkout by the disgruntled workers was a failure, the Journal referring to them as "cowards".[69]

Local issues took a backseat to State and national politics during the Fall 1898, but the conflict with Rapid Transit resurfaced on March 1899. McGuire once more demanded payment of back taxes, declaring its overcrowded cars a health menace and demanding the ouster of its president. It was rumored McGuire was in league with Sim Dunfee and Richard Croker, the Tammany boss, in a scheme to replace the company. McGuire imposed a license fee for each car of the Transit Company which would generate about $8000 for the city offers.[70] With no settlement in sight, an enflamed citizenry, "with McGuire's sanction" began what became known is "The Butternut Street Riot" in late April 1899.

A crowd armed with crowbars and tools supplied by McGuire, began tearing up the tracks laid in violation of city ordinances in the German section of Butternut Street. Not only did the mayor supply the tools, but he promised no interference from the police, despite company demands for protection. McGuire was on the scene, encouraging rioters who ripped out over 300 feet of rails and demolished switches. Stones were thrown at railway cars and three people were injured in the melee.

In a later conference with the mayor and the North Side Citizens Association, the Company again demanded police protection. A sharp exchange followed: McGuire asserted the people were right, but declared he would do what he could to protect property; President Allen of the Transit Company called the members of the North Side Association "anarchists" and blamed beer as the reason for the riot. The North Side Association, mostly German, regarded it an ethnic slur. It later passed a resolution demanding the company attend a public hearing, calling themselves law-abiding citizens, absolving the mayor of any involvement. It further regretted not having tied the railroad executives to the rails and thrown them into the dump, threatening to tear up more rails if their demands were unmet and asked the Common Council to rescind the company's franchise. The Citizen's Association blamed the company for igniting the incident when one of its motormen, jumped off a car and grabbed a boy by the throat. The Transit Company, in turn demanded the names of the rioters and threatened not to run any cars in the Butternut-Street route until its property was duly protected.

Throughout the crisis, McGuire seemed non-plussed. He said Syracuse was cursed by franchises passed over his veto. The rioters he said, were good citizens and taxpayers and he repudiated the Anarchist label stating the crowd was "enthusiastic and orderly", having no option but to tear up the tracks to show their indignation. McGuire denied he encouraged the attacks, but acknowledged it was done with his tacit consent and support, since the rails had no legal warrant to be there and the company had ignored for years orders to have them removed.[71] McGuire obtained a permanent injunction sought by the North Side Association preventing the company from laying any more rails on Butternut Street. As to revenue, the issue was resolved at the state level when Governor Theodore Roosevelt, overcoming objections of his own party, passed the Ford Bill, allowing municipalities to tax franchises as real estate.[72] McGuire was elated, believing the new source of revenue would eliminate the need for a major tax hike given the deficit under which he was operating. But the local Republican machine which had been so critical of him was not about to be outdone.

Within a week, the Rapid Transit Company conceded defeat, offering once again the pay its back taxes. However, residents of Butternut Street demanded annulment of the franchise since the company had made public no plans for improving the line in its area, vehemently protesting McGuire's demands it lay concrete. Another stalemate between the Mayor and the Company was the result.[73]

McGuire, running for re-election in 1899, and aware of the budget shortfall, sought to alleviate the problem by proposing a railway bond scheme of $2 million funded at four percent for twenty years. The Common Council was reluctant to endorse it, unless the term of indebtedness was 30 years.[74] McGuire blamed the opposition to his bond scheme by the Republican combination of Frank Hiscock, Francis Hendricks, Jacob Amos and others, predicting the "ring of millionaires will be buried in an avalanche of disgruntled voters in November". McGuire's efforts to obtain support for the railroad bond refunding scheme were defeated, the Republicans obtaining an injunction against their issuance by the end of July 1899.[75] McGuire had to admit defeat for the present, pursuing to appeal at a later date. For the time being, he now had to focus on being re-elected.[76]

In addition to other railway companies seeking lucrative franchise and contracts, other public utilities and businessman also sought a favorable review. These included sanitation, telephone and electricity and would create further discord between himself, his party, the Republicans and the Common Council. One asphalt paving company he initially fought against. But after his failed bid for a fourth term as mayor, he became strongly identified with-and tarnished by it, bringing disrepute to himself and his brother George H. McGuire.

Related to the issue of asphalt, which not only eliminated issues of muddy streets, was that of public sanitation. It entailed clean streets, ease of transportation, sewage and public health.

McGuire had always maintained an interest in public sanitation.

It was not simply for politics and patronage. In many urban areas of the era, disease was rampant and Syracuse was no exception. For example, during his tenure as mayor, there were outbreaks of typhoid fever, diphtheria, scarlet fever and smallpox.[77] Concern for eliminating these scourges led him to push for improvements in public hygiene-paving streets, street cleaning, building sewers and sanitary facilities, and public baths. It also generated more political infighting over control of the franchises.

Strongly associated in the public mind with McGuire and sanitation were his famous "White Wings", a corps of 60 men wearing white uniforms would sweep the estimated 40 miles of paved streets of the city. Costs to Syracuse were estimated at $1500. The largest cost was the purchase of wagons, carts and receptacles. In addition, there were to be eleven sprinkling inspectors to insure the street were kept in pristine condition. His critics complained of costs and whether the employees were really doing their jobs.[78] In addition, some of the equipment needed was supplied by McGuire's Syracuse Hardware and Iron Company, an issue which helped tarnish his reputation in a subsequent bid for mayor.

The two issues which drew the most fire were those of awarding the contract for garbage treatment and asphalt paving got him into trouble with Frank Matty and his allies Sim Dunfee and Eugene Hughes.

By the late 19th century, concern over urban sanitary conditions consumed many tax dollars. Iron pipes, pumps and filtration systems improved water quality and hence removed the threat of typhoid. The dense city populations increased demands for more water and better drainage and sewage systems. And despite improvements, disease was not eradicated in part because municipalities continued to dump sewage into nearby ponds, lakes and creeks.[79] Syracuse, as a growing industrial city, was subject to the same demands and pressures to modernize. In the process, it also generated political in-fighting between the Mayor James K. McGuire, the president of the Common Council and their respective allies. This issue of a garbage treatment facility began within months of McGuire's first term as Mayor. After reviewing the legality of the previous contract to build a treatment facility, the Mayor voided it. The awarding of the contract was stonewalled by the Board of Health which had not reviewed the plans. Frank Matty claimed McGuire was in a hurry to award the contract, that it needed prior approval from the Common Council and, that it had been let at a price $8000 above the previous bid. Both rivals claimed the other had a vested interest in different companies being awarded the contract. The Journal was more blunt: "The mayor of late is as dumb as an oyster on the garbage question." The one existing plant was burdened by overload, had shut down six times and was unable to keep up with amount of trash generated. At a subsequent meeting the problems were admitted by the contractor, who promised to build a second plant twice as large to accommodate the waste. Until a second plant was in operation, the mayor was criticized by the Board of Health for dumping garbage illegally in Salina and polluting the near-by creek.[80] An injunction to prevent continued dumping was prepared by the law firm of Hiscock and Doheny and ordered by Judge Frank H. Hiscock. The refuse was then dumped in Manlius which it resented, the Board of Health having temporarily abandoned the notion of a garbage reduction plant.[81]

The apparent beneficiary of these municipal squabbles was Sim Dunfee, a self-made millionaire, whose political connections gave him several lucrative franchises in Syracuse-electricity, telephones and now trash. His company was awarded a contract for ten years at a cost of $410,000 over the veto of James K. McGuire with only one dissenting vote. It was essentially a done deal largely because Dunfee had support from Frank Matty who was reportedly "looking out for Dunfee's interest in the Common Council". It was alleged the costs of Dunfee's contract were inflated from two to three times what costs were for cities of similar size, generating him profits of $30-$40,000 annually. McGuire stubbornly refused to sign the pact until ordered to do so by the courts.[82]

The issue revived again two years later when the pact was up for renewal. Dunfee wanted to both collect and dispose of the city's trash, but again faced opposition from the Mayor. Dunfee had a ten year deal for disposal, but sought to enlarge his operations. This was direct challenge to McGuire's control over the dispensing of patronage jobs in the Board of Health, turning them over instead to a private contractor.[83]

Like McGuire, Dunfee was a Democrat and a second generation, self-made Irishman. It would appear two would be natural allies, but like McGuire, Dunfee would do whatever was necessary for his own political or pecuniary advantage. For example, he was a confidante of Republican James Belden and political ally of Democrat Frank Matty. Dunfee's name was also tarnished with allegations of bribery.

The garbage issue exacerbated McGuire's political problems during his re-election bid in 1901. In response to a lawsuit brought by residents of Hiawatha Boulevard, Judge W.S. Andrews ruled the city could not run refuse into Onondaga Creek. The judge said the plaintiffs had a right to prevent pollution of the creek and all city sewers must conform. McGuire expected the decision, but dreaded its implications. Over the last six years he had built over 30 miles of sewers used by 70,000 residents, with Onondaga Creek as its drains. The noxious odors and fears of epidemics brought legal action. It was imperative the city move towards the Gray sewage system. Initiated in the States by Samuel Merrill Gray, it emulated a system popular in Europe, having interconnected sewer pipes collect waste from various neighborhoods and sent to central processing plant for treatment. The issues McGuire faced were the ripping up of streets to build the connections and the cost of a treatment plant. City Engineer Sweet estimated the costs at $750,000.[84] Obviously this was not good news to the mayor, who was already under fire for his financial problems. It may also have contributed to his electoral defeat in November 1901.

The issue which defined McGuire's private sector career after he left public office in 1902 was asphalt. And much of it involved a local business, Warner-Quinlan and Empire Contracting, the latter owned by Sim Dumfee. With railways being built, through the city, it meant streets were uprooted to lay rails and then had to be repaved. Often the three issues-sewers, railway franchises and paving contracts were interwoven, as were allegations of bid-rigging, fraud and corruption. The city would contract for the paving then bill the company for the work done. By May 1897 complaints as to the cost and quality of pavement laid were being heard. The mayor, running for re-election in 1897, claimed to have smashed the paving ring, reducing rates by one-half to two-thirds of what they were previously blaming them for increased assessments. Using this as a political plank, McGuire asserted his need for re-election was imperative to keep such "jobbers" at bay. "These birds of prey hover over City Hall to harvest contracts for paving in 1898 when the sewers will be laid".[85] The issue was again raised by the Mayor in mid-March 1898 when he condemned the City Council for letting paving bids without obtaining specifics as to the type of asphalt used, angering both residents and transit companies upset with construction delays.[86]

McGuire, as mayor had always endorsed competition between rival asphalt companies to obtain the lowest prices for the city despite bringing him into conflict with Alderman Frank Matty. Editorials in the Syracuse Herald condemned the lack of competition as inimicable to the public interest, especially in view of the fact that specifications written by the City Engineer were over-ridden by the Common Council. The Aldermen responded to such criticism by saying it could not approve of an inferior grade of asphalt. Matty had a resolution passed specifying only "genuine Trinidad Asphalt from the island of Trinidad".[87] A see-saw battle ensued between the City Engineer, who kept returning the bid specifications to the Common Council, and the latter which continually rejected them.[88] Matty's dictatorial control over paving materials was publicized in both editorials and cartoons in the Herald.[89] In April Warner-Quinlan, the major competitor to the "Asphalt Trust", took the issue to the courts, claiming its asphalt equal in quality to that accepted by the Common Council. It's lawsuit claimed the narrow wording of the Common Council resolution was designed to limit competition, especially since it had been the low bidder. City Counsel and McGuire ally, Melvin Z. Haven, said the Common Council resolution was illegal because it exceeded its authority. It could not exclude any paving material. Thus, the asphalt issue re-ignited the Matty-McGuire feuding of the recent past. Matty attempted an end-run around Haven by having a plebiscite whereby local residents would designate the paving materials for their neighborhoods. Matty sensed his cause was doomed since another competitive bidder and "Asphalt Trust" rival, the Warner- Quinlan Company, had asphalt claims a mere 2000 feet away from that deemed acceptable by the Common Council. In the end he need not have worried. The "Asphalt Trust" won its lawsuit overruling the temporary injunction obtained by the Warner-Quinlan Company, the court reasserting the principal of the sanctity of contracts.[90] The <u>Herald</u> condemned the decision in both articles and cartoons. McGuire, again trying to bring both sides together, drafted a resolution incorporating Matty's concept of giving local residents a say in the selection of paving materials and insuring the contract went to the lowest bidder. The Common Council ignored it.[91] The Mayor claimed the Syracuse had become a national scandal, with its record-breaking prices for asphalt contracting. He claimed credit for competition having brought down prices to under $2 per square yard, saving the city over $60,000.[92] Perhaps-or was there something else going on? With an eye towards re-election to a fourth term as Mayor, did McGuire align himself with Sim Dunfee? It was Dunfee's firm, the Empire Contracting Company, which was the low bidder of 13 of 15 contracts. Dunfee was a political ally of Matty's. The remaining six contracts were awarded to five other companies, including Warner-Quinlan and Barber Asphalt, Barber being part of the "Asphalt Trust". This parceling out of contracts may have served to keep the issue dormant until after the election of November 1901. Nonetheless, the debate continued through June. The Common Council rescinded all bids from companies using California asphalt which had the lowest price. Matty sought to maintain the monopoly of Trinidad asphalt. McGuire realized his veto would be over-ridden, but he refused to sign the ordinance ousting bids with California asphalt. The awards became operative without the mayor's signature. McGuire pinned his hopes for rejection on the Board of Contract and Supply which he assumed would not award the higher bids.[93] An editorial cartoon in the <u>Herald</u> aptly summed up the issue. Entitled the "Paving Despot", it depicted Matty smoking two cigars, igniting papers labeled "paving specifications", enthroned in a chair labeled "Common Council" with a two figures ("the public") groveling at his feet.[94] The Board of Contract and Supply approved the California asphalt McGuire had also endorsed, but the Council refused to let bids until it got what it wanted. To make sure there was no misunderstanding, the Common Council spelled out in detail what it would accept: "Asphaltum used shall be equal to that obtained from Pitch Lake on the island of Trinidad and to be refined, and as far as possible, freed from organic and mineral matter and oil, and must contain 60 percent bituminous soluble in bisulphide of carbon".[95]

Matty was adamant that only Trinidad asphalt be used. McGuire was reluctant to veto it, knowing from past experience, it would be overridden by the Common Council. Obviously Matty and his allies sought to eliminate competition and exclude the low bidders. McGuire had the City Engineer William Sweet on his side in the debate who said there was no disparity in quality between California and Trinidad Asphalt.[96]

Sweet was not a pliant tool of the mayor. In fact, he was among his critics, especially in the closing months of the 1901 mayoralty campaign. In an interview with journalist Edith Cornwall, he called the McGuire administration the "the greatest curse on the city", claiming everyone from the mayor on down was dishonest and incompetent.[97] The City Engineer claimed refusal to use California asphalt was a conspiracy against the public. McGuire essentially capitulated, although he obtained a compromise-the asphalt applied had to be the same grade and quality as Trinidad, the "competition" occurring between those residents wanting brick or asphalt.[98] His claims to having "smashed the paving ring" were obviously premature, but, first he had an election to win.

McGuire, running for a fourth consecutive term was compelled to mend fences since his struggle against Republican Jay Kline was going to be difficult. This was also McGuire's introduction into the dark side of asphalt paving. When his public career was over, he soon became publicly identified with the "Asphalt Trust" and worked hard to maintain it's monopoly using the same arguments Frank Matty used against him. The details of that story are yet another chapter in the "political lives of James K. McGuire."

Notes

1 For example, see "Js. K. McGuire: States Biggest Democrat". Post Standard 10 November 1899. The article claimed his successful bid for a third term was a "victory for a wide-open town".

2 "Parkhurst, Charles Henry" (1842-1933). In Malone, Dumas (ed.) Dictionary of American Biography vol. 14 (New York: Charles Scribners Sons, 1934), 244-246.

3 Farragher, John Mark, Buhle, Mary Jo Cziton, Daniel, Armitage, Susan. Out of Many: A History of The American People 4th ed. (Upper Saddle River, New Jersey: Prentice-Hall, 2003), 590-591: Carnes, Mark C., Garraty, John A. American Destiny: History of A Nation 3rd ed. (New York: Pearson-Longman, 2008), 528-529.

4 "Opening Game," Syracuse Journal. 1 May 1896:6.

5 "Two Players Arrested." Syracuse Journal 3 May 1897:6.

6 Robert G. Ingersoll (1833-99), known as the "great agnostic", was the son of a clergyman, a distinguished free thinker, a prominent lawyer, a Civil War veteran, Attorney-General of Illinois and splendid orator. Probably most famous for his nomination speech favoring James G. Blaine in 1876, he later made his living lecturing on various topics, including religion, literature and politics. "Ingersoll, Robert Green," In Malone, Dumas (ed)., Dictionary of American Biography, vol 9, (New York: Charles Scribner's Sons, 1932) 469-470.

7 "Sunday Baseball," Syracuse Journal 10 May 1897:6.

8 Fredric Dan Huntington was a New England Episcopal clergyman, theologian, educator and long-term bishop of the Syracuse diocese. He was founder and president of what became known as the Manlius School. Bishop Huntington On Baseball". Syracuse Journal 17 May 1897:6. Patrick A. Ludden was an Irish-born Catholic priest, ordained in Albany, New York and chosen by Pope Leo XIII to be the first bishop of the Syracuse diocese. He was an ardent baseball fan and enthusiastic supporter of the Syracuse State league team. His successor was Rev. Grimes. "Bishop Ludden Dead at 76." New York Times 7 August 1912.

9 "Syracuse Satisfied" Sporting Life 15 May 1897:10. http://www.lg84.org/SportsLibrary/SportingLife/1897/vol29NO08/SL2908010.pdf

10 "Rev H.N. Kinney on Sunday Baseball," Syracuse Journal 10 May 1897:6.

11 "Sunday Ball Games" Syracuse Journal 14 May 1897:6.

12 "The Pulpit's Voice," Syracuse Journal 24 May 1897:6; "Sunday Baseball," Syracuse Journal 7 August 1897:6.

13 "City Maps Will Be Big Expense". Syracuse Journal 25 May 1898:5.

14 "Appeal To The Courts". Syracuse Herald. 22 June 1901:6; "Sunday Ball Games". Syracuse Herald. 28 June 1901:6.
15 "Editorial: Sunday Baseball". Syracuse Herald 12 July 1901:4.
16 Cornwall, Edith. "Guy Galligher-Reformer." Syracuse Herald 14 July 1901:1.
17 Reiss Steven. "The Baseball Magnates And Urban Politics In The Progressive Era: 1895-1920". Journal of Sport History. vol I, no 1, 1974: 41-62.
18 "Raines, John". Malone, Dumas (ed). Dictionary of American Biography vol 15 (New York: Charles Scribner's and Son's, 1935), 326-327.
19 Peters, John T.. "Suppression of Raines Law Hotels", Annals of the American Academy of Political and Social Science vol. 32. November 1908, 86-96.
20 Ibid., 87.
21 "Was No Bribery," Syracuse Journal. 18 May 1896:8.
22 "Broad Changes" Syracuse Journal 22 February 1897:6. The accuser was Rev. Thomas J. Villers of the First Baptist Church.
23 "Alderman Matty's Little Side Entrance". Syracuse Journal. 21 June 1898:6.
24 "Model Mayor Described". Syracuse Herald 2 May 1898. Using a Biblical example, Rev Main suggested the model be Nehemiah, reform Mayor of Jerusalem 2300 years ago, whom he claimed was a "patriot", not a politician". Rev. Main described McGuire's lack of reform effort, made him an "enemy of the public good".
25 "Matty and His Saloon". Syracuse Journal 13 August 1898:6; "Frank Matty's Doors Barricaded". Syracuse Journal 20 December 1898:6.
26 James Roscoe Day (1845-1923) was a New England Methodist clergyman. He spent five years in the West as a lumberman, stage-driver, cowboy and roustabout claiming to have not visited "the saloon or its precincts". He became a minister, ordained in 1872 and became Chancellor of Syracuse University in 1893 which was at the time linked to the Methodist Episcopal Church. Under his leadership it grew in reputation, numbers and facilities, although he ran up huge deficits and his faculty was underpaid. He was a feisty and outspoken on social issues, particularly trusts and the decline in public morality. "Day, James Rosoe." The National Cyclopedia of American Biography, vol XII (New York: James T. White and Company, 1904), 418; "Day, James Roscoe." Dictionary of American Biography, vol 5 (New York: Charles Scribner's Sons, 1930), 160-161.
27 "Dr. Day's Answer" Syracuse Journal 23 October 1897:5. In return, Matty promised an investigation into the city's role in the management of university affairs. "Seeking Revenge." Syracuse Journal. 29 December 1897:6.
28 "Editorial: Strong Words By A Brave Man". Syracuse Journal 22 May 1900:4; "They Are Slaughter Houses For Our Young." Syracuse Journal 24 May 1900:6. John R. Grimes wan an Irish-born priest who became full-time pastor of St. Mary's in Syracuse in 1890, making it the largest Catholic

Church in Central New York. For his efforts, he was made bishop in 1912. "Grimes, John R" The National Cyclopedia of America Biography, vol II. (New York: James T. White and Company, 1921), 447-448.

29 "Matty Rails At Both". Syracuse Herald 16 April 1901:7.

30 "Vice In Syracuse". Syracuse Herald 7 May 1901:6. Peck noted the vice rates of Syracuse were 50 percent less than that other municipalities. McGuire told Orne to visit San Francisco, Las Vegas, Tuscon, Denver or Sacramento if he though Syracuse was bad. The Herald, to its credit, claimed such charges slandered the city. "Editorial: Good Word For Syracuse" Syracuse Herald 9 May 1901:6.

31 "Anti-Gambling Crusade". Syracuse Herald 11 May 1901:6.

32 Cornwell, Edith. "Guy B. Galligher-Reformer." Syracuse Herald 14 July 1901:1. Galligher was a Methodist Episcopal minister from Elmira, active in various charities and the Anti-Saloon League.

33 "Editorial: Proceed Against Peck". Syracuse Herald18 October 1901:4.

34 "Editorial: As To Slots". Syracuse Herald 25 July 1901:4; "Slot Machines Popular With Young And Old". Syracuse Herald 6 October 1901: 27.

35 "List For In Peck". Syracuse Herald 23 July 1901:6.; "Slot Machines". Syracuse Herald 24 July 1901:6. "Machines Out". Syracuse Herald 25 July 1901:46; "Their Sunday School Lesson". Syracuse Herald 28 July 1901:1.

36 "Peter O'Neill Says He Is Persecuted". Syracuse Herald 28 June 1900:7; "Editorial: The Case of Peter O'Neill". Syracuse Herald 29 June 1900:4. O'Neill had been a Democratic ward-heeler.

37 "When In The History of This City Have You Had A More Liberal Mayor Than I?" Syracuse Herald 16 October 1901:1.

38 "Christian Endeavorers" in Hastings, James (ed) Encyclopedia of Religion and Ethics, vol. III. (New York: Charles Scribner's Sons, n.d.) 571-573.

39 "Christian Endeavor Meet in Syracuse". Syracuse Herald 23 October 1901:7. Howard Hyde Russell was the son of a Midwestern preacher, who became a lawyer, clergyman, author and reformer. He founded the intersectarian Anti-Saloon League in 1883 which within two years had become a nation-wide organization. See "Russell, Howard Hyde". National Cyclopedia of American Biography, vol XIII (New York: James T. White and Co., 1906), 330.

40 Farragher, John M.; Buhle Mari Jo; Armitage, Susan H. Out of Many: A History of The American People, 4th ed. (Upper Saddle River, New Jersey, 2003) 608.

41 Harring, Sidney. "Class Conflict And The Suppression of The Tramps In Buffalo, 1892-94". Law and Society Review Summer, 1977), 873-911.

42 "McGuire Heard From". Syracuse Journal 5 October 1896:6.

43 "City Boards". Syracuse Journal 8 January 1897:6.

44 The Dingley Tariff, the brainchild of Republican Congressman Nelson

Dingley of Maine was passed in 1897 increasing tariff rates by almost 50 percent. Supposedly it would protect American manufactures from foreign competition. McGuire assumed that would stimulate productivity and create jobs

45 "Hard Times". Syracuse Journal 23 July 1897:6.
46 "Dey the Winner". Syracuse Journal 25 October 1897:6.
47 "In Response to Kline". Syracuse Herald 19 October 1897:7.
48 "Editorial: Astounding Charges". Syracuse Herald. 1 November 1901:1.
49 "McGuire Worth $18,000". Syracuse Herald 1 November 1901:6.
50 "Campaign". Syracuse Herald. 1 November 1901:7.
51 "Won't Have Any Colonizing". Syracuse Herald 1 November 1901:6; "Tramps Imported". Syracuse Herald 1 November 1901:9.
52 "City Payrolls". Syracuse Herald 21 October 1901:6; "Eight Men Arrested". Syracuse Herald 5 November 1901:9.
53 "All Just Correct". Syracuse Journal 11 May 1896:5.
54 "Those Street Railway Assessments". Syracuse Journal 12 August 1896:5. McGuire's commitment to bringing railroads under control was noted early as his first inaugural address to the city council on 3 January 1896. In Common Council Manual of The City of Syracuse, 1896 (Syracuse: E. M. Grover Company 1896), 49-57.
55 "500 Men Wanted". Syracuse Journal 5 October 1896:6; "With Jeers And Scoffing". Syracuse Journal 6 October 1896:6; "Matty-Belden Combine". Syracuse Journal 13 October 1896:1.
56 "A Hearing Tonight". Syracuse Journal 1 May 1896:6.
57 "And Still They Kick". Syracuse Journal 5 May 1896:5; "More Sensations". 5 May 1896:8. A lawsuit by the concerned residents to prevent the construction of the railway was filed and an injunction followed. "Unexpected Turn". Syracuse Journal 21 May 1896:6; "Injunction Goes". Syracuse Journal 8 June 1896:6.
58 "Syracuse City Hall Ring". City Government. January 1897 8:-11. The City Government article cited the West Shore Railway as the culprit, whereas it was more likely the New York Central and Hudson River Railroad which had been running through the city for a dozen years preceding McGuire's administration.
59 Common Council Manual... 1896, op.cit 44-57. McGuire wanted two per cent from all franchises granted by the city with a bond sufficient to guarantee that amount. It would bring $2000 to the city treasury. "About franchises". Syracuse Journal 15 May 1896:8.
60 "They Mean Business". Syracuse Journal 13 May 1896:8; "Significant This". Syracuse Journal 14 May 1896:8; "Is It Bribery"? Syracuse Journal. 15 May 1896:1; "There Was No Bribery". Syracuse Journal 18 May 1896.

61 "Park Employees". Syracuse Journal. 20 May 1896:6; "Lost A Franchise" Syracuse Journal. 4 August 1896; "In The Council". Syracuse Journal 11 August 1896:6.

62 "Franchises May Not Pass". Syracuse Journal 21 November 1899:5; "Common Council Grab Bag". Syracuse Journal 21 November 1899:6.

63 The safety issue was noted in McGuire's first inaugural address, in 1896. See Common Council Manual For The City of Syracuse, op. cit., 1896:53.

64 Farragher, John Mack et al. Out of Many: A History of The American People, 4th edition (Upper Saddle River, New Jersey, 2003) 582;583; Carnes, Mark C. and Garraty, John. American Destiny, 3rd edition. (New York: Pearson-Longman, 2008), 525-526.

65 "To Repudiate". Syracuse Journal 26 September 1896:5; "For Taxpayers Interest: Syracuse Journal 28 September 1896:6; "Mayor Was Hasty": Syracuse Journal 13 March 1897:6; "No Common Center". Syracuse Journal 22 March 1897:6. Part of the problem was the company had been refused permission by the Common Council to run a power wire since it had no franchise for the area. To get to the city center, the trains had to move at full speed, thus endangering pedestrians.

66 "A Quiet Meeting" Syracuse Journal 23 March 1897:6; "Citizens Committee". Syracuse Journal 23 March 1897:6. "City Gets This". Syracuse Journal 15 May 1897:5; "Offer Accepted". Syracuse Journal 15 May 1897;6. "Quarter of A Mill". Syracuse Journal 21 July 1897:6. McGuire vetoed the proposal, but it was over-ridden.

67 "Strike Is On". Syracuse Journal. 5 August 1898:8. "Both Men And Company Are Firm. State Mediator In City". Syracuse Journal 6 August 1898:5; "Trolley Cars Again Speed Over Streets". Syracuse Journal 8 August 1898:6."

68 "Pitched Battle At Noon". Syracuse Journal 12 August 1898:6; "State Arbitrators Here Again." Syracuse Journal 13 August 1898:6: "Amicable Settlement". Syracuse Journal 16 August 1898:5.

69 "Recent Tack By Rapid Transit". Syracuse Journal 21 September 1898:5. "Strike Sure". Syracuse Journal 17 November 1898:6; "A Fiasco". Syracuse Journal 18 November 1898:6. Apparently only 20 of 270 workers walked out.

70 "Unpaid Railroad Taxes". Syracuse Journal 23 March 1899:6; "Retaliate". Syracuse Journal 24 March 1899:6; "Mayor McGuire's Railroad Scheme". Syracuse Journal 28 March 1899:6; "Overcrowded Street Cars". Syracuse Journal 29 March 1899:5; "Mayor's Attempt To Enforce Law". Syracuse Journal 1 April 1899:5; "Railway Fight Resumed", Syracuse Journal 11 April 1899:6.

71 "Unable To Make Settlement". Syracuse Journal 22 April 1899:6; "Mayor McGuire's Attitude". Syracuse Journal 24 April 1899:6.

72 "Injunction Will Be Asked For". Syracuse Journal 27 April 1899:6; "New York

CONFLICTS AND CRISES 45

Legislature". New York Times 12 April 1899, "Franchises To Be Taxed". New York Times 29 April 1899; "Taxing of Franchises". Syracuse Journal 3 May 1899:8.

73 "Rival Railroad Scheme Offered". Syracuse Journal 5 May 1899:6; "To Annul Franchise". Syracuse Journal 8 May 1899:5; "McGuire And Railway Company". Syracuse Journal 21 June 1899: 6; "Rapid Transit Will Refuse". Syracuse Journal 7 July 1899:6.

74 "Railroad Bond Issue". Syracuse Journal 11 July 1899:8. "Mayor McGuire's Gets Personal". Syracuse Journal 12 July 1899:6. McGuire claimed Onondaga Savings Director President Charles Stone as hating him for blocking payment of $30,000 for his legal services to the Municipal Water Board. Charles Clark, the bank's president was called a hypocrite who has originally initiated the city's first railroad bonds in 1869 for $1 million, but allegedly the city had to pay out over $2 million. "Bond Resolution Defeated", Syracuse Journal 25 July 1899:8.

75 The injunction was presented by George Doheny of the Hiscock law firm. McGuire wanted bonds issued at four percent, but various banks were willing to underwrite the costs at three percent. The court stated the bonds should not be issued if the cheaper rate was available. "City Enjoined From Issuing Railroad Bonds" Syracuse Journal 27 July 1899:6; "Refrained From Issuing Railroad Bonds At Four Percent". Syracuse Journal 1 August 1899:6.

76 The railroad bonds were delivered a month after McGuire's re-election in December 1899. "Railroad Bonds Delivered". Syracuse Journal 29 December 1899:5.

77 "Jefferson Street Residents Threatened With Malaria". Syracuse Journal 29 May 1898:6. "The Blame". Syracuse Journal 15 December 1898:6; "City's Sanitary Conditions Today". Syracuse Journal 1 March 1899:6; "Testimony In Typhoid Cases". Syracuse Journal 16 November 1899; "No Need For Alarm". Syracuse Herald 24 January 1899:6.

78 "Street Cleaning And Flushing". Syracuse Journal 7 March 1899:5; "Unsprinkled Streets Taxed". Syracuse Journal 8 March 1899:5; "Sprinkling Tax Muddle": Syracuse Journal 10 March 1899:6.

79 Farragher, et al, op. cit., 583.

80 "A Time To Explain". Syracuse Journal 6 May 1896:6; "Shut Down Again". Syracuse Journal 7 July 1896:5. "Three Boards To Meet". Syracuse Journal 7 August 1896:6. "They Mean Business". Syracuse Journal 23 May 1896:5. "Matty and Belden Combine" Syracuse Journal 13 October 1896:1; "Building Fences". Syracuse Journal 18 February 1897:6.

81 "Flies On Salina Farm" Syracuse Journal 3 June 1896:6; "Injunction Goes". Syracuse Journal 8 June 1896:6; "Garbage Ghost". Syracuse Journal 23 March 1897:6.

82 "John Dunfee". Syracuse And Onondaga County, New York: Pictorial and Biographical (New York: J.S. Clark Publishing Company, 1908), 89-95; "Dunfee Again". Syracuse Journal 6 August 1897:6; "$410,000" Syracuse Journal 7 August 1897:5. For insights into the micro politics of this franchise deal, see "Fight Is A Hot One". Syracuse Journal 2 August 1897:5. "End Is Not Yet". Syracuse Journal 30 August 1897:5. "Latest Blow". Syracuse Journal; "McGuire Must Sign". Syracuse Journal October 1897:6.

83 "Dunfee Has Another Scheme". Syracuse Journal 13 December 1899:5; "Big Contract Grab Attempted". Syracuse Journal 16 December 1899:5.

84 "Gray, Samuel Merrill (1842-1921) The National Cyclopedia of American Biography, vol xix (New York: James T. White and Company, 1926), 175-176. Gray was a city engineer for Providence, Rhode Island. In the mid-1880's he studied municipal sewage systems in Europe and came back to incorporate their ideas not only in Rhode Island, but throughout the United States and Canada. "Means Big Cost". Syracuse Herald 9 July 1901:6; "Editorial Sewer Problems" 10 July 1901:4.

85 "Work To Go On" Syracuse Journal 17 November 1896:6; "Never Said A Word". Syracuse Journal 18 May 1897:6; "The Mayor's Harangue" Syracuse Journal 5 June 1897:5.

86 "Against Asphalting". Syracuse Journal 16 March 1898:6; "Merchants Angry". "Syracuse Journal 25 May 1898:5; "Asphalt Paving Full Width". Syracuse Journal 31 August 1898:5; "A Temporary Injunction". Syracuse Journal 15 July 1899:6.

87 "Competition In Paving". Syracuse Journal 8 August 1899:5;

88 "Both Sides Stand Firm". Syracuse Herald. 25 June 1901. 6. There was a potential conflict of interest in this dispute. Frank Hiscock was a attorney for the Warner-Quinlan Company which was the enemy of the "Asphalt Trust" which had a monopoly on Trinidad Asphalt. The Warner-Quinlan Company at the time was involved in extensive litigation with the Asphalt Trust over its claims to asphalt in Venezuela. See, "Cooked Up By Trust". Syracuse Herald 23 January 1901:6; "Syracusans Influence Government". Syracuse Herald 25 January 1901:6.

89 "Mayor On Paving Prices", Syracuse Herald 20 May 1901:6. Paving Depot". Syracuse Herald 16 June 1901:1; "Overzealous Council" Syracuse Herald 19 June 1901:4; "Paving Contest", Syracuse Herald 19 June 1901:6; "St Matty". Syracuse Herald 21 June 1901:4; "Editorial: Arbitrary And Illogical". Syracuse Herald 21 June 1901:4; "Editorial: Paving Hold-up". Syracuse Herald 22 June 1901: 4. The interesting point here is that the rejected bids were California asphalt, a type already in use in numerous cities, and according to McGuire, those which had been in use for several years.

90 "Taken To Courts". Syracuse Herald 21 April 1901:1; "Asphalt Combine".

Syracuse Herald. 24 April 1901:6; "That Paving Ordinance". Syracuse Herald. 27 April 1901:6; "Editorial: Matty vs. Haven." Syracuse Herald 31 April 1901:6; "Contracts Upheld". Syracuse Herald 5 May 1901:1.

91 See "Up Against It". Syracuse Herald 7 May 1901:1; "Editorial Paving Contracts." Syracuse Herald 7 May 1901:4. "Trying For Low Bid". Syracuse Herald 15 May 1901:6; "Fat Man On The Common Council". Syracuse Herald 16 May 1901:9.

92 "Prices Smashed". Syracuse Herald 21 May 1901:9. "Dunfee, John". National Cyclopedia of American Biography. Vol XIV. (New York: James J. White and Company, 1910), 504. This brief biography says one of the many businesses he owned was the Empire Contracting Company which laid asphalt pavement in Syracuse. "Let Repairs Be Made". Syracuse Herald 22 May 1901: 1; "Repairs At Public Expense." Syracuse Herald 26 May 1901:1.

93 "Mayor Will Not Sign It". Syracuse Herald 11 June 1901:6.

94 The Paving Despot: Syracuse Herald 22 June 1901:1.

95 "Editorial: Paving Hold Up". Syracuse Herald 22 June 1901:4.

96 "Both Sides Stand Firm: Syracuse Herald 25 June 1901:6.

97 Cornwall, Edith, "The McGuire Machine". Syracuse Herald 30 June 1901:1.

98 "Council's Desire". Syracuse Herald 21 July 1901:1.

CHAPTER I - C
The Boy Mayor, 1895-1901: Patronage, Graft, Deficiency, Defeat

So what was it that brought down a popular three-time Democratic mayor of Syracuse, New York? In addition to him alienating significant elements in the Democratic Party at both the state and national levels, there was increasing criticism of McGuire's administration. Especially telling were the issues associated with patronage, his personal business contracts with the city and allegations that Syracuse was a "wide-open town", a virtual cesspool of sin according to his most vehement critics.

Patronage was widely practiced by both parties at all levels, reaching its apogee in New York during the last quarter of the 19th century under the auspices of William M. Tweed, the man who marked the emergence of Tammany Hall as a significant force in New York City and New York State politics. In itself, patronage was not necessarily bad, but became so under corrupt municipal bosses. Often, the party out of power would use the label to tarnish its opponents in the hopes of obtaining political office. At the municipal level, patronage was used to create party loyalty among those elected to office to ensure their support and hence continued employment. Municipal control was made easier by lack of a secret ballot until the later reforms of the Progressive era. From the onset of his first term, McGuire condemned the abuse of patronage. In his inaugural address, the mayor stated, "We are the servants of the people...We are not here to make easy berths for friends at public expense".[1] Nonetheless, some of his most significant political battles were fought over the use of patronage.

James K. McGuire used patronage throughout his terms as mayor, but the level of criticism increased each time he beat his Republican rivals in mayoralty elections. For example, within months of his first election victory, McGuire sought to oust the incumbent Police, Fire and Health Commissioners and appoint his own men to the positions. Interestingly, one of his first appointees was Charles F. Baldwin, his opponent on James J. Belden's reform ticket which split the Republicans giving McGuire his victory.[2] A week later McGuire appointed "loyal Democrats" to sinecures as custodians in City Hall and as watchmen for the city parks.[3] McGuire explained his actions in subsequent interviews in the Syracuse Journal, noting their salaries were not extravagant, two simply replacing others who had left and complaining the Journal had made an issue of pointing out they were all Irish.[4]

A year later, McGuire ran into opposition with his appointments, given his limited influence among the 19 aldermen and the firm opposition of Frank Matty. According to the Syracuse Journal, despite McGuire's claim to a reformist label, he was trying to build a political machine. Traditionally appointments were made by the Common Council and they resented McGuire's efforts to usurp their power. With a Democratic majority of one on the Common Council, Matty opposed McGuire's appointments especially on the Board of Health given its potential for numerous patronage jobs. There were also rumors circulating McGuire had ties to a garbage reduction company. If he controlled the Board of Health, he could award the contract to his business associate. In order to obtain the appointments, McGuire had to rely on Republican votes controlled by James J. Belden.[5] Syracuse was treated to the spectacle of a McGuire-appointed Fire Marshall, not being allowed to take office by the incumbent who claimed only the Common Council could rule on his tenure. Interesting, in the struggle over Fire Marshall, Mayor McGuire openly claimed," to the victor belong the spoils" urging the incumbent turn over his office. The issue as to which branch of government has the power of appointment was ultimately relegated to the courts.[6] By mid-1897, McGuire was running for a second term. By then, the feud between him and Matty was intense. The confrontation between the two received notoriety in an article first published in City Government in January 1897 and republished almost verbatim in The Syracuse Journal.[7] McGuire was at the time involved in a series of fights with "franchise-grabbers". The article described the problem, in part, as due to the indifference on the part of the better class of citizens on primary elections resulting in the election of aldermen "from a class of ward politicians of unsavory order in private life: making them "unworthy of public confidence". Further, Frank Matty was specifically named as a key person responsible for many franchise giveaways, exercising greater influence than the mayor. Mentioned as franchise-grabbers were William B. Kirk and Eugene Hughes, in addition to the alderman who voted approval of the measures. A portion of McGuire's speech denouncing "Mattyism" was also reproduced. The article praised McGuire as a reformer deserving of re-election because he fought the franchisers and jobbers who made huge profits with no return to the city. Given the fact that McGuire's political enemies were named the Journal implied McGuire had written the article, as self-serving, a charge the mayor denied. The Journal further alleged the charges were without foundation and hence hurt the City's reputation.

The Mayor was condemned for allegedly coercing city employees to subscribe to his newspaper, The Courier. A letter sent to employees blatantly played the patronage card-"The Courier must have the active support of its friends. If we lose it, we are certain to destroy our chances of party success. Subscribe to its stock at $10 per share". McGuire was condemned in the partisan Post for requiring poor workers to subsidize the Democratic Party. "The mayor awaits the reply of every victim [sic], and he is a dull man who does not know what that signifies. It means chip in or get out".[8] McGuire was also criticized for appointing policemen who had not taken the civil service exam. Appointees to the Board of Health were considered "incompetents".[9] In addition to the criticisms of patronage, McGuire's chances were not enhanced by divisions within the Democratic Party. He need not have worried. They captured the city in a landslide.[10]

McGuire immediately mended political fences by rewarding Matty political ally Sim Dunfee as water Commissioner. The micro politics of this situation are as follows: McGuire held up additional patronage appointments in order to obtain support for his candidates to the Board of Health, two of whom were Republicans which he needed to keep the Beldenites happy; Matty sought re-election as President of the Common Council so he could appoint the City Treasurer; Matty and Dunfee were both political allies and were partners in a scheme to have Dunfee's firm awarded the city's garbage contract; McGuire needed a united Democratic party to win re-election.¹¹ McGuire, playing up to Republican votes, got his main political supporter, M.Z. Haven to resign as City Clerk and have his successor appointed by the Republican majority on the City Council.¹²

On the eve of McGuire's attempt to win a third term as mayor, M.Z. Haven noted almost $64,000 was expended from the Highway Fund. The Journal charged the money was used to employ hundreds of men just prior to the election, who do nothing but owe their useless jobs to the McGuire machine.¹³ Following his election, McGuire purged many employees in the city water, treasurer, public works and engineering departments, citing their appointments were illegal under civil service law.¹⁴ Ultimately, he was able to put many of his own people in these positions.

During his final term as mayor, allegations of abuse in civil service appointments surfaced again, some with lower scores being placed over more successful candidates. The Civil Service Board heard complaints alleging candidates had no need to take the exam if they had pull with Mayor McGuire. Four persons had been tested but 32 were already in salaried positions.¹⁵ An editorial in The Syracuse Journal suggested that the Mayor has unusual powers of divination–he made appointments before his candidates took the exam and after taking it, they miraculously appeared a the top of the civil service lists.¹⁶

McGuire's insistence on his own appointees without regard to Democratic Party wishes alienated him from many. For example, his steadfast determination to have Patrick Ryan appointed City Court Judge riled critics within his own party. Some assumed McGuire thought himself the whole Democratic Party, noting such was a bad precedent as what happened with Croker insisting on Judge Daly and its attendant bad publicity.¹⁷ It was this kind of Machiavellian politics which led to the controversial selection of Frank Matty as Common Council President on the 77ᵗʰ ballot with its resultant indictments, arrests and scandals, with both Matty and McGuire dreading the publicity of an investigation.

Once again revealing his political survival skills, McGuire caved in to political demands by his "new" political ally, Sim Dunfee.

Dunfee sought and obtained from the mayor the removal of an inspector who had been critical of Dumfee's work for the telephone company's subway system after threatening to build a competing line.[18][19]

In return for such patronage McGuire expected untiring efforts and loyalty as noted in this undated and unsigned letter, apparently in reference to his re-election bid in 1897.

John Dunfee
Syracuse Businessman
(Source: National Cyclopedia of American Biography, 1910)
Public Domain

James J. Belden
(1825-1904)
New York Congressman
(Source: Autobiographies of the President, Supreme
Court and Fifty-Fifth Congress, Vol. I, 1899)
Public Domain

Dear Jerry

Take off your coat and get to work. Two years ago I was elected Mayor and the fight for mayor pulled the whole ticket through the Board of Aldermen.

Indirectly the fight I made for Mayor carried 3 doubtful wards. Add a result, the Common Council was Democratic and you got a position which has netted you nearly $2000. In addition to that, I prevented the appointment of Malone by refusing to sanction the (certification) of 2 Democrats and Republicans who wanted to make him Sealer of Weights and Measures. And if the Common Council is to be Democratic again, it is I who must pull most if the Alderman through. Besides it is in your business interests to work for me. Meagher says he will take care of your brother in due (time). But your family through yourself has (been) pretty well recognized and I want you to get to work (and) hustle for the whole ticket.[20]

The "Jerry" was Jeremiah Carey. It reveals McGuire was feeling desperate as to his chances for re-election given the division within the Democratic party and, it reveals his adherence to the principles of patronage. In this context, his obituary stated correctly,… "he kept control through special favor, carefully distributed".[21]

In addition the publicity surrounding his alleged abuse of patronage, McGuire was also criticized for his business contracts with the city of Syracuse. As noted, he was the owner of the Syracuse Printing Company, a partner in the Syracuse Hardware And Iron Company, and the Charles M. McGuire Insurance Company, all of which obtained lucrative city contracts, especially during his third run for mayor. For example, as early as June 1897, it was alleged McGuire's insurance company obtained $66,500 of $327,000 worth of insurances on the city's school houses, with twenty other agents each obtaining awards of under $20,000 each. The Journal said the Board of Education let the contracts go to the highest bidder, costing urban taxpayers' an additional $1146. The Board was controlled by Commissioner Kiely, allegedly a McGuire "henchman".[22]

Two years later, the Mayor's ties to insurance contracts were lampooned in a cartoon in the Syracuse Journal.[23] During his third re-election bid, the Journal noted again the amounts of insurance awarded to his brother's insurance company, including not only the city's school buildings, but other property as well, such as the city's street sweeper's, horses, elevators, boilers, City Hall and its contents, in addition to the city's hospitals. The Journal reported McGuire's company had replaced the agent which had previously insured City Hall. This was a prologue to the role the McGuire Brothers and their insurance company would play in the asphalt scandals to which they were linked in 1914.[24]

His Republican critics desperate to overthrow him, also attacked McGuire for his hardware contracts, especially during the campaign of 1899. Alleging a whole host of financial irregularities, his enemies claimed the Mayor had illegally transferred funds from one budget line to another, one of which was paid to the Syracuse Hardware and Iron Company.[25] In addition, it was claimed McGuire awarded contracts on items over $75 without competitive bids in violation of the City Charter. It was proclaimed "a shocking and reprehensible state of affairs". Over $3000 in city funds went to his firm in 1898-99 in violation of state law forbidding public officials from being involved in the sale of goods to municipalities charging all contracts must be let to the low bid. A hardware company official responded simply stating there was a clerical error.[26] Especially telling to his critics was the fact that the brand of lawn mower purchased by the city was the one for which the Syracuse Hardware and Iron Company had a monopoly. The Journal investigated and found it could purchase none for the price allegedly paid to McGuire's Company, and could locate none of the horse drawn mowers. It was also stated the city was over-charged more than twice the price for such mundane items as files, manure forks, wheel barrow rims, and tools, allegedly selling lawnmowers and sawdust shovels to the city in winter. Following his electoral victory in 1899, McGuire resigned as Director and Treasurer of the Syracuse Hardware and Iron Company, calling the criticism an unnecessary distraction from city affairs.[27]

Financial skull-duggery was also charged against McGuire in the area of property assessments. In one instance, he was accused of removing himself from the tax rolls, even though in previous years he had been assessed on property worth $3000. The evidence was the official tax records which revealed his name fraudulently erased from the books, which, if held up to the light could be shown to have included his name. McGuire had sworn on an affidavit that he owned property. The Journal concluded McGuire was a hypocrite-for going after those who didn't pay their taxes, and, of inciting class prejudice, presumably claiming to be "propertyless" in the search for working class votes.[28]

While the above charge was serious it was not as damning to McGuire's career as were those alleging his administrations property assessments were bogus, padded upwards of $2 million in order to keep the tax rates low. In essence, assessments were made on nonexistent properties and individuals. A thief and embezzler, Charles DeGraw, was held responsible for pushing up the property assessments. Prosecution of both McGuire and DeGraw was considered a possibility. McGuire admitted the error, but claimed it was unintentional, and that such mistakes in other municipalities were not uncommon.[29] Despite his critics' attacks, McGuire was able to obtain yet another term as mayor, although the financial scandal would continue to plague him and ultimately lead to his undoing.

Financial shenanigans had been a consistent problem throughout McGuire's terms of office. Beginning with his first administration, questions were continually raised as to his fiscal policies. Initially no fiscal mismanagement was found in his administration.[30] In his bid for re-election in 1897, McGuire claimed the city was in good financial shape,[31] although there was a ripple of discontent. A local businessman questioned how the city's books could balance since there was no record of his payment.[32] By January 1898, the Journal, no friend of McGuire, condemned the deplorable state of city finances[33] His detractors increased throughout the Mayor's remaining tenure, especially the office of City Treasurer, who either could not or would not answer questions concerning an alleged deficit. There was talk of an official investigation, but McGuire found support in Frank Matty, who proclaimed McGuire was not solely responsible for it in its entirety.[34] At the end of his third term, McGuire was forced to appeal to the state legislature for financial support to pay for the city's deficit. The Mayor claimed state mandates had put his administration into a financial hole. The publicity surrounding this led to more calls for an audit of city accounts which McGuire refused considering it a blatant attempt to a make "political capital" on the part of his Republican critics. Ultimately the Mayor capitulated, in part due to the negative publicity surrounding the Butternut Street riot.[35] McGuire attempted to explain the deficit in order to preempt the threat of an investigation. Failing that, he put forward a bond scheme to pay back the deficit over a 30 year period. McGuire retreated from the bond plan since the interest rate was considered excessive, but pressure on him continued in his bid for re-election in the fall, 1899.[36]

McGuire attempted to ease deficiencies in some departments by transferring funds into them from others, an issue which got him into legal trouble. A judge ordered an injunction against such actions. The Republican press was jubilant given McGuire's fiscal problems and believed he could be unseated in November. Ads damned McGuire for successive deficits, allegedly increasing over ten fold-from $20,000 in 1896 to $200,000 in 1899.[37]

Despite the controversies, McGuire won by over 2000 votes, but fiscal scandals dogged his administration into its third term. For example, in February the Mayor had to admit the deficit was really $350,000-$150,000 more than was admitted to during the campaign.[38] McGuire responded by claiming his electoral victory vindicated him, proving the people approved of the deficit. Nonetheless, the criticism led to state investigation of Syracuse's finances by the Assembly Committee on Cities. The publicity was especially damning, since the City Treasurer could not account for the deficiency. McGuire was called to testify. Especially problematic were accounts in the Poor Department whose administrator, Jacob Sehl, could provide few details, other than political affiliation, for their obtaining work tickets. He conveniently could not be found when process servers sought his records. Sehl later testified that he awarded permits without fully investigating the claimants, assuming he was dealing with "honest men". Poor Department expenses increased from $54,000 in 1896 to $140,000 in 1899. Sehl claimed he had insufficient help to investigate all the claims. The Journal damned his statements as a testament to the waste and extravagance of the McGuire administration whose primary purpose was to obtain patronage jobs for them in exchange for votes, a charge Sehl did not refute. In addition to discrepancies in the Poor Department, the Assembly Committee found Commissioner Edward DeGraw's assessments inflated an excess of $4 million. The Committee found various no-show jobs, as well as some municipal employees having two jobs. McGuire's past business dealings in both insurance and hardware were resurrected as were his abuses of civil service law in his appointments to city jobs.[39] The upshot of it all was that a special grand jury was impaneled to investigate the municipal malfeasance of Mayor James K. McGuire. The Assembly Committee found him personally liable for the poor financial condition of Syracuse and alleged that serious criminal and civil offenses had been committed such that they should be taken up by the Grand Jury of Onondaga County, the Governor appointing extraordinary term of the Onondaga County Supreme Court to supervise it work. An interesting precedent occurred during this interlude. As would happen over a decade later during the asphalt scandals, Tammany Hall came to McGuire's assistance. Despite its often tenacious relationship with McGuire, he was at the time the head of the Democratic State Committee, and a some-time ally of Tammany rival David B. Hill for control of upstate Democrats. Possibly "Boss" Richard Croker thought he was winning McGuire over, or perhaps he sought to forestall any additional investigations of his own activities. Nonetheless, this time it was Assembly Democrat Patrick F. Trainor, who sought to derail the investigation by having his minority report minimizing the impact of McGuire's culpability accepted as the majority committee report. The Republican-controlled Assembly voted it down.[40] The Journal editorials used the Assembly Committee report to castigate the "rottenness" of McGuire's administration, and for inciting "class war" in Syracuse. McGuire defended himself claiming his critics were vengeful Republicans intent on his overthrow, asserting should an official investigation occur, "many fingers would get burned".[41]

After an initial flurry of activity, the issue of McGuire's indictment lay dormant for months, much to the dismay of Syracuse Journal readers and Onondaga Republican leaders – James J. Belden, Frank Hiscock, Francis Hendricks and Horace White.[42] By May, Judge William S. Andrews discharged the Grand Jury because he saw no reason to impanel one given that Governor Theodore Roosevelt appointed New York Supreme Court Justice Wilmot Smith as head of an extraordinary Grand Jury investigation into the city's finances.[43] Mayor McGuire, under oath, was unable to recall many details, but newspaper accounts imply that Frank Matty was the real target. It was rumored that 15 aldermen, the mayor and Commissioner of the Poor Jacob Sehl were to be indicted. McGuire's response was to charge a Republican conspiracy was out to destroy him and ruin his chances for a fourth consecutive term as mayor. He named Republican party boss Frank Hiscock; Francis Hendricks, owner of three banks and the State Superintendent of Insurance who was linked to Republican State "Boss" Thomas Platt in Albany; John S. Kenyon, Secretary of the State Railroad Commission; State Senator Horace White and Austin C. Chase for singling him out for making "small profits" in both insurance and hardware companies, claiming similar charges could be leveled at other municipal officials, such as the Water Commissioner, or members of the Board of Education, the Library Board or the Plumbing Board. John S. Kenyon, party stalwart, in turn defended his Republican colleagues referring to the mayor as a "hypocrite, a sensationalist and a demagogue".[44]

By July, Attorney General John C. Davies was petitioned by

Attorney Francis B. Gill to commence legal action against McGuire for illegally doing business with the city in violation of the White Charter. The deposition listed his ownership of stock in the Syracuse Hardware and Iron Company, his issuance of insurance policies from the firm of McKeough and McGuire, his holding stock in the <u>Evening Telegram</u> which printed the official proceedings of the city and, his ownership of a $100,000 worth of stock in the Syracuse Printing Company which had several contracts with the city.[45] McGuire alleged the charges had been reviewed previously and he was exonerated by a vote of 18-4. The Mayor cleverly fought back claiming that Merchants Bank earned $5,000 annually doing city business. Interestingly, the counsel for Merchants Bank was Ceylon Lewis, the attorney who initially bought the charges against McGuire. The charges against Controller Adolph Manz were dropped since he had been ordered to pay bills by city Counsel Melvin Z. Haven. It was also found McGuire had not been involved in the Syracuse Printing Company and the Syracuse Hardware and Iron Company since 1900, that insurance policies went directly through the United States Guarantee and Fidelity Company of Maryland for which affidavits were supplied.

Interestingly, the Republican Superintendent of Insurance, Francis Hendricks, used his political influence to prevent the indictments of McGuire and the aldermen from reaching the Attorney General, convincing the new Republican Governor Benjamin B. Odell, Jr. the proper venue for legal action was the Onondaga County District Attorney's office. At the time its incumbent was Republican Jay Kline. McGuire loudly claimed it was malicious prosecution, the charges against him having been dismissed by previous Governor Theodore Roosevelt and Judge Wilmot Smith. This ended attorney Ceylon Lewis' ties to the case, extricating him and Merchants Bank from any taint of political revenge. Governor Odell asserted should Kline refuse to take up the McGuire case, he would pursue it nonetheless, even though he did not want the State underwriting the costs of a special counsel for an issue that was best served at the local level. McGuire's fiery retorts brought criticism from Common Councilor

Frank Matty who believed such vitriole hurt the chances of aldermen who were also indicted.⁴⁶ After much political wrangling; the charges against McGuire were dropped.⁴⁷

There may be some truth to McGuire's contention of a Republican conspiracy. The <u>Syracuse Herald said</u> as much, referring to the charges as "trivial, especially in lieu of the prior investigations which went nowhere". The article further stated it was a plot by his enemies to break him and his reputation, the work of "partisan ghouls carrying politics to extreme lengths".⁴⁸

The vendetta was continued by his Republican enemies. McGuire was distracted by Democratic state politics, his gubernatorial bid having been sabotaged by Richard Croker and David B. Hill. Meanwhile there was the problem of obtaining a budget for Syracuse, approval of which required 15 votes on the city council. McGuire obtained only 12 of 19 but proceeded as if it was legally adopted. The Republicans led by Hiscock charged the budget was in excess of what was allowed under the White Charter and sued to keep the budget to a maximum of $1,167,000.⁴⁹ McGuire referred to the charges as "cowardly politics of the Hendricks machine" since Republican predecessors Kirk and Andrews had left deficiencies as well. McGuire claimed a minimum $1,500,000 was necessary to function effectively, without which government services would be curtailed.⁵⁰ A legal ruling by Judge Frank Hiscock declared the budget was illegally adopted forcing the common council to limit it $1,524,935.⁵¹ Much of the struggle was overshadowed by state and national elections. Both McGuire and David B. Hill, loyal party men, came out strongly for William J. Bryan. This may have signaled a rapprochement between the two, since they had been divided over the silver issue. By 1900, McGuire had apparently retreated from his endorsement of silver but stubbornly clung to his ambition of state-wide political office.⁵² Apparently both Hill and McGuire were allies of convenience; the goal uniting them was an effort to keep downstate Tammany from gaining control of upstate. This effort to prevent a takeover was supported in both editorials and cartoons in the <u>Syracuse Herald</u>.⁵³

Given the criticism he faced, as early as December 1900 he began playing the coy candidate, asserting he would not run again, putting forward the names of several alternatives.[54] Despite the dynamics of intra-party strife, it was economics – particularly the looming deficit and the machinations of the Republicans at the local and state level which destroyed McGuire's public service career.

As noted previously, McGuire's claim of a minimum budget of $1.5 million was the basis of considerable opposition. The mayor claimed there could be no reductions, given the increased costs of public services and debt service.[55] Led by aldermen Frank Matty and Republicans Regan and Mack, some members of the common council sought to place the entire $400,000 deficit in the current budget which would balloon the tax rate. This was the seed of McGuire's undoing; the deficiency was the focus of editorials and articles in the papers in the ensuing months. In March, the Common Council reversed itself. Bonds would be issued for the full amount, listed by Controller Adolph Manz at $402,379 and paid out in five installments so it would not impose any onerous tax burden on the city's property owners. A bill pending in the legislature, sponsored by Republican Senator Horace White of the Cities Committee, sought to have the entire $400,000 put on the tax roles and be paid off in one year. McGuire astutely called it "a Republican outrage" in order to have the Republican machine carry the city in the next election. The deficit covered municipal debts dating back a dozen years. McGuire claimed "the Hendricks gang want[ed] to break the Democrats", reiterating his vetoes on numerous expenditures, saved the city thousands of dollars.[56] In McGuire's absence, City Counsel Melvin Z. Haven appeared before the Governor claiming the deficiency bill unconstitutional, later stating he believed the Governor would not sign it. The bill passed and Haven was forced to bring suit to nullify it. The claim to unconstitutionality was the bill's illegal delegation of powers from city commissioners to the legislature.[57] The court rejected Haven's claim so the entire $400,000 deficit was put into the municipal budget, a move the <u>Herald</u> once again denounced as "a folly expedient…with taxpayers being used as pawns in a selfish political game", calling the Republican machine the same "arrogant", blundering oligarchy it was years ago".[58]

The Democrats abandoned their attempt to keep the deficit out of the budget by July 1901, about the time there was increasing pressure on McGuire to declare himself a candidate,[59] yet he continued to distance himself from a bid for a fourth term. Positioning himself for a later run, he watched the Republican machine embarrass itself scrambling to find an acceptable candidate, initially sabotaging District Attorney Jay Kline's effort,[60] encouraging M. E. Driscoll to run.[61] But like McGuire's first effort, Kline was aggressively campaigning without machine support.[62]

The deficiency of 1899, after an extensive audit, was found to be $314,000 which resulted in a tax rate of $21.30, an amount considered excessive for a city the size of Syracuse. This was the issue Republican would use to club the Democrats during the campaign.[63] Both parties had no endorsed candidate as late as September.[64] The issue was resolved when both parties chose their leading candidates. Republicans gave Jay B. Kline the nod; Democrats selected incumbent James K. McGuire.[65] Immediately following their selection, the campaign went into full swing. McGuire fought to defend his record. He tried to shift blame for the deficit on others – the Water Board having to borrow $40,000 for interest due on bonds, for pairing contracts let prior to his administration; for increased costs in sanitation. He claimed the Common Council was at fault, spending lavishly despite his attempt to limit it by vetoing proposals, which were often over-ridden. McGuire responded to Republican assaults by acknowledging problems of the past, but claimed his previous Controllers for the problems. There were no deficiencies since the current incumbent Adolph Manz was in charge. He claimed his was an administration of progress, the Republicans one of stagnation. A brochure listed his accomplishments – more schools, students, firehouses, policemen, electricity – all done while maintaining a "relatively low" tax rate. McGuire claimed his Republican opponents charged him with an excessive salary list, yet many were the creation of the White Charter, a product of Republican State Senator Horace

White.⁶⁶ To Kline's charges of an inflated salary structure, McGuire noted how Kline's salary had been increased from $2000 to $5500 annually. As to inefficiencies, the Mayor claimed that for his salary increase of 250 percent, the number of prosecutions of his office had decreased and he had not filed reports for the last two years as required by the Board of Supervisors. McGuire was especially vitriolic as to Kline's role in issuing the indictments against him and the aldermen, yet was now running on the same ticket as those he indicted.⁶⁷ Admitting increased expenditures, McGuire claimed significant urban improvements, that "living in a high-class city" was worth the cost.⁶⁸

Kline simply attacked McGuire's budget, claiming the city could be run well on $1,350,000. He condemned waste, corruption in various public service departments. He also finally managed to obtain verbal support from the Republican machine, although the promised funds were not forthcoming. He alleged the Democrats had ample money because they "squeezed" city employees for contributions. At a large public rally, Congressman M. E. Driscoll lambasted the McGuire administration, particularly City Counsel Haven and the excessive tax rate. What Kline was unable to do, was demonstrate where he could reduce the budget by $210,000. As a man who sought the office of mayor for over eight months, the <u>Herald</u> noted, he was not able to come up with a plan, nor did he give one throughout the campaign.⁶⁹

One prominent supporter of McGuire was George W. Driscoll, a long-time Democrat and brother and law partner of Congressman Michael E. Driscoll, the outspoken critic of the mayor⁷⁰. He supported McGuire because he believed Kline unable to control the swarm of hungry office holders. The only issue keeping Republicans together was the common goal of ousting McGuire. Driscoll condemned the Republican machine for everything "low and corrupt" in the campaign. He prophesied if such men regained power, Syracuse would decline as a city. He further condemned Kline as a hypocrite, running for office on a ticket with men he had indicted two years previously.⁷¹

On the eve of the election, the campaign became more disorderly, with hecklers disrupting speakers, carrying away the oppositions' banners.[72] In addition, an editorial in the Journal condemned an editorial in the Republican Post-Standard laying two criminal charges on the Mayor – that he purchased corruptible voters for the election, and that he used his office for political gain. The Journal noted how the Post-Standard had previously praised McGuire as an "honest man". The Post further claimed life under Tammany Hall was almost virtuous compared to Syracuse under McGuire. The Journal demanded proof of the charges, because, if false they were libelous. If corruption in voting occurred, it was the job of the District Attorney to prosecute the offenders. It was astounding, that since the District Attorney was aware of the charges, no prosecutions had occurred. The Herald having investigated McGuire's personal finances found him never to have benefitted personally from any franchise, contract or bid. And the letter purporting to know of McGuire's campaign paying $15 per vote was proven to be a forgery. The Herald went on to level charges of its own, claiming Republicans had brought in numerous floaters from the "criminal classes" – rape fiends, burglars, thugs, thieves, pickpockets and scurvy lawbreakers" – all under indictment who District Attorney Kline released on bail. The Herald article concluded: "[The Republicans] are dragging the dives and gutters for votes."[73] A McGuire campaign advertisement echoed the charge: Kline was weak, loose, defiant of decency, supported by thugs, fences and riffraff. It urged voters to smash Kline, save little girls, orphans [from evil], save property owners from burglars. McGuire, claiming the moral high ground asserted his campaign was that of "Decency vs. Deviltry".[74]

Kline claimed McGuire imported hordes of hoodlums, one group of which attacked him with stones as he was to address a campaign rally. The Herald endorsed the re-election of McGuire, saying he had lifted the city out of a rut and calling Kline a "weakling candidate" controlled by the Hendricks machine.[75] McGuire was considered the favorite in the balloting but he and other Democrats came up short, Republicans winning the city, the county and a majority on the Common Council. McGuire was graceful in defeat, announcing his retirement from public office.[76] He would move full-time into the private sector but scandal would follow in his wake within a decade. It revolved around asphalt paving contracts, something of which he had inside knowledge as mayor. Only in the interim, McGuire did a complete turn-about, this time not fighting against the "Asphalt Trust", but advocating for it.

Notes

1 "Address.". Common Council Manual Of the City of Syracuse, 1896. (Syracuse: E. M. Grover, 1896), 44-57.
2 "Looking for Gore". Syracuse Journal 11 May 1896:5.
3 "Offices Created". Syracuse Journal 18 May 1896:8.
4 "McGuire's Interview". Syracuse Journal 19 May 1896:6. McGuire complained, that when he ran for mayor the Journal had criticized him as a "radical and a Hibernian". "Park Employees". Syracuse Journal 21 May 1896:6.
5 "They Are Filed Now". Syracuse Journal 16 February 1897:6; "Building Fences". Syracuse Journal 18 February 1897:6; "Belden And Matty". Syracuse Journal 23 February 1897;6.
6 "Mayor's Politics". Syracuse Journal 3 May 1897:6; "Mayor's Charges". Syracuse Journal 4 May 1897:6; "He Won't Get Out". Syracuse Journal 4 May 1897:6; "Now Who's Who?" Syracuse Journal 5 May 1897:6; "A Stay On Salary". Syracuse Journal 19 May 1897:6.
7 "Syracuse City Hall Ring". Municipal Government (January 1897) 8:9-11; See "An Adv[sic][For The City". Syracuse Journal 19 January 1897:6. Ironically, the Municipal Government article praised Jay Kline as a reformer and an enemy of corruption. It would be Kline's campaign issues against McGuire when the latter ran for mayor for a fourth term in 1901.
8 "Mayor's Circular". Post-Standard 30 June 1898.
9 The Syracuse Journal was vitriolic in its condemnation of McGuire. McGuire had been sued for $10,000 by a patronage appointee of Matty, but (since he and Matty were now allied) the lawsuit was dropped. Such machinations were critiques as part of the mayor's "deceitful nature". See "McGuireism". Syracuse Journal 8 July 1897:6.
10 "It Was A Landslide". Syracuse Journal 3 November 1897:6.
11 "Dunfee Is Named". Syracuse Journal 19 November 1897:6; "Deals With Deals". Syracuse Journal 6 December 1897:6;
12 The Republicans, after a month's delay chose George Metz. "Lively Balloting But No Choice". Syracuse Journal 23 April 1899:7; "George Metz, City Clerk". Syracuse Journal 9 May 1899:6. Haven was later made City Counsel.
13 "The Herald Then And Now". Syracuse Herald 1 November 1899:3.
14 "Army of Men Discharged From Water Department". Syracuse Journal 13 January 1900:5.
15 "Must Have Pull With Mayor McGuire". Syracuse Journal 29 June 1900:1; "A Farce". Syracuse Journal 16 March 1898:6; "Make A Poor Case". Syracuse Journal 17 March 1898:6. The Library's Boards' choice was a graduate of Wellesly and a former teacher. The other candidates had backgrounds as clerks, attended high school, and one had attended Syracuse University.

"More Of A Farce". Syracuse Journal 19 March 1898:6; "Mayor McGuire's Bundle of Christmas Gifts". Syracuse Journal 22 December 1899:5; "Why McGuire Gave Out Appointments". Syracuse Journal 27 June 1900:5;.

16 "Editorial: Civil Service Methods". Syracuse Journal 28 June 1900:2.

17 "Democracy Dissatisfied". Syracuse Journal 19 August 1899:6.

18 "Mayor's Plan". Syracuse Journal 17 January 1898:6.

19 "New High School". Syracuse Journal 25 February 1898:6.

20 Undated Letter, James K. McGuire File. Onondaga County Historical Association.

21 "Obituary"., James K. McGuire File, Onondaga County Historical Association. Undated.

22 "Mayor And His Rule". Syracuse Journal 11 June 1897:6. The Charles M. McGuire Insurance Company was controlled by the mayor's brother.

23 "Sidetracked". Syracuse Journal 8 June 1899:1.

24 "McGuire's Insurance". Syracuse Journal 23 October 1899:6.

25 "Funds Juggled Any Old Way". Syracuse Journal 12 October 1899:6.

26 "McGuire's Private Snags". Syracuse Journal 21 October 1899:6; "Lampwich Charge". Syracuse Journal 26 October 1899:6.

27 "Facts About Lawn Mowers". Syracuse Journal 28 October 1899:6; "Bargains In Lawn Mowers". Syracuse Journal 31 October 1899:4; "More Hardware Prices". Syracuse Journal 31 October 1899:5; "Lawn Mowers In Winter". Syracuse Journal 4 November 1899:3; "Resigns". Syracuse Journal 17 January 1900:5.

28 "McGuire Tax Dodger". Syracuse Journal 1 November 1899:8.

29 "Fraud And Corruption". Syracuse Journal 31 October 1899:6; "Astounding" Syracuse Journal 1 November 1899:6; "McGuire's Myths" Syracuse Journal 2 November 1899:5; "Desperate Fake of Discredited and Defeated McGuireites". Syracuse Journal 3 November 1899:4; "A Bold Fake". Syracuse Journal 3 November 1899:4; "Fraud Upon Fraud". Syracuse Journal 4 November 1899:4.

30 "Just Correct". Syracuse Journal 11 May 1896:5.

31 "The Mayor's Harangue". Syracuse Journal 5 June 1897:5.

32 "How Is This?" Syracuse Journal 12 June 1897:5; "The City's Books". Syracuse Journal 10 August 1897:6.

33 "A Chapter of Local History". Syracuse Journal 21 January 1898:6; "McGuire Admit's It". Syracuse Journal 1 March 1898:6; "Mayor Won't Sign". Syracuse Journal 2 March 1898:6; "The City Scandal". Syracuse Journal 3 March 1898:5; "Of Public Interest". Syracuse Journal 5 March 1898:6; "Allen's Statement". Syracuse Journal 8 March 1898:6; "City Officials Severely Criticized". Syracuse Journal 26 July 1898:6; "Mayor's Great Deficit". Syracuse Journal 7 September 1898:6; "Juggling City Budget". Syracuse

Journal 13 September 1898:7; "City Finances Badly Depleted". Syracuse Journal 12 November 1898:6.

34 "Mayor McGuire's Latest Move". Syracuse Journal 3 March 1899:6; "Why Not Open City Books?" Syracuse Journal 8 April 1899:6; "City Books To Be Examined". Syracuse Journal 16 May 1899:6;

35 "M'Guire Admits Extravagance". Syracuse Journal 13 June 1899:6. The Mayor alleged the major overdrafts were in assistance to poor expenditures. "Mayor M'Guire's Bond Scheme". Syracuse Journal 22 June 1899. The 30 year payback was illegal under the recently passed White Charter. For details on the Butternut Street Riot, see pp.

36 "Bond Resolution Defeated". Syracuse Journal 25 July 1899:8.

37 "Mayor McGuire's Deficiencies". Syracuse Journal 6 September 1899:5; "Slates Made By Democrats". Syracuse Journal 16 September 1899:6; "Won't Pay His Debts". Syracuse Journal 19 September 1899:5; "Funds Juggled Any Old Way". Syracuse Journal 12 October 1899:6; "Republicans Are Confident" Syracuse Journal 18 October 1899:5; "Mayor McGuire's Defiats" Syracuse Journal 21 October 1899:5;

38 "Editorial: Mayor McGuire's Humiliation Statement". Syracuse Journal 23 January 1900:4. Subsequent editorials condemned the size of the deficit, unfavorably comparing Syracuse to other similarly-sized cities in terms of expenditures. "Syracuse Over Albany By More Than $70,000". Syracuse Journal 23 January 1900:6; "City's Deficiency Nearly $400,000". Syracuse Journal 3 February 1900:5. "Editorial: Dionysius The Tyrant And McGuire". Syracuse Journal 16 February 1900:7.

39 "Deficiency Bill Gets Very Hard Rap". Syracuse Journal 21 February 1900:4; "Investigate: Syracuse Journal 22 February 1900:6; "Investigating Committee After Facts, That's All". Syracuse Journal 26 February 1900:5; "Editorial: Mayor McGuire's Opportunity". Syracuse Journal 7 March 1900:4; "Misappropriations of Public Funds". Syracuse Journal 2 March 1900:6; "Queer Facts Learned By Investigations". Syracuse Journal 16 March 1900:5; "Jacob Sehl Very Much Wanted". Syracuse Journal 29 March 1900: 1, 6, 8; "Editorial: What Are Your Going To Do About It?". Syracuse Journal 31 March 1900:4. P.J. Enright, for example was both grading inspector and supervisor of McGuire's white wings sanitation men. Of eleven sprinkling inspectors, it was determined only three did any work. See "Law Was One Thing, Methods Another". Syracuse Journal 31 March 1900:6. There was also the possibility of a conflict of interest in McGuire's appointments. Rev. Ira M. Van Allen was employed by the city as a Sewer Inspector and was also in the employ of a contractor. "Syracuse's Municipal Investigation". New York Times 25 March 1900.

40 "Special Grand Jury To Investigate". Syracuse Journal 5 April 1900:1. Patrick

F. Trainor (1864-1902) was a Scots-born Catholic whose parents immigrated to America. He became a lawyer and a Tammany loyalist serving six terms in the State Assembly. Possibly as a reward for his efforts in the McGuire investigation he was his party's choice for State Senator in 1900, serving one term until his death two years later. "Senator Trainor Dead". <u>New York Times</u> 26 December 1902.

41 "Editorial: Game of Politics". <u>Syracuse Journal</u> 7 April 1900:4; "Editorial: McGuire's Latest Gallery Play". <u>Syracuse Journal</u> 11 April 1900:4; "Editorial: What Next?" <u>Syracuse Journal</u> 14 April 1900:4.

42 See, "Editorial: Who Is Responsible". <u>Syracuse Journal</u> 23 April 1900:4; "Editorial: Let There Be Action". <u>Syracuse Journal</u> 24 April 1900:4. Editorials of April 25, April 26 carried the same theme as well. "Editorial: City Is Safe". <u>Syracuse Journal</u> 7 May 1900:4.

43 "Three Grand Juries Want To Investigate". <u>Syracuse Journal</u> 10 May 1900:6; "Now No Guilty May Escape". <u>Syracuse Journal</u> 31 May 1900. Of those impaneled, five of 21 were Democrats; "Grand Jury's Secrets Have Been Divulged". <u>Syracuse Journal</u> 20 June 1900:6.

44 "Mayor McGuire In Ugly Mood". <u>Syracuse Journal</u> 23 June 1900:6; "John Kenyon Replies To McGuire". <u>Syracuse Journal</u> 25 June 1900:6. Austin C. Chase was President of the Syracuse Chilled Plow Company, a director of the Syracuse Savings Bank and former Postmaster for the city.

45 "Action To Remove Mayor McGuire". <u>Syracuse Herald</u> 16 July 1900:6; "The Case of Mayor McGuire". <u>New York Times</u> 20 July 1900. For a brief biography of Ceylon Lewis see, <u>The American Bar</u>. McGuire was defended by City Counsel Melvin Z. Haven. "Political Persecution". <u>Syracuse Herald</u> 17 July 1900:4. A copy of Gill's deposition can be found typed on index cards in red ink in the James K. McGuire File, Onondaga County Historical Society. The date is 17 July 1900.

46 "In Kline's Hands". <u>Syracuse Herald</u> 18 January 1901:6; "Odell Sarcastic Says McGuire Owes Him No Thanks". <u>Syracuse Herald</u> 23 January 1901:5. "Angry At McGuire". <u>Syracuse Herald</u> 24 January 1901:6. Matty claimed McGuire failed to obtain enough votes to pass the budget. He also claimed he and the other aldermen have no issue with Hendricks even if McGuire did. The political in-fighting was depicted in a <u>Syracuse Herald</u> cartoon of 27 January 1901. Entitled "Shooting In The Air", it portrayed McGuire shooting over crouching aldermen behind a box labeled "alleged conspiracy case". Aldermen were shouting, "Come off, you'll draw their fire".

47 "Manz All Right". <u>Syracuse Herald</u> 20 July 1900:7. "to Be Dismissed". <u>Syracuse Herald</u> 15 August 1900:6. "To Oust Syracuse's Mayor". <u>New York Times</u> 17 July 1900.

48 "Political Persecution". <u>Syracuse Herald</u> 17 July 1900:4.

49 "City Council Fails To Approve Budget". Syracuse Herald 23 September 1900:1; "Will Fight Budget". Syracuse Herald 27 September 1900:6; "May Sue Former Mayor". Syracuse Herald 28 September 1900:1; "McGuire On Litigation". Syracuse Herald 30 September 1900:1.
50 "McGuire On Budget". Syracuse Herald 1 October 1900:2.
51 "Declares It Illegal". Syracuse Herald 9 October 1900:6. "Work Of Budget". Syracuse Herald 15 October 1900:5; "Budget Adopted". Syracuse Herald 24 October 1900:6.
52 "Spoke For Bryan". Syracuse Herald 3 November 1900:9; "McGuire's Views'. Syracuse Herald 8 November 1900:6. David B. Hill wanted Bryan to lose in order to have Tammany Boss Croker shoulder the burden of blame for the Democratic disaster, hence strengthening his efforts to maintain control of upstate Democrats. In addition, it also tarnished upstate rival McGuire, who was, at the time, head of the Democratic State Committee and Campaign Manager for New York State. For more information see political cartoons – "Who Was Told To Mine The State", But Now Is In The State of Mind: McGuire". Syracuse Herald 11 November 1900:5 showed a frustrated McGuire reviewing state election campaign returns. "An Opportunity for Chairman McGuire To Mine His Genius". Syracuse Herald 18 November 1900:1 portrayed a perplexed mayor trying to re-assemble a mule. On 25 November 1900:1 the Syracuse Herald ran a cartoon entitled "He Won't Be Really Thankful Until He Gets It" reveals McGuire, hatchet in hand, approaching a turkey labeled, "Upstate Democratic Leadership". The chance of McGuire obtaining state-wide office were considered minimal at best, given the opposition by both Croker and Hill. See cartoon "What Santa Has For Town's Good Politicians: A-Z". Syracuse Herald 23 December 1900:27. Under "M": McGuire in his head has a germ, what politicians know by the term of governoritis. It's easy to kill unless he gets "glad hands" from Croker and Hill". His chances were poor because he had limited campaign funds and was largely unknown outside Central New York. See cartoon, Syracuse Herald 17 December 1900:1, "The Wizard of The Cue" showing McGuire atop a pool table aiming at the corner pocket labeled political contributions.
53 "Editorial: Hill And Tammany". Syracuse Herald 7 December 1900:4. The editorial praised Hill's efforts to form an upstate Democratic organization to contest Tammany Hall was referred to as "a great service in resistance to Crokerism". In a cartoon, "Aha-The Hour Is Ripe" in the Syracuse Herald 8 December 1900:1, portrayed a David B. Hill, emerging from bed, with a gun in hand. Bells in the background chimed "Tammany Must Go". The new political love-fest between two previous rivals was lampooned in a Syracuse Herald cartoon of 11 February 1901:1. It depicted Hill as a puppet wearing a "sign" May I Be Your Valentine" with McGuire holding the strings.

54 "Not To Run Again". Syracuse Herald 1 December 1900:6. "Mayor's Decision". Syracuse Herald 2 December 1900:1; "McGuire Wants Meagher". Syracuse Herald 1 February 1901:3. Meagher was McGuire's Commissioner of Public Works at the time. A follow-up cartoon in the Syracuse Herald of 3 February 1901:1 entitled, "Draping The Model" pictured Meagher as McGuire's heir apparent. Keeping speculation alive as to his political intentions, as the election drew closer, McGuire mentioned both Daniel Rosenbloom from the Board of Education or John S. Moffitt from the Water Board as possible candidates. "Men For Mayor". Syracuse Herald 5 May 1901:1; "Political Gossip". Syracuse Herald 12 May 1901:1; "Cornwall, Edith". "Interview With Mayor McGuire". Syracuse Herald 19 May 1901:1; "Mayor Under Fire". Syracuse Herald 9 June 1901:1.

55 "City Budget". Syracuse Herald 7 January 1901:6.

56 "Will Talk With White". Syracuse Herald 12 February 1901:1; "Deficiency Again". Syracuse Herald 13 March 1901:4; "Not In Lump". Syracuse Herald 13 March 1901:6. The Syracuse Herald supported McGuire's allegations of a Republican plot. See "Editorial: Double-Edged Sword". Syracuse Herald 18 March 1901:4. See cartoon "Debtortown To Creditville" Syracuse Herald 20 March 1901:1.

57 McGuire at the time was traveling through the Southwest, visiting Las Vegas, Nevada, New Mexico and California. "Heard Before Governor". Syracuse Herald 10 April 1901:6; Cornwall, Edith. "Mel Haven, City Attorney, Gives His Opinion, Legal And Otherwise". Syracuse Herald 14 April 1901:29; "Haven Bring Suit". Syracuse Herald 17 May 1901:6.

58 "Editorial: The Deficiency Again". Syracuse Herald 1 June 1901:4; "Editorial: Worth Considering". Syracuse Herald 26 June 1901:4. The Herald of 26 June 1091:1 re-enforced their comments with a cartoon entitled, "One Who Feels The Blow" depicting the Republican machine hitting a person labeled "Taxpayer". "Editorial: Machine vs. Machine". Syracuse Herald 28 June 1901:4.

59 "Tax Rate About $20". Syracuse Herald 3 July 1901:6. The increased focus on McGuire's political ambitions were featured in numerous cartoons in the Herald. See "Nurses Quarrel And Youngster Get Worst Of It". Syracuse Herald 30 June 1901:1 depicting two nurses quarreling over a wrecked baby carriage labeled "city government". "A Horse May Be Known By The Hat He Wears". Syracuse Herald 7 July 1901:1; "Shadowed", Syracuse Herald 10 July 1901:1 showing McGuire holding a petition labeled "Appeal From The Public For A Fourth Term" "Maneuvering For Position In The Upcoming Municipal Race". Syracuse Herald 14 July 1901:1, "Having Ears, He Hears Not". Syracuse Herald 28 July 1901:1.

60 "Political Gossip". Syracuse Herald 15 April 1901:1. Kline was not part of the

Hendricks machine. It was feared should he obtain the nomination, they would lose control of their current organization and its patronage. In other words, they would be in the same position as Democrats prior to McGuire winning office in 1895. Kline, as District Attorney, was criticized by his own party for not closing down saloons and gambling dens. "Political Gossip". Syracuse Herald 21 April 1901:1. Kline had also spoken out against the Deficiency Bill claiming the city should not be made to suffer from the Republicans also. Cornwall, Edith. "How Jay B. Kline Refused To Talk Politics With Me". Syracuse Herald 21 April 1901:23.

61 "Driscoll's Boom". Syracuse Herald 16 June 1901:1. McGuire ridiculed the Republicans' efforts to obtain a viable nominee, even though he had declared himself a non-candidate. See "Here's An Irish Tip For Hendricks And His Sad Machine Appendix, Straight It Comes From McGuire, Is It Heaping Coals of Fire". Syracuse Herald 11 August 1901:1. It was elaborated two days later in a cartoon entitled, "Jimmy's Shillelagh". Syracuse Herald 13 August 1901:1.

62 "Kline The Only One" Syracuse Herald 26 August 1901:1.

63 "Audit Completed". Syracuse Herald 15 August 1901:6; "Editorial: Tax Rate" Syracuse Herald 26 August 1901:4; "Tax Rate, $21.^{30}". Syracuse Herald 23 September 1901:4; "McGuire On Tax Rate". Syracuse Herald 24 September 1901:7. For an example of its use in a Kline campaign advertisement, see "The Little Homes of Syracuse" which portrayed the homes of toiling men of Syracuse sacrificed to the usurions tax rate of $21.^{30} Syracuse Herald 2 November 1901:7.

64 Editorial: "A Mayoralty Candidate". Syracuse Herald 12 September 1901:4; "It Is Too Early". Syracuse Herald 20 September 1901:6.

65 "Kline Wins Nomination". Syracuse Herald. 10 October 1901:1; "Editorial: Mayor McGuire". Syracuse Herald 11 October 1901:4. The Herald included a series of cartoons of both candidates preceding their respective party's selection. On Kline, see "Kline Racing Ahead of Kline" 10 October 1901:1. Included was a poem: Hooray! Hooray!/In Hustling Jay/The Only Man Living/Who Can Beat James K." For McGuire, he was seen clinging to a tree, being nipped by a donkey. It was entitled, "What Can A Poor Man Do?" 8 October 1901:1.

66 "Advances In Six Years". Syracuse Herald 18 October 1901:13; "In Response To Kline". Syracuse Herald 19 October 1901:7; "Who Is To Blame For This Deficit?" Kline Campaign Advertisement 30 October 1901:7.

67 "Mayor In The Fifth". Syracuse Herald 22 October 1901:10. McGuire, in condemning Kline on the indictments specifically referred to E. J. Mack and Alan Fobes, the latter serving as Foreman of the Grand Jury which served the indictments. "1700 Indictments". Syracuse Herald 29 October 1901:6.

68 Campaign Advertisement. "To The Citizens Of Syracuse". <u>Syracuse Herald</u> 23 October 1901:7; Campaign Advertisement. "To The People". <u>Syracuse Herald</u> 28 October 1901:7.

69 "Kline And Driscoll On The Issues". <u>Syracuse Herald</u> 18 October 1901:12. "Editorial: Lets Have The Facts". <u>Syracuse Herald</u> 19 October 1901:4; "Will Stir It Up". <u>Syracuse Herald</u> 20 October 1901:12. As to assessing employees for contributions, it was a tradition used by the party in power in order to maintain itself. See "Editorial: Political Assessments". <u>Syracuse Herald</u> 21 October 1901:4; "These Are The Facts". <u>Syracuse Herald</u> 30 October 1901:1; "Editorial: Tracking on Kline". <u>Syracuse Herald</u> 30 October 1901:4.

70 "Editorial: Let Us Have The Debate". <u>Syracuse Herald</u> 24 October 1901:4; "M'Guire Willing". <u>Syracuse Herald</u> 24 October 1901:6; "Kline Will Not Debate". <u>Syracuse Herald</u> 26 October 1901:2.

71 "Why He Supports M'Guire". <u>Syracuse Herald</u> 27 October 1901:6. This open endorsement of McGuire in such a hotly contested election may have been the reason for his laudable biography in The Democratic Party In The State of New York James K. McGuire (ed.) (New York: United States History Company, 1905) vol. III, 26-27.

72 "Kline Is Severe, Too". <u>Syracuse Herald</u> 30 October 1901:10.

73 "Editorial: Astounding Charges". <u>Syracuse Herald</u> 1 November 1901:1. The <u>Post-Standard</u> editorial reviewed was entitled "Our Venal Vote". The outside voters was referred to as "tramps", "colonists" or "floaters". Their use was not uncommon in municipal elections.

74 "Mayor Worth $18,000". <u>Syracuse Herald</u> 1 November 1901:6; McGuire Campaign Advertisement, <u>Syracuse Herald</u> 1 November 1901:7; "Tramps Imported". <u>Syracuse Herald</u> 1 November 1901:9. McGuire Campaign Ad. "Decency Against Deviltry". <u>Syracuse Herald</u> 3 November 1901:7.

75 "Editorial: To Independent Voters". <u>Syracuse Herald</u> 2 November 1901:4; "Kline And Machine". <u>Syracuse Herald</u> 2 November 1901:7.

76 "McGuire Is Favorite". <u>Syracuse Journal</u> 3 November 1901:1; "Editorial: Results In Syracuse". <u>Syracuse Journal</u> 6 November 1901:4; "Republicans Make Clean Sweep". <u>Syracuse Journal</u> 6 November 1901:9. McGuire lost by 1435 votes. The <u>Herald</u> writing his obituary in 1923 reported his loss at 700 votes. "James K. McGuire". <u>Syracuse Herald</u> 30 June 1923.

Chapter 1 - d

The Dream Denied:
Failure to Win State-Wide Office

In the decade, between his fight against the Hill faction in 1895 and his massive three-volume history, <u>The Democratic Party of the State of New York</u> in 1905, McGuire become an admirer of his former rival, referring to Hill as the most prominent figure of the State in Democratic politics[1] What events transpired in that decade to turn McGuire around? The answer can only be found in reviewing the events of that decade which saw both men fall from the political grace of Tammany Boss Richard Croker. Like McGuire, Hill began his career as a newsboy, on railroad cars in the Southern Tier. He became a lawyer, entering practice with John Stanchfield, a man who would later become his political rival.[2] During his early term in the state legislature, Hill formed a close relationship with fellow Democratic Samuel Tilden.[3] Like McGuire, Hill was a popular reform mayor of Elmira, New York who was elected lieutenant-Governor in 1882 with Grover Cleveland as Governor. McGuire says Hill was one of the few men who actively sought the nomination as Lieutenant-Governor, it being usually considered a consolation prize for those who failed to obtain more lucrative or more powerful posts.[4] When Cleveland moved on to the Presidency, Hill became Governor. Because he was opposed to civil service reform, Hill was able to obtain support from Tammany Hall and keep its rival Kings County Democracy at bay, in part because he made sure reform measures dealing with affairs in cities, especially New York City, were side-lined.[5] Hill consistently opposed reform measures including a bill to prevent bribery in elections and another establishing the Australian (secret) ballot (The Saxton Bill). In fact, Hill regarded the Saxton Bill as "an unnecessary and mischievous innovation", "a mongrel foreign system" ill-adapted to the American republic. The <u>New York Times</u> reported Governor Hill's justification for vetoing the bill was "laborious and painful", since he benefitted from the current system by "controlling masses of ignorant or subservient voters through the liquor saloons and political "heelers".[6] This was an obvious reference to Hill's Tammany Hall connections. Recall that McGuire was in favor of the secret ballot. In addition, McGuire had spoken out against boss rule, "where every name and move is approved in advance... Minorities must be conciliated and are entitled to representation in Democratic enclaves".[7] Hill, on the state level, like McGuire in Syracuse, had to contend with a legislature controlled by the opposition. The Republicans were in control of both legislative branches, one job of which was to elect Senators to Congress. Direct election of Senators would only come during the Progressive reforms of 1912. Both parties fielded candidates. The results were inevitable. The Republicans defeated the Democrats receiving 19 Senate votes, 73 Assembly votes to the Democrats 13 in the Senate and 52 in the Assembly.[8] The lesson was not lost on Hill. His manipulation of electoral results favorable to his entry into the Senate would create a scandal during his subsequent administration. As McGuire noted, Hill was "an active and conspicuous figure in Democratic politics and was unremitting in his efforts to gather in his own hands all the reins of party government".[9] McGuire would be similarly criticized, albeit on a smaller stage, and with less spectacular results.

Hill easily won renomination for Governor in 1886, but fissures were showing in the Democratic Party, one element supporting reform and Hill leading the opposition. The division in the party was so great that Hill obtained a candidate for Lieutenant-Governor and a campaign manager with great difficulty turning down one nominee and two others, Roswell Flower and Henry W. Slocum,[10] refusing to serve. He won the Governor's chair with both Tammany and Kings County Democracy support by concessions to labor and the Catholic vote. Despite his wins, the Republicans controlled the legislature. Hill installed William F. Sheehan of Erie County as minority speaker.[11] The Governor and the Legislature disputed the methods for enumerating the state census, each party endorsing a formula favorable to its own constituents. Both Republicans and Democrats, in a blatant bid for the Irish vote, passed resolutions condemning the wrongs inflicted by the British on Ireland.[12] Ireland would become increasingly important in the career of James K. McGuire.

The prevailing harmony of the Democratic State Convention was broken over the issue of civil service reform. A compromise was reached whereby the convention agreed to support existing civil service law but rejected the concept of a merit system. Despite a strong showing by Democrats, the Republicans retained control of both houses of the Legislature.

The <u>New York Times</u> condemned Hill's nomination in 1888 stating:

> From such uncleanness as the New York Democracy put upon itself at Buffalo yesterday there is but one purification-the fires of defeat. In nominating David B. Hill for Governor, the Democratic Convention did not merely touch the pitch and pass by with soiled garments, it went boldly into the pool of defilement and wallowed. For the first time, in its history the party entrusted the work of choosing its candidates by its basest members.[13]

Hill's nomination was tainted by the New York aqueduct scandals. In 1883 New York City constructed an aqueduct to obtain water from Croton Lake, thirty miles north. Five years later, rumors were rife of irregularities in the awarding of contracts. An investigation was launched by Thomas Platt, Republican boss and rival to Tammany Boss Richard Croker and David B. Hill. Platt's front man to head the investigation was J. Sloat Facett, who confirmed many of the suspicions about the project. Mirroring McGuire's political maneuvers, contracts were often awarded to firms that were not the lowest bidders. This was linked to a second scandal. One of the companies which benefitted from these inflated awards, Clark and O'Brien, had apparently paid off Democratic campaign expenses. The head of the Democratic State Committee during Hill's 1885 gubernatorial campaign was John O'Brien, President of Clark and O'Brien.[14] While some of the facts may be in dispute, it was an obstacle Hill had to overcome in order to win a second full term as governor. Like McGuire's mayoralty successes, Hill's was due to a divided Republican party and a united Democratic party, bringing upstate and downstate groups together. In addition, Hill won the governorship once again with support of liquor dealers despite the fact that Cleveland lost the state and the Presidency. Cleveland's loss was blamed on Hill's close alliance with Tammany Hall, both of which opposed civil service reform. It widened the breach between Hill McGuire and Cleveland. McGuire attributed Cleveland's defeat to Republican distortion of Cleveland's message of tariff reform and to the incredulity of the voting public. [15]

Hill, by seizing control of local organizations, was able to dominate 26 of 34 state committeemen and was aiming at consolidating power in a bid for the Presidency by moving into the Senate.[16] By 1890, Hill had acquired a reputation as a successful political strategist, had brought the Democrat's divergent factions together and was a successful two-term Governor. This time Hill, who had to previously fight a Republican-controlled Legislature now had a Democratic majority. The win gave Democrats a chance to select a Senator. In addition, it would increase Hill's standing nation-wide. The Democrats had won the Assembly and sought a majority in the Senate, so they could choose the new federal Senator. The selection of the nominee was Hills. The alternative to his own candidacy was one who could not obtain Tammany support. Hill chose himself, eyeing the Senate seat as a convenient stepping stone to the Presidency, if not in 1892, than possibly four years later. It was one of several factors that led to his downfall. He held two political offices until December, 1891-Senator and Governor, using the latter to ensure the State party was under his control to reinforce his presidential bid in 1892.[17]

While Governor, Hill's blatant attempt to retain political control of the party resulted in the "most striking abuse of election machinery since 1792," in which the Republican votes of several counties were thrown out on technicalities. When the Republican County Clerk refused to certify the fraudulent returns in Dutchess County, he was removed and replaced by a pliable Democrat, John Mylod. This incident is more aptly called, "The Steal of the Senate".[18] The dispute ended up in the courts, with the Democrats obtaining control of the

Senate, 17-15. Ultimately it was found the Deputy Attorney-General, Isaac Maynard, had been guilty of taking documents from a public official to permit a fake canvass of votes resulting in a fraudulent majority for his party in the State Senate.[19]

Hill's aggressive pursuit of the United States Senate, and his role in the Mylod decision were all damaging blows to his Presidential aspirations. A third issue which undermined his goal, was the "snap convention" of 1892. Its goal was to ensure a solid New York delegation for David Hill as President.

As Senator, Hill became familiar with and popular among Southern legislators. Believing with their support and with his own machine in New York State, he could win the presidential nomination, Hill convened the "Snap Convention" in 1892. It was called early in February, the usual time being later in the Spring. The Cleveland (Reformist) wing of the party claimed it did not have fair representation.

The convention delegates were instructed to nominate David B. Hill as President, as a "Democrat who had led his party from victory to victory for seven successive years and has never known defeat". Cleveland Democrats had their own convention in Albany. As a result of the schism, and due to his declining popularity among Southerners who had their own "favorite son", Hill was never a serious contender. Tammany was hostile to Cleveland using its eloquent spokesman, W. Bourke Cochran, to try to stem the tide to no avail. The resultant protest injured Hill's plans for the Presidential nomination and Cleveland was selected. The defeat in Chicago left Hill a bitter and disappointed man but after nursing his wounds, he campaigned for Cleveland.[20] At the time of the controversy, James K. McGuire had proclaimed his allegiance to the reformist/Cleveland wing of the Democratic Party,[21] bringing him into conflict with David B. Hill. Both the reelection of Maynard as Judge of The Court of Appeals and the means by which he obtained his original appointment were key issues for the Democrats in 1893. A large contingent of "Anti-snappers" tried to make their resistance known but Hill and Croker were in command. One protestor against Maynard's nomination,

Robert Weiderman, declared: "His act was a crime and if it was to be rewarded it has been rewarded enough". He was not allowed to finish his speech. Thomas F. Grady stated: "He stood by us and it is for us to stand by him." Maynard was nominated by acclamation, with only one vote cast against him.[22] The obvious lesson was the importance of party loyalty to the spoils system. It was a lesson James K. McGuire learned well during his multiple terms as Mayor of Syracuse.

Hill also alienated the reformist wing of the Democratic Party by using his position on the Senate Judiciary Committee to twice block President Grover Cleveland's nominees to the Supreme Court. Both men were reformers who had taken prominent roles condemning Hill's actions in the Maynard decision.[23] Maynard was the issue in the elections of 1894 and it destroyed the political career of David B. Hill. At the same time, James K. McGuire was beginning to actively move into Onondaga County and Syracuse City politics. The man chosen by the Democrats to succeed Hill as Governor was Roswell P. Flower. James K. McGuire was beside himself in his praise:

"The confidence of the people in Mr. Flower, his widespread and justly deserved personal popularity, his notable official record and invaluable party service, combined to create an almost universal demand that he should be the nominee for Governor in 1891. To this command the convention bowed, and with practical unanimity he was declared his party's choice".[24] In fact, the decision was made by Tammany Boss Croker, William Sheehan, a Hill ally and later a Tammany stalwart, Speaker of the State Assembly and a power in the Erie county Irish Democratic machine, and Edward Murphy, Jr. Murphy was the son of Irish immigrants who established a successful brewery in Troy, New York, was a Fordham graduate, Democratic leader for Renssalaer county, leader of the State Committee and a United States Senator.[25] Although Flower was not his first choice, Hill assented because Sheehan an upstate Democrat, would be Lieutenant Governor.[26]

Flower was a Democratic party loyalist, whose marriage to the daughter of a successful businessman made his later business ventures profitable. Prior to his tenure as governor, Flower had been a rival to Grover Cleveland, both for President and for Governor, instead being elected to Congress.[27] Flower sternly handled striking railroad workers in New York in 1892, calling out the National Guard to suppress them.[28] For one who portrayed himself as a champion of the worker, McGuire makes no mention of the brutality used in containing the strike, noting only the troops had done their work well, applauding Flower's "courage and resolution."[29] A series of events during Flower's administration compelled the party to replace him as gubernatorial nominee in 1894 – the Maynard scandals, the perception that he was Hill's puppet, the Lexow Commission investigating the degree of political corruption in New York City, the Panic of 1893, and the schism within the Democratic party over the silver issue. In addition, Flower was unwilling to run. McGuire astutely assessed the party's plight. The Democratic Party at state and national levels was in a shambles…. "laying supine and had lost its wonted energy and hope".[30] Hill as Chairman of the State Democratic convention in Saratoga, "chose a slate of lambs to be led to certain slaughter at the polls". Hill sought to rebuild its fortunes by making concessions to the reformist wing of the party, but he was opposed in this by Tammany leader Croker and Brooklyn leader McLaughlin. Hill was nominated for Governor, despite his own opposition.[31] McGuire accurately described Hill as acceding to the wishes of the convention given his loyalty to the Party. Even in his acceptance speech, Hill expressed regret over his nomination and his failure to heal and harmonize the factions within the party. "Recollecting that the Democratic Party has honored me in the past when I solicited its favors, in the days of its sunshine and prosperity, I cannot desert it now in the hour of its danger and this great emergency".[32] Hill's past worked against him. "He knew it was a sacrifice and he made it".[33] The Republicans chose Levi Morton as their candidate. Merchant, banker, Congressman, diplomat and former Vice President of the United States in 1888, Morton was a popular anti-silver advocate.[34] The Democrats, identified with scandals in both New York City and by Hill's maneuver's, lost heavily. Croker left the city for his

Irish estate, returning three years later to supervise the election of the first mayor of Greater New York.

McGuire did not endear himself to either Hill or Croker by critical comments as to boss rule. In particular, he singled out Hill for his role in the Mylod decision.

A good healthy opposition within the party before the convention is a good thing on election day. The voters are growing distrustful of conventions and primaries, where every name and move is prepared in advance and the cut-and-dried tickets no longer carry the day when voting time comes. I believe that every important element and faction should be represented in Democratic committees and conventions… Minorities must be conciliated and are entitled to representation in Democratic enclaves. If my memory serves me rightly, but one voice was heard against Judge Maynard and one delegate was unceremoniously bowled down. But election day demonstrated that if the protest of this one delegate had been heeded, New York would have remained in the Democratic column.[35]

Ironically, McGuire would soon find himself linked to Hill in the latter's machinations to dominate State politics. This was the world of Democratic state politics which James K. McGuire was about to enter. By then, he had already been elected to municipal office and after two terms as Mayor, he was eyeing the governor's chair. His plans were derailed because he alienated two major players in Democratic state politics – upstate leader David B. Hill and Tammany Boss Richard Croker, neither of whom wanted a strong upstate rival to wreak havoc with their plans.

Now a force in state politics, McGuire used his new power to second the nomination of William Sulzer for Governor in 1896.[36] The Democratic Party was divided between gold and silver factions. Sulzer was at the time a Tammany loyalist and a member of the State Assembly, having the honor of being elected its youngest speaker. Leading the anti-silver faction was David B. Hill, whose efforts at limiting the party's endorsement of a silver plank were a failure. The Democrats backed William Jennings Bryan. On the state level, Hill and Tammany both opposed the silver issue, but "with perfectly frank cynicism", supported Bryan and the Chicago platform, producing a split in the party at the State level.[37]

McGuire plunged into the Bryan campaign, speaking for free silver as fervently as he did for low tariffs. He was an ardent supporter of Bryan.[38] This, plus his reformist image, may have been factors widening the breach between Hill and McGuire. For example, McGuire acknowledged that he was the only delegate at the 1892 convention who supported Cleveland, all others were solidly behind David B. Hill.[39] The elections of 1896 were a disaster for the Democrats at the State and national levels. Two years later, after having won re-election as Mayor of Syracuse, James K. McGuire attempted to win his party's nomination for Governor. McGuire wanted the gubernatorial nomination in 1898. He had proven his political mettle, winning re-election as Mayor of Syracuse in 1897, despite the Republicans landslide of the previous year.

McGuire initially portrayed himself as a reformer. The Syracuse Journal called him a "social revolutionist" whose "radical positions alienated even some Democrats". During his honeymoon, McGuire had attended the Democratic Convention in Chicago. McGuire openly supported Bryan whose silver position was an anathema to both David B. Hill and Grover Cleveland. McGuire also endorsed the pro-labor politics of Illinois Governor John P. Altgeld, whose pardoning of four men convicted of murder in the Haymarket Square riot was extremely controversial. Altgeld protested the use of federal troops in the Pullman Strike of 1894, and, like McGuire, Altgeld was a silver Democrat. The Syracuse Journal concluded, "we are sorry the young mayor had his head turned by wild theories of western populists".[40] Subsequent articles in the Journal referred to McGuire, because of his open endorsement of William J. Bryan as a "member of the Populist branch of the Democratic party", tarnishing him with the anarchist label and implying he was inciting class war. McGuire simply argued he was anti-imperialist and anti-trusts.[41] As a result of his electoral victory, McGuire controlled both the Syracuse and the Onondaga County Democratic Party which made him a force in state politics. McGuire had begun his campaign for Governor in 1897 by selective leaks to the media and by making popular appearances. For example, John F. Gaynor, an Onondaga County Democrat, stated his county's support for McGuire's gubernatorial bid. "The Democrats are going to elect the next Governor. If Syracuse has her way, McGuire will be the man".[41] He was wrong on both counts. McGuire had recently been elected to a second term as mayor and had become a new member of the Board of Trustees of the Catholic Club, a group that sponsored lectures on a variety of topics of civic interest.[42] Aware of the changing diversity of Syracuse, McGuire astutely courted the ethnic vote. For example, although listed on the program as "I. K. McGuire" [sic] he was present at the dedication of Hebrew Free School in 1897.[43]

McGuire was always careful to play the humble people's candidate, attributing his wins to a popular groundswell of opposition to "machine politics as usual". For example, in a speech celebrating his second win as mayor in 1897, McGuire noted:

His administration pleased the people, however, who admired his courage, as well as his ability and his activity, and in 1897 at the close of his term, the Democratic City Convention gave him a unanimous nomination. The Republicans had taken the alarm by this time, recognizing that they had no ordinary antagonist to deal with, so they changed their tactics, relegated their party hacks to the rear and nominated a reputable businessman against him. It was all to no avail, however, it had proved so refreshing to the voters to see a man of independence and pluck at the head of municipal government, that McGuire again covered the city by a sweeping majority.[44]

Unlike many white candidates for political office at the time, McGuire campaigned openly for the black vote. For example, McGuire was known to have clambered onto the hot asphalt to shake hands with a black laborer who was laying pavement for him. In fact, McGuire was keynote speaker at the state convention of the United "Colored" Democracy in October, 1898. Its leader, Edward E. Lee was known as the "black" Croker because of the numerous patronage jobs the Tammany boss had distributed in return for the 42,000 black votes Lee was able to deliver on election day. McGuire noted how blacks were avid supporters of the Democratic Party and how he as mayor had recognized "colored" people who in turn had twice supported him in his bid for mayor. A key order of business was the passing of a resolution extolling the bravery of "Negro" troops during the Spanish-American War and denouncing their inferior treatment by the War Department. This was no doubt a retort to aspiring Republican gubernatorial candidate Theodore Roosevelt's racist comments concerning black troops during the Spanish-American War.[45]

Long after he abandoned politics and Syracuse, his image as champion of the downtrodden persisted. His obituaries make constant references to him as "a true Social Democrat". At his funeral mass, common laborers in overalls and hob-nailed boots were in attendance along with the rich and powerful.[46] McGuire apparently nursed his image of humble public servant, distributing quarters to the unfortunates of the city from his meager salary reportedly even marrying a young couple, dispensing with the customary $5 fee. On New Year's Day 1899, he hosted a dinner for 3500 children. When called to address the group, he credited its success to merchants, waitresses and laborers, admonishing the children, "as the advance guard of Syracuse, the future of the city is in your hands – be kind to animals, do good to your mother, be faithful to your teachers, study hard, keep good company and come home early".[47] McGuire continued to appeal to "the people" throughout his terms as mayor, In 1899, he held a family picnic for 6000 people at Kirk Park. Campaigning in Geddes in November 1899, McGuire handed out pennies and lozenges to the crowd. One yelled out, "T'ree cheers for Jimesy Maguires".[48] In looking at his political track record, we see in McGuire a kind of political ambivalence necessitated by politics. He exacted concessions from recalcitrant businessmen and politicians where he could, made inter- and intra-party alliances as necessity demanded and ultimately may have been ensnared by the corruption of those who surrounded and may have influenced him. Three such persons where Democrats David B. Hill, Frank Matty and Republican James. J. Belden.

With Hill's forces in disarray, and with the local Republicans divided, James McGuire saw an opportunity to move more effectively into politics in the early 1890's, serving as delegate to the Democratic State Conventions and initially showing himself as a populist reformer and leader of the anti-Hill faction in upstate Democratic politics.[49]

McGuire was critical of boss rule and like his later political rival, Thomas Ryan,[50] urged party unity in the face of common obstacles. McGuire had already acquired a reputation for eloquence. His speaking tours of behalf of Grover Cleveland won him a chance at the consular service which he declined.[51] He continued his activities on behalf of Democratic candidates by contributing articles and making speeches throughout the State, stumping for the Roswell Flower/William Sheehan ticket. He made speeches in Ohio and elsewhere endorsing the Cleveland/Stevenson ticket. Two years later, McGuire took an active part on behalf of David B. Hill's unsuccessful campaign.[52] In Syracuse, the local Republican Party was bitterly divided between Francis Hendricks and James Belden. Hendricks, despite limited formal schooling, was a successful businessman, banker, former two-time mayor of Syracuse, a state legislator and Collector of Customs for the Port of New York under the Harrison administration. The chapel at Syracuse University was a gift of his estate. He was, under Governor Theodore Roosevelt, the State Superintendent of Insurance.[53]

Syracuse politics were a microcosm of events on the state level, reflecting a resentment over "bossism", whether that of Democratic David B. Hill or that of Republican Thomas C. Platt, both of whom shared two traits; a vitriolic hatred of reformers from within and without their respective parties, and; a belief that the ultimate political sin was disloyalty to the party.

McGuire's predecessor as Mayor, Jacob Amos, revealed the political divisions within Syracuse Republicans. Amos was a prominent Republican businessman who inherited, expanded and sold his father's flour milling business, moving into banking, transportation, paving, coal and plaster.[54] His first election as mayor in 1892 was the result of a united Republican Party antagonistic to the dictates of Democratic

Boss and Governor, David B. Hill. Hill's Syracuse representative, William Kirk, had selected George Penn, a local businessman, who was soundly defeated. Amos' second victory in 1894 was over Jay B. Kline, a Republican candidate of the Belden faction and Duncan Peck, the Democratic candidate. Peck, a lifelong Syracusan, had been an unsuccessful candidate for mayor and state legislature. He became Commissioner of Public Safety during McGuire's third term as mayor. A dozen years later he linked McGuire to the scandals associated with the Asphalt Trust. Amos' victory was perceived as a repudiation of "bossism" of State Republican leader Platt and his agent, James Belden.[55] Apparently Amos' victory was engineered by reformist elements within the Republican party led by Francis Hendricks. Hendricks was aided in his efforts by Howard G. White, wealthy businessman, stockbreeder, former member of the State Assembly and owner of the Syracuse Standard. An additional ally was Frank Hiscock, former Onondaga County District Attorney and Senator. An important journalist on Amos' side was Carroll E. Smith, owner and editor of the Syracuse Journal, former county clerk and state assemblyman.[56] The local, state and national impetus for reform against "bossism", as well as the factionalism within the major parties had a profound impact on the political fortunes of James K. McGuire.

James Belden was a successful banker, newspaper owner, and former two-term mayor of Syracuse. He was elected to replace Frank Hiscock and served as Congressman for four terms, 1887-1895. His estate bequeathed monies to help establish a Hospital For Women and Children in Syracuse. Belden apparently became wealthy as result of his fraudulent dealings with the Canal Ring of the 1870's, various construction and railway projects and through his exploitation of cheap labor, particularly blacks and Italians, whose low wages forced them into decrepit housing and meager diets. Belden allegedly bought off criticism by giving to charities.

The feud between the Belden-Hendricks factions accelerated after Belden's forces lost control of the Republican State convention in September, 1894 and Belden went on a European vacation. He was widely assumed Belden had retired from active politics. The New York Times reported as much, assuming Belden at 65, would spend the remainder of his years in travel. However, it held open that Belden was still able to mount a formidable campaign, having some of the most able men of the county bar on his side. Belden's paper, the Post, had criticized the city administration, charging it with corruption and high taxes. A faction within the Republican party nominated Belden "in absentia", but he declined. Failing to obtain Belden's consent, his faction had problems fielding a candidate for mayor. The President of the Businessman's Association, E. A. Powell, Chairman of the Beldenite convention, was selected but he refused to run, despite pleas from his supporters. All the while, there were rumors alleging that should Belden's faction not obtain a candidate, it would endorse the Democrat, James K. McGuire.[57] At the last moment, they were able to decide on a candidate. They chose Charles Baldwin, neighbor to Democratic candidate James K. McGuire. The two rivals shared a duplex on Green Street in Syracuse, McGuire living at 201 and Baldwin living at 203.[58] Ironically, Baldwin had been linked to the Hendricks faction and it as assumed he would use those ties to pull votes away from Charles E. Saul, a man who had never held elective office other than that of School Commissioner. He was written off by The New York Times as a "thoroughly hide-bound machine Republican who would obey Mr. Hendricks implicitly". Because of the split, Hendricks was concerned that McGuire would win.[59] McGuire's candidacy was initially considered a joke by the old guard members of the party, but hard work in the caucuses gave him an insurmountable lead, forcing rival Democratic candidates out of the race, winning a unanimous nomination and in the process unifying the party. A reform candidate was wanted. McGuire was quick to assume that position, running his own campaign independent of the Democratic old guard of William Kirk, Henry J. Mowry and Thomas Ryan who were followers of David B. Hill. McGuire's plurality was 3166 votes.[60] Writing a decade later, McGuire reported the reasons for his electoral triumph. "[He] went immediately to work, however, delivering more than sixty speeches and making a canvass remarkable for its vigor and determination. Indeed its strenuousness made it a phenomenal Democratic campaign in the Republican Gibraltar of Syracuse, and the result was the triumph of the young Democratic Napoleon by more than 3000 majority over his Republican opponent, receiving one of the largest votes ever recorded a Mayoralty candidate in Syracuse".[61] His eloquence was allegedly so great that it "won the heart of a farmer's daughter named McGuire living at Forestport, New York, whose family, though not related, had come from the same part of Ireland as had James K. McGuire's. They married in June 1896.[62]

McGuire, inaugurated on 2 January 1896, lost no time in consolidating power, eliminating machine Democrats because they had been closely associated with the politics of David B. Hill. The Syracuse Herald Journal reported the new mayor was running amuck, taking the axe to current office holders, wanting to install his own people. Interestingly, one of his new appointees was Charles Baldwin, his recent rival in the mayoralty contest, as Police Commissioner, who as Belden's candidate, split the Republicans and made McGuire's victory possible.[63] Some critics have charged that McGuire was successful in ousting the Hendricks machine because it had been fattening on the spoils of City Hall, much to the delight of James J. Belden, who was instrumental in bringing the change about. Belden, apparently for his crime of defying the party in the mayoralty election which gave the office to James K. McGuire, was denied the official Republican endorsement but was nonetheless re-elected to Congress as an Independent Republican in 1896. Belden got Democrat party support, not only for his Machiavellian politics, but because he was a free silver Republican. Hence, Belden, McGuire and Bryan were politically aligned on the silver plank.[64]

In the immediate post-election period, Belden was a frequent visitor to McGuire's office. He was admitted immediately, whereas McGuire made old Guard Democrats seeking patronage, cool their heels. Rumors were rife as to whether "the Boy Mayor" would stand up to both Belden and Matty. Essentially the struggle was over who would control key patronage jobs in Syracuse. Frank

Matty, as President of the Common Council, appointed members to key committees – highways, sewers, finance, assessment and franchises. Belden soon betrayed McGuire obtaining Republican votes on the Common Council to elect Frank Matty president.⁶⁵ Despite having lost the battle for control of the Common Council, McGuire's inaugural address outlined a series of reform measures: a condemnation of patronage, municipal ownership of the electric lighting and water plants, a new high school, free public baths, regulation of public franchises and their use as a source of revenue for the city and a moderate program of public works. The "Boy Mayor" also noted the city was close to its limits of indebtedness and urged the Common Council limit expenditures.⁶⁶ The tone was thus set for McGuire's multiple terms as mayor – struggles with the Common Council and political machines, franchises, public spending and the political alliances McGuire forged in order to maintain power. It would set precedents for his behaviors both in the private sector and in his role as Irish Nationalist as well.

McGuire's relationship with Belden did not end after the former's election to his first term as mayor. Belden, having supported a Democrat as mayor, was considered a pariah among the Republican establishment. Belden continued to alienate his party machine by having local Democrats and his own Onondaga (Republican) chief nominate him for Congress. He also had the support of Democrat James K. McGuire. McGuire was allegedly "hot" for the Democratic nomination for Congress, but apparently found he had little support, needing Belden's Onondaga Club to win. Belden's Club would only support their man. McGuire had to lick his wounds and with Common Council rival Frank Matty, endorse Belden for Congress. Belden also obtained support from the McKinley League, a group of dissident Republicans, after which rumors of bribery and patronage ran rampant. The Republican machine wanted Belden defeated, but acknowledged how the incumbent Congressman had garnered Democratic support to win his seat four times in the past. The Syracuse Journal openly proclaimed a deal between McGuire and Belden and saw it as payback for Belden's support for McGuire as mayor. Both denied any complicity, each claiming his campaign was against their respective party machine. In his speech seconding Belden's nomination, McGuire revealed, despite his public profession to be a reformer, that he was an astute and pragmatic politician.

In the midst of a hostile surrounding, and a new political environment, we must confound our enemies by adopting a line of policy which will strengthen our party in other directions. You are familiar with our local politics…[o]ur hope lies in the continued division in their ranks..[W]e must have sense enough to act in the interests of our party by utilizing political expediency…[W]e have all to gain and nothing to lose by adopting the course I am about to propose… I would not endorse a Republican if I did not believe our party materially benefitted…I am convinced my action will be vindicated at the proper time…[Belden] is fighting the machine, our deadly foes and to support Belden is to weaken our enemies and strengthen Democrats…[67]

During the campaign, Belden and McGuire were condemned by critics, both because they were allegedly squeezing their employees to contribute to Belden's campaign and threatened with job loss should they fail to do so. In addition, McGuire was condemned for campaigning for Democrat William J. Bryan and for Republican James Belden, while ignoring city business. Part of McGuire's admitted deal with Belden, was to obtain Belden's support for Democrat State Assembly seats.[68] Not only was McGuire involved in Belden's campaign, but so too were Democrats Sim Dunfee, Frank Matty and William Kirk. Dunfee was a business associate of Belden; Matty had obtained campaign contributions from Belden, and Kirk, Democrat Boss of Onondaga County prior to McGuire's assumption of power, who in the past supported Belden for Congress; in return, Belden had endorsed Kirk for mayor. This inter-party political collaboration was lampooned in several Syracuse Journal cartoons and articles.[69] The interesting point to this campaign was that Democrat rivals McGuire, Kirk, Matty and Dunfee were brought together to support a Republican in the name of Democratic party unity. By thus keeping the Republicans divided, McGuire could once again slide into the mayor's office. The problem was that Belden, as he had done to McGuire earlier in his first election bid as mayor, was ready to abandon him at the first opportunity.[70]

The McGuire deal with Belden apparently fell through. The result of the elections of 1896 were a Democratic disaster at the federal and state level. McKinley won the Presidency hands down, and Republican Frank Black became Governor. Belden was elected to Congress, and no Democrats were elected to the State Assembly. The headlines of the Syracuse Journal summed up the Democrats dilemma: "Belden Got The Democrats And The Democrats Got Nothing". Along with allegations of electoral fraud and vote-buying, McGuire was reluctant to admit he had been out-smarted, attributing the Democratic defeat to the McKinley landslide.[71] As with the politics of Irish Nationalism, as will be shown in subsequent chapters, McGuire was outmaneuvered by those who were more astute political players.

Meanwhile, Belden consolidated his power by buying out the Syracuse Standard, a newspaper which had been in existence since 1829. Belden merged it with his Post, thus eliminating a paper that was both a competitor and a critic of his policies. Ever the political animal, Belden announced the merger "will strengthen forces working for municipal reform".[72]

For his re-election bid in 1897, McGuire was once again counting on intra-party strife among Republicans to help him win. It was also rumored that Belden's McKinley League would unite with the Democrats to ensure McGuire a second term, which after wavering, it ultimately did although Belden publicly backed Donald Dey, the Republican nominee. Syracuse Democrats were divided between McGuire and his new ally William Kirk versus Sim Dunfee and Frank Matty.[73]

Despite optimistic promises of a Republican victory,[74] allegations of electoral fraud, and a bitter campaign which denounced McGuire's politics and policies, the Democrats won in a landslide capturing the mayor's office and the county, but fell short of a majority on the Common Council.[75]

McGuire declared his win as a victory for the people of Syracuse, claiming he was confident of victory when he saw the "eager, upturned faces of the people in the thousands who were not deceived by sham reformers..."[76] McGuire was now forced to align himself with Frank Matty in order to consolidate his gains. It would lead to further criticism as an alleged reformer who was now openly consorting with the old guard Democratic machine.

In 1898 both Belden and McGuire flirted with nominations of their respective parties, Belden for re-nomination as Congressman and McGuire for Governor. Both were to be denied. Michael E. Driscoll became the Republican choice for Congress, Theodore Roosevelt ousted the incumbent Frank S. Black. As noted below, McGuire lost his bid for Governor, due to the firm opposition of David G. Hill and Richard Croker.

The Democratic State Convention of September 1898 was held in Syracuse. It was a virtual declaration of war between the two factions – upstate Democrats for whom David B. Hill was the nominal leader, and downstate, under the control of Richard Croker, recently returned from his three-year hiatus in Ireland. McGuire had every reason to believe the time was right for him to obtain the gubernatorial nomination. The event was in his town and many upstate Democrats were in key positions and several were only nominally tied to David B. Hill. The Convention Chairman, Frederick C. Schraub, was a lawyer from Northern New York, former District Attorney for Lewis County and New York State Commissioner of Agriculture.[77] Several leading contenders came from upstate, including McGuire, Robert Titus of Buffalo and John Stanchfield of Elmira, a former law partner of David B. Hill. Hill's initial choice was Elliott Danforth, an upstate lawyer, banker, former State Treasurer and Chairman of the Democratic State Committee.[78]

Hill won contested delegates from Erie and Monroe Counties with the help of Kings County Democracy. Hill sought to win Tammany support for an upstate candidate by not mentioning the silver issue, excoriating the Republican candidate, Theodore Roosevelt and the Republican party's involvement in the Erie Canal scandals as well as the recent election law authorizing the State Superintendent of Elections to appoint extra commissioners in order to prevent illegal voting in Greater New York.[79] Hill was zealously guarding his power base and patronage in upstate New York. Croker sought D. Cady Herrick of Albany, a lawyer and former district attorney from Albany County and New York Supreme Court Justice.[80] Hill suggested Herrick was unacceptable to upstate New York. Croker's second suggestion was Robert van Wyck, Tammany's mayor of Greater New York. Hill parried the suggestion, saying there was much upstate prejudice against downstate and a candidate from the city would prejudice the success of the ticket. Croker was also resentful of Hill's reference to him as a "race-track statesman".[81] Croker was aided by Senator Edward Murphy, Jr. of Troy, and by Anthony N. Brady of Albany. Brady was a successful businessman with interests in construction, transportation, gas and oil.

Richard Croker
(1843-1922)
Tammary Boss
Library of Congress LC-ggbain 01082
No Known Copyright Restrictions

David B. Hill
(1843-1910)
Governor, Senator from New York
Public Domain
(Source: http;//www.hallof governors.ny/DavidHill)

He was a business partner with Ex-Governor Roswell Flower and Senator Edward Murphy, Jr. His net worth at his death in 1913 was estimated conservatively at $50 million.[82] Brady essentially told Hill that upstaters had to get over their downstate prejudices. Hill was losing his advantage. Hugh McLaughlin's agents at the convention were James Shevlin and State Senator Patrick H. McCarren. Neither Hill nor Croker could reach consensus, Hill refusing Mayor Robert van Wyck, and McCarren refusing to endorse anyone from upstate. McLaughlin's agents suggested Augustus van Wyck, the mayor's brother and McLaughlin's legal advisor. A southern educated lawyer, van Wyck later became a Supreme Court Judge in New York and was active in the Democratic Party in Brooklyn.[83] This nomination came as a surprise to both him and to Hill. It signified to Hill his loss of McLauglin's machine. Van Wyck's sole credentials were the fact that he was not linked to the urban political problems of Greater New York and he had the prestige of judicial office. Hill gracefully accepted defeat, winning the Lieutenant Governor slot for Eliott Danforth, his ally in the Mylod scandals.[84] McGuire was nominated by Melvin Z. Haven, his political ally in his first bid as mayor of Syracuse, whose ultimatum to Hill demanding McGuire as the[85] party's candidate for Governor, was an empty gesture.[86] The final balloting gave van Wyck 351 votes; John Stanchfield, 41; Robert Titus, 39; James K. McGuire, 19.[87] McGuire thought the nomination could have been his. The convention was in Syracuse, and the Republicans were divided between Roosevelt and Black factions and had he obtained Croker's endorsement, he may have beaten Theodore Roosevelt, since the latter's margin of victory was only 8000 votes. Later Croker admitted that had he pushed McGuire more forcefully, it might have aborted Roosevelt's bid for the Presidency.[87] Croker blamed David B. Hill for opposing McGuire's nomination, a point downplayed by McGuire who claimed Eugene Hughes, then a McGuire ally, went to New York City and guaranteed Croker $50,000 for the campaign. McGuire, probably was correct naming Senator Edward Murphy, Jr. as the reason Croker rejected him as a candidate, although the advice of Anthony Brady was undoubtedly a factor as well.[88] Murphy, Jr.

had been a friend of Hill and had worked to obtain support for Hill's Presidential bid with trips to various western and mid-Western states and was one of the inner circle of Croker, Murphy, Sheehan along with Hill who set up the nomination of Roswell P. Flower. Murphy, Jr. was Tammany's choice for Senate in 1892 when Hill grabbed the slot for himself. Murphy urged Hill not to do so believing it would endanger Hill's plans for the Presidency. Nonetheless, he worked for Hill's Presidential nomination, but his efforts were no match for Cleveland's allies, who won the nomination. Murphy, Jr.'s reward was his election as United States Senator, 1893-99 through the combined efforts of Hill and Croker and over the strenuous objections of President Cleveland. Murphy, Jr. was a leader in getting Hill to acquiesce to the party's demand that he run for Governor in 1894.[89] By then, it appears that Murphy, Jr. had moved closer to Croker and Tammany and away from Hill. As shown above, this was obvious from the support Murphy, Jr. gave Croker in the decisions of the State Convention in 1898. The loss of a previously strong ally must have been a bitter pill for Hill to swallow.

Croker was obviously trying to discredit his political enemy, David B. Hill. Hill threatened to denounce Croker and the Ice Trust from the floor, wresting a concession from Croker that equivocated on the silver issue. Hill was even suggested as Bryan's vice-presidential running mate. The move was rejected by Hill, although had he wanted the vice president slot, it could have been his. Hill realized this was a blatant attempt to humiliate him by Croker, by making him stand for policies in which he did not believe. Croker, delivered the New York delegation for Bryan, placating downstate Democrats and destroying the influence of upstate Democrats.[90] As noted, Hill was adamant in trying to obtain an upstate candidate for Governor, but the combination of the loss of McLaughlin's machine support and the close business and political ties of Edward Murphy, Jr., Anthony Brady and Richard Croker gave them the advantage. In addition, McGuire's envoy's offer of $50,000 may been considered a paltry sum relative to Brady's $50 million net worth.

McGuire reveals a shift in his attitude towards David B. Hill.

McGuire was critical of Croker's control of the convention. "It cannot be doubted that the Democrats would have been successful under Hill's leadership, but Croker was the dominant leader that year. Had Croker desired the defeat of the party, he could scarcely have gone about attending that end more adroitly.[91] The selection of two Tammanyite brothers, Croker's blatant attempt to obtain upstate political advantage and the controversy of Judge Daly,[92] allowed Roosevelt to make Croker the issue in his campaign. Croker, demanding complete obedience from Supreme Court Justice Joseph F. Daly, refused to re-nominate him for the position. When it became public and was defended by Croker, it was a ready-made opportunity for Roosevelt. "My object was to make the people understand, that it was Croker, not the nominal candidate, who was my real opponent: that the choice lay between Croker and myself".[93]

Both Hill and McGuire, despite their disappointment, played the "loyal Democrat". They asked the convention to make the resolution unanimous on the von Wyck nomination. McGuire remarked Van Wyck was "the ideal candidate," piloting him through applauding crowds and creating the impression van Wyck was a strong administrator.[94] Because of the split in Democratic ranks over the silver issue, neither David B. Hill nor Richard Croker played an active role in the Bryan campaign. Croker sought to mollify McGuire by offering him the position of Lieutenant-Governor. McGuire refused, choosing instead to be Democratic State Committee Chairman and running for a third term as Mayor of Syracuse. He defeated Republican Theodore Hancock, a successful candidate for New York State Attorney General.[95] Beating Hancock was no small feat, encouraging speculation that he would run for Governor in 1900 against Roosevelt. By then, however, the taint of scandal would destroy his aspirations.[96] McGuire's win may have been due to a split in Republican ranks and was alleged to be a victory for the principle of a "wide open town". The scandals which destroyed McGuire's political career are addressed in previous chapters.

McGuire settled to run again for a third term as mayor. 1898 – at the state and local level, was a Republican year. Driscoll went on to serve six terms in Congress, failing to be re-elected in 1912. Theodore Roosevelt went on to become "the accidental President" in the wake of William McKinley's assassination at the Buffalo Exposition in 1901. Two years later McGuire once again tried to rally his forces for an attempt to be the first Catholic Governor of New York, but his efforts came to naught. He was out of office as mayor and he had his political base within the party undermined by Croker.[97]

McGuire's chances for obtaining his party's nomination for Governor were not enhanced by the widening rift between himself and "Boss" Croker. First, despite his being on the Democratic State Committee, Croker had reasons to distrust McGuire. In addition to his maneuvers with Croker rival David B. Hill, McGuire was allegedly involved in an internal Democratic party plot against Croker. His political allies were Oliver Hazard Perry Belmont and Norman Mack of Buffalo. Apparently the feud began when O. H. P. Belmont replaced his brother Perry as the favorite of Richard Croker in New York City Democratic circles. Perry Belmont had supported Croker in the bitter convention fight against Hill in August 1900, refusing to vote for McGuire as Temporary Chairman. As noted, Croker's forces won the convention and gradually usurped McGuire's powers and funds as Chairman of the Democratic Campaign Committee. In an effort to show party unity, McGuire was among a select number of Democrats who attended a William Jennings Bryan banquet in New York City, many of whom he opposed at the recent convention. David B. Hill was not mentioned.[98]

After the disastrous Democratic results in the elections of 1900, Perry Belmont resigned from the Democratic Club of which he had been a member since 1872, allegedly to take part in the anti-Croker campaign of David B. Hill. Nonetheless, at a subsequent dinner in December 1900, both Hill and Perry Belmont were present but McGuire and O. H. P. Belmont were not.[99] In addition, by then McGuire had been publicly identified with scandal in awarding contracts to businesses in which he had an economic interest.[100] He had also angered David B. Hill by giving in to Croker's demand the State Democratic Convention be held in Saratoga. Hill wanted it in

New York City.¹⁰¹ And despite declaring himself not a candidate, he aroused Croker's suspicions after he called a meeting of Democratic city chairmen to discuss the campaign without Croker's knowledge. In response to Croker's demand McGuire publicly state he was not a candidate, McGuire was evasive. Even so, McGuire openly endorsed Bird Coler, the candidate supported by David B. Hill.¹⁰² Assemblyman Patrick Trainor, noted previously, complained McGuire was using Tammany money for upstate politics. Croker demanded the mayor either change course or retire from the State Committee.¹⁰³ In the midst of the political brawl between Hill/Croker factions, C. S. Harvey, Mayor of Hudson, New York began a "boom" for McGuire.¹⁰⁴ By then, the State Party was divided between Hill/Coler/McGuire and Croker/Murphy, Jr. factions, the latter declaring this was "war to the end". Cartoons in the Herald made fun of the Democratic debacle.¹⁰⁵ Possibly McGuire, having won the mayoralty by exploiting divisions within his own party thought he could come out as a compromise between the two rival camps. However, he was too closely identified with Hill who further provoked Croker by criticizing him in a speech in Troy, New York. The rivalry degenerated into a shouting match, Hill having called Croker "corrupt, ignorant and arrogant". Croker's response was equally vindictive, referring to Hill as "a deceitful, untruthful sneak".¹⁰⁶

As noted previously, the party's selection of gubernatorial candidate was in the hands of Hugh McLaughlin's Brooklyn democracy. McGuire, as he would later when the Irish Nationalist movement in America was rent by factionalism, brokered a meeting between Hill and McLaughlin trying to have the latter endorse Coler. Ultimately, McLaughlin sided with Croker. In a convention floor fight, the Democrats chose Stanchfield.¹⁰⁷

As to McGuire's candidacy, John F. Gaynor of Onondaga County declared for Croker, openly questioning whether McGuire – or any Democrat – could carry the state. An article in the Herald summed up McGuire's gubernatorial bid – "M'Guire Candidacy Flat". Having not openly sought it, with Croker and Hill hostile, McGuire received only a few token votes. By adhering to Coler, and projecting an electoral disaster for the Democrats, Hill sought to burden Croker with the blame. He rationalized his position on McGuire stating, "he is young and will have another chance".[108] Despite his efforts to stem his boom, a small number of delegates voted for McGuire.[109] Despite Hill's statements, and the <u>Herald</u> editorial, McGuire's political career had peaked.

Given his involvement in Democratic state politics, it is interesting to note James K. McGuire's assessment of David B. Hill. McGuire's massive three volume history of the party was defensive about Hill, alleging there must be some balance to the criticism of the man.[110] With reference to Hill's use of the spoils system, McGuire wrote: "Being a Democrat, he legitimately inherited the theory of Jackson and van Buren: 'To The Victors Belong The Spoils' and he not only assumed the heritage but guarded it…jealously… McGuire applauded Hill's organizing ability that was unmatched since the time of the Albany Regency".[111] And as to the disputed senatorial seat of 1891, in response to the media criticism that Hill stole the senate, McGuire responded: "To those who live under revered laws this coup d état must seem admirable, however much they object. In the study and practice of law he was compelled to subordinate right to expediency. Such an education fits man for intrigue and intrigue is the soul of politics".[112] McGuire, in retrospect, with his political ambitions shattered, may have perceived strong parallels between his and Hill's political careers. Starting out as newsboys they became excellent orators, upstate Democratic mayors, both used convenient political alliances to advance their respective careers. Hill would ally with Tammany Hall, in opposition to the Bronx County Democracy. Later, to thwart Tammany's bid to control upstate, Hill flirted with McLaughlin's County Democracy. McGuire, as noted above, voted with both Republican and Democratic rivals in the common council for political advantage and like Hill, was hostile to Tammany's plans to control upstate. Both shamelessly used patronage. Both had unique organizing abilities, building coalitions to push their own agendas. In that context, McGuire's praise of Hill could well be applied to himself. "Hill was a major politician and his business was to win through the strategy and tactics which are the recognized weapons of political warfare," calling him "an American Machiavellian."[113] Two years later McGuire was still trying to be a player in state politics supporting Bird Coler for governor who ultimately became the party nominee.[114] Coler lost, and so too, did McGuire and Hill. Ultimately, so did Croker. McGuire resigned his position as chairman of the Executive Committee of the Democratic State Committee in July 1902, The New York Times reporting that he was not a member of the Democratic State Committee. His humiliation was complete when his attempt to obtain the nod for Lieutenant Governor in 1902 on the Democratic ticket, a position he snubbed in 1898, was aborted.[115] McGuire left public life and went into private business beginning an association with the "Asphalt Trust" which would lead to his second indictment. In his nominating speech for Coler, Hill ironically spoke out against political dictatorship, remarks aimed at "Boss" Croker. The Republicans won the governorship of New York State and the Presidency as well, weakening Croker's hold on the party, leaving Hill and McLaughlin in temporary control. It was a short-lived truce. The new dictator of Tammany Hall was Charles Murphy. Ultimately both McGuire and Hill were undone by those who knew better how to manipulate power to their own advantage. There was still one other mentor in the political lives of James K. McGuire-Frank Matty.

Frank Matty (1850-1939) was a farmer, saloon-keeper and Democratic alderman in the city of Syracuse, who, like James J. Belden and David B. Hill, was both ally and adversary of James K. McGuire. Their initial relationship was confrontational. It was this initial dispute which gave McGuire his reputation as a reformer, fighting against the "city hall ring" dominated by Frank Matty.[116] After his election, McGuire sought his own man as president of the common council, Howard Lincoln. The new mayor charged Matty with attempted bribery: Matty demanded an official investigation. In return, Matty used his influence with the aldermen to block McGuire's policies.[117] The confrontation centered on the awarding of various franchises by the "city hall ring" to Eugene Hughes and Company which turned no revenue over to the city.

The contentious relationship persisted throughout McGuire's terms as mayor. For example, as the issue of granting franchises grew more heated, McGuire stated Matty's third ward was so corrupt it was "bought like sheep" and that Matty belonged in Sing Sing. The Matty-McGuire confrontation worsened, fraying McGuire's relationship with Republican James J. Belden who initially backed McGuire's choice of patronage appointments. The fight degenerated into vicious name-calling, McGuire's referring to Matty as a "ballot box stuffer" and "the John Y. McCane of Syracuse." Matty responded calling McGuire a "yellow dog."[118]

An even bigger struggle ensued over Matty's reelection as President of the Common Council in January 1898 following McGuire's election to a second term. Matty was re-elected on the seventy-seventh ballot by a vote of 10-9. The council consisted of 11 Republicans and eight Democrats. All of the Republicans swore to support Republican E.J. Mack and all swore they had done so. Indictments were issued for conspiracy against all the alderman. Apparently two Republicans voted for Matty, the Democrats put in one vote each and Matty was elected. Charges went to a grand jury and indictments were brought against all the alderman. Rivals Mack and Matty promised to preside at common council meetings. City business was at a standstill and McGuire's efforts to obtain a compromise were ineffective. But this time Matty and McGuire were political allies because the latter allegedly did not want the city account books opened for inspection. He was also maneuvering for the Democratic gubernatorial nomination and hence wanted no scandal. The squabble persisted for months, polarizing the parties on the common council and holding up city business.[119] In addition McGuire with Matty and Melvin Z. Haven support, continued to be a silver Democrat much to the consternation of David B. Hill. After much delay, the court found in favor of Frank Matty who took his position as President of the Common Council.

To solidify their alliance, Matty hosted a party at his saloon, the official reason stated was the growth of McGuire's hardware business. The real reason was to heal the rift within the Democrats so McGuire could have a united party in the upcoming fall elections. The reason for dissension within the party was the mayor's decision to remove the farmers' market from Clinton Square on the North Side to the Hughes Stone Yard on the South Side, a move disputed by Frank Matty. McGuire was also casting about for a more compliant candidate for President of the Common Council, playing up to the German ethic vote.[120] In addition, William Kirk and McGuire were distanced from one another, Kirk threatening a run as an independent against McGuire.[121] The mayor exuded confidence at his chances of re-election, claiming bipartisan support would give him his greatest majority ever. He was aided by the fact the Republicans were having a problems fielding a candidate.[122] The void was filed by a reluctant Theodore E. Hancock, lawyer, former Onondaga County District Attorney and Attorney-General of New York State. Republicans accused McGuire of favoritism in his business, obtaining lucrative city contracts, corruption, allegations of abuse of patronage and fraudulent assessments to maintain low tax rates. Theodore E. Hancock and the Republicans were confident of victory. Despite the allegations of malfeasance, McGuire once again came out ahead, winning with a plurality of 2063 votes, almost a thousand more than his previous victory. Not only did McGuire win the mayor's office, his candidates became President of the Common Council, City Comptroller and Municipal Court Judge.[123] His victory was sweetened by the fact his campaign made inroads into traditional Republican strongholds and William J. Bryan referred to him as a "rising star" in the Democratic Party.[124] Although he astutely avoided the silver issue in his campaign, McGuire was a silver Democrat, an issue which aborted his efforts to obtain the Democratic bid for Governor.

Despite his wins, McGuire continued to face opposition from Frank Matty. Matty, supported by contractor Eugene Hughes, got his candidate chosen as City Clerk. McGuire refused to get involved in the issue. Instead his candidate was selected as Deputy Clerk.[125] McGuire, during the campaign and in the months following, was pummeled by his critics over the mounting city deficit which ultimately led to a state investigation. The official report condemned the city's accounting methods as "shocking and deplorable." Indictments were encouraged by Republican leaders James J. Belden, Francis Hendricks and Frank H. Hiscock. The worsening scandal involved Frank Matty who conveniently disappeared to avoid being served a subpoena. McGuire's regular press statements throughout the controversy angered Matty who feared the publicity would hurt his and other aldermem's chances of election.[126] As the campaign reached its climax in November 1899, McGuire found a convenient scapegoat, Edward F. DeGraw, an alleged embezzler who he accused of falsifying the assessments. Later the Mayor shielded DeGraw, claiming the bogus assessments were unintentional.[127]

As these examples reveal, McGuire was usually able to put himself above the fray of internal political squabbles and come out relatively successful, at least for his first three terms as mayor. In his fourth attempt, the scandals had become widely publicized and McGuire was abandoned by all but a few of his politically faithful. A determined and unified Republican party was able to forge a coalition with the assistance of a Republican-dominated State legislature that ended McGuire's efforts to obtain a platform by which he could launch another attempt to become Governor. In addition, his alienation of Richard Croker as a result of his political maneuvers to maintain separation between upstate and downstate Democratic parties was no small factor in his undoing. McGuire also antagonized David B. Hill on the State level and many Gold Democrats including Grover Cleveland, by his staunch solidarity with William Jennings Bryan on the silver issue. Collectively, they ended the first of the political lives of James K. McGuire.

Notes

1 McGuire James, (ed) History of The Democratic Party In The State of New York: (New York: United States History Company 1905), vol. II, 55. David Bennett Hill (1843-1910) was an upstate Democrat, lawyer, lieutenant-Governor, Governor and federal Senator. As will be shown, Hill was regarded by his contemporaries, including James K. McGuire, as a shrewd political manipulator.

2 Ibid, 79.

3 "Hill, David Bennett". National Cyclopedia of American Biography (New York: James T. White and Company, 1898), vol. I, 453-4.

4 McGuire, op.cit., 81 McGuire had refused the Democratic nomination for Lieutenant-Governor in 1898.

5 Ibid.

6 "The Governor's Progress." New York Times 14 January 1890.

7 "Conciliate The Minorities." New York Times. 5 August 1894: 1.

8 McGuire, op.cit., 55.

9 Ibid., 59.

10 Ibid.,59; Smith Ray B. and Brown Roscoe C.E. History of the State of New York: Political and Governmental. 1922., vol. III; 316-17; 319 Roswell Flower was a Jefferson County Democrat, wealthy businessman, Congressman and Governor of New York State, 1892-94. Henry W. Slocum (1826?-1894) was a native of Onondaga County, a successful Civil War general and Democratic Congressman, 1869-73; 1883-85.

11 Smith and Brown, op.cit., vol. III, 321.

12 Ibid., 327-331.

13 New York Times 12 May 1999, cited in Smith and Brown, op.cit., 345.

14 Smith and Brown, op.cit., 346; 351; Bass, Herbert J. I Am a Democract": The Political Career of David Bennett Hill (Syracuse, New York: Syracuse University Press, 1961), 102-109.

15 McGuire, op.cit., 70.

16 Smith and Brown, op.cit., 3352; 353.

17 Bass, op.cit., 157-160; 169; 174.

18 Smith and Brown, op.cit., 365-6; Bass, op.cit., 196; 299-311; McGuire, op.cit., 83-85.

19 Isaac Maynard was a Democrat party loyalist and lawyer from Delaware County, serving in the State Assembly in 1875, being elected judge two years later. He ran unsuccessfully for Secretary of State in 1883. In 1884 he was appointed by Attorney General O'Brien as First Deputy Attorney-General. He later moved to Washington and served under President Cleveland in the Treasury Department, resigning in 1889 when Harrison became President.

Returning to New York, Maynard was appointed by Governor David B. Hill as a commissioner to revise the general laws of the state (http://www.denyhistory.org/books/brevie12.html). Maynard sent out feelers to put his name forward for Attorney-General in 1891 ("Judge Maynard's Record", New York Times 28 August, 1891). The new Democratic Governor, Roswell Flower, appointed him Judge of the Court of Appeals and he was confirmed by the Senate. Flower was beholding to Hill who continued to have a controlling interest in State Democratic politics, patronage and legislation. It was Hill who pushed Flower to appoint Maynard (Bass op.cit., 215). As a result of Maynard's advice, the disputed results of 1891 in Onondaga and Dutchess Counties were awarded to Democrats. The Times was outraged, referring to Maynard's "reprehensible conduct", the judgeship called "the reward bestowed by Governor Flower on Hill's subservient tool". ("Maynard Gets His Pay". New York Times January 20, 1892).

20 McGuire, op.cit., 85-86; 102-103; Bass, op.cit., 217-235; 236; 237.

21 "Mr. Cleveland's Attitude". New York Times 24 October 1900:7.

22 Smith and Brown, op.cit., 387-388.

23 The candidates were William B. Hornblower, a corporate attorney, legal scholar and former ally of David B. Hill. Another was Wheeler H. Peckham, a member of the American Bar Association which condemned the Maynard decision. In Smith and Brown, op.cit., 403-405.

24 McGuire, vol. II, op.cit., 122.

25 Ibid. vol. III, 19-25.

26 Bass, op.cit., 487; Smith and Brown, op.cit., 365.

27 McGuire, op.cit., 121.

28 For Flower's controversial role in maintaining law and order in the face of the strike, see Foner, Philip. History of the Labor Movement in the United States: From The Founding Fathers of the AFL to the Emergence of American Imperialism (New York: International Publishers, 1975), 253-54; Harring, Sidney. "Class Conflict and the Suppression of Tramps in Buffalo", 1892-94". Law and Society Review, (Summer 1977), 873-911.

29 McGuire, op.cit., 123.

30 Ibid., vol. II, 87.

31 Bass, op.cit., 243; Smith and Brown, op.cit., 406.

32 McGuire, vol. II, op.cit., 87; New York Tribune 7 October 1894 cited in Smith and Brown, op.cit., 406.

33 Bass, op.cit., 243.

34 Men of Affairs in New York: A Historical Work. (New York: Hammersly and Company, 1906), 5-6.

35 "Minorities Must Be Conciliated". New York Times 12 October 1894:3.

36 "Nomination For Governor". New York Times 18 September 1896:2. McGuire

would obtain his second indictment as a result of the asphalt scandals which come to light during Sulzer's aborted term as governor in 1913. See pp _____.

37 Smith and Brown, op.cit., IV, 29; 31; 32.

38 "Deaths of the Day": James K. McGuire "23 June 1923, Article fragment. James K. McGuire File, Onondaga County Historical Association.

39 "Mr. Cleveland's Attitude". New York Times 24 October 1900:7.

40 See for example, "Local Popocrats". Syracuse Journal 21 August 1896:6; "Bryan Circus". Syracuse Journal 26 August 1896:6; "Mayor's Bad Break." 27 August 1896:6; "Nobody Is Willing". Syracuse Journal 5 September 1896:5;. "Won't Yield On 16:1 Point." Syracuse Journal 21 April 1899:6; "He Is Not A Candidate." Syracuse Journal 10 August 1900:6.

41 "Mayor McGuire for Governor" New York Times 9 November 1897:3.

42 Syracuse Elects A Women." New York Times 5 November 1897.1; "Catholic Summer School." New York Times 29 January 1898:5.

43 Rudolph, Bernard. From Minyan To Community A History of The Jews of Syracuse (Syracuse: Syracuse University Press, 1970), 167.

44 McGuire, James K. The Democratic Party of the State of New York (New York: United States History Company vol. II, 1905), 446.

45 "Body of James K. McGuire on Train." 1 July 1923 article fragment. James K. McGuire File, Onondaga County Historical Association; "Black Croker Comes To Town". Syracuse Journal 3 October 1898:4; "Colored Democrats to Meet." New York Times. 5 October 1898:2. Having initially praised their bravery, Roosevelt bowed to white prejudice, believed that such flattery would make them forget their "place". Roosevelt made his situation worse by saying blacks were dependent on their white officers and black non-commissioned offices lacked the ability to command men like the best classes of whites (Powell, Anthony. "An overview: Black Participation in the Spanish-American War" www.SpanAmWar.com/AfroAmericans.htm). There is reason to question McGuire's commitment to racial equality. For example, he made several racist remarks upon his return from Santo Domingo in 1913.

46 McGuire, Democratic Party... op.cit, vol II 446-447; 73 1959. James K. McGuire." Syracuse Herald 30 June 1923. "James K. McGuire File", Onondaga County Historical Society; "150 Police and Fireman In Uniform Escort Funeral Cortege." 2 July 1923 article fragment. "James K. McGuire File. Onondaga County Historical Association; "James K. McGuire In Happy Days." Syracuse Journal 1 May 1896:6.

47 "Babel Was Never In It". Post Standard 1 January 1899. McGuire's admontion to the children be good to their mothers apparently was based on his own close ties to his mother, Mary Jane who he believed was responsible for his success. She had been an invalid for years, had developed consumption and passed away on 20 January 1899. "Death of Mrs. McGuire." Post Standard

29 January 1899. Dinners to orphans and the poor were a political staple in McGuire's politics. See "McGuire's Dinner Party." Syracuse Journal 1 December 1898:5; "Ton of Turkeys for Mayor's Dinner." Syracuse Journal 23 December 1898:6; "Big Juvenile Outing." Post Standard 30 August 1899,.

48 Untitled article fragment. Post Standard 1 November 1899 James K. McGuire File Onondaga County Historical Association.

49 "Syracuse City Caucuses," New York Times 17 September 1895:3.

50 Thomas Ryan was born in Ireland, coming to the United States at age five, obtaining an education in Syracuse public schools. A Civil War veteran, he became a cooper, a restauranteur and a brewery-owner. Also like McGuire, he challenged the Republican incumbent, only for State Assembly. The results were controversial, giving his opponent a narrow margin. Ryan refused to contest the results. He was later a three-term Mayor of Syracuse (Notable Men of Central New York XIX and XX Centuries: Dwight Stoddard, 1903, 241); Kingsley, J., Knanber J.C., Neville, CC, A.C. Buckenleger (eds.) Political Blue Book of Syracuse, New York (E.M Grover, 1902), 198. McGuire praised Ryan in his History of the Democratic Party in New York State (III 1905, 411-412), noting his origins in Ireland his humble roots, his patriotism and his devotion to hard work which made him a success both as a business-man and as a Democratic mayoralty candidate in a solidly Republican city. Ryan, like McGuire, also edited a newspaper, The Syracuse News, a Democrat mouthpiece.

51 "James K. McGuire", National Cyclopedia of American Biography (1897, 19).

52 McGuire, James K. op.cit,. (vol. II 1905) 445, "General Harrison At Flag Raising", New York Times 28 July 1895:5; "Mr. Hill Open the Campaign." New York Times 12 October 1894:3.

53 "Francis Hendricks." National Cyclopedia of American Biography XXI (1931), 326; Francis Hendricks Will Succeed Payn". New York Times 27 January 1900. James J. Belden was a successful banker and contractor and twice-elected mayor of Syracuse and a three term Republican Congressman. Upon his death in 1904 he left an estate worth $6 million. "Belden's Political Ways." New York Times 17 October 1887; "Mrs. J.J. Belden Dies In Hotel Manhattan" New York Times 27 December 1910; roots web acncestry.com/~nyononda/hospital/syrhospwomenchildren.html.

54 "Jacob Amos" Syracuse and Onondaga County New York Pictoral And Biographical (New York: S.J. Clarke, 1908), 191-93.

55 "Syracuse Charter Election". New York Times 17 February 1892:5; McGuire James K. History of The Democratic Party... op.cit 384; "Symptoms At Syracuse." New York Times 22 February 1894:4.

56 "Hendricks Francis" National Cyclopedia of America Biography, vol V (1907), 39-40. "Hiscock, Frank". National Cyclopedia of American Biography, vol

XII (1904), 352. "Smith, Carrol Earl." National Cyclopedia of American Biography, vol IV (1897), 490; "Belden's Man Defeated, "New York Times 21 February 1894:1.

57 "Belden's Public Generosity". Daily Journal 31 October 1896; "A First Voters Inquires." 1896 18 October 1896. Articles incomplete. "J.J. Belden File". Onondaga County Historical Association, Belden Gives Up The Fight". New York Times 12 September 1894: 4; "Belden Will Not Run For Mayor". New York Times 16 October 1895. Belden's career is reviewed in Kingsley, et.al., op.cit, 193-194.

58 "Mayor Rivals Neighbors", Syracuse Herald 20 April 1947. "James K. McGuire File" Onondaga County Historical Association.

59 "A Three-Cornered Fight". New York Times 3 November 1895.

60 "Captured By Young Men". New York Times 9 October 1 1895; 9; "Syracuse Machine Ousted". New York Times 7 November 1895; 5.

61 McGuire, James K. History of The Democratic Party ...op.cit, 445-6.

62 "Bonds Keep Him At Home". New York Times 2 July 1895; 1. McGuire Democratic Party... op.cit, 447. The marriage story maybe exaggerated and the details are cloudy. One source alleges she was the daughter of a Booneville lumberman "Body of James K. McGuire on Train Arriving Today: City Will Bow In Tribute". July 1923 no title, n.p. JKM File Onondaga County Historical Association. Another states that one of his printed lectures on the cause of Irish freedom came into the hands of an Oneida County farmer named Philip McGuire who invited James to visit his home. He married the farmer's daughter, Francis Gertude, becoming heir to $5000 ($50,000? Obscured) "Poor Newsboys Who Have Been Elecred to High Political Offices: Two Mayor's" New York World, 1898 (n.d.d.p). "JKM File" Onondaga County Historical Association.) More became known as his father-in-law's will was made public. The articles support the details noted above. "The McGuire Will". Syracuse Journal 19 May 1896:6. Two things are obvious: both families shared a common name and place of origin in Ireland, and James K. McGuire had access to a sizeable inheritance which may have made it possible to run again for public office. Details of McGuire nuptials are found in "McGuire-McGuire". Syracuse Journal 24 June 1896; 6.

63 "Looking For Gore". Syracuse Journal 11 May 1896; 5., "McGuire First Day". Syracuse Post 2 January 1896. McGuire was apparently grateful appointing Belden's nominees wherever a Republican was needed. McGuire's ties to Belden during his first term as mayor were extremely close, having visited the Republican in New York City after the election and apparently acceding to Belden's demands. Disagreements between the two would soon follow, however, especially over the choice for President of the Common Council and policy issues. Belden preferred Democratic Frank Matty to whom McGuire

was initially opposed. See, "Queer Talk: Rumors of Bribery and Corruption at City Hall". Syracuse Daily Journal 3 January 1896:5. Alleged Bribery". Syracuse Journal 4 January 1896:5. "Mayor Visitors" Syracuse Journal 4 January 1896:6. "McGuire vs. Matty". Syracuse Journal 6 January 1898:6. "McGuire's First Day". Post 2 January 1896.

64 "Belden's Public Generosity". Daily Journal 31 October 1896, "James J. Belden File". Onondaga County Historical Association.

65 "The Young Mayor". Syracuse Journal 7 January 1896:5.

66 "President Matty". Syracuse Journal 7 January 1896:8. Additional comments are noted in Dick Case, "There's Nothing New Under the Limestone Arches of City Hall". Syracuse Herald 1 September 1980. "James K. McGuire File". Onondaga County Historical Association.

67 "Local Politics". Syracuse Journal 10 September 1896:6; "Belden Names". Syracuse Journal 12 September 1896:5. "Queer Politics". Syracuse Journal 14 September 1896:6.

68 "Belden On Money". Syracuse Journal 3 October 1896:5.

69 For cartoons see "McGuire and Belden: Tire is Punctured". 22 October 1896:1; "William J. Kirk Says Belden Is Good Enough Democrat For Me". Syracuse Journal 28 October 1896:1; "Boodle, Boodle, Who Got The Boodle, Sim Dunfee Agent". Syracuse Journal 19 October 1896:1; "Vote For Me Or Lose Your Job-JJB". Syracuse Journal 30 October 1896:1. "Mutual Friends". Syracuse Journal 23 October 1896:1; "The Two Jims". Syracuse Journal 24 October 1896:1; "Two Steps Down For Every One Up". Syracuse Journal 26 October 1896:1; For articles, see "Belden's Boomers" Syracuse Journal 27 October 1896; "Belden Repudiated". Syracuse Journal 28 October 1896. For Belden's anti-Republican stance see, "Poole For Congress". Syracuse Journal 9 1896. For Belden's anti-Republican stance see, "People For Congress". Syracuse Journal 9 October 1896:4. "Matty and Belden Combine". Syracuse Journal 13 October 1896:1. In this article, Matty flatly states Belden's past service must be repaid. The Journal castigated Belden, Matty and McGuire for their being "the incarnation of all that is evil and corrupt in city life".

70 "Last Hours of Canvass". Syracuse Journal 2 November 1896:1.

71 "Local Election results". Syracuse Journal 4 November 1896:6. Votes were allegedly bought for $3-$15 each. "After Election". Syracuse Journal 5 November 1896:6.

72 "Consolidated". Syracuse Journal 24 February 1897:6. The Post Standard essentially became Belden's house organ. Both papers had been losing money, but Belden was a millionaire and could absorb the losses. The merger left only one Democrat paper, The Courier still functioning.

73 "How It Looks Today". Syracuse Journal 3 September 1897:6. Donald Dey For Mayor". Syracuse Journal 4 September 1897:6. "Democrats Are Glum".

CONFLICTS AND CRISES

Syracuse Journal 13, September 1897: 6, "McGuire and Kirk". Syracuse Journal 20 September 1897:6. "Political Outlook". Syracuse Journal 21 September 1897:6. "Fusion Ticket". Syracuse Journal 22 September 1897:5; "McGuire As Boss". Syracuse Journal 28 September 1897:6. For Belden's McKinley League rationale endorsing McGuire, see "Fusion Completed". Syracuse Journal 5 October 1897:5. The McKinley league was itself divided, with one faction supporting the Republican candidate for mayor; Donald Dey, the "radical" wing choosing McGuire. An attempt by Republicans to unite the dissidents in the McKinley League with the regular Republicans was a failure. See "Republican Harmony". Syracuse Journal 12 October 1897:6; "The Agreement Repudiated". Syracuse Journal 16 October 1897:5; "Belden Talks Politics". Syracuse Journal 18 October 1897:5.

74 "Dey the Winner". Syracuse Journal 25 October 1897:6; "Dey To Victory" Syracuse Journal 27 October 1897:6; "By The People, For The People". Syracuse Journal 29 October 1897"6; "Looks Suspicious". Syracuse Journal 5 November 1897:6; "May Be A Recount". Syracuse Journal 8 November 1897:6.

75 For a sample of the mudstinging against McGuire, see "Issues of Campaign Set Forth". Syracuse Journal 19 October 1897:8; "Dr. Day's Answer". Syracuse Journal. 23 October 1897:5; "McGuire All At Sea". Syracuse Journal 27 October 1897:6. "It Was A Landslide". Syracuse Journal 3 November 1897:6. McGuire won with a plurality of almost 1231 votes.

76 "It Was A Landslide". Syracuse Journal 3 November 1897:6.

77 "W.F. Porter Moved Up". New York Times 29 September 1898:1; McGuire Ii, op cit., 440-443.

78 Robert Titus was a lawyer, Civil War veteran, a Democratic State Senator and judge. "Titus Robert". National Cyclopedia of American Biography, vol. VII. (New York: James T. White and Company, 1897), 421-422. John Stanchfield was an Elmira lawyer, partner of David B. Hill, district attorney and mayor of Elmira, New York. Stanchfield was a Democratic member of the New York State and Assembly, unsuccessful candidate for Governor in 1898. He won the nomination in 1900 but was defeated. He was extremely critical of William Jennings Bryan at the Democratic Convention of 1912. "Stanchfield, John Barry". Dictionary of American Biography, vol. 17 (New York: Charles Scribner's Sons, 1935), 499. Danforth, Elliott was a Chenango County lawyer, banker, and two-term New York State Treasurer. "Danforth, Elliott". The National Cyclopedia of American Biography, vol. I. (New York: James T. White and Company, 1898), 364-365. Other sources saw the convention as already under Croker's control. See, "All Under Croker's Hat". Syracuse Journal 27 September 1898:1. "Boss Croker's Convention". Syracuse Journal 28 September 1898:1.

79 Smith and Brown, op.cit., vol. IV, 312.

80 "Herrick, D. Cady". Who Was Who In America, vol. I. 1887-1942, (Chicago: Maguis Who's Who, 1943), 555.
81 Alexander Stanwood, De Alva. Four Famous New Yorkers: The Political Careers of Cleveland, Platt, Hill and Roosevelt, vol. IV. Political History of the State of New York, 1882-1905 (Port Washington, New York: Holt, Rhinehart, Winston, 1923). Croker had a stud farm in Ireland. One of his horses won the Irish sweepstakes.
82 "Brady Nicholas Anthony". Dictionary of American Biography vol. 2, (New York: Charles Scribner's Sons, 1929), 581-582; "Brady, Nicholas Anthony". National Cyclopedia of American Biography, vol. XVI, (New York: James T. White, 1918), 149.
83 Augustus Van Wyck, Jurist Dies at 71". New York Times 9 June 1922.
84 Smith and Brown, op.cit., vol, IV, 56; Alexander, op.cit., IV, 315.
85 "The Silver Democrats". Syracuse Journal 28 September 1898:6.
86 Smith and Brown, vol. IV op.cit., 56; McGuire, vol. III op.cit., 446-447. McGuire's tallies are different, giving Van Wyck 350 and himself 21. Melvin Z. Haven was a member of the Democratic State Committee, and a successful lawyer in Syracuse. (In McGuire, vol. III, op.cit., 192-193.
87 "James K. McGuire, 1868-1923 Obituary". Article fragment James K. McGuire File, Onondaga County Historical Association; Brewster, Arthur Judson. Life Was Never Dull (Syracuse, New York: Syracuse University Press, 1953), 40.
88 "Croker On McGuire: Believes Syracusan Could Have Beaten Roosevelt". Article fragment. James K. McGuire File, Onondaga County Historical Association.
89 Bass, op.cit., 87; 145; 197; 241; 243.
90 Smith and Brown, op.cit., 73; Connable and Silberfarb, op.cit., 221.
91 McGuire, vol. II, op.cit., 88. Writing in 1905, McGuire was apparently still embittered by the results.
92 Daly was a Democrat, a jurist of 28 years experience whose legal expertise won for him bipartisan respect. Daly had earned Croker's ire by refusing to nominate a clerk at Croker's dictation. Croker's response was a major tactical blunder. "Judge Daly was elected by Tammany Hall, after he was discovered by Tammany Hall and Tammany Hall had a right to expect proper consideration at his hands", later defending his remarks by disparaging Daly's character referring to him as "not an upright judge". The Bar Association united behind Daly. This gave Roosevelt his campaign issue and reinforced fears of domination by Tammany Hall. If Croker could dominate the mayor of New York City, the Governor of the state and control the judiciary, it made Croker and Tammany corruption the focus of his campaign. "Daly, Joseph F." National Cyclopedia of American Biography, vol. I, (1898,) 181; Brown and Smith, vol. 4, op.cit., 57-58; Alexander, vol. IV op.cit., 319-320.

93 Cited in Connable, and Silberfarb, op.cit, 220.
94 McGuire, vol. II. op.cit., 176; Alexander vol. IV, op.cit., 317; "The Silver Democrats". Syracuse Journal 28 September 1898:6.
95 "Hancock, Theodore". National Cyclopedia of American Biography, vol. XLIX, (New York: James T. White and Company, 1966), 351.
96 "James K. McGuire: States Biggest Democrat". Post-Standard 10 November 1899.
97 "Some Local Gossip". Syracuse Journal 1 August 1898:6; "McKinleyites To Go It Alone". Syracuse Journal 20 August 1898:5; "The People Want Col. Roosevelt". Syracuse Journal 23 August 1896:1; "Roosevelt Will Be Nominated". Syracuse Journal 26 September 1898:1; "The Split". Syracuse Journal 7 October 1898:8; "All Under Croker's Hat". Syracuse Journal 27 September 1898:1. This was James Belden's last effort at obtaining public office, refusing his party's nomination for mayor of Syracuse on 1899. Belden apparently turned on his former Democratic ally, urging McGuire's defeat for a third term, condemning his "recklessness and extravagance". "Mr. Belden Not A Candidate". Syracuse Journal 20 April 1899:1; "Talk With Belden". Syracuse Journal 14 August 1899:8. Belden died six years later, leaving an estate of over S6 million. "Mr. J.J. Belden Dies in Hotel Manhattan". New York Times 27 December 1910.
98 "McGuire In New Role: The Bryan Democrat Talks of Croker Plot". Post Standard 29 May 1899. Oliver Hazard Perry Belmont (18958-1908) was the son of August Belmont. His mother was the daughter of Matthew Perry, the US navy commodore responsible for opening up Japan. He inherited a fortune from his father, became a banker and newspaper publisher. He was a delegate to the Democratic national Convention in 1900 and served one term in Congress, 1901-1903. "Belmont, Oliver Hazard Perry". Who Was Who In America. vol I, 1897-1942. (Chicago: A.N. Maquis Company 1943), 81; "Hill Loses on First Test of Strength". New York Times 17 August 1900:1; "Hill Men In Rear". New York Times 14 October 1900; "Mr. Croker's Bryan Banquet: New York Times 14 October 1900.
99 "Democratic Love Feast." New York Times 23 December 1900. Perry Belmont (1850-1947) was a lawyer, diplomat Democratic Congressman and author of numerous books on politics and international affairs. As Congressman, he had the reputation of a reformer. He may have been enticed back into the Democratic fold in December 1900 by Croker's promise of a "New Democracy" and the presence of previously bitter enemies at the "love-feast".
100 "The Case of Mayor McGuire". New York Times 20 July 1900.
101 "McGuire And Smith". Syracuse Herald. 5 August 1900:1.
102 "Evaded A Reply". Syracuse Herald 15 August 1900:1.
103 "Tammany Men Criticize McGuire". Syracuse Herald 16 August 1900:1.

For a cartoon see, "Rocks Ahead" <u>Syracuse Herald</u> 19 August 1901:1. It portrayed a stormy sea with Croker's face as the ocean, with D.B. Hill at the tiller and McGuire trying to patch the sails.

104 "Harvey Booms For McGuire". <u>Syracuse Herald</u> 21 August 1900:4; "McGuire's Boom," <u>Syracuse Herald</u> 4 September 1900:3.

105 "Tammany Plans Separate Campaign". <u>Syracuse Herald</u> 23 August 1900:1. For cartoons, see "Tammany Democracy" <u>Syracuse Herald</u> 23 August 1900:1. "Champion Hard Hitter" <u>Syracuse Herald</u> 25 August 1900:1. "Crazy Quilt of Political State Fair." <u>Syracuse Herald</u> 26 August 1900:1.

106 "Croker's Heated Reply To Hill's Troy Speech." <u>Syracuse Herald</u> 4 September 1900:2; "Editorial Hill Versus Croker". <u>Syracuse Herald</u> 5 September 1900:4. Croker also impugned McGuire as a servant of Hill. "Croker Reminiscent" <u>Syracuse Herald</u> 4 September 1900:3.

107 "Arranged By McGuire". <u>Syracuse Herald</u> 5 September 1900:4. A cartoon depicted McLaren as "The King of King's County." <u>Syracuse Herald</u> 6 September 1900:; "Hill Will Force Croker to Defeat Coler," <u>Syracuse Herald</u> 9 September 1900:1.

108 "Stanchfield and Mackay." <u>Syracuse Herald</u>. 7 September 1900:1; "Hill Will Force Croker... op.cit; "McGuire Candidacy Flat", <u>Syracuse Herald</u> 11 September 1900:1; "Hill Says Nominee Will Be Defeated". <u>Syracuse Herald</u> 11 September 1900:2. An editorial in the <u>Syracuse Herald</u>, "McGuire in State Politics" 12 September 1900:4, indicated there was a bright political future for McGuire.

109 "Took off McGuire Badges". <u>Syracuse Herald</u> 11 September 1900;2. After the convention, a cartoon depicted McGuire peddling his convention badges at 50 cents each. It was entitled," Sell'em Out Cheap" <u>Syracuse Herald</u> 13 September 1900:1.

110 McGuire, vol. II op.cit., 80.

111 Ibid, 81.

112 Ibid, 83.

113 Ibid, 84.

114 "Ex-Gov Hill confers with Many Leaders." <u>New York Times</u> 27 September 1902:14.

115 "James K. McGuire's Successor." <u>New York Times</u> 10 July 1902:2; "Mr Platt And Mr. Coler." <u>New York Times</u> 28 September 1902:3.

116 "Syracuse City Hall Ring". <u>City Government</u>. January 1897:9-11. Matty was born in Mexico, Oswego County in 1852. He moved to Syracuse operated livery business, but was best known for operating a saloon, being representative for the Third Ward beginning in 1883, and President of the Common Council for most of his tenure. "Frank Matty". In Kingsley, h.J., Knawler,

J.C., Neville, J.J. (eds.) The Political Blue Book of Syracuse, New York (E. N. Grover, 1902), 26-30.

117 "Matty Is Willing". Syracuse Journal 1 May 1896:6.

118 "Talks At Bunco Game". Syracuse Journal 23 December 1896:6. John Y. McKane owned a construction company in New York City. He became associated with corrupt politics in the 1870's when Coney Island became a haven for Tammany Hall politicians, with its attendant vices-gambling, pickpockets, prostitution. McKane maintained power by controlling the Common Council and delivering favors to his friends. McKane was politically linked to Brooklyn Boss Hugh McLaughlin, who protected McCane in a subsequent investigation. McKane's influence was so persuasive, he helped win New York for Cleveland in 1888, later deserting the Democrats for Republican Benjamin Harrison in 1892. The violence and fraud he used in this last election proved his undoing. A subsequent trial sentenced him to six years in Sing Sing, hence the relevance of McGuire's remark. McKane died one year after his release from prison in 1899. See "Coney Island- John McKane" http://www.westland.net/coney/articles//mcKane.htm. Retrieved 27 May 2010; "Belden and Matty". Syracuse Journal 23 February 1897:6.

119 The scandal even reached the pages of the New York Times. See "Syracuse Council Organized". New York Times 5 January 1898. For a representative sample of articles, refer to: "The New Council". Syracuse Journal 3 January 1898:6. "Matty Again". Syracuse Journal 4 January 1898:6; "Serious, This". Syracuse Journal 5 January 1898:5; "11 Under Seal". Syracuse Journal 8 January 1898:5; "The Council Muddle". Syracuse Journal 4 February 1898:6; "Disgrace And Corruption". Syracuse Journal 24 March 1898:6.

120 "Democratic Politicians" Syracuse Journal 28 August 1899:6; Declines Nomination; Syracuse Journal 4 September 1899:5. The Democrats ultimately settled on Martin L. Gann. "Democratic Convention". Syracuse Journal 9 October 1899:6.

121 "Mayor McGuire's Blow-Out". Syracuse Journal 31 May 1899:6. "North Siders Up In Arms", Syracuse Journal 12 May 1899:6. "Politics Warming Up" Syracuse Journal 1 June 1899:6; "McGuire Appeals To Democrats: Syracuse Journal 21 July 1899"5.

122 "Mayor McGuire Confident". Syracuse Journal 17 June 1899:6. Neither District Attorney Jay Kline nor former Congressman James Belden were interested. Theodore E. Hancock, a lawyer and state attorney-general was a reluctant nominee. "T.E. Hancock Will Accept", Syracuse Journal 23 August 1899; "Hancock Heads Ticket". Syracuse Journal 11 October 1899:5. "Hancock Theodore E. National Cyclopedia of American Biography vol XLIX (New York: James T. White and Company, 1966), 351.

123 The scandals associated with McGuire's tenure as mayor are dealt with

elsewhere. On the election, see "Republicans Are Confident". Syracuse Journal 18 October 1899:5; "Republican Orators Nail Campaign Lies". Syracuse Journal 24 October 1899;8; "McGuire's Record Will Surely Defeat Him". Syracuse Journal 26 October 1899:6; "Heavy Vote Being Case". Syracuse Journal 7 November 1899. To his credit, Theodore E. Hancock was magnanimous in defeat. See "Mayoralty Candidates Remarks". Syracuse Journal 8 November 1899. The Post-Standard blamed the defeat on "factional bitterness" among Republicans. "Genius For Handshaking". Post-Standard 10 November 1899.

124 "Democrats and Patronage". Syracuse Journal 10 November 1899:5. There was a growing anti-silver insurgency among New York Democrats, led in part by Bourke Cochran, who at the time, was a Tammany spokesperson. This also aligned David B. Hill with the downstate Democrats and virtually destroyed McGuire's gubernatorial chances as he was an outspoken silver advocate. See "Movement Against Silver". Syracuse Journal 4 January 1900:5. "Cochran's Reply to Bryan". Syracuse Journal 9 January 1900:6.

125 "City Clerkship Contest Over". Syracuse Journal 9 January 1900:5.

126 "The City Is Safe Editorial" Syracuse Journal 7 May 1900:4. "Grand Jury's Secret Have Been Divulged". Syracuse Journal 20 June 1900:6; "Angry At McGuire". Syracuse Herald 24 January 1901:6. The Herald lampooned Matty's statements in a cartoon, "Shooting In The Air" in which McGuire, armed with a pistol in each hand, was aiming over the heads of crouching aldermen who were yelling, "Come Off, You'll Draw Their Fire". Syracuse Herald 27 January 1901:1.

127 "Astounding", Syracuse Journal 1 November 1899:6; "Desperate Fake of Discredited McGuireites". Syracuse Journal 3 November 1899:4; "A Bold Fake". Syracuse Journal 3 November 1899:4; "Fraud Upon Fraud". Syracuse Journal 4 November 1899:3.

Chapter II - A

"The Asphalt Jungle": Post-Mayoralty Meddling and a Marriage of Convenience

As noted in the "Introduction", James K. McGuire's multiple careers often overlapped each other. There was no clearly established end to one and start of another. His financial and political interests, forged in his early years, defined the man throughout his life.

James K. McGuire's pursuit of elective political office ended after his failed attempt for Mayor of Syracuse for a fourth consecutive term, although he continued to play a cameo role in State politics for almost 20 years. By 1905, he had re-made himself and his reputation. The year is significant because he had been publicly identified by Senator Thomas F. Grady as being a lobbyist for the Asphalt Trust. McGuire was so labeled for trying to prevent a bill "requiring a fair and reasonable opportunity for competition" before any pavement was laid in New York City.[1] That portion of his story will be dealt with in detail in subsequent sections of this chapter. It should be noted that Senator Thomas F. Grady, also known as "a silver-tongued orator", was a loyal Tammanyite whose corruption was so widely known that as early as 1883, Governor Grover Cleveland successfully requested Tammany Boss "Honest" John Kelly not renominate him a State Senator.[2] The reasons for this attack on McGuire are unclear, but it infers Murphy and McGuire were at odds at this point. McGuire's attempts at fence-mending may have been his three-volume history of the Democratic Party and his endorsement of Tammany-backed candidates in subsequent years.

Having won the factional struggle against David B. Hill, and his ally McGuire, Tammany Boss Richard W. Croker sought harmony after the November 1900 elections by a holding unity banquet, inviting his defeated enemies. McGuire's fall from grace was obvious by the fact that his name was not even listed in the <u>Times</u> article under "Prominent Persons Present".[3]

Tammany Boss Richard W. Croker effectively quashed McGuire's political aspirations. The selection by the party of John B. Stanchfield as the Democratic candidate for Governor rather than himself was his last major effort at a public career. It was also the twilight of "Boss" Richard Croker. William Jennings Bryan's presidential bid did capture New York City and the South. But he lost the West and the entire East, including New York State. Croker's influence on the national, state and local Democratic organizations was severely weakened. Croker returned to his Irish estate announcing that he was out of politics. His main concern now was to win the Irish Derby.[4] He left behind a broken organization and vestiges of political scandal. Although he would return for an occasional battle in the city's urban politics, his efforts to reinstate the power of Tammany under his leadership were a failure. Croker's successor was Charles Francis Murphy, who would rebuild Tammany as a state and national power. He would also provide avenues of opportunity for those loyal to him. One of them would prove to be James K. McGuire.

Even after he was vindicated, McGuire's name continued to be tarnished in public. One of his assailants was a notoriously corrupt cop, William Devery, whose links to Tammany became a public embarrassment. This was the same Devery who had part ownership of the Syracuse baseball team during the tenure of Mayor James K. McGuire. "Big Bill" Devery controlled New York gambling houses in conjunction with "Big Tim" Sullivan.[5] The close alliance was demonstrated when the State Legislature abolished the Office of Chief of Police. This was followed by a succession of raids on their gambling dens. Sullivan wired Croker, the gist of which was that if Devery was not reappointed, Croker would lose the political contributions of Sullivan's gaming houses. Croker had his pliable mayor, Robert Van Wyck, appoint Devery to a new position but Devery was not pleased.[6] Devery publicly castigated Croker and challenged Charles F. Murphy, the new leader, for the control of Tammany. Devery won election as leader of the Ninth District, but was refused a seat at the Democratic Convention ironically based on allegations of fraud and corruption.[7] McGuire, his homage to Tammany now complete, was a leader of this effort. Devery lambasted him: "McGuire is more crooked than Pearl Street…Now McGuire in 1898 got state money to spend in Syracuse and the city was Republican by 3,300 and in 1897 it went Democratic. Let him explain that. Let him make an accounting of what he has done with the funds…let him go back to Syracuse and tell the people what he did with all the money he spent when mayor…"[8] McGuire was still a player in state politics supporting Bird Coler in 1902 for governor who ultimately became the party nominee,[9] but McGuire's elective political career was over. He officially resigned as Chairman of the Executive Committee of the Democratic State Committee in December 1902, even though it was widely acknowledged that his term as Chairman expired two years earlier. His place was rumored going to be filled by Bird Coler or Senator P. H. McCarren.[10] His humiliation was complete when his attempt to obtain the nod for Lieutenant Governor in 1902 on the Democratic ticket, a position he snubbed in 1898, was aborted.[11] McGuire left public life in 1902 and went back full time into the private sector, including publishing several Catholic newspapers.[12] Here again, there is some ambiguity in the record. One source suggests that because of his meager salary, McGuire left public office with a debt of $4000 which he eventually paid off.[13] Another suggests McGuire was highly successful in business[14]. The allegations of bid-rigging in supplying printing services, insurance and supplies from his various businesses in the city of Syracuse suggest he was prosperous. Nonetheless, with his options limited in Syracuse, James K. McGuire moved downstate to New Rochelle in 1902. That same year he became associated with the Barber Asphalt Company.[15] McGuire's brief autobiography, written in 1905 noted, "He is still a young man, and it would be safe to predict that many high public honors are yet in store for him."[16] He would obtain publicity for his efforts, but not the acclaim or power that he so earnestly sought. He would become linked once more to Tammany politics and political scandal.

McGuire's political reputation was sullied even further in very public disputes over control of the Democratic party in Syracuse and Onondaga County, first with Sim Dunfee, then with former political ally Melvin Z. Haven, and last, with William H. Kelley.

Dunfee, like McGuire, had Irish roots, a Syracuse upbringing and a struggle upward from poverty, ultimately becoming a successful contractor, owner of several public utilities and a prominent realtor.

Dunfee was also a Democratic State Committeeman and the debate between the two was rife with recrimination. McGuire had apparently moved closer to the new "Boss" of Tammany, Charles F. Murphy, who was trying to build a power base for his organization upstate. McGuire had called Dunfee, a "drunk" and a liar". Dunfee, as a Democratic State Committeeman was in a strong position, given the money he contributed to Democratic coffers which endeared him to David B. Hill. McGuire, in fact, stated it was only Dunfee's money that got him the job as State Committeeman, bribing the Onondaga County delegates with $300 each. Finally McGuire urged the ouster of Dunfee because there had been no Democratic electoral victories under his leadership. McGuire called Dunfee a "Jonah" for not supporting him in his last bid for mayor, Dunfee responding by calling McGuire a "political blackleg, a liar, and a hypocrite" who had destroyed the party by driving out its old warriors" – Ryan, Kirk and Lane – "with no more influence in state politics than a ward committeeman." Dunfee alleged that McGuire "milked (demanded kickbacks) everyone under him, even the scrubwomen in City Hall and he would have swallowed that if he could have held the carcass".[17] Dunfee stated he had been a backer of McGuire when he was Mayor but was angry because McGuire never put money for improvements into Dunfee's ward. Dunfee further alleged that in McGuire's absence, it was Mowrie and Kirk who made the Democrats effective winning the City of Syracuse for Governor Roswell Flower and Lt.-Governor William Sheehan, putting John Ryan and Duncan Peck in the Assembly. The upshot was that dissident Democrats formed the nucleus of a new organization to wrest control from the two feuding factions. Waiting in the wings were Duncan Peck, James Meagher, Adolph Manz and William Kelley.

Scandal would follow McGuire through both his public and private sector careers. McGuire abandoned elective politics at the time his nemesis, Richard Croker, was pushed into retirement in part by his bold attempt to make Tammany a state-wide player, not just a New York City power. This was one of four events that brought Croker down. The publicity surrounding these efforts gave

Theodore Roosevelt an issue that assured his victory as governor in 1898. Croker's attempts to recoup his political fortunes by supporting William Jennings Bryan's second bid for President in 1900 by obtaining New York State votes would have brought him significant power beyond the Hudson, but Bryan did not carry the state. A third investigation commission, the Mazet Committee,[18] revealed the depths of Tammany graft and corruption in the city. Croker had lost control over his machine, allowing district bosses such as "Big Tim" Sullivan become too powerful and independent. A coalition of groups sponsored a reform candidate for mayor, former president of Columbia University, Seth Low, who was victorious. Croker did not want to go quietly nor did he, but Tammany defeats in the New York City mayoralty race of 1901, and scandals linking the organization to prostitution, gambling and police corruption[19] contributed to his political demise. He no doubt found some comfort on his Irish estate, his stable of thoroughbred horses, the arms of his Cherokee Indian bride fifty years his junior and several millions of ill-gotten dollars.[20] By then, "Boss" Charles F. Murphy was working to control both upstate and downstate political machines. Previously, an alliance between Hugh McLaughlin of Brooklyn and David B. Hill, ruler of the upstate Democratic faction, was able to keep Tammany at bay. That alliance was now in disarray. Murphy forced the colorful William J. "Fingy" Conners of Buffalo from control of the State Committee and replaced him with the reliable John Dix. By 1902, Murphy was in undisputed control of the Democratic Party and the state legislature and hence could elect a national senator as well.[21]

The year 1905 was significant for James K. McGuire in another way. William Randolph Hearst entered politics in New York City as a reform candidate for Mayor. His papers pilloried the Murphy machine, but Murphy's candidate, George B. McClellan, was re-elected for a second term. At the Democratic State Convention the following year, apparently Murphy and Hearst had struck a deal to get Hearst Tammany support for the gubernatorial nomination. Murphy was aided by Buffalo Democrats William J. "Fingy" Conners and Norman Mack. In Syracuse, ex-Mayor James K. McGuire was leader of the pro-Hearst forces and successfully got out large numbers to register. The Herald reported that it was McGuire's goal to take over the party. His political foes declared the Hearst supporters had been absorbed by McGuire, making the disparaging remark, "that Democrats can be bought like cattle", a probable throwback to his Sim Dunfee feud of the previous year. Ironically, a political ally during his years as Mayor, Melvin Z. Haven, now a State Committeeman, was his political antagonist. Haven was still a loyal supporter of David B. Hill.[22] Haven predicted Hearst ally McGuire would be defeated having "earned the enmity of all he called ingrates". He condemned McGuire for having the nerve to return after an absence of four years to try to run things. William H. Kelley, later linked to asphalt scandals, was Chairman of the Haven committee. The first district was lost by McGuire's faction, 25-23; the third district went pro-Hearst. In the second district, the chairmen unseated two pro-Hearst delegates. McGuire's faction bolted, held its own convention and sent a protest delegation to Buffalo. Haven apparently lived up to McGuire's praise of him as an organizer of the highest skill, "one of the sharpest and shrewdest politicians in the state".[23] Despite massive rallies and prominent speakers such has Bird Coler, McGuire lost badly. Haven had obviously outwitted his mentor. Democrats of the 39th Congressional District nominated McGuire for Congress but it came to naught.[24] A reluctant convention followed Murphy's dictates and Hearst was nominated. In a bitter campaign, Hearst lost to Republican Charles Evans Hughes, who had just completed investigating corrupt insurance companies in New York. Persistent rumors alleged that Murphy did not actively campaign for Hearst and Brooklyn Boss, Senator Patrick H. McCarren, worked with upstate Democrats against Hearst.[25] But two things were obvious: Murphy was in control of the Democrats, upstate and down, and; McGuire had deserted Hill, fellow Hill supporter Melvin Z. Haven, the Upstate Democrats and was now allied with "Boss" Murphy and Tammany Hall.

During Murphy's tenure, "Tammany politicians had gone in heavily for contracting as a business during the early years of the twentieth century, and the control of the state was profitable for the contractors and their associates".²⁶ McGuire and others had stumped for various candidates of the Democratic Party, as had fellow Irishmen Bourke Cochran and Thomas O'Grady. Another popular speaker for the Tammany organization was William Sulzer whose career would link him, along with McGuire and Tammany Hall with scandals on the canals and highways.

This oratorical tradition was traceable to the early years of Tammany during the late 18th Century, the annual "Long Talk". It would have speakers extol the virtues and achievements of the organization. "Down to the days of Senator Robert Wagner, the Long Talker was Tammany's shiniest ornament, holder of an honor next only to the Grand Sachemship".²⁷ While their contributions to the party were noted, these "showmen" were never as well-rewarded, for the men used by Tammany as actors and orators had never received the respect or remuneration paid to contractors or asphalt manufacturers, a point openly acknowledged by Tammany lieutenant, George Washington Plunkitt.²⁸

With his public political career over, James K. McGuire pursued avenues in the private sector. His brief biography notes he focused on three areas: an insurance business, as lobbyist for the Barber Asphalt Company and as President of the Syracuse Printing and Publishing Company, which published The Catholic Sun.²⁹ Each of these business interests are relevant in so far as we pursue the other political lives of James K. McGuire - asphalt scandals and Irish Nationalism. By 1905, he was openly referred to as the Barber Asphalt lobbyist. This opens the second of his political lives. However, before we can assess that second career, it must be noted that, aside from McGuire's acknowledged role in asphalt contracting in 1905, that same year saw the publication of his massive three volume history, The Democratic Party of The State of New York. His purported goal was to impart historical information and "portray an impartial record of the Democratic Party. The growth, work, achievements, successes, and reverses of the party have been traced with an eye single to the evolution of the truth, so far as it could be ascertained or understood". The author's stated aims - "its pages will not be found to consist of panegyrics upon Democratic achievements nor critical disquisitions on the conduct of other parties".[30] However, by what it says and by what it omits, the text reveals McGuire had abandoned his former political allies and became an apologist for the Tammany machine. This is not to condemn the man, but instead to reveal his multiple political lives during a dynamic period in American history. Half of the three volumes are biographies of prominent Democrats. And his history of the party gives us insights into the man and his motives. Both the history and the biographies are significant not only for what and who are included, but for their omissions as well. Some of the passages reveal glaring contradictions of the man and his use of history.

For example, McGuire sings the praises of the Democratic Party as "having fought for the rights of the individual, the states and it tenets are dictated by the disinterested regard for the rights of the people. It is a party that has never sold or bartered its birthright".[31] Further, the author states the party's commitment "to advance the condition of the people, as well as the state, had always been a noticeable and highly commendable feature of the legislation and work of the party."[32] McGuire criticized the Federalist Party as one which "never appreciated the intelligence of the masses.[33] In the same volume, in his treatment of Martin Van Buren, McGuire states: "He [Van Buren] thoroughly, honestly, and without demagoguery believed in the common people and their competence to deal wisely with political difficulties.".[34] Further, after praising Samuel Tilden, who urged the people review the currency question, McGuire, a silver advocate at one point, said he believed the people of the United States have too much reason to experience the truth of this far-seeing question".[35] Similarly, in praising Governor Lucius Robinson, McGuire said Robinson still believed, that in the end, "the sober judgment of the people was the safeguard of the Republic.[36] Yet despite these compliments towards the interest and intellect of the common man, McGuire betrays an elitist intellectual bias. For example, in referring to Cleveland's failure to win re-election, McGuire blamed Cleveland's adherence to tariff reductions as the vehicle whereby to curtail the power of the trusts by encouraging competition from overseas. In this context McGuire wrote: "It seems unquestionable that he [Cleveland] must have had implicit confidence in the intelligence of the masses and entertained the belief that the country at large would understand his statesmanlike attitude. Unfortunately, he gave the masses credit for more intelligence than they possessed". Furthermore McGuire states: "The over-confiding belief of some who were really great statesmen in the general intelligence of the public is one of the great surprises of history".[37] Was he assuming Cleveland was naive or that politics was best left to political Machiavellians such as David B. Hill or, "Boss" Charles F. Murphy and himself? This was the same Democratic party, "historically the most important party [which endorsed] the creed of man, the fruit of Liberty organized to secure and maintain the rights of the citizens".[38] Yet by his own admission, the man who proclaimed "I am a Democrat" and on whom McGuire lavished much praise, David B. Hill, was opposed to civil service reform, vetoed bills outlawing bribery in elections and the use of the Australian [secret] ballot as well as bills calling for a more appropriate reapportionment based on up-to-date census figures.[39] Hill could thus hardly be an advocate of the common man. McGuire, in his assessment of David B. Hill, suggested the latter's inability to remember names and faces "gave rise to unintended slights to many pigmies[sic] every one of whom the government permits to vote."[40]

There was religious intolerance in McGuire as well. This seems surprising, given the fact his paper, <u>The Catholic Sun</u> in numerous articles reported on the bigotry against Catholic in the United States.[41] Having praised David B. Hill's efforts to allow Catholic priests greater access to inmates in correctional facilities[42], McGuire assailed Mormonism. It was, he said, "a religion with features of sincerely immoral character such as massacres of enemies of the faith and with a grotesque fiction of marriage as a security for admission to eternal life. It is the result of a crude, ignorant credulous impulse to make a scheme of religion from Bible record in which [slaughter and polygyny] was authenticated as a subject of divine revelation.

It was not a case of simple and honest religion to be tolerated, but a case of dangerously low superstition, of insensate reversion to barbarism in social law and criminal subversion of [a] just order of organized welfare".[43] Mormonism had its origins in Central New York during the 1820's. Its adherents suffered much persecution for their beliefs and migrated to Utah in the 1840's after its founders had been murdered. Friction between the Mormons and the federal government, coupled with Indian unrest, led to the massacre of a party of immigrants in 1857. Abandonment of polygyny in 1890 brought the state into the union six years later. McGuire's condemnation may reflect the misunderstanding of many Americans of the time as to the tenets of the Mormon religion. Or it could well reflect the outrage he felt for his Roman Catholic co-religionists in America and in Ireland, whose belief systems were held in contempt by their respective WASP establishments. There was, in fact a rising tide of nativism in the United States, especially against the Catholic Church, some of which would reach a fever pitch in the decade after 1905. This was also reflected in the growing sectarianism between Northern and Southern Ireland over the issue of Home Rule.[44]

McGuire's visceral response to Mormonism could also have been rooted in the mass Irish immigration projects of the 19th century. Reacting to the nativist response to Irish Catholics in eastern cities, there was concern about maintaining their cultural and religious integrity in the secular, industrial, urban environment, urging a mass immigration to such western states as Wisconsin, Illinois, Nebraska and Minnesota. The Catholic Church hierarchy, dominated as it was by Irish clergy, was bitterly-divided over the issue, its critics fearing a cultural and political isolationism that contributed to the problems the Mormons faced in the ante-bellum period. These Irish immigration experiments met with mixed results, yet they continued into the twentieth century. One was advocated in 1904, the year prior to McGuire's publication of <u>The Democratic Party In New York State</u>. Another was encouraged as late as 1917 in honor of Sir Roger Casement, martyred hero of the Easter Rising.[45] Hence, McGuire may have been motivated by two inter-related concerns - any focus on the Irish and separatist communities might jeopardize the groups emergent power and status in urban, industrial America, a power based on Irish control of urban, political machines from which James K. McGuire and other Irish had benefitted.

Another ambiguity apparent in McGuire's work is his attitude towards trusts, to which he devotes an entire chapter.[46] Having portrayed the Democratic Party as the champion of the people and opposed to trusts, he said protectionist policies allowed America to become covered with trusts, "bearing a striking resemblance to the castles of the feudal barons of old who ruled and exacted tribute from their vassals".[47] McGuire referred to them as monopolies, with no competition and price-fixing which had robbed and oppressed the American people, a policy McGuire attributed to the Republican Party. In the same breath of condemnation, McGuire lists political corruption, "a universal curse in all monarchal and aristocratic governments" which has "no place in democratic institutions". Against these ravages of corruption, "the Democratic Party is the only well organized defense".[48] The trusts named by McGuire included Standard Oil, The Sugar Trust, The Steel Trust and the Beef Trust. The trust issue was the principle issue in the Presidential campaign of 1904.[49] Yet, while McGuire admitted the examples he gave were but a "few illustrative instances out of hundreds that might be given", there was no mention of the Asphalt Trust of which he was a prominent of member and beneficiary. Nor was there any mention of the Ice Trust controlled by Tammany Boss Charles Murphy. The Ice Trust had a monopoly on the ice supplied to New York City. It jacked up the price so high as to make it unavailable to the poor.[50] The workings and problems of these trusts had been in the papers for years, so the glaring oversight begs the question, "Why"?

Another point must be noted. Chapter XXXIX of Volume II, "Tammany Hall and Its Relation To The Democratic Party of the State" reveals a distortion of historical fact, idealizing the organization to which he now belonged and by this writing perhaps revealing loyalty to its new Boss, Charles F. Murphy. For example, McGuire attributes the formation of Tammany Society in May of 1789 to

William Mooney, an upholsterer by trade and a native-born American of Irish descent.⁵¹ True, partially. However, the society predates William Mooney going back at least to William Penn in the late 17th Century and itself is shrouded in myth. The Chief's name was Tamanend, of the Delaware tribe, some of whom lived in New York State. Apparently Tamanend gave his people wisdom, truth, charity, hospitality, the domestication of agriculture, including beans, apples, corn, tobacco, onions and the cures for snakebite and syphilis.⁵² Tamanend allegedly had an exhausting battle with the Evil Spirit. The epic struggle gave birth to many of the geographic features of the Northeast-rivers, mountains and waterfalls. The bout ended in a draw. No doubt the irony of the patron saint of Tammany Hall as a leader in the struggle of good versus evil was not lost on McGuire's contemporaries.

The symbol of a fight between the forces of good and evil was politically expedient during the American Revolution when numerous Indian societies sprung up, one of which was present at the Boston Tea Party. St. Tammany's Day was established in Philadelphia (May 1) and may have been used as a counterpoint to Loyalist groups such as the Sons of St. George. The venerable chief may not have been a good candidate for sainthood: he allegedly died by his own hand having set fire to his wigwam when he was drunk.⁵³ After the Revolution, the group was incorporated at Barden's Tavern in New York City. McGuire would have you believe William Mooney was "a clear-sighted intelligent man" who detested British domination and its aristocratic form of government and who sought to disseminate Democratic doctrines throughout the country.⁵⁴ A more apt assessment, given what was to transpire during McGuire's involvement, is mentioned in Connable and Silberfarb. "It was said of William Mooney, that he was also a deserter from the Revolutionary Army. He joined the British forces in New York and for a year he wore the kings uniform. Such gossip did not become credible until he was caught taking four thousand dollars from the City Treasury to purchase, in his words, "trifles for Ms. Mooney".⁵⁵ Tammany was thus established on democratic principles to represent the anti-monarchist middle class, but the actions of its founders suggests that looting the public purse was also significant.

Chief Tamanend was allegedly entrusted with power because his constituents held he would not abuse it. The organization was divided in thirteen tribes directly responsible to Tamanend's Great Wigwam. McGuire, Silberfarb and Holly agree the society engaged in beneficent activities.[56] A major difference in interpretation is that McGuire alleges the members were pledged "to hold in check the overweening power of the Central Government (States Rights)."[57] Connable and Silberfarb assert such is only a half-truth. The members also had to affirm they were attached to the Constitution of the United States insofar as to "secure and perpetuate the equal and inalienable Rights of man".[58]

Essentially the author appears to be an apologist for Tammamy Hall, it having recently weathered scandals and exposures as a result of the Mazet Committee and the Lexow investigations. McGuire's own words serve to indict him.

In recording the history of the Democratic Party of the State, it is manifest that in considering the history of Tammany Hall we are legitimately confined to the organization's influence on State politics. That influence has certainly been great for almost a century. Today the great strength of the Democratic Party in the State lies in Tammany Hall. It is the most powerful and most wonderful political club in this country, or the world at large, has ever been, and has attained such an influence with the Democratic Party, not only of the State, but of the whole country, that it has become a factor in Presidential contests and can make its power felt in Democratic National Conventions.

To the outside world, Tammany has been painted in somber colors. The virtues of the organization have been too much ignored, its faults too often magnified and distorted. Ulterior aims and motives are attributed to the organization.[59]

So much for the lack of panegyrics.

Such laudatory praise for a predatory organization serves to bolster the case that McGuire had sold out to Tammany and may have been using the book to both score points with his new bosses and to serve as a counterweight to Gustavus Myers' exposé, <u>The History of Tammany Hall,</u> originally published in 1901 by private subscription. No publishing house was willing to risk retaliation in any form from Tammany Hall, despite their reviewers' positive recommendations.[60] Even when published, its limited edition of 1000 copies "was mysteriously bought up, presumeably by the Wigwam's friends to retire all outstanding copies of the book."[61] McGuire stated he used all key histories of New York in his research, yet Myers is not among them. Surely it is inconceivable that such a well-read individual would not have been aware of it. In contrast to McGuire's praise of Tammany, noted above, it is interesting to compare Myers' assessment.

If my narrative furnishes a sad story for the leaders and chieftains of the Tammany Society and the Tammany Hall political organization, the fault is not mine, but that of a multitude or incontestable public records [which] show that a succession of prominent Tammany leaders were involved in some theft or swindle, public or private...From the early active beginning of its political career, Tammany leaders, with generally brief interruptions, thus continued to abstract money from the City, the State and the Nation- the interruptions to the practice generally coinciding with the periods when Tammany in those years was deprived of political power...

The records show that Tammany was thus from the beginning, an evil force in politics.[62]

Other questions are pertinent, too. McGuire's contemporaries as Tammamy bosses included "Honest" John Kelly, boss from 1878-86, Richard W. Croker, boss from 1886-1902, and; Charles F. Murphy, boss from 1902-24. Only the first two are given passing mention and the last one is noted not at all. Was this a conscious effort on the part of the author to evade the issue of bossism which had been a recent issue of political significance – the New York State gubernatorial contest of 1898, the Presidential election of 1900 and, the New York City mayoralty race of 1901- all political disasters for Tammany Hall, and no small reason for the political demise of Richard W. Croker?

In essence what we have in McGuire's book is the written equivalent of "The Long Talk". The virtues and achievements of the organization are extolled, but it is certainly no impartial record of the Democratic Party as was the author's stated intent. And while there is much interesting information, it amounts to little more than propaganda. McGuire would write two other books in a similar vein in his role as Irish nationalist and paid agent for the German Information Service That is the subject of a subsequent chapter.

During the height of the Whitman - John Doe 1914 asphalt proceedings, the split between McGuire and Tammany linked Onondaga County Boss William H. Kelley was aired over the appointment of an internal revenue collector, each seeking to seat his own candidate. McGuire's intervention according to his critics was holding up approval of Kelley's candidate. McGuire denied those charges in addition to reports alleging he was about to re-enter local politics. McGuire also criticized his brother George for attacking Kelley, complimenting Kelley for his support during his "recent troubles". With the recent passage of the Sixteenth Amendment mandating a federal income tax, it made this an important fight for control of federal patronage.

McGuire intervened once more a year later in Onondaga County politics, again challenging Kelley's candidate for Deputy United States Marshal for the Northern District of New York.[63] McGuire continued to meddle in Onondaga County politics despite his protestations of friendship to William Kelley.

The appointment of an anti-Kelley candidate as Assistant United States District Attorney for Northern New York in January 1915 reignited the simmering feud with McGuire. Kelley had assurances from several Congressmen and the United States District Attorney for Albany that his candidate would be chosen. Kelley believed McGuire was behind the move as part of a strategy to replace him as Democratic State Committeeman. For McGuire it was a forlorn hope.[64] By then McGuire has become deeply enmeshed in the intrigues associated with Irish nationalism and German subversion and propaganda.

When World War I ended, the two rivals buried their political hatchet seeking common cause in the effort to have Tammany Democratic Al Smith unseat two-time Republican Governor and former crusading District Attorney, Charles S. Whitman.

This eight-year intra-party feud between the two rivals ended when McGuire's brother, George H. McGuire, assured State Committeeman, William H. Kelley, they would work with him to insure the election of every Democratic candidate at the State and local levels. McGuire had not been active in campaigning since 1910 but now was lending both financial and moral support to all party candidates.[65]

By 1918, McGuire was described as having taken only a "passing interest in State politics of late" and would not take part in the gubernatorial campaign, having advised William R. Hearst not to run against Al Smith.[66] Apparently, James K. McGuire's political involvement had reached its nadir. A brief three-line article in the Herald noted: "For the first time in more than twenty years James K. McGuire was missed at a State convention".[67]

The recent events, coupled with his intra-party feuding, were apparently wearing on McGuire. He was quoted in the Herald as stating:

"I think I have all the excitement I need- investigations, trials, federal, State and New York City, lawsuits, injunctions, enormous expenses with heavy traveling and while I am always glad to assist friends, local differences at home over an office look pretty small to me.[68]

McGuire continued to meddle in Onondaga County and Syracuse city politics for over a decade mixing it with his economic interests in asphalt paving. McGuire's mayoralty record was assailed by new political rivals. Republican candidate for Mayor of Syracuse and former alderman, Eugene J. Mack, condemned his predecessor's granting of various franchises. McGuire responded the accusations were neither fair nor true, noting his many vetoes on franchises were overridden by a coalition of Democrats and Republicans, with Mack's support for many of his vetoes.[69]

Despite controversies surrounding them, the McGuire brothers attempted to create an insurance syndicate based on their current holdings. The move was not surprising. The McGuire Insurance Company had been actively increasing its services to which advertisements in the <u>Herald</u> attest. Their goal was to purchase a large majority of the capital stock of a major life insurance company. If successful, plans were to bring its operations and jobs to Syracuse. The un-named company reportedly had assets of $25 million with annual revenues of more than $3 million.[70] No follow up data could be ascertained as to the success of this venture. However, it appears it was not to be. James K. McGuire's moves into active and open support for the German cause during the Great War may not have boded well for its success. Within one month of publicizing the launching of this insurance business, the Syracuse Board of Contract and Supply rescinded its resolution awarding an insurance bid to McGuire and Company. The bid was withdrawn, according to the McGuires, because the rates had increased and the company was unable to fulfill the terms of the contract.[71] But could it have been tied to an increasing swell of anti-German feeling that was permeating America at the time? Undoubtedly these were due to a variety of factors-Allied propaganda, German military and diplomatic blunders and the publicity given to German subversive activities. But McGuire, through his pro-German books and speeches, may have sealed the fate of this business venture. All this is substance for the third chapter in the political lives of James K. McGuire.

So except for some sporadic incursions into Onondaga County and Syracuse City politics, essentially by 1905, McGuire was tied to the fate of Tammany Hall. Within a decade, he would be involved in political scandal, linked to Tammany politics, corporate greed and accusations of criminal behavior. The strands of this complex tale come together in 1912, with elections of Woodrow Wilson as President and controversial but short-lived Democratic Governor William Sulzer of New York. This is the second of the political lives of James. K. McGuire.

Notes

1 "Grady James McGuire As Asphalt Lobbyist" <u>New York Times</u> 4 June 1905. In 1905 rivals to the Asphalt Trust received 80 percent of the paving awards in Manhattan by Borough President Ahearn. Previously he stated the product of the Asphalt Construction Company did not meet specifications because it came from California. Ahearn reversed himself when city engineers approved the samples submitted. The Barber Company reportedly received only "a few contracts". See "Asphalt Trust's Rival Gets Most Contracts". <u>New York Times</u> 19 July 1905. This issue over contract specifications would plague urban politics for at least another decade and suggests McGuire, as a Barber lobbyist, had legitimate cause for concern and actively sought to maintain its near monopoly of lucrative contracts by bid-rigging, a move he contested vigorously as Mayor of Syracuse.

2 "M. Murphy and Senator G." <u>New York Times</u> 22 December 1910. Governor Grover Cleveland requested Tammany Boss "Honest" John Kelly not to renominate Grady as State Senator in the best interests of the party. Grady was temporarily removed, but returned to power by Tammany Bosses Richard W. Croker and Charles F. Murphy. In 1910 Grady's name was linked to an illegal gambling parlor. A decade of receipts revealed the Senator obtained over $43,000 from this operation. The <u>Times</u> published this "flagrant indecency" four years later because Boss Charles F. Murphy was considering pushing Senator Thomas F. Grady as Majority Leader of the Senate.

3 "Democratic Love Feast" <u>New York Times</u> 23 December 1900; 3.

4 Connable Alfred and Silberfarb, Edward. <u>Tigers of Tammany: Nine Men Run Who Ran New York</u> (New York: Holt, Rhinehart, Winston, 1967) 222; 227. Croker managed to win the Derby, but that success failed to win his acceptance by British royalty. He also reputedly aided Irish nationalists, supplying the movement with cash, and endorsing the concept of Home Rule. As a result, he won the ire of Britain, whose occupation army raided Croker's estate at Glencairn, but found no evidence of Croker's financial aid to the rebels. When Croker died in 1922, his pallbearers were revolutionary leaders, including the founders of Sinn Fein. IRA soldiers snapped to attention as his body was interred. Unlike James K. McGuire one year later, his passing was noted by luminaries in the struggle for Irish freedom.

5 Kramer, Rita. "What Are You Going To Do About It?" <u>American Heritage</u> 2005); Werner, M.R. <u>Tammany Hall</u> (New York: Garden City Publishing Company, 1928,) 480; Connable and Silberfarb, <u>Tigers of Tammany</u>, 228; 229.

6 Connable and Silberfarb, <u>Tigers of Tammany</u>, 222; 225. Devery, a New York City native had risen through the ranks of the New York City Police Department

and despite several indictments for corruption, blackmail and extortion, he was acquitted because of his close ties to Tammany Boss Richard Croker. He became the first police chief in the newly unified New York City in 1898. He was relieved of office in 1901 and became wealthy in real estate using his fortune to acquire a film distribution company and several baseball teams, one of which became the New York Yankees. "Big Bill" Devery Dies of Apoplexy." New York Times 21 June 1919; "Film Exchange Profits" New York Times 9 July 1913 "The Big Fishes and The Sharks" http://www.oldandsold.com/articles01/article923.shtml; "Harvey Frommer on Sports" http://www.trave-watch.com/janyankee1.htm.

7 Werner, Tammany Hall, 491.

8 "Devery In Defiant Mood" New York Times 26 August 1902; Connable and Silberfarb, Tigers of Tammany, 238-39.

9 "Ex- Governor Hill Confers With Many Leaders" New York Times 27 September 1902. Bird Sim Coler was born in Illinois. His family moved to Brooklyn. Well-educated, Coler moved into the family banking and brokerage business. He was active in the Brooklyn Democracy and after Greater New York was formed in 1898, he was elected its first Controller. He opposed the Ramapo Aqueduct scheme and the methods of Tammany Boss Richard Croker in an article entitled "Commercialism In Politics". He was nominated for Governor in 1902, but lost to Benjamin Odell by a narrow margin. Coler later was elected Brooklyn Borough President in 1906 and continued his reform efforts. "Bird Sim Coler". Men of Affairs in New York: An Historical Work (New York: L.R. Hamersley and Co. 1906), 223-24.

10 "James K. McGuire's Successor" New York Times 10 July 1902. McCarren was an unlikely choice. Patrick McCarren (1847-1909) was born of Irish parents in Massachusetts. He moved to Brooklyn to work in the sugar refineries. McCarren moved into politics and was elected State Senator in 1881, holding that position for 18 years. He was known for his public works projects and for being a pawn of the oil and sugar interests. Successor to Hugh McLoughlin as Democratic Boss of Kings County, McCarren had an on-off relationship with Tammany Hall, thwarting Boss Murphy's attempt to obtain the governorship for William Randolph Hearst in 1908. "Hill and McCarren Peace Treaty." New York Times 30 March 1902; "McCarren To Murphy: Bring On Your Charges." New York Times 18 August 1904.

11 "Mr. Platt and Mr. Coler," New York Times 28 September 1902:3.

12 Cath. Encyclo.newadvent.org/cathon/11692 a.htm, 4; Robert Bond. The Press of Syracuse: Onondaga Centennial 1896, 563-75.

13 "Mayor Rivals Were Neighbors" Syracuse Herald 2 April 1947.

14 "Deaths of the Day: James K. McGuire", 30 June 1923. McGuire File. OCHA.

CONFLICTS AND CRISES   141

15 McGuire, James K. The Democratic Party In New York State (New York: United States History Company, 1905) Vol II, 447.
16 Ibid.
17 "McGuire With Them" Syracuse Herald 26 February 1904. McGuire was supposed to refrain from party politics as it was the "policy of men involved in the asphalt business." "Democratic Turmoil:" Post-Standard 17 February 1904; "John Dunfee at French Lick Lays Bare McGuire Methods." Post-Standard 26 February 1904. "Democrats Form Nucleus For New Organization." Post-Standard 16 February 1904. John Dunfee's (1851-1904) parents emigrated from Ireland during the famine years. His mother died when he was young and the family lived in poverty along Canal Street in Syracuse. In true Horatio Alger style, he worked as a newsboy. He sold apples and worked as a driver on the Erie Canal, buying his own canal boat and becoming a lock tender and horse trader. He was appointed Fire Commissioner by mayors Ryan, Burns and Kirk and he was a friend of future Democratic Presidential contender, Alton B. Parker. His wealth came from his successful contracting business in such diverse places as Boston, Massachusetts, New York City, Albany and Virginia. Dunfee was a promoter of the Syracuse Electric Light and Power Company and had a controlling interest in several other local and regional companies. He later became involved in real estate. Dunfee generously contributed to local charities, churches and hospitals. "John Dunfee". Syracuse and Onondaga County New York: Pictorial and Biographical (New York: S.J. Clark Publishing Company, 1908), 89-95).
18 The Mazet Committee investigations, beginning in 1899, disclosed that every member of Tammany or its Executive committee, held public office or was a favored contractor. Many city contracts were awarded without bidding. City payrolls were padded. The most prominent scandals uncovered were the Ice Trust, the Ramapo project and Croker's ties to the city government. The Ice Trust monopolized the sale of ice, maintaining such a high price so as to keep it from the poor. The Ramapo project was an attempt to extort outrageous rates on New York City for supplying water. Under examination, Croker admitted his influence in Albany, that judges were assessed kickbacks to be paid to Tammany. For details, see Myers, Gustavus, The History of Tammany Hall (New York: Burt Franklin, 1917), 280; 284-89.
19 Werner, Tammany Hall 473,474; Brown, Roscoe, in Smith, Ray (ed.). History of New York State 1896-20 (Syracuse, New York: Syracuse Press, 1922) vol. IV, 83.
20 Connable and Silberfarb, Tigers of Tammany, 26.
21 "Murphy Controls Senate Selection" New York Times 31 December 1901.
22 "A Hill Man To Head State Committee". New York Times 25 April 1904; 2. William J. Fingy" Connors rose from an impoverished cabin boy on the

Great Lakes steamers, to a saloon owner who controlled the employees on the docks in Buffalo by monopolizing the freight handling and grain elevator business through violence and intimidation. His union power was broken in a great strike of 1898-99. He switched his allegiance from Republican to Democratic in 1890's, and acquired two newspapers. He had also aligned himself with Tammany Boss Charles Murphy and in the process becoming State Chairman in 1906. Irwin Will. "The Rise of 'Fingy' Conners": orig. Colliers Magazine 1908. http://www.buffalonian.com/history/articles/1901-1950/1908conners/1908conners.html. Norman Mack was born in Canada and attended public schools in Ontario. He lived with relatives in Michigan where he began his career in publishing. Within two years, he established a newspaper in Jamestown, New York and legally changed his name from MacEachern. Mack later moved to Buffalo and established The Evening Times, the only Democratic daily paper in Western New York. A staunch Democrat connected to William Sheehan's Erie County machine, Mack served as a state committeeman, national committeeman, and was national chairman after 1908. McGuire described Mack as "forceful, energetic leader in the state and nation," "a Democrat of national reputation, a recognized power in the organization." Mack remained active in politics through the Franklin D. Roosevelt administration. http://www.online biographies.info/ny/erie/my/mack.ne.htm. "Mack, Norman Eugene: National Cyclopedia of American Biography vol XXVI (New York: James T. White and Company, 1937), 43. "To Control Party". Syracuse Herald 2 September 1906.

23 McGuire, James. The Democratic Party in New York State. Vol III, 192. "To Control Party" Syracuse Herald 2 September 1906.
24 "Fear A Light Turnout." New York Times 14 October 1906:3; "Fears Fight At Syracuse." New York Times 21 September 1906:2; "James K. McGuire For Congress". New York Times 9 October 1906;2.
25 Myers, Gustavus, The History of Tammany Hall (New York: Boni and Liveright, 1917,) 311.
26 Werner, Tammany Hall, 519.
27 Connable and Silberfarb, Tigers of Tammany, 29.
28 Werner, Tammany Hall, 530.
29 McGuire, The Democratic Party in New York State, Vol. II, 447.
30 Ibid, Vol I, 5-6.
31 Ibid. Vol I, 18. For more on this, see Willis Holly, "Tammany: A Glance At Some of Its Representative Activities, And A Brief Discussion of Its Political Character". In Smith, Ray (ed.). History of The State of New York: Political and Governmental, vol. 5 (Syracuse: Syracuse Press, 1922), 398-99.
32 McGuire, Vol I, 71.
33 Ibid. Vol I, 46.

34 Ibid. Vol I, 227.
35 Ibid. Vol I, 461.
36 Ibid. Vol II, 27.
37 Ibid. Vol II, 70.
38 Ibid. Vol I, 19.
39 Ibid. Vol II, 65;75;82.
40 Ibid. Vol II, 93.
41 For example, The Catholic Sun criticized the demands by Protestants to retain Bible readings in the public schools. See "Hiberians Request Bible To Be Abolished in Schools" 6 April 1900: 1; "Bishop Ludden Is Very Pain Spoken". 27 April 1900:1; "King James Put Out of Schools". 8 June 1900:1. General references to Anti-Catholic bias in America are found in the following Catholic Sun articles: "Bishop Ludden Says Bigotry Rules 27 January 1911; "Bigotry Alive Again In America" 10 March 1911: 1,4.
42 McGuire, Vol II, 325.
43 Ibid. Voll II 325.
44 For example, Bishop Patrick A. Ludden reported the rising tide of bigotry as evidenced by the New York State Democratic political party over the fight by its reformist wing to deny a senate seat to William Sheehan of Buffalo, the hostility of the Post Standard to the St. Patrick's Day parade, the growth of Freemasonry, the popularity of the scurrilous stories of ex-nuns and the populist oratory of Tom Watson. See, "Bishop Ludden Says Bigotry Rules." Catholic Sun 27 January 1911; "Bigotry Alive in America. "Catholic Sun 10 March 1911: 1, 4. There was some truth to Catholic's tracing negative attitudes of their faith to the British colonial past in the United States. See Higham, John. Strangers In The Land: Patterns of American Nativism, 1860-1925. (New Brunswick, NJ: Rutgers University Press, 1955), 175-193). Especially galling was the emergence of a new group, the Guardians of Liberty begun in 1912. See "Deny Sympathy To Guardians of Liberty." Catholic Sun 27 September 1912: 1; "Religious Issue Factor at Buffalo." New York Times 27 October 1914. On the importance of sectarianism in Ulster, see "Ulster Bigotry And Intolerance", Catholic Sun 16 February 1912:1.
45 For details, see Wittke, Carl. The Irish In America (Baton Rouge, La: Louisiana State University Press, 1956), Chapter VII, "The Irish as Farmers", 62-74.
46 James K. McGuire, Vol II, Chapter XXXXXVI.
47 Ibid. Vol II, 185.
48 Ibid. Vol II, 185, 186; 187; 188.
49 Ibid. Vol II, 193.
50 Myers, Gustavus. The History of Tammany Hall (New York: Bart Franklin, 1917), 286; Brown, Roscoe in Smith, Ray (ed.) History of the State of New

York: Political and Governmental vol. IV, 1896-1920 (Syracuse: Syracuse Press, 1922), 73-74. The scandal involved everyone from Mayor Robert van Wyck to leading Tammany officials and had to be resolved by Republican Governor, Theodore Roosevelt.

51 McGuire, History....vol. II, 208. Willis Holly however, downplays Mooney's role, noting only that he was often regarded as the founder of the Tammany Society and its Grand Sachems in 1789. However, Holly suggests that Mooney was best known as a friend and creditor to Aaron Burr. Instead, Holly attributes the formation of Tammany to John Pintard – merchant, scholar, newspaper editor, member of the New York City Council and Assemblyman. Pintard was active in the social, charitable and educational work of Tammany, originating its museum and historical society. Pintard's influence waned during Dewitt Clinton's era, both favoring the construction of the Erie Canal, with most of Tammany opposing it. For details, see Willis Holly, "Tammany: A Glance...." in Smith, Ray (ed.), History.... Vol.5 370; 374; 376-391.

52 Connable and Silberbarb, Tigers of Tammany, 21-22; 23-24. With reference to the Indian Chief Tamanend, Holly writes: "The legendary Indian chieftain chosen as the tutelary saint of the Tammany Societies, and the vague and various traditions of his heroism and his wisdom, need not concern us in connection with this record. There is too much confusion and contradiction in them to justify the hasty acceptance of any of their phases and they have too little relation with the history of the Society in New York to warrant the labor and effort of sifting out the truth concerning him either as a warrior or a philosopher, as a friend of the White man or the out-traded and out-bargained representative of the red" (368). Citing Edwin Patrick Kilroe, Holly suggests the deeds of Tamanend were "confounded" with the "great Iroquois Hiawatha" (368).

53 Ibid. 23-24,

54 McGuire, The Democratic Party In New York State, Vol II, 208.

55 Myers, History of Tammany Hall, 1.

56 Ibid, 6; James K. McGuire, The Democratic Party In New York State, Vol. II, 210-211; Connable and Silberfarb, Tigers of Tammany, 31; 32-33; Holly, Wills, "Tammany: A Glance...", in Smith, Ray (ed.) History....., 377; 398.

57 McGuire, The Democratic Party In New York State, Vol II, 209.

58 Connable and Silberfarb, Tigers of Tammany, 29.

59 McGuire, The Democratic Party In New York State, Vol. II, 212. Holly urged an even handed approach in assessing Tammany. Holly, Willis. "Tammany: A Glance....." in Smith, Ray (ed.) History in, 358-59; 364-66.

60 Myers, History of Tammany Hall, X-XI, XIII.

61 "Tammany's Evil Ways Are Told In A New History" New York Times 28 October 1917.
62 Myers, History of Tammany Hall, vii.
63 "McGuire Denies He's Holding Spillane's Job." Syracuse Herald. 14 April 1914:3; "Brewster Or Dillon Will Get Place, Says M'Guire." Syracuse Herald. 24 July 1914:12; "Clancy Insists Upon Spillane Being Appointed." Syracuse Herald. 11 April 1914:6. 108-109. McGuire's choice as candidate for the position, Neal Brewster, was chosen over the objections of both Kelley, a power in Onondaga County politics linked to Tammany Hall and J.R. Clancy. John Richard Clancy, a famous manufacturer of theatrical hardware, (1859-1932) was the local Congressman, 1913-1915, failing to be re-elected for a second term. Thus, despite his protests to the contrary, McGuire was involved in behind-the-scenes politics in Syracuse and Onondaga County. See, "J.K. M'Guire Out Of Local Politics." Syracuse Herald 18 August 1913:6.
64 "Kelley Machine Shattered, Claim of Insurgents". Syracuse Herald. 28 January 1915:2. See "Asphalt Jungle III", pp., fn. 59.
65 "News of Politicians". Syracuse Herald. 11 August 1918:17. The alliance between the McGuires and Kelley was reinforced in August, 1918. Both politicians sought the ouster of the incumbent from the third ward, apparently because he would not support the Democratic candidate for Senator. "3rd District Fight Most Bitter Yet" Syracuse Herald 28 August 1918:6.
66 "News of The Politicians". Syracuse Herald 31 July 1918:26.
67 "In The Wake of The Convention". Syracuse Herald 26 July 1919:6.
68 "M'Guire Denies He's Holding Spillane's Job." Syracuse Herald 14 April 1914:3
69 "Former Mayor M'Guire Is Incensed Over Statements About His Administration." Syracuse Herald 16 October 1913; 6; "Mack's Record As Alderman Might Have Been Better". Syracuse Herald 18 October 1913: 7.
70 See for example, advertisements for automobile insurance. Syracuse Herald. 20 February 1916:28.
71 "Syracusans Seek Control of Big Insurance Co." Syracuse Herald. 2 March 1916:6. "To Ask For New Bids." Syracuse Herald. 14 April 1916.

CHAPTER II - B

The "Asphalt Jungle": Barber Asphalt, Bribery and The Brothers McGuire

McGuire's biography suggests that he maintained close ties to the state Democratic Party, advising its leaders and framing planks in the party platform.[1] The documentary record is limited but it reveals his involvement with the party at least until 1914. McGuire was associated with the Barber Asphalt Company beginning in 1902, which begins the second major chapter in his life. A dozen years later, McGuire's name surfaced once again and was linked with asphalt in another corruption scandal.

As noted in the chapter on his career as mayor, McGuire was involved in controversies about asphalt contracting, particularly his last administration.

His main opponent was long-time rival Frank Matty. Matty's dictatorial control over paving materials was parodied in editorials and cartoons in the Herald.[2] At this time, McGuire encouraged competitive bidding as the vehicle whereby lower prices resulted, benefitting both the taxpayers and the city, stating, "As a result of intense competition, the city government came out with flying colors and there will be no paving scandals to conjure up during the next administration."[3] Sim Dunfee's companies were awarded 13 of 15 contracts.[4] The dispute centered on bid specifications calling for Trinidad asphalt. All contractors, save Warner-Quinlan, specified the use of Trinidad asphalt. Warner-Quinlan used asphalt from California, an emerging source of competition for the Barber Company. Matty used his control over the Common Council to rescind all bids not specifying Trinidad asphalt, a move opposed by Mayor McGuire.[5] Despite his vocal opposition, McGuire refused to veto it, assuming his veto would be over-ridden by the Matty-dominated Common Council. This was the beginning of McGuire's long association with the "Asphalt Trust." In order to place these events in the proper context, a brief overview of asphalt and its use in America is essential.

Asphalt is found in most crude petroleum and is most often used for paving streets and for lining reservoirs and irrigation canals.[6] The product is distilled creating topped crude which can be used as fuel or further refined into asphalt cement used in paving. It can be found in natural deposits in pits and lakes. Two of the best known natural deposits are in Pitch Lake, Trinidad and at Lake Bermudez, Venezuela.[7] The growth of urban America's need for paved streets and reservoirs, its increasing use of automobiles, the growth of business monopolies, America's expansionist policies and the cities' domination by political machines, made for an unsavory combination that was ripe for corruption. In the midst of all of these developments was James K. McGuire.

The American most commonly identified with the asphalt industry was Amzi Lorenzo Barber (1843-1909). Graduating from Oberlin in 1867, he was hired by O.O. Howard to take charge of the Normal Department of Howard University. Barber left the university five years later to enter the private sector. He made a fortune in real estate. In 1876, the federal government was reviewing materials that could be used to pave the streets of the capital. Barber saw the financial possibilities, abandoned real estate and in 1877 started A.L. Barber and Company, incorporating it five years later as The Barber Asphalt Paving Company.[8] For paving the streets of Washington, D.C., Barber had to work through General Francis V. Greene, West Point graduate, author of several volumes on military history and at the time, municipal engineer for the capital district. The reason for this was the Board of Public Works had been thoroughly discredited and President Grant gave planning of the project to the Army Corps of Engineers. In addition to Greene, Barber cultivated contacts with Clifford Richardson, inspector of asphalts and cements in the nation's capital beginning in 1887. Richardson resigned in 1897 to work for Barber. His successor was Allen Dow, a man who had been a chemist for the Barber Company. Richardson's experiments improved the quality of asphalt and hence its demand. This combination of Barber associates in the higher circles of government, a relatively undeveloped technology and scrupulous disregard of principle save economic gain, gave Barber a monopoly for over a decade.[9] Greene resigned from the Army and became Vice-President of the Barber Asphalt Company.[10] As did many 19th century American capitalists, Barber sought vertical integration, not only manufacturing the materials, but controlling the sources of supply as well. Barber bought his materials from Pitch Lake, Trinidad beginning in 1877 from a group of small lease holders whom he felt were being exploited by the British Colonial Government. Barber negotiated to buy out the small lease holders, obtaining the entire Pitch lake concession in 1888.[11] He was called the "Asphalt King" because he controlled the chief source for over twenty years. Thus he bought pitch from his own subsidiary, manufactured the asphalt and sold the finished product by having the specifications rigged by compliant politicians.[12] For a while, Barber was able to insure his monopoly as the other sources of "natural" asphalt suffered from limitations, such as extensive costs for transportation to lucrative eastern markets, and problems of access, since they were located in remote or mountainous regions.[13] Essentially what McGuire witnessed in Syracuse in 1901 had precedents in numerous American cities prior to McGuire's involvement with the Asphalt Trust. McGuire, as his public political career reached a low point, established a working relationship with the Asphalt Trust and would apparently follow the same methods used by others in obtaining asphalt contracts. As his own experience had shown, bids were awarded by politicians-aldermen, mayors and politically-appointed city engineers. This nexus of politics and profit would engulf him, his brother and business partner, George, the "Boss" of Tammany Hall, Charles F. Murphy, the Governor of New York, William Sulzer and his fellow Irish Nationalist, James M. Sullivan, among others.

Barber moved his headquarters to New York City and formed a front company to avoid any problems of doing business in a British territory. Four years previously, his subsidiary, The Trinidad Asphalt Company, acquired the Venezuelan property of The New York and Bermudez Company about the time McGuire's predecessor as mayor, Jacob Amos, was beginning urban improvements in Syracuse. Barber wanted control of the Venezuelan deposits because if it was allowed to prosper it would compete with his company. Even though it was not at peak production, the Venezuelan deposits had the potential for becoming a major producer, threatening Barber's monopoly.

The company in control of the Venezuelan asphalt was the New York and Bermudez Company. When the Bermudez Company won a contract to pave streets in Washington, D.C., Barber sued, claiming the company was negligent and was using an inferior material. Because of the recession of 1893, the Bermudez Company found itself strapped for cash. Barber bought it under favorable circumstances. The Spanish-American War depressed asphalt prices. Guided by General Francis V. Greene, the Barber Company sought to monopolize the world asphalt business, establishing the Asphalt Company of America in 1899.[14]

The "Asphalt Trust" was the result of the National Asphalt Company absorbing the Asphalt Company of America which had previously taken in the Trinidad Asphalt Company in 1888 and the New York and Bermudez Company. By 1900, Barber controlled 80 percent of the asphalt companies in America. These were, in turn, taken over by John Mack, a Pennsylvania politician who formed the National Asphalt Company in 1899. Within two years Amzi Barber sold out his holdings and retired. At that time, the Asphalt Trust was experiencing financial difficulties because of its acquisitions and because of the "ruinous competition" it faced from the Warner-Quinlan Company of Syracuse. According to John Moody, the Warner-Quinlan syndicate obtained paving contracts for over one million square yards of asphalt in such diverse places as Washington, D.C.; Albany and Syracuse, New York; Chicago, Illinois; Alleghany, Pennsylvania; Cleveland, Ohio; Jersey City and Newark, New Jersey.[15] These developments pushed the Trust into expensive litigation, intense competition and intervention in the internal affairs of a sovereign state. For example, the Warner-Quinlan Asphalt Company, a prominent competitor of the Asphalt Trust refused to be at the mercy of one supplier. It's agents obtained a claim in Venezuela in 1900. Warner-Quinlan was sued by a trust subsidiary, the New York and Bermudez Company, involving it in Venezuelan politics, bribery and intrigues with the United States Department of State. Warner-Quinlan used the good offices of former Republican Senator and political rival to James K. McGuire, Frank Hiscock. Perhaps Warner-

Quinlan thought it politically pragmatic to use a former Republican Senator with Republican Theodore Roosevelt serving as President. However, it was the same Roosevelt, who as Governor of New York two years previously, unsuccessfully sought out his Spanish-American War colleague, and fellow Republican, General Francis V. Greene, to be the Empire State's Superintendent of Public Works. At the time of the Venezuelan controversy, Greene was the President of the newly-reconstituted Barber Asphalt Paving Company. Since its claims were considered legally weaker, the New York and Bermudez Company, in an attempt to monopolize the Venezuelan deposits, funded a revolt against the incumbent President which led to the loss of 12,000 Venezuelan lives.

Amzi L. Barber
(1843-1909)
"The Asphalt King"
(Source: http://72.52.242.201/
~washingt/sites/default//files/se_1107.pdf.washington, 1902)
Public domain

General Francis Vinton Greene
(1850-1921)
Soldier, Businessman, NYC Police Commissioner
Public Domain

Because of its meddling in Venezuelan politics, the government demanded $5 million in compensation from the New York and Bermudez Company and confiscated its property. The Venezuelan government needed an agent to market its pitch, choosing the retired Amzi L. Barber's newly established Barber Asphalt Company. The incumbent President was subsequently overthrown in 1908 and the United States rushed in warships to guarantee the new government. The thankful successor reduced the fine to $60,000, the Bermudez property was returned and Lorenzo Barber was cut off from his source of supply. Barber's search for an alternative source brought him to California. The exertions of exploration contributed to his death. A new trust, The General Asphalt Company, was formed in 1903 absorbing 54 of 69 firms, controlling 80 per cent of the market. It consisted of four divisions: The A. L. Barber Paving Company; The New Trinidad Asphalt Company; The South American Asphalt Paving Company; and, The New York and Bermudez Company.[16] It was this organization's subsidiary, The A. L. Barber Paving Company which employed James K. McGuire.

This same Warner-Quinlan Company would implicate James K. McGuire in asphalt scandals a decade later. This interconnection of fraud, corruption and foreign intrigue was best summarized by John Carlisle, a New York State Commissioner of Highways, under indictment for graft in 1913 who said: "The public should remember that this is the unclean thing of the industrial eye in America. It has left its grimy trail of graft across the continent, and has corrupted, or attempted to corrupt, officials in nearly every city in which it has done its work. Not content with this, it has financed revolutions and overthrown governments, and today is a subject of international complications."[17]

Monopoly control, like that of other industries, brought with it a stench of scandal. Because of the intense competition among asphalt producers, as early as the 1890's, there were charges of collusion, favoritism, bid-rigging, questionable trips and vacations to select politicians, the same charges that were leveled at the Syracuse Common Council under McGuire's tenure as Mayor. It also was great fodder for the reading public as the scandals were given ample coverage in the urban press. Barber Asphalt usually got the bids, or had previous bids thrown out, even though its prices were 20-40% higher, because the job specified "Trinidad Asphalt" obtained from Pitch Lake, on the island of Trinidad. The quality was allegedly worth the difference in price. This gave it a virtually monopoly. Various cities, such as Syracuse under McGuire, were rocked with scandals and exposés. Others included New York City, Trenton, Newark, and, Jersey City, New Jersey.[18] These would set the precedents for 1913 investigations that brought about the second indictment of ex-Mayor James K. McGuire. The trust would have its subsidiaries bid against each other,[19] maintaining a facade of competition, but in reality, all profits went to the Asphalt Trust. By the turn of the century, twenty million yards of Trinidad Asphalt pavements had been laid in eighty cities in the United States, at a cost of over $60 million dollars. The Trinidad Asphalt Company had supplied nearly all of the material for this work, and the Barber Asphalt Company had done upwards of one-half of it. The remainder was done by about thirty companies in which neither of the two firms had any interest beyond supplying the material. The pavement laid by these companies, especially the Barber Company, was so acceptable that it became the standard pavement of the United States.[20]

By 1902, James McGuire had relocated to New Rochelle, close to the borders of urban New York. He began his long association with the Barber Asphalt which by now, like similar American business combinations of the time period, had become a "trust", and like them, was linked to near-monopoly business practices and political scandals. As Deming notes, "There is probably some truth in the allegation that political collusion was used to insure the adoption of 'Trinidad Lake' asphalt to the exclusion of other asphalts… The method used pursued to artificially maintain prices was to secure the adoption of city specifications excluding all asphalts except Trinidad Lake, a course of action frequently involving collusion with city officials and prolific of vindictive opposition, litigation, heavy expense and graft."[21] As subsequent investigations would reveal, and as Syracuse city politics has shown, this company report was accurate. For example, Fillmore Condit, chief witness against the McGuire brothers in the New York paving scandals stated, "Up to the present time, it has been practically impossible for the [Union Oil] Company to get its products accepted by anyone doing work for the State, as the specifications of the New York Highway Department have been drawn in such a way as to exclude the products of the [Union Oil] Company. The Barber Asphalt Company has furnished practically all of the oil and asphalt used on the state highways of New York to the exclusion of the products of other companies, of which my company was one".[22] This simply mirrored the trust's practices of two decades. The comfortable monopoly enjoyed by the Asphalt Trust was challenged by the emergence of new technologies that endangered its hold on both asphalt supply and application. For example, The Union Oil Company, established in California in 1890, processed asphalt from crude oil. This was so-called "artificial" asphalt. Prior to the completion of the Panama Canal in 1914, its product was shipped around Cape Horn, or by railroad. The country's booming rail network gave the Union Oil Company and others quick and cheaper access to Eastern Markets, and dropping costs from $3.36 per square yard to $1.52. Booming oil industries had no use for the petroleum residue used for artificial asphalt and were selling it for seven cents a gallon. Union Oil sent its first shipload of "artificial" asphalt to the East Coast in 1896, threatening the Barber monopoly which controlled the Trinidad Lake deposits.[23]

The natural asphalt of the Asphalt Trust began to see its market share drop after 1901. For example, in 1900 virtually all asphalt in America was "natural" from Venezuela or Trinidad. Seven years later it dropped off by 80 percent.[24] The cost of extracting and shipping "natural" asphalt was expensive, as it was the softening process needed to make it usable on American roads. In addition, it often had unwanted natural ingredients, such as stones and vegetation. Amzi Barber had suspected there was viability to natural California asphalts, but initial reports indicated insufficient quantities for commercial gain.[25] Years later, Barber employee Fred Warren, discovered its commercial potential and began independent operations around 1900.[26] The company obtained a patent the following year for hot mix asphalt, calling it Bitulithic (bitumin/asphalt and lithic/stone) as compared to sheet asphalt which used sand. The variable size of stones in the mix gave Bitulithic asphalt greater strength.[27] Challenged by the Asphalt Trust, the court validated the Warren Brothers patent. When the Trust cut off the Warren supply of natural asphalt, the brothers began to process coal tar, later joining industrial giant Standard Oil in the production of artificial asphalt.[28] These developments meant increased competition. Hence, there was need for people who could use their political connections and social networks to limit inroads into the monopoly the "Trust" was trying so hard to maintain. Such a man was James K. McGuire.

Until 1920, urban America still largely used the horse for transportation. The strength, stability and cost of asphalt made it the preferred surfacing for the nation's growing road network.[29] This preference continued as the country moved towards automotive transport. Woodrow Wilson's Federal Aid Road Act of 1916 increased national demand for asphalt, but by then James K. McGuire had left the asphalt business and was engaged in propaganda activities for the Imperial German Government, beginning yet another chapter of his political life.

McGuire re-enters our chronology in 1905, for two reasons: 1) he wrote a three volume history of the Democratic Party in New York State, and; 2) he was singled out for criticism by Senator Thomas Grady as "being a lobbyist of the Asphalt Trust" because he was trying to prevent a bill "requiring fair and reasonable opportunity for competition" before any pavement could be laid in the City of New York.[30] The irony here is that McGuire, in a short span of four years, had done a complete turnaround. As mayor, publicly at least, he favored competition as the vehicle to lower prices in the public interests. Now, as Barber Asphalt lobbyist, he opposed it. What conditions occasioned this reversal? The answers are found in the subsequent chapters. As will be seen, McGuire would be involved in a political scandal tying him and his brother George to Tammany politics, corporate greed, and accusations of inappropriate behavior resulting in his second criminal indictment. The strands of this complex tale come together with the elections in 1912 of Woodrow Wilson as President and the controversial, but short-lived Governor of New York, William Sulzer.

Notes

1 James K. McGuire. The Democratic Party In New York State. (New York: American History Book Company, 1905), 445; "Grady Names M'Guire Asphalt Lobbyist", New York Times 16 May 1905:6.
2 "Paving Despot". Herald 16 June 1901:1; "Overzealous Council". Herald 19 June 1901:4; Paving Contest". Herald 19 June 1901:6.
3 "Mayor on Paving Prices". Herald 20 May 1901:6.
4 "Dunfee Awarded 15 Contracts". Herald 26 May 1901.
5 "Mayor Will Not Sign It". Herald 11 June 1901:6.
6 The use of asphalt for these purposes dates back to ancient Mesopotamia. "History of Asphalt", http://hotmix.org/index.php?option=com_content &task=view &idzi&Itemid=57m.
7 In Europe, the use of asphalt is quite ancient predating the Christian era. Spaniards wrote about Trinidad asphalt during the first quarter of the 16th Century. Sir Walter Raleigh used it for caulking his ships in 1595, after which it was really forgotten until the late 19th Century. The National Asphalt Pavement Association lists Belgian chemist Edmund de Smedt as the person who first successfully used asphalt in the United States, paving a street in Newark, New Jersey in 1870. Desire for a more modern healthy, hygienic and aesthetic capital, and to help offset the Depression 1873, led to concern for improvements in street construction under the Grant administrations. Dan McNichol. Paving The Way: Asphalt In America (Lanham, Maryland: National Asphalt Pavement Association, 2005), 35; 41;51; 99-100; 231 N.G.Lay, Ways of the World A History of the World's Roads And The Vehicles That Made Them (New Brunswick: Rutgers University Press, 1992); 208; 231; (http://www.hotmix.org/index.php?optiom=com_content &task=view&id=21&itemid=57)
For the best overview of the history and technology of asphalt during this period, see, 1.B Holley. "Blacktop How Asphalt Paving Came To the Urban United States". Technology and Culture: October 2003; 44:4 Research Library, 703-33.
8 "Scenes From the Past". The Informer. November 2007, 13. For a good brief biography of Amzi Barber, see McNichol, chapter 5: "The Asphalt Tycoon", 57-69.
9 Lay, Ways of the World... 233-36.
10 "Major General Francis V. Greene". New York Times 4 September 1898. Greene came from a distinguished military family. A West Point graduate, Greene served in the Corps of Engineers. He was involved in the survey which formalized the USA-Canadian boundary. He was observer of many campaigns after which he was an engineer in charge of public works in the

nation's capital, 1879-85. He resigned from the army to work with the Barber Asphalt Company serving as its President, 1892-1900. During his connection with Barber Asphalt, he authored articles on the history, use, merits and manufacture of asphalt, especially extolling the virtue of the product of Pitch Lake, Trinidad, over which Barber had a monopoly. Having joined the New York National Guard upon his retirement from the military, when it was activated during the Spanish-American War, he served as a Brigadier-General in the Philippine campaigns. An active Republican, Greene served as New York City Police Commissioner from 1903-04, later becoming President of the Niagara-Lockport and Ontario Power Company, retiring in 1915. "Greene, Francis Vinton". National Cyclopedia of American Biography vol. XXIII (Ann Arbor, Michigan: University microfilms 1967), 23; "Francis Vinton Greene". http://www.arlingtoncemetery.net/fvgreene.htm; F.V. Greene, "Asphalt and Its Uses". Transactions of The American Institute of Mining (Buffalo: 1888), 355-75. See also McNichol Paving..., 67-68.

11 McNichol, Paving...63.

12 "Barber, Amzi Lorenzo". Dictionary of American Biography vol. I (1931), 586-587. Deming, Arthur. Corporate Promotions and Reorganization (Cambridge: Harvard University Press, 1914), 412-63. A good example of the political machinations of Barber is noted in McNichol. A competing company, North American Asphalt, found a promising supply source on an Indian Reservation in Utah and was negotiating leases with the tribe. The Indians, their Congressman and North American Asphalt wanted to make a deal, but they were thwarted by the Secretary of the Interior who supported Barber Asphalt. The Secretary exempted portions of the reservation claiming they had never been ceded to them as "permanent" and thus had no right to the property, threatening their reservation lands would be reduced by 90 percent, from two million to 200,000 acres, should they resist (McNichol, 59-60). Thus was pattern set for domestic politics in Barber's attempts to maintain a monopoly that would ensnare James. K. McGuire. For details, see I.B. Holley, Blacktop 710-11.

13 McNichol, Paving... 64.

14 Ibid. Upon his acquisition of the Venezuelan deposits they were miraculously no longer "inferior".

15 Moody, John. The Truth About Trusts (New York: Moody Publishing Company, 1904), 300. According to the National Asphalt Paving Association, until about 1900, almost all asphalt used in the United States came from Pitch Lake in Trinidad and Lake Bermudez in Venezuela. It was a "natural" asphalt, but by 1907 refined asphalt was becoming more accepted. Intense competition allowed cities to establish stringent requirements for their roadways, including warranties on workmanship and materials. (http://

www.hotmix.org/Index.php?=com+content&task=view&idzi&Itemid=57);
McNichol, Paving 64-67

16 Mcbeth, Brian S. Gunboats, Corruption and Claims: Foreign Intervention In Venezuela, 1899-1908 (Westport, Conn: Greenwood Press, 2001), 41-50; 63-266 McNichol Paving…67-8; "ExSenator Hiscock Defends Venezuela", New York Times 23 January 1901; "Latest In Asphalt War." New York Times 30 June 1901 "Asphalt Trust In Hands of Receivers." New York Times 29 December 1901. "Asphalt Trusts Financial Condition" New York Times 31 December 1901; Amzi Barber Dies of Pneumonia" New York Times 19 April 1909; "Has Title To Asphalt Lands." New York Times 26 December 1909; "Barber Had Income From J.J. Albright." New York Times 19 April 1913. In a subsequent Government investigation of the affair, Amzi Barber absolved General Greene of any involvement, taking full blame for the events. See. "Revolution Backed By Asphalt Company. "New York Times 19 October 1905. For the dictator's overthrow, see "Nations Aiding Foes of Castro". New York Times 18 December 1908. For an overview see I.B, Holley Blacktop 711-713. Charles M. Warner was a prominent Syracuse businessman and loyal Republican. He held only two public offices in his life, despite party entreaties to become more involved. He was Postmaster in his native Jordan, New York and later Fire Commissioner of Syracuse under Mayor Jacob Amos. "He was connected with many gigantic enterprises which employed thousands", including the Warner-Quinlan Asphalt Company, flour milling, lumber, railroads, banking and brewing. His name would figure prominently in the asphalt paving scandals of the following decade. See M. J. Kingsley, J. C. Knauber, J. J. Neville, A. C. Buckenberger The Political Blue Book of Syracuse, New York (E.M. Grover, 1902), 259.

17 "Carlisle Fights Back", New York Times 22 November 1913:2;

18 "Demands Proof of Charges", New York Times 11 November 1892;9; "Trinidad Asphalt or None", New York Times 15 May 1893:12; "New Jersey Public Jobbers", New York Times 5 June 1893:9; "Mayor Gilroy Makes Reply", New York Times 17 January 1894:9; "Wants An Investigation", New York Times 22 January 1894:2; "A Public Works Scandal", New York Times 4 October 1898 "Trenton Paving Scandal" New York Times 5 May 1908:16.

19 "Mr. Townsend On Pavements", New York Times 15 January 1894:2.

20 McNichol Paving… 58

21 1906 G.A. Co. Rep. 7; cited in Deming, 417. Barber would also "paid hirelings" such as engineer Clifford Richardson who would write in engineering journals that Barber asphalt was the only material worth laying. Richardson was a Harvard-educated chemist who worked for Barber, 1896-1900, 1913-21. He authored two books on asphalt pavement and under his auspices Barber laid 30-40 million square yards of pavement. Supposedly the Barber Company

bought up all copies of Richardsons 1905 textbook to prevent disclosure of its trade secrets. I.B. Holley. <u>Blacktop</u>...712; "Richardson, Clifford <u>National Encyclopedia of American Biography</u>, vol. xxxiii (Ann Arbor) University Microfilms, 1967), 253; Lay, <u>Ways of</u> ...237.

22 "Seeks To Indict James K. M'Guire", <u>New York Times</u> 24 November 1913;1-2.
23 McNichol, <u>Paving</u> ... 77-78; Lay, <u>Ways of The World</u>... 244.
24 <u>Ibid</u>, 90.
25 <u>Ibid</u>, 80.
26 McNichol, 86; Holley <u>Blacktop</u>... 720.
27 McNichol 88; Holley, 720.
28 McNichol, 90; 108; Lay, <u>Ways of The World</u>... 244; Holley, 723.
29 McNichol; 94; Holley 727.
30 "Grady Names M'Guire As Asphalt Lobbyist", <u>New York Times</u> 6 April 1905:6.

CHAPTER II - C

"Asphalt Jungle": "Boss" Murphy, the Brothers McGuire – Mistakes and Miscalculations, 1912- 13"

As in 1901, and again in 1905, the year 1912 marked a watershed in the career of James K. McGuire. Now closely tied to Tammany Boss Charles F. Murphy, McGuire's career would mirror the ebb and flow of Murphy's political fortunes. In terms of their impact on McGuire, Murphy had to deal with several issues: 1) he unsuccessfully backed "Champ" Clark against Woodrow Wilson for the Democratic nomination for President; 2) the depths of Tammany corruption were revealed once again in the Becker-Rosenthal murder case, one outgrowth of which was the appointment of Irish nationalist and McGuire associate James M. Sullivan as Ambassador to Santo Domingo, and; 3) Murphy backed William Sulzer for Governor of New York, whose independent stance rankled Murphy and ultimately exposed McGuire's machinations in bid-rigging and bribery for paving contracts in New York State.

The Progressive split within the state Republican party, gave the Democrats control of both houses. By 1912, "Commissioner" Murphy had firm control of the state and sought to use that as a vehicle to force his choice of Democratic candidate for President, James Beauchamp "Champ" Clark at the national convention in Baltimore. He was resisted by Franklin Roosevelt who pushed for Thomas Woodrow Wilson. Wilson had made his political career by defying the political bosses who had helped make him Governor of New Jersey. Likewise, Roosevelt, in 1910, had taken on and successfully blocked Murphy's candidate for senator, William Sheehan, supporting instead, Brooklyn reformer, Edward Shepard. After five weeks of deadlock, the two parties agreed on a compromise candidate, James A. O'Gorman, who turned out to be a Murphy loyalist.[1] At the national level, William Jennings Bryan, realizing his nomination was impossible, threw his support behind Wilson, forcefully denouncing an alleged deal between Tammany Hall and financiers J. P. Morgan, Thomas Fortune Ryan and August Belmont, to push for the candidacy of "Champ" Clark. Murphy could not swing Tammany to support Wilson, earning the ire of Wilson in the process and ultimately depriving Murphy of federal patronage jobs. Theodore Roosevelt bolted the national Republican party, splitting it and giving a narrow victory to Wilson. FDR went to Washington as Assistant Secretary of the Navy. Bryan, in return for his support for Wilson, was made Secretary of State[2] and in that capacity was responsible for appointing James M. Sullivan Ambassador to Santo Domingo. Sullivan would lure McGuire to Santo Domingo with promises of asphalt paving contracts, in a scandal that tarnished them, Tammany Hall and the asphalt industry.

A second serious scandal to confront Murphy, was the Becker-Rosenthal murder case of 1912. It would bring to prominence James M. Sullivan, leading to his appointment as ambassador to Santo Domingo; it would mark the emergence of District Attorney Charles W. Whitman, who would not only serve as prosecutor in the case, but also as prosecutor in the ensuing corruption scandals associated with James K. McGuire and other individuals linked not only to Tammany Hall politics, but to the cause of Irish freedom as well.

A major issue "Boss" Murphy faced in 1912 was finding an acceptable candidate for governor. His previous pick, John A. Dix, was largely a compliant tool of Murphy's machine. However, he undoubtedly evoked Murphy's ire by supporting insurgent Democrats led by Franklin D. Roosevelt who resisted Murphy's pick for United States Senator, William Sheehan, Speaker of the New York Assembly. Murphy needed a new face to go against Theodore Roosevelt's Progressive Party Candidate, Oscar Straus. He chose William Sulzer. Sulzer was a two-time unsuccessful candidate for governor. In 1896 he was supported by Syracuse Mayor James K. McGuire.[3] He failed to win the nomination a second time a decade later. Sulzer, had a career as member of the State Assembly and while not obtaining the nomination for Governor, he was elected to Congress in 1896. McGuire referred to Sulzer as a "brilliant orator" with a "national reputation" whose services were in demand in state and national campaigns.[4] The two would become political enemies in the asphalt scandals of 1913-14. With Murphy's backing, Sulzer was successful in 1912. Sulzer was a faithful machine man, yet he nursed a stubborn streak of independence. He perceived himself to be a "man of the people", championing industrial and social reforms, and earning strong support from radicals and labor.[5] Martin Glynn, a loyal protégé of "Boss" Murphy, wanted the nomination, but had to settle for Lieutenant-Governor. However, even before the election, Glynn held out to his confidantes the possibility that Sulzer would be removed.[6] It was alleged that the Democratic candidate for President, Woodrow Wilson, who made his reputation defying the political bosses in New Jersey, was Sulzer's idol. If true, this did not augur well for Murphy-Sulzer relations, nor for James K. McGuire. Sulzer won the election with a 200,000 vote plurality.[7] Sulzer tried to put some distance between himself and Charles F. Murphy. The "Boss" offered financial assistance to Sulzer but it was turned down. The Governor-elect refused to approve of Murphy's suggestions for appointive office. Sulzer told Murphy he was going to be Governor, to which Murphy allegedly replied, "Like hell you are".[8] Given the importance of kickbacks in construction and paving contracts, Murphy was especially insistent that Jim Gaffney of the New York Contracting and Trucking Company be appointed State Highway Commissioner. The New York Contracting and Trucking Company was started by John J. Murphy ("Boss" Murphy's brother), James Gaffney, an Alderman, and Richard J. Crouch (one of Murphy's political lieutenants) when the "Boss" was appointed New York City Docks Commissioner during the Van Wyck administration. In this position "Boss" Murphy amassed a fortune of over $1,000,000. The trucking company averaged a profit of $200 a day from dock properties. It later was awarded a contract for $2,000,000 for excavating the site of the New Pennsylvania Railroad Station. Interestingly, the Board of Alderman, controlled by Tammany, had steadfastly refused to vote for a franchise giving the railroad the use of the streets for its tunnel approaches. The bid was awarded to the New York Contracting and Trucking Company even though its bid was $400,000 higher than its nearest competitor. Later, the company was awarded a $6,000,000 contract for building improvements for the New York, New Haven and Hartford Railroad. By 1905, the New York Contracting and Trucking Company had been awarded contracts totaling $15,000,000, all from corporations benefitting from New York's municipal government.[9]

Murphy sought to have Eugene McManus made Commissioner of Labor, and [John] Gavin as Public Service Commissioner.[10] The Public Service Commission was a body with significant authority in the granting of public franchises. It had been ruled by political independents. Since numerous subway franchises were to be awarded, Tammany wanted control. Its compromise candidate was Edward E. McCall. Sulzer found Murphy's insistence on Gaffney particularly objectionable. The Boss responded. "It will be Gaffney or it will be war".[11] To Murphy control over these appointments was imperative since the Highway Commission was composed of the State Engineer, the State Superintendent of Public Works and the Superintendent of Highways. New roads had been authorized in a bond issue by the people of New York creating a fund of $50 million for that purpose.[12] The State Superintendent of Public Works was former Syracuse Mayor James K. McGuire's Commissioner of Public Safety, Duncan W. Peck. In his <u>History of The Democratic In New York State</u>, McGuire praised Peck's administrative abilities.[13] Peck's activities at the state level were tainted with scandal. He was in charge of Erie Canal patronage and his activities on behalf of Charles Murphy were well-known from Erie County to New York City in all counties affected by the canal. The re-appointment of Peck by Sulzer in January 1913 shocked Sulzer's friends.[14] At that time, Sulzer had not openly broken with Tammany and he may have been doing some political fence-mending. Whatever the reason, Peck, like McGuire, would reveal his close ties to Charles Murphy in the impeachment crisis of Governor Sulzer. This was the first of three fateful missteps for the governor.

Governor Sulzer also sought legislation reforms, such as a direct-primary bill, an anathema to both Murphy and Republican party Boss William Barnes, Jr. He did manage to pass a highway reorganization bill, but Murphy's henchmen, Assembly leader Al Smith and Senate Majority Leader Robert Wagner were in total control and Sulzer was without support from Republicans. Because of the deadlock, legislation and appropriations were at a standstill. Instead of caving in to Murphy, Sulzer appointed a commission headed by John N.

Carlisle of Watertown, an independent, anti-Tammany Democratic, and John H. Delaney of Brooklyn, a life-long friend of the governor, leader of the Typographical Union and opponent of the Patrick H. McCarren machine, as members of a special commission of inquiry with the goal of purging useless expenditures, abolishing sinecures and promoting honesty in the interests of the taxpayers. Pressure to desist came from Tammany, fearing widespread disclosures detrimental to its interests.[15] This pair was joined by J. Gordon Lynn of the Department of Accounts of New York City, a veteran of previous municipal investigations. In addition, Lynn was joined by John T. Norton, Deputy Attorney General, a former state assemblyman from Rensselaer County.[16] Forrest and Malcolm asserted that Lynn and Delaney were "Tammany men".[17] This was especially true of Delaney who would later betray his "friend", William Sulzer. The position of Executive Auditor was given by Sulzer to John A. Hennessy, a New York journalist, without obtaining Murphy's prior approval.[18] Hennessy, an Irish immigrant, got his training in journalism from his father. He was elected a Democratic State Assemblymen twice, often taking positions opposed to the Tammany machine. He was considered a friend and mentor to William Sulzer. His independence aborted a political career, having been beaten twice for the Assembly. Hennessy then abandoned politics for about 15 years, focusing on his career in journalism. Having successfully uncovered waste in Mayor William Jay Gaynor's administration, his close association with Sulzer made him a natural selection when the Governor needed someone to head an investigation into corruption on the state level. Hennessy's documented accounts of the widespread graft and corruption is found in his <u>What's The Matter With New York?: A Story of the Waste of Millions</u>.[19] Hennessy estimated that the state got thirty cents in value for every dollar spent on its roads later stating, "As these cases develop, the electors of New York will learn that the political organization, so-called Democratic, captained by Charles F. Murphy in New York City, by William Fitzpatrick in Buffalo, and by William H. Kelley in Syracuse, is organized to loot the treasury and regards every honest man as its enemy".[20]

Obviously Sulzer's choice of members of his investigating commission were personal friends and, he thought, anti-machine Democrats. He apparently accepted "Boss" Murphy's declaration of war and was determined to fight back. It was a fatal error. Hennessy's testimony in front of the investigating committee concerned the graft and corruption uncovered in contracts for the restoration of the burned portions of the state capital. These revelations led to the forced resignation of Herman W. Hoefer, the state architect, and a reorganization of that department. To Tammany, this was political treason and unpardonable.[21] Sulzer removed Hoefer, citing padded payrolls, cost over-runs, and questionable contracts. In addition, an independent panel of architects condemned Hoefer as a man who by training, ability or experience was "incompetent" for the job. Hoefer was removed by Sulzer despite attempts at interventions by John H. Delaney, by Senator James F. Frawley and Robert Wagner who voiced their objections in the name of Charles F. Murphy.[22] Sulzer's political error was compounded in Tammany's eyes when he removed C. Gordon Reel as Highway Commissioner in March, 1913, "in the interests of public service and the general welfare" replacing him with Deputy Superintendent, James H. Sturtevant. Ironically, he retained Duncan W. Peck, Superintendent of Public Works and John A. Bensel, State Engineer and Surveyor, the latter possibly because the Barge Canal was undergoing serious modifications at the time.[23] Sulzer used Reel's removal to publicize the deplorable condition of the Highway Department as exposed by his Commission of Inquiry, promising to eradicate waste, corruption and inefficiency. Reel felt he was being scapegoated by Sulzer since his two colleagues remained on the Highway Commission and the changed specifications began under the previous administration. Reel was removed two weeks after State Architect Herman Hoefer. Sulzer's refusal, despite Charles F. Murphy's insistence, that another "organization man", James E. Gaffney, replace the disgraced Reel, led to an open break between the two rivals.[24] Gaffney was co-owner with Murphy of the New York Contracting and Trucking Company, a man who took $30,000 in bribes from one of the aqueduct contractors. Previously Gaffney had extorted money for awarding a bid to a contractor on the Catskill Aqueduct. Sulzer noted that even Senator O'Gorman said the appointment of Gaffney "would be a disgrace to the state and ruin [Sulzer's] political career".[25] Sulzer stumped the state appealing to the people, writing articles on "The Paradise of Graft" in Albany[26] urging passage of his direct primary bill and condemning boss rule. As a result of Hennessy's investigation, Tammany loyalist State Senator Stephen J. Stilwell was tried and convicted for accepting a bribe in January, 1913.[27] Other Tammany allies were also tried including the powerful Justice Daniel Cohalan, a long-time Murphy ally, Irish nationalist and friend of James K. McGuire. Cohalan was tried by the Legislature for extortion. John A. Connolly, allegedly paid Cohalan $4,000 to obtain public office. Connolly said Cohalan demanded 55 percent of the profits of contracts he obtained from the city. Cohalan refused to appear before the Grievance Committee of the Bar Association which confirmed every charge made by Connolly. The Bar Association was anxious to investigate urging Governor Sulzer encouraged them to pursue the matter. Neither the Governor nor District Attorney Charles S. Whitman were interested in pursuing the case since it involved a disgruntled office seeker who bribed Cohalan prior to his being elevated to the Supreme Court.[28]

Charles F. Murphy
(1858-1924)
Tammary Boss, 1902-1924
Public Domain
(Source: The World's Work:http://archive.org/stream/
worldswork07 gard#page n17/mode/20p)

Charles S. Whitman
(1868-1947)
Governor of New York District Attorney
Public Domain
Library of Congress IGggbain.04989
No Known Copyright Restrictions

William Sulzer
(1863-1941)
New York Assemblyman, Governor
Public Domain
(Source: Life and Speeches of William Sulzer, 1902)

"Big" Tim Sullivan
(1862-1913)
Tammany Politician, Congressman
Library of Congress Document No 1177
Public Domain

John A. Hennessy
(1859-1951)
Investigative Journalist
Library of Congress LC-B2-2878 2
No Known Copyright Restrictions

Martin H. Glynn
(1871-1924)
Governor of New York
Public Domain
Library of Congress ID ggbain 07770
No Known Copyright Restrictions

The governor then made a second major mistake. Sulzer possibly wanting to get "Boss" Murphy to back off by doing a favor for Murphy's legal advisor, granted Cohalan's request to be tried by the judiciary committee of both state houses, a move allowable under the New York State Constitution. One of the presiding judges was from the Bar Association. He was incredulous that a lawyer and judge submitted to committed blackmail over a two-year period and later manufactured false evidence to explain it away. He called Cohalan "blameworthy" and guilty of shattering public confidence and demanded his removal.[29] Nonetheless, the outcome was never in doubt. Tammany loyalists, Assembly leader Alfred E. Smith and Senate Majority Leader Robert F. Wagner were in control. Cohalan was exonerated. In the Senate, the vote was 31-8; in the Assembly, it was 112-8.[30] And whereas the governor might have assumed he was obtaining the good will of "Boss" Murphy, the very opposite occurred. The "Boss" declared war on the governor. The effort would ensnare not only the governor, but his investigators, District Attorney Whitman and the brothers McGuire as well.

Edward E. McCall, a Supreme Court Justice, was Murphy and Sulzer's compromise candidate for Public Service Commissioner. His efforts kept the two from an open break until April, 1913.

Sulzer was determined to get a direct primary bill and refused to call off the Hennessy investigations. "Boss" Murphy held an "impeachment court" at Delmonico's Restaurant in May, 1913. His regional political bosses were there – Norman E. Mack of Erie County, Patrick McCabe of Albany, Edward E. McCall, William Fitzpatrick of Buffalo, Martin Glynn, John H. McCooey, Thomas Foley, Robert F. Wagner, Senator James A. Foley, Alfred E. Smith, Aaron Levy and James Frawley. Murphy demanded they "get something" on Sulzer to have him removed from office. The Frawley Committee was established in July 1913 with that goal in mind. Its mandate was: "To examine into the financial administration and conduct of all institutions, societies or associations of the state which are supported in whole or in part by state monies". The committee employed Matthew F. Horgan as its secretary. Horgan had been intimately tied to the Sulzer campaign in 1912. He had access to the Governor's private papers and his home. He was later denounced by Sulzer as a "spy".[31] The primary purpose of the Frawley Committee was to offset the investigations of Hennessy but apparently its initial efforts bore little fruit. It appeared as if Sulzer was going to have his way, but then he took a third fateful step that lead to his undoing.

In June, 1913, Governor Sulzer called a special session of the legislature to discuss amending the Corrupt Practices Act. The Frawley Committee seized on this to increase its mandate as follows: "The whole subject of any wrongful or unlawful influence aforesaid, and of receipts and expenditures of candidates for elective office to be filled by votes of the electors of the whole state, be referred to a certain joint legislative committee of the senate and the assembly to examine into the methods of financial administration".[32] This gave the Frawley Committee the green light to delve into Sulzer's campaign expenditures. It was this investigation of Sulzer that enveloped James K. McGuire and his other associates in asphalt contracting.

Then Sulzer's enemies went for the kill. They investigated Sulzer's character and charges of unprofessional conduct as a lawyer in Vermont. The investigation of the Frawley Committee revealed that Sulzer reported $6,540 in expenses from 68 persons but actually obtained $12,405 from 94 persons which was put into a private account and used to purchase stock. Sulzer's explanations, that funds came in and were disbursed without his knowledge, that he trusted monetary outlays to his assistants assuming they were accurate, and that the money given to him was to be used as he saw fit, fell on deaf ears. At least one check was endorsed by Sulzer acknowledging it as a campaign contribution.[33] Tammany made a strenuous effort to get as many Democrats to the Legislature as possible during their summer break and finally managed to muster enough votes for impeachment on eight articles. It passed, 79-45.[34] One of the witnesses against the Governor was former McGuire associate Duncan Peck who stated that Sulzer asked him to conceal the fact that Peck had given him a $500 contribution.[35] Sulzer's eleventh hour attempts to reach an accommodation with "Boss" Murphy came to nothing.. The decision was rendered in October 1913. The vote was 43-12 to remove Sulzer from public office for violation of three of the eight counts against him.[36]

While Murphy won and showed his precedent-setting power in removing a sitting governor, he also lost. Sulzer was considered a martyr by his Assembly constituency. He was re-elected and used his position as a platform to expose Tammany corruption. Murphy's role in Sulzer's ouster was widely publicized and public revulsion of his abuse of power was shown in the elections of 1913. With few exceptions, virtually every Tammany man who voted for Sulzer's impeachment was voted out of office.[37]

The repercussions of the Sulzer impeachment haunted Tammany's efforts in maintaining control over both the municipal government of New York City and the state. For example, Mayor William Gaynor, who obtained the office with Tammany support, proved too intractable and independent for a machine that placed loyalty and compliance above competence.[38] Gaynor's untimely death opened the way for other reformers including John Purroy Mitchel, whose exposés of municipal contract corruption led to the removal of Tammany-puppet borough Presidents in Manhattan, Queens and the Bronx by Republican Governor Charles Evans Hughes. Mitchel was subsequently elected President of the Board of Alderman. Mitchel, at the young age of 34, became the Fusion reform candidate. Like McGuire, Mitchel was referred to as "The Boy Mayor". Tammany chose Edward E. McCall, a former judge and head of the Public Service Commission to run against him. McCall was noted for three things: his girth, his geniality and for being a good Tammany loyalist.[39] Especially damaging to McCall's candidacy was Hennessy's testimony from lobbyist Eugene Wood that McCall paid $25,000 to Tammany to be nominated as Supreme Court judge. "Boss" Murphy was opposed but "Big Tim" Sullivan pushed McCall's nomination and it was approved.[40] Charles S. Whitman, crusading district attorney and hero of the Becker-Rosenthal murder case obtained endorsement for district attorney from both Fusion and Tammany. Mitchel won with a 124,262 vote plurality. Not only did Tammany lose City Hall, but it also lost control of the state legislature, as well.[41]

The graft revelations were now pursued with vigor by District Attorney Charles Whitman who looked into Highway Department frauds. Whitman was hampered by jurisdictional issues, which limited him to New York County, hence he was unable to proceed in rural areas unless he was appointed an Assistant Attorney-General. Governor Glynn was reluctant to appoint Whitman to that position. It should have come as no surprise. Martin H. Glynn as Governor, sought to carve a middle path between the Tammanyites and the reformist wings of the party. For example, Glynn had initially urged passage of a direct primary bill in 1909 when he was editor of the Albany Times-Union, and as Lieutenant-Governor, wanted Sulzer to come out strong for it. Later, he refused to help Sulzer get it passed. Glynn also urged Sulzer to appoint Patrick E. McCabe, Glynn's political mentor and Charles F. Murphy's "factotum" in Albany County, as Public Service Commissioner. One of his first announcements as Governor, following the impeachment of Sulzer, was to urge the cessation of "government by investigation".[42] Glynn, in the wake of the strong public reaction to Sulzer's impeachment, once more endorsed the direct primary law, as well as the direct election of United States senators and a workmen's compensation bill.[43]

Glynn was encouraged to use his new power to end the widespread corruption. The pressure came from Attorney-General Thomas Carmody, an anti-Tammany Democrat thoroughly disgusted with the State administration.[44] In addition, Glynn was presented with formal charges against Highway Commissioner John Carlisle and James K. McGuire by District Attorney Charles Whitman. Upstate Democrats were demanding action. As a result, Governor Glynn announced his own state-wide investigation under the leadership of James W. Osborne.[45] The use of a parallel investigation commission was not unique in New York State politics. A similar attempt was made under the administration of reform Governor Samuel J. Tilden who was investigating corruption in the Canal Ring during the 1870's. One of those figuring prominently in the scandal was Republican

James Belden of Syracuse. Canal interests in the Assembly, fearing an investigation would expose their involvement, established a parallel committee to discharge the same duties as the Governor's. The Assembly Committee then sought to join the Governor's Commission in order to divert or derail it, but their efforts were declined and "the committee abandoned all pretense of making an investigation and passed out of public view".[46] Several indictment were handed down, all but two of whom were Democrats. Nevertheless, though the efforts at recovery and punishment came to little, the canal ring was broken. Such was to be the outcome of the highway investigations of 1913-14 as well.

Nevertheless, Governor Glynn refused to appoint Whitman as Deputy Attorney-General to overcome the jurisdiction[47] problem, hinting that Whitman was trying to enhance his reputation to make a run for higher office. Interestingly, Glynn asserted that Whitman's "messenger boys" in this endeavor were Henry A. Rubino, attorney for the Warner-Quinlan Company and James W. Osborne, his special investigator into highway scandals. It was the dogged determination of Whitman which highlighted the role of James K. McGuire and others involved in bribery, corruption and illegal campaign contributions. The issue that Tammany tried so hard to bury during the Sulzer impeachment, was about to engulf its leaders. For example, a Tammany district leader was jailed for his part in a Rockland County road swindle. The Democratic State Treasurer, John J. Kennedy under questioning by Whitman in the on-going graft inquiry, committed suicide. Kennedy had come up from the ranks, rising from saloon keeper, to alderman to Democratic State Treasurer in 1911. His business interests included an insurance bonding company connected to Tammany. The company was tied to Charles F. Murphy, Jr., nephew of "Boss" Murphy, the same business partner of the McGuire brothers. The insurance company, the United States Fidelity and Guaranty Company of Baltimore, was known as a "Tammany concern" whose men wielded great influence as officials or directors. It was this company that floated the bail bond for James K. McGuire upon his second indictment. And though Kennedy resigned his position as vice-president of the company in Buffalo prior to becoming State Treasurer, he was under investigation by District Attorney Whitman for favoring his company with deposits of state money. A rival bank, The Fidelity Trust Company, lost $700,000 when its account was switched to Kennedy's company four months after he took office as State Treasurer. Similar to George H. McGuire, Kennedy was humiliated in his public testimony by Whitman. He was reluctant to undergo a second crucifixion. Whitman was reportedly going to use this to leverage Kennedy into revealing the workings of the Democratic party and had Kennedy subpoenaed. Kennedy allegedly committed suicide because he feared being indicted for perjury. His son was also under indictment in connection with bonding contracts on state canal and highway projects. This was the same insurance company to which the McGuire brothers and Charles Murphy, Jr. were connected. It was mentioned this too, was a factor in Kennedy's suicide.[48] Rumors of collusion and bid-rigging during the brief tenure of Governor Sulzer began to surface in June, 1913. Michael J. Walsh, Acting State Controller, refused to honor highway bids let by John N. Carlisle, Highway Commissioner. Walsh noted such practices were the reason for Sulzer's instigation of a Commission of Inquiry into the Highway Department. This was the rationale for the removal of its Tammany Commissioner, C. Gordon Reel and the passage of a state law requiring competition on all bids over $1000. Both Carlisle and Sulzer, against Tammany opposition, advocated for greater discretionary power for the Superintendent of Highways in letting paving bids. Walsh further noted the collusion between representatives of the Highway Department and contractors which encouraged favoritism in awarding contracts. The Acting Controller also reported the specifications called for a patented material controlled by a "well-known politician", a practice which had been universally condemned. Essentially, Carlisle was repeating the sins of his predecessors when the Highway Department was totally under Tammany control.[49] George H. McGuire had previously told Hennessy he knew of no illegal contributions made by contractors that had not been recorded.[50] Despite this transparent lie, Hennessy cited McGuire as the source of information about graft on the states highways and canals, the knowledge of which contributed to the defeat of Tammany candidates throughout the state. George McGuire gave Hennessy a list of contractors who had all paid blackmail amounting to hundreds of thousands of dollars. The money was divided among Tammany politicians, using dummies to conceal the contributions. In his testimony, Hennessy tied McGuire to 43 corporations, including the Barber Asphalt Company. Hennessy's other informant was Eugene Wood, a lobbyist in Albany long associated with the Democratic party and its scandals. Wood was spilling Tammany's downstate secrets about the Delmonico meeting to impeach Sulzer.[51] Wood's motive was revenge. He had business ties to electric power companies in Albany and Troy, and to Anthony N. Brady, the gas and electric power magnate. Both wanted to make sure a bill of 1913 to authorize the production of electric power at low cost to municipalities was defeated. Wood went to "Boss" Charles F. Murphy who promised it would fail but Murphy reneged. Brady and Wood were outraged and promised to get even. Wood urged Sulzer to veto the bill because if he did, Sulzer would obtain his and Brady's support in his fight with Murphy. In addition, "Fingy" Conners, former Democratic State Chairman deposed by Murphy because he was too independent, also testified to Hennessy that he was ordered by "Boss" Murphy to get big contributions from state contractors. Wood was later subpoenaed to testify in person by District Attorney Charles Whitman.[52] After examining Wood and George H. McGuire, Whitman anticipated calling James K. McGuire to testify.[53] James K. McGuire was moving quickly towards his second indictment.

The accusations of graft surrounding James K. McGuire centered around an alleged secret meeting on 5 July, 1913 at Cooperstown, New York where decisions highly favorable to the Barber Asphalt Company were reached. Participants at the meeting were Governor William Sulzer, State Highway Commissioner John N. Carlisle and George H. McGuire. Soon after Highway Commissioner Carlisle took office, efforts were allegedly made by him to "squeeze" the

Warner-Quinlan Company, a major competitor of the Barber Asphalt Company. The specifications were drawn up by "a panel of advisory engineers" appointed by powerful Democrats, including James K. McGuire. Carlisle had appointed a Board of Consulting Engineers, composed of Harold Parker, George C. Diehl and William De Hertburn Washington to reorganize the Highway Department with an eye towards greater efficiency. The Commissioner's report projected a net savings of $300,000 to $500,000 annually.[54] This Board of Consulting Engineers was allegedly also at the 5 July 1913 Cooperstown meeting. Their appointments suggest collusion on the bid-rigging scheme. Washington was selected by Sulzer upon the recommendation of James K. McGuire; the other two by businessmen interested in State highway contracts. Parker was allegedly a stockholder in the Hassam Compressed Concrete Company to which the State had paid royalties for the use of a paving process. These engineers received $50 per day plus expenses for their efforts from May through November 1913. Two of them resigned their positions as a result of these revelations.[55] A damning piece of evidence of the meeting was the record of a long distance phone call to the office of the Highway Department on that same day. It was alleged the receiver of the call, James K. McGuire, "the Barber Asphalt Company man," was in the office of the Highway Department for the "very purpose of receiving the call". Details of the meeting were provided to District Attorney Whitman by Henry A. Rubino, attorney for the Warner-Quinlan Asphalt Company, a major competitor with Barber Asphalt for paving contracts.[56] Warner-Quinlan, the losing bidder in the Syracuse paving contract awards of 1901, was about to exact revenge. In subsequent testimony, George H. McGuire told of an unreported campaign contributor of $500 he gave to Sulzer the day after he won the gubernatorial nomination. McGuire also admitted giving Hennessy $2500 to help Sulzer out of his money problems. Hennessy said the larger amount was to defray the cost of his investigation, since the Legislature refused to fund it. Hennessy's assertions as to the purpose of the $2500 were supported by Henry L. Stoddard, editor of the <u>Evening Mail</u>, and treasurer of a committee of citizens who wanted the graft investigations to continue.[57] Hennessy also stated George H. McGuire, in giving him the larger sum, was "double-crossing" his own party managers, supporting the regular party organization in Onondaga County and aiding Sulzer's attempt to break Murphy's power upstate, a charge George H. McGuire denied. To support his claims, Hennessy produced the "M" telegram,[58] allegedly sent to him by George H. McGuire. Dated 27 October 1913, and addressed to Hennessy, it said Everett Fowler came to Syracuse, and made his headquarters at William Kelley's office. Kelley was the Democratic Boss of Onondaga County who replaced James K. McGuire. Kelley helped Fowler shake down contractors.[59] Kelley also purportedly monopolized all the road repair work through the intercession of Duncan W. Peck, and C. Gordon Reel. George H. McGuire denied any connection to the telegram and further denied giving Hennessy a list of contractors' contributions, including the Barber Asphalt Company, to which his brother James was connected.[60] For their efforts at exposing Tammany corruption, both District Attorney Whitman and Hennessy received threatening calls. Some advisors were urging Whitman desist since there was no evidence of crimes committed in New York County. Whitman responded that money sandbagged from contractors upstate was ultimately divided and used downstate. Even if the grafters went unknown, Whitman was determined at the very least to indict some conspirators for perjury. George H. McGuire, it was rumored, would be that person if he did not own up to his role. Whitman played his hand carefully, laying a trap for McGuire. Whitman had obtained testimony from the Western Union clerk at the Syracuse railroad station, as well as from McGuire's own secretary, that McGuire was the writer of the "M" telegram. When brought to the stand again and confronted with both his own typewriter and the expert witness who said it was the machine on which the telegram was written, McGuire "refreshed" his recollection and admitted authorship. Prior to his testimony, George H. McGuire had retained Henry A. Wise, former U.S. Attorney-General as his counsel. After testifying, McGuire collapsed, his lawyer denying that his distraught client had later attempted suicide.[61] Whitman pursued his quarry, obtaining an indictment against Everett Fowler, based on the "M" telegram which mentioned Fowler as the main bagman for the Democratic party in the office of Tammany's political boss in Onondaga County, William H. Kelley. Fowler, according James K. McGuire, was a lawyer of prominence with a long interest in the party organization having filled a number of local positions in Kingston, New York.[62] Fowler, according to George H. McGuire's testimony, was in a meeting in 1911 in Albany with Governor John A. Dix, G. Gordon Reel, former head of the Highway Department, and Tammany's Erie County leader, Norman E. Mack. It was here that Fowler was designated as one of the upstate collectors of campaign funds.[63] Fowler obtained his money from contractors by threatening them their work would not pass inspection if they did not do as he asked. Interestingly, Kelley left a paper trail of his misdeeds – signed letters to area contractors insisting they meet with him. This was reinforced with the publication of a letter from Arthur A. McLean, Treasurer of the Democratic State Committee, acknowledging their contributions. However, not all of the contributions were reported to the Secretary of State as required by law. It was important to Whitman's case to prove a conspiracy existed. The fact the check had been cleared by a New York City bank showed a crime had been committed in New York County and would thus eliminate any jurisdictional issues.[64] The following week George H. McGuire was on the stand again, this time reading into the court record a 20 page statement "correcting" his previous testimony alleging what he said previously was only "hearsay." George H. McGuire did indicate that he and his brother James K. McGuire received a commission on all sales of Barber Asphalt Company products made to the state and to state contractors. Both brothers he admitted, were stockholders in Barber Asphalt amounting to $70,000 and they had talked with Governor Sulzer and Highway Commissioner Carlisle urging them to favor Barber Asphalt. State Highway Commissioner John N. Carlisle admitted knowing the McGuires were representatives of Barber Asphalt and meeting them "on business", but he denied being at the Cooperstown meeting.[65] McGuire also noted that his brother James had left for South America three days earlier,[66] but given his record of untruthful testimony, Whitman was unwilling to believe him until it had been confirmed by other sources. James K. McGuire was not simply avoiding testifying before District Attorney Whitman. He went to Santo Domingo on business, ostensibly at the invitation of the American Ambassador, James M. Sullivan, his associate in Irish nationalist politics. Given that several of his companions on the trip were also being investigated, as was the ambassador himself, this "Sojourn to Santo Domingo" provides additional insights into Tammany politics, asphalt scandals and international intrigue.

CONFLICTS AND CRISES 185

Notes

1 Connable, Alfred and Silberfarb, Edward, Tigers of Tammany: Nine Men Who Ruled New York (New York: Holt, Rhinehart, Winston, 1967) 250-52, Brown, Roscoe, in Smith, Ray (ed.) History of the State of New York: Governmental and Political, 1896-1920. vol. IV (Syracuse: Syracuse Press, 1922), 193-9. Werner, M. R. Tammany Hall (Garden City, New York: Garden City Publishing Company, 1928), 518. "Statesmen Warmly Welcome O'Gorman". New York Times 3 April 1911.
2 Connable and Silberfarb, 252; Brown IV, 215-217; Werner, 529.
3 "Nominations For Governor". New York Times 18 September 1896:2.
4 McGuire, James K. The History of The Democratic Party In New York State, (New York: American History Book Publishing, vol. II, 1905), 505;506.
5 Brown, Roscoe E. In Smith(ed.), vol. IV, 30:131-135; Connable and Silberfarb, Tigers of Tammany...252-3; Werner, 231. Thomas, Samuel Bell, The Boss Or The Governor (New York: Truth Publishing Company, 1914), 14-35.
6 Thomas, 101-102; Forrest, Jay W. and Malcolm, James. Tammany's Treason: The Impeachment of Governor Sulzer (Albany, New York: Jay H. Forrest, 1913), 51.
7 Werner, 532; Connable and Silberfarb, 252.
8 Brown IV, 229.
9 "Tammany's Evil Ways Are Told In A New History". New York Times 28 October 1917.
10 Thomas, 100; Werner, 533; Brown IV, 231.
11 Myers, Gustavus. History of Tammany Hall. 2nd ed. (New York: Boni and LIveright, 1917), 362. Brown IV, 231; Werner, 535.
12 "Big Problems That Face New York's Governor". New York Times 10 January 1913.
13 McGuire, vol. III, 384.
14 Forrest and Malcolm, 58.
15 "Picks Two Investigators". New York Times 3 January 1913.
16 "Graft Commission Begins Work Today". New York Times 7 January 1913.
17 Forrest and Malcolm, 48.
18 Brown IV, 230; Werner, 235; "Hennessy, Who Turned The City's Campaign Topsy-Turvy". New York Times 2 November 1913.
19 Hennessy, John A. "What's The Matter With New York?; A Story of The Waste of Millions (New York: O'Connell Press, 1916).
20 Werner, 535; Connable and Silberfarb, 253.
21 Forrest and Malcomb, 48.
22 "Ousted For Ending Tammany's Graft". New York Times 22 October 1913.
23 Whitford, Noble, E. History of the Barge Canal of New York State (Albany:

J. B. Lyon Company, 1922), 229-45; "Sulzer Removes C. Gordon Reel", New York Times 8 March 1913.

24 "Ousted For Ending Tammany's Graft". New York Times 22 October 1913.

25 Myers, 366;368.

26 Thomas, 111. Places visited included Syracuse, Buffalo, Corning, and Elmira. Two of the Assembly members of the Onondaga County delegation who were to greet him were supporters of Sulzer's direct primary bill. The Governor was counting on S. Gay Daley and P. J. Kelley for support in his showdown with "Boss" Charles F. Murphy. He would be disappointed. "We'll Win, Says Governor Sulzer". Syracuse Herald 19 May 1913: 2: "Onondaga Men Go With Tammany". Syracuse Herald 12 August 1913:9.

27 Brown IV, 231.

28 Ibid., 239-5; Myers, 383-4. According to Myers, Cohalan was appointed as judge as the result of a deal between Tammany "Boss" Murphy and Governor Dix. Cohalan began his career as a lawyer whose career prospered as a result of his ties to Tammany Hall. By 1908, he was a Grand Sachem. When Murphy failed to get Cohalan (and later Billy Sheehan), a federal Senate seat due to opposition from insurgent Democrats, a compromise candidate was arranged in the person of Judge James A. O'Gorman. Cohalan was appointed Justice of the State Supreme Court to replace O'Gorman

29 Myers, 334.

30 Brown IV, 234-5; Forrest and Malcolm, 112-113; "Bar To Investigate Cohalan Charges". New York Times 30 May 1913; "Waits For Sulzer In Cohalan Case". New York Times 3 June 1913.

31 Forrest and Malcolm, 107-108.

32 Ibid., 108.

33 "Find Checks Paid To Sulzer Himself". New York Times 4 September 19013. Onondaga County Assemblyman S. Gray Daley and P. J. Kelley voted with the Frawley Committee. It would be safe to assume there was pressure on them to do so from William H. Kelley, political boss of the county. Kelley, as would soon be made public, had been a "bagman" for Charles F. Murphy. The fact the Frawley Committee Report was "hammered" through the Assembly without giving its members an opportunity to read it gave the procedure all the earmarks of a "political lynching". "Onondaga Men Go With Tammany". Syracuse Herald 12 August 1913:9.

34 These included: (1) filing a false statement with the Secretary of State regarding campaign expenditures; (2) perjury in swearing the account was accurate (3) bribery of witnesses before the Senate Committee; (4) suppression of evidence; (5) preventing a witness from testifying; (6) larceny for using campaign contributions for personal purposes; (7) using the power of his

office to intimidate legislators to support his bills, and; (8) concealing his interests in Stock Exchange transactions. In Brown IV, 238; Myers, 537-38.
35 Brown IV, 238; Forrest and Malcolm, 162.
36 Myers, 554; Brown IV, 240-41. Several sources believe the verdict, while politically motivated, was just. See Brown IV, 241; Weiss, Nancy. "Sulzer, William". In Edward T. James (ed.) Dictionary of American Biography, Supplement Three, 1941-45 (New York: Charles Scribner's and Sons, 1973), 751.
37 "Buffalo Landslide Against Murphy". New York Times 5 November 1913.
38 Gaynor had been a judge of the New York Supreme Court where he earned a reputation for vigorous enforcement. He resigned from the bench to become a Tammany-endorsed candidate, despite his reputation for municipal reform. Gaynor was not pliable to Tammany purposes, filling city offices with experts and those chosen from civil service lists, cutting down on the patronage so essential to Tammany success. It was this war on corruption that led to his attempted assassination. A discharged employee, James J. Gallagher, shot Gaynor in the throat. Gaynor never fully recovered, but his popularity made him a possible candidate for Governor and hence a potential candidate for President. Gaynor refused the nomination insisting on serving out his term as Mayor, a decision that assisted Woodrow Wilson in obtaining the Democratic presidential nomination in 1912. Tammany refused to renominate him as Mayor. He was nominated by Independents for a second term, but died before the election was held. "Gaynor, William Jay". National Cyclopedia of American Biography vol. XVI Ann Arbor: University Microfilms, 1967), 353-4; "Gaynor William Jay". In Johnson, Allen and Malone, Dumas. Dictionary of American Biography (New York: Charles Scribners, 1931), 200-201.
39 "Tammany's Mayoralty Candidate, Edward D. McCall, At Close Range". New York Times 31 August 1913.
40 "M'Guire Owns Up" New York Times. 12 November 1913.
41 Maeder, Jay. "John Purroy Mitchel, Boy Mayor". Daily News 30 May 1913, Part I; Brown IV, 245. For details on the Becker-Rosenthal Case, see "Sojourn To Santo Domingo" Chapter, pp.
42 Forrest and Malcolm, 47; 50; 83; 143; Brown IV, 247.
43 "Martin H. Glynn: Accomplishments and Contributions" http://www.valatielibrary.org/glynnbio-print.htm
44 "Carmody To Quit State Law Office". New York Times 21 July 1914.
45 "Gov. Glynn's Opportunity". New York Times 22 November 1913; "Glynn Makes New Rules". New York Times 25 November 1913.
46 Smith (ed.), vol.III, 175; 176; McGuire, I, 426.
47 Brown IV, 246; "Gov. Glynn Opens Fire On Whitman". New York Times 22

December 1913. "Another Hearing On Carlisle Charges". <u>Syracuse Herald</u> 19 December, 1913:12.

48 "Kennedy's Rise To Power". New York Times 16 February 1914; "Acts of Kennedy Were Under Fire". <u>New York Times</u> 16 February 1914; "Three Kennedy Inquiries". <u>New York Times</u> 17 February 1914; "Kennedy Feared Charge of Perjury". <u>New York Times</u> 17 February 1914; Myers, 389-90.

49 "Vetoes Road Plans of Sulzer's Board". <u>New York Times</u> 25 June 1913. It would be interesting to speculate as to whom Walsh was referring. He was circumspect but the phrase "patented material controlled by a well-known politician" points towards James K. McGuire who, as noted, had already been tied to Barber Asphalt. Interestingly, two months previously, George H. McGuire had been with Governor Sulzer and the two had taken a three-hour walk. McGuire would not divulge what was discussed. "G. H. McGuire Takes Walk With Sulzer". <u>Syracuse Herald</u> 16 April 1913:6.

50 "George M'Guire Explains". <u>New York Times</u>; November 1913. This item was given major coverage in a Herald article. "Hennessy Says George H. M'Guire Was Informant". <u>Syracuse Herald</u>. 1 November 1913.

51 "Gene Wood Told Wigwam Secrets: Tammany At Bay". New York Times 1 November 1913; "Who Was Eugene Wood?" www.albanylaw.edu/media/user/wood.pdf. Apparently, not only contractors were solicited for campaign contributions. <u>The New York Times</u> reported numerous judges and many businesses contributed money that was not reported to the Secretary of State as required by law. Interestingly, one of the concerns was Barber Asphalt, giving $5000. For the complete list, see "Will Call M'Guire In New Graft Hunt". <u>New York Times</u> 6 November 1913:5.

52 Forrest and Malcolm, 89; "M'Guire Owns Up" <u>New York Times</u> 12 November 1913. "Gene Wood Told..." <u>New York Times</u> 1 November 1913; "Wood Subpoenaed By Whitman's Men" <u>New York Times</u> 5 November 1913. Anthony N. Brady (1843-1913) was born in France and when he was young his family moved to Troy, New York. He received an elementary school education and moved into retailing at a young age. He later moved into supplying building materials, contracting and obtaining franchises in public utilities in New York City becoming known as the "traction magnate", expanding his operations into Washington, D. C. and Philadelphia. His business interests were linked to Standard Oil, the Albany Gas and Light Company and the American Tobacco Company. He was the richest Catholic in the United States leaving a fortune estimated at $50 million. "The American Tobacco Company" http://smokershistory.com/ATC.htm# Anthony N Brady. "Brady, Anthony Nicholas "in Johnston, Allen (ed.), <u>Dictionary of American Biography vol. 2</u> (New York: Scribners, 1929), 581-82; "Brady, Anthony Nicholas". <u>National Cyclopedia American Biography vol. XVI</u>, 1918), 149.

CONFLICTS AND CRISES 189

53 "Will Call James K. M'Guire To Testify". <u>New York Times.</u> 6 November 1913.
54 "Hennessy To Front Asphalt Inquiry". <u>New York Times</u> 4 November 1913; "Show How To Save Millions On Roads". <u>New York Times</u> 2 November 1913.
55 "Accuses Carlisle In Asphalt Deal". <u>New York Times</u> 28 November 1913; "Hennessy To Front..". <u>New York Times</u> 4 November 1913.
56 "Phone Call Trail to Highway Graft". <u>New York Times</u> 23 November 1913.
57 "Warn Whitman In Graft Inquiry". <u>New York Times</u> 8 November 1913.
58 <u>The Syracuse Herald</u> printed the full text of the telegram. Addressed to Hennessy, it read: "Election here looks close. Because of big Bull Moose vote important you make in speech the right reference to William H. Kelley. When Everett Fowler came here, 1911 and 1912, he made his headquarters at Kelley's office and Kelley helped him set up and shake down contractors on State work. In the M [obscured] statement filed with the Secretary of State, Kelley's name appears putting up $2,000 but he never put up eight cents of his own money. He also monopolized the road repair work and has big road contract, upon which several supplementary agreements have been allowed through Peck and Reel. Local papers will copy what you say in speech. You will know what to say for effect in the local city election. Should be done immediately.
M."
"Typewriter Expert Before Grand Jury Gives Damaging Evidence Against M'Guire". <u>Syracuse Herald</u> 12 November 1913:3.
59 William Henry Kelley (1867-1943) traces his paternal roots to Ireland. His father worked in the stone quarries of the Onondaga Indian Reservation for fifty years. William Kelley's playmates were Onondagas. He learned their language and employed them whenever possible in his later business ventures. Educated at the Onondaga Academy and at Mead's Business School, he was involved in the grocery business and as a coal dealer. He was a member of the Democratic State Committee from 1910 until his death. He moved into banking during the 1920's, and served on the boards of several corporations and charities in Syracuse. "Kelley, William Henry". <u>National Cyclopedia of American Biography vol. 33</u> (New York: William White, 1947), 410-411. What is not mentioned, was Kelley's ties to Tammany as its bagman for upstate New York.
60 M'Guire Balks At Graft List", <u>New York Times</u> 7 November 1913; "Typewriter Expert Grand Jury Gives Damaging Evidence Against M'Guire". <u>Syracuse Herald</u> 12 November 1913:3.
61 "M'Guire Owns Up: Taken Off Stand". <u>New York Times</u> 12 November 1913. "Clark Describes Scene When M'Guire Collapsed At YMCA Meeting". <u>Syracuse Herald</u> 17 November 1913:7. "Whitman Wants M'Guire To Make Clean Breast". <u>Syracuse Herald</u> 19 November 1913:1.3.

62 McGuire, James K. vol. II, 431. The surety company that signed Fowler's bond was the one that George H. McGuire was the upstate agent for – the United States Fidelity and Guaranty Company of Baltimore, Maryland. Martin W. Littleton was Fowler's attorney. Littleton was a Tennessee-born, self-educated lawyer who become Democratic Brooklyn Borough President, 1903-05 and won, despite his independent-stance. He had a reputation for being a formidable criminal attorney, having won several high profile cases. At the time of Fowler's indictment, Littleton was completing his first and only term as a United States Congressman. Alvin Harlow. "Littleton, Martin Wiley". In Harris E. Starr (ed.). Dictionary of American Biography vol. XI Supplement One (New York: Charles Scribner's Sons, 1944), 501-502. "Fowler Says He Will Fight Indictment". Syracuse Herald 17 November 1913:1,2.

63 "M'Guire Opens New Lead On Campaign Funds". New York Times 20 November 1913.

64 "Whitman Snares A State Bagman". New York Times 15 November 1913. The failure to accurately report campaign funds was one of the stated reasons for the impeachment of Governor William Sulzer. The four upstate contractors were named in the Syracuse Herald, as well as the details of the Cooperstown meeting. "Four Contractors Say They Gave Up Money To Fowler In Syracuse". Syracuse Herald 21 November 1913:1,2.

65 "Carlisle Fights Back". New York Times 22 November 1913. "The M'Guires Own $70,000 Stock In Asphalt Company". Syracuse Herald 27 December 1913:1,3.

66 "M'Guire Opens New Lead…." New York Times 20 November 1913.

Chapter II - D

Asphalt Jungle: Subpoenas, Sullivan and Santo Domingo

James K. McGuire left New York City during the Whitman John Doe investigations to pursue business interests in Santo Domingo. As with other aspects of his life, the trail is rather complex, tying in the various strands of his political lives – Tammany politics, Irish nationalism, and asphalt paving. His connection to the island republic was in the person of James M. Sullivan. In order to better appreciate McGuire and his involvement in Santo Domingo, it is necessary to understand his relationship to Sullivan, a Tammany lawyer who was appointed Minister to Santo Domingo.

James M. Sullivan (1868-1933) was born in Ireland. The facts about his early life are unclear. His family believes that Sullivan was actually born in 1863 but changed the date when he went to Yale Law School so as not to appear so much older than his fellow classmates. Sometime when James was very young, his parents immigrated to Massachusetts. The family says Connecticut, but the New York Times and the New York World place his early years in Brooklyn.[1] He may have completed his high school education in Palmer, Massachusetts, but again, family lore has it that he had to leave school when his father died to help support the family. He may have become a journalist working for the Hartford Courant and later the Waterbury American,[2] but his granddaughter says it is more likely he sold subscriptions. As a reporter, he was referred to as "Legs," because he would walk anywhere to get a story. It was during this early phase of his life he met William Jennings Bryan, also a newspaperman, who later sponsored him politically.[3] In fact, one version of his early years tells of his finding an ingenious, if unethical, way to "get rich quick." In selling subscriptions, he may have advised already subscribing customers to cancel them and sign up again with him.[4] As in the novel Emigrant Dreams by his granddaughter, novelist Mary Rose Callaghan, the facts of Sullivan's life are often merged with fiction. The National Cyclopedia related that he worked as a hotel night clerk in New Haven and attended Yale University. Logan insists Sullivan was sent to Yale by a "well-fixed cousin", Tim Sullivan, obtaining his law degree in 1902.[5] The New York Times says he was involved in prize-fighting. As a promoter,

Sullivan was charged with absconding with the box office receipts, allegedly used to fund his Yale law school education. It was these links to the gambling underworld that brought him into contact with "Bald Jack" Rose, a man whose involvement in the Becker-Rosenthal murder would bring a change of fortune for the aspiring attorney.[6]

James Mark Sullivan's law career began in Connecticut in association with Edward J. Maher. Later he moved to New York City where he maintained a "struggling practice" based on his Tammany Hall connections and his intimacy with underworld and gambling interests.[7]

While McGuire was becoming more outspoken on the Irish nationalist issue in the context of the early 20th century, the record as it pertains to James M. Sullivan is sparse. Aside from his birth in Ireland and his brothers' activities on behalf of Parnell, there was his marriage into an activist Sinn Fein family in 1910.[8] Perhaps he was too concerned with earning a living, hanging on the margins of Tammany society and the urban underworld of New York City. Yet his ties, while, indirect, reveal associations with some leaders of the Irish nationalist community, especially John Goff and James K. McGuire. Sullivan used his Yale-learned oratorical skills as a speaker for the Democratic Party from 1896-1912 during the heyday of William Jennings Bryan, the three-time Democratic candidate for president. Sullivan was known as the man "with the golden voice" focusing his efforts among Irish-Americans in the Northeast, working under the tutelage of James K. McGuire, three-time Democratic mayor of Syracuse.[9] The nickname may have confused Sullivan with Bryan, the latter known as "The Boy Orator of the Platte."[10] Further, the confusion may have stemmed from Sullivan's long-time association with James K. McGuire, whose eloquence won for him the title, "The Silver-Tongued Orator of Onondaga".[11] Meanwhile, Sullivan's law practice in New York may have brought him some prominence, but again accounts differ. Callaghan says that her mother, Sheila Sullivan Callaghan, told her that Sullivan had worked on the Harry K. Thaw case, perhaps as a junior lawyer under Daniel O'Reilly. But the New York Times reports of the Harry Thaw-Stanford White murder case of 1907 mention O'Reilly only once, and then only to say that he was the first lawyer to council Thaw and was very soon replaced by other attorneys. Sullivan's name is not mentioned at all. If he was involved, it was only tangentially and for a short time. According to <u>The Phelan Report</u>, "Mr. Sullivan found that O'Reilly's practice was highly sensational and unpleasant, but it appears that he divided some fees with him and remained associated with him for nearly two years". Subsequently O'Reilly was disbarred and imprisoned. He reportedly had an affair with his client Harry Thaw's wife, the famous Evelyn Nesbitt Thaw.[12]

The year 1912 was a turning point in Sullivan's career. Not only did he campaign successfully for Woodrow Wilson, but he achieved some notoriety as a result of his role in the Becker-Rosenthal case. Sullivan's connection with the Becker-Rosenthal case provided him with the contacts he needed. The case also reveals the nature and extent of Tammany Hall in police corruption, bribery and graft. Some leaders in the cause of Irish nationalism – W. Bourke Cockrane, Daniel Cohalan, Judge John Goff,[13] John C. McIntyre,[14] James M. Sullivan and James K. McGuire – were also intimately tied to Tammany politics. The most penetrating analysis of this case has been told elsewhere, but a brief overview is necessary to understand how McGuire, asphalt and Santo Domingo are linked.

Policeman Charles Becker was simply the product of a corrupt system that included individual police officers, entire police departments, lawyers, judges, prostitutes, informers, dope addicts, saloon-keepers, bordello operators, politicians and "legitimate" businessmen, as the asphalt and other trust scandals have shown. Appointments to the force were purchased, as were promotions. Once rookies learned that merit was irrelevant, they went into debt to finance their careers. To do so, they were drawn into a system of graft, becoming ever more greedy and brutal. Becker was connected to the local Tammany machine through "Big Tim" Sullivan (1863-1913), a state senator whose fortune was made in prostitution, gambling and prize-fighting. Becker was thus able to play both sides of the law to his own advantage. Becker was even praised for his law enforcement efforts.¹⁵ "Big Tim" Sullivan, Becker and gambler Herman Rosenthal were partners in a gaming parlor. As "Big Tim" was suffering from increasing bouts of insanity, Becker sought to supplant him. Becker assessed Rosenthal a $500 contribution for a colleague's legal fees. Rosenthal refused to pay and threatened to expose the whole scheme of police corruption to District Attorney Charles S. Whitman. To prevent exposure, Becker allegedly got "Bald Jack" Rose to hire some hit men to eliminate Rosenthal. James M. Sullivan got Rose to finger Becker. Rose had been an acquaintance of James M. Sullivan when they were both associated with gambling houses, prize fights and vaudeville shows in Connecticut, ostensibly when Sullivan was working as a journalist. The relationship continued sporadically after both moved to New York City. According to Andy Logan, by then Sullivan had a "thriving practice" due to his ties to Tammany Hall. After Rosenthal was murdered, Rose sought Sullivan's advice and the two conferred. Sullivan then allegedly reported these developments to "Boss" Murphy. After Rose was booked, Sullivan held another conference with his client, claiming the police were at the bottom of the murder.¹⁶ But Tammany was not united in its condemnation of Becker. John C. Fitzgerald, former state senator and a current member of the state assembly, was a political ally of "Big Tim" Sullivan. He stood firmly behind Becker. "Murphy Men", lawyers Aaron Levy and James M. Sullivan, condemned Becker, suggesting "Boss" Charles Murphy was anxious to have Becker take the blame.¹⁷ The politically ambitious District Attorney, Charles S. Whitman, also sought to use Becker to further his own career. The Tammany connection was made even stronger by having its puppet, Governor John Dix, select Judge John Goff to preside at the trial. Goff, based on his involvement in the Lexow Committee investigations of 1894 into police corruption, had no love of the New York City Police Department.¹⁸ Once again, the Tammany-Irish nationalist ties are revealed. The attorney who got Becker off in his first trial was John C. McIntyre, a Tammany lawyer and Clan-na-Gael member who was paid $13,000 from a Tammany account with the understanding to keep "Big Tim" Sullivan out of it.¹⁹ Becker's guilty conviction was reversed on appeal. His second trial was initially handled by W. Bourke Cockran, another man tied to both Tammany Hall and Irish nationalism. Cockran, initially skeptical, was later convinced of Becker's innocence. However, prosecuting attorney Charles G. Whitman and presiding Judge Samuel Seabury refused to take Cockran's arguments seriously. Seabury later secured Tammany support in his successful bid for Judge of the Court of Appeals.[20] Cockran, in a rage, said, "This is not a trial, but an assassination", leaving his assistant Martin Manton, to handle the case.[21] Seabury's instructions to the jury were prejudicial to the defense, despite Manton's objections. After deliberating four hours, the guilty verdict was delivered. Governor William Sulzer, also a protegé of "Big Tim" Sullivan, was allegedly going to pardon Becker, believing him innocent. By the time the Court of Appeals reversed the decision in the Becker's first trial, Sulzer had been impeached by "Boss" Murphy. Martin Glynn replaced the disgraced Sulzer as Governor, but he was not re-elected in 1914. Instead, he was replaced with crusading District Attorney Charles S. Whitman and the new governor was not about to reverse himself nor show mercy. "Big Tim" Sullivan, who may have had doubts about Becker's guilt, was suffering from paresis, a degeneration of the brain caused by syphilis, and was confined to an asylum.[22] Although the circumstantial evidence suggests otherwise, Charles Murphy denied any ties to the Becker-Rosenthal case, an advocate proclaiming, "No one can justly say that there has been any connection between the police and Tammany in the division of such sordid spoils while Murphy has been leader, no matter what conditions existed before he came into the leadership. Murphy is the mortal enemy of the grafting cop, and you have heard little of red lights since he has been at the head of the organization".[23]

How does all this fit in the context of McGuire, Irish nationalism, asphalt scandals and Santo Domingo? The answer, given below, weaves together the tangled strands which constitute a vital part of the second of the political lives of James K. McGuire. Because of William Jennings Bryan's support for his candidacy at the hotly contested Democratic convention of 1912, following his election, Woodrow Wilson appointed Bryan as Secretary of State. Wilson delegated the duties of awarding patronage to his personal secretary, Joseph Tumulty, an Irish-Catholic political ally from his days as Governor of New Jersey. "Frequently 'exigencies of the situation' forced them to overlook the intrinsic merits of the candidate in order to strengthen Wilson's forces".[24] Tammany wanted "Champ" Clark and lost; Wilson lost New York State in the election of 1912 and it was possibly thought politically expedient to throw the party regulars some patronage.[25] The Phelan Report states that soon after the election of 1912, James M. Sullivan sought public office. "Under the direction and leadership of James K. McGuire, Mr. Sullivan was on guard to prevent Mr. Wilson from losing any Irish-American votes through misrepresentation." Sullivan first sought to be a United States District Attorney in New York, but influenced by men who wanted a Minister to Santo Domingo who would be friendly to their interests, he applied for the position in May 1913, was appointed in July, confirmed in August, and arrived at his post in September, 1913.[26] Some choices for ministers and ambassadors were no better or worse than in previous administrations, but the choice of James M. Sullivan would prove to be an embarrassment. According to the Phelan Report, Sullivan admitted his lack of diplomatic experience could be problematic given the dynamics of the country's politics. The Report also noted his inability to speak Spanish. Sullivan's stated purpose in obtaining the position: "I was anxious to secure this post for the purpose of getting even by means of the good salary that goes with the place".[27] Nonetheless, "the exigencies of the situation" won him the appointment. Sullivan did have some powerful friends on his side. For example, District Attorney, Charles Whitman, endorsed him, as a reward for his assistance in the Becker-Rosenthal case, as did James A. Hamill, a long-time New Jersey associate of Joseph Tumulty. So too did Judge George Gray of Delaware, Yale Alumnus Homer Cummings, Coordinator of the Democratic Speakers's Bureau in the election of 1912. Also in his cheering section was James K. McGuire.[28]

There were some critics who referred to his "unsuitability" and shady background as reason for his exclusion,[29] but their efforts were to no avail and Sullivan was confirmed. After his confirmation, Sullivan hastened to Syracuse to thank former Mayor James K. McGuire for his support, the Mayor taking time away from a family vacation at his in-law's home in Forrestport for the occasion.[30] Given what was to be exposed in a subsequent investigation, since they visited for a "few hours", it might justifiably be assumed more than compliments were exchanged.

Santo Domingo, had a long, chaotic history marked by the dramatic failure of self-government and democracy. For example, there were 19 constitutions promulgated between 1844-1918. Of 43 Presidents only three completed their terms – the others either killed, deposed or resigned. There had been 23 revolutions in the territory since 1844. Its leaders' plans for development meant borrowing large sums from foreign investors. Continued chaos meant debt payments were often in arrears. President Theodore Roosevelt used this as a pretext for seizing the country in 1905, and placing the United States in control of the country's customs revenues.[31] It was into this political maelstrom that Sullivan and James K. McGuire were drawn. Soon after his appointment as ambassador, Sullivan was being urged to resign.

James M. Sullivan
(1873-1935)
Library of Congress ggbain 13754
public domain
No Known Copyright Restrictions

Charles Becker
(1870-1915)
New York Lieutenant
Library of Congress ID ggbain 13426
No Known Copyright Restrictions

"Bald Jack" Rose
(1876-1941)
Mobster
Library of Congress ggbain 15864
No Known Copyright Restrictions

James D. Phelan
(1861-1930)
Senator From California
Library of Congress ID hec17102
No Known Copyright restrictions

As early as December 1913, the New York Times reported rumors of Sullivan's corrupt activities, the same time as his associate James K. McGuire was in Santo Domingo to investigate business opportunities at the invitation of the American minister. The New York World and The New York Times made a number of allegations against Sullivan, focusing on his unfitness for the job and various "importunities".[32] One was the alleged corruption involving the awarding of contracts for various public works projects. All these events were unfolding at the time of the Hennessy-Whitman investigations. And like those, it involved James K. McGuire, and others tied to similar scandals in New York State. The accusations paralleled those noted in the Hennessy-Whitman investigations. In return for a payment of $5000 to businessman William C. Beer, contracts would be awarded. Contractors Thomas Hassett, Tim Sullivan, John Mann and W. Lee Sisson acknowledged that bribery in bidding was a common practice. Tim Sullivan admitted receiving $3000 for expenses, stating that he and James K. McGuire were sent for by Sullivan because "the pickings were good and he wanted to keep it all in the family."[33] Timothy J. Sullivan was allegedly head of a multi-million dollar construction company and was second cousin to James M. Sullivan. According to the Phelan Report, the full extent of Tim Sullivan's "contracting" experience was that of a section boss on the Boston and Albany railroads and later being a coal dealer.[34] Tim Sullivan was to be rewarded for paying for the ambassador's education by being awarded several construction projects. The ambassador, allegedly said, "Tim, I always told you I'd make good. How'd you like to go to Santo Domingo and make a bunch of money?... I'm going to be the appointed minister down there and you can be the head of a $20,000,000 firm, if you will. It may be my last chance to help you, Tim and I've got four years at least to work on. I'm going to clean up all I can."[35] Sullivan repudiated these claims: "I have no sympathy with anyone who attempts to gain influence with the Dominican government through me".[36] Others who were allegedly in on the deal were Secretary of State Bryan, then Lt.-Governor Martin Glynn of New York and New Jersey Congressman James A. Hamill, the latter very active in obtaining Sullivan's appointment.[37] According to Tim Sullivan, James M. Sullivan, the ambassador, was to receive a percentage of the profits from all contracts thrown to McGuire and that he, Tim Sullivan, was to see that the minister "got his bit". The bank that facilitated the scheme was "solid" with Secretary of State William J. Bryan. Tim Sullivan allegedly received a loan from this bank through the influence of his cousin, the American minister, who endorsed the note. Part of the quid-pro-quo was the note would never have to be repaid as the amount would be part of the Minister's "rake-off". Assuming the scheme went through, James M. Sullivan's cut was to be $100,000.[38] Boston businessman James Byrne, in Santo Domingo to build a power plant, was told by Tim Sullivan that James K. McGuire of New York was the contractor for the job. Any work he obtained would have to share a percentage of the profits with Sullivan.[39]

James K. McGuire sailed for the Dominican Republic in October 1913, at the time the Whitman John Doe probe was becoming more intense.[40] His brother, George H. McGuire, was unsure of the date of his departure as he was with details of his testimony on other facts in dispute. In his absence, District Attorney Charles S. Whitman filed an indictment against James K. McGuire.[41] McGuire returned from Santo Domingo via Puerto Rico to face charges. In addition, there was a probe by Governor Glynn's special investigator, James W. Osborne. McGuire vigorously denied the charges against him.[42] One of McGuire's associates on the journey to Santo Domingo included Lee Sisson, a contractor, whose appointment as investigator for the island's Department of Public Works was encouraged by Minister Sullivan.[43] Sullivan, in the name of efficiency and economy, supported the work of the new Director of Public Works in Santo Domingo, while denying that he ever recommended anyone for the position. Nonetheless, despite James M. Sullivan's denial, both rampant rumors on the island and subsequent testimony in the Phelan Report confirm otherwise. Minister Sullivan allegedly told his cousin Timothy J. Sullivan he could have that position if he wanted it.[44] The importance of this position, as noted in the previous chapter on New York State, for awarding contracts with its attendant graft and patronage cannot be understated. Lee Sisson was head of the Sisson Construction Company, a front company organized by special interests who obtained Sullivan's appointment as minister for the express purpose of obtaining contracts in Santo Domingo.[45] Further, Lee Sisson testified that:

[James M.] Sullivan brought him [Tim Sullivan] down here to get public works contracts…O'Neil, Sullivan's brother-in-law is coming and we must take him and Timothy J. Sullivan and M. Sullivan himself into the company and pay the Minister five or ten percent interest in the company, as he can throw contracts at us.[46]

Upon his return to New York, James K. McGuire made light of the charges against him. In a cable to the NY Times he wrote: "I am sailing for home tomorrow. My indictment is on incident of the fight between the asphalt companies. I will answer effectively. Please agitate for lower cable rates. "McGuire referred to the charges lodged by Whitman-conspiracy, bribery, larceny, extortion, soliciting or accepting contributions from corporations"- as "a despicable frame-up". McGuire said he went to Santo Domingo on business at the invitation of the American minister.[47] This assertion was a lie as noted in the Phelan Report:

James McGuire, former Mayor of Syracuse, a very close friend of Mr. Sullivan and one of his chief supporters for this appointment, is a contractor. He wrote to Mr. Sullivan in Santo Domingo asking about contracts and went down in October, 1913, and stayed at the legation for a week. He says he made a $600,000 proposal to the Government, and I am personally frank to say that the fact that Mr. Sullivan was a minister to Santo Domingo naturally made me feel more willing to go to Santo Domingo than otherwise.[48]

If there was no collusion between McGuire and Sullivan, why the contradictions in McGuire's statements regarding his visit to Santo Domingo? The New York Times reported McGuire as one of several businessmen "who used Mr. Sullivan to further their hunt for concessions in San Domingo," an assertion denied by McGuire in a letter to Secretary of State William Jennings Bryan and published in the <u>Times</u>. In it McGuire responds that he and his brother-in-law, Frank J. McGuire, were engaged in contracting work. They noticed an announcement in our engineering papers the Dominican Republic was about to engage in a considerable amount of road work. McGuire allegedly wrote to Minister Sullivan who encouraged him to review the proposed projects in November as the climate was more pleasant at that time. McGuire asserted they visited five cities on the island and that Minister Sullivan took no interest in his work, "not even introducing him to the [Dominican] Minister of Public Works". McGuire stated all the Dominican officials he met- from the President on down-spoke of the American minister in the most favorable terms. The <u>Times</u> story noted two discrepancies between this statement and one made a week earlier. For one, McGuire said that Sullivan initiated the correspondence as to public works projects, and; that he stayed at the legation as there was no fit hotel. Secretary of State Bryan, the discrepancies notwithstanding, used McGuire's second statement to defend his appointment of Sullivan "The letter just reivd[sic] from Mr. McGuir[sic] shows (t)he unfairness and injustice of the criticism which has been directed against Minister Sullivan on account of Mr. McGuire's visit to Santo Domingo.[49] Both McGuire and Bryan, having advocated for the appointment of Sullivan in the first place, were obviously justifying their choice as Minister. As events will later show, these same statements would reflect badly on them both and further tarnish their careers. McGuire went to Santo Domingo with two other businessmen, Thomas Hassett and John Hamilton. Thomas Hassett, former Secretary of The Board of Water Supply and connected to New York State Engineer John A. Bensel, had been a focus of the Whitman investigations. Hassett allegedly tried to solicit a bribe of $50,000 from Anthony C. Douglass, a contractor, for work on the Catskill Aqueduct.[50] McGuire should have been more astute and avoid any public connections to men whose lives were being investigated by government officials - Hassett, in New York State, and Sullivan, by the federal government. Perhaps both felt secure - they were, in Secretary of State Bryan's words, "deserving Democrats". Both were wrapped in the political security blanket of Tammany's embrace. They may have shared a sense of invulnerability given their friends in high places. This sense of security was soon to evaporate in the growing scandals that would tarnish their lives, linking both ever closer to the cause of Irish nationalism. McGuire may not have received any contracts for work in Santo Domingo because of the island's political unrest, because of federal government scrutiny of Minister Sullivan's conduct and because he had to return home to deal with the indictment from the John Doe investigation under District Attorney Charles Whitman. However, the machinations of the various parties suggests McGuire had few moral qualms vis-a-vis obtaining contracts under dubious circumstances from which he could personally benefit. It also gave greater plausibility to the charges levied against him in the Whitman proceedings.

The political lives of James K. McGuire will return briefly to Santo Domingo and fellow Irish Nationalist James H. Sullivan, but that is the subject of the following chapter. The point is, that McGuire was involved with, in Whitman's words, "leaders of our invisible government." That opinion was undoubtedly reinforced when McGuire, upon returning to the United States to deal with his indictment in the Whitman John Doe proceedings, posted a $1500 bond backed by the United States Fidelity and Guaranty Company of Baltimore, Maryland. This was the same insurance company that was reportedly "friendly" to Tammany interests. Its involvement with the bonding business on public highways and canals was connected to Tammany affiliated machines at both ends of the Empire State-Murphy in New York City and Kennedy in Erie County. Its agent in Central New York was the McGuire Insurance Company.[51] Sullivan would have about year left to his sojourn in Santo Domingo. James K. McGuire returned home to deal with his indictment. Sullivan would later be forced to resign in the wake of a second special investigation which destroyed his public service career. However, while the ostensible reason were allegations of corruption, the real motive may have been his ties to Irish nationalism and the international intrigues associated with it. Sullivan, like McGuire, was in league with German designs which compromised President Woodrow Wilson's stated goal of neutrality. The evidence is a letter from the German Foreign Office Archives dated 20 January 1915 in which the German consul reveals its contents to the Imperial German Ambassador to Haiti and Santo Domingo, Dr. Fritz Perl. In it, Sullivan inveighs against British rule in Ireland and offered his services to the German government. The proposal was refused given the fact Sullivan was being investigated by the Phelan Commission. The Germans were unsure as to the results of the probe since he had weathered a similar investigation several months previously. Nonetheless, Sullivan had raised his hand against the government he had sworn to defend.[52] And while it was not acknowledged publicly, this may have been the principal reason for his removal. This is pertinent to the next chapter on McGuire's third political life, as Irish Nationalist. For now, we must return to McGuire's indictment in the Whitman John Doe investigations

Notes

1 "James M. Sullivan Ex-Diplomat Dead", New York Times 17 August 1935: 13; "British Seize A.M Sullivan On Irish Soil", New York Times 5 May 1916: 1. This has been discussed earlier by the auther. See Schultz, Daniel. Tarnished Hero: James Mark Sullivan and His Fight For Irish Freedom. New York: Page Publishing, 2017, Chapter III, pp. 63- 126.

2 Logan, Andy. Against The Evidence: The Becker-RoMuch of this has been writtesenthal Affairs (New York: McCall, 1970), 76; "Sullivan, James Mark", The National Cyclopedia of American Biography.

3 Callaghan email to author 10 September 2002.

4 Knight, Melvin. Americans In Santo Domingo (New York: Vanguard, 1928). 53; Phelan, James D. Santo Domingo Investigation: Copy of The Report, Findings and Opinions (Washington, D.C.: Gibson Brothers, 1916), 5.

5 Logan, Andy, Against..., 76. "Lawyer Wins Heiress", New York Times 19 September 1910.

6 Knight, Melvin. Americans ... 54; Phelan Report, 5; "May Be Samuel Schepps". New York Times 22 July 1912.

7 "Sullivan, James Mark". The National Cyclopedia of American Biography, 362. Phelan Report, 6; Logan, Andy, 76; Link, Arthur. The Struggle For Neutrality, 1914-15 (Princeton, N.J.: Princeton University Press, 1960), 107.

8 "Lawyer Wins Heiress". New York Times 19 September 1910.

9 "Phelan Reported Sullivan Unfit". New York Times 27 July 1915:5; "Sullivan, James Mark", National Cyclopedia, 362; Phelan Report, 6-7; Link, Neutrality, 107

10 Callaghan email to Author 9 October 2002.

11 McGuire, James K. National Cyclopedia of American Biography (1897) 19.

12 Phelan Report, 6.

13 John William Goff (1848-1924) was an Irish immigrant who overcame poverty by hard work, attending night school and apprenticing as a lawyer. He was admitted to the bar in 1876. An ardent member of the Irish Land League in 1874, he organized, with John Boyle O'Reilly, an expedition to free his imprisoned companions. Given his ties to Fenian organizations, many of his compatriots were also his clients. He was made an Assistant District Attorney in 1888 for New York City. His attempt to be elected District Attorney was a failure as a result of electoral fraud. Goff was chief counsel to the Lexow Committee. In 1906, he was elected to a 14-year term as Justice to the New York Supreme Court. "Goff, John William" in Johnson Allen and Malone, Dumas. Dictionary of American Biography Vol IV (New York: Charles Scibner's and Sons, 1932) 359-60; "Goff, John William". National Cyclopedia of American Biography Vol XV (Ann Arbor: University

Microfilms, 1967) 254. The National Cyclopedia of American Biography noted Goff's selection by Governor Dix as a "special judge in the Rosenthal murder case", and it was generally noted that a jurist better fitted for this particular task could not have been selected. It charitably stated that one of Goff's chief characteristics is a disposition to disregard minor technicalities in the admission of testimony when a strict adherence to the letter of the law of evidence would defeat the ends of justice" (254). The DAB more accurately notes ... "Goff was not profoundly learned in the law, and after his admission to the bar his professional and other interests precluded any extended study " (360). Hence, Goff probably was not the best choice of judge in this matter. A full narrative of Goff and the rescue of the imprisoned Fenians is found in Stevens, Peter F. The Voyage of The Catalpa (New York: Carroll and Gray Publishers, 2002)

14 With Becker in jail and "Big Tim" incapacitated "Big Tim's" empire fell to Tom Foley, former Sheriff of New York County and member of the Sullivan clan. Later, serving on the State Highway Commission, Foley's name was implicated in the asphalt paving scandals along with James K. McGuire. Foley negotiated to have John McIntyre serve as Becker's lawyer. In addition to his Tammany Hall and Clan-na-Gael connections, John C. McIntyre had a history of association with Irish nationalism. His grandfather had been exiled in 1878 for participation in the Irish cause in 1896, McIntrye acquitted a Fenian in London on trial for trying to blow up the House of Parliament and kill Queen Victoria. McIntyre failed to win acquittal for Becker, but the decision was reversed on appeal, winning Becker a second trial. Even here, the shadow of Syracuse played over the case. The presiding judge who wrote the opinion was Frank Harris Hiscock, who honed his legal skills in the office of his uncle, and McGuire's political nemesis, Frank Hiscock. Hiscock's opinion noted the "prejudicial character of (District Attorney Whitman's) statements, but it bitterly condemned Goff's rulings as "erroneous, not as a matter of discretion, but as a matter of law, his actions constituting grounds for reversal". Mcintyre went on to become a Justice in the New York State Supreme Court (Andy Logan 317-32). "Hiscock, Frank Harris", Cyclopedia of National Biography, vol. A (Ann Arbor: University Microfilms, 1967) 110.

15 "Work of Strong Arm Squad". New York Times 2 September 1911.

16 Logan, Andy 75-77, "May Be Samuel Schepps". New York Times 22 July 1912.

17 Ibid., 80.

18 Ibid., 87.

19 Ibid., 151; 157-60.

20 "Seabury, Samuel". Dictionary of American Biography: Supplement Six, (New York: Scribers and Sons 1980), 569-70. Seabury resigned from the bench to unsuccessfully run as Democratic candidate for Governor in 1916.

His fame rests in his criminal investigations of Tammany Hall during the administration of Mayor Jimmy Walker in the 1930's.
21 Logan, Andy, 256-58.
22 Ibid., 86; 307; 154-57; Connable, Alfred and Silberfarb, Edward. Tigers of Tammany: Nine Men Who Ruled New York (New York: Holt, Rhinehart, Winston, 1967), 250-2; Werner, H.R. Tammany Hall (Garden City; New York: Garden City Publishing Company, 1928), 438-39.
23 Warn, Axel. "Charles Francis Murphy: Human Being" New York Times. 22 February 1914.
24 Blum, John. Joe Tumulty and The Wilson Era. (Boston: Houghton Mifflin, 1951), 33.
25 Ibid., at 111.
26 Phelan Report, 7;10; "Phelan Reported Sullivan Unfit", New York Times, 27 July 1915: 5; "Hurries To Santo Domingo." New York Times 9 September 1913. "Dominican Tangle Under Inquiry". New York Times 10 December 1913. According to this article, one of the major reasons for Sullivan's appointment to the Ministerial post in Santo Domingo was because he "stumped the state of Maine for Mr. Bryan is one of his several campaigns and thereby created a political obligation which Mr. Bryan, with characteristic generosity, promptly recognized".
27 Ibid., 7;8.
28 "Phelan Reported Sullivan Unfit". New York Times. 27 July 1915:5 James A. Hamill attended the same small Jesuit college as Wilson's advisor, Joseph Tumulty. Their long friendship made him an ally when Wilson rewarded Hamill with patronage jobs. Hamill was a central figure in the Santo Domingo scandals. Blum, 11-14. Judge George Gray of Delaware thought Sullivan's efforts among Catholic voters on behalf of Wilson should be rewarded. Gray was also reportedly a good friend of Secretary of State Bryan Blum, 111; The Santo Domingo Scandal". New York Times 26 January 1915. Homer Stiles Cummings, Yale Law 1893, was a mayor of Stanford, Connecticut and States Attorney for Fairfield County. As Director of the Democratic Speakers' Bureau in 1912 probably came into contact with Sullivan. He was Vice-Chairman of the Democratic National Committee, 1913-19, and a United States Senator at the time of Sullivan's appointment as Minister. "Cummings, Homer Stiles" in John Garraty (ed). Dictionary of American Biography: Supplement Six, 1956-60 (New York: Charles Scriber's Sons, 1980), 136-38; "Cummings, Homer Stiles". Cyclopedia or American Biography vol. D (1934) pp.
29 Welles, Sumner. Naboth's Vineyard: The Dominican Republic, 1844-1924 (Savile Books, 1966), 718-719.

Rodman, Selden. Quisqueya: A History of The Dominican Republic (Seattle: University of Washington Press, 1964), 19.

Rippy, J. Fred. The Caribbean Danger Zone (New York: G.P. Putman's Sons, 1940), 195.

Wriston, Henry Merritt. Executive Agents In American Foreign Relations (Baltimore: Johns Hopkins University Press, 1929) 182.

30 "Ministers Came Here To Thank Mcguire". Syracuse Herald 28 July 1913:5. The second minister McGuire supported was former Tennessee Governor Benton McMillen (1845-1933) another "deserving Democrat". McMillen was a well-educated lawyer and judge. He served as a Congressman from 1878-99, resigning to become Governor. He was a reputed expert of monetary affairs and was a Bryan (pro-silver) Democrat. He failed to be re-elected to Congress in 1912. In the interm 1903-12, he was active in the insurance business. McMillen was appointed to Peru in 1913, a country also noted for political instability and at the time undergoing modernization. It suggests perhaps fortuitous business opportunities, through the intervention of grateful ambassadors, was an item for discussion. This suggestion is made more plausable by the fact that after McGuire was exonerated in the wake of the John Doe investigations, he planned a trip to South America upon his return from a visit to Europe. James K. McGuire hosted a dinner honoring his "good friend Benton McMillen" in August 1913, prior to his departure for Peru. There was no mention of James M. Sullivan. "Brewster or Dillon will get Place, says M'Guire". Syracuse Herald 24 July 1914; Robison Daniel, "McMillen, Benton in Schuyler, Robert Livingston (ed.) Dictionary of American Biography, Vol XI, Supplement One (New York: Charles Scribner's Sons, 1988, 533-34. "Benton McMillen" The Tennessee Encyclopedia of History and Culture. http://tennesseeencyclopedia.net/imagc gallery.php? Entry ID=h054 McMillen was appointed Ambassador to Guatemala, 1919-22 a time when The United Fruit Company dominated the country. "J.K. M'Guire Out Of Local Politics". Syracuse Herald 16 August 1913:6. "Tennessee Democrats Nominate Candidates" New York Times 30 May 1902.

31 Schoenich, Otto. Santo Domingo: A Country With A Future (New York: Macmillion Company, 1918), 304-06. Logan, Rayford 50-57 Haiti and The Dominican Republic (New York: Oxford, University Press, 1968), 50-57. Fagg, John Edwin. Cuba, Haiti and The Dominican Republic (Englewood Cliffs, New Jersey. Prentice Hall, 1965), 51-54.

32 "Says Sullivan Got Bryan Whitewash", New York Times 13 January 1915; "Bryan's Grapejuice In Sullivan Inquiry" New York Times 19 January 1915; "Religion Bryan Aid In Affairs of State", New York Times 22 January 1915.

33 "Says Sullivan Got Bryan Whitewash", New York Times 13 January 1915;

"Says Bryan Ignored Sullivan Scandal". <u>New York Times</u> 17 January 1915; Blum, 112.
34 <u>Phelan Report</u>, 15.
35 "Says Bryan Ignored..." <u>New York Times</u> 17 January 1915.
36 "Bryan Declares Changes Against Sullivan Unjust" <u>New York World</u> 12 January 1913, 6:1.
37 Blum, 11-14; 57;71; "Phelan Reported Sullivan Unfit" <u>New York Times</u> 27 July 1915.
38 "Says Bryan Ignored Sullivan Scandal" <u>New York Times</u> 17 January 1915:9; "Bryan's Name Used In Rake Off Talk". <u>New York Times</u> 21 January 1915. "Contracts Were Controlled By Former Mayor". <u>Syracuse Herald</u> 17 January 1915: 1,2. Among Those to be subpoenaed was James K. McGuire.
39 "Says Bryan Ignored." <u>New York Times</u> 17 January 1915:9 "Contracts Were Controlled By Former Mayor" <u>Syracuse Herald</u> 17 January 1915:1,2.
40 M'Guire Admits Trying To Hold Up". <u>New York Times</u> 22 November 1913.
41 "Seeks to Indict James K. M'Guire". <u>New York Times</u> 24 November 1913; Bench Warrant For J.K. M'Guire" <u>New York Times</u> 25 November 1913.
42 "J.K. M'Guire Found In Porto Rico". <u>New York Times</u> 27 November 1913:1 "McGuire Denounces Charges As Lie" <u>New York Times</u> 4 December 1914:1.
43 <u>Phelan Report</u>, 16.
44 <u>Ibid</u>.
45 <u>Ibid</u>., 14;16.
46 <u>Ibid</u>., 17.
47 "J.K. M'Guire Calls Charges Incident", <u>New York Times</u> 28 November 1913; "Asphalt Oil Men Out To Ruin Him", <u>New York World</u> 8 December 1913.
48 <u>Phelan Report</u>, 16-17.
49 "M'Guire Defends Sullivan To Bryan". <u>New York Times</u> 14 December 1913:S4.
50 "Whitman Clears Thomas Hassett", <u>New York Times</u> 13 June 1914: 10; "Hassett Joins M'Guire" <u>New York Times</u> 5 December 1913: 2.
51 "M'Guire Provides $1500 Bail". <u>New York World</u> 9 December
52 Hohlt to Perl. German Foreign Ministry Archives. 20 January1915; Perl to Bethman-Hollweg, German Foreign Ministry Archives 2 June 1915. Perl was German ambassador to Haiti and Santo Domingo. Bethman-Hollweg was Chancellor of Germany at the time. For details, see Schultz, Daniel F. <u>Tarnished Hero: James Mark Sullivan and His Fight For Irish Freedom</u>. New York: Page Publications, 2018, Chapter III, pp. 61-124.

Chapter II - E

"Asphalt Jungle": The Investigations Conclude-Bosses, Bagmen, Bribery, Buncombe

James K. McGuire's allegation, that his problems were the result of competition between rival asphalt companies, carried with it an element of truth. It was this premise, along with partisan politics, that resulted in his beating the second indictment. His chief accuser was the Syracuse-based Warner-Quinlan Asphalt Company. According to C.B. Warner, of the Warner-Quinlan Asphalt Company, there was no such wording as "natural solid asphalt" in the state specifications until after the July 5, 1913 Cooperstown meeting.[1] District Attorney Whitman produced Fillmore Condit, the New York representative of the Union Oil Company of California. Condit, a successful inventor, realtor, Methodist and member of the Anti-Saloon League, made an extremely credible witness.[2] Condit alleged that it was practically impossible for his company to get its products accepted by anyone doing work for the State, since the specifications were drawn to favor the Barber Asphalt Company.[3] Condit stated both McGuire brothers asked him and representatives of three other oil companies in August 1912 for campaign contributions for the Democratic State Committee. This was in violation of section 44 of the General Corporations Law making it a misdemeanor, punishable by a year in jail and a $5000 fine, to solicit a campaign contribution from a corporation, a fact admitted to under oath by George H. McGuire.[4] According to Condit, McGuire told him specifications as drawn by the Highway Department, could let his be one of five companies in on the construction of 500 miles of roads if "it would agree to terms." Those five were corporations were Barber Asphalt, Union Oil, Warner-Quinlan, U.S. Asphalt Refining Company and Warren Brothers. The terms were a $5000 campaign contribution and a commission of one cent per gallon on all products furnished to the paving contractors payable to George H. McGuire of McGuire and Company, Syracuse. That would amount to an additional $15,000. Arrangements were to be finalized with George H. McGuire, but Union Oil refused the terms. Condit came forward voluntarily when the investigations became public. George H. McGuire testified receiving a gift of $750 from James Johnson, sales agent of the Barber Company of Philadelphia, as a partial reimbursement for a gift of

$2500 to Sulzer.⁵ It was documented, however, that the company with which McGuire had long been associated, the Barber Asphalt Company, contributed $5000.⁶ George H. McGuire admitted under oath that he had made such a proposal. He also named Charles F. Murphy, Jr., nephew of the Tammany boss, as his partner in the bonding business on State canals, aqueducts, subways and highways, reportedly obtaining 80 percent of such business in state jobs.⁷ Several Syracuse area contractors admitted having made contributions to either Everett P. Fowler or William H. Kelley, believing they thought it would help their business if they did contribute. As a result of his testimony, George H. McGuire was immune from any prosecution that might grow out of the investigation. It was further determined by Whitman, that both McGuire brothers shared in the commissions on the sale of asphalt oils and other road materials to the State or to contractors on State jobs. The brothers' joint bank account showed deposits greater than those admitted to under oath by George H. McGuire. The money came from several businesses during the Sulzer administration, one of which was the Barber Asphalt Company. Shortly thereafter, District Attorney Whitman indicted James K. McGuire, allegedly one of the most powerful Democratic politicians of the state, on the basis of testimony from George H. McGuire and Fillmore Condit.⁸ As shown when he was in trouble as Mayor of Syracuse, McGuire had a habit of being "out of town" for health or business reasons. Apparently this dodge was in widespread use. Of 62 subpoenas by District Attorney Whitman, only eight were served. The excuse given to process servers, "He's out of state on business".⁹ In the interim, Whitman put a guard on duty to watch the home of James K. McGuire pending his return to face the indictment. A warrant was issued for McGuire's arrest but it was determined that he had departed for the West Indies. He was later reported returning via Puerto Rico. However, the plot thickens. Arthur B. Chamberlin was employed by Condit for a short time to act as an agent for his Union Oil Company. When Condit told Chamberlin of the McGuire brothers' offer, Chamberlin expressed doubt it had been endorsed by Tammany "Boss" Charles F. Murphy. The interesting tie here is that Chamberlin was a friend of "Boss" Murphy and his nephew, Charles F. Murphy, Jr., was a business partner of the McGuire brothers. Chamberlin was apparently working as Murphy's contact with Condit, encouraging him to pay the bribe. This assumption is probably valid since Chamberlin was in Condit's employ for less than three weeks.[10] It was during this short interval, the McGuire-Condit exchange took place.

On the witness stand, Chamberlin threw doubt on whether Condit's affidavit was accurate, reporting Condit's note specifically asked for a "campaign contribution", but nothing was said about the Democratic party.[11] In addition, Condit's statement was shown to have been written months after Chamberlin ceased his employment with Condit.

The McGuire brothers were not alone in sandbagging contractors. Others told similar stories about being shaken down by Murphy bagmen in Albany, Cortland, Fulton, Rochester, Buffalo and Syracuse. George H. McGuire testified he knew of a $500 contribution to the Sulzer campaign. George H. McGuire also gave Hennessy $2500 to help Sulzer out of his legal troubles after he was impeached.[12] Chamberlin reported the Sulzer-McGuire connections in August 1913 when the Frawley Committee was digging for evidence to discredit Governor Sulzer, but dropped the matter fearing disclosure would expose too many high-ranking Tammany officials. Hence, the McGuire data was never used in the Sulzer impeachment trial. "Boss" Murphy was attempting damage control, but the scandal could not to be contained. Apparently Tammany had no problem sacrificing the McGuire brothers whose loyalty to the organization was open to question. However, it was feared that disclosure would expose high-ranking Tammany officials, an issue Charles F. Murphy was working strongly to prevent.[13] The McGuire brothers found out about the Condit memo the day before George H. McGuire was going to take the stand in the Whitman John Doe investigations. Chamberlin volunteered no information about the statement, leaving George H. McGuire vulnerable to Whitman's cross-examination. It was reported that Tammany would assert that James K. McGuire had nothing to do with the organization.[14] Perhaps the links were indirect, but they were present. For example, in the indictments against Everett Fowler and James K. McGuire, the company which put up their bail money was the United States Fidelity Guaranty Company, for which the McGuire brothers were agents as were other Tammany Hall politicians. In addition, the McGuire indictment lists Tammany lawyers John B. Stanchfield and Isidor J. Kresel as his attorneys.[15] While the ties between Tammany and the McGuires were obvious, it suggests that the organization was trying hard to cover its major players from exposure. In the process, the McGuires were obviously expendable.

James K. McGuire, in an interview in Havana en route to New York City, vigorously denied the charges claiming that it was based solely "on the animosity of powerful oil and asphalt interests which had been unable to control him". McGuire discounted his brother's testimony as unreliable due to his physical and mental condition.[16] He denounced Condit as "consummate liar", and "a tool of powerful interests". McGuire stated further he was not in a conspiracy with Sulzer, nor was he present at the Cooperstown meeting. McGuire denied going to Santo Domingo to flee District Attorney Whitman's jurisdiction, stating emphatically his absence was strictly for business reasons. McGuire dismissed the charges as simply the outgrowth of an ongoing struggle between two competing asphalt companies – the so-called "Asphalt Trust" of which he was a member and the Warner-Quinlan Company.[17]

Chicanery was afoot, however. Important documents were reported missing from the files of Secretary of State Mitchell May, possibly to derail Hennessy's investigation of graft in all state departments. State Highway Superintendent John N. Carlisle was to be interrogated to explain his actions, allegedly favoring Barber Asphalt interests. The missing records might have included the campaign lists of receipts and expenditures. Hence, the paper trail tying Tammany leaders to illegal campaign contributions was now gone. James K. McGuire surrendered a week later after pleading not guilty and posting $1500 bail.[18] Later, John A. Hennessy denounced Governor Glynn,

Attorney-General Carmody and James W. Osborne for obtaining papers essential for him to convict a number of paving contractors throughout the state in a raid on the evening of December 1. Calling it a "Tammany trick", and "a political burglary", Hennessy said the evidence would have implicated several of Charles Murphy's State Committeemen. For all intents and purposes, any real investigation into the highway frauds was an at end. It was alleged by Hennessy the Osborne investigation was nothing but a smokescreen to derail his probe. On December 5, Hennessy appealed to Governor Martin Glynn for an honest inquiry into the highway scandals, demanding that charges be brought against himself and other individuals and not as part of a general investigation of Highway Department scandals. Testimony from the Warner-Quinlan Company alleged that it had revamped its asphalt plant, after reaching an agreement with the previous Highway Commissioner that its materials would be suitable for use on New York State roads. The decision was later overturned by Commissioner Carlisle. Hennessy called the owners of the Warner-Quinlan Company, which had brought charges against Carlisle, "a couple of crooks" and their attorney, Henry A. Rubino, as "a disreputable lawyer". The latter responded he "had never taken money from McGuire". Rubino planned on calling the two McGuire brothers as witnesses.[19] Hennessy said that Governor Martin Glynn was on the "Murphy side of the fence" and had been in constant contact with Murphy's "messenger boys", Robert Wagner, Al Smith and John Delaney. Glynn was also stonewalling, suggesting the case against Highway Commissioner John N. Carlisle need not be submitted to a commission other than that headed by James W. Osborne.[20] Apparently, a Tammany whitewash was in process.

Osborne had issued the subpoena and it was carried out by his assistant, Arthur T. Warner, and two deputies from the Attorney-General's office. And whereas the records were subsequently returned, as they had not been bound. Items could have slipped out of, or been taken from, the folders. Hennessy urged Governor Glynn appoint a committee to investigate the matter, barring any members of Tammany Hall from serving. Since Osborne had been busy on private business, he could not have reviewed the files to ascertain their relevance. Hence, since the stolen records dealt with materials used by the highway engineers, no collusion between them and contractors could be proven. Hennessy had offered his services to both Glynn and Osborne, but neither took him up on it. Hennessy queried as to why now, after sixteen months of inactivity, did the Attorney-General not take action? In response to Hennessy's demand for action, Governor Glynn urged patience. A new Republican-dominated Assembly was believed willing to pressure Glynn to actively pursue the investigations.

The two commissions were obviously rivals to one another, and Hennessy's complaints are most plausible, despite Governor Glynn's denials. "It was pointed out that in his investigation Mr. Osborne might call a witness from New York County (Whitman's jurisdiction), and then this witness would be able to claim immunity from prosecution by Mr. Whitman.[21] It was noted further by the attorney for the liquid asphalt interests that the books of the Barber Company were in Philadelphia and New York had no jurisdiction over them".[22] By December, James K. McGuire and several other alleged bagmen for the Democrats were indicted by District Attorney Charles Whitman. Whitman obtained several indictments – Arthur A. McLean, Everett Fowler[23] and James K. McGuire. The District Attorney anticipated trying the former Syracuse Mayor first, in February 1914. Whitman continued his investigation in January 1914 calling ex-Governor Sulzer as a key witness. Within a month, plaintiffs and defendants were involved in a war of words, at one point almost coming to blows.[24] Whitman uncovered further evidence of Tammany corruption in the awarding of contracts on the New York State Barge Canal. Sulzer had recommended the contracts be held up because one bid of $1,487,701 was awarded to P. McGovern and Company, whose officers included Tom Smith, Secretary to Tammany Hall and Phil Donohue, Tammany Treasurer. The bid was $200,000 more than the State Engineer's estimate. Contractor James C. Stewart alleged that Tammany confidante James E. Gaffney tried to extort a $135,000 bribe in exchange for the winning of a Barge

Canal contract bid, an offer he refused, despite making previous pay-offs to Tammany Hall.[25]

James W. Osborne, after conferring with Governor Martin Glynn, refused Hennessy's request to pursue charges against him as an individual, instead continuing his investigations into various departments of state administration. Hennessy won a partial victory, however. Having been criticized for the schedule of Saturday interviews given his private workload, Commissioner Osborne cleared his agenda to devote full time to his investigations. This may have had less to do with Hennessy than the fact that Governor Glynn was unhappy with Osborne's slow progress. Glynn threatened him with removal and replacement by District Attorney Charles Whitman unless the pace of investigations accelerated.[26] Osborne interviewed James K. McGuire making two rulings favorable to the defendant. As McGuire was under indictment for illegally soliciting campaign contributions, Osborne ruled no questions could be asked of McGuire relating to that issue. Second, Henry Rubino, attorney for the Warner-Quinlan Company, tried to show McGuire was still connected to the Barber Asphalt Company as late as Summer 1913 despite McGuire's assertion he had severed all ties to that organization two years previously. Osborne also cut off that line of inquiry.[27] McGuire admitted owning $35,000 worth of Barber stock, however. As Whitman's investigation continued, the McGuire name resurfaced. A road contractor, John W. Flynn, testified receiving letters from James K. McGuire and Charles F. Murphy, Jr., requesting he give them his bonding business. The letters purportedly contained inside information regarding engineers' estimates and contractors' bids for various construction jobs.[28] This opened up the McGuires to additional charges of graft on public contracts.

By mid-January, 1914, Commissioner James W. Osborne sent testimony involving the Highway Commission to the District Attorney of Albany County. Those named included former Highway Superintendent C. Gordon Reel, John A. Bensel, State Engineer, Duncan W. Peck, State Commissioner of Public Works and, Charles F. Foley, Deputy Commissioner of Highways. All were "friendly to

Tammany". The evidence was presented in part, to allay suspicion that Osborne and Governor Martin Glynn were protecting Tammany interests. The charges assert Foley was essentially given carte blanche in the awarding of over 300 contracts and the Highway Commission acted simply as his "rubber stamp". Highway Commissioner Carlisle was instructed to search his files and send relevant information to the District Attorney. The defendants responded saying what was done was simply past practice.[29]

This development followed in the wake of District Attorney Charles Whitman backing away from pursuing the misdeeds of Arthur A. McLean, Democratic State Treasurer since 1897 and personal advisor to "Boss" Charles F. Murphy. In exchange for pleading guilty to accepting illegal campaign contributions, Whitman supported McLean's appeal for clemency alleging McLean was "the victim of a custom, thoroughly bad, but for which he himself is not primarily responsible.[30] The second indictment against McLean was dropped. The New York Times suggested an arrangement was made. In return for leniency, Whitman would have McLean give evidence against Tammany, an unlikely prospect according to McLean's colleagues. Supposedly, prominent Republicans, "whose names were known throughout the nation", interceded on McLean's behalf, "trying to knock the props from under the graft investigation". Everett Fowler, the other Tammany bagman under indictment, pleaded not guilty. His lawyer promised a long legal battle on the issue of jurisdiction, which could last for over a year. It is possible, it was pointed out, that Whitman might be elected to some other office before the highest court had passed on the case.[31] Given the comments about the role of prominent Republicans and of Whitman's desire to be Governor, it suggests that other agendas might have been at work. Either way, the fact is one of McGuire's attorneys, John B. Stanchfield, was one of the lawyers representing A. A. McLean. This augured a positive outcome for McGuire's indictment as well. Stanchfield, it will be recalled, had David B. Hill as his mentor and law partner, was a former District Attorney, a member of the State Assembly and unsuccessful Democratic candidate for Governor in 1900. More importantly, he served as one of the counsels to the Assembly Committee that successfully impeached Governor Sulzer.[32] Given Stanchfield's close association with Tammany Hall, his actions on behalf of James K. McGuire suggest that, contrary to Tammany's assertions, McGuire was still close to the organization – at least insofar as it sought to make sure no "higher ups" were brought to the bar of justice. In addition to District Attorney Whitman's John Doe proceedings and James W. Osborne, Governor Glynn's special investigator, a third inquiry was initiated by John H. Delaney, Commissioner of Economy and Efficiency who, like the others, was looking into allegations of highway graft. Delaney's appointment was interesting, given that former-Governor Sulzer had named him, along with George H. McGuire and United States Senator James A. O'Gorman, as being involved in graft relative to State Barge Canal bids.[33] Sulzer had also sent a telegram at the instigation of George H. McGuire, who sought to have a bid awarded to James E. Stewart when the latter refused payment of a $135,000 bribe to Tammany Hall. Sulzer said Delaney urged Stewart to go see "Boss" Murphy to clear up the matter. Supposedly, Stewart went to his attorney, George Gordon Battle, law partner to Senator James A. O'Gorman, to try and rectify the situation. If this was accurate, the Times article would have been correct in its assessment that Sulzer's testimony would cause great uneasiness in Tammany as it would expose its corruption to public view.[34] At this point in the investigations, the work of Osborne and Whitman complimented each other, Osborne encouraging the former to subpoena the bank records of all major players in the investigation including Sulzer and numerous Tammany officials.[35] One of the accounts being pursued was that of Duncan W. Peck, former Commissioner of Public Works when James K. McGuire was Mayor of Syracuse, and more recently, a witness for the prosecution in the impeachment trial of ex-Governor William Sulzer. Whitman's John Doe proceedings were further supported by the Republican majority of the New York State Assembly which sought to grant him state-wide authority so he could pursue his investigations unhampered, thus removing Osborne from the scene. Ostensibly it would also strengthen Whitman's gubernatorial ambitions. In order to avoid the cash-flow problems encountered by the Hennessy Commission under ex-Governor William Sulzer, the Assembly sought money from a contingency fund, thus eliminating the need for approval from the Democratically-controlled Senate. Under the proposed plan, Whitman's assistant, John K. Clark, would head the investigations, overriding Osborne's authority, and utilizing John A. Hennessy as counsel. Indictments in Onondaga, Erie and Warren Counties would follow, the goal of which was to send the "looters" to prison and get at their superiors. If carried out, Whitman would have the power to pry into the affairs of every state official and avoid the jurisdictional disputes which had hampered his efforts. Whitman had even included the name of one prominent Republican whose bank accounts were subpoenaed since it was alleged that both party machines worked together to loot the State Treasury and divide the spoils. The Republican bagman was allied to Party Boss William Barnes, Jr.[36] The man who was to tie Tammany Hall directly to the graft, James C. Stewart, would not positively identify James E. Gaffney as the man who demanded a bribe of the five percent of a $3 million contract. This was a major blow to Whitman's case, but it is logical to assume that O'Gorman, a Tammany loyalist, urged Stewart to "disremember" Gaffney so as not to link the bribery allegations to "Boss" Charles T. Murphy.[37] The same Times article noted James W. Osborne's attempt to pursue charges against Ex-Highway Commissioners John A. Bensel, Duncan W. Peck and C. Gordon Reel on the grounds they violated their oaths by allowing Deputy Commissioner Charles F. Foley to let over 300 contracts without public bidding. This was prevented by Attorney General Carmody and the District Attorney of Albany County. Despite finger-pointing and accusations among the defendants, Osborne's case was blocked when District Attorney Alexander of Albany County refused to present the case to a grand jury citing lack of evidence.[38] With much of Whitman's case hanging on Stewart's identification of James E. Gaffney, the District Attorney was trying to find a picture that accurately represented Gaffney at the time of the alleged bribe took place, since Gaffney's appearance had apparently changed since their first meeting. It was also reported the trial of James K. McGuire would be coming up soon.[39] Whitman continued to probe deeper into corruption scrutinizing the decision of Attorney-General Carmody pertaining to the James C. Stewart Canal bid, and his ruling that Highway Commission members Peck, Reel, and Bensel were not negligent in their duties, relegating decision-making on highway bids to Charles F. Foley. Attorneys for Thomas Hassett, former Secretary of the Board of Water Supply and later Secretary to State Engineer John Bensel, who was indicted for soliciting a bribe of $50,000, were attempting to have charges against their client dismissed.[40] Hassett's lawyers were fighting the indictment and it was ascertained that Whitman was willing to cut Hassett a deal in return for turning state's evidence.[41] In the wake of all this investigations came the suicide of John K. Kennedy, Democratic State Treasurer, who was the target of three separate investigations, one of which conducted by District Attorney Whitman, linked him to the "bonding clique" with Charles W. Murphy, Jr. and the McGuire brothers.[42]

As far as the Osborne probe into the affairs of James K. McGuire was concerned, it all hinged on whether the attorney for the Warner-Quinlan Company, Henry A. Rubino, could substantiate the charges against John A. Hennessy. McGuire, Highway Commissioner Carlisle and Hennessy all took an active part in the proceedings, which were essentially anti-climatic. Osborne demanded proof of a conspiracy between Hennessy, Carlisle and the McGuires that worked to the detriment of the Warner-Quinlan Company and for the interests of the Barber Asphalt Company. After some hesitation, Rubino withdrew all the charges, except the one accusing Hennessy of accepting contributions from George H. McGuire to be used for illegal purposes. Hennessy countered with charges that Rubino received $10,000 from the Warner-Quinlan Company which he divided with John H. Delaney, Commissioner of Efficiency and Economy, to upgrade the ratings of road materials of the Warner-Quinlan Company so as to make them acceptable to the State Highway Department. Testimony of State Superintendent of Maintenance,

Joseph Curren, led to the January 1914 convictions of Bart Dunn, Tammany leader in Rockland County. He paid a $500 fine and served six months in jail. This incident was followed by John H. Delaney retaliating by initiating charges against Curren for falsifying data on his civil service application, a charge Curren denied. Delaney had been referred to by ex-Governor Sulzer as [Tammany Boss] "Murphy's messenger".[43] This was the same John H. Delaney who, with support from Tammany Senators James Frawley and Robert Wagner, sought to prevent Governor Sulzer from ousting State Architect Herman Hoefer. This reinforces the suspicion that Hennessy's accusations had merit. The multiple investigations and countercharges were an elegant smokescreen to mask the extent of Tammany corruption to protect its higher-ups from prosecution. It also explains why the McGuire brothers schemes played no role in the Sulzer impeachment trials. Hennessy threatened to implicate Governor Martin Glynn as well as Rubino and other officials in a civil lawsuit should the charges be withdrawn. Hennessy later asserted that because Governor Glynn purposely delayed action for months on road investigations urged earlier by Hennessy, the conditions as to their initial repair could not be investigated. The legislature would later endorse the administrative changes Hennessy had urged the Governor to implement months previously. Testimony from the Whitman John Doe proceedings was read into the record reiterating George H. McGuire had given Hennessy $2500 at the suggestion of Governor Sulzer. Hennessy explained the money was to be used to continue his investigations into corruption since the Tammany-controlled legislature refused to advance funds for that purpose. The logic is interesting. Why would the McGuires contribute money to a probe that would uncover their misdeeds in the asphalt contracting and bonding business? In addition, it laid them open to charges they were attempting to undermine Tammany rule. The mysterious phone call to Highway Superintendent Carlisle and the subsequent release of information regarding the use of asphalt materials was never addressed. The net result was the charges against James K. McGuire were withdrawn.[44]

Alfred Smith
(1873-1944)
Tammany Politician, Governor of New York
Library of Congress ID bec 21487
No Known Copyright Restrictions

James A. O'Gorman
(1860-1943)
Tammany Politician, Judge
Library of Congress ID ggbain.10914
No Known Copyright Restrictions

CONFLICTS AND CRISES

Robert F. Wagner
(1877-1953)
Tammary Politician, U.S. senator
public domain

What did all these investigations accomplish? Governor Sulzer was impeached. Most critics believe it was a correct judgment but public sympathy and recently-elected Democratic President Woodrow Wilson were for Sulzer. It backfired on Tammany Hall and Charles Murphy, leading to its temporary loss of control of City Hall and the state legislature. Sulzer was elected to the Assembly for one term on the Progressive ticket and ran unsuccessfully for Governor on the American and the Prohibition Party ticket in 1914. He made Governor Martin Glynn the target of his wrath. Both lost subsequent gubernatorial bids to crusading District Attorney Charles Whitman. Sulzer's political career ended two years later when the Prohibition Party refused him as their candidate for President. Sulzer declined the American Party nomination. He retired to his private law practice, dying in obscurity in 1941[45].

Governor Martin Glynn, trying to walk the tight rope between the Tammany machine and its reformist wing led by the deposed Sulzer, was caught in the crossfire. Glynn regarded himself a Party man, but would appoint only competent personnel, not party hacks to public office. On the national scene, William J. Bryan and President Wilson were outraged at Sulzer's impeachment. By December 1913 Glynn had joined the "get Murphy" movement. He considered himself leader of the State Democratic Party, but got little support for his effort from Wilson.[46] Glynn was bitterly disappointed by his loss to Whitman in 1914 since he was linked in the public mind to Tammany corruption. Glynn's political reputation was revived in 1916. Woodrow Wilson hand-picked Glynn to deliver the keynote speech at the Democratic National Convention. Wilson's campaign slogan, "He kept us out of war", was attributed to Glynn's oratory.

Some smaller fry of Tammany were brought to the bar of justice- Bart Dunn, Stephen J. Stillwell and John J. Kennedy for example, but the higher-ups did not suffer. After months of hearings by James W. Osborne into the affairs of C. Gordon Reel, John Bensel, Duncan W. Peck and Charles A. Foley, District Attorney Alexander of Albany Country refused to hand down any indictments.[47] In addition, both John A. Bensel and Duncan Peck kept their jobs under Governor

Martin Glynn. Peck later sued a northern New York paper for libel for printing the charges Hennessy larged against him. Bensel was cleared by the Tammany-controlled Frawley Committee.[48] Charges brought against James K. McGuire were dropped, but would be resurrected a decade later.

There were rumblings of discontent with Murphy's leadership. Former Boss Richard W. Croker condemned his successor: "The Hall will not win under Murphy's management", he is reported to have said.[49] In February 1914, yet another investigating committee would continue to probe allegations of fraud in the State Highway Department initially brought by both Hennessy and Osborne. This one was led by John Leo Sullivan, an anti-Barnes machine upstate Republican Assemblyman. His mandate was to scrutinize the acts of Governors Dix, Sulzer and Glynn. In addition, it was to investigate the office of State Engineer, especially during the tenure of John A. Bensel as well as the work on the State Barge Canal. Hearking back to scandals of McGure's mayoralty years, the Sullivan Committee was to investigate the "printing ring". This was the alleged link between prominent politicians from the Albany area and lucrative state government printing contracts. Prominent among those named was William Barnes, Jr. and Martin Glynn. The data covered much old ground and suggests a Republican reprisal for what may have been considered a Democratic whitewash in the recently concluded highway investigations. This investigation would be stonewalled, as was its predecessors, by rank partisanship. The Republicans refused to allow any Democrats to serve on the committee, based on their distrust of the previous investigations. Democrats refused to fund it without representative on the committee.[50]

With his election secure in 1912 and with anti-Tammany John Purroy Mitchel as Mayor, President Woodrow Wilson sensed a chance to undermine "Boss" Charles Murphy's rule. Wilson organized a political insurrection with Secretary of State William Jennings Bryan and his appointed Collector of Customs of the Port of New York, Dudley Field Malone.[51] This office was a vehicle for federal patronage in New York City. A Committee of 150 was formed to challenge Tammany. At the Democratic National Club, City Judge Edward F. O'Dwyer called Murphy "the ruin of the party". In March 1914, Charles F. Murphy and several of his by lieutenants were ousted from the Democratic Club, allegedly for non-payment of dues. They were all reinstated a month later. Everything else soon fell back into place as well. For example, Murphy was able to elect the Board of Alderman in New York City and the District Attorney's office. Elected Sheriff was Tammany stalwart Alfred E. Smith. President Wilson, seeking re-election in 1916, heeded the advice of his Secretary, Joseph Tumulty, to desist from further attacks on Tammany. Wilson made peace with Murphy in return for his tacit support.[52] The following year Murphy's candidate, Judge John F. Hylan, won the New York City mayoralty race and would remain in office until 1925. And in 1918 Al Smith defeated Charles S. Whitman for Governor. "I have always outwaited them," Murphy said.[53] Murphy was back in power. So it was also for his regional subalterns-Arthur Murphy of the Bronx, William Fitzpatrick in Buffalo and William Kelley in Syracuse.

McGuire's ties to Tammany may have been broken, but it did not seen to limit his business options. The investigations apparently had little impact on his fiscal fortunes. In an interview in January 1914, he told reporters that he had "many irons in the fire" including the McGuire Contracting Company which did business in North Carolina. McGuire listed himself as Vice President of the Cape Fear Gravel and Sand Company, a partner with his brother-in-law in a steam shovel plant in North Carolina and a vice –President of the Canadian Magnicite Company. In addition, he continued his association with the McGuire Insurance Company and listed himself as agent of the United Fidelity and Guaranty Company as well as President of the Syracuse Printing and Publishing Company.[54]

Nonetheless the spectre of the asphalt scandals of the past continued to haunt James K. McGuire for a decade after. Perhaps it was the "return to normalcy" that permeated America in the post-War era. Reaction is perhaps the best term for the period, given the veritable worship of business prosperity, the decline of labor militancy, the persecution of racial and ethnic minorities. Al Smith, a reform Governor, won election in 1918 over incumbent Republican Charles S. Whitman, a move which brought Onondaga County political rivals James K. McGuire and William Kelley together. Smith's first two terms (1918-20, 1922-24), spanned the final years of both James K. McGuire and "Boss" Charles F. Murphy. During his first term, the State, like the country was involved in a campaign against radicalism. The legislature determined qualifications of its members and in 1920 had refused to seat five Socialists, despite Smith's opposition. It also established the Lusk Committee to investigate "enemies of government", gathering an enormous body of data on suspected radicals. It was part of the larger Red Scare then prominent in America. On the federal level, there was a Senate Investigation On Brewing and Liquor Interests and German and Bolshevik Propaganda which had pointed out McGuire's ties to the Imperial German Government. It also tended to discredit the "wets," a cause embraced by both Al Smith and Charles F. Murphy.

Smith's re-election bid in 1920 fell a victim to isolationist sentiment, prohibitionism and reaction in the Republican landslide of 1920. A Republican governor, Nathan Miller, was elected in New York by 74,000 votes.[55] A conservative, Miller, in the name of efficiency, slashed the state bureaucracy, trimming 2000 jobs, claiming a $20 million saving during his administration. Perhaps Miller, sensing the ebb of the Republican tide which had put him and President Harding in office, was looking for a campaign issue. Possibly noting the fame of his Republican predecessor as Governor, Charles Whitman, in the asphalt probes of 1913, Miller may have resurrected the McGuire scandals to garner public support for his re-election bid. The third McGuire indictment was dated January 1923 suggesting legal paper work was initiated during the waning days of the Miller administration. The Republican Governor may have had an agenda. The District Attorney of New York County was Joab H. Benton,[56] Democratic ally of Mayor John F. Hylan, who had ties to Tammany Hall. Governor Miller railed against the prevalence of crime in New York City, admonishing Benton and other officials to make the city a safe place in which to live. So, McGuire's prior links to Tammany and the scandals could discredit "Boss" Murphy and his machine. Even though Miller was out of office by the time McGuire was indicted for a third time, he may have been, as in the asphalt investigations, left to be a fall guy for the Murphy machine. McGuire had made public comments favoring Prohibition, an issue close to the heart of both Charles F. Murphy and newly re-elected Governor Al Smith. Murphy, who by his treatment of Governor Sulzer, showed his vindictive side, may have allowed the third indictment against James K. McGuire to proceed. Murphy men controlled the Board of Alderman, the District Attorney's office, the New York City Mayor and the Governor. An indictment was filed against McGuire 22 January 1923 for violation of General Corporation Law, sec. 44 dating back to the asphalt scandals of 1913. McGuire was charged with soliciting money from a corporation doing business with the State to aid a political party. The indictment once again specified the Union Oil Company and the $5000 bribe, citing his brother George H. McGuire and Filmore Condit as witnesses against him. The original indictment dated October 24, 1913 was simply edited, the dates changed and the name of former District Attorney Charles S. Whitman crossed out and the current incumbent, Joab H. Benton, stamped over it. Both the original, annotated indictment and a typed memo from the court stenographer record the death of McGuire. Each recommended the legal action against him be "abated".[57]

By then, the asphalt wars had concluded and the competing concerns essentially merged. The power of The Asphalt Trust declined as the amount of "natural" asphalt on the nation's roads decreased. More manufacturers produced "artificial" asphalt, which by 1920 had become the standard for American highways. Patents began to expire, road-building equipment had become more affordable and more contractors entered the business.[58] Producers began to recognize a need to improve their image and promote their product to the general public. In 1919, J. R. Draney of the U.S. Asphalt Refining Company and W. W. MacFarland of Warner-Quinlan took the lead in the formation of the Asphalt Association. It provided technical information to states, cities and counties on the application of asphalt materials. The Association reduced the number of grades from 102 to nine and the number of manufacturing plants to six.[59] The ruinous competition which generated the "Asphalt Wars" of a decade earlier was over. This was simply part of a trend of post-World War I America. Large corporations, aware of the negative publicity of their abuse of monopolistic power outweighed any economic gains, sought stability and fair prices that would maximize profits in the long run. The decade became an era of "regulated competition" through such trade groups as the Asphalt Association, which discussed policies, exchanged information and "administered" prices in their respective industries. The conservative Republican governments of the 1920's encouraged these moves[60] which contributed to the era's overall prosperity. James K. McGuire would be a part of that for a short time, working for several corporations, using his social and political networks for their advantage. He would also utilize those connections in the cause of Irish freedom.

Murphy's tenure continued through the Great War, Wilson's struggle over the Treaty of Versailles and the rancor which polarized Irish America in the factional strife between Daniel F. Cohalan and Eamon deValera to control the funds and the organizations backing the struggle for Irish independence. These issues also provided opportunities for James K. McGuire who had long been identified with the cause of Ireland. Those endeavors would lead him into a variety of activities some of which compromised President Wilson's efforts to maintain American neutrality in the years 1914 - 1917. As with the "Asphalt Jungle", this chapter in his life is a complex web of intrigue, politics and propaganda.

Notes

1 "Whitman Hears of State Road Deals". New York Times 21 November 1913; "McGuire Admits Trying To Hold Up". New York Times 22 November 1913; "Accuses Carlisle In Asphalt Deal". New York Times 28 November 1913:1 "Four Contractors Say They Gave Up Money To Fowler In Syracuse". Syracuse Herald, 21 November 1913:1,2

2 "Condit, Fillmore." Political Graveyard: Index of Politicians From Conte to Condoleeza". http://politicalgraveyard.com/bio/comte-conditt.html.; "FillmoreConditt." http://findagrave.com/cgi-bin/fg.cgi?page=gr&GSln=Cindit&GScnty=1913&Grid=…

3 "Seeks To Indict James K. M'Guire". New York Times 24 November 1913. Apparently this was not McGuire's only legal entanglement with asphalt contracting. In April 1914 the Herald quoted him in reference to the appointment of a local internal revenue collector: "I have not urged Attorney General McReynolds that a lawyer be named internal revenue collector. My business with his department concerned solely certain alleged asphalt charges reported to exist against me by federal authorities in restraint of trade. I was informed that no charges have been made by the department and I am not being investigated. The Oklahoma matter was dismissed." "M'Guire Denies He Is Holding Up Spillane's Job". Syracuse Herald 14 April 1914:3.

4 "Phone Call Trail To Highway Graft" New York Times 23 November 1913. There were, in fact, two counts in the indictment against James K. McGuire: the first was for illegally soliciting from a corporation doing business with New York State; the second dealt with illegally soliciting a bribe to aid a political party or organization. Witnesses listed against him were both his brother George and Fillmore Condit. See, "Court of General Sessions of The People In And For The County of New York: The People of The State of New York Against James K. McGuire. Supreme Court No. 97158, December 5, 1913, 1-3.

5 "Seeks To Indict James K. M'Guire," New York Times 24 November 1913; "Bench Warrant For James K. M'Guire". New York Times 25 November 1913 1:3.

6 "Will Call M'Guire In New Graft Hunt." New York Times 6 November 1913; "Whitman Hears of State Road Deals". New York Times 21 November 1913: 1; "M'Guire Admits Trying To Hold Up". New York Times 22 November 1913: 1.

7 "Phone Call Trail To Highway Graft". New York Times 23 November 1913

8 "M'Guire Admits Trying To Hold Up". New York Times 24 November 1913; "Seeks To Indict James K. M'Guire". New York Times 24 November 1913 1:2.

9 "Seeks To Indict James K. M'Guire" New York Times 24 November 1913 1:2. "James K. M'Guire Under Indictment In New York On Charges of Illegally Soliciting Contributions For Political Campaign" Syracuse Herald 24 November 1913. This article noted 50 of 62 contractors, who were solicited for contributions left town to avoid testifying.

10 "Whitman Will Call Special Grand Jury". New York Times. 29 November 1913: 3. "James K. M'Guire Under Indictment In New York On Charge of Illegally Soliciting Contributions For Political Campaign" Syracuse Herald 24 November 1913: 1, 3. The source of the indictment was the written memo from Fillmore Condit. Apparently Condit was warned not to mention the Democratic Party if he was called to testify. There was another interesting Syracuse connection here. The man was Paul McLoud, former Chief Engineer in the Department of Highways. Chamberlin, working for Condit at the time, was told the Union Oil Company product did not meet state specifications. He showed a sample to McLoud, and it was accepted. As noted previously, Barber was working hard to maintain its monopoly in the fact of increasing competition from manufacturers of "artificial" asphalt, such as the Union Oil Company and the Warren Brothers. Perhaps this is why McGuire was willing to work with Condit and others in exchange for certain "considerations"? "District Attorney Whitman Puts Guard Over New Rochelle Home of Former Mayor J.K. M'Guire". Syracuse Herald 25 November 1913: 1,3.

11 The indictment against McGuire reads the sum of $5000 was to be paid "for and in aid of a certain political party and organization for a political purpose…" See, "People of New York Against James K. McGuire". Supreme Court No. 97158, December 5, 1913, p. 1.

12 "J.K. M'Guire Calls Charges An Incident." New York Times 28 November 1913: 3; "Bench Warrant For J.K. M'Guire". New York Times 25 November 1913 1:3; "M'Guire Admits Trying To Hold Up". New York Times. 22 November 1913:1.

13 "Says Tammany Knew M'Guire Terms" New York Times 26 November 1913:4; "Tammany Knew of Demand On Asphalt Co." Syracuse Herald 26 November 1913: 1.

14 "Why Chamberlin Got Memo." New York Times 27 November 1913.

15 "People of the State of New York Against James K. McGuire". For Stanchfield see fn32. Kresel, an Austrian immigrant, was educated in the public schools of New York City and graduated from Columbia Law School in 1900. He served as Assistant Attorney-General from 1902-10. Both he and Stanchfield served on the Legislative Committee that impeached Governor Sulzer. In addition, both Stanchfield and Kresel were defense attorneys for Judge Daniel F. Cohalan's bribery trial in 1913. For Kresel, see "Kresel, Isidor Jacob". Who Was Who In America, vol. 3 (Chicago: Maquis – Who's Who, 1960), 490.

On the Cohalan issue, see "Cohalan Calmly Faces His Accuser". New York Times 9 July 1915.

16 "M'Guire Blames Brother Mania." New York Times 8 December 1913. "J.K. M'Guire Says George Is Mentally Unbalanced" Syracuse Herald 8 December 1915: 1,3. George H. McGuire was reportedly on the verge of collapse after being grilled by District Attorney Charles S. Whitman. At his second hearing he was visibly ill. A third report indicated he was quite sick and in seclusion in Atlantic City. It was George H. McGuire's testimony that resulted in the indictments of his brother, James K. McGuire and Everett Fowler. The question is, was his illness feigned? "George H. M'Guire Seriously Ill At Atlantic City." Syracuse Herald 26 November 1913:6.

17 "M'Guire Denounces Charges As Lie." New York Times. 4 December 1913:1. "Indictment Due To Asphalt Fight J.K. M'Guire Says". Syracuse Herald 28 November 1913:3.

18 "J.K. M'Guire To Surrender" New York Times 7 December 1913; "Calls Six To Tell of Wide Conspiracy "New York Times, 9 December 1913; "Some Records Take Flight". New York Times 20 November 1913. Mitchell May (1870-1961) was a Brooklyn-born lawyer and politician. He served a two-year term in Congress during the turn of the century. May served as Assistant District Attorney for Kings County and as New York Secretary of State, 1913-14, ending his career as a New York State Supreme Court Justice. Brown, Roscoe in Smith, Ray (ed). History of the State of New York: Political and Governmental vol. IV (Syracuse: Syracuse Press, 1922), 224;248.

19 "Hennessy Appeals For Real Inquiry". New York Times 5 December 1913. Thomas Carmody (1859-1922), a Democratic lawyer, politician and Cornell alumnus, had experience as a District Attorney and member of the State Civil Service Commission during the 1890's. Carmody served twice as delegate to the Democratic National Convention and as New York State Attorney-General, 1910-15. He resigned from public office, allegedly disgusted by the rampant fraud and corruption practiced by Tammany Hall. "Carmody Will Quit State's Law Office". New York Times 21 July 1914. Did his disgust and resultant resignation emanate from inside knowledge or complicity with the lost records? The question cannot be answered, but the notion is intriguing. "Thomas Carmody Dies". New York Times 23 January 1922.

20 "Hennessy Assails Glynn For Raid". New York Times 7 December 1913; "Glynn Counsels Patience". New York Times 7 December 1913.

21 "Whitman Hears of State Road Deals". New York Times 21 November 1913:1; "Glynn Counsels Patience". New York Times 7 December 1913.

22 "Graft Inquiry Delayed". New York Times 29 November 1913:3. The issue of jurisdiction had been ongoing from the outset of District Attorney Charles S.

Whitman's "John Doe" investigation, both sides claiming their interpretation of the law as correct.
23 There are two indictments on record against Everett Fowler. The first was filed in November 1913 alleging contractor Seneca Hull paid a bribe of $250 to obtain payment of $23,568 for highway work done in Cortland County which Fowler had threatened to withhold if the bribe was not paid. See "Court of the General Sessions of the People In And For County of New York: The People of the State of New York Against Everett Fowler" Cal. No. 12508. No. 96849 14 November 1913, 1,2. The second was filed in January 1914 giving more details of the Seneca Hull extortion count, naming Norman Mack as Chairman of the Democratic State Committee and Arthur A. McLean as Treasurer of the Democratic State Committee as signers and depositors of the check from Hull on the Fourth Bank of the City of New York. This act, since it was done in New York County, gave District Attorney Whitman jurisdiction over this criminal matter. See, "Supreme Court, Count of New York: The People of New York Against Everett Fowler" No. 968491/2 8 January 1914, 1-7. Fowler's bail bond of $5000 was paid by the United States Fidelity and Guaranty Company.
24 "Indicts A.A. M'Lean In State Graft Case". New York Times 5 December 1913:1; "Seeks Old Picture of 'Jim Gaffney'". New York Times 1 February 1914; "Sulzer Today To Tell of Graft". New York Times 21 January 1914:6; "Get Near To Blows At Graft Inquiry". New York Times 22 February 1914:20. Whitman found that a favorite method for extorting campaign contributions was "boosting". That is, contractors would order additional layers of stone underlayment. The additional sum which they received for this was equal to the amount of the political contribution that was demanded. "Lawyer Halts John Doe Probe". Syracuse Herald 17 December 1913:4.
25 "Accuses Gaffney of Hold-Up". New York Times 17 January 1914; Whitford, Noble. History of the Barge Canal of New York State (Albany: J. B. Lyon and Company 1921). Appendix: Tables of Contracts, /#12 on page 558 lists Stewart's Company.
26 "Osborne May Go Unless He Acts". New York Times 23 December 1913.
27 "Glynn Indorses [sic] Osborne's Plan". New York Times 27 December 1913. "M'Guire Appears At Asphalt Probe". Syracuse Herald 26 December 1913:6.
28 "C. F. Murphy, Jr. Was Active In Bonding". New York Times 13 January 1914.
29 "Seeks To Prosecute Old Highway Chiefs". New York Times 18 January 1914.
30 "A. A. M'Lean Guilty: Sentence Stayed". New York Times 14 January 1914.
31 Ibid.
32 John Barry Stanchfield (1855-1921), the Amherst-educated son of a physician from Elmira, New York, studied law under David B. Hill. He served as District Attorney and mayor of his hometown and later served in the State

Legislature, and was unsuccessful Democratic nominee for Governor in 1900. In 1905, he moved his law practice to New York City. Hostile to Bryan's nomination in 1912, he later served as one of lawyers in the impeachment trial of Governor William Sulzer. "Stanchfield, John Barry". <u>Dictionary of American Biography</u> vol. 17, 1935, 499. "John B. Stanchfield, Lawyer, Dies at 66". <u>New York Times</u> "Stanchfield, John Barry". <u>The National Cyclopedia of American Biography.</u> (Ann Arbor: University Microfilms, 1967), 360-61.

33 According to ex-Governor William Sulzer, John H. Delaney carried $10,000 given him by Sulzer to "Boss" Charles Murphy from Allan Ryan, the son of Thomas Fortune Ryan, the Tammany-linked financier, transportation and tobacco magnate. In Myers, Gustavus. <u>The History of Tammany Hall</u>, 384. On Ryan, see "Ryan, Thomas Fortune'" in Malone, Dumas. <u>Dictionary of American Biography</u> vol. 16 (New York: Charles Scribner's Sons, 1935) 265-68.

34 "Sulzer Anxious To Tell Of Graft". <u>New York Times</u> 19 January 1914. "Call Sulzer Today To Tell Of Graft". <u>New York Times</u> 21 January 1914.

35 "Digs For Graft In 16 Accounts". <u>New York Times</u> 26 January 1914.

36 "Plans Graft Hunt By The Assembly". <u>New York Times</u> 27 January 1914. William Barnes, Jr. was the Albany-based Republican State Chairman. Harvard-educated, owner of the <u>Albany Evening Journal</u>, Barnes fought against the reformist tendencies in the Republican party spearheaded by ex-President Theodore Roosevelt, working hard to ensure the re-nomination of William Howard Taft in 1912. Barnes supported Charles Whitman for Governor in 1914. The Barnes-Roosevelt rivalry culminated in a lawsuit brought by Barnes alleging Roosevelt had slandered him, linking Barnes and Tammany Boss Charles F. Murphy in crooked business and political deals. The venue was changed from Albany to Syracuse to lessen the chance of having a jury impaneled favorable to Barnes. Roosevelt's attorney was Stewart F. Hancock. The jury decided in favor of the defendant. Wesser, Robert. <u>A Response To Progressivism: The Democratic Party In New York Politics</u>, 1902-1918 (New York: New York University Press, 1986), 75-78; Brewster, Arthur. <u>Memories of Clinton Square And Other Tales of Syracuse</u> (Syracuse: Syracuse University Press, 1951), 97-108. Brewster was the reporter for the <u>Post-Standard</u> who covered the trial.

37 "Met By Stewart, Gaffney Balks". <u>New York Times</u> 31 January 1914.

38 "Carlisle And Peck Both Seen To Go". <u>New York Times</u> 6 February 1914.

39 "Seeks Old Picture of 'Jim Gaffney'". <u>New York Times</u> 1 February 1914.

40 "Mack As Bagman To Contractors". <u>New York Times</u> 5 February 1914.

41 "Hassett Demurs". <u>New York Times</u> 20 February 1914.

42 "Kennedy Says He Is Ready To Testify". <u>New York Times</u> 8 February 1914; "Three Kennedy Inquiries". <u>New York Times</u> 17 February 1914.

43 "Graft Committee Hits At Governor Glynn". New York Times 1 March 1914; "M'Guire Says He Was Offered Job By C. M. Warner". Syracuse Herald 29 December 1913:3.

44 "Get Near Blows At Graft Inquiry". New York Times 27 February 1914; "Sues Hennessy For $50,000". New York Times 5 March 1914.

45 "Sulzer, William". Dictionary of American Biography, Supplement Three, 1941-45 (New York: Charles Scribner's Sons, 1973) 751-2.

46 Lizzi, Dominick. Governor Martin H. Glynn: Forgotten Hero (New York: Valatie Press, 2007), 61-62. McGuire's Catholic Sun gave favorable reviews of McGlynn when he assumed office in the wake of Sulzer's impeachment. This is not surprising. McGlynn was the Empire State's first Roman Catholic governor and at the time both McGuire and McGlynn were closely allied with Tammany Hall. See "Glynn Now Governor of New York State". Catholic Sun 17 October 1913:2; "New Executive of Empire State". Catholic Sun 24 October 1913:1. In his bid for re-election against District Attorney Whitman the following year, both had apparently severed their ties to Tammany Boss Murphy. McGuire's paper ran a half-page advertisement urging McGlynn's re-election citing his efficiency, reforms and reliance. "Honorable Martin H. Glynn: Candidate For Governor:" Catholic Sun 30 October 1914:1.

47 Myers, Gustavus, The History of Tammany Hall (New York: Burt Franklin, 1917), 391.

48 "Peck's $30,000 Libel Suit To Be Tried Tomorrow". Syracuse Herald 29 November 1915:3; "Assembly to Rake Record Of Glynn". New York Times 20 February 1914.

49 Werner, M. R. Tammany Hall (New York: Garden City Publishing Company 1928), 556-57.

50 "Assembly to Rake Record Of Glynn". New York Times 20 February 1914; "Hunt Ring Of Graft For Highway Work". New York Times 23 March 1914; "Assembly Extends Graft Inquiry". New York Times 6 May 1914. "Glynn Urged To Aid In Primary Reform". New York Times 7 May 1914.

51 Dudley F. Malone (1882-1950) was an Irish Catholic anti-Tammany Democratic lawyer who married the daughter of Senator James A. O'Gorman. His efforts on behalf of Wilson won him the post as Collector of Customs of New York City, a position he sought to use to break Charles F. Murphy's hold on city politics, a view then compatible with Wilson's. Malone was ultimately made to back off. Controversy surrounded him, similar to that of James K. McGuire. He was accused of not keeping the port neutral in the wake of the sinking of the Lusitania, which he admitted allowing to load ammunition for the Allies. Malone's later political career was somewhat erratic, embracing several liberal causes which alienated him from Wilson. During the 1920's, he embraced the causes of Polish and Irish freedom. See "Malone, Dudley

Field". In Garraty, John and James, Edward T (eds) <u>Dictionary of American Biography: Supplement Four</u> (New York: Charles Scribner's Sons, 1974), 541-3.

52 Connable, Alfred and Silberfarb, Edward, <u>Tigers of Tammany: Nine Men Who Ran New York</u> (New York: Holt, Rhinehart, Winston, 1967), 255. The authors appear to confuse the matter of the opposition leader, referring to him as John O'Dwyer. See also, "To Crush Murphy, Amend Primary Law". <u>New York Times</u> 15 February 1914; "Glynn Urged To Aid In Primary Reform". <u>New York Times</u> 7 May 1914. "Murphy Taken Back Into Democratic Club". <u>New York Times</u> 15 August 1914. Wilson's fence-mending was to no avail. He had earned the enmity of the German-and Irish-Americans who feared Wilson's political tilt towards the Allies. In addition, there was the previous history of animosity between Murphy and Wilson and its resultant lack of patronage to the "Boss". Tammany refused to give the President any delegates from Manhattan or the Bronx. A quid-pro-quo was arranged. In return for Tammany's support in the election, Wilson would not intervene in the New York City mayoralty contest. It was a sham. Wilson got a small majority in the city, but not enough to offset the traditional upstate Republican lead. But he won California and the election. (Connable and Silberfarb, 257-259).

53 Cited in Lizzi, <u>Governor Martin H. Glynn</u>, 62.

54 McGuire's Varied Interests". <u>Marcellus-Observer</u> 9 January 1914 James K. McGuire File. Onondaga County Historical Association.

55 "Miller, Nathan. <u>National Cyclopedia of American Biography</u>. Volume D. (New York: James T. White and Company, 1934), 70-71; "Miller, Nathan". John Garrity, ed. <u>Dictionary of American Biography, Supplement Five</u> (New York: Charles Scribner's Sons, 1977), 493-94.

56 "Benton Urges New Federal Auto Law". <u>New York Times</u> 12 May 1922; "Asks 'Blue Sky' Law To End Bucketing". <u>New York Times</u> 20 February 1922.

57 "Court of the General Sessions of the Peace In and For The County of New York: The People of the State of New York Against James K. McGuire". Cal. No. 37644 No. 97158 22 January 1923 (5 pp). "Court of The General Session of the Peace, City and County of New York, Part VII. Indictment Filed November 23, 1913. John F. Daley; official Stenographer" (2 pp.).

58 McNichol, <u>Paving.</u>. 151; "Asphalt Institute: Celebrating 90 Years of Service to the Asphalt Industry"; <u>http://www.asphaltmagazine.com/singlenews.asp?ite_ID1680&comm=0&list_code_int.pnl</u>

59 McNichol, <u>Paving.</u>, 167; "Asphalt Institute…", 1.

60 Carnes, Mark C. and Garrity, John A. <u>American Destiny: Narrative of a Nation</u>, 3rd edition (New York: Pearson-Longman, 2008), 709-10.

Chapter III - A

Shamrocks, Subversion, Sabotage and Sedition: Anglophobia and The Celtic Renaissance in America

Irish Nationalists, like McGuire, would use American history as a vehicle to show our relationships with Britain had usually been hostile. These Irish leaders were often men of intellectual achievement who used their talents to provide unity and direction to the Irish in America. So too, did revolutionaries from India who yearned for freedom from British rule. Similar to the Irish, many Indian Nationalists were well-educated, often expatriates, who used America and other countries as a base for propaganda and sabotage. In the much-publicized Hindu-German conspiracy trials of 1917-1918, the defendants, like the Irish, used America's fight against Britain during the American revolution as part of their defense.

As will be shown, there was an alliance between the Indian and Irish revolutionaries in terms of ideals, activities and mutual support systems using the same networks of personnel to aid and abet their schemes against their common enemy. James K. McGuire was undoubtedly aware of these activities given the fact that a number of his associates in the Clan-na-Gael and the Friends of Irish Freedom were involved and he was functioning as a paid propagandist for the Imperial German government.

Indian Nationalists praised the Irish as the model by which freedom could be achieved going so far as to adopt a variant of the Irish tricolor as their flag. One of their organization's initals, Friends of Freedom for India (FFI), had the ring of the American Irish organization, the Friends of Irish Freedom (FOIF). The nature and extent of these inter-connected organizations will be explored in a subsequent chapter.

Ever since the American Revolution, Irish had hoped trouble with England would stir a movement for Irish independence. Miller reports that in its attempt to win freedom from Britain, Benjamin Franklin shipped revolutionary propaganda to Ireland, the Continental Congress established a standing committee to correspond with Ireland and, John Adams predicted in 1780 that Ireland would win its independence before the United States.[1]

The French Revolution was celebrated in Ireland and Irish volunteers went to the Continent to aid in the revolutionary cause.[2]

The revolutionary contagion spread to Ireland and inspired the Rising of '98 and another in 1803. Both risings were promptly suppressed but they had a long-term impact. They created martyrs such as Robert Emmet and Theobald Wolf Tone; they created political refugees, many of whom came to the United States to agitate for Irish independence, and; it forged the Union of England and Ireland in 1801. Many of the refugees also escaped to France or Canada. A shipload of 400 put in at Norfolk, Virginia,[3] a port that received notoriety in the Gladstone incident of 1914 which involved James K. McGuire. The "Men of '98" were revered as heroes and eulogized in the Irish press in America, especially McGuire's Catholic Sun.[4]

European rebellions a half century later spread to Ireland. Like its continental counterparts, there was an Emerald Isle organization similar to "Young Italy" and "Young Germany". The United Irishman urged violence and there was talk of Irish-American volunteers coming to their aid. But the poorly-armed and disorganized rebels were put to route and the number of Irish political refugees to the United States increased, joining others waiting for the next opportunity to rise against Britain.[5] The Irish in America nourished their grievances, using growing political power and emergent middle class status to influence policies favorable to Ireland. Any slight to British arms and honor was hailed by Irish in America. For example, they applauded the Sepoy Mutiny of 1857 against British rule in India.[6] They nurtured their hatred following the Civil War. Forming the Irish Revolutionary Brotherhood, the Fenians hatched a plot to conquer Canada and hold it hostage until Britain had freed Ireland. Although there was some encouragement for their cause in America because of British support for the Confederacy, Secretary of State William Seward condemned the two failed attempts as a violation of American neutrality.[7]

The Fenians also financed the building of two submarines by Irish-born John Holland for the intended purpose of destroying British warships in American harbors. Although two were successfully built, a dispute between the two parties prevented their implementation.[8]

Irish loathing of the British was nourished in America by four key figures - John Devoy, O'Donovan Rossa, John Boyle O'Reilly and Patrick Ford.[9] Their efforts were aided and abetted by visits of Irish nationalists to America, such as Michael Davitt and Charles Parnell.[10] The Irish fear and hatred of Britain was such that even seemingly innocuous events were perceived as part of a British conspiracy to influence American foreign policy. For example, when the opening of the Brooklyn Bridge was mistakenly set for Queen Victoria's birthday, Irish-Americans mobilized mass meetings and threatened to blow it up.[11] On a local level, McGuire's <u>Catholic Sun</u> condemned the journey of the Syracuse militia to Canada to celebrate the Queen's birthday, noting how long Ireland had suffered under British rule and condemning those Irish who would sell their souls to the devil by toasting to a Queen who had done little to alleviate the suffering in Ireland, whose forefathers ravished their women, butchered their ancestors, depopulated the land and desecrated their altars.[12] Many Irish-Americans believed the Rhodes' Scholarships were a subtle attempt to create a generation of pro-English youth in America.[13] Perhaps they perceived the world through their own conspirational eyes.

Unfortunately for Irish Nationalists as their Anglophobia was increasing – and perhaps caused by – a thawing in United States – English relations, initially marked by the resolution of the <u>Alabama</u> claims.[14] The American-Irish responded by sabotaging the Bayard – Chamberlain Treaty of 1888[15] and by complicating American diplomacy in other international disputes as well. Two well-documented instances of Irish Nationalist antipathy towards Britain were shown in the Venezuela boundary disputes and their open and vociferous support for the Boers in the Great South African War.

As early as 1895, Irish-Americans were urging war with Britain over the Venezuela boundary dispute. Having annexed British Guiana in 1814, the British in 1885 arbitrarily increased their land claims 30,000 square miles into Venezuela, a region where gold had allegedly been found. The Venezuelan government broke off diplomatic relations. A decade later, the United States demanded a settlement under the aegis of the Monroe Doctrine. Tensions between

Britain and the United States were brought to a fever pitch. "A wave of jingoism swept over the entire country……The Irish National Alliance pledged 100,000 volunteers and the Society of the Friendly Sons of Saint Patrick pledged its support to fellow member, President Grover Cleveland".[16] Interestingly, South African issues played a role in the successful resolution to the Venezuelan crisis, but precipitated yet another one for American foreign policy. The British, by then facing problems in South Africa and under pressure from America, agreed to arbitration and a treaty followed in 1899 giving most of the disputed territory to Venezuela.

With the outbreak of the Boer War, there was strong sentiment among the Irish for the Dutch farmers. Three massive demonstrations were staged in the nation's capital in favor of the Boers, promoted and financed by the Ancient Order of Hibernians and the Clan na Gael.[17] Speakers for the New York Committee to Aid the United Republics of South Africa, evoked images of Spanish atrocities in Cuba, portraying starving women in the far off Transvaal, demanding freedom for the Boers. They reminded their American audience of long-standing British-American rivalries. Speakers vented their hatred for Britain, warning Britain would not hesitate to destroy the American Republic if it had the power.[18] The Irish press in America was universal in its condemnation of Britain. Among them was The Catholic Sun, published by James K. McGuire. For example, McGuire cited Michael Davitt's speech condemning British misrule in Ireland and the Transvaal, proclaiming, "England is the enemy of Liberty".[19] Articles and editorials in the Catholic Sun decried the British soldiers as "cowardly butchers"[20] and prophesied a British defeat.[21] The articles also denounced the use of Irish troops to fight against the Boers, a foreshadowing of similar efforts against Irish recruitment by the British in World War I. These efforts went further, explaining the "Irish" regiments in South Africa weren't really "Irish" – the British were simply using the fearsome "Irish" label to intimidate the Boers.[22]. Only one percent were "Irish". When shown later that many were Irish-born, they were scorned as "the progeny of penury, dirt and debauchery, a hand-to-mouth class, the dregs and scum of the social body".²³ They were condemned as "worse than Hessians", "a disgrace" for putting the Irish nationalist cause in a bad light – "for how could Irish in America, who support the South Africans, ask that wrongs be righted when our fellows wage war on Boer patriots?"²⁴

In addition to journalistic support, the Irish raised money and volunteers to back the Boer struggle. For example, The Ancient Order of Hiberians pledged to raise $1 million to equip and transport troops to South Africa, pledging to do all it could to support them without violating United States law.²⁵ Resolutions passed by the United Irish Societies condemning Britain were endorsed by prominent congressmen, including Representatives William Sulzer, Thomas Marion Jetty of Illinois, Senator William E. Mason of Iowa, Judge John W. Goff, W. Bourke Cochran and Syracuse Mayor James K. McGuire.²⁶ McGuire revealed his oratorical skills, outlining Boer history in South Africa, how greed for gold and imperial control were the motivating factors in the war, comparing Boer leader Paul Krueger to George Washington and introducing a resolution in support of the South African Republics.²⁷ Nationalist involvement was not limited to speeches and fund-raising. A sixty-person "ambulance corps" was dispatched to aid the Boers by the United Irish Societies of Chicago. Supposedly non-combatants, the "noble band" suffered several casualties, much preferring muskets to litters and bandages. After numerous adventures, they returned home as heroes on the German Hamburg-America line.²⁸ The Boers, encouraged by international support, delayed the end of the war until 1902.²⁹ In addition to the volunteer ambulance corps, radical Fenians saw a chance to strike a blow for Irish freedom in America. Luke Dillon, John Walsh and John Nolan planned to dynamite the locks of the Welland Canal, ostensibly to prevent Britain from sending troops and supplies to aid in the war effort. The explosion did some limited damage. The conspirators were soon arrested, tried, convicted and sentenced to long terms in prison.³⁰

The cause of the besieged republics was given new life by two developments, both interrelated and given full coverage in McGuire's papers. Michael Davitt, resigned his seat in Parliament in protest against the war. Speaking to the United Irish Societies in Chicago, Davitt indicated all Irish members of Parliament supported the Protestant Boers cause in the name of Home Rule, the British having taken it from the South Africans by force as they had from the Irish.[31]

The other prominent speakers in defense of the South African Republics were Maude Gonne, "Ireland's Joan of Arc" and John McBride, leader of the Irish Brigade in South Africa. Gonne, an Irish activist since the 1880's, organized protests against Queen Victoria's Diamond Jubilee and by 1900 had established the "Daughters of Erin", a revolutionary women's society. To protest the Boer War, Maude Gonne carried the Boer flag through the streets of London. She and McBride arrived in April 1901 to encourage support for both Irish and South African freedom. With British forces reduced in Ireland and committed to the war, she said now was the time to strike for Irish freedom.[32] Despite valiant guerilla tactics, a combination of numbers, widespread use of concentration camps and total war, the British were able to overcome the Boers.

1898 saw increased activism on the part of various Irish groups in the United States, due in part to the centennial of the "Rising of '98" and the outbreak of the Spanish-American War. And while the Irish Catholic press in general condemned the war, when Theodore Roosevelt formed the "Rough Riders", many Irish joined its ranks. New York's regiment, "The Fighting Sixty-Ninth" mustered over a thousand volunteers for the conflict. The SOFSOSP adopted the regiment as its own and raised funds to support it.[33] This increased activity by Irish nationalists on behalf of Irish freedom-in America, Great Britain, South Africa – was not without a touch of paranoia. Irish organizations were warned against infiltration by those sympathetic to British rule. As natives of Ireland, "rich in brogue and suave in manner, they are members of the Royal Irish Constabulary", as a body they are mean with allegiance to British [Free] Masonry.[34] This premonition would prove accurate as the British were able to successfully infiltrate many of the Irish Nationalist organizations during the Great War.

Given the extent of Irish activity, it is no wonder it led to a resurgence of intense Irish nationalism. This renewed animosity to England was demonstrated in three areas - hostility to the symbol of British aggression, Queen Victoria; a renewed interest in revising negative attitudes towards the Irish in America; and forging an alliance with German-Americans who were equally Anglophobic.

The death of Queen Victoria in 1901 revealed the growing rift between Irish-Americans and Great Britain. Much of the United States was in mourning and "eloquent tributes were paid to the virtues of the dead sovereign".[35] Some members of the Irish press in America were less than sympathetic. McGuire's <u>Catholic Sun</u>, for example, said the Queen had been a mental wreck for months because of the Boer War. At social functions she was in a daze, would often fall asleep and was in the final stages of "senile decay".[36] Syracuse Mayor James K. McGuire refused to lower the flag at Syracuse City Hall in tribute. "No: the flag on the Syracuse City Hall will not be lowered on account of the death of any potentate, foreign ruler or any member of a royal family."[37] In an unsigned hand-written note attached to the clipping, someone wrote: "I am pleased to preserve this expression from an Irish boy of American birth and now a mayor of an American city with the appreciation of the courage to act and to reason like an American".[38]

Charles Stewart Parnell
(1846-1891)
Irish Nationalist
Library of Congress LC BH 826-460
Public Domain
No Known Copyright Restrictions

Queen Victoria
(1819-1901)
Public Domain
(Source: National Portrait Gallery NPG x95802)

Maude Gonne Mac Bride
(1866-1953)
Irish Nationalist
Public Domain
Library of Congress LC-DIG-ggbain-00617

Major John Mac Bride
(1868-1919)
Irish Nationalist
Public Domain

The Society of the Friendly Sons of St. Patrick had become increasingly hostile to British policies with respect to Ireland. Previously its members had toasted to the reigning sovereign of Great Britain and Ireland. However, it became evident that the years of struggle to win freedom from Britain had taken its toll. In response to a British invitation to attend a memorial service for Queen Victoria, the SOFSOP took no official action. The organization's position was made clear by its President, James A. O'Gorman. "As he put it, to Englishmen, Victoria was a great queen, but the Irish could take no part in the manifestations of grief and sorrow following her death without the grossest betrayal of their own nationality.[39] Irish – America's negative sentiment towards Queen Victoria was reciprocal. According to Jerome ann de Weil, Victoria did not like the Irish, their national character or their religion. She hated Parnell, the Nationalist party and opposed Home Rule[40].

A second response was renewed interest in physical force nationalism. Irish volunteers were formed to send soldiers to South Africa in 1895, the goal of which was to harass Britain in case of entanglements with other countries. An estimated 22,000 volunteers were in America. Major Thomas Lynch of the "Fighting 69th" urged the Volunteers continue their drilling despite calls for their abolition after the Spanish-American War.[41] And, although leaders of various Irish societies denied it, the visit to the States of Maude Gonne and John McBride fanned the flames of physical force nationalism. Leader of the New York Irishmen, J. J. Jennings, refused to discuss details raising the spectre of schism within the Irish community as to the appropriate tactics to use to win Irish independence. Michael Kennedy, spokesman for the United Irish League endorsed Parliamentary methods, not violence.[42] The Catholic Sun published an article favorable to John Redmond, yet on the same page reported John McBride being awarded a sword by a committee of Irishman. In accepting it McBride commented: "I am the symbol of honest opposition to Britain. I am seeking funds to arm the Irish", but when pressed, he refused to divulge details.[43]

At the same time their abhorrence of Britain was increasing, the Irish in America displayed two almost contradictory attitudes – one was an increasingly strong identity with the "Auld Sod" and its problems. In addition, they had also had begun to acquire a stake in their new homeland as they began to move forward and upward. From 1870-1900 marked a period of slow advancement, but after the turn of the century there was significant increase, the Irish establishing themselves firmly in the middle class.[44] Their changing material circumstances allowed them to contribute sizeable sums for Irish suffering during the famine of 1880 when an estimated $5 million was raised[45]. Charles Stewart Parnell traveled to America in 1880 addressed numerous mass meetings and even the House of Representatives. Patrick Ford, editor of <u>The Irish World</u> for over four decades, organized American Land League branches which raised over $343,000.[46]

The Irish Land Leagues were popular in America, obtaining the endorsement and financial support of non-Irish and non-Catholics, including Wendell Phillips and Henry Ward Beecher. Its efforts were endorsed by the Irish-American press as well.[47] Irish Nationalist leaders would continue to tap the pockets of Irish in America. Many of the leaders of the Irish community in America were the more educated and sophisticated type – educators, editors, idealists – who sought to remake Ireland in the image of America. They saw a renascent Irish republic with its own institutions, constitution and educational system. All this activity encouraged Irish leaders to build organizations, to read, write articles and speak out in favor of Irish freedom. In the process, it accomplished two purposes for the Irish. It furnished a rationale as to their low status. Any Irish weakness could be explained away by English exploitation and misrule. In addition, it provided a bond that tied American Irish together – first and second generations, the various regions of Ireland. Their newspapers, edited by Irish nationalists, gave them a common outlook and unity in a nativist, Protestant, Anglo-Saxon world.[48]

Simultaneously with the efforts to improve conditions in Ireland were efforts to revive the Irish language and culture, both in Ireland and the United States, a movement referred to as the "Gaelic

Renaissance". Interestingly, much of the Gaelic revival owed its origins to continental European academics, such as German scholar Kuno Meyer, who praised the "beauty and antiquity of ancient Gaelic."[49] Gaelic societies in America preceded those in Ireland by a generation. It was part of an effort to prove Ireland had an ancient and civilized culture. As early as 1857, the <u>New York Irish-American</u> printed a column in Gaelic and soon various societies began publishing Gaelic manuscripts, followed soon by concerts of Gaelic songs. The Ancient Order of Hibernians endowed a chair in Gaelic at the Catholic University in Washington, D. C.[50] It was hoped this linguistic and cultural revival would improve their status. In the United States, the movement was more broadly-based including songs, recitations, dancing, picnics, and sports.[51] Their activities were given widespread coverage in the Irish press. In addition, it sought the teaching of Irish history in both public and parochial schools, it wanted to correct the negative stereotypes associated with the "stage Irishman" and prevent further emigration from Ireland.[52] By creating a "respectable culture", it would unite Irish-Americans in a common cause. One outgrowth of this effort was the creation of the American Irish Historical Society in 1897, the goal of which was to condemn the "Anglo-Saxon Shibboleth". It also sought to keep British propaganda out of American history books and create a more balanced treatment of American history. For example, the Society wanted inclusion of the sacrifices made by Irish regiments in America's wars, especially the Fighting 69th. It also encouraged scholarship in Irish history through journals, field trips and essay contests.[53]

This renascent ethnic pride reached fever pitch in the Abbey theater production of Synge's, <u>Playboy of the Western World</u> and in campaigns to erase the negative image associated with the "stage Irishman". Second and third generation Irish deeply resented the caricatures of their culture. Such purposeful representations were popular in the late 19th century, but especially galling to the Irish were the gorilla image, the dirty clothes, the short-stemmed pipe, the shillelagh and the alleged fondness for drink. By 1900, the

AOH launched a campaign to oust the infamous stereotype of the "stage Irishman".[54] The Irish press was intimately involved in the attempt to create a more positive image of the Irish in the wake of the groups new-found unity, power and status. The <u>Catholic Sun</u>, owned by James K. McGuire, was part of this effort. For example, an article entitled, "The Stage Irishman" referred to it as a "disgusting monstrosity" which should not be encouraged as it degraded the Irish character. Further, it stated, "as a caricature, it perpetuates prejudice with its "cheap buffooneries", usually portrayed by those who had never been to Ireland.[55] The AOH threatened boycotts of theaters and booking agencies, and encouraged a hissing campaign by any who were in attendance. At a celebration honoring martyr Robert Emmett, the Deputy Commissioner of Public Safety in Syracuse, New York, Edward Ryan, said such measures were necessary to oust this negative image, urging Irishman in the name of self-respect and manhood to organize and eliminate the simian stereotype it so often portrayed. Reportedly, his remarks drew widespread applause.[56] Possibly typical of the attitude of the now upwardly mobile Irishman was this description of Syracuse Democrat, successful businessman and ardent Irish nationalist, John McCarthy:

[He] was a professional Irishman. Proud of his ancestral Emerald Isle, he lost no opportunity to whoop it up for the Irish for whom nothing was too good. He loved every county of Ireland – Donegal, Clare, Kilkenny, Limerick, Tipperary, Cork. He loved the lakes of Killarney and the Blarney Stone. He loved the old songs like "Mother Macree" and "Where The River Shannon Flows". He resented any real or fancied insult to his Gaelic colleagues. Especially did he resent the caricatures of Irishmen seen on the vaudeville stage of that period. His mind was all conditioned for an explosion which needed only a spark to set it off.[57]

By 1904, the Ancient Order of Hibernians announced a similar campaign against inaccurate Irish images in magazines and newspapers. Despite its best efforts, the stereotype persisted. Protests peaked in the massive AOH demonstrations in 1912 against Synge's <u>Playboy of the Western World</u>. Ironically it was an attempt by Yeats,

Shaw and Synge to create a positive image for Ireland and enhance its prospects for independence. Instead, it had the opposite effect. The Irish press, especially the <u>Gaelic American</u> and the <u>Irish World</u> were extremely outspoken in their condemnation.[58] There was a positive side to these efforts. Irish songs of the 19th century resuscitated a latent feeling of what many immigrants felt they left behind, albeit romanticized and demonizing Great Britain for all of its problems. An additional response by Irish Nationalists was to bind themselves with other immigrant groups of like mind. German-Americans and Indian revolutionaries had good reason to be suspicious of British designs as well. This is the focus of the subsequent section.

Notes

1 Miller, John C. Triumph of Freedom, 1775-1783. (Boston: 1948), 412-414.
2 Hayes, Richard. Ireland and Irishmen In The French Revolution (London, 1932).
3 Wittke, Carl. The Irish In America (Baton Rouge: Louisiana State University Press, 1956), 164.
4 Especially numerous were articles on Robert Emmett, the Manchester Martyrs and the Rising of '98. For example, see, "Editorial", Catholic Sun 26 July 1895; "Men of '98", Catholic Sun 16 July 1897:1; "Irish Rebellion". Catholic Sun 10 February 1898:1; "In Empire Hall". Catholic Sun 26 November 1897:1; "God Save Ireland: Last Words of Manchester Martyrs". Catholic Sun 19 November 1897:1; "Ireland's Hero, Robert Emmett". Catholic Sun 4 March 1898,1;5,6; "Emmett and His Epitaph". Catholic Sun 2 March 1900:1; "Irish Famine" Catholic Sun 8 October 1897:1. As a businessman, James K. McGuire was not beyond profiting financially from his promotion of Irish nationalism. Advertisements in the Catholic Sun encouraged the sale of patriotic memorabilia, including pictures of its martyred heroes, such as Robert Emmett, Brian Boru, Theobald Wolfe Tone and Daniel O'Connell for 75¢ each. Pictures entitled "The Trial of Robert Emmett", "The Execution of Robert Emmett" sold for $1 each. See, "Beautiful Pictures For The Catholic Home". Catholic Sun 7 December 1911:4.
5 Wittke, The Irish. . . .81.
6 Ibid. 162.
7 Duff, John B. The Irish In The United States. (Belmont, California: Wadsworth Publishing Company, 1971), 66.
8 Ibid. "Holland's Great Wonder". Catholic Sun 8 April 1898:8.
9 John Devoy had been a member of the Young Ireland Movement, the Irish Republican Brotherhood, and had served in the French Foreign Legion. Imprisoned in England for terrorism, he was released on condition he exile himself to the United States where he continued his agitation for Irish freedom as editor of the Gaelic American and as a leading conspirator in Clan-na-Gael activities. Other radical Irish-American journalists included John Boyle O'Reilly, editor of The Boston Pilot. Also included was Patrick Ford, a journalist and editor of the Irish World from 1870 until his death in 1913. In that capacity he was an uncompromising opponent of Home Rule and a member of several Irish nationalist organizations including the United Irish League and the Ancient Order of Hibernians among others. In Duff, The Irish. . . 67.
10 Michael Davitt (1846-1906) personally experienced the worst of 19th century famine – plagued Ireland. Faced with eviction, his family emigrated to

England. He lost an arm in a factory accident, and began reading Irish history and politics. Joining the Fenian movement, Davitt was arrested for arms smuggling and served only seven of a 15 year sentence due to the intervention of Charles S. Parnell and the Amnesty Association. Davitt traveled widely as a publicist for the Nationalist cause, meeting John Devoy and other Clan-na-Gael leaders in America in 1878. Davitt worked with Parnell in Ireland to encourage land reform, the former earning another prison term for his efforts. Davitt was banned from the IRB in part because of his denunciation of physical force politics. He worked with, but was critical of, Parnell's methods. As with other Irish Nationalists, he was hostile to the Boer War. His was a legacy of criticism of British rule in Ireland, the topic of his numerous books and essays. http://multitext.ucc.ie/d/MichaelDavitt. The efforts of Charles Stewart Parnell (1846-1891) on behalf of Irish freedom are well-known, as is the scandal that split the Irish Parliamentary party in 1889. For a brief biography, see http://www.historylearningsite.co.uk/charles_stewart_parnell.htm.

11 Gibbon, Florence E. The Attitudes of The New York Irish Towards State And National Affairs, 1848-1902 (New York: 1951); 375-77.

12 "The Queen's Birthday". Catholic Sun 21 April 1899:1; "In Empire Hall". Catholic Sun 26 November 1897:1; "Shame On Such Irishmen". Catholic Sun 18 November 1898:7.

13 Wittke, The Irish. . .163.

14 These were monetary claims for damages done by British blockade runners during the Civil War. A commission awarded the United States $15,500,000 in gold. Bemis, Samuel Flagg. A Diplomatic History of the United States (New York: Henry Holt and Company, 1942), 412.

15 Thomas F. Bayard was a Secretary of State under Grover Cleveland and Ambassador to Great Britain. The treaty was an attempt to resolve fishing rights of American vessels within British territorial waters. The issue was eventually resolved by international arbitration in 1909. In Bemis, A Diplomatic.... 429.

16 Bailey, Thomas. A Diplomatic History of The American People (New York: Appleton-Century Crofts, 1964), 434-37; Murphy, Richard and Marmion, Lawrence. History of The Society of the Friendly Sons of Saint Patrick in The City of New York, 1784-1955. (New York, 1962), 375.

17 Downing, Rossa F. "Men, Women and Memories" in William G. Fitzgerald (ed.), The Voice of Ireland (Dublin: John Heywood, Ltd. 1924), 215.

18 "A Meeting In Boston, Massachusetts". Journal of The American Irish Historical Society II (1899), 119.

19 "Mr. Davitt's Excoriation". Catholic Sun 27 October 1899:1.

20 "Editorial: English Jingoism". Catholic Sun 5 November 1899:4.

21 "Boers Are In The Right". Catholic Sun 24 November 1899:1.
22 "The Fighting Irish", originally a term of disdain because of their alleged proclivity for crime and violence, was turned around after the bravery shown by Irish recruits in the Civil and Spanish-American Wars. The positive image was reinforced by Joseph Ignatius Constantine Clark (1846-1925) whose poem, "The Fighting Race" glorified the tradition of the Celtic warrior-hero in an American context. See Joseph J. C. Clark, The Fighting Race And Other Poems And Ballads (American News Company, 1911), 33-36. The popularity of Irish pugilists, John L. Sullivan, James J. Corbett and James Fitzsimmons gave Irish aggression a more positive image. In fact, Mayor James K. McGuire proudly displayed a horseshoe given him by Fitzsimmons in Nevada in 1897 inscribed with the following: "To James K. McGuire, a fighter in politics as I am in boxing". "James K. McGuire Gets Horseshoe". Catholic Sun 1 February 1901:5. "Irish Fusilliers". Catholic Sun 24 November 1898:8.
23 "Those Irish Regiments". Catholic Sun 2 March 1898:1.
24 "Irish Hessians". Catholic Sun 9 March 1900:4. This article was in response to Queen Victoria's praising of the "valor, dash and courage" of the Irish troops in South Africa. The comments were no doubt a response to those made about the use of Irish troops in the Transvaal as well as to lay the groundwork for the Queen's visit to Ireland later that year, a prospect condemned by the Nationalist Press. "Why She Is Not Welcome" Catholic Sun 6 April 1900:1. Initially praised in the Irish press for his leadership of the Irish Parliamentary Party, John Redmond undermined much of his support shortly thereafter by welcoming Queen Victoria on her visit to Ireland in 1900. In Wittke, The Irish. . .,168.
25 "Hibernians And Boers". Catholic Sun 29 December 1899:1; "Hibernians To Aid Boers". Catholic Sun 19 January 1900. James E. Dolan of Marcellus, National Vice-President of the AOH was present at a massive rally in support of the Boers in Washington, D.C.
26 "Hibernians and Boers". Catholic Sun 29 December 1899:1; "Eight Thousand Cry Sympathy For Boers". New York Times 30 October 1; "Honorable Cockran to M'Kinley. Catholic Sun 15 September 1899:1; "Cockran Himself Again". Catholic Sun 13 October 1899:1,2; James McGurrin. Bourke Cockran: A Free Lance In American Politics (New York: Scribner's and Sons, 1948), 197-203. "Senator Mason and The Boers". Catholic Sun 15 December 1899:3.
27 "Boer Mass Meeting". Catholic Sun 2 March 1900:1.
28 Duff, The Irish. ...67. "The Chicago Hibernians". Catholic Sun 9 November 1900:1; "They Fought For Boers". Catholic Sun 25 November 1900:1. There was more to the story. There were 53 men in the unit and their activities were

being monitored by Joseph Chamberlain. He wanted no incident that would encourage a surge of Irish volunteers aiding the South African republics. Apparently, the Clan-na-Gael executive had chosen to remain neutral in this struggle. John Finerty, leader of the United Irish League, had Clan connections and feared the Clan was deserting the Irish Brigade fighting for the Boers in South Africa. He wanted to get these volunteers to the Brigade without incurring the wrath of the Clan, the United States government and the British. Hence, they were disguised as Red Cross men, who dropped their bandages and picked up guns when they joined the Irish Brigade covering the Boer retreat to Pretoria. The group had allegedly been approved by Clara Barton, after being assured the men would do no fighting. "The Chicago Ambulance" http://penandspindle.blogspot.com/2007/12/Chicago-ambulance.html; "Going To Nurse Boers". Catholic Sun 16 February 1900:1.

29 "Boer Representative". Catholic Sun 24 January 1902:1. Hercules Vilgoen, Boer representative to the United States, addressed a packed meeting at Turn Hall in Syracuse.

30 Luke Dillon's family moved to England to escape the worst of the famine years, later migrating to the United States. Having served in the US military, Dillon settled in Philadelphia and became active in Clan na Gael activities. Involved in the dynamite campaign in England during the 1880's, he returned to the States, taking sides with Devoy against the O'Sullivan wing of the Clan. The plot to blow up the Welland Canal was allegedly hatched by the Napper Tandy camp of the Clan na Gael in New York City, since two of the conspirators were members of that group. The Clan officially denied any involvement in the plot. Convicted of the Welland Canal Plot, Dillon refused appeals by Clan leaders to confess and a request clemency. The Clan applied pressure to the various presidential candidates during the election of 1908 to have Dillon released but nothing came of their efforts. President Taft was besieged with appeals in 1910-11 and negotiations were undertaken with the Canadian government. The timing was appropriate – Edward VII was about to be coronated and the United States – Great Britain arbitration treaty was in Congress. For Taft, Dillon's release might secure Irish-American support for the treaty. The treaty was defeated as a result of joint German – and Irish-American pressures, but ultimately, as the prospect of war with Germany loomed, Dillon was released in 1914. For details, see Alan J. Ward, Ireland and Anglo-American Relations, 1899-1921. (Toronto: University of Toronto Press, 1969), 62-69. Dillon remained an ally of John McGarrity in Clan activities. "Luke Dillon" Fenian Graves http://irishfreedom.net/Fenion%20graves/Biographies/Third%20...; "Irish Leader Said To Be A Life Convict In Canada". New York Times 29 March 1902; "That Welland Canal Plot". Catholic Sun 25 May 1900:1.

31 "Michael Davitt Is Now In The United States". Catholic Sun 8 August 1901:1.
32 There is a brief biography of both in "Irish" Joan of Arc' Will Be Here April 11". Catholic Sun 20 March 1901:1. See also "Maude Gonne" http://www.spartacus.schoolnet.co.u//ACgonne.htm; "Maude Gonne MacBride 1865-1953 Revolutionary http://www.irelandseye.com/irish/people/famous/mgonne.shtm.
33 Murphy, Richard and Marmion, Lawrence History of The Society of The Friendly Sons of St. Patrick In The City of New York, 1784-1955 (New York, 1962), 383.
34 "Right In Our Midst British Spies Are Flooding The United States". Catholic Sun 19 November 1897:1. The article urged caution in recruitment of members, recalling the alleged infiltration of a police spy which aborted a conspiracy to dynamite British property in 1896. Interestingly, one of the key conspirators, Edward J. Ivory, had as part of his defense team, American lawyer John F. McIntyre, the Tammany lawyer prominent in the Becker-Rosenthal murder case. On the Ivory case, see "Edward Bell Remanded". New York Times 18 September 1896; "The Dynamite Conspiracy". New York Times 25 September, 1896; "Edward J. Ivory On Trial". New York Times 19 January 1897.
35 "Grief At Queen's Death Voiced In This City." New York Times 25 January 1901:2.
36 "Queen Victoria Dead". Catholic Sun 25 January 1901:2.
37 "Would Not Lower Flag". New York Times 25 January 1901;2. "Why Flag Wasn't Lowered." Syracuse Herald-Journal 9 February 1901.
38 Clipping, James K. McGuire File, OCHA.
39 Murphy and Marmion, A History of the Society.. 397. A brother of James K. McGuire, Edward, was an officer in the SOFSOSP, 1895-99. James K. McGuire was listed as an active member of SOFSOSP as late as 1922. Murphy and Marmion, 52; 374; 395.
40 40. Aan de Wiel, Jerome. The Irish Factor, 1899-1919: Ireland's Strategic and Diplomatic Importance for Foreign Powers. Dublin: Irish Academic Press, 2008, 7-8.
41 "Clan-na-Gael Recruiting". Catholic Sun 5 January 1902:2.
42 Talk of Using Physical Force Against England". Catholic Sun 9 August 1901:1.
43 "Ireland Is Preparing". Catholic Sun 15 November 1901;1.
44 Duff, The Irish... 44; Shannon William V., The American-Irish (New York: MacMillan 1963), 143; Irish In America" Catholic Sun. 24 August 1900:1; "Irishmen In The United States." Catholic Sun. "October 1911:1,3.
45 Wittke, The Irish... 164. A second famine generated a letter from Patrick Ford and Maude Gonne published in the Catholic Sun urging support for "starving Ireland" and a Syracuse Irish Famine Relief Fund was established.

In response to their appeals James K. McGuire contributed $10. See, "An Appeal" Catholic Sun 15 April 1898:1; "Tetters From Maude Gonne," Catholic Sun. 22 April 1898:1; "Irish Famine Relief Fund" Catholic Sun 29 April 1898: 1. Letters of support as well as amounts contributed by donors were published.

46 Wittke, The Irish... 164-65; Shannon, The American-Irish...134.

47 Wittke, The Irish..., 165-66. The endorsement of Wendell Phillips (1811-84) and Henry Ward Beecher (1813-87) was significant. Both had embraced liberal causes-women's suffrage, Native American rights, abolition, temperance. Their elevated social status as members of the Protestant elite gave increased credibility to the Irish Nationalist cause. Beecher, in fact was a critic of the Chinese Exclusion Act of 1882, comparing them favorably to the Irish, arguing that excluding the former while allowing entrance to the latter was unjust. For brief overviews of their lives, see "Wendell Phillips http://www.answers.com/topic/wendell-phillips; "HenryWardBeecher" http://www.answers.com/topic/henry-ward-beecher.

48 Shannon, The American-Irish, 133.

49 "German Students And Irish Language". Catholic Sun 25 November 1901:1. Much of this revival was due to the scholarship of Kuno Meyer (1858-1919), a German scholar of Celtic language who founded the School of Irish Learning in Dublin in 1903. On the eve of World War I, he left Germany and toured the United States giving numerous lectures. His activities come into our story of James K. McGuire as Irish Nationalist in a subsequent section. For a brief biography, see "Kuno Meyer" http://www.answers.com/topic/kuno-meyer. "Kuno Meyer Coming". Catholic Sun 15 March 1912:1.

50 Una Ni Bhromheil. "The Creation of An Irish Culture In The United States: The Gaelic Movement, 1870-1915". New Hibernia Review 5:3 (Autumn, 2001), 87-100.

51 For examples of Celtic pride in language and sports, see "Lords Prayer In Irish". Catholic Sun 10 May 1901:7; "Celt As Athlete Leads the World". Catholic Sun 20 September 1901:3; "Hurling, Ireland's Game". Catholic Sun 28 December 1900:1; "Characteristics of the Celt." Catholic Sun 24 November 1911:2. Supposedly the goal of the Gaelic movement was to retain the Irish language, but there was a strong Nationalist emphasis. "English is foreign in spirit; a return to Gaelic is a return to purity." The role of Maynouth in the language revival was duly noted. "The Gaelic Movement." Catholic Sun 17 March 1911:1.

52 Bhromheil, "The Creation...," 98.

53 Wittke, The Irish..., 170-171. "69th Regiment's Anniversary". Catholic Sun 21 April 1911:1,4; "Irish Regiments Are Ignored". Catholic Sun 10 November 1911:1.

54 Wittke, The Irish..., 260; 262; "Movement For Suppression of Stage Irishman". Catholic Sun 16 May 1902;1,5.
55 "Stage Irishman". Catholic Sun 20 October 1901:48. This article credits Irish playwrite Dione Bouccicault for helping to destroy this Irish stereotype. See also Wittke, The Irish... 255; 263; "Home Life In Ireland". Catholic Sun 5 January 1911:11.
56 "Stage Irishman". Catholic Sun 9 March 1900:1; "Sully On Stage Irishman". Catholic Sun 23 March 1900:1. "Boycott The Play With Stage Irishman". Catholic Sun 2 march 1900:1.
57 Brewster, Arthur Judson. Life Was Never Dull (Syracuse: Syracuse University Press, 1953, 193.
58 Wittke, The Irish...263. For details, see "Irish-American Nationalists, The Playboy Controversy, and the Development of American Free Speech Ideology".
http://64.233.179.104/search?q=cache:7QfxXSm6d-kJ:millercenter.virginia.edu/pubs/dissertation_chapters/2005/brunner.pdf+stage+irishmanEhl=en.

Chapter III - B
Shamrocks, Subversion, Sabotage, Sedition: McGuire's Irish Nationalist Pedigree

James K. McGuire's Irish nationalist credentials are extremely strong. His early speeches contained many Irish and Irish-American themes.[1] He claimed to have been an ardent nationalist since 1886. According to John Devoy, McGuire joined both the Clan-na-Gael and the Land League in the early 1880's.[2] His commitment was publicly demonstrated at an Irish convention in Chicago in 1891, when escorted by Clan-na-Gael Guards, Hibernia Rifles and the Emmett Guards,[3] he was the main speaker. In his address, McGuire repudiated Home Rule and omitted any mention of Parnell because he had become disenchanted with Home Rule given the repudiation of Parnell in the wake of the Kitty O'Shea divorce scandal.[4] During his speech, a bulletin circulated among the crowd, praising past Fenians for their loyalty and sacrifice, and urging unity for the sake of Irish freedom. McGuire's address revealed his thorough knowledge of Irish resistance to British rule, a recurrent theme in his Nationalist rhetoric and writings. Initially, McGuire embraced Home Rule as espoused by the Irish Parliamentary Party under the leadership of John E. Redmond, later repudiating the latter's leadership when Redmond endorsed support for Britain during the Great War. However, unity was an important issue at the time, given the fissures in the I.P.P. in the wake of the Parnell-O'Shea divorce scandal and the split in the American Clan-na-Gael between Alexander Sullivan and John Devoy. Perceived as too moderate by some, Devoy had lost control of the Executive Council of the Clan and a radical triumvirate led by Alexander Sullivan took over, initiating a period of terrorist activity. Devoy allied with Dr. Patrick Cronin to oust "the Triangle" which culminated in Cronin's murder in 1889. McGuire, apparently disgusted with the internal dynamics and violence of the Clan, dropped out, rejoining it in the years prior to World War I. This type of behavior would characterize McGuire's action's three decades later, when he withdrew from The Friends of Irish Freedom after it broke with Eamon DeValera in 1920.[4]

Four years later, McGuire addressed a rally of Irish at the Grand Alliance Convention in 1895. The principal speaker, Congressman John Finerty of Chicago, eulogized the Manchester Martyrs, a favorite topic of McGuire's Catholic Sun. It was at this time, both McGuire and James Mark Sullivan, another politically-connected Irish Nationalist, were speakers for the Democratic Party and enjoyed "twisting the lion's tail". Cuddy lists McGuire, along with John T. Ryan, John Devoy, Daniel Cohalan and Joseph P. O'Maloney among the prominent Irish-America nationalists of the day.[5] McGuire used his newspapers as a forum for his views, particularly The Catholic Sun of Syracuse, New York. He would maintain a controlling interest in the business for almost thirty years. It was one of several newspapers of what later became known as the "McGuire Group",[6] but its official title was the Syracuse Catholic Publishing Company, established in 1892 with James K. McGuire as Secretary and Treasurer. A printing business was also carried on in connection with the paper. It was this connection which contributed to McGuire's political problems and his failure to be re-elected mayor in 1901. The Sun also circulated as the Catholic Chronicle in Albany, and the Catholic Light in Scranton, Pennsylvania.[7] On several occasions he wrote admiringly of the key events and individuals in Irish history – the famines, the aborted revolutions, the evils of British occupation, current Irish issues and nostalgic remembrances of The Auld Sod. His appeals were also on a practical level, urging financial contributions to elect Nationalist candidates to the British Parliament and for Irish famine relief.[8] In fact, one of the many obituaries to him stated, "McGuire was Sinn Fein in sympathy as soon as Sinn Fein undertook its task".[9]

Early in his Nationalist career, McGuire was hostile to the I.P.P., but he soon re-embraced the concept of Home Rule, and its leader, John Redmond. The Catholic Sun carried numerous articles on the man, the movement, and his activities. For example, in 1910 McGuire got John Redmond to speak in Syracuse, New York, referring to him as a "great leader". James K. McGuire was on the Executive Committee for the event. His brother Edward S. McGuire, was one of several vice-presidents for the occasion.[10] The Catholic Sun published a huge advertisement for Redmond's appearance, urging its readers turn out and give the Irish leader a "hearty welcome", later reporting his speeches in Syracuse and Utica in great detail.[11] McGuire's paper also carried numerous articles predicting the inevitable success of Home Rule, featuring articles by both Redmond and T. P. O'Connor. In addition, like much of the Irish press, The <u>Catholic Sun</u> closely followed events detailing the Home Rule Movement. It carried a series entitled, "Notes On The Irish Home Rule Campaign".[12] Another series dealing in depth with the issue was called, "Home Rule By Clauses", an item-by-item analysis of the various parts of the Home Rule Accord.[13] McGuire's activities also included fundraising for the United Irish League, for which he received praise from its President, Michael J. Ryan.[14] McGuire hosted, along with later political rival William Kelley, a meeting to celebrate the passage of the Home Rule Bill in Parliament.[15] Syracuse responded once again to appeals for funds to encourage Home Rule raising $1600 after a speech by Michael J. Ryan, President of the U.I.L. The McGuire brothers, George, Charles, and Edward, giving $100, $50 and $10 respectively. James' contribution if any, was not noted.[16] The cash would be needed. The Home Rule Bill failed in the House of Lords, 326 – 69, after which McGuire's papers, like most of the Irish press, took a distinctly negative tone. Prior to the bill's failure, the <u>Catholic Sun</u> had a conciliatory attitude towards Ulster. Especially noted was its large Catholic population. Five of nine counties were predominantly Catholic, accounting for 44 percent of the population. Irish freedom, it argued, was a Nationalist issue, not a sectarian one, a forlorn attempt to allay Protestant fears of Roman Catholic domination.[17] The Irish press and people in America were initially divided at the outbreak of World War I. Wittke summarized the issues:

In 1914, <u>The Irish World</u> still supported Redmond, home rule, and Parliamentary procedures. Devoy's <u>Gaelic-American</u>, on the other hand, was convinced that England would never voluntarily surrender control of Ireland. The Ancient Order of Hibernians favored complete independence, and the Clan-na-Gael, in convention at Atlantic City, denounced Redmond for promising aid to England in her hour of distress. Eventually <u>The Irish World</u> came around to the position of <u>The Gaelic-American</u> and broke with Redmond.

The Ancient Order of Hibernians were sharply divided on the proper policy to follow toward England. Differences of opinion among Irish groups in New York, Chicago, and other cities became so acute that considerable rowdyism marked some of their meetings; funds were solicited for conflicting objectives; and charges were made that much of the money failed to reach its proper destination. Personal rivalries and the ambitions of certain leaders who sought prestige among the Irish-American group greatly aggravated their differences of opinion.[18]

As the resistance to Home Rule in Ulster hardened, the tone of McGuire's paper shifted, calling its resistance "bigoted", "intolerant", "virulent".[19] The Catholic Sun believed a north/south civil war a limited possibility, predicting Sir Edward Carson and his followers would be imprisoned. Further, it cast the Orangemen in a negative light: "The Belfast warrior is a knight with a nightmare, a K-nut with a small screw, a much-libeled, narrow-minded, moderately honest man who says when he is angry there are a million men to fight Home Rule, when only one-quarter of that number, including crippled and old-age pensioners, who says he hates, loathes and detests his countrymen when he really does nothing of the sort".[20] The hopes of the Nationalists were dashed when in September 1912, Sir Edward Carson introduced the Ulster Covenant, excluding the province from Home Rule. The Conservative party allowed the Northern counties to opt out of the provisions of the Home Rule Bill.[21] Heavy recruitment in 1913 of paramilitary volunteers in the North was responded to by similar moves in the South. These ominous developments were overshadowed by the outbreak of World War I. The war would turn Irish Nationalists from Redmond, the U.I.L. and the I.P.P., alienate many of its former supporters and foster a growth of extremism that found itself enmeshed in intrigues with Indian revolutionaries, Mexican insurrectos and the German Imperial Government. James K. McGuire would be an important part of those developments. Before moving into that, more of McGuire's Nationalist pedigree must be known to understand his embracing extremism in the cause of Irish freedom.

McGuire as Irish Nationalist belonged to numerous organizations and took a leading role in many of them. For example, Patrick McCartan, initiated as a Clan-na-Gael member in Philadelphia in 1901, asserts that McGuire was a "high-ranking" member of the Clan, as does Golway.[22] In addition, McGuire not only admitted having met Casement in Washington, D.C. in 1913, he was actively involved in the plot to get him into Germany.[23] At the time, Sir Roger was negotiating with the Hamburg-America Steamship Line to put in at Irish ports since the British had abandoned Ireland as a port of call with a disastrous effect on Irish commerce.[24] The Clan-na-Gael became more active in domestic political affairs of the United States in the early years of the 20th century. It established its own paper, The Gaelic American, in 1903 with Daniel F. Cohalan as President of the Board of Directors and with John Devoy as editor. During 1911-12, the Clan sought to defeat the Anglo-American arbitration treaty, seeing it as one more example of British domination of American foreign policy and a potential threat to the economic concerns of Irish-Americans.[25]

Home Rule, initially triumphant in May 1914, was widely celebrated in both Ireland and by Irish-Americans, but it was a hollow victory. By September it had been suspended as a result of the outbreak of World War I.[26] The Irish press was particularly bitter about its suspension and became vitriolic in its condemnation of England's choice as Under-Secretary of Ireland, Sir Matthew Nathan. The Catholic Sun was no doubt typical. Nathan, it reported, had prior experience governing British colonies in Africa and in Hong Kong. He was deprecated as a "sometime governor of yellow and black races", as a "Jew and a Mason". "Ireland has an ex-nigger, ex-Mongol, inexperienced, English-Jewish governor planted in Dublin Castle". The article urged all Irishmen, Protestant and Catholic, to demonstrate against this "gross government outrage".[27]

By March 1915, the slaughter resulting from trench warfare brought both revulsion and suspicion of English intentions. Why, Irish-Americans asked, were Orange volunteers kept at home while thousands of good Catholics were dead in the trenches as the Conservative Party plotted secretly to undo Home Rule.[28] By August, Great Britain had exiled Sinn Fein leaders Ernest Blythe, Liam Mellows, and H. J. Pim for speaking out against British troop recruitment in Ireland.[29] That same month Irish-American militant Patrick Ford, editor of the Irish World, printed a series of letters he had written over the years to William Gladstone, collectively referred to as "the trail of the serpent", later published as a book entitled The Criminal History of the British Empire. It was widely advertised in The Catholic Sun.[30]

McGuire and the Irish Nationalists even went so far as to endorse women's suffrage in the hope of garnering support for Irish freedom. For example, an advertisement in the Catholic Sun of October 1915 urged a "yes" vote on the referendum in November. Prominent Americans listed as in support of the resolution included "W. Wilson, Sec. Garrison, P.J. Tumulty, Rabbi Wise, Mayor Michael McAnemy, George McAnemy, J. K. McGuire, W. J. Bryan, Thomas Edison." The ad said the public should bow to the inevitable: "Suffrage is Bound To Come". And linking the denial of votes for women to Ireland, it further stated: "Every argument used against womens' suffrage was used against manhood suffrage in Ireland and against Catholic emancipation."[31] In the same month the Catholic Sun article was published, the idea of an Irish Race Convention was discussed by Daniel F. Cohalan, Jeremiah O'Leary, former American consul in Munich, T. St. John Gaffney and several others. There was need for a public organization that would attract mainstream politicians, writers, clergy in a non-revolutionary society to serve as a front for Clan activities. It's goal was to speak with a united voice, repudiating Redmond and Home Rule. McGuire, in charge of convention arrangements and credentials, made sure it was given significant coverage in the Catholic Sun, calling it a "splendid gathering of the clans" with over 3000 in attendance "from every state and territory". The major figures in the struggle for Irish freedom were present: Victor Herbert, President of the Society of the Friendly Sons of St. Patrick, opened the meeting. Thomas Addis Emmet set the tone for the occasion, echoing the words of the Manchester Martyrs, "God save Ireland: make her free and punish her enemies". John Goff, temporary chairman, urged Irish-Americans to unite in the great struggle, lambasting British tyranny, calling Home Rule "an empty formula", urging Britain "and every nation blighted by her alliance be beaten…" in the war. John Redmond, formerly highly-regarded in the McGuire papers, now found his name hissed by those in attendance. Other speakers included John Devoy, who urged using "bullet and sword" against "perfidious Albion" and a resolution compelling the United States to export arms to Ireland. James K. McGuire, using data from his book, <u>The King, The Kaiser and Irish Freedom</u>, addressed the issue of the economic decline of Ireland under British rule. Daniel F. Cohalan, long the major voice for Irish freedom in America, ominously closed the session saying, "We must do more than make speeches".[32]

Sir Edward Carson
(1854-1935)
Architect of Northern Ireland
Library of Congress ID cph 3c3537k4
Public Domain

Michael J Ryan
(1862-1943)
Irish Nationalist
Public Domain
LC-ID ggbain15451

William Bourke Cockran
(1854-1923)
Congressman, Irish Nationalist
Public Domain

John P Holland
(1841-1914)
Inventor of the Submarine
Public Domain
(Source: http:// en.wiki/image: John Philip Holland)

John Redmond
(1856-1918)
Leader of the Irish Parliamentary Party
National Library of Ireland
Public Domain
(Source: John Redmond's Last Years, 1919)

Thomas P O'Connor
(1848-1929)
Journalist, Irish Nationalist
Library of Congress ID ggbain 04319
Public Domain

Sir Matthew Nathan
(1862-1939)
Under Secretary For Ireland
Public Domain

John Goff
(1848-1934)
Judge, Irish Nationalist
Public Domain
(Source: The World's Work, 2013)

Many of these speakers were high-ranking Clan-na-Gael members who were already collaborating with the German Imperial government to stage a rebellion against British rule in Ireland. The remarks were obviously a foreshadowing of events to come, setting the stage for its acceptance and support among Irish-Americans.

The First Irish Race Convention of March 1916 also launched a new organization, The Friends of Irish Freedom, the goal of which was to foster the independence of Ireland. The name itself suggests Clan domination. During initiation into the secret society, a candidate would knock on a closed door and members would answer, "Enter Friends of Irish Freedom". Of the 17 members of the FOIF Executive Committee, 15 were members of the Clan.[33] FOIF was, in effect, the National Auxiliary of the Clan which served several functions: to rally public support for the Easter Rebellion and later to protest its brutal suppression by the British. Signatures to the invitation convoking the Irish Race Convention included Daniel F. Cohalan, George M. Cohan, Thomas Addis Emmet, James K. McGuire and others. It endorsed principles of the Gore-McLemore resolutions calling for impartial defense of American rights, for laws preventing Americans from booking passage on belligerents' ships and further urging the torpedoing of an Allied vessel was insufficient cause for war.[34] Other resolutions encouraged American neutrality and paid homage to Irish pride. For example, one resolution called on the U.S. government not to curtail the use of the submarine which was essential part of America's defense. This was a tribute to Irish-born John Holland (1841-1914) whose successful efforts to develop a submarines were supported by the Fenians in America. Later, the U.S. Navy assisted his successful efforts in the 1880's.[35] In line with its goal of unity, moderates such as Congressman William Bourke Cochran and militants such as John Goff and Daniel F. Cohalan shared the platform. After an emotional appeal to aid Ireland in its hour of need, Devoy collected $10,000 and wired it to Ireland. Once again revealing his close ties to the nationalist movement, James K. McGuire was appointed head of the Executive Committee of FOIF.[36] Later, the Executive Committee of FOIF established a

European Bureau with pro-Irish, pro-German, former U.S. Consul to Munich, T. St. John Gaffney in charge.[37] Possibly because of their identification with the cause of Germany, during the first week of April 1916, Devoy and several other members of the Revolutionary Directory of the Clan were investigated as to pro-German activities in the United States, including their ties to Franz von Papen and Wolf von Igel, two of their key contacts as to the details of the Easter Rising.[38] The Secret Service would soon raid von Igel's office. The captured papers exposed a vast network of German espionage, subversion, sabotage and close ties to Indian revolutionaries and Irish- and German-American organizations to which James K. McGuire was associated.

Shortly before the Easter Rising of 1916, McGuire authored an article in the Catholic Sun. In it, he noted the increased number of arrests of members of the Irish Volunteers found with arms and munitions. He suggested there was widespread disaffection among troops stationed in Ireland who were selling their guns to soldiers of the Irish Volunteers, who openly drilled and demonstrated throughout the country. McGuire, like other Nationalists, urged the 11,000 police who were watching "Nationalist shirkers and traitors" be sent instead to fight in Europe. His separation from John E. Redmond was complete, referring to him as completely "subservient" to Lloyd George, for begging the latter to establish war industries in Ireland as well as condemning Redmond's position on recruitment.[39] Given his high positions with the Clan-na-Gael and the Friends of Irish Freedom, their collaborations with Imperial Germany and Roger Casement on the Easter Rebellion, his publications suggest this was more than a premonition, that he had direct knowledge of the events before they were to unfold.

With the greater legitimacy as Executive Director of FOIF, McGuire embarked on a speaking tour demanding Irish independence and American neutrality.[40] He sponsored a rally of the Syracuse chapter of FOIF featuring Jeremiah O'Leary, who at the time was a member of its Executive Committee. McGuire featured an article with a picture of O'Leary in the Catholic Sun, calling him a "Friend of Irish liberty, a brilliant lawyer, orator, a fighter for truth, an imposing figure at the Irish Race Convention, the foremost leader of the Celtic race."[41] This close relationship would become distant following America's declaration of war against the Central Powers. O'Leary refused to be silenced by the increased repression of the Wilson administration, McGuire instead strategically choosing a pragmatic patriotism.

In line with FOIF's goal of establishing groups throughout the country, the Syracuse branch of FOIF was named after Brian Boru, the legendary 11th century King who sought to free Ireland from Danish occupation. The meeting was addressed by both Edward Ryan and James K. McGuire. Ryan addressed the reasons for the uprising and announced the slogan of the new society: "Complete freedom from English rule and control". McGuire's remarks focused on the distinctions between the FOIF program and that of the I.P.P.[42] The details of the meeting were reported in more depth by the Syracuse Herald which revealed McGuire's divorce from Redmond. Responding to a letter from John F. Redmond, referring to those "who have tried to make [Ireland] a cats-paw of Germany as an "insane, anti-patriotic movement while they remain safe in the remoteness of American cities" who were guilty of "a double treason" – against innocent American blood shed by Germany [by sinking unarmed merchant vessels with US citizens aboard] and against Britain. By the time they addressed the FOIF members, the rebellion had been suppressed. Both Edward Ryan and James K. McGuire expressed concerns that America was getting distorted reports of the war, the result of British censorship and because New York newspapers were owned by "English capitalists". Ryan hoped for a day, "When England's flag will be trailed in the dust" pledging we will do what we can to put it there." Taking full aim at Redmond, Ryan said, "Some of our friends who pretend to represent Ireland tell us this is treason. Well, if it be treason, we stand ready to make it good." Ryan suggested the reason for the Rising was an attempt by Britain to disarm the Irish Volunteers. He praised the efforts of the revolutionaries and condemned provisions of the Home Rule

Act. McGuire, claiming adherence to the cause of Irish freedom dating to 1886, once again demonstrated his knowledge of Irish history. He stated the rebels chose Easter Sunday to commemorate the Battle of Clontarf of 1014 when Brian Boru defeated another foreign invader, the Danes. McGuire, like Ryan, condemned the Home Rule Act as crippling to its domestic and foreign policies. Echoing Ryan, he praised the rebellion, noting the fate of Ireland depended on the defeat of England by Germany, and once again reprising the theme that Britain had been the historical enemy of America. McGuire lauded the efforts of Roger Casement who early had foreseen an Anglo-German confrontation.[43] The meeting, and the naming of FOIF branch after Brian Boru was a significant, substantive, symbolic break from the polices of the now disgraced John E. Redmond. McGuire continued his tirades against Home Rule. He published a statement on behalf of FOIF condemning the new compromise pact, castigating its provision as recognition that the bloody reprisals of the British during the Rebellion made Americans more sympathetic to their cause. McGuire scorned the provision as a set-up by the representative of the British government and members of Ireland's Ancient Order of Hibernians. He was particularly hostile to the idea of partition, condemning the loss of its most prosperous provinces and the cultural heartland of St. Patrick, Armagh, to Ulster. He perceived such a plan as weakening Ireland, making its economically poorer sections dependent on the British crown, preventing internal development and external trade.[44] McGuire's comments were supported by Seamas MacManus, Irish dramatist, poet and writer, whose works contributed to the rise of Irish National literature. In an address to the Syracuse Chapter of the Friends of Irish Freedom, MacManus condemned the Home Rule Act as a "counterfeit compromise" and an out-in-out iniquitous hoax. Speaking before a monument to the sixteen executed martyrs of the Easter Rebellion, MacManus condemned the current Home Rule Act as the substitution of English blood-sucking leeches for Irish ones. He recited the past sins of British rule in Ireland, declaring "who accepts home rule is not a man nor an Irishman".[45]

McGuire's escalating outspokenness, the foreign intrigues with his associates in Irish Nationalist organizations andtheir allies, coupled with the increasing hostility of the Wilson administration, had repercussions on other McGuire associates as well. The asphalt scandals, as noted previously, implicated James K. McGuire with the American Ambassador to Santo Domingo, James M. Sullivan, another active Irish Nationalist. As noted previously, Sullivan's activities on the island were subsequently investigated by Democratic Senator James D. Phelan of California.[46] Publicly, the greatest scandal surrounding Sullivan was the alleged corruption in awarding contracts for various public works projects. It was this that formed the basis of the <u>Phelan Report</u> of 1915 which led to Sullivan's resignation as ambassador. However, Sullivan's Nationalist credentials hint that perhaps there were other motives at work. For example, his two brothers, Timothy and Alexander, were active in the <u>Young Ireland</u> movement, editing its official organ, <u>The Nation</u> (1842-92). Timothy was Lord Mayor of London, associated with the Land League and later served as a member of Parliament. James M. Sullivan delivered a speech on Republicanism at the grave of Wolfe Tone in 1911 at a ceremony organized by Arthur Griffith and the IRB. At the time, this was no small thing. National independence appeared to be a distant dream. Yet, under the calm surface, a current of resentment was stirring. There was labor union unrest under the leadership of Jim Larkin. There was also a resurgent nationalist culture, and a growing Unionist threat of partition under Sir Edward Carson. Nationalist demonstrations against the visit of King George V in June 1911 were overshadowed by the thousands lining the streets to view his procession.[47] And like other Nationalists, Sullivan had protested the production of "Playboy of The Western World".[48]

According to his grand-daughter, Sullivan was always intensely Irish, often traveling between New York and Ireland. His wife was an O'Mara, the daughter of a Parnellite M.P. Her two brothers were prominent in DeValera's rise to power.[49] McGuire at the time with close ties to the Wilson administration, was prominent in urging Sullivan's appointment to the position of Ambassador, praising his

Irish origins, his Yale law degree and his prominence in the Irish Nationalist movement.[50]

There may be grounds for suspecting his dismissal may have been more than allegations of corruption. They tie him, like McGuire, to intrigues with the Imperial German Government. First cleared by Secretary Bryan, as the charges against him mounted, there was an official investigation by Democrat James D. Phelan. Sullivan was allowed to resign before the report was made public. By then the briefcase of Dr. Heinrich Albert was stolen by Secret Service agents who had been keeping Albert under surveillance. The papers revealed a $40 million spy, sabotage and propaganda ring in the United States. Wilson decided to publish the contents in the hopes of curtailing such activities. In the wake of these discoveries, the Wilson administration expelled Franz von Papen, Captain Boy-Ed and the Austrian Ambassador, Constantin Dumba.[51] One additional reason for Sullivan's dismissal may have been the fact that many Irish-American Nationalists favored a German victory in the war. As will be shown later, many Irish-Americans leaders such as James K. McGuire of FOIF and Jeremiah O'Leary's American Truth Society, carried on ceaseless anti-Allied propaganda. Both McGuire and O'Leary worked with German agents and were recipients of cash from the Germany embassy. Sullivan was also involved. According to reports in German Foreign Office archives, Sullivan intrigued with German diplomats in Haiti and Santo Domingo.[52] Obviously, these activities were an open challenge to Wilson's stated policy of strict neutrality. These machinations, coupled with the <u>Gladstone</u> incident, hint that perhaps there was more than business on the agenda of these two Irish Nationalists when they met in Syracuse and in Santo Domingo. Sullivan's granddaughter, Mary Rose Callaghan, recalled her mother saying Sullivan failed as an ambassador because he was so anti-British. He refused to allow British ships to refuel in Santo Domingo.[53] But Wilson was by then leaning toward support for the Allies, becoming less tolerant of the "hyphenate" position in American politics. Perhaps Wilson was sending a message to the leaders of militant Irish-American organizations. Is it coincidence that within months of Sullivan's dismissal, he demanded the resignation of T. St. John Gaffney, American consul in Munich? Gaffney was ousted by Wilson because of his public support for the German cause and because of his pro-Irish policies. It was alleged that Gaffney received secret messages from Irish nationalists in America via the Austrian government and that he had associated with Roger Casement. Gaffney also carried on correspondence with Denis Spellissy, treasurer of the American Committee of Irish Volunteers. Established in June 1914, its goal was to buy arms for Ireland.[54] A year later Gaffney was a leader of the American Independence Conference with Daniel F. Cohalan and Jeremiah O'Leary, an organization of German-and Irish-Americans working for a Republican victory in 1916.[55] In 1917, Gaffney was back in Berlin where he co-founded the German-Irish Society, publishing a monthly journal supporting the cause of Irish independence. He was Irish representative at the International Socialist Peace Conference in 1917, where he published papers on behalf of FOIF. Prior to Casement's departure on his ill-fated journey to Ireland, he wrote to his German contact von Wedel, that leaving care of the Irish Brigade in Gaffney's hands. Gaffney apparently had limited contact with the brigade which by the war's end led to demands by its members that he be replaced by Ferdinand Hansen, a German-American.[56] Wilson was undoubtedly using a psychology of escalating pressure against St. John Gaffney and other militant Irish nationalists. Both Gaffney and Sullivan may have been pawns in Wilson's delicate attempt to appear genuinely neutral. These events link Sullivan to the militant, pro-German Irish nationalist movement of which James K. McGuire was a part. Subsequent events reveal that Wilson, both before and after the election of 1916, would have his revenge in full measure against those who opposed his policies.

Sullivan, having resigned his ambassadorial post under a cloud, returned to Ireland. Reinforcing his ties to Irish Nationalism, he established The Film Company of Ireland in 1916,[57] a mere six weeks before the Easter Rising The company's offices were burned during the Rebellion. Sullivan was interned and because of his American citizenship, freed. The British, with their involvement in the Great War were loathe to further alienate American public opinion, especially its increasingly vocal Irish-and German-American populations. James K. McGuire had links to these individuals and events given his membership in the Clan-na-Gael and the Friends of Irish Freedom and other organizations. His employment as propagandist by the German Information Service and his previous associations with Sullivan put a cloud of suspicion over their activities on behalf of German interests, not only in the Caribbean, but also in Ireland and the United States as well. The fact that Sullivan was vociferously defended by John D. Moore, National Secretary of The Friends of Irish Freedom and Joseph W. Gavan, a lawyer indentified as associated with various radical Irish-American organizations,[58] suggests that Sullivan, like McGuire, was intimately involved in the events of the last week of April 1916.

Notes

1 McGuire, James K." National Cyclopedia of American Biography vol. VIII (New York James T. White and Company, 1897), 19; McGuire, James K. The Democratic Party In New York State, vol. III 1905, 445.

2 "Fenian Chief's Estimate of James K. McGuire." Catholic Sun 19 July 1923.

3 Militia companies were established by many immigrant groups in the United States prior to the Civil War since they were unwelcome in those organizations established by Nativists. Some Irish leaders thought such groups would eliminate factional and regional rivalries. Irish units had a variety of names often named after revolutionary heroes and martyrs – Robert Emmet, Napper Tandy, John Mitchel. Colorful outfits, flags, military drills and parades were commonplace.

4 Numerous sources document the Parnell episode. See for example, Harrison, Henry Parnell Vindicated: The Lifting of The Veil (London: Constable, 1931). Devoy documents Clan-na-Gael issues in the Gaelic American 29 November 1924. It was widely reported in the American press as well. "Cronin Grand Jury". New York Times 29 June 1889; "Irish National Agitation". New York Times 25 July 1884. See, "Kerwin and the Clan-na-Gael". New York Times 17 July 1894. Wittke, Carl. The Irish In America (Baton Rouge, Louisiana: Louisiana State University Press, 1956), 52-54. McGuire, James K. What Could Germany Do For Ireland? (New York: Wolfe Tone Co., 1916), 278-80. "Talking To Irishmen". Sun Times 16 August 1891. James K. McGuire File, OCHA; "McGuire In New York". Catholic Sun 29 November 1895:1; "Fenian Chief's Estimate of James K. McGuire". Catholic Sun 19 July 1923. A critical assessment of McGuire written by John Devoy a month after McGuire's death, the author states it was McGuire who informed Devoy DeValera had dispatched a hit squad from Dublin to assassinate Devoy "for betraying the Republic". For details pertaining to the Cronin murder, see "The Cronin Conspiracy". New York Times 31 May 1889; "Kerwin and the Clan-na-Gael". New York Times 17 July 1894.

5 Cuddy, Edward. "Irish American Propagandists and American Neutrality, 1914-17. "Mid-America 49 (1967), 252-275. James K. McGuire was listed as an active member of the Ancient Order of Hibernians. "Talking To Irishmen" Sun Times 16 August 1891.

6 Brewing and Liquor Interests And German And Bolshevik Propaganda: Report and Hearings of The Subcommittee on the Judiciary United States Senate. Vol. II. (Washington, D.C. Government Printing Office, 1919), 1392.

7 Catholic Encyclopedia Periodical Literature In The United States/Newspapers 12 pp. 11/3/05 http://www.Newadvent.org/cather/11692a. htm.p 4; Robert

Bond, "The Press of Syracuse" in Dwight H. Bruce (ed). Onondaga' Centennial (Boston: History Company 1896, vol I, 563-75).

8 For example, see "Irish Famine" Catholic Sun 8 October 1897:1; "The Irish Question" Catholic Sun 26 July 1895: 1; "An Appeal For The Starving In Ireland" Catholic Sun 15 April 1898:1.

9 Syracuse Post-Standard article fragment. James K. McGuire File, OCHA. Sinn Fein was formally established in the same year McGuire published his book, The Democratic Party in New York State and was publicly identified as a lobbyist for the Asphalt Trust (1905). This reveals the overlap and interests of the man's many careers. Sinn Fein was an amorphous group of like-minded radical Nationalists and played a secondary role to Redmond and the I.P.P. until World War I. Almost insolvent, it was galvanized into action by the Easter Rising of 1916. See MacDonncha, Michael. Sinn Fein: A Century of Struggle (Dublin: Sinn Fein 2005).

10 "John Redmond To Speak In Syracuse". Catholic Sun 24 June 1910:5; "United Irish League Convention". Catholic Sun 30 September 1910; 4.

11 "Friends of Ireland Hear Honorable John E. Redmond". Catholic Sun. 28 October 1910:7; "Redmond Thrills Great Audience". Catholic Sun 4 November 1910:2.

12 "Home Rule Gaining". Catholic Sun 17 March 1911:1,4,; "Home Rule Defended". Catholic Sun 17 March 1911;1; "Home Rule For Ireland Assured". Catholic Sun 28 July 1911;1,2; "Home Rule Position Grows Stronger". Catholic Sun 30 August 1912:1; "All To Unite For Ireland's Just Demands". Catholic Sun 3 July 1912:1. Thomas Power O'Connor (1848-1929) was an Irish-born journalist who, like McGuire, was fluent in German. He was elected to Parliament as an Irish Nationalist (I.P.P.) and served until his death. Like McGuire, he founded a weekly newspaper called The Sun and was the author of numerous books on Irish history and politics. (http://spartacus.schoolnet.co.uk/Joconnor.htm) "Notes On The Irish Home Rule Campaign". Catholic Sun 12 April 1912:1; 28 February 1913:2; 28 March 1913:1; 12 May 1913:1; 11 July 1913:1; 15 August 1913:1.

13 "Home Rule By Clauses". Catholic Sun 6 December 1912:8; 13 December 1912:2; 27 December 1912:2.

14 "United Irish League Convention". Catholic Sun 30 September 1910:1,4. Encouraged by John Redmond, it was initially organized under John Finerty in Chicago in 1901. The group took its name from a parent organization in Ireland that was formed to heal the wounds created by the Parnell scandal. John Finerty (1846-1908), was an Irish-born Democratic Congressman from Chicago, Civil War veteran, correspondent and owner of a weekly Irish paper, The Citizen. Described as a "radical advocate of Irish independence", Finerty supported fellow Chicagoan Alexander Sullivan in his struggle with

Devoy to control the Clan-na-Gael. The U.I.L. was an effort to heal the divisions in the Nationalist cause. It was successfully used by Redmond as an American fund-raising organization, collecting hundreds of thousands of dollars up to the eve of World War I, an imperative since until 1911 members of Parliament were unpaid and most Irish Parliamentary Party members needed assistance. In Michael F. Funchion (ed). Irish American Voluntary Organizations (Westport, Connecticut: Greenwood Press, 1983), 272-3. See also, Funchion, Michael. Chicago's Irish Nationalists, 1881-1890 (New York: Arno Press, 1976), 84-86. "Finerty, John Frederick". The National Cyclopedia of American Biography vol. XIII (New York: James T. White Co., 1906), 324.

15 "United Irish League". Catholic Sun 6 December 1912:5.
16 "Over $1600 For Home Rule Fund". Catholic Sun 23 January 1913:5.
17 "Some Striking Irish Statistics". Catholic Sun 3 February 1911:4; "Do Not Fear Catholic Ascendancy In Ireland". Catholic Sun 11 January 1913:1.
18 Wittke, Carl. The Irish In America. (Baton Rouge: Louisiana State University Press, 1956), 274.
19 "Ulster Bigotry and Intolerance". Catholic Sun 16 February 1912:1; "Ireland's Home Rule Campaign". Catholic Sun 9 February 1912:1.
20 "Will Ulster's Next Step Be Taken July 12?" Catholic Sun 12 July 1912:1,4.
21 "Home Rule". Catholic Sun 17 January 1913:2.
22 McCartan, Patrick. With DeValera In America. (New York: Brentano, 1932), 12-14; Golway, Terry. Irish Rebel: John Devoy and America's Fight For Ireland's Freedom (New York: St. Martin's Press, 1998), 203-204. McCartan was involved in the formation of Sinn Fein. He emigrated to Philadelphia and edited Irish Freedom. He returned to Ireland and worked with the Irish Republican Brotherhood, and was arrested during the 1916 Rising. He escaped and was elected as a Sinn Fein member to the Irish Parliament. Appointed as Sinn Fein representative to the United States, he allied with Joseph McGarrity against Cohalan and Devoy over control of The Friends of Irish Freedom (FOIF) and was instrumental in establishing the American Association For The Recognition Of The Irish Republic. Returning to Ireland, he gave his reluctant support to the Anglo-Irish Treaty of 1921. "Dr. Patrick McCartan" http://wwwnationmaster.com/encyclopedia/Dr.PatrickMcCartan. See Chapter IV, pp…
23 Cronin, Sean. The McGarrity Papers: Revelations Of The Irish Revolutionary Movement In Ireland And America, 1900-1940 (New York: Anvil Books, 1972), 53; Golway, op.cit., 203-4.
24 "Uprising In Ireland". Catholic Sun 5 May 1916:1,2.
25 Doorley, Michael. Irish-American Diaspora Nationalism: The Friends of Irish Freedom 1916-35 (Four Courts Press, 2005), 27. With its roots in

Fenianism of the 19th century, the Clan-na-Gael was an attempt to unify divergent factions. The brainchild of civil engineer Jerome Collins, it began in New York City in 1870. Among its early leaders were John Devoy and Dr. William Carroll. Nationalism was its focus and it often attracted middle-class, respectable, prominent (and often Protestant) Irishmen to its ranks. It became more activist in the 1870's with the Catalpa rescue and the establishment of a "skirmishing fund" to support terrorist activities. The Clan initiated the "new departure" under Devoy, advocating cooperation with both the Land Leagues and the IRB. Militants under Alexander Sullivan took over in 1882 and the Clan's involvement in terrorist activity began in earnest, initiating a dynamite campaign in England. The murder of Dr. Patrick Cronin in 1889, a critic of Sullivan, created a division within the organization that was not healed until 1900 by John Devoy and Luke Dillon. Ruddy, Michael. "Musings on The Origins of the Clan na Gael". http://freepages.generalogy.rootsweb.ancestry.com/~mruddy/clanorigins.htm; "Luke Dillon (1850-1930) in Fenian Graves http://www.irishfreedom.net/Fenian%20graves(Biographies/Third%. Dillon was later convicted of a 1900 attempt to blow up the Welland Canal locks to prevent Canada from sending troops to aid Britain in the Boer War, being released in 1914.

26 "Home Rule Wins Triumphant Victory In House of Commons". Catholic Sun 29 May 1914:1,6. "Irish Home Rule And European War", Catholic Sun 11 September 1914:1; "King Withholds Assent To Bill Angering Liberals And Nationalists". Catholic Sun 11 September 1914;1. "Operation of Home Rule Suspended", Catholic Sun 18 September 1914:1; "Irish People And Suspension Act". Catholic Sun 30 October 1914;1.

27 "Comment On Nathan, Secretary of Ireland". Catholic Sun 20 November 1914:1, 4. The comments in the Catholic Sun, were vitriolic, anti-Semitic and incorrect. Nathan came from a prominent Jewish family, was educated at Sandhurst and had a distinguished military career. He was Acting Governor of Sierra Leone, Gold Coast, Hong Kong and Natal, and was Chairman of the Board of Revenue for Ireland prior to his appointment as Under-Secretary. His superior was Augustine Birrell, Lord Winborne, who was stationed in London. Nathan was the effective head of administration in Ireland. He worked with the I.P.P. to promote Home Rule. Nathan also sought to suppress nationalist activities, such as the drilling of the Irish Volunteers and their recruitment activities. He suppressed seditious newspapers. Nathan was in charge when Casement was arrested. He requested authorization from Lord Winborne to raid headquarters of the Irish Volunteers, but the Easter Rising occurred before it could be granted. A Royal Commission investigating the Uprising resulted in the resignation of both Nathan and Birrell. For details, see O'Broin, Leon. Dublin Castle and the 1916 Rising (London: Sidgewick

and Jackson, 1970), 12; 19-23; 32-42; 161. In an article predating his book, O'Broin gives a more favorable view of Nathan. In fact, he states his being Jewish was an asset in a country divided by Christian sectarian rivalries. O'Broin, Leon. "Birrell, Nathan and The Men of Dublin Castle" in Martin, F.X., Leaders and Men of the Easter Rising (Ithaca, New York: Cornell University Press, 1967), 1-14.

28 "Has Sacrifice Of Irish Lives Made Home Rule Safe?" Catholic Sun 23 March 1915:1.

29 "Irish Leaders Exiled". Catholic Sun 6 Auburn 1915:4; "Banish Irishmen For Opposing War". New York Times 17 July 1915. Ernest Blythe (1889-1975) was the son of a Protestant Unionist farmer. He joined the Gaelic League and the Irish Volunteers and spent two years as an agricultural laborer learning Irish. Blythe was imprisoned, led hunger strikes and spent the Easter Rising in prison. He later supported the Anglo-Irish Treaty of 1923 and was a controversial Minister of Finance in the Cosgrave government. He was an author of Irish poems and several volumes dealing with issues of partition. "Ernest Blythe: Life, Works, Criticism, Notes" http://www.pgil-eirdata.org/html/pgil_datasets/authors/b/Blythe,_Ernest/life.htm Pim was the author of several books under the pseudonym A. Newman. For Mellows, see Greaves, C. Desmond. Liam Mellows And The Irish Revolution. Belfast: Foilseachain an Ghlior Gafa, 2004.

30 "The Criminal History of The British Empire". Catholic Sun 6 August 1915:8. There were a series of five letters: "What Has The British Empire Done For The People Of England?"; "Ireland Under The Curse Of The British Empire"; "The British Empire In America"; "The Curse Of The British Empire In Africa And Asia"; "A Summary Of British Infamies". Ford scored the British on its alleged outrage over the "rape of Belgium", noting it has done much worse many times over to Ireland in the course of two centuries. Advertisements for the book were carried in issues of the Catholic Sun 3 December 1915:6 and 11 December 1915:14.

31 Advertisement: "Frank P. Walsh, Chairman of the United States Commission On Industrial Relations". Catholic Sun 22 October 1915:5.

32 "Irish Race Convention". Catholic Sun 3 March 1916:5; "Friends Of Irish Freedom At Convention". Catholic Sun 10 March 1916:6. "Irish Race Convention". Catholic Sun 18 February 1916:2. Golway 219; Doorley, 36-37; O'Brien, William and Desmond, Ryan Devoy's Post-Bag, 1871-1918 (Dublin: C. J. Fallon, 1948) Vol. II, 480-81.

33 Doorley, 13:37; Funchion, 120. The Board of Directors of FOIF included Daniel F. Cohalan, James K. McGuire, Joseph McGarrity, Robert Ford, John O'Dea, Luke Dillon, Jeremiah O'Leary, Dennis Spellisy, Edward Ryan of Syracuse, Dr. William Carroll and John T. Ryan of Buffalo. The Executive

Committee consisted of seven from the Board of Directors: Cohalan, O'Dea, McGuire, McGarrity, Ford, O'Leary and John T. Ryan "Permanent Officers of Friends of Irish Freedom". Catholic Sun 10 March 1916:1.

34 Blum, John M. Joe Tumulty And The Wilson Era (Boston: Houghton-Mifflin, 1951), 99. May, Ernest. The World War And American Isolation, 1914-17. (Cambridge: Harvard University Press, 1959), 188-89.

35 O'Brien and Desmond, Vol. I, 470-471; Vol. II, 514-18; Doorley, 39; Devoy, John. Recollections of An Irish Rebel (Dublin: Irish University Press, 1969), 40.

36 Carroll, Francis M. American Opinion And The Irish Question, 1910-23 (New York: St. Martins Press, 1978), 82. "Appointed Chair of Executive Committee of Friends of Irish Freedom". Catholic Sun 28 August 1916:2. Devoy, however, states that McGuire never attended a meeting of the National Council to which he was elected and re-elected. One of the reasons for his absence was his business activities kept him away from New York. See "Fenian Chief's Estimate of James K. McGuire" Catholic Sun 19 July 1923.

37 Tansill, Charles C. America And The Fight For Irish Freedom, 1866-1922 (New York: Devon-Adair, 1957), 189. Gaffney, T. St. John. Breaking The Silence (New York, 1930). Thomas St. John Gaffney (1869-1944) was an Irish-born Nationalist who emigrated to the United States. Active in the Republican Party in New York State, he was rewarded with diplomatic posts in Germany, 1905-1913. A prolific author, Gaffney contributed numerous articles to various journals on a variety of topics. He was a member of the American-Irish Historical Society and The Gaelic Society. "Gaffney, T (Thomas) St. John". Who Was Who In America, vol. 2 (Chicago: A.N. Marquis Company, 1963), 202. Gaffney was dismissed from the diplomatic service by President Wilson for his pro-German sentiments and later served as FOIF representative in Germany.

38 Golway, Terry. Irish Rebel: John Devoy And America's Fight For Ireland's Freedom. New York: St. Martin's Press, 1998, 221.

39 "Unrest In Ireland Shown By Press". Catholic Sun 15 April 1916:10.

40 "Great Rally At Fenueil Hall". Catholic Sun 28 April 1916:6.

41 "Meeting of Friends of Irish Freedom". Catholic Sun 26 May 1915:2; "Friend of Irish Liberty". Catholic Sun 17 March 1916:2. Jeremiah O'Leary was a pro-active Nationalist whose satirical anti-British journal Bull was later banned by the United States government. He was described as "an active Sinn Feiner and pro-German propagandist" and was allegedly involved in sabotage, espionage and treason. "Jeremiah O'Leary Is Under Arrest". New York Times 16 June 1918.

42 "FOIF Perfect Organization". Catholic Sun 14 April 1916:5. "FOIF Complete Organization In Syracuse". Catholic Sun 5 May 1916:2.

43 "M'Guire To Answer Redmond Attack On Irish-Americans". Syracuse Herald 29 April 1916:6; "Freedom of Ireland, Downfall of England, Is The General Theme of Irish Banquet". Syracuse Herald 2 May 1916:6.

44 "McGuire Says Home Rule Act Is Not Satisfactory". Syracuse Herald 7 July. 1916:7

45 "Who Accepts Home Rule Is Not A Man Nor An Irishman". Syracuse Herald 8 December 1916. McManus would later write a series of articles on conditions in Ireland in The Catholic Sun during the 1920's.

46 James Duval Phelan (1861-1930) was a banker, a reform mayor of San Francisco, and spearheaded efforts to rebuild the city in the wake of the earthquake of 1906. Phelan served one term as Senator (1915-21). James K. McGuire may have visited Phelan on his trip out West. Phelan also belonged to several Irish Nationalist organizations including the Society of the Friendly Sons of St. Patrick and the Ancient Order of Hibernians. The close ties to McGuire and Irish nationalism may have resulted in the mild tone of the report investigating the conduct of McGuire associate James M. Sullivan in Santo Domingo. "James Duval Phelan". National Cyclopedia of American Biography vol. VIII. (New York: James T. White and Company, 1924) 478-9; "Phelan, James Duval". Dictionary of American Biography vol. 14 (New York: Charles Scribner's Sons, 1934), 523-4.

47 "What Was Dublin Like In 1911?" http://www.census.nationalarchieves.ie/exhibition/Dublin/main.html.

48 Felter, MaryAnn and Schultz, Daniel. "James Mark Sullivan and The Film Company of Ireland". New Hibernian Review 10:2 (Summer 2004): 24-40

49 Callaghan email to author 27 June 2002. For details on the O'Mara family, see Lavelle, Patricia. James O'Mara: Staunch Sinn Feiner, 1873-1948. (Dublin: Claymore and Reynolds, 1961).

50 "President Wilson's Excellent Appointments". Catholic Sun 1 August 1913:1. The article noted Sullivan had been McGuire's guest the previous Sunday. Devoy lists McGuire's associates in the Wilson administration's as William G. McAdoo, Secretary of The Treasury; Josephus Daniels, Secretary of The Navy, and; Albert S. Burleson, Post-Master-General. "Fenian Chief's Estimate of James K. McGuire," Catholic Sun 19 July 1923.

51 Wittenberg, Ernest. "The Thrifty Spy On The Sixth Avenue El". American Heritage December 1965, no. 1 60-64; 100-101.

52 Link, Arthur. The Struggle For Neutrality, 1914-15. (Princeton: Princeton University Press, 1960), 107.

53 Callaghan email to author 14 January 2003.

54 Carroll, 32. Gaffney, T. St. John, 94-95; 99; 101; "Irish Here Demand Volunteers Arm". New York Times 6 July 1914. The Times article noted the growing rift between militants and John Redmond, urging him not to

agree to partition. The American Fund Volunteer Committee promised to "put a gun in the hand of every volunteer who stood ready to fight for Ireland 'undivided and free'". Denis Spellisy was listed as Treasurer of the organization.

55 Esslinger, Dean. "American, German and Irish Attitudes Towards Neutrality". Catholic Historical Review. 53 (1967): 194-216.

56 Ward, Alan. Ireland And Anglo-American Relations, 1899-1921 (Toronto: University of Toronto Press, 1969), 143. "Gaffney, T. St. John". Marquis Who's Who?; Gaffney, T. St. John, Breaking... 212-215; 235-40.See also,:T. St.John Gaffney (186401945) http://www.irishbrigade.eu/other-men/gaffney/gaffney.html 9 pp. Hansen was aGerman national, who became a naturalized American citizen in 1891. He made a fortune in the caviar business. He was active in the Friends of Peace, an offshoot of the American Truth Society whose goal was to prevent American entry nto the Great War. Its members included Jeremiah O'Leary, Bernard Ridder, John D. Moore and James K. McGuire all of whom signed a letter to President Wilson in October 1916 demanding peace. Untitled document: Https://www.irishbrigade.eu/other-men/hansen/hansen.html.

57 Rockett, Kevin, Luke Gibbons and John Hill. Cinema and Ireland (New York: Syracuse University Press, 1988), 16; 116 fn 1. Golway, Terry. Irish Rebel: John Devoy And America's Fight For Irish Freedom (New York: St. Martins Press, 1998), 220. "James Mark Sullivan Arrested For Complicity In Revolt". New York Times 5 May 1916:1,3; "Four More Irish Chiefs Put To Death". New York World 9 May 1916:2; "James J. Sullivan, Once US Minister Arrested As Rebel". New York World 5 May 1916:1-2; "Sister Pleads For Sullivan". New York Times 8 May 1916:6; "James Mark Sullivan Arrested For Complicity In Revolt". New York Times 5 May 1916: 1,3.

58 "British Seize AM[sic] Sullivan On Irish Soil". New York Times 5 May 1916:1.

Chapter III - C

Shamrocks, Subversion, Sabotage, Sedition: The Hyphenates Alliance, 1907-1917

German and Irish American cooperation in trying to influence United States domestic and foreign polices prior to WWI evolved over several decades, given the fact of their cultural and political differences. Wittke notes such issues in temperament-sober, thrifty Teuton versus the prodigal, not always sober Celt; politics-Irish favored Democrats and many Germans leaned Republican; Irish sentiment favored Catholic France during the Franco-Prussian War; each competed with the other in the tight job markets of the recessions of late 19th century America. The Protestant religion of most German immigrants also created tensions. In addition, German Catholics resented Irish hegemony of the Catholic Church in the United States.[1]

However, there were some commonalities that laid the basis for future cooperation. Both had initiated plans for widespread colonization in the United States.[2] Despite some initial mutual animosity, both groups faced persecution and bigotry from Nativist groups which forced them into a united front. Relief funds for both groups were solicited in the German language press and they often worked together to oppose prohibitionism and Blue laws.[3]

By the turn of the century approximately one-third of the German population was Catholic and Germans by then outnumbered Irish as adherents to the Roman Catholic faith. Acknowledgement of the increased German presence in the Church was the establishment at the turn of the century of a chair of German literature at Catholic University.[4]

Prior to the United States entry into World War I, German and Irish-American groups organized in order to influence American foreign policy and call attention to problems in their respective homelands. Irish-and German-Americans focused on efforts to have the United States maintain strict neutrality, as President Wilson had indicated at the outset of hostilities.

Like the Irish, the Germans were one of the oldest and largest ethnic groups, had become assimilated into American society and had experienced a high degree of upward mobility. Wittke noted there were over 8,282,000 Americans who claimed Germany as their country of origin, 30 percent of which had been born overseas, and most of the remainder had one or both parents born in Germany. They took pride in their accomplishment in their adopted land, but were also pleased with the progress made by their Fatherland in the decades following unification on 1870. As with the Irish, this found expression in the fostering of a German language press and in their efforts to preserve their art, music, culture and literature in America.[5] By 1890, there were 800 German language papers in America representing over 50 per cent of the country's foreign language press.[6]

Similar to the Irish, as noted in the references from the Catholic Sun as to the neglect of Irish history and culture in American history books, the German-Americans also felt slighted. To correct this, The National German-American Alliance in 1915 urged the adoption of a text that paid more attention to Germanism so that American children might be taught the names of great men of American history who were of German origin. As the war progressed, in order to combat what they considered a "Pro-British bias" in the major newspapers, they encouraged public access to their ethnic press. For example, Wittke reported the local German-American Alliance of Pasaic, New Jersey in 1916 forced the public library to renew its subscriptions to both the Gaelic American and The Fatherland. In addition, English translations of German classics were published at bargain prices by the German Publication Society of New York.[7]

Like the Irish, the Germans were not unified by religion or politics, nor did their organizations reflect a common outlook on social or political issues. Nonetheless, the leaders of various German-American organizations were often taken as speaking for the group as a whole. As with the Irish, the outbreak of the Great War posed some serious problems for the Germans. Their loyalty, previously unquestioned, was now suspect. Activities once regarded as harmless were perceived by many as a plot to win American public opinion for the German cause. What German-and Irish-Americans simply regarded as "fair play" and legitimate counterpropaganda, were now received with suspicion and hostility.[8] As will be shown, both German-

Americans and Irish-Americans were not blameless. Revelations of their activities published by the Wilson administration indicated a widespread network of subversion, sabotage and propaganda. While undertaken by only a minority, their activities were assumed to represent ethnic groups in their entirety. One such activist was Irish Nationalist and German propagandist, James K. McGuire.

Both German-and Irish Americans were united by Anglophobia. For Ireland, it was England's war-an attempt to monopolize world trade by eliminating competition and exploiting its Empire. Britain was, to Irish-Americans, the "Perfidious Albion." Irish propaganda hammered at the idea that Great Britain had never fully rejected the idea thatAmerica was no longer a British colony. Their reunion was a nefarious plot between Cecil Rhodes and Andrew Carnegie. Rhodes' will established a fund to establish and promote a secret society the aim of which was the extension of British rule throughout the world. Carnegie allegedly predicted a reunion of the two countries, stating, "I say that as surely as the sun in the heavens once shone upon America and Britain united, so surely it is one morning to rise, shine upon and greet again. The reunited States, the British American Union".[9] This attitude was exemplified when George Sylvester Viereck interviewed Daniel F. Cohalan asking his assessment of German propaganda efforts in the United States. Cohalan, replied:

In America England's retiring garrisons left behind them an Army of Troy civilians who never for an instant surrendered the idea of regarding America politically and metaphysically as a dominion of the British crown. This army of occupation has been in the United States so long that most of us do not realize that they are still at the heart Englishmen. This element dominate[s] the Wilson Administration and the Councils of Big Business.[10]

For Germans too, the conspiracy was based on contemporary issues perceived through their version of history. It was a struggle between Germanic civilization and "Slavic barbarism" reflecting a Pan-German bias with traditional animosity towards Russia.[11] Their issues with Britain concerned commercial dominance, naval supremacy and colonial rivalries. Hence, both groups were united in the idea of a vast international British conspiracy to create a world order with itself in control.

Some rapprochement between German and Irish-Americans began to coalesce in 1898 when rumors of a secret American-English alliance surfaced. By the turn of the century, both Irish-Americans and German-Americans had established their own national organizations with the goal of America first - to avoid entangling alliances unless their adopted country was the primary beneficiary. As early as 1898, Wittke states that Irish-Americans insisted that Britain was involved in a campaign of lies to create anti-German sentiment in America. Conversely they praised Germany's opposition to America's pro-British foreign policy.[12] The Catholic Sun reflected the opinions of both groups, noting opposition to such an alliance by such prominent Syracusans as John Cummins, Melvin Z. Haven, Frank Matty and Edward Joy. A second article reported similar criticism from a German-American convention in Chicago.[13] This joint criticism continued with increased intensity in following years. For example, The Catholic Sun reported a meeting of German-Americans in Buffalo. The group expressed concerns the United States would be lured into an Anglo-American alliance.[14]

As early as 1902, The Catholic Sun foreshadowed events of the coming decade, declaring in the wake of the Boer War, that England was American's natural enemy, Germany was our friend. Professor Ernest Von Halle, a German economist with close ties to the Kaiser, was often the featured speaker, insisting that bad German-American relations were part of a British plot.[15]

Similar to the Irish, the Germans also founded organization to foster pride in their culture and to improve their image in their adopted country. The most prominent association was the National German-American Alliance formed in 1901 under the leadership of Charles Hexamer, receiving a national charter from Congress six years later.[16] The charter, as approved by Congress, endorsed its goals as a patriotic and educational organization. The Germans, too, like the Irish, were concerned about resurgent nativism which they believed would further reduce German immigration to the

United States, a process that had been noticeable since the turn of the century. New immigrants from the old country were perceived as a necessary source of recruits to keep alive the cultural ties to the Fatherland.[17] Foreign affairs also permeated the thoughts of Germans in America. As with the Irish, the Boer War, and the Venezuela Affair of 1902-03 created some suspicions of British intentions. Like the Irish, by responding positively to the plight of the Boers, the Imperial German Government incurred the enmity of the British.[18] A similar provocation in Morocco, 1905-06, was the result of a bungled attempt by Germany to disrupt a Franco-English rapprochement. The result was deteriorating relations with Britain and reinforcement of the alliance system which encircled Germany.

The Irish-German coalition was formalized in 1907 when the Ancient Order of Hibernians and The National German-American Alliance in Philadelphia agreed to oppose any and all foreign alliances and prevent any laws restricting immigration and prohibiting personal freedom.[19] Soon after, many joint boards of mutual cooperation sprang up between the two ethnic groups. The collaboration between the National German-American Alliance and the Ancient Order of Hibernians in 1907 was referred to by the latter as "a master stroke in Irish Affairs". Claiming the two groups were 57 percent of the American people, the AOH sanctioned the display of the German flag on German holidays.[20] Both groups sent petitions of protests to Washington. "German-Americans signed Irish petitions, and respected Irish leaders like Patrick Ford, Mayor James A. [sic] McGuire of Syracuse, National President P. J. O'Connor of the [Ancient Order of] Hibernians, Judge James A. O'Gorman of New York, Thomas A. Emmet, and Patrick Egan reciprocated by signing German petitions".[21]

That same spirit of inter-ethnic collaboration was reinforced with the publication of Friedrick von Bernhardi's, <u>Germany and the Next War</u> in 1911. It advocated a policy of ruthless aggression combining Social Darwinism with Machiavellian politics. Conquest was a law of necessity to Bernhardi and was regarded by many as Kaiser Wilhelm's rationale for war. In it, Bernhardi noted, "The German-

Americans have formed a political alliance with the Irish and thus united, constitute a power in the state with which the American government must reckon". Bernhardi also pointed out, should there be a war with Britain, Islamic and Bengali revolutionaries in India could be used to German advantage. During the war, the Imperial German government made an effort to recruit Muslim POW's, with about 3,000 going to serve in the mid – East. And given its involvement with the Ghadarite movement, despite attempts to get Sikhs to join, most remained loyal to Britain.[22] Given Bernhardi's status as a military veteran, historian and member of the General Staff in Berlin, he was in a position to know its strategies in the event of war. His book was given widespread coverage in the American press and when the war began it was considered prophetic.[23] In addition to Bernhardi, <u>Vampire of the Continent</u>, written by Count Ernst zu Reventlow also increased suspicion as to Germany's motives. It essentially blamed the war on England's desire to eliminate its commercial rival, proclaiming British supremacy was really based on piracy, a policy which continued to the present. The Irish connection is George Chatterton-Hill who wrote the "Introduction". Chatterton-Hill was a social Darwinist and an Irish Nationalist who spent World War I in Germany, was an associate of St. John Gaffney and a founder of the German-Irish Society and corresponded with Roger Casement.[24] Chatterton-Hill's "Preface" encouraged Americans to read the book. His tone was ascerbic, referring to Britain's "insatiable greed", as an "international Shylock", "a venomous serpent devouring it's colonies for its own enrichment". He railed against British maritime supremacy proclaiming it could only be destroyed when Ireland is free. His comments as to the strategic location of Ireland, the British destruction of flourishing Irish industry and it's proud cultural traditions were reminiscent of the remarks made by James K. McGuire in his two books written in his role as propagandist for the German Information Service. Taken together, these works publicized the alliance between Germany and Irish revolutionaries and their respective allies in America. It would also cast both groups under the pall of suspicion and disloyalty as the United States moved towards involvement in the Great War.

These collaborations continued. On the eve of WWI, the Clanna-Gael, the American Truth Society and other Irish and German organizations, implemented agreements to join forces.[25] In line with this increased collaboration, The Catholic Sun praised the visit to America in 1912 by Kuno Meyer, the German Celtic scholar. "The Irish regard him as one of their own despite his German citizenship" noted McGuire's paper.[26]

Despite their efforts, the German-Irish connection was not solidified until after hostilities began. For example, in August 1914 at a gathering in Celtic Park, thousands of Irish-American gathered to hear anti-Redmond speeches. There were cheers for the Kaiser and German flags were openly displayed. Similar demonstration were held in New Jersey a week later where John Devoy and Jeremiah O'Leary addressed the crowd.[27] According to Gustavus Ohlinger, the following year the German-and Irish-Americans were "fraternizing ostentatiously with one another on St. Patrick's Day". Such was not always the case. In years past, the two groups had brawled with one another on the same holiday. In subsequent years, following their new-found unity, joint celebrations honoring the birthdays of their respective culture heroes – Otto von Bismarck and Robert Emmett were held.[28]

Charles J Hexamer
(1862-1921)
Pro-German Activist
Public Domain
(Source: Library of Congress/Bain)

George S Viereck
(1884-1962)
Author, pro-German activist
Library of Congress ID cph 3b227115
Public Domain

Louis Hammerling
(1870-1935)
Head of the American Association of Foreign Language Newspapers
Public Domain
(Source: American Leader, 1912)

Arthur Zimmermann
(1864-1940)
German Foreign Minister
Public Domain
(Source: de: image Arthur_Zimmermann.png)

Dr. Heinrich Albert
(1874-1960)
German Spymaster
Bundsarchiv, Bld 102 134486/CC BY-SA3 0

James Gerard
(1867-1951)
American Ambassador to Germany
Public Domain

Richard Barthold
(1855-1932)
Pro-German Activist
BundeArchiv, Bld 137 25348/CC BY-SA 3 0

Konstantin Dumba
(1856-1947)
Austro Hungarian Ambassador to the United States, 1913-1915
Library of Congress IDnpcc 19942
Public Domain

When Austria declared war against Serbia, John Devoy proclaimed it as "Ireland's Ally" indicating where the sympathies of the physical force Nationalists lay.[29] A German-Irish Committee was formed under Saemus O'Sheel,[30] in order to correct the pro-British bias of the American press. Louis Hammerling, President of the American Association of Foreign Language Newspapers, allegedly manipulated the majority of its papers to favor Germany for a "handsome fee".[31] Hammerling was called "the most dangerous German agent in America" by British secret agents. His notoriety came from the large number of ethnic newspapers whose content he controlled. In particular there was a visceral reaction to his publication of "An Appeal to the American People" in April 1915. The article urged the United States to suspend manufacturing arms and munitions and refrain from shipping them to the Allies because of the widespread devastation to inncocent civilians. It further urged American workers to to show their opposition by leaving their jobs in protest. Allegedly financed by small voluntary contributions, it was instead fronted by Edward Rumely who received funding from Heinrich Albert. Hammerling was vilified in the press and later investigated by the same Overman Commission which looked into the pro-German activities of James K. McGuire. Other pro-Irish, pro-German tracts were distributed in the United States as well, including the writings of Irish and Irish-Americans such as Patrick Pearse, Roger Casement, Jeremiah O'Leary, and Frank Harris,[32] all of whom blamed Britain for the war, condemned British imperialism in general, and in Ireland in particular. Among those noted were the works of James K. McGuire.

In addition to the German language press and the efforts of Louis Hammerling, several German-American writers and professors embraced the dual cause of Irish Freedom and pro-German propaganda, including such intellectuals as Frank Koester and Professor Edwin J. Clapp.[33]

To counteract the Allied stereotype of Prussian militarism, and its Bernhardian summons to unalterable laws of nature and to man's baser instincts, an intellectual appeal to American sympathies was made. A manifesto was signed by 93 prominent Germans whose contributions were recognized throughout the world. They included Ernst Haeckel, Max Planck, Wilhelm Wundt and many others. The document alleged the German invasion of France through neutral Belgium was justified. It complained the barbarous Allies were summoning the black and yellow races and the equally uncivilized Slavs to destroy the homeland of Goethe and Beethoven.[34]

These efforts were undermined by the actions the Central Powers - the sinking of the Lusitania, the seizure and publication of the papers of Dr. Heinrich Albert detailing a major network of German subversion and sabotage in America and their links to Irish-American organizations and front groups and the expulsion of several diplomats - all resulted in a climate of opinion that was decidedly pro-Allied. A wave of anti-German hostility and hysteria rolled across America. Often, pro-German was perceived as synonymous with disloyalty. Paranoia was rampant. For example, General Francis V. Greene of Barber Asphalt fame, wrote in February 1915 of the need for American preparedness. Discounting Japan and Britain as potential belligerents, Greene believed Germany already had a feasible plan for the invasion of America's east coast. Once New York City was taken, John D. Rockefeller, Andrew Carnegie, George F. Baker, Jacob H. Schiff, Franklin A. Vanderbilt, Henry C. Frick, Vincent Astor, would be held for a ransom of $5 billion. Greene did not think it would occur if the United States was adequately prepared.[35] Even former President Theodore Roosevelt succumbed to this invasion hysteria which in part, explains his vehement anti-hyphen stance.[36] In addition, there were rumors of a German invasion of Canada using German reservists in America. Things were no better in Berlin. Arthur Zimmerman, under Secretary in the Foreign Office was having lunch with Ambassador James W. Gerard. Zimmerman warned if there was trouble between the United States and Germany there were a half million trained Germans in America who would join the Irish and start a revolution. Gerard scoffed, allegedly saying, there are a half million lampposts to hang them on.[37] Unfortunately such rumors were given credence by the arrest of the German-Consul-General in San Francisco and several members of his staff for attempting to organize a military expedition, gun-running and sabotage in collaboration with Indian and Irish nationalists.[38] This latter activity led to the Hindu-German conspiracy trials of 1917-1918.

Such flights of journalistic license only enflamed anti-German feeling in the United States so that Henry Weismann was compelled to address it at the groups convention in Buffalo in July 1916. Weismann condemned the persecution, suspicion and hatred targeting Germany and German-Americans who stood, not with a radical, subversive minority, but simply for fair play and in international affairs in its conduct of an education campaign on behalf of the Central Powers.[39] These events would coalesce in the wake of the Irish Race Convention, the Easter Rebellion and the attempt on the part of German-and-Irish Americans to overthrow the Wilson administration in the election of 1916. Meanwhile the German-and Irish Americans reinforced their collaborations. The National German-American Alliance, now numbering over 2 million members, endorsed Home Rule for Ireland.[40] Irish-Americans encouraged support for Roger Casement's efforts to replace Cunard and White Star steamship lines which had vacated Queenstown Harbor with ships from the Hamburg-Amerika line. Dismay was widespread when Germany, fearing British reprisal, withdrew from any such commercial commitment to Ireland. In addition, the Clan-na-Gael supported various projects to benefit Ireland, one of which brought Bulmer Hobson to America in 1914 to inform John Devoy and through him, the German government, as to developments in Ireland. Along with Patrick Pearce, who was also in America at the time, Hobson spoke at Clan gatherings throughout the country.[41]

As was noted previously, a split developed in Irish-American public opinion centered on John Redmond's decision to support the British war effort. Many United Irish League members and Ancient Order of Hibernians supported Redmond. Some thought it would create a breach between the Irish and the Germans in America violating America's declared policy of neutrality by supporting one of the belligerents. At the time, Redmondite Home Rulers were still the dominant force in Irish-American thinking, a feeling which soon eroded. The outbreak of war, and the subsequent postponement of the Home Rule question, the emergence of partition and subsequent arming of the Ulster Volunteers, complicated American politics at home and abroad. The Irish Volunteers also armed. Redmond was able to gain control of the organization, but his support for Britain in the war effort was repudiated by Irish-America,[42] assuming it a pretext for recruitment for troops to serve in the British army. The net result was the disintegration of the United Irish League. President Michael J. Ryan urged its dissolution.[43] James K. McGuire, Clan member, resigned from the UIL in protest.[44] Michael J. Ryan, in a complete turnabout, warned Redmond he could no longer expect Irish-American support. "Americans of Irish and German blood, live together in America in harmony; they intermarry; and together, for the last twenty years at least, they have been the formidable force that has prevented an entangling alliance with Britain".[45] Ryan donated $100 to the German cause and openly declared his support for Germany. Two years previously, Ryan, endorsed Redmond's leadership and lent him significant financial support.[46] Redmond's political base in American was rapidly dwindling.

President Woodrow Wilson's proclamation of neutrality in 1914, was initially greeted with support and commendation by many German-American leaders and the German language press. It began to change as his administration's actions belied his professions of neutrality. For example, Wittke noted the Wilson administration censoring German news dispatches received at their Long Island wireless stations, its acceptance of orders for supplies by Allied powers, his admonition of the activities of German and Irish Americans in America, and his acceptance of a Belgian delegation protesting alleged German atrocities but his refusal to give audience to German-Americans protesting America's un-neutral behavior.[47]

Protests increased as both German-and-Irish Americans encouraged a munitions embargo, initiated by the National German-American Alliance in October, 1914. The Alliance received support for such a policy from Irish-Americans in nation-wide demonstrations held in Chicago, New York, New Orleans, St. Louis, Philadelphia, Baltimore, Cleveland, Cincinnati, Davenport, Iowa and elsewhere. One held at Chicago in 1915 hosted 18,000 hyphenate advocates of genuine American neutrality.[48] Richard Bartholdt and Henry Vollmer championed a resolution in Congress prohibiting the exporting of arms and munitions from any American seaport and were promised support for a similar resolution from Senator Gilbert M. Hitchcock of Nebraska.[49] Bartholdt summoned Americans with pro-German sympathies to a conference in Washington in January 1915 to agitate for freedom of the seas and real neutrality. Among those present were Dr. Charles J. Hexamer, John Devoy and Edward von Mach. Despite much agitation, the embargo resolution was not passed by Congress. William Jennings Bryan, originally castigated in the hyphenate press as a "faker", "a grape-juice clown", and a "ward politician", was particularly disliked for his stand in favor of Prohibition.[50] Hyphenate attitudes towards Bryan softened after he endorsed Irish Home Rule in 1913. The Secretary of State incurred the wrath of Britain "for violating diplomatic protocol", but he became a darling of the Irish press for his "manly defense of an oppressed people".[51] He resigned his cabinet position in June 1915 to protest what he believed was a violation of the Wilson administration's policy of neutrality in the wake of the Lusitania incident. After his resignation, Bryan was lauded by Indian nationalists for his condemnation of British colonialism in his pamphlet "British Rule In India". Initially published in 1906 when he was an active member of the Anti-Imperialist League, it had been reprinted by Indian revolutionaries and was being redistributed in multiple languages. He disclaimed any responsibility for its republication claiming it distorted his views[52], but it made him a popular speaker. Bryan spoke at a major rally at Madison Square Garden under the auspices of the Friends of Peace, an organization of German-and Irish-Americans, the German Alliance of Greater New York, The United Irish Societies, the American Truth Society, The American Independence Union, The American Humanity League, American Women of German Descent, and the German American Peace Societies of the State of New York.[53] Allegedly members of the

German diplomatic corps were present, including Franz von Papen, Captain Karl Boy-Ed, and Dr. Constantine Dumba.[54] The overriding concern of the delegates was to have the United States strictly adhere to its policy of neutrality. Several members of the sponsoring societies served on the boards of directors of multiple pro-German/pro-Irish Nationalist organizations. For example, the Friends of Peace included Michael J. Ryan of the United Irish League, Robert Ford, John Devoy, Jeremiah O'Leary of the American Truth Society, Daniel F. Cohalan and James K. McGuire of the Clan na Gael, Mary McWharter of the AOH Ladies Auxiliary, Henry Weisman of the National German-American Alliance, and Richard Bartholdt of the American Independence Union. In addition to those noted, Ohlinger added the American Neutrality League.[55]

Irish-American and German-American groups co-operated in other ways as well. For example, German and Irish-Americans protested the biased reporting in the Anglo-American press. It was also at this time high-ranking members of the Clan-na-Gael met with representatives of the Imperial German government to discuss preparations for a rising in Ireland. Also, many prominent Irish-American such as Jeremiah O'Leary, Timothy S. Hogan, and Robert Burke[56] were figured prominently as speakers at "German Day" gatherings. The Irish reciprocated, having Dr. C.J. Hexamer, President of the National German-American and Dr. Julius Hoffman address Irish groups.[57]

James K. McGuire, Clan-na-Gael leader and member of the Executive Committee of the Friends of Irish Freedom, was an active participant. For example, speaking in Syracuse to the Federation of German Catholic Societies, McGuire praised the thoroughness of German youth which made possible the unification of Germany, creating an empire more powerful than that of Rome. He lauded the work of German universities and their thorough training. Noting the ethnic roots of his audience, McGuire stated that Charles Steinmetz, not Thomas Edison, was the "Greatest Electrician". Further, he said Andrew Carnegie learned all about steel from ideas first initiated in Germany. Given the current world crisis and its repercussions on world trade, McGuire said access to quality products was now impossible. This country would have to rely on an "inferior product made in America".[58] McGuire continued to work the German-American speech circuit in the ensuing years. He was the principal speaker at the annual German Day picnic in Syracuse in August 1916.[59] While he stressed American neutrality, McGuire noted the tenacity of German fighters on the eastern and western fronts which gave his German audience much to celebrate. McGuire's speech left no secret as to his sympathies. Referring to "British executioners" at the reprisals in the wake of the Easter Rebellion, McGuire predicted the fall of Verdun to German arms, and praised the voyage of the Deutschland,[60] a commercial submarine, which made two successful voyages to the United States. He also noted the failure of the British offensive on the Somme, exalting German determination in what he perceived as an uneven struggle. "Gaunt famine, enemies seven to every defender one, the money and munitions of America, the very seas are arrayed as enemies of Germany…[A]nd there stands Germany, unconquered and unconquerable, holding on grimly to hundreds of thousands of square miles of the richest territory torn from her enemies and no serious dents of great military importance along her thousands of miles of front." McGuire further assailed the Lusitania policy as giving Germany the "worst" of the decision without requisite concessions from England. McGuire scored the British for posing as "Saviors of Belgium", yet committing atrocities in Ireland. He believed American public opinion was becoming more suspicious towards England, noting such pro-British plays as "The Savior of Belgium" and "Hands Across The Sea" had packed up and returned to England.[61] As events turned out, this was, like his prophecy of a German victory, nothing more than wishful thinking.

German-and-Irish Americans continued their collaborations until America's entry into the war. For example, in October 1916, The New York Times reported on the groups' united efforts to raise money for the Irish Relief Fund in the wake of the Rising of 1916. President of its fund-raising committee, John J. O'Leary, brother of Jeremiah, leader of the American Truth Society, declared this effort was the "foundation of the confederation of the German and Irish peoples of America". Other German-American members of the American Truth Society included George Sylvester Viereck, Bernard Hermann Ridder and Frederick Franklin Schrader.[62] O'Leary's efforts were aided by Alphonse G. Koelbe, a prominent Catholic layman and President of the United German Societies of New York, and numerous German-Americans conspicuous in journalism and religious societies. The Irish segment consisted of Daniel F. Cohalan and Edward G. Moore, among others.[63]

Initially, the German press was favorable towards Wilson given his proclamation of neutrality. Their efforts focused on trying to correct the negative stereotype of Germany as a militaristic power, with an antiquated form of government led by an autocratic warlord. Their attempts to portray the Kaiser as "knight without fault or blemish" had little support, a position they blamed on a diabolical plot by Britain. The National German-American Alliance was urged to protest the slanderous attacks by the "Tory press".[64] The official bulletin of the National German-American Alliance stated it was "waging war against Anglo-Saxonism, against the fanatical enemies of personal liberty and political freedom; it is combating narrow-minded known-nothingism, the influence of the British, and the enslaving Puritanism which had its birth in England.[65]

The German papers launched a diatribe against all things English. Protests were held in various parts of the country and despite a growing dislike by many Americans for all things German, readership of the German press in America actually increased by almost 20 percent.[66] Echoing comments similar to that of the Irish-American papers, the German-American press used American holidays and heroes to advocate for their cause. George Washington's birthday and the Fourth of July were used to warn the Wilson administration against European alliances. As with the Irish papers extolling the bravery of its fallen heroes in America's wars, so too did the Germans remind Americans of their debt to Baron von Steuben who helped win independence from the same enemy Germany was currently fighting. Reflecting again on American-British hostilities in years past, some German papers believed the British Orders-in-Council prior to the War of 1812 interfered with America's shipping rights as a neutral urging declaration of war as the solution.[67] The protests were fruitless. In the end, British violations meant the loss of America property, whereas Germany's resulted in the loss of American lives. The difference was decisive; for the hyphenates, especially the leaders of their nationalist organizations, disastrous. Among the casualties, was James K. McGuire.

Notes

1 Wittke, Carl. The Irish In America (Baton Rouge; Louisiana State University Press, 1956), 120-121; Cuddy, Joseph. Irish-American And National Isolation, 1914-20 (New York: Arno Press, 1976), 37. The religious conflict between the two ethnic groups resulted in Cahenslyism. Named after German Peter Cahensly, it advocated ethnic parishes and parochial schools, a move opposed by the Irish Catholic hierarchy who saw it as a divisive force in the American Church. For details, see Meng, John. "Cahenslyism: The Second Chapter." Catholic Historical Review XXXII (October 1946), 302– 40.

2 For Irish colonization schemes, see Wittke, The Irish... op.cit. Chapter VII, "Irish As Farmers", especially pp.66-74. For German plans, see Hawgood, John A. The Tragedy of German-America: Germans In the United States of America During the Nineteenth Century and After (New York: G.B. Putnam's Sons, 1940. especially Part II, "New Germanies On American Soil," chapters IV-VII, pp 93-224.

3 Wittke, The Irish..., 182; 183; Cuddy, 38.

4 Colman, J. Barry. The Catholic Church and German-Americans (Milwaukee, 1953), 7; 249-51.

5 Wittke, Carl. German-Americans And The World War (Columbus, Ohio: Ohio State Archeological and Historical Society, 1936), 3.

6 "A German-American Chronology". http://www.lib.iupui.edu/kade/adams/chrono.html.

7 Wittke, German-Americans..., 27; 28, 29.

8 Wittke, Carl. The Irish..., 273; 274.

9 Viereck, George Silvester. Spreading Germs of Hate (New York: Horace Liveright, 1930), 215-217.

10 Viereck, Spreading Germs.... 117-118.

11 Wittke, The German-Americans...6.

12 Wittke, The Irish...,274.

13 "Anglo-American Alliance". Catholic Sun 15 July 1898:1; "Chicago's Best Germans". Catholic Sun 29 July 1898:1.

14 "Hyphenated Americans". Catholic Sun 17 March 1911:2.

15 "Is Our Natural Enemy". Catholic Sun 4 April 1902:1. Von Halle (1868-1909) was a German economist who traveled extensively in the United States. He was an expert on the cotton culture of the South, the economics of the West Indies and Venezuela and on the business enterprise of Germans in the United States. This is relevant insofar as Germany and the United States had – and would have – tense relations in both the West Indies and Venezuela. Von Halle was a friend of the Kaiser and as an advocate of a large German navy

helped author several naval bills for the Imperial Government. "Ernst von Halle Dead". New York Times 29 June 1909.

16 Johnson, Charles Thomas. Culture At Twilight: The National German-American Alliance, 1901-1918 (New York: Peter Lang, 1999), 37. The NGAA was a federation of German ethnic associations and at its height claimed more than two million members. Its activities were investigated by Congress in 1917. Hexamer resigned his presidency and its charter was revoked the following year.

[16] Ibid., 39.

17 Ibid., 39.

18 These developments were noted in McGuire's paper, The Catholic Sun. See, for example "Irish Are In Boers Camp". Catholic Sun 13 October 1899:1. "Ireland And Germany Make It Unpleasant For England". Catholic Sun 29 November 1901:1. There were an estimated 2675 volunteers from ten countries. Germans outnumbered the Irish by more than 3:1. Kugel, Frank. "Nordic Volunteers In The Anglo-Boer War". Posthorn, August 2007, 6 -9. Proposed Imperial German intervention in the Boer War embittered relations between Britain and Germany. See Vagts, Alfred. "Hopes and Fears of An American-German War, 1870-1915" Political Science Quarterly, vol. 55, No. 1 (March 1940), pp. 53-76; Roberts, Edward. Ireland In America. (New York, 1931), 189-90.

19 Wittke, German-Americans..., 19; 36; O'Dea, John. History of The Ancient Order of Hibernians and Ladies Auxiliary, Vol. III (Philadelphia: Keystone Printing Co., 1923), 1387-88. Personal freedom was a metaphor for anti-Prohibitionism.

20 O'Dea, Ancient Order...vol III 1388; Wittke, German-Americans...276. An agreement was signed three years later reaffrirming the pledges. Charles Hexamer of the NGAA and the Anglophobe President of the AOH, Mathew Cummings. With Home Rule by then an apparent reality, Cummings was replaced by a moderate Redmondite, James Regan. Some members of the Clan believed Cummings was trying to dominate its activities which may have been the real reason he was replaced. Aan de Weil, op. cit., 143;145;263)

21 Wittke, The Irish...,274.

22 Waters, Florence. Germany's Grand First World War Jihad Experiment" https://www.telegraph.co.uk/culture/museums/11022199/germany's-grand-WW1-jihad-

23 O'Connor, Richard. The German-Americans: An Informal History (Boston: Little, Brown and Company, 1968), 378-79. Von Bernhardi, Friedrich. Germany and the Next War. Berlin: J. G. Cotta, 1911, 96. See also Fraser, Thomas. "German and Indian Revolutionaries, 1914 – 1918" Journal of Contemporary History, 12 (2) April 1977, 255 – 272. Bernhardi went on to

be a decorated commander in the Eastern front during the war. The British Foreign office, as part of its propaganda efforts, made sure that all works of extreme German nationalists and militants were published in English as a means of letting the Germans portray themselves as "barbarians". See Epstein, Jonathan. "German and English Propaganda in World War I" Paper given at NYMAS 1 December 2000.
Bernhardi (1849-1930) was a Prussian general and military historian whose book was considered a contributing cause to World War I. His book and its impact were treated in, "War Is Right, Peace Is Wrong, Says German General" <u>New York Times</u> 21 April 1912; "Opposes Peace Idealism; Gen. Bernhardi's Book To Be An Attempt To Justify War". <u>New York Times</u> 21 May 1911; "When Bernhardis Govern The World" <u>New York Times</u> 21 December 1916; "German Army General Foretold German's War Plans" <u>New York Times</u> 14 August 1914.

<u>24</u> Count Ernst zu Reventlow was a Commander in the German navy and a writer on naval history and politics. The initial copies of the book, shipped from Berlin to New York, were intercepted by the British and destroyed. A subsequent copy was sent over on the German merchant submarine, <u>Deutschland.</u> It was translated by George Chatterton-Hill, who endorsed a projected alliance between Ireland and Germany. The book was made available to the general public. "Reventlow Calls England Vampire of Continent". <u>New York Times</u> 26 November 1916; "Viereck Got $100,000 From Germans". <u>New York Times</u> 26 July 1918. Chatterton-Hill's credibility is suspect. According to Sir Charles Curry, Chatterton-Hill was born in Ceylon of an Irish father and a native mother. He had never set foot in Ireland (Curry, Sir Charles. Sir <u>Roger Casement's Diaries: His Mission to Germany and the Findley Affair.</u> Munich: Archie Press, 1922, 219-226). Chatterton-Hill's praise for Reventlow may not be due to the embrace of his prose. Rather it was possibly an effort to have Casement intervene with the German government to free him from an internment camp which was accomplished in April 1915, after Chatterton-Hill swore he "was true to the cause of Ireland". Later Reventlow sponsored him to the D I G (German-Irish Society) where he was joined by Matthias Erzberger, Thomas St.John Gaffney, Kuno Meyer and Theodor Schiemann. (ann de Weil, op. cit., 306-307.) It's goal was to have a unified front in German, Irish, Irish-American, German-American propaganda. Schiemann had entertained the notion of a German-Irish alliance as early as 1904. He also corresponded with George Freeman, an Irish nationalist employed by John Devoy with ties to Indian revolutionaries. It was Schiemann who encouraged Kuno Meyer's lecture tour of the United States. Meyer's talks were given extensive coverage in James

K. McGuire's Catholic Sun. See also "George Chatterton-Hill: http://www.irishbrigade.eu/other-men/chatterton-hill/chatterton-hill.html.

25 Child, Clifton. German-Americans In Politics, 1914-17. (New York: Arno Press, 1970), 77.

26 "Kuno Meyer Coming". Catholic Sun 15 March 1912:1.

27 Carroll, F. M. American Opinion and The Irish Question, 1910-23 (New York: St. Martin's Press, 1978), 47.

28 O'Conner, Richard. The German-Americans...394, citing Ohlinger, Their True Faith and Allegiance. For a brief biography of Ohlinger, see fn. 33.

29 Wittke, German-Americans..., 276; Ward, Allan J. Ireland And Anglo-American Relations, 1899-1921 (Toronto: University of Toronto Press, 1969), 91.

30 Saemus O'Sheel was a third-generation Irish-American. Born James Shield he changed his name to a more Gaelic form. A staunch Irish Republican who never visited Ireland, he wrote anti-British propaganda during World War I, much of it published in The Fatherland, a publication subsidized by the German government and edited by German-born George Sylvester Viereck. O'Sheel worked for Democratic Senator James A. O'Gorman (1913-16) and claimed to be author of the McLemore Resolution banning Americans from traveling on foreign ships in a war zone. O'Sheel met Viereck, a fellow poet and journalist whose works were in vogue from 1907-12 after which he became a confirmed Germanophile. See, "Shaemus O'Sheel" http://viereckproject.wikispaces.com/Shaemas-OSheel. For Viereck, see "George Sylvester Viereck" http://www.lib.viowa.edu/spec-coll/Bai/johnson2htm.

31 Ward, 91. Louis N. Hammerling (1870 – 1935), born in Galacia, had limited formal education. He went to America and worked at various jobs-on a plantation in Hawaii, as a restaurant worker, a coal miner in Pennsylvania, and later as a journalist.. This position connected him to politicians and in 1904, he was asked to coordinate activities of foreign language newspapers for the Republican election campaign. Four years later he was a delegate to the Republican National convention. In 1908 he organized the American Association of Foreign Language Newspapers, the goal of which was to deliver advertising from American businesses to various ethnic papers in return for which the papers would endorse the policies of their advertisers. This allowed for commission of graft and fraud, making Hammerling wealthy in the process. His deeds are covered in Park, Robert, The Immigrant Press and Its Control (New York: Harper Brothers, 1922), Chapter XVI, "The Manipulations of Hammerling," 377-410. Hammerling, like McGuire, was investigated by the Senate Committee on Brewing and Liquor Interests and German and Bolshevik Propaganda. Report and Hearings of the Subcommittee on The Judiciary. United States Senate, vol I (Washington, D.C. US Government

Printing Office, 1918), 465-472. Some of Hammerling's activities allegedly involved soliciting information as to worker discontent in munitions plants in various locations throughout the country. One informant said she was paid off to keep silent about Hammerling's financial connection to the German and Austrian governments. See Berkley Hudson. and Karen Boyajy, "The Rise and Fall of an Ethnic Advocate and American Huckster". Media History, vol.15, No.3, 2009, 287 – 302; M.B.B. Buskupski. The Most Dangerous German Agent In America: The Many Lives of Louis N. Hammerling. Northern Illinois Unversity Press, 2015, Chaps. 5,6, 53 – 92.

32 Frank, Harris (1856-1931) was an Irish-born American journalist, writer and editor of various periodicals, who had some formal education in German universities. During World War I, he edited Pearson's Magazine (1916-22) which, like other pro-German publications after America's entry into the war, was harassed by the United States Post Office and its publication eventually suspended. There are several in-depth biographies of Harris, but a brief version can be found in "Frank Harris" http://www.answers.com/topic/frank-harris.

33 Koester (1876-1927) was a German-born engineer and author who emigrated to the United States in 1902, obtaining employment with a series of American companies, becoming an expert on civic improvements for several American municipalities. Naturalized a decade later, Koester wrote tracts favorable to the German cause, especially Secrets of German Progress in 1915. ("Koester, Frank". Who Was Who In America Vol. I. 1897-1942 Chicago: Marquis Who's Who, 1943), 690.

Professor Edwin J. Clapp was author of Economic Aspects of The War (New Haven: Yale Univ. Press, 1915). Clapp ostensibly endorsed American neutrality, but his comments were pro-German, condemning the British blockade, believing it ineffective, and its seizure of American cargoes illegal. See, "America's Part In Europe's Conflict: Professor Edwin J. Clapp Discusses In A Forthcoming Book: Some Economic Aspects of The War That Involve This Country's Neutral Rights". New York Times 5 September 1915.

34 O'Connor, Richard. German-Americans...,384. Others who signed the manifesto were Max Rheinhardt, the actor and theater director; Hermann Suderman, the German dramatist and novelist, Gerhardt Hauptman, German dramatist and Nobel laureate, and Rudolph Christoph Eucken, a philosopher, author and Nobel Prize winner. It was obviously designed to appeal to American intellectuals.It's racism and calls for Teutonic supremacy are apparent.

35 "How Germans Might Capture New York". New York Times 21 February 1915.

36 Viereck, George S. Spreading Germs of Hate (New York: Horace Liveright, 1930), 254-257.

37 Tuchman, Barbara. The Zimmerman Telegram (New York: Ballantine Books, 1958); cited in O'Connor, op. cit., 402.
38 Ohlinger, Gustav. "German Propaganda in The United States." The Atlantic Monthly, 1916, 534-547. Gustavus Ohlinger (1877-1972) was the son of German missionaries in China. He traveled widely, graduating from the University of Michigan Law School in 1902. Ohlinger established the Michigan Law Review and later practiced law in China. He returned to the United States in 1906. Ohlinger practiced and taught and authored several books and articles on civil procedures. He served in the US military, 1918-19. Ohlinger wrote two books critical of German-Americans, Their True Faith and Allegiance (1916) and The German Conspiracy In American Education (1919), as well as numerous articles. In them, Ohlinger asserted German-Americans supported Germany through subversion. His works were highly regarded by Theodore Roosevelt with whom he carried on an extensive correspondence. Ohlinger testified against the National German-American Alliance before the Senate Judiciary Committee in 1918. "Gustavus Ohlinger: Biographical Sketch". Ward M. Canaday Center University of Toledo, n.p.,n.d. "Ohlinger, Gustavus". The National Cycolpedia of American Biography, vol. 58 (Chifton, New Jersey. James T. White Company, 1979), 574-75. Franz Bopp was Consul-General in San Francisco. He and his colleagues were accused of delaying or destroying military cargoes destined for Russia, in addition to plotting to blow or a tunnel of the Canadian Pacific Railroad to delay supplies dustined for the Russian front. He and his accomplices were tried, convicted and sentenced to imprisonment after one of them turned State's evidence they tried to instigate a rebellion against British rule in India. Bernstorff, Count Johann, My Three Years In America (New York Scribners, 1920), 112:120-21.This formed part of the prosecution in the Hindu-German conspiracy trials of 1917-1918.
39 "German Alliance Head Criticizes President". New York Times 3 July 1916. Weisman was a German-born, former baker, labor union activist, lawyer and businessman. He would later reverse himself, urging support for President Wilson's policies a month prior to American entry into the war. "Pledges German-Americans" New York Times 5 March 1917.
40 "German Alliance In Favor of Home Rule" Catholic Sun 24 October 1913:1.
41 Bulmer Hobson (1883-1969), abandoned his Quaker faith and espoused violence in the cause of Irish independence. He was a founding member of the Irish Volunteers and organized the Howth gun-running episode, but his willingness to give John Redmond control over the Irish Volunteers and his belief the Easter Rising was premature, alienated him from the Nationalist leadership. For details on Hobson, see Hay, Marnie. Bulmer Hobson and The Nationalist Movement In Twentieth-Century Ireland

(Manchester University Press, 2009). Padraic Pearse's (1879-1916) career is much better known. A leader in the Gaelic League, he sought to re-ignite cultural awareness, establishing St. Enda's school for that purpose. The School stored arms for the Irish Volunteers. In 1913 he was initiated into the Irish Republican Brotherhood and was at the initial meeting of the Irish Volunteers. Pearse read the proclamation establishing the Irish Republic during the Easter Rising of 1916. He was among the 14 leaders executed by the British. For a full treatment, see Edwards, Ruth D. Patrick Pearse: The Triumph of Failure (London: Gollancz, 1977).

42 Cuddy, Joseph Edward. Irish-America and National Isolationism, 1914-1920. (Arno Press, 19776), 46.

43 Gwynn, Denis. The Life of John Redmond (London, 1932), 419; Devoy, John. Recollections of An Irish Rebel (New York, 1929), 409.

44 "Uprising In Ireland". Catholic Sun. 5 May 1916: 1,2; "Friends of Irish Freedom Complete Organization In Syracuse". Catholic Sun. 5 May 1916:2.

45 Gwynn, The Life..., 418. Such was not always the case. A century earlier, Dr. Ernest Ludwig Brauns denounced Germans who intermarried with Irish, fearing a loss of Germanic language and a diluted German culture. In O'Connor, op. cit., 76-77.

46 "Promises Aid To Redmond". New York Times. 25 June 1914; "Pledge $97,000 For Irish Nationalists". New York Times 17 July 1914.

47 Wittke, German-Americans..., 46.

48 Ibid., 59.

49 Ibid., 61. Gilbert Monell Hitchcock, was a lawyer and newspaper editor from Iowa. He spent two years as a student in Germany. Previously having served as a Congressman, he was Iowa's first Democratic Senator. He was often critical of Wilson's policies and supported an arms embargo to all belligerents through 1916. Wittke reports that he was considered as a nominee to run against Wilson in 1916 (88). "Hitchcock, Gilbert Monell". Dictionary of American Biography Vol. XI Supplement One (ed. R.L. Schuyler) (New York: Scribner's & Sons, 1944), 410-411. Bartholdt was a German-born, naturalized American citizen. He was a journalist, lawyer and Republican Congressman from Missouri, 1893-1915. He was actively involved in the peace movement until World War I. He joined the American Independence Union, an organization dedicated to maintaining American neutrality. "Urges America To Stay Neutral". New York Times 2 June 1915. Vollmer was a lawyer, a former mayor of Davenport, Iowa and a one term Democratic Congressman. He was tied to pro-German sympathies by his advocacy of an arms embargo and the actions of his brother who violated the provisions of the Espionage Act following America's entry into World War I. "Vollmer,

Henry". Biographical Directory of The United States Congress http://bioguide.congress.gov/scripts/biodisplay.pl?index=voool3.
50 Wittke, German-American..., 49.
51 Mr. Bryan's Home Rule Address". Catholic Sun 21 March 1913:1.
52 Dignan, Don K. "The Hindu Conspiracy in Anglo – American Relations During World War I". Pacific Historical Review 40 (1) February 1971,57 -76.
53 "Excuses Lusitania Horror". New York Times 26 June 1915. "Ridder On Bryan Meeting". New York Times 26 June 1913.
54 McMaster, John B. United States In The World War, 1914-1918. (New York: D. Appleton and Co., 1918), 113-115. Dumba was the Austro-Hungarian ambassador, later expelled from the United States for his subversive activities.
55 Ohlinger, "German Proganda", op.cit., 543.
56 Timothy S. Hogan was an Ohio lawyer, Democrat and State Attorney-General, 1911-1915. He ran unsuccessfully for Congress against Republican Warren G. Harding in 1914, in a campaign noted for its vicious anti-Catholicism. Hogan was also Ohio State President of the Ancient Order of Hibernians. http://www.ohioattorneygeneral.gov/about/past_ags/hogan.asp." Warren G. Harding^.
http://virtualology.coin/uspresidents/presidentharding.com/ Robert Ernest Burke was an Illinois Democrat, who rose from poverty by selling newspapers becoming a contractor and a power in Chicago politics. His role as campaign manager for Mayor Carter Harrison won him appointment as City Oil inspector. He was referred to as "Chicago's Richard Croker", suggesting the criminal charges of embezzlement which led to his political demise had credibility. "Robert E. Burke of Chicago Indicted". New York Times 6 October 1901; "Chicago's Richard Croker". New York Times 13 October 1901; "Robert E. Burke Dead". New York Times 30 July 1921.
57 Wittke, German-Americans..., 277. Julius Hofmann (1882-1965) was Minnesota-born Democrat and Roman Catholic, who earned a doctorate in forestry. He worked as a university professor, for the U.S. Forestry Service and authored numerous articles on scientific agriculture and forestry management. "Hofmann, Julius". The National Cyclopedia of American Biography, Vol. 53 (New York: James T. White and Company, 1971), 91-92. Charles John Hexamer, born in Philadelphia, Pennsylvania had a love of German language and culture. He was organizer and idealistic leader of the National German-American Alliance until 1917.
58 "Urges Importance of Specializing In Work". Syracuse Herald 18 November 1914.
59 "Plans Complete For German Day". Syracuse Herald 6 August 1916: 22. German Day celebrations were annual affairs in many cities with a large German population. Initiated in 1902 following a visit from the German

Crown Prince Henry in February, they were organized by Dr. H. A. C. Anderson, President of the United German Societies. Anderson was born in Germany, and educated in the United States. He worked as a bacteriologist in the New York City Health Department. Anderson presided over the first German Day celebration. His initial address stressed the goal of the celebration was to work closely with all Americans in "closer friendship". Then President Theodore Roosevelt was soundly cheered. The German Charge d' Affairs in Washington, D.C. and Dr. Kuno Franke of Columbia University addressed the audience. The following year, Anderson noted hostility to the celebration in the Anglo-American press. As the World War unfolded, Theodore Roosevelt would be an outspoken critic of German ethnic solidarity. See "Prince Henry's Escort", New York Times 7 February 1902; "First Celebration of German Day". New York Times 10 November 1902; "German Day Celebration". New York Times 23 November 1903. "Dr. H. A. C. Anderson's Death" New York Times 6 January 1909. As the war progressed, German Day celebrations became increasingly "political", raising funds for the German Red Cross, a front for German propaganda, and endorsing resolutions of American neutrality. Activities were curtailed as anti-German hostility increased following America's entry into the war. See Wittke, German-Americans..., 35; 59-60; 171.

60 The Deutschland was a blockade-running submarine owned and operated by the North German Lloyd line. Captained by Paul Koenig, it would submerge to avoid British patrols. It successfully landed its cargo of dyes, medicines and gemstones at Baltimore in July 1916. In addition, it carried propaganda materials to be used by the German Information Service. "Viereck Got $100,000 From The Germans". New York Times 26 July 1918. An obvious chink in its blockade of Germany, Britain protested its use arguing it could not be stopped and searched as was the case with ordinary surface marine vehicles. Pressure by various groups alleging the United States was showing pro-Allied favoritism forced the government to reject this argument, stating as long as they remained unarmed they would be regarded as merchant vessels. The Deutschland returned to Germany with a cargo of tin, rubber and nickel. The merchant submarine made a second successful crossing in November 1916 after which its captain wrote a popular book, Voyage of the Deutschland, The First Merchant Submarine (New York: Hearst International Library Co., 1916) in an effort to sway public opinion in favor of Germany. It was extremely popular when published in the United States in 1917. After America entered the war, the Deutschland and five other merchant submarines were converted into battle cruisers and outfitted with torpedo tubes and deck guns. The Deutschland's career as a raider lasted from June 1917 to Novemeber 1918 having sunk 19 Allied merchant ships.

It was surrendered as part of the armistice in 1918. "U-Boat to Convoy the Deutschland". New York Times 4 November 1916; "The Submarine Deutschland". http://coloranthistory.org/SubmarineDeutschland.html. The Deutschland had a brief reprise in McGuire's life following the Easter Rising and the execution of Sir Roger Casement.

61 "Predicts Fall of Verdun This Year". Syracuse Herald 8 August 1916: 7.

62 Bernard Herman H. Ridder (1851-1915), was a New York City-born insurance salesman turned editor for the leading German newspaper in the United States, the Staats-Zeitung. He was an anti-Tammany Democrat and a reformer. See "Ridder, Herman". Dictionary of American Biography Vol. 15 (New York: Charles Scribner's Sons, 1935), 590-91. Frederick Franklin Schrader (1857-1943) was a German-born journalist and writer. He was co-editor and founder of The Fatherland. Schrader wrote several pro-German works, England In The Witness Stand, (1915), and Germans In The Making Of America (1923) among other works in addition to several plays.

63 "Germans Capture Irish Bazaar". New York Times 4 October 1916.

64 Wittke, German-Americans…, 11-13.

65 Ohlinger, Gustav, "German Propaganda"… op.cit, 541.

66 Ford, Nancy Gentile. Americans All (College Station, Texas: Texas A and M Press, 2001), 18.

67 Wittke, German-Americans… 48; 50. Richard Bartholdt had spoken at the unveiling of the statute of Baron von Steuben in Washington in 1910. A year later he presented a replica at Potsdam, Germany. Faust, Albert B. "Bartholdt, Richard". Dictionary of American Biography Vol. XI Supplement One. Robert L. Schuyler (ed.) New York: Charles Scribner's Sons, 1944,), 53-54.

Chapter III - D

The Teutonic Embrace- Espionage, Sedition, Subversion and Sabotage on Three Continents, 1890-1918

An Irish Political Paradigm Shift

During the time of "official" American neutrality, 1914-1917, the Imperial German government established a Secret War Council. Its efforts were two-fold involving legal and peaceful activities, such as fund-raising, obtaining essential war materials and propaganda. The dark side of the mission involved its agents, diplomats, businessmen and sympathizers in acts of subversion, espionage and sabotage. James K. McGuire, through his participaqtion in one of the Council's agencies, was an active partner in both endeavors from 1914 until American entrance into the war in April 1917. Council members included Heinrich Albert, nominally the Director of Purchasing; Military Attache Franz von Papen; Naval Attache Karl Boy-Ed; Count Johann von Bernstorff, the German Ambassador to the United States; Dr. Bernard Dernburg, head of the German Red Cross; George Silvester Viereck, editor of the pro-German newspaper, The Fatherland; Dr. Karl Alexander Feuhr; Hugo Munsterberg, psychology professor; William Bayard Hale, American journalist and former aid to President Woodrow Wilson; Prince Hatzfeld, representing the German embassy; Hans Tauscher, agent for Krupp armaments, and Matthew Claussen representing the Hamburg-America Shipping Company (HAPAG).[1] Another member may have included Felix Sommerfeld, whose activities almost precipitated a war with Mexico. Their efforts were global in scope, reaching not only into the United States but Canada, Mexico, the Middle East, the Far East, India and Europe. Germany faced an uphill battle in its efforts as the day after war was declared, the British cut the transatlantic cable. Hence, they had to use elaborate and time-consuming codes, ciphers and couriers to maintain contacts with their agents. But first, in order to access willing collaborators, the Germans had to initiate contacts with groups previously ignored, but which shared a common grievance against a common enemy – Britain. It is no small irony, that colonized peoples turned to a major colonizer - Germany - for assistance in their efforts at liberation.

For Irish nationalists, the man who inaugurated the Teutonic embrace was Frank Hugh O'Donnell. His career discloses early ties to Irish nationalists, Indian revolutionaries and the German government. It reveals the Germans did not have to start from scratch, but that were able to tap into pre-existing subversive networks in Europe, India, Mexico and the United States. O'Donnell was a politician who apparently reveled in controversy. Early in his university career he showed his hostility to British colonialism in a speech denouncing its creation in the 16th century by Queen Elizabeth I for which he was censured. He moved to London and began a career in journalism, later being elected to Parliament. In 1875, he established the Constitutional Society of India which demanded Home Rule for the colony. His ultimate goal was to establish a confederation of discontented members of the British Empire in the hope of ending it. These efforts link O'Donnell to other Irish and Indian revolutionaries who, with Germany, would use the Great War as a vehicle for pursuing their goals. As early as 1901, he advanced a proposition to the German Empire to forge a bond between it and the Irish, essentially abandoning Ireland's traditional anti-British alliance with France. Initally rebuffed, the Germans became interested when Britain and France signed the Entente Cordiale in 1904. While some German cabinet ministers showed interest others thought it unwise and it was again shelved. O'Donnell had a contact who was a confidante of the German Kaiser in the person of Dr. Theodor Schiemann. He was a prominent historian who was also connected to Irish affairs through his correspondence with George Freeman. Freeman was an Irish nationalist, a soldier of fortune and a journalist who immigrated to America and was employed as a foreign affairs correspondent with John Devoy's Gaelic American. Devoy was also sympathetic to the cause of Indian nationalists.[2]

Another Irish-American who espoused similar ideas was Myron Phelps, a Yale-educated lawyer. His employment with a rubber company gave him cause to travel extensively to India and Ceylon where he became enamored with the culture and religions of the East. It also made him acutely aware of the common experience of

British imperialism shared by both India and Ireland. In his "Letters to the Indian People" published in 1907-1908, Phelps, like William Jennings Bryan, was extremely critical of British rule in India. Using a technique later embraced by McGuire, Phelps compared events in pre-Revolutionary America with those occurring in contemporary India urging its peoples unite in a common struggle to overthrow British control. He condemned the drain of wealth from the subcontinent to England. To further this goal in the United States, Phelps founded India House in 1908, based on one established in England three years before. Its ostensible purpose was to assist Indian students, but according to one historian, its purpose was to "inculcate sedition".[3] As a result of his activities, Phelps came under scrutiny by British agents who concluded his efforts were harmless.

While the direct effect of these efforts in the short-run was minimal, it did generate discussion as to the role of Britain's colonial policies. Between 1906-1908, William Jennings Bryan and Theodore Roosevelt debated the merits of British rule. Bryan, a member of the Anti-Imperialist League was critical, whereas Roosevelt applauded their efforts.[4]

Of the three Irish-Americans noted above, possibly the most significant was George Freeman, an Irish immigrant who had been active during the 1880's in the Irish Land League. He later moved to Canada where he urged its separation from the British Empire. Freeman later relocated to New York to link his movement with the Clan-na-Gael, becoming foreign affairs editor of the Gaelic American. The Clan had made contact with Indian revolutionaries in New York as early as 1905. Like the others, Freeman was interested in the fate of India, forming the Pan-Aryan Association in 1906. He had articles from the radical journal, The Indian Sociologist, printed in his paper, as well as assisting Hindu nationalists write their own journal, Free Hindustan, and having it printed on the Gaelic American press.[5] It was Freeman who used his influence to have German government officials turn down O'Donnell's offer of an Irish-German alliance believing him to be a charlaran and an opportunist. In his decade long correspondence, he fostered a strong connection to Dr. Theodor Schiemann, keeping him informed as to the state of Irish affairs. It was Schiemann who served as Sir Roger Casement's liaison to the Berlin government.[6] Through Schiemann, Freeman had the Kaiser's ear as well and the Emperor retained a strong interest in Irish affairs. For example, it was Schiemann who believed the social unrest in Ireland would prevent Britain from entering the war, especially after the killings in the wake of the Howth gun-running episode. Schiemann believed Britain was too focused on Ireland and its threat of a civil war to be concerned with events in the Balkans. Hence, Berlin backed the Austrian ultimatum.[7]

East Meets West: The Indo – Irish – German Connection

Similar experiences against a common enemy forged a German-Irish-Indian nexus which played itself out on a global stage and was reflected in the politics of the United States, politics that James K. McGuire, through his connections, contacts and actions would play an important, if often ignored, role. The Indo-Irish connection would continue into the post-war period, suggesting a political bond stronger than merely Realpolitik.

Much of the information in this section may be thought peripheral, though it is not unimportant. It reveals the national and international contexts, connections and commitment of James K. McGuire and his associates in the cause of Irish freedom.

Swami Abhedananda
(1866-1939)
Indian Nationalist
Public Domain

Lala Har Dyal
(1884-1939)
Indian Nationalist
Public Domain

Frank H. O'Donnell
(1846-1916)
Public Domain
(Source: NYPL)

Bernhard Dernburg
(1865-1957)
German propagandist
Bundsarchiv, Bld 102 12088/CC BY-SA 3 0

James K McGuire From His Book, The King,
The Kaiser and Irish Freedom, 1915

Picture of McGuire from Book Title, King Kaiser
and Irish Freedom Public Domain

William Bayard Hale
(1869-1924)
Pro-German Publicist
Public Domain
(Source: World's Work 1914)

Title Page From James K McGuirre
What could Germany Do For Ireland? 1916
Public Domain

Sir Roger Casement
(1864-1916)
Explorer, Human Rights Activist, Irish Nationalist
(Source: National Library of Ireland on the Commons)
No Known Copyright Restrictions

Theodor Schiemann
(1847-1921)
German Historian
Public Domain
(Source: http://www.sammlungen.hh.berlin.de/dokumente/12827)

Kuno Meyer
(1858-1916)
German Scholar, Linguist, Propagandist
Public Domain
(Source: http://en.wikipedia.org/wiki/File K _meyer.jpg)

Franz von Rintelen
(1878-1949)
German Spy Saboteur
Public Domain
(Source: https://archive.org/details/throttleedthe dete00tunnmiss)

Events in India of the 19th century paralleled those in contemporary Ireland.

For example a pamphlet for the Independent Hindustan dated December, 1920 lists the members of the Board of Directors of the Friends of Freedom for India. It reads like a "Who's Who" of the American left. The activists represented every geographical region of the USA except for the Southeast. Along with Indian revolutionaries Tarak Nath Das and Sailendra Ghose, it included intellectuals and social critics such as Dr. Franz Boas a prominent critic of racial and cultural stereotypes prevalent at the time, Dr. W E B Dubois scholar and critic of American racism, Robert Herrick and Upton Sinclair, novelists critical of contemporary American society. Also listed were prominent trades union and social critics such as suffragist and writer Sara Bard Field, lawyer and journalist Arthur Le Seuer James Maurer, socialist, pacifist and labor advocate Abraham Lefkowitz, a founder of the NYC unit of the American Federation of Teachers and numerous others of a similar outlook. Probably most important for the topic of this manuscript were spokepersons for Irish Independence including John D. Moore, former National Secretary of FOIF, Peter Golden, prominent member of the IPL. In addition to them, other important Irish-Americans also known to McGuire also included Edward F Dunne whose family immigrated to Illinois. Dunne became lawyer a reform mayor of Chicago during the time Upton Sinclair exposed the horrors of the meat-packing industry (1905). He was later elected Governor, endorsing women's suffrage and actively combatting a resurgent KKK. As will be shown, Dunne served on the American Committee on Conditions in Ireland and was its representative at the Paris Peace Conference after the war. There was also Frank P. Walsh a lawyer from Missouri who served on the War Labor Board. Like Dunne, Walsh also served on the American Commission on Irish Independence. The report was critical of British policy and caused Walsh to fall out of favor with the Wilson administration. Interestingly, another prominent American member of the FFI Board included Agnes Smedley, journalist and teacher, who became involved in the Hindu-German Conspiracy, later joining

Ghose in Germany after her prosecution under the Espionage Act of 1918. In addition, there was Dr. Gertrude Kelly, and Irish-born naturalized citizen who earned an MD. She was as a labor activist and suffragist, extremely involved in Irish Nationalist politics. Her brother, Dr. John Forrest Kelly, was a prominent electrical engineer, an associate of Thomas Edison, an Irish Nationalist and critic of James K McGuire. She was strongly opposed to the treaty ending the Irish War of Independence. Like McGuire she was surveilled by federal agents. Another activist not especially known for his Irish leanings was theologian Norman Thomas. He addressed meetings of the IPL along with Liam Mellows, Peter Golden and Norah Connolly during the AAIR convention held in Syracuse, New York. Thomas was an active member of the Protestant Friends of Ireland. This group was actively involved in the <u>East Side</u> incident, an effort to smuggle Thompson submachine guns into Ireland during the Irish Civil War. And of course there is the 32 page pamphlet <u>India and Ireland</u> written by McGuire ally Eamon DeValera comparing the colonial histories of the two countries and published by the FFI in 1920.

Moderates established the Indian National Congress to press for increased autonomy not unlike Parnell's Irish Parliamentary Party. More radical groups emerged urging the use of violence, similar to the Irish Revolutionary Brotherhood. Many activists in both India and Ireland fled to the United States or Canada when investigated by British authorities. For Indians, Vancouver, New York and San Francisco were centers of activity. It was in San Francisco where the German-Irish-India connection was most apparent. Many Irish and Irish-American nationalists were involved, all of whom were associates of James K. McGuire. They included Sir Roger Casement, John Devoy, Eamon De Valera, Father Peter Yorke, John McGarrity, and Larry DeLacey[8]. Some would reappear in a later chapter of McGuire's life, as de Valera partisans in a major gun-running episode during the 1920's.

The leader of the Indian revolutionaries in New York was Swami Abhedananda. Known mostly as a religious scholar, he was also an Indian patriot, advocate for its freedom and an ardent defender of its culture as shown in his his "Brooklyn Lectures" of 1905. He published <u>Free Hindustan</u>, the editor of which was Taraknath Das, an anti- British Bengali revolutionary and international scholar who worked closely with George Freeman, Devoy's editor of the <u>Gaelic American</u>.[9] The British regarded Abhedananda as a "seditonist" and put pressure on the American government to have his paper shut down which was accomplished by 1910.[10] The center of Indian Activity then moved to the West Coast - Vancouver, Seattle and San Francisco. The main organization was the Ghadar Party. Established in 1913 under the leadership of Lala Har Dayal, a well-educated Punjabi who had traveled extensively, ending up in California after hearing of the discrimination faced by his fellow Indians.[11] His radical anarchist and anti-British writings cost him his university position. He fled to Germany after being arrested by American authorities for disseminating anarchist literature. His successor as leader of the Ghadar movement was Ram Chandra.[12] Ghadar means revolution. It was to be an exclusively Indian organization, a view encouraged by Irish nationalists in an unsuccessful effort to prevent British infiltration. Leading Ghadar spokesmen openly acknowledged German sympathy for their movement by late 1913, often in the presence of representatives of the German Imperial government. By March of 1914, German newspapers reported on the gloomy situation in India for England as the result of outside assistance. Despite their best efforts at secrecy, British agents penetrated the party and were more than willing to share their information with American authorities which led to Dayal's arrest in March 1914. He jumped bail and ended up in Germany as an active member of the Berlin Committee (the Indian Independence Committee) for the duration of the war.[13] Its goal was similar to that of the German-Irish Committee, whose members were associates of James K. McGuire. Dayal's successor, Ram Chandra, was involved in gun-running and sabotage which culminated in the Hindu-German conspiracy trials of 1917-1918. The German consul in San Francisco, Franz Bopp, vice-consul Wilhelm von Brincken and naval attache

E.H. von Schack were his co-conspirators.[14] John Devoy was an outspoken supporter of Indian revolutionaries. Militant Ghadarites such as Abdul Mohammad Barakatullah appeared on stage at Irish nationalist gatherings. Barakatullah was a founding member of the Pan Aryan Association, linking him to both the Clan -na - Gael and Anglophobe lawyer Myron Phelps. He was later associated with Tarak Nath Das in the Ghadar party and joined him in exile in Germany where he indoctrinated Indian POWs with anti-British propaganda.[15] Like Casement with the Irish, they tried to recruit Indian POW's into a fighting force against Britain.

Possibly the most notable gun-running effort of the Hindu-German alliance was the <u>Annie Larsen</u> conspiracy, an attempt by Indian revolutionaries, aided and abetted by German government officials and Irish nationalists, to smuggle arms into India for Ghadar revolutionary activities in direct violation of American neutrality laws. McGuire associate John McGarrity arranged to have a sizeable shipment of arms sent via an Irish shipping company to Galveston, Texas then on to San Diego. According to de Rosa,[16] it was Sir Roger Casement, who had lived with McGarrity while in the United States, who recommended McGarrity for the job. Larry DeLacey was responsible for forwarding the cash for the arms[17]. Despite elaborate planning, the ships designated to make the transfer were unable to rendezvous. They were interned by the American government and their cargos impounded. German authorities claimed the guns were for their troops in East Africa. The ship owners said they were destined for Mexican revolutionaries.[18]

The day after the United States entered the war, 105 conspirators were arrested. The American social climate would make a fair trial difficult at best. Already there were reports of German agents sabotaging railroads; there was the Black Tom explosion; the exposure of German subversion in the Von Igel papers and the efforts to stir up labor unrest on the docks in New York City by Jim Larkin and James K. McGuire. In order not to further stir up the Irish - Americans, the United States government scrupulously avoided any mention of involvement by Irish in the plots. Its official propaganda agency, the Creel Commission, simply referred to it as a "Hindu-German Conspiracy"[19]. But the evidence shows how deeply the Irish were involved. For example, Franz von Papen's Memoirs reports on the many connections to Irish and Indian plotters.[20] Irish support for the conspiracy went deeper than simply logistics and propaganda. Not only did the Irish bail several defendants out of jail, their legal defense team consisted mostly of Irish-Americans, some of whom were closely tied to Irish nationalist organizations. Possibly the most prominent was defense attorney Daniel O'Connell who had a long history of involvement in Irish republican activities. He was an active propagandist for Germany, he was a leader in the Democratic party in California, and like McGuire, had strong ties to William Jennings Bryan.[21] O'Connell also defended Larry De Lacey, a McGuire ally in a later gun-running episode during the Irish Civil War. In this case De Lacey tried to assist several defendants to escape to Mexico before their trial. Hence his trial was rushed forward prior to the others. He was sentenced to two years in prison[22]. In addition, there was George McGowan, a militant Irish nationalist, who defended his son-in-law, Wilhelm von Brincken, vice-consul to the German legation who served as key liaison to the Indian revolutionaries in San Francisco.[23]

The trials ended in April 1918. Of the 105 indicted, 29 were convicted, three pleaded guilty, one went insane and two were shot dead while in court[24]. The conspirators were sentenced to terms in jail ranging from two months to two years and fines ranging from $ 1000 to $7500. The presiding judge followed the government's script placing on the blame solely on the "Prussian military system"[25].

Thus was the Hindu-German-Irish conspiracy shut down on the West Coast, at least for the duration of the war. But the trials could never have taken place without the assistance of British intelligence agents, a point acknowledged by chief prosecutor, US Attorney John W. Preston.[26] Germany and Irish-America were also deeply involved on the East Coast. It is here where the involvement of James K. McGuire was most pronounced.

McGuire's East Coast Machinations

The German Foreign Office established a propaganda agency, the German Press Bureau and Information Service (G.I.S.), in August 1914. Initially it's head was Dr. Bernhard Dernburg, former Colonial minister who came to the USA as a representative of the German Red Cross.[27] Dernburg, a former banker, had been Colonial Secretary in the German government. He spoke excellent English, and had banking connections in the United States. In reality, he was there on what was ultimately an unsuccessful effort to arrange a loan of $150 million and sell German war bonds. He later focused his energies on propaganda, primarily through speeches, interviews and editorials. Jones and Hollister suggest that Dernburg's role was to stir up labor strife among stevedores on the East Coast,[28] a project involving James K. McGuire and James Larkin among others. The German Red Cross was ostensibly the recipient of $886,000 in contributions collected by the National German-American Alliance under the leadership of Charles Hexamer. The German embassy supplied the headquarters for the Alliance. It was later revealed the money was turned over to count Bernstorff, the German ambassador, and $700,000 was used for propaganda purposes.[29] Among the organizations that were recipients of German Red Cross cash was the Irish Relief Fund. Supposedly the money never left the United States, and a similar sum was allegedly set aside for those purposes in Germany. This was the basis for the allegations of its use for propaganda, a charge later denied by Bernstorff.[30]

Dernburg's first assistant was Matthew B. Claussen, New York press agent for the Hamburg-America Line (HAPAG). Claussen's official duty was to circulate bulletins and news releases to the American press. However, he was listed by Dr. Heinrich Albert, along with Alexander Fuehr, as one of the chief stockholders of the American Correspondent Film Company, the purpose of which was to correct American misperceptions of Germany's war efforts, especially in the wake of the alleged atrocities committed in Belgium by German troops. It was formally established in April 1915.[31]

In his capacity as publicity director for HAPAG, Claussen's public relations campaign highlighted the intense rivalry between Great Britain and Germany in the in the pre-war luxury liner trade. The person who was produced many of the pictures for brochures used by Claussen was Albert Dawson, an Indiana-born American who started a career in photography at a young age, moving from the midwest to New York in 1910. His work so impressed Claussen, his company received an exclusive contract with HAPAG. This connection formed the basis of what became known as the American Correspondent Film Company.[32]

The GIS early recognized the need for publicity showing a German perspective of the war, especially in the wake of negative publicity following the invasion of neutral Belgium. Dawson was chosen by Claussen as the man for that job. Through Claussen, Dawson secured a letter of introduction from Ambassador von Bernstorff and along with journalist Edward Lyell Fox was in Germany by December 1914.[33] The two Americans obtained the appropriate permits and were soon at the Western Front, where their cinematic efforts were initially well-received by German officials.

By February 1915, Dawson needed more cash for his work, despite the fact he was funded through HAPAG. He obtained it through the intervention of politician Mathias Erzburger, head of the semi-official propaganda agency, the Zfa, the Central Administration for Services Abroad. This bureau worked under the Foreign Office, had its own news department, and publicity agency with responsibility for foreign propaganda.[34] Meanwhile Dr. Fuehr, Dernburg, Claussen and the GIS planned the formation of the American Correspondent Film Company which came into existence in April 1915.

The American Correspondent Film Company may have been one of the more successful propaganda efforts of the Imperial German government in the United States. Claussen made a point to emphasize its production was made by "neutral" Americans.[35] Claussen, as an American, was basically a front man with little experience in cinema. Claussen, like Dawson, was made a minority shareholder. Claussen's vice-president, Felix Malitz, with prior experience in film, received a sizeable share of the company's stock and a lucrative contract as well. Malitz was responsible for editing the several films the company produced. Malitz hired two others – Gustav Engler and Albert Sander – whose involvement would scandalize the company and bring about its demise.

Sander set up a front company, The Central Powers Film Directory, ostensibly to import pro-German films. In reality, the goal was to recruit spies for Germany.[36] Malitz and Engler also set up a front company, The Piedmont Pictures Corporation, for smuggling rubber through a courier system used by the American Correspondent Film Company. All three were ultimately arrested, charged and imprisoned, but the negative publicity was the death knell for the ACFC.[37]

On the way to the front, Dawson struck cinematic gold by filming McGuire associate Sir Roger Casement who was then in Berlin trying to recruit Irish POW's to fight against the British. In addition, given the Hindu-German conspiracy noted previously, it was significant that Dawson was also granted permission to film the the "model" POW camp at Zossen established to encourage Islamic and Indian soldiers to enlist in the German army.[38]

Dawson was a difficult personality who clashed with Prussian military officials, yet he was able to complete a number of successful documentaries. Ultimately his cinematic efforts were frustrated by military authorities who resented his interference to the extent he was investigated by German military intelligence. Despite efforts by Fuehr to prevent it, the GIS was asked to terminate his contract which occurred in May 1916. Upon his return to the United States, Dawson, like McGuire, was surveilled by Department of Justice agents who considered his films suspect. Yet he was later employed by both George Creel's Committee on Public Information and the United States Signal Corps[39] His career came to an abrupt end when he was ensnared in the negative publicity during the trials of Malitz, Engler and Sander. He was charged with embezzlement and court-martialed in March 1918.⁴⁰ Ironically Dawson was investigated by the same Senate committee which inquired into the activities of fellow-GIS employee James K. McGuire.

Dr. Alexander Fuehr's previous post was at the Imperial Embassy in Tokyo. His office was opposite that of another G.I.S. member, George Sylvester Viereck, whose newspaper, The Fatherland, was heavily subsidized by Dr. Heinrich Albert, since it performed much of the editorial work for GIS publications. Dernburg was a major contributor to The Fatherland.⁴¹

The major figure on the GIS was Dr. Heinrich Albert whose official title was head of the German Purchasing Commission.

Yet another American member of this committee was William Bayard Hale, a former minister and a distinguished journalist whose career included being literary editor of the New York Times, editor of World's Work. As special correspondent for the Hearst papers he had written an insightful interview with Kaiser Wilhelm in 1908. Hale had also been advisor to Wilson prior to the prominence of Colonel House and was the author of a biography of Wilson in 1912. An anthology of his speeches followed two years later. Hale was Wilson's confidential agent in Mexico whose subsequent report was used by Wilson to refuse diplomatic recognition to Huerta's regime.⁴² After a disagreement with the President, what had apparently been a warm friendship later turned into a bitter hatred. When hostilities broke out, Hale demanded fair play for Germany. His closeness to Wilson, his German-American wife, and his journalist credentials made him a logical choice for GIS propaganda, for which he was paid $15,000 a year.⁴³

It was Hale, who during a discussion with the German Information Service, suggested posting a warning to American passengers not to board the Lusitania, a warning written by Bernstorff himself.⁴⁴ But it was the rash insertion by Viereck in The Fatherland of, not only a warning, but what was regarded as a prophecy: "The Gulflight" carrying contraband through the war zone, paid the penalty of her foolhardiness. Before long, a large passenger ship like the Lusitania, carrying implements of murder to Great Britain, will meet with a similar fate". When the Lusitania was sunk, the British complained to the State Department that Viereck had foreknowledge of the event.[45] Despite later revelations the Lusitania was carrying contraband, America was seething with anger. Nonetheless, prominent Americans such as Vice President Thomas R. Marshall, Senators William J. Stone, Gilbert M. Hitchcock and William Borah and Congressman A. Mitchell Palmer tried to bring a balance to the issue.[46] Hale was also charged with writing Dernburg's speech justifying the sinking of the Lusitania, although Hale claimed he simply edited it.[47] It was this crisis and Dernburg's defense of German policy which led to his recall.[48] With the departure of Dernburg, Albert became the head of the German Press Bureau and Information Service.

It was into this dangerous company that McGuire was drawn. It was reported in 1915 that James K. McGuire met with Dr. Alexander Fuehr, Dr. Heinrich Albert and several other pro-Germans, including George S. Viereck, Edward Rumely and Dr. William Bayard Hale. Rumely was an Indiana-born physician, educator and journalist who received his education at Notre Dame University and his MD from the University of Freiburg in 1906. He was pro-German during the Great War. Outraged by what he saw as a British bias in the newspapers, he purchased the New York Evening Mail allegedly with funds from the German government. Later he was charged and jailed in 1918 under the Trading With The Enemies Act. He was later pardoned by President Wilson.[49] This committee chose McGuire to be involved in its propaganda efforts. The men met frequently in New York City with Dr. Albert and Dr. Dernburg.[50] Under Fuehr's direction, James K. McGuire organized the Irish Press and News Service for the Germans, furnishing articles to a number of Catholic newspapers, including his own. Numerous articles in McGuire's Catholic Sun are titled "Irish Press and News Service", often containing the subtitle, "Special to This Journal". McGuire's connection to Catholic papers predated his ties to the German government. However, in his subsequent employment by the G.I.S., the information for his weekly news releases came directly from Fuehr and were decidedly pro-German. His books were financed through Dr. Heinrich Albert's office, and were circulated by the G.I.S. as propaganda. McGuire also arranged for their printing in both Germany and in Austria-Hungary. They were so highly regarded by Albert that he refused to publish another one, Ireland and We, written by Prince Hatzfeld, head of the German Red Cross, member of the German Embassy and part of the Secret War Council, saying that McGuire's work covered the same ground and was more effective and suitable for American readers.[51] Obviously, McGuire's efforts on behalf of Germany were highly regarded.

Bernstorff does not mention McGuire by name, but states simply that, "Now and then, an Irishman would appear before the [propaganda] cabinet with plans for Irish-German cooperation".[52] McGarrity, McGuire, Cohalan, Devoy, John T. Ryan-the individual is not mentioned, but it reinforces the fact that prominent Irish-Americans, McGuire included, were intimately involved in collaboration with the Imperial German government.

The propaganda cabinet also encouraged publications of books and articles without a "German label." Articles by Americans without obvious German associations were immediately seized upon and redistributed. Many works by Dr. William B. Hale, Shaemus O'Sheele and others were disseminated in significant quantities. "Books by James K. McGuire linking the fate of Germany and Ireland, were distributed on a large scale". Apparently, McGuire was on such good terms with Dr. Heinrich Albert to present him personally with a copy of his second book, What Could Germany Do For Ireland?[53]

McGuire was in Ireland in 1914 doing research for his pro-German books.[54] McGuire's first effort, The King, The Kaiser And Irish Freedom (1915), was endorsed by the editor of a German language newspaper from his home town of Syracuse. Noting his early ties to the German community, the editor wrote that McGuire's first education was in a German school in the basement of a Lutheran Church in Butternut Street, Syracuse. The author went on, "During the thirty years he lived in our midst, no man occupied a warmer place in hearts and affections of the German people…[H]e always held the support of the German people, irrespective of party ties. It is perfectly natural for him to defend German ideals and causes, for he is a student and writer in German history, philosophy and poetry, as well as a firm friend and son of Ireland with an international reputation (Signed) Alex E. Oberlander".[55] The book was dedicated to "the millions of men and women of German blood in this country-who form the bulwarks of American civilization"- going on to praise the Germans who fought with Washington, and Andrew Jackson, in the Civil War to preserve the Union and in the Spanish-American War - "to all the vast Teutonic elements of the Unites States whose efforts have placed our nation to the forefront in education and in all arts and sciences-a noble people from whom Americans learn to be efficient and thorough-to the thrifty, useful, industrious, patriotic children of the Fatherland".[56] His book largely reiterates the revolutionary nationalists' programs and policies, castigating Redmond for his loyalty to Britain and for his recruitment of Irish soldiers to die for England.[57] McGuire, in a complete reversal of his previous attitude, puts Redmond in the same category as earlier generations of "weak leaders, traitors and informers…., the work of martyrs and patriots checked or destroyed by treason in their own ranks".[58] Recent German naval victories had made British claims of invincibility seem hollow-"The Invasion of England and Ireland are reasonable probabilities…". He compared the current sad state of Ireland with the martyrs and patriots of an earlier generation, reserving his harshest invective for Redmond ("an agent of the British Crown In Ireland"), comparing him to Benedict Arnold and his ally Joseph Devlin as "a spectacle of slavish submission."[59] In contrast, he lauds the work of Sir Roger Casement, contrasting his efforts on behalf of Ireland with Kitchener and Wellington, who "fought for England alone".[60] McGuire traced British-American hostilities to the early 19th century, showing how such rivalries destroyed American commerce.[61] He contrasted the prosperity of [the conquered territories] of Alsace and Lorraine under German rule with Ireland's poverty under Britain.[62] Echoing Thomas Paine, McGuire claimed Europe was the "Mother" country of America, not England.[63] He evoked the names of Germans prominent in American history - von

Steuben, de Kalb and Carl Schurz. McGuire praised Germany's social security system and industrialization to counter British charges of Teutonic barbarism. McGuire also played the religious card, attesting to the Catholic religiosity of German solders attending mass at a French church. The implication-how could such good Catholics be responsible for the atrocities lodged against them?[64] McGuire's answer to the question, "What Could Germany Do For Ireland'? Was two-fold: commerce and industrialization. This again contrasts with later chapters castigating British rule, showing how colonial laws destroyed Ireland's native industries.[65] McGuire ended the chapter stating, "There is no chance for Irish prosperity under English rule, unless the yoke of bondage is thrown off and the nation becomes free and independent and works out her destiny with the aid of her successful sons and daughters throughout the world, and establishes a friendly alliance with a country which is not a national or logical rival and is not interested in her exploitation.[66] He deprecated British propaganda extolling German atrocities and compared them to the documented massacres in Ireland during the Cromwellian period.[67] McGuire noted the disproportionate number of Irish casualties in the trenches and criticized the British for their censorship of Irish patriotic newspapers, perhaps anticipating what would happen to his works after America entered the war on the Allied side. Not surprisingly, McGuire concluded: "Liberty for Ireland can only be won through the triumphs of Germany-Austria."[68] McGuire, echoing sentiments expressed by Rumely, defended his book in the Syracuse Herald, stating it was a necessity given the "studied violation of neutrality on the part of certain Anglo-American newspapers, by the misrepresentation of the Irish nationality at home and abroad, by the vilification of Germany and above all by the growing probability that this section of unfair America, by no means in a majority, will destroy all hope of the United States becoming the arbiter at the end of the war". The Herald article complimented McGuire on the vast amount of research on a wide variety of subjects.[876] An advertisement for The King, The Kaiser and Irish Freedom appeared in a 16 March 1915 article in the Syracuse Herald, noting the book had taken New York

City by storm, with over 18,000 volumes sold in nine days, breaking all sales records. The article stated the work was being published in Berlin in German, in Vienna in "Austrian" and in South America in Spanish. The review praised McGuire as a keen observer who "arraigns the British Empire from cover to cover".[69]

It is important to note here that McGuire had not yet openly broken with the Wilson administration. Recall McGuire's involvement in the Wilson election campaign of 1912, his role in recommending Catholic candidates to the Wilson cabinet and Secretary Bryan's endorsement of Home Rule. The breach would widen, becoming outright hostility to his former ally, President Woodrow Wilson, moving McGuire firmly towards subversion, if not sabotage.

<u>What Could Germany Do For Ireland</u>? was James K. McGuire's second propaganda effort. Its "Introduction" was written by Dr. Thomas Addis Emmett,[70] surgeon, nationalist and vitriolic critic of British rule in Ireland who referred to the author as "my friend". The title of McGuire's second volume was a statement from chapter XII in his first book that he turned into a question. It was dedicated to John Mitchel[71] and all patriots "who dared face and contest in the name of liberty, hostile majorities at home and abroad".[72] It breaks little new ground, reiterating and elaborating on themes noted earlier – blaming Britain for the famine destroying Irish industries,[73] condemnation of Home Rule,[74] predicting German assistance in the cause of Irish freedom,[75] questioning British motives for becoming involved in the conflict,[76] condemning Redmond's recruitment policies and countering reports of German atrocities. For example, in this volume McGuire referred to the "rape of Belgium" as a "red herring", simply propaganda bait to obtain Irish recruits to fight against Germany.[77] The book also excoriated British censorship and the betrayal of patriots by traitors.[78] Interestingly, McGuire suggests that, given the existence of 18,000 armed constabulary and 5000 retired police and a standing army of 30,000, and the fact that the British control all the customs and the ports, the Irish could never import sufficient arms for a successful rebellion.[79] Since the book was published in December 1915, was McGuire trying to disarm

British intelligence with these comments, given the fact members of the Clan-na-Gael had enlisted German support for a rising a year earlier? Advertisements for McGuire's second book were carried both locally in the Syracuse Herald and nationally in the New York Times.[80] and The Fatherland.

1916 then, was a pivotal year for Irish nationalists. Their propaganda machine was gearing up, links were intensified with German-American societies, plans laid for German government support for an uprising and it was the year of the first Irish Race Convention. What Could Germany Do For Ireland? contains a significant amount of detail about the natural resources of Ireland. Of particular interest is Chapter VI, "The Gateway of Europe", which opens with homage to Admiral Thomas Thayer Mahan and his concept of geopolitics, noting "Ireland is the natural connecting link between Eastern and Western worlds".[81] Later, he refers to its commodious harbors, [and] numerous rivers, a fact not unknown to the German Admiralty as well as England. These harbors offer an almost irresistible temptation, an invaluable prize to the power that desires to possess and retain mastery of the high seas. Ireland lies 60 miles from England and only 13 miles from Scotland. "The occupation of Ireland by a world power, such as Germany, and its conversion into a naval and military base, would bring about speedily the downfall for all time of England from the rank and status of a first class world power".[82] He further noted how Germany's use of the Irish coast for submarine warfare on British shipping inflicted damage to England's reputation as "Mistress of the Seas".[83] Was this a premonition, a prophecy or something else? Given the fact that 15 of 17 members of the FOIF Executive Committee were Clan members, including McGuire, and the Clan was active in planning the rising as early as 1914, it infers the presence of McGuire in Ireland in 1914 was more than simply academic research.

McGuire, now in the employ of the German Information Service, used his newspapers to advertise his publications. The Catholic Sun carried multiple ads for his The King, The Kaiser and Irish Freedom. The paper bound edition sold for 50 cents, a cloth edition was priced at $1.50, and a deluxe edition with gold letters and a leather binding went for $3.00. Reinforcing the hyphenates' alliance, the <u>Sun</u> called it, "The ideal gift for your Irish-American or German-American friends", calling it the largest, circulated book of the year.[84] In early 1916, <u>What Could Germany Do For Ireland?</u> was published. The <u>Catholic Sun</u> dutifully carried advertisements for his second effort. It sold for $1.35. The <u>Catholic Sun</u> edition of 18 February 1916, not surprisingly, carried a review of his book initially published in the <u>Irish World</u> of 5 February 1916, along with articles announcing the First Irish Race Convention. The review called McGuire's work "timely and valuable", claiming the goal of British rule in Ireland was its "absolute ruin". Summarizing much of its content, the reviewer reiterated McGuire's stance denouncing Home Rule as a "mockery, a delusion and a snare" because it had to be made palatable to Sir Edward Carson and the Unionists.[85] Not surprisingly, it was reported that McGuire's books had been endorsed by the "German Official Agency" which was in itself reason enough for reading them.[86]

McGuire's two major works were in large measure an echo of what Roger Casement wrote in <u>The Crime Against Ireland and How The War May Right It</u>, a 96 page pamphlet based on seven essays written between 1911-1914, predating McGuire's publications, printed and circulated by the German Foreign Office".[87] Casement consigned to Germany the high moral purpose of liberating Ireland, a position held by Catholic Spain during the 16th and 17th centuries, and as McGuire briefly noted in his first volume, by France during the late 18th.[88] Just as McGuire's articles in the <u>Catholic</u> Sun praised the prowess of Gaelic warriors and athletes, so too did Casement.[89] Both condemned the use of Irish troops to maintain an oppressive empire, Casement going so far as to damn any Irishman in the British army as a traitor.[90] McGuire repeats Casement's argument as to the strategic value of Ireland,[91] blaming Britain for destroying Irish trade and commerce.[92] In addition, both McGuire and Casement indicate strong sympathy and support for the German "race",[93] believing the true alliance, because of their common history of hostilities to England, was a union of Germany, Ireland and the United States.[94]

After the publication of Casement's pamphlet, McGuire was in Ireland ostensibly researching his own books. By then, McGuire and other leaders of the Clan-na-Gael were in negotiations with the German ambassador and Sir Roger Casement to fund and arm an insurrection against their common enemy, England. According to Jerome ann de Weil, Casement's writings were already known to German sources, especially Theodor Schiemann, influential policy advisor to the Kaiser and key contact with Irish nationalists, Hugh O'Donnell and George Freeman[95] McGuire's advantages were probably his American citizenship, his status in the Clan na Gael and FOIF, his Irish newspaper chain and his then current good ties to the Wilson administration. Given those positions, it may have been supposed McGuire would attract a wider readership.

Because of McGuire's speeches, writings and activities on behalf of Irish nationalism and a German victory, he was described by Edward Cuddy as, "one of the most active propagandists of his day" and his name was tied to other prominent Irish-American nationalists including Joseph McGarrity of Philadelphia, John T. Ryan of Buffalo, John Devoy, Daniel F. Cohalan, Joseph P. O'Mahony and others.[96] In addition, David P. Hirst, while limiting his description of McGuire's efforts to a paragraph, lists his two books and described his direction of the Irish Press and News Service saying... "he was a directing force in many other phases of the propaganda campaign".[97]

All however, were not convinced of McGuire's importance. For example, Henry Landau stated that at the outbreak of the war, James Larkin was the one sought out by the Germans as the one who had the greatest potential for the nationalist movement. "O'Leary, McGarrity, Keating, MaGuire, [sic] and Devoy, famous Irish leaders at the time, were working closely in this country with the Germans; but Larkin had qualities which none of them possessed".[98] Peterson is even more dismissive of McGuire's efforts. Remarking about the propaganda work of various German-language newspapers which reached only a limited public, Peterson noted, there should be added to the list... the group of unimportant Irish-American papers owned by James K. McGuire (<u>The National Catholic</u> in NYC, <u>The Truth</u> in Scranton and <u>The Light</u> in Albany)...As far as influencing Americans was concerned, however, they can be completely discounted. Their editors wasted their ammunition on captured forts".[99] Reinforcing Peterson's comments, Link referred to McGuire's two books as "typical" of the Irish-American tracts.[100]

Shane Leslie, in <u>The Irish Issue In Its American Aspect</u>, described McGuire's, <u>The King, The Kaiser and Irish Freedom</u> as "naively preposterous and figured in the literature of the prison camp in Germany". This reference was to Casement's ill-fated effort to raise an Irish Brigade for the Easter Rebellion among Irish POWs in Germany. Firm in his moderate views of Irish nationalism, Leslie believed the Irish press in America did not represent Irish opinion in the United States. Leslie condemned the Clan-na-Gael and Daniel F. Cohalan as fanatics and the Irish Race Convention of 1916, with its pro-German stance, as a source of ridicule by leading Irishmen.[101] A review in the <u>New York Times</u> of 16 May 1915 noted there was little about the King or the Kaiser, but there was much about Ireland, especially McGuire's condemnation of Home Rule, Redmond and the destruction of Irish industry under Britain. The reviewer called it a biased argument, appealing only to "irreconcilable Irish in America".[102] And, despite McGuire's claims to his books' popularity, his periodic appearances in his former home town and his publications in The <u>Catholic Sun</u>, his fame as an author was apparently not well-received in Syracuse, New York. For example, in an article in the <u>Post-Standard</u>, on a list of local authors who reflected credit on the City of Syracuse, McGuire was not listed. In addition, McGuire was not included among authors in a display at the local library, nor in a subsequent library bulletin.[103]

Despite the increasingly heated rhetoric, it was the <u>Lusitania</u> crisis that heightened tensions between Germany and the United States. Hostilities were averted by Wilson's "Too Proud To Fight"[104] speech, a move which antagonized both Allies and domestic critics who sought a more rigorous stance towards Germany. Two political casualties of this incident were Secretary of State William J. Bryan, who thought Wilson too strongly anti-German in his response and resigned in protest, and; Dr. Bernard Dernburg, whose inept justification for the sinking led to his recall.[105]

In an attempt to avert another crisis that might push the United States into the Allies camp, Irish and German-Americans tried to prevent United States citizens from sailing on belligerents' ships. The effort was supported by the American Embargo Conference, an organization which supplanted Labor's National Peace Council. Established by Bernstorff in November 1915, it attempted to lobby Congress to formulate and direct trumped-up sentiment in favor of an embargo on munitions and against the right of American citizens to travel on British ships.[106] It served as the basis of the Gore-McLemore resolutions, which, because of Wilson's firm opposition, went nowhere. Nonetheless, the hyphenates continued to apply pressure to Wilson to remain strictly neutral. For example, not only were McGuire and other Irish-Americans active in the pro-German cause, there were also German-Americans, such as George Sylvester Viereck and Charles John Hexamer, involved in making speeches and writing articles. So too were many German and Irish nationals. They included Dr. Bernard Dernburg, "the unofficial mouthpiece of Germany".[107] There was also Dr. Kuno Meyer, the distinguished scholar on the Gaelic language. Kuno Meyer was one of the earliest links between Germany and Irish nationalists. He founded the School of Irish Learning in Dublin in 1903. The following year he assisted Arthur Griffith in organizing Sinn Fein. Meyer's Celtic scholarship won him academic honors in Ireland and in Germany. A decade later, under instructions from his government, he was associated with the Clan-na-Gael in America. In The United States, while a lecturer at Columbia University, he gave a pro-German speech to a Clan-na-Gael meeting on Long Island in December, 1914. It's contents, and his letter to the New York Times responding to its condemnation of his speech, made it clear he supported Germany's war efforts and the cause of Irish freedom. He resigned his academic position and went on a speaking tour of the United States in 1915.[108] The British were convinced that he collaborated with Roger Casement, assisting in his writing of anti-British pamphlets which he translated for publication in Germany. It was alleged that Meyer's brother Richard conducted Casement from Norway to Germany in 1914.[109] There was also talk that Kuno Meyer was a co-conspirator along with Ram Chandra and Larry De Lacey in the Hindu-German plot to ship arms to the Indian revolutionaries.[110] However this involvement is questioned by O'Luing who noted that by 1915 Meyer was old, ailing, injured and recently married to a young American woman[111].

Plowman believes the "Kuno Meyer" involved in the Hindu-German conspiracy was a pseudonym for German military attache in San Francisco Wilhelm von Brincken who as liaison was actually involved in the gun-running effort.[112] McGuire's ties to the Clan and FOIF whose members were involved suggest he was certainly aware, if not complicit in these activities.

Many Irish-American orators joined the pro-German lecture circuit, one of whom was James K. McGuire. As early as 1914, McGuire was making pro-German speeches, asserting that "Germany has always been Ireland's friend. Ireland's destiny is written in Germany". The following year, he was even more outspoken. "Remember it is England that declared war on Germany on the false claim of Belgian neutrality. Only through Germany is her [Ireland's] hope of an alliance which would make Ireland strong and prosperous. The British Empire is [en] dangered by the more competent, [...] resourceful and efficient Germany.[113] Later that year, McGuire, in an interview in the Syracuse Herald, endorsed Germany's plan, in the wake of the sinking of the Lusitania, to keep Americans "off British ships carrying munitions of war for the enemies of Germany". McGuire affirmed the Imperial German Government's position that it must maintain its submarine warfare until Britain allows America to ship supplies to Germany, a policy that did not violate treaty rights and for which it should not be censored.[114] Essentially, McGuire was parroting the neutralist line that the real threat to peace was the fact Americans sailed on belligerents' ships. Hence free travel, "freedom of the seas", had to be sacrificed in the name of world peace, a position Wilson refused to accept. Despite Wilson's stonewalling on the issue, the German-and Irish-Americans persisted by forming organizations to pressure the government to remain neutral. One of them was the Friends of Peace.

McGuire was a member of this organization established in June 1915 during a rally of the National German-American Alliance held at Madison Square Garden. The meeting was called to order by George Von Skal, German journalist and friend of John Devoy who earlier had organized American support for the Boers during the South African War. Von Skal also joined Devoy in protests against the Arbitration Treaty of 1911. Von Skal was employed by the German consulate at this time, a paid agent of Franz von Papen. Devoy met with von Skal and von Papen regularly through 1914-15.[115] The von Skal–Devoy connection probably went on even longer. For example, in August 1916 the British intercepted a message from Von Bernstorff which read in part: "Von Skal maintains relations with the Irish for which he has special qualifications in his many relationships in those circles and has their complete confidence".[116] The Friends of Peace was established to impress the fact on Wilson that the bulk of Irish-and German-Americans were opposed to war with Germany. According to others however, the organization was the work of a German agent, Albert Sander, employee of the American Correspondent Film Company whose espionage activities were noted earlier. In conjunction with the Clan-na-Gael and a "German society", the American Truth Society, they formed the Friends of Peace. Its primary purpose was to keep America from entering the war.[117] Jones and Hollister describe its peace efforts as "insincere". Wittke disagreed, stating the goal of the movement was not to aid Germany, but to prevent American entry into the war.[118] The Friends of Peace coordinated the activities of a variety of pro-German groups.

In addition to James K. McGuire and other prominent hyphenates, the President of the Friends of Peace, Henry Weisman, was also head of the German-American Literary Defense Committee, the purpose of which was to prepare pamphlets and articles for distribution. Its Executive Secretary was Albert Sander, the German spy. Sander got Dr. Heinrich Albert to send Reginald Rutherford, an officer of the American Truth Society, to Holland to act as a spy for the German government. James K. McGuire was, at the time, one of the Directors of the American Truth Society.[119] It was for The Friends of Peace that Bernstorff, in January 1917, then in Germany, requested $50,000 from the Imperial Government, to lobby Congress to pass a resolution in support of Irish independence. The following month, Sander was arrested and later imprisoned as an enemy agent.[120] The Press Committee of The Friends of Peace included George Von Skal, John Devoy, Robert Ford, George Viereck and several others.[121]

Additional evidence suggests that McGuire and The Friends of Peace were playing in subversive company. For example, the work of Frank Buchanan, Congressman from Illinois, reveals a complex connection to Franz Rintelen, whose mission in 1915 was to wreak havoc with America's munitions industries by sabotage and by encouraging labor strife. Rintelen unwisely chose David Lamar as his accomplice. Lamar's questionable background included an attempt to defraud John D. Rockefeller, Jr. Not only did he defraud Rockefeller, but he had his driver, James McMahon, who was going to testify against him, so savagely beaten by members of the notorious "Monk" Eastman gang, McMahon was unable to bear witness against him. At the time Rintelen contacted him, Lamar was under indictment for impersonating a United States senator in hopes of making a speech to drive down steel prices. His maneuvers brought him wealth, an estate in New Jersey and a mansion on Fifth Avenue. But Lamar was driven more by the need to gain power and recognition. While his case was on appeal, he met Rintelen who employed him in April 1915. Lamar secretly informed on Rintelen to the Justice Department which encouraged Lamar's covert operations. According to historian Barbara Tuchman, Lamar spent over $500,000 promoting work stoppages. The reports of their success were largely products of his imagination.[122] Lamar met Buchanan and ex-Congressman Robert Fowler of Illinois. In Chicago, they formed a labor union, Labor's National Peace Council, among stevedores in all major ports. Buchanan as its President, tried unsuccessfully to enlist the support of Samuel Gompers.

Gompers may have represented a logical choice. In the past, he had been supportive of both pacifism and Irish Nationalism. For example, Gompers, from the 1890's to the beginning of World War I was an active and outspoken pacifist who later became an ardent advocate of preparedness. In addition, Gompers had known many Irish Nationalists, including Patrick Ford, O'Donovan Rossa, Michael Davitt, Charles Stewart Parnell and T.P O'Connor through whom he was actively identified with the cause of Home Rule. Over the years the relationship was strained, especially when the German-Irish connections became public.[123] This was especially true with Labor's National Peace Council. Its goal was to get dissident German and Irish dock workers to cause trouble, hence delay getting supplies from America to the Allies. Activity focused on the New York City docks. Despite the upward mobility of the Germans and Irish since their arrival in America, many still earned a living on the docks, residing in the tenements of Hell's Kitchen. The President of the International Longshoremen's Association was an Irishmen, Dick Butler. He told how German agents working in collusion with Irish sympathizers, tried to obtain a strike of the 20,000 longshoremen in the Port of New York and thus prevent the loading of food and supplies for ships bound for Allied ports. Butler was allegedly offered a million dollars for his union and ten dollars per week for each longshoreman by a group of wealthy Boston Irishmen. Butler refused the offer, but the word leaked out and the story was covered in the major dailies.[124] While not specifically mentioning Larkin by name, Butler implicated him and a wealthy anti-British Boston Irishman, Mathew F. Cummings, in the plot to have a long work stoppage in the New York docks. T.V. O'Connor, President of the International Longshoreman's Association, allegedly received monetary advances from Cummings to organize the strike. Cummings' connection to the cash was Dr. Bernard Dernburg, McGuire's boss in the G I S. O'Connor related details of the plot to Secretary of Labor William B. Wilson who informed the President, the Treasury Department and the Secret Service. The plan was aborted in the wake of the <u>Lusitania</u> controversy and the deportation of Dernburg. Also implicated in the plot was George S. Viereck and Dr. Edmund von Mach, the Harvard-educated art historian. Credit for foiling the plot was given to Gompers, T.V. O'Connor, "Big Dick" Butler, William Flynn of the Secret Service who was tied to the stolen Dr. Heinrich Albert papers, and Paolo A. Vaccarelli (Paul Kelly), at the time, a vice president of the International Longshoremens' Association.[125] Wilson, by praising brave, honest, patriotic labor leaders was both wooing the labor vote and appealing to the loyalty of American voters.

Captain Paul Koenig
(1867-1933)
Captain of the Submarine Deutschland
Book no longer in copyright

Submarine Deutschland
Public Domain
(Source: Journal of United States Artillery, vol. 46, 1916)

Dudley Field Malone
(1882-1950)
Lawyer, reform Democrat
Library of Congress ID cph 3c18913
Public Domain

David Lamar
(1877-1934)
Financier, "The Wolf Of Wall Street"
Public Domain
(Source: the World's Work, 1919)

John Devoy
(1842-1928)
Irish Nationalist, Leader of the Friends of Irish Freedom
Public Domain
Library of Congress
No Known Copyright Restrictions

Franz von Papen
(1879-1964)
German Military Attache
Public Domain
Library of Congress/ Bain

Edward Rumely
(1882-1964)
German Propagandist
National Archives 533461
Public Domain

Joseph P Tumulty
(1879-1954)
Secretary to President Woodrow Wilson
Library of Congress ID CPH cb 45344
Public Domain

Samuel Gompers, leader of The American Federation of Labor, was convinced the United States would become involved in the World War. He also believed that German-American societies were fronts for German propaganda. Many locals in the American Federation of Labor had a large majority of German members. Gompers had been on good terms with German ambassadors von Sternburg, von Speck and von Bernstorff. Apparently the source of Gompers' information about Germany's labor efforts were two British labor representatives to the A.F.L. convention of 1914, James Sneddon and Albert Bellamy. Both were British Trade Unionists and members of the Labor Party. These two men toured the United States and Canada. From Sneddon, Gompers avers he learned much about German propaganda methods which he staunchly resisted from becoming entrenched in American labor unions, especially the Longshoremen.

By 1915 Labor Peace Councils had been formed in several major port cities including Washington, Chicago and Baltimore. German agents were trying to organize stationary engineers as a means of controlling industrial production. These people supervise the boilers, pumps and turbines in factories, ships and warehouses. In control of such strategic positions, a strike by them would cripple production and services in those industries. According to Gompers that was the plan-to tie up American productivity for a few weeks to allow Germany to win the war. Gompers refused to have anything to do with the organization, branding its chairmen, John B. Walker and Henry Weisman, as tools of German militarism who had been sent to buy out American labor leaders.[126] According to Reinhard Doerries, strike action was initiated by von Papen and von Igel in collaboration with John Devoy, James K. McGuire and Jim Larkin.[127]

CONFLICTS AND CRISES 359

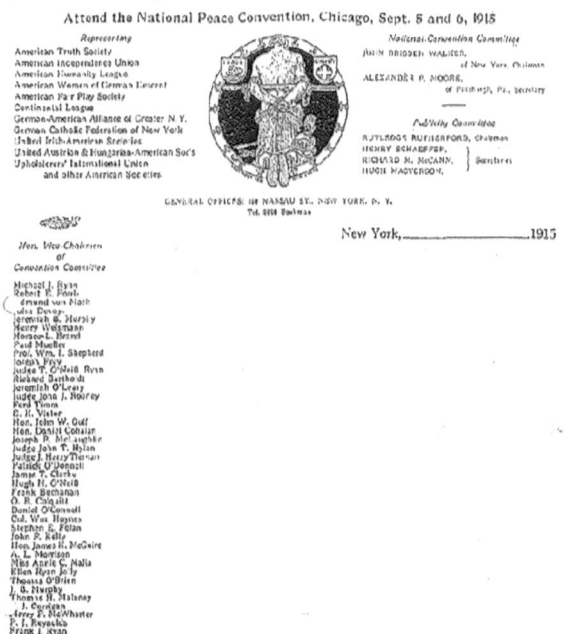

Source: John P. Jones, Paul M. Hollister: The German Secret Service In America, 1914 – 1918. Boston: Small, Maynard and Company 1918, p. 250. Book No Longer In Copyright. Note McGuire's name is 13th from the bottom.

Count Johann H von Bernstorff
(1862-1939)
German Ambassador to the United States and Mexico, 1908-1917
Public Domain
Library of Congressggbain03440
No Known Copyright restrictions

William Jennings Bryan
(1860-1925)
Politician, Anti-Imperialist, Secretary of State
of the United States, 11913-1915
Public Domain
Library of Congress
No Known copyright restrictions

Wolf von Igel
(1888-1970)
German Agent
Public Domain
Library of Congress/ Bain

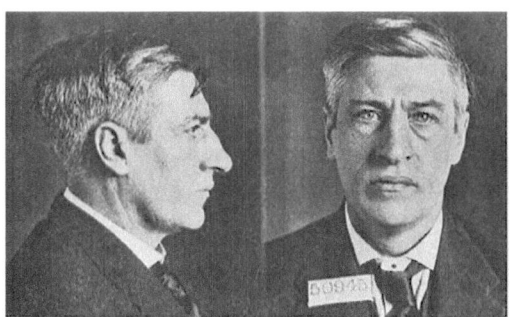

Jim Larkin
(1876-1947)
Socialist, Labor Leader, Irish Nationalist
Public Domain
(Source: Revolutionary Radicalism: It's History,
Purpose, tactics. N.Y.: J. Lynn and Co., 1920)

An additional source of confidential information for Gompers was John R. Rathom, editor of the <u>Providence Journal.</u> Rathom, an Australian immigrant, was pro-Allied and it was later proven his sources were contacts in the British embassy. It is no wonder the pro-Germans believed there was a Tory press in operation, especially given what was noted previously about <u>The New York Times</u>.[128] After one short-lived strike, the movement collapsed in the wake of the publication of Dr. Heinrich Albert's papers in August 1915 and internal schism. Buchanan resigned from the council, but along with Lamar and Rintelen, he was later convicted of violating the Sherman Anti-Trust Law and sentenced to one year in prison. The attempt cost the Imperial German government between $500,000-$800,000 and was given widespread coverage in the German language press and <u>The New York Times</u>.[129]

Labors National Peace Council, despite its over-all failure, did publicize the non-neutrality of the Wilson administration. It filed suit in Chicago against the Cunard Steamship Line and Collector of the Port of New York, Dudley Field Malone, alleging he allowed the <u>Lusitania</u> to leave with a cargo of explosives in violation of American neutrality laws.[130] Malone was allegedly involved in conspiring with Woodrow Wilson, J.P. Morgan and New York Senator James A. O'Gorman. Malone was at the time married to O'Gorman's daughter. He was also a political friend and ally of Wilson, having campaigned for him in 1916. It is alleged that Malone turned a blind eye to the practice of allowing contraband to be shipped aboard neutral vessels during war, in violation of U S neutrality laws. Using a technicality which considered artillery shells to be labeled "non-explosive" because they had no fuses, they were not registered on the ship's manifest. Malone, as head of customs in the Port of New York, could then legally clear these ships. J.P. Morgan was owner of International Mercantile and Marine (IMM) whose subsidiaries were both the Cunard and White Star lines. Morgan was also sole purchaser of munitions for the British government and was paid a commission of one per cent on all sales. Wilson wanted the arms trade to increase American prosperity but he was hamstrung by his policy of neutrality.

It thus became standard practice to file fraudulent manifests, be certified as compliant and then file a supplemental manifest when the ship was at sea. Malone had a history of questionable dealings and was not above being complicit in such transactions. Public manifests revealed that ships of the IMM were regularly sailing with cargoes of tons of ammunition for the Allies[131].

This reveals Wilson's ambiguity when dealing with the neutrality issue It was this same law which led to the prosecution of members of the Hindu-German conspiracy. Apparently Wilson was willing to turn a blind eye to such dealings when it suited his purposes

Other efforts by Germany to subvert American labor included the attempt to recruit James Larkin, who had come to America in 1914 at the behest of James Connolly to obtain guns for a rising and to raise money for Irish labor unions. He "presented the Clan and the Socialists with a dynamic, popular and persuasive figure who traveled throughout the country on behalf of those organizations attacking Redmond and Home Rule and preaching revolutionary Irish nationalism and socialism."[132] Larkin was an advocate of Irish independence which brought him support from Tom Clarke of the IRB. Clarke wrote a letter of introduction for Larkin to John Devoy who arranged a speaking tour for Larkin during which he emphasized their close ties to German-Americans. Larkin and Devoy were present at the home of Daniel Cohalan when Dr. Kuno Meyer arrived to present Casement's proposal for raising a division of soldiers among Irish POW's in German prison camps. He was later introduced to both German and Austrian consuls[133]. Dorries lists Larkin's high-ranking contacts in America as Franz von Bopp, the German consul in San Francisco, who was deeply involved in gun-running and sabotage on the West Coast. In addition, another was Lothar Witzke, a key player in the Black Tom explosion.[134] Others included Franz von Papen, Karl Boy-Ed, Wolf von Igel, Kuno Meyer and Bernard Dernburg.

Larkin, in extreme financial duress, asked Devoy to arrange a meeting for him with German diplomats. "Larkin...was prepared to take a German offer of cash in exchange for his support of the

German war effort". Carroll stated that Larkin refused an offer to be on regular salary by Captain Karl Boy-Ed. Larkin continued organizing dock workers after his lecture tour proved financially unsuccessful, later becoming an agent for the Western Federation of Miners in Butte, Montana. Because of his financial problems, Larkin used Devoy to connect him to German agents, one of whom was Dr. Bernard Dernburg. In a subsequent interview, with "James K. MaGuire [sic] a close associate of John Devoy" present, Dernburg urged Larkin to become involved in sabotage. Larkin once again refused. The Germans wanted Larkin to organize sabotage in American ports. Von Igel took Larkin on a visit to its sabotage centers in Hoboken and showed him various incendiary devices. Larkin again refused to supervise sabotage operations on the East Coast, but he was willing to continue stirring up labor problems and he maintained contacts with von Igel and the militant Irish Nationalists. Larkin supposedly had a meeting scheduled with von Igel on the day Secret Service agents raided his office. Larkin left when he saw the swarm of G-men. When Larkin was in New York, he often sat in on meetings with the Clan's leading triumvirs-Cohalan, Devoy and McGarrity-and hence was privy to their deliberations.[135] His headquarters were the center for smugglers and saboteurs who cooperated with the German government for the benefit of Irish freedom and Irish-American labor leaders and longshoremen who passed on information about the contents and destinations of ships bound for Europe. O'Connor suggests one of his main henchmen was the editor of German language Socialist paper Volkszeitung, Ludwig Lore, who was liaison between von Papen, the German embassy and the Irish. Despite Larkin's assertion he was not involved in sabotage, others believe Larkin and his associates were responsible for the Black Tom explosion in New York Harbor, 30 July 1916, destroying $25 million worth of equipment and munitions, killing six and injuring thirty-five.[136] Called "Black Tom" because of its resemblance to a tomcat with it's back up, it was a peninsula pointing out from New Jersey towards the Statue of Liberty. It was a tempting target. There were 24 warehouses, and seven piers with over a thousand tons of munitions, dynamite, TNT and gasoline.[137] Larkin, interviewed years later, admitted organizing strikes and labor disturbances to improve the lot of the longshoremen, and to prevent supplies from reaching the Allies. He was present when German sabotage agents planned the Black Tom explosion,[138] but he adamantly denied any involvement. Circumstantial evidence suggests otherwise, but there is no evidence linking him to the explosion. But Larkin met frequently with smugglers and saboteurs and Irish-American labor leaders. Dorries asserts that McGuire was also tied to strike action on the docks in the Fall of 1915, along with other plotters John Devoy, Franz von Papen, Wolf von Igel, and James Larkin[139]. Larkin relied on Ludwig Lore, editor of a Socialist daily newspaper, for assistance in obtaining arms for Irish rebels. As noted, Lore was the intermediary between Franz von Papen and the Irish. Also, the explosion followed soon after the arrest and conviction of Roger Casement and the execution Larkin's friend and mentor, James Connolly.[140] It would take decades to identify the perpetrators. Ultimately no one was ever prosecuted or convicted of the explosion[141].

As noted above, James P. McGuire, was involved in labor agitation. Dr. Heinrich Albert applauded McGuire's efforts to disrupt America's war production through subversion. In praise of McGuire's efforts Albert wrote:

One of these Irish gentlemen, McGuire, has written a very readable book on the war, whose circulation in the United States was furthered by Excellency Dernburg. Under the guise of publishing this book still further, Mr. McGuire is now giving us assistance is suitable fashion in labor questions, to which I, in agreement with the Ambassador (Bernstorff) and Mr. Von Papen (military attaché), am giving my special attention.[142]

There were no additional details, but if true it suggests that McGuire had crossed the line from propaganda to subversion and to sabotage. McGuire, along with other leading Irish-Americans, was moving in dangerous directions. For example, from a cable intercepted from the German General Staff to its embassy in Washington on 26 January 1915, Sir Roger Casement recommended three ranking Irish

Nationalist for involvement in sabotage-Joseph Mc Garrity, John P. Keating and Jeremiah O'Leary, although there was no direct evidence of their involvement. Landau suggests there were instructions relative to sabotage in the United States prior to the sending of his message.[143] Nonetheless, despite sporadic work stoppages, only some of which could be directly attributed to sabotage, the German effort to create labor strife in order to stifle American war production was a costly failure. Despite widespread agitation by the hyphenate press and the German Information Service, there was limited support for the Central Powers. Germany was suspect in eyes of many Americans because of recent rivalries over spheres of influence in the Caribbean and the Pacific. Many Catholics were appalled by Protestant Prussian militarism and its alleged mistreatment of neutral Catholic Belgium. Any protestations honoring the independence of small nations was viewed by them with skepticism. All that changed, however, with the Easter Rebellion of 1916.

The Rising of 1916 created ferment for months in diplomatic relations with Britain and Germany and was a vehicle for vehement denunciation of British rule in Ireland by the hyphenate press. It made the Irish in America close ranks, pushed moderates in Ireland into the radical camp and virtually destroyed John Redmond's credibility and organizations in both countries. Even the moderate Ancient Order of Hibernians at its 50th convention in July 1916 condemned Redmond's pledge of support for the English cause, demanded no compromise on the issue of Home Rule and expressed its horror and rage at the execution of the rebel leaders, raising large sums to relieve the suffering of the victim's families.[144] Intimately involved in events leading up to the Rising, McGuire used his positions as German propagandist and Irish Nationalist to further their interests.

After the failure of the Easter Rebellion, Larkin, along with other Irish Nationalists, such as James K. McGuire, organized public demonstrations in support of the insurrection. Larkin went to San Francisco where he met the German consul Franz von Bopp and American labor radical Tom Mooney,[145] who had been active in creating labor problems so as to prevent American supplies from reaching the Allies. Larkin returned to New York shortly before the deadly Black Tom Explosion.[146] His ties to groups and individuals involved in sabotage, labor agitation and Irish Nationalism made Larkin extremely vulnerable. He later was informed by James K. McGuire, the German government wanted him to go to Mexico, then return to San Francisco and engage in sabotage, an offer he again refused. [147] Apparently angry at Larkin's stubborn refusals, his German associates may have turned against him. He was thrown out of his hotel. Penniless, he was sleeping on a park bench. Later he sought better lodgings. A tramp who took his place on the bench was later found murdered. He eventually made it back to New York with the assistance of the Clan-na-Gael[148]. Larkin was subsequently arrested in 1919, not for sabotage or subversion but due to his affiliation with radical organizations which were a target of the Red Raids. He served four years for criminal anarchy, was deported to Ireland where he received a hero's welcome.

McGuire and Post-Rising Reactions

In the wake of the failed uprising of 1916, McGuire's paper, like most of the Irish press, produced several articles endorsing the rebellion, praising Sir Roger Casement, condemning John Redmond and British Rule. McGuire, along with many extreme Nationalists, was quick to defend the work of Casement. An article in the Catholic Sun featured a large front-page picture of Casement and an interview with James K. McGuire. Noting his two books on Irish freedom, the article referred to McGuire as being "intimately acquainted" with Casement. McGuire indicated he met with Sir Roger Casement the year before he embarked on his journey to Berlin. Casement, had in fact traveled widely in the United States, addressing the convention of the Ancient Order of Hibernians at Norfolk, Virginia in July 1914. He spoke of the need for arms and aid for the Irish Volunteers. Over 5000 Hibernian Riflemen proposed sending their guns and uniforms to the Volunteers.¹⁴⁹ In his article, McGuire compared Casement to Wolfe Tone and Robert Emmet, who also died as patriots to revolution in Ireland. He compared Casement to abolitionist John Brown, an American martyr, whose execution furthered divisions in the United States, accelerating the nation's move towards Civil War. McGuire went on to briefly outline Casement's efforts to form an Irish Brigade of the German Army from British prisoners of war. McGuire elaborated on the press censorship, the riots and the continuing unrest in Ireland. Calling the uprising "premature", McGuire predicted the execution of Casement and other leaders would simply further the cause of Irish freedom.¹⁵⁰ Other articles in the <u>Catholic Sun</u> alluded to a "well-laid" plot on the part of Germany to hit England in a three-pronged effort-invasion from the East by German warships, a Zeppelin air attack and an internal revolution by anti-English patriots.¹⁵¹

In a subsequent article, McGuire wrote in more depth on the Uprising of 1916, noting the number of Irish casualties both in the Easter Rebellion and in the trenches of Europe. Perhaps suspecting his activities were being monitored, McGuire pronounced his loyalty to the United States as well as his devotion to the Irish cause. He portrayed Woodrow Wilson as sympathetic to Ireland because in his five-volume <u>A History of The American People</u> (1902), he favorably described the Fenian raids on Canada in the post-Civil War era. Wilson had written about the love of "liberty [which] could not be torn from the breasts of Irish-Americans." Revisiting a recurrent theme, McGuire wrote, "Americans are prone to forget their history, noting that since only one-third of Americans supported the American Revolution, there could have been no hope of success without intervention from France, just as there could be no hope of Ireland's success without German assistance". McGuire compared Sir Roger Casement to George Washington. Casement, he wrote, is considered a traitor because he was in British diplomatic service. Following that logic, so too was Washington, who fought under Braddock in the French and Indian War.¹⁵² McGuire endorsed the Rising, calling Sinn Fein the organization devoted to saving the

Irish race and culture. Interestingly, McGuire, again evoking lessons from American history, compared the Irish Rebels with the heroic resistance of American Patriots at Bunker Hill who also fought until their ammunition ran out. Those not killed or captured rose again to successfully oust British rule in America, as would the Irish, should Germany bring aid to them.

McGuire was walking a political thin line. At the time, he was still ostensibly pro-Wilson, having openly supported him for election in 1912. He was solicitous to Wilson when the President chose Irish Catholics for his Cabinet. McGuire reaped the benefits of this collusion by having his candidates for federal patronage jobs in upstate New York chosen over those of the Tammany Boss of Onondaga County, William Kelley. And apparently, his close ties to Irish irreconcilables and pro-German causes were unknown or ignored by the Wilson administration.

McGuire had good cause to laud the efforts of Sir Roger Casement, given his dual roles of Irish Nationalist and German propagandist. He was intimately involved in the plot to get Casement into Germany, admitted having met Casement in 1913 when he came to America to raise money for Irish Volunteers. With John Devoy and other leading Nationalists, they protested the killings by the British Army in the wake of the gun-running incident at Howth.[153] In collaboration with Kuno Meyer, Casement authored several pamphlets calling for a German-Irish alliance.[154] The I.R.B., in close touch with the Clan-na-Gael, believed the time was right for a rising. Devoy used these developments to obtain support for his revolutionary program. Devoy, Jeremiah O'Leary, head of the American Truth Society, Daniel Cohalan and other Clan leaders on August 14, 1914 met with German Ambassador von Bernstorff and members of his staff-Wolf Von Igle, Bernard Dernburg, Franz Von Papen and George von Skal. A request for officers and arms was made by Devoy. The strategy of the Rising and its diversionary importance was emphasized. Plans for the Rising were formulated. It is certain that the Clan-na-Gael was involved, that Devoy was liaison to von Papen and Tom Clarke of the I.R.B. The Clan sent substantial sums to Dublin prior to Easter week, 1916.[155]

The German Imperial Government was happy to accommodate Casement. He was a knight of the British Empire and a prominent convert to the Nationalist cause. The Clan-na-Gael, despite some reservations by Devoy, agreed to supply Casement with money and a false passport under the name of James Landy, a New York businessman and a co-conspirator in the plan. Since his photograph had been published as a result of his protest of the Howth gun-running deaths, Casement shaved his beard. Landy supplied a pair of his glasses and coached him as to his mannerisms to assist in Casement's disguise. He was also given a letter attesting to Landy's character on State Department letterhead which "was probably supplied by a Philadelphia lawyer named Michael F. Ryan, who was a friend of both Secretary of State William Jennings Bryan and a high-ranking Clan member named James K. McGuire, a one-time mayor of Syracuse, New York".[156] Cronin states Landy gave Casement several letters including one from the Assistant Secretary of State who was a friend of James K. McGuire.[157] Hence, McGuire's ties to the Rising are obvious.

Devoy and Cohalan were a bit unsure of Casement because he had taken moderates Bourke Cockran and John Quinn into his confidence. They were correct to be concerned, especially about Quinn. Although he temporarily sheltered Casement in 1914, he held moderate Home Rule views and publicly supported the Allies. According to Spence, Quinn may have been a British agent[158]. Nonetheless, because of Joseph McGarrity's strong endorsement, and Casement's appeal to the Kaiser, his mission was approved and financed by the Clan.[159] The stage set for what has been called "the most successful failure in Irish history." Involvement by Irish-Americans in the events before and after the ill-fated rebellion would prove embarrassing to President Wilson in terms of domestic and international politics. As noted, one of the key players in those incidents was James K. McGuire. McGuire was involved in a number of activities on behalf of the cause of Ireland, but not always to the liking of high-ranking Clan members. One of them was the Brogan affair.

Casement's tribulations in Germany are well-documented. Like the East Indians, his efforts to recruit volunteers among British prisoners in Germany were largely unsuccessful. The Germans were skeptical of Casement. However they realized the military advantage of a diversionary effort against Britain, offering Casement 20,000 rifles, ten machine guns and quantities of ammunition, but no German officers. Casement was not informed as to the Rising's details until they were finalized. In fact, realizing German support for the Rebellion was luke-warm at best, Casement attempted to abort the effort, sending Irish-American John McGoey to Ireland to have the leaders cancel it. Neither McGoey nor the message arrived.[160]

The Brogan Affair

Casement's position was made even more difficult by his erstwhile supporter, James K. McGuire. The episode was recorded by John Devoy in his Recollections of an Irish Rebel. The title of the chapter, "Butting in on the Clan -na- Gael:…Pet Schemes of Unauthorized Men Endangered Our Position" reveals the divisions of opinion over policies within the Clan, and also raises questions as to McGuire's motivation.

In his book Devoy relates the stories of three individuals who "butted in". Two schemes emanated from idividuals who mailed their proposals to German ambassador von Bernstorff who in turn forwarded them to John Devoy for approval. The first sought to start a newspaper friendly to the German cause. It was dismissed since several such publications already existed. A plan to start a magazine in Ireland opposing recruitment of Irish troops for the British Army was also reviewed. Devoy, always suspicious of British infiltration and spying, feared if discovered, it would discredit the IRA leadership as paid German agents. To prevent such occurrences, the Clan refused German money and the overture was rejected[161]. The third proposition involved McGuire and according to Devoy "might have resulted in irreparable harm".[162]

The project involved Edward Rumely, a pro-German American, who disliked the pro-Allied bias of most newspapers in the United States. With German money, he purchased the New York Evening Mail to assist the German cause. Rumely met Anthony J. Brogan when both attended Notre Dame University in Indiana. In the interim, Brogan had apparently obtained control of the Irish-American, a nationalist newspaper.[163] Devoy had slight regard for Brogan's attachment to the Nationalist cause. Apparently Rumely, with support from James K. McGuire, who according to Devoy, "should have known better", sent Brogan to Germany to assist the German cause. Additional details about Brogan were supplied by Jeremiah Joseph O'Leary, a member of Sinn Fein, in a document from the Bureau of Military History. O'Leary, then living in London, indicated he had contact with Roger Casement in May and June of 1914. He described his connection to Brogan in the Summer of 1915.[164] Brogan's cover was that of a salesman of outboard motors. His goal was to assist Germany in its intelligence operations. While in Germany, he met Casement who in turn gave him O'Leary's address to be used as a London contact. Brogan had by then traveled to London in the company of a German officer, Hans W. Boehm. Boehm had been assigned to assist Casement's efforts in recruitment of Irish POW's. Casement spoke no German but Boehm was conversant in English, had an American wife and a number of Irish friends so he was considered a good contact. But Boehm was periodically pulled away from Casement and assigned to the United States which leaves one with the impression the Irish Brigade was not a significant part of his assignment. In that sense, Boehm typified the attitude of the German Foreign Office towards Casement.[165] Boehm was regarded as a "high level German spy"[166], whose goal was to obtain information on British military preparations, especially Kitchener's "new Army". The Irish-born Horatio Herbert Kitchener was then Secretary of War in the British Cabinet with a long history of battlefield success in both the Sudan and in the Boer War. Contrary to prevailing opinion, he believed the war would be a long, drawn-out affair. He saw the need for well-trained and well-led divisions organized on a scale unprecedented in British history. His methods brought him into conflict with other cabinet ministers. From an ill-equipped and ill-prepared army, he was able to forge a sizeable force of proficient recruits.[167] Brogan accurately told O'Leary his estimate of 2 million troops for Kitchener's army was "fairly accurate".[168] This turned out to be correct so it appears Brogan did have access to truthful information.

Dorries, in his <u>Prelude to the Easter Rising</u>, records a letter from Casement to Joseph McGarrity on 1 March 1915 urging the use of Devoy's <u>Gaelic American and Brogan's Irish –American</u> to present a united front in the cause of Irish freedom[169] The following day, a top secret memo from Boehm indicated he and Brogan needed to go to Ireland immediately to "make preparations", the purpose of which was not stated in the document[170] The request was denied[171] and restated in a subsequent memo[172] One of the signatories was Richard Meyer,[173] the person who escorted Casement into Germany from Sweden. All Casement's correspondence went through Meyer. It is Meyer and other members of the German Foreign Office who sought to use Brogan "for the purpose of securing the nationalist movement in Ireland."[174] That implies the Germans sought to control it. Despite misgivings from Devoy, Casement continued to trust Brogan, urging he be given access to the Irish POW's. As late as March 1915, Casement, in two letters revealed his continued trust in Brogan believing criticisms of him were "unfounded" and that he would act in a "loyal and straightforward way to the Irish cause".[175] An incensed Devoy wrote to McGarrity claiming such actions on Casement's part were "folly" and "they must stop that kind of thing or I will drop the whole business"[176] Again the intent is unclear but could that be a threat by Devoy to stall the rising? There was a subsequent meeting with Sean MacDermott, Michael Collins and Jeremiah Joseph O'Leary and Brogan.[177] It was determined Brogan had no credentials, was not an active member in good standing wth any of the nationalist organizations and was "distrusted" by them. He was considered a free-lance journalist who had come to Europe to act as a German spy. Dick Connolly urged the IRB to have no connection with Brogan, although he would not prevent others from doing so. Another fact was British agents were aware of Brogan's presence in Ireland but were unsure as to his intentions.[178] Dorries' last letter relative to Brogan is dated 24 June 1915 in which Brogan encouraged support for Casement's Irish Brigade project, a Rising and the need for strengthening Irish friendship abroad. Boehm supported Brogan, believing he was beginning to establish useful contacts with the Irish in England.[179] Boehm typified German Foreign Office attitudes towards the Irish. He used Casement to promote contacts with Irish nationalists in America to wreak havoc on American munitions and supply operations. He met with Devoy and John Kenny,[180] the latter a long-time Fenian and past President of the New York chapter of the Clan. As Clan envoy to Germany, Kenny won its acceptance of a plan to support an Irish insurrection against Britain and supply arms for the effort. He also served as a courier for messages from the IRB to the Clan. Given his prominence in both the Clan and FOIF, it is logical to assume McGuire was aware of and complicit in Kenny's activities.

Following Casement's arrest, his attorney Gavan Duffy[181] told Jeremiah Joseph O'Leary, Casement had become suspicious of Brogan. Duffy was in possession of documents from Casement giving details about Brogan, but he refused to share them. Still, O'Leary maintained contact with Brogan, introducing him to James Johnston of Belfast, a prominent Fenian. Aside from another meeting with Brogan about obtaining arms for the Irish Volunteers, contact was apparently broken off with him as a result of pressure from Devoy and his allies. Irish Nationalists eschewed further contact with Brogan but apparently Boehm, then in America, hired him for sabotage work, "as Brogan was ready for anything, he hated England".[182]

This begs the question, what was McGuire trying to accomplish from his involvement? Was he trying to strengthen his credentials with German-Americans via Rumely? Was he trying to use his position within the GIS to leverage his visibility and worth to his German handlers? Was he trying to undermine Devoy who was wary of him given his late attachment to the cause of Sinn Fein and the fact he was a paid German agent, the type who Devoy mistrusted. This explains, in part, why Devoy published a letter extremely critical of McGuire following his death in 1923.[183]

This incident has parallels to the earlier Freeman – O'Donnell – Schiemann incident noted previously. Both reveal schisms within the Irish Nationalist movement and their efforts to maintain a united front and keep free-lance opportunists, eager to obtain German gold, at arms length. Of note is the fact that Freeman was Devoy's representative for the <u>Gaelic-American</u> in Europe. He used the same arguments against O'Donnell as Devoy did against Brogan. And if the reports of Boehm using Brogan as a saboteur in America are accurate, it reveals that Germany on more than one occasion was pursuing a course independent of the wishes of Irish Nationalists. Worse – they could backfire on them as did the case with David Lamar.[184]

McGuire apparently received Casement's testimony to the fact he tried to forestall the rebellion in letters obtained from Casement sent via the merchant submarine <u>Deutschland.</u> With them came the request that McGuire edit the letters, write an introduction and have them published in this country. On its return voyage to Germany, the <u>Deutschland</u> carried the German language edition of <u>What Can[sic] Germany Do For Ireland</u>? In addition, there was a pamphlet written by McGuire entitled "American Impressions of The World Struggle".[185] The man, his trial, assessing who was to blame for his capture, and the execution of Sir Roger Casement consumed a significant amount of space in the Irish press. James K. McGuire's <u>Catholic Sun</u> was no exception. McGuire praised Casement and put him on the pedestal of such luminaries to Irish Nationalism as Wolfe Tone and Robert Emmet, accurately predicting Casement's execution would only aid the rebel's cause. A similar glowing account of Casement's life and martyrdom followed in August, 1916.[186] The full text of his speech from the dock was printed in the <u>Catholic Sun</u>

in July 1916,[187] as was the notice of his death the following month, accompanied by his portrait.[188]

Following the Uprising, by far the biggest issue which involved James K. McGuire in the Casement affair was assessing the blame for his capture and in attempts to obtain clemency. There were persistent rumors the United States government had leaked information about the Rising and Casement to British authorities. Reprinting an article from The Fatherland, the G.I.S. subsidized German-American paper of George S. Viereck, The Catholic Sun, citing John Devoy, suggested the arrest of Wolf Von Igel and seizure of his papers by the United States Secret Service in April 1916, was the source for information later sent to the British Government alerting it to The Easter Rebellion. It denounced American government involvement as a "fatal American treachery".[189] Richard Spense suggests that perhaps ordinary diplomatic channels were by-passed in the leaking of information, similar to the manner in which it was done in the suppression of the Hindu-German conspiracy. British agents had infiltrated both Hindu and Irish organizations with which Imperial Germany had established ties. The head of the British Secret Service in America was Sir William Wiseman. A member of the lower nobility he worked as a banker. He enlisted when the war broke out, was wounded and was later asked to establish an intelligence network in the United States to monitor the activities of Irish and Hindu revolutionaries. Wiseman leaked that information about their activities to American authorities. The question: was there a quid pro quo as to the von Igel papers which contained details of the Easter Rising? Perhaps. Wiseman was in close contact with Colonel Edward House, Wilson's most trusted advisor and is is not unreasonable to assume information passed between them. All three were Anglophiles. The British had broken the German code and were in possession of useful information as to German designs[190]. This perspective was prevalent in the Irish press in America, but it may not be accurate. According to Hartley, the archives of the British Foreign Office reveal the government was not given copies of the von Igel papers. The only message leaked to the British was a note sent by rebel leaders to delay the gun-running expedition. It arrived too late to prevent the ship's departure. Given the heightened tensions between Britain, Wilson, Germany and the Irish, perceptions may have determined their view of reality. McGuire was no exception. He simply made Casement a victim and the British government appear as villains. This was far from accurate and it was used by Britain to portray the plot simply as a German conspiracy[191].

The charges were vehemently denied by Secretary of State Robert Lansing, William Jennings Bryan's replacement. Lansing "flatly denied" the allegations of John Devoy, although the government did not dispute it had knowledge of Casement's activities. Information of plans made in Germany to invade Ireland were not communicated to Great Britain. The seized papers of von Igel were said by the State Department, to be of "little value."[192]

Because of Casement's prominence, the Irish press and many mainstream papers pleaded for clemency. It was an uphill struggle. As with the Hindu-German conspiracy trials, Irish lawyers were key players in his defense. On Casement's team of lawyers was an American, Michael F. Doyle, a former secretary to William Jennings Bryan and legal counsel to the Department of State. He carried $1000 in Clan-na-Gael money to assist in Casement's defense. Doyle's presence created problems for the British. He had been a high-ranking member of the State Department and he was being bankrolled by the Clan. Upon his arrival, he accused the British of ill treatment, condemning Casement's prison conditions. British law forbade foreign lawyers from representing clients in British courts. Hence Doyle could only visit Casement with a British lawyer present

Casement was tried for high treason, found guilty and sentenced to death. The sentence received a mixed reaction in the United States largely because the British initiated a smear campaign. Excerpts from his Black Diaries revealed his homosexuality, a factor which contributed to his guilty verdict. The Catholic clergy was largely silent, despite Casement's recent conversion to Catholicism.

Following Casement's conviction, Doyle organized the movement to grant him a reprieve, getting both the United State Senate and the

Papacy to intervene. Doyle wrote to Joseph Tumulty, President Wilson's Secretary, to see if the President would intercede on Casement's behalf, a request initially rejected by the President.[193] Under pressure from The Friends of Irish Freedom and Joseph Tumulty, the White House relented, sending a message urging compassion. It arrived too late to have any effect. FOIF, Tansill, McGuire and the Irish Press were convinced the message was delayed purposely to insure Casement's death.[194] McGuire's <u>Catholic Sun</u> undoubtedly reflected Irish opinion on the matter. Accompanying the article. "Roger Casement, Patriot", The <u>Catholic Sun</u> published the full text of McGuire's telegram to President Wilson, protesting the delay of five days between the passage of the Senate resolution and the 24 hours delay between Wilson's signing the request for clemency and it being received by the British government. McGuire alleged the message was sent at 8 o'clock London time. Casement was executed one hour later. The British Foreign Office claimed it did not receive the message until after Casement was executed and buried. McGuire, in his capacity as Chairman of the Executive Committee of the Friends of Irish Freedom, demanded an investigation as to why there was such a delay especially since the cable routes on both sides of the Atlantic were controlled by Great Britain. McGuire was confident that such an investigation would be forthcoming. Officially, the Government said the message was sent in a timely manner; unofficially there is reason to suspect the delay was intentional.[195] Both the ethnic press and mainstream papers responded vehemently to Casement's death. However, Frank Polk, State Department counsellor, revealed the British Foreign Office refused to grant clemency despite the United States Senate resolution. Nonetheless there was little doubt that Casement's "moral character" was a instrumental in causing his execution.

The <u>Catholic Sun</u> reprinted articles from <u>The New York World</u>, <u>The Washington Post</u> and <u>The Baltimore Sun</u> condemning his execution.[196] The <u>Catholic Sun</u> echoed these statements, noting that British officialdom ignored the United States Senate resolution and a petition by prominent writers requesting clemency for Casement.

The writers' reprised the example of Northern leniency to Southern leaders at the conclusion of the Civil War, noting in that instance a seemingly irreparable breach [was] happily healed over." Signatures included G.K. Chesterton, Israel Zangwill, Sidney Webb, Sir Arthur Conan Doyle, John Galsworthy and several others.[197]

Following the Easter Rebellion of 1916, many Irish and German-Americans held a rally supporting the revolt. McGuire's name was not noted among the speakers. Many of those with whom he was in contact and in sympathy with were. They included John Devoy and John D. Moore, National Secretary of FOIF.[198] Given his intimate ties with the men and the movement, it would be logical to assume McGuire was involved. All prominent Irish-American nationalists, to whom McGuire had strong associational ties, condemned the hasty execution-Daniel F. Cohalan, Joseph W. Gavan of The Friends of Peace, Robert Ford, Jeremiah O'Leary in his capacity as head of the United Irish Societies of New York, and John D. Moore.[199]

In line with other protests, McGuire arranged for the Brian Boru branch of The Friends of Irish Freedom in Syracuse, New York to stage a massive rally in June 1916. Over 300 attended. The featured speakers were prominent Irish Nationalists, John W. Goff and Jeremiah O'Leary.

Both Goff and O'Leary were reportedly given a long ovations after their introductions by Edward Ryan. Their speeches were described as a "masterly indictment of British government in Ireland as dishonest, brutal and murderous." They repeated the standard litany of Irish Nationalist grievances-biased press reports of the war, the United States was merely an "English dependency", the British sabotage of Home Rule, the misguided leadership of Irish politicians, the noble sacrifice of past and current martyrs, whose ideas would live on. There was also praise for John Holland, "a Fenian" whose invention of the submarine was to challenge British naval supremacy.[200] This was an apparent justification for its use by Germany against the hated British.

Not all Irish-Americans endorsed the FOIF program. Moderate Irish spokesman Patrick Egan condemned FOIF as an, "organization made in Germany [that was] an audacious attempt to get a plank [establishing the an independent Irish Republic] on the platform of the Republican Party is the work of German agents... being friendly to the Irish Republic and being friendly to Germany is one and the same thing... Real Americans who love Ireland should resent such efforts."[201] It was this same Egan, former minister to Chile, in the wake of the executions of the leaders of the Rising who said, if England should have executed anyone, it should have been John Devoy and his associates. Presumably this included McGuire given his strong ties to the Clan and FOIF. It was they who planned and directed the rebellion from New York, obtaining money and arms from the Germans. Egan denounced Casement, Devoy and the Clan as a paid German agents. This was obviously applicable to McGuire in his capacity as employee of the German Information Service, but German money was lavishly spent on others as well.

Despite Egan's protest even moderate Irish opinion was incensed by the hasty execution of the rebel leaders. For example, Bourke Cockran, long and admirer if English law and culture, less than a month after the insurrection reversed himself, stating he had been wrong urging his countrymen to forgive and forget the oppression of the past. Recent events had shown the refutation of his position. "The foulest deeds that ever discredited English rule are exceeded in this recent massacre".[202] At least temporarily, the Irish in America closed ranks, repudiating Redmond and calling for an end to British rule.

McGuire's paper, like much of the hyphenate press, carried detailed stories about the Easter Rebellion for months after the events of April 1916. Several articles in the Catholic Sun were authored by James K. McGuire[203] Especially notable were the articles covering the execution of rebel leaders. They reflect several themes-the heroic resistance of the Irish rebels, the atrocities and hasty executions committed by the British in its suppression, and the idea that the revolt was instigated by Britain as a means of suppressing the Irish Volunteers and the Citizens' Army.[204] In numerous articles, interviews with survivors and the speeches of those sentenced to death, were published verbatim.[205]

In addition to his own journalistic efforts, McGuire in his role as FOIF leader and G. I. S. employee, made sure that lurid tales of survivors of the Easter Rising received widespread coverage well into the Fall of 1916. All stories published from the Irish Press and News Service, were from refugees who escaped execution and/or imprisonment, or were surviving family members of the participants. The Irish continued to publicize the plight of those suffering in the wake of the Easter Rising and to maintain pressure on the Wilson administration by organizing a series of bazaars. Speakers, such as Nora Connolly, the daughter of James Connolly and Agnes Newman, Casement's sister, were featured as were Irish art and handicrafts. Prominent among the exhibits was the one of the submarines invented by John P. Holland. Funds raised by these fairs were denied access to Ireland by the British government. Other exiles recently admitted to America in addition to those named above, including Liam Mellows, Robert Monteith, Patrick McCartan, and Diarmuid Lynch. Many of them joined other expatriates such as Luke Dillon, Padriac Colum, and James Larkin on speaking tours and writing tracts condemning British rule in Ireland.[206]

Typical of such efforts was the interview of the aged mother of executed rebel Michael O'Hanrahan. Mrs. O'Hanrahan said the British "murdered Ireland's best and bravest, shot them down like dogs, without trial have thrown hundreds of other brave men into prison where they are treated like the scum of the earth". Lamenting the bad food, and the dirty cells filled with rats, Mrs. O'Hanrahan fervently believed God would punish England, and praised her sons' efforts to free Ireland. The journalist concluded: "In her brave grief this poor old woman was the symbol of Ireland".[207] Such emotional pieces in the Catholic press undoubtedly generated widespread support for the Irish cause.

There were also reports published in the <u>Catholic Sun</u> by Helen Russell, a veteran of the rebellion and an escapee, living in New York. Her article proclaimed Britain's goal was nothing short of genocide through conscription–military and economic. Believing Ireland the granary of England, Russell urged an economic boycott–farmers should refuse to sell their produce to Britain, so a repeat of the famine of 1840's would be averted. To further her point, Russell said British starvation of Boer non-combatants was the reason it won the South African War. Ending her report, Russell stated, "England knows how to use a famine. Let Ireland be aware and on her guard".[208] The point was conceded by none other than John Redmond who said it was government policy to control prices or prevent export in the interests of Ireland. "If potatoes follow the meat and grain to England, Ireland will again know the hunger and fever of famine...Some millions of people will be practically foodless by St. Patrick's Day".[209]

Another interview appearing in the Catholic Sun was of the widow of James Connolly, whose handful of fighters, outnumbered by more than 15-to-one, held the British army and Irish constabulary at bay. The author's description of the plaintive wails of Connolly's wife and children was extremely emotional, the eight children praying for their father and for God to punish England. As with Sheehy-Skeffington, the British government denied her permission to leave Ireland, although one daughter avoided the authorities and made it safely to New York.[210]

Another widow given coverage in McGuire's Catholic Sun, was the wife of Edward Kent. She praised her husband's efforts on behalf of Ireland, lamenting the fact the authorities would not release his body to her, reiterating the fact that Ireland would never rest until it was a free, independent nation. Raising points noted by other militant nationalists, the widow claimed it was noble to die in the streets for Irish freedom rather than be butchered in a foreign land fighting for England and a mythical Home Rule. The treatment of the leaders of the Irish Rebellion, she emphasized, made a mockery of British statements it had entered the war to defend helpless Belgium from German atrocities.[211]

Possibly the best propagandist endorsed by FOIF was Hannah Sheehy-Skeffington, widow of the Irish patriot, writer, suffragist and pacifist. Both she and her husband had previously been imprisoned by the British for their anti-recruitment activities in 1915. After her husband was murdered under suspicious circumstances, she was forbidden to leave Ireland but escaped to America in December 1916. She spent two years publicizing conditions in Ireland before a variety of groups—women's societies, pacifists, suffragists, giving The Friends of Irish Freedom significant publicity.[212] Her impact on public opinion in the United States was such that Shane Leslie, the British propagandist, referred to her as "a most damaging personage."[213] McGuire's Catholic Sun published the description of her husband's death months before her arrival in America.

In addition to the "survivor stories", The Catholic Sun also published poems and eulogies to the heroes of the 1916 Uprising. Other ambassadors of revolution who publicized the travails of Ireland were some of its leading intellectuals, including Padraic Colum and Seamus McManus. Colum was a writer involved in the Gaelic League, the Abbey Theatre and associated with many Irish literati of the period, including James Joyce and revolutionaries such as Patrick Pearce, Thomas McDonagh and Roger Casement. He collected Irish folk songs, including several that were printed in the Catholic Sun. They included the "Shan Van Vocht", "The Wearin' O' the Green" and "Billy Byrne of Bally-Manus". The works published reflected back on the failed rebellion of 1798 and the George III's forbidding of wearing green, a symbol of the United Irishmen. To informed Irishmen, the parallels between the events of 1916 and 1798 were extremely evident.[214]

MacManus, like Colum, was active in promoting the rise of Irish literature. And, like Colum, he popularized Irish folklore both in Ireland and the United States. Instead of his usual light-hearted message of simple, happy peasants, his presentations this time had a more serious theme—the destruction of Irish culture under England. In the first of two lectures in Syracuse, the poet gave a slide show presentation to the Men's Club of the Fourth Presbyterian Church. McManus revealed the ancient academic traditions of Ireland, the production of scholars who educated many of early European monarchs, followed by centuries of decline under English rule. His second lecture was a carbon copy of his first, sponsored by the

Friends of Irish Freedom, the proceeds of which went to the Irish Relief Fund.[215]

In addition to publicizing events and personalities of the Easter Rebellion. McGuire's paper carried advertisements for <u>Poems of The Irish Revolutionary Brotherhood</u> featuring the works of Patrick Pearse, Thomas MacDonough, Joseph M. Plunkett and Sir Roger Casement for 55 cents a copy printed by the Syracuse Printing and Publishing Company-<u>The Catholic Sun</u> Press. Other timely memorabilia featured in the <u>Catholic Sun</u> were advertisements for his own books, and "The Latest and Best Portrait of Sir Roger Casement, Ireland's Latest Martyr, 16 x 13 inches, framed for only one dollar."[216] In addition, James K. McGuire also used the <u>Catholic Sun</u> to not only advocate the Nationalist cause, but also to advertise the products of his printing businesses. Previously noted were ads for memorabilia on Irish heroes, his books and those of other writers, published by the Syracuse Printing Company or The Wolfe Tone Press. Following the Easter Rebellion, the <u>Catholic Sun</u> advertised Republican flags which sold for 25 cents to $2.50, depending on size. The ad encouraged patrons in large capital letters to "unfurl the Flag of the Irish Revolt.[217]

Following the Easter Rebellion and the executions, was the attempt by Irish-Americans to extend relief to the Irish people who were suffering in the wake of its suppression. On 20 May 1916, the Irish Relief Committee was established with Thomas Addis Emmett as President. It had extensive support from the Catholic Church in America, with three Irish -American and one Irish Cardinal as honorary officers. John D. Moore of FOIF was Secretary, and Bourke Cockran served as Vice-President.[218] Its efforts were supported in the Irish-American press including McGuire's <u>Catholic Sun</u>. An article from July 1916 documented the difficult conditions under which people were living in Dublin. "Gaunt and emaciated figures of men and women stalk the streets. The children of the tenements suffer. Hospital reports show an alarming increase in the mortality rate of infants". Unemployment and, a rising cost of living bring "the people face to face with ruin and starvation in the poorest quarters".[219]

Peter Golden, a writer and singer prominent in Irish-America, was recruited to emphasize that privations noted above were the direct result of violent suppression of the insurrection.[220] Various groups of Irish-Americans competed to raise the largest amount of money, encouraged by the publication of their contributions.[221] There were also suggestions to groups to send funds to "the only authorized Irish relief fund" of which Thomas Hughes Kelly is Treasurer. The article specifically warned against sending money to "the enterprising Lady Aberdeen" as they will not reach the "destitute families of the victims of the Irish Revolution".[222] Despite the confusion, the fund-raising was apparently successful. Within a month, $100,000 was raised. A committee consisting of John Archdeacon Murphy of Buffalo, and John Gill of New York City was given permission to enter Ireland. However, a second delegation headed by Thomas Kelly and Joseph Smith was detained by the British in Liverpool. The American State Department urged that Kelly and Smith be allowed to proceed but the British refused. The British regarded Smith as a Sinn Fein agitator in disguise. They found a dinner invitation for Smith from Mayor James Curley of Boston, claiming Smith was to distribute relief funds and gather data for a second rebellion.[223] Kelly was the Treasurer of FOIF. In addition, the British uncovered a memo from von Bernstorff urging "The (Relief) Committee here will proceed to Ireland taking with them money for relief and gather information."[224] Hence the British refusal to allow their passage to Ireland. The official British explanation was that Murphy and Gill were sufficient personnel to do the job. James K. McGuire, a member of the Executive Committee of the Irish Relief Fund, and John D. Moore, protested this injustice on behalf of the committee.[225]

The British tried to counter stories of Irish privation with reports of how Ireland had prospered during the war. They found themselves in a quandary-to allow an Irish relief tour was a tacit admission of suffering, but to them Irish fund distributors raised security issues. If admitted to Ireland it would increase hostility to Britain by the Nationalists. The British refused admission to Smith and Kelly. British Intelligence found the true object of their visit was to assess whether Ireland was ready for another Rising, believing post-revolution unrest was the result of the Irish-American relief organization[226]

Upon their return, Murphy and Gill reported on the misery and destitution of Ireland, conditions which forced starving peasants into the British Army.[227] Murphy, in a formal statement, quoted imprisoned and soon-to-be executed rebels, as to the severity of destitution and destruction in Dublin as well as in the West and South of Ireland. He praised the Irish Relief Fund for its "generous action". John Archdeacon Murphy, while noting that most victims were Catholics, said the Rising was a united effort of Protestants, Catholics, socialists and aristocrats. Thus the British were embarrassed by the public exposure of the misery extant in Ireland, yet refused permission of members of a relief commission to distribute aid. It was obvious, also, that their bloody reprisals unified Irish opposition to them in both Ireland and in America.[228] The net result was in increase in sympathy and support for the Irish cause and a move towards more radicalism with the formation in January 1917, of the American Sinn Fein. Launched by FOIF, its officers included both O'Leary brothers, Peter Golden, Dennis Spellisy, John D. Moore, Robert Monteith of Irish Brigade fame, who had escaped from Ireland and was in America, and James Larkin, founder of the Irish Citizen Army, also living in America. At its conference a month later, Daniel Cohalan condemned the idea of intervention on the Allied side as simply a vehicle to keep Ireland under British control.[229] British suspicions of the Irish Relief Fund mission were justified when the Irish Revolutionary Directory of the Clan requested arms and troops from Germany for a second uprising in September and again in December 1916. The Executive Committee of FOIF in December, of which McGuire was the head, demanded Germany declare its position on Irish independence.[230] Militant Irish opinion was beginning to suspect Germany's intentions as to the issue of freedom for Ireland. In December 1916, Germany issued peace proposals which failed to include Irish aspirations. It was this which led to McGuire's demands regarding Germany's plans for Irish independence.

The public statements of FOIF urging a common cause with Germany may have had a negative impact in the interests of Irish freedom. Some of its leaders, noting an increased hostility towards Germany, by the Fall 1916 were making statements distancing themselves from their erstwhile ally, Germany. For example, Doorley noted remarks of both John J. Curley and Judge John Goff to that effect. The latter bluntly stated: "Pro-Germanism is not wanted...". Goff's remarks indicated the Irish-German collaboration was an alliance of convenience... "we are with them when they are against England".[231] These remarks may reflect Irish Nationalists' perspective on Germany given its luke warm support of the Easter rising and its reluctance to fully a support a subsequent rebellion.

President Wilson's patient diplomacy with Germany was eventually rewarded in May 1916 with the Sussex Pledge. Germany agreed to revert to the old international policy of warning merchant ships and provide safe passage for passengers and crewmen. This, despite the fact that Britain used armed merchant vessels which often rammed vulnerable submarines on the surface. These diplomatic maneuvers from May 1915 to February 1917 prevented an outbreak of hostilities for almost twenty months. It gave Wilson a hiatus in which he could focus on the election of 1916. But there were other international distractions. Not only were there problems of German subversion and sabotage on the East and West Coasts, but issues surfaced in Mexico and the Caribbean as well.

South of The Border...Mexico As America's Ireland

Given Germany's abandonment of unrestricted submarine warfare as a result of the Sussex pledge, its limited options were subversion and sabotage. Events on the East and West coasts have been noted but Germany was active in Mexico and the Caribbbean. Several of the participants were associates of McGuire. In his capacity as propagandist for the GIS and in his roles as key member of FOIF and the Clan-na-Gael, he had to be aware of their activities.

Concern for the security of the Panama Canal brought American intervention in Haiti and Santo Domingo. This was, in part, a function of McGuire's "deserving Democrat", Tammany associate, fellow Irish Nationalist and ambassador to Santo Domingo, James Mark Sullivan. Sullivan was investigated twice for corruption with regard to his activities in the unstable country. Ostensibly this was the rationale for his removal but his Irish Nationalist credentials contained an anti-British bias that made him, like McGuire, pro-German. Documents from the German Foreign Office dated 15 January 1915 from the German consul reveal conversations in which Sullivan railed against British rule in Ireland, encouraged a German invasion wrest its control from Britain and offered his services to effect that change. Sullivan even suggested "exploiting" the French ambassador's wife, an ethnic German, who despised her adopted country. Correspondence and contacts continued through June of 1915, but nothing came of them.[232] In other words, Sullivan was actively courting treason with German diplomats at the time his activities in Santo Domingo were under investigation. This may have been the reason the Germans kept him at a distance, since a prior inquiry had gone nowhere and they feared a similar result this time as well. But the incident does show McGuire and his associates were willing to cross the line from collaboration to subversion to sabotage to treason. Similar events, also involving McGuire colleagues occurred in Mexico.

Although McGuire's boss in the GIS, Dr. Bernard Dernburg, had a brief tenure, he was largely responsible for intitiating German policy vis-à-vis the United States and Mexico. The goal was to provoke a war between the two countries to provide a diversion of troops and material in the same way the Irish uprising was contemplated. As noted previously, the German diplomatic corps in San Francisco was involved arms shipments to factions in Mexico. Dernburg's primary agent in Mexico was Felix Sommerfeld, a German national who had worked for assassinated President Francisco Madero and who was currently acting as a spy and arms agent for Pancho Villa. Sommerfeld worked with Woodrow Wilson's Special Envoy to Mexico, William Bayard Hale in negotiations with current President Venustiano Carranza. At the time Hale was a close confidante of Wilson but he later was an employee, like McGuire, of the GIS. When Hale broke with Wilson, it was Sommerfeld, through his connections to Dernburg, who got Hale a job as a correspondent for the Hearst newspapers in Germany.[233] This was in addition to Hale's salary as a member of Germany's Secret War Council.

Pancho Villa
(1878-1923)
Mexican Revolutionary Leader
Library of Congress ID -LC DIG-npcc 19554
Public Domain

General John J Pershing
(1860-1948)
Library of Congress ID ggbain 21134
No Known Copyright Restrictions

Francisco Madero
(1873-1913)
President of Mexico, 1911-1913
Public Domain

Venustiano Carranza
(1859-1920)
President of Mexico 1917-1920
Public Domain
(Source: World's Work, 1915)

Victoriano Huerta
(1850-1916)
President of Mexico, 1913-1914
Library of Congress ID ggba1n 13949
No Known Copyright restrictions

Henry Lane Wilson
(1857-1932)
Ambassador to Mexico, 1910 1913
Public Domain

When Madero and his accomplices overthrew dictator Porfirio Diaz, Sommerfeld joined him, rising to become head of his secret service, an organization which included Mexican nationals and foreign adventurers. In the wake of Madero's subsequent murder and the coup d'etat by Victoriano Huerta in 1913 had the tacit support of United States ambassador Henry Lane Wilson. Sommerfeld, with the aide of German ambassador to Mexico Paul von Hintze, went to Washington, D. C. He obtained funds from American lawyer and lobbyist Sherburne Hopkins[234] whose clients included major figures in American finance and questionable activities with several Central American dictators. Hopkins had a background in the Navy and he was an informer for United States Military Intelligence (MID)[235]. One of his Central American clients was Francisco Madero who used Hopkins' funding to arm his troops. Hopkins' network of subversion was uncovered after a break-in of his Washington, D.C. office, allegedly by Huerta supporters, which obtained documents revealing his connections to Huerta rivals, Venustiano Carranza and Pancho Villa and American oil and railroad interests[236]. In the wake of the ensuing scandal, Felix Sommerfed filled the void, filing reports to US military intelligence from 1914-1918. Yet Sommerfeld was playing double agent. When Carranza and Villa split by the Spring of 1914, he joined Villa, moving to New York as his agent, connecting with German Naval Attache Karl Boy-Ed, to obtain arms for his Mexican client. Through German Ambassador Bernstorff, Heinrich Albert opened several bank accounts in various American cities, including one used by Sommerfeld to purchase arms[237]. The source of arms was the Bridgeport Projectile Company, established by Franz Rintelen in 1915. It's purpose was to manufacture arms and ammunition which would then be destroyed to prevent them from being used by the Allies. The delay in filling orders and their purposeful destruction was designed to assist in a German victory which the Germans thought possible by late 1915.[238] A second aspect of the plan was to pay extremely high wages to create labor unrest and recruit workers from other plants[239] the goal of Rintelen's National Peace Council, of which McGuire was a member.

A further link to Sommerfeld was German agent James Manoil who purchased arms for him from the Western Cartridge Company. The company was established in 1898 by industrialist Franklin Olin in East Albion, Illinois[240]. It was Manoil who deposited funds in a St. Louis bank for Sommerfeld which were then used to purchase weapons from the Western Cartridge Company. All this was done a few months prior to Villa's Columbus, New Mexico attack. Interestingly, Manoil's address was the same as German Military attache, Franz von Papen, the same address which also housed the management of the Bridgeport Projectile Company.[241] The manager behind the scenes was Carl Heynen, a representative of the German-Amerika shipping line (HAPAG), aide to Heinrich Albert and personal friend of Felix Sommerfeld. When questioned later by Department of Justice agents, Sommerfeld could not answer why $340,000 from an account he had in the St. Louis bank, was the exact amount in the same bank in which the German embassy had opened an account. After the arms were purchased and sent to Villa, both accounts were closed on the same day. Were these arms designed to have a German surrogate, Villa, instigate an incident that would divert American arms and men from participation in the Great War on the Allied side?[242] A bizarre conspiracy which was an outgrowth of Mexican frustrations and international intrigue referred to as the San Diego Plan, or sometimes as the Bandit War. Its origins are obscure and its goals changed over time. It was allegedly the outgrowth of German efforts to provoke a war between Mexico and the United States. According to the plan,-there was to be an uprising against Anglo domination in the Soutwest - Texas, New Mexico, Arizona, Colorado and California. All Anglo males over the age of 16 were to be killed. Each state would have the option of of becoming an independent republic or joining Mexico.There was some sporadic cross-border violence which engendered severe reprisals by the Anglo community. The crisis worsened with Wilson's recognition of the Carranza regime angering his rival Pancho Villa. To make matters worse, the United States allowed Carranza to transport troops across American territory resulting in a major defeat for Villa's forces, destroying his army and turning him into a guerilla leader. Needing supplies and a victory to consolidate his power, Villa invaded Columbus, New Mexico in March 1916. According to historian Friedrich Katz, Villa's decision was a political act, not the rash decision of a crude bandito leader. He was unwilling to accept American rapprochement with Carranza and hopeful of incurring the wrath of the United States against Mexico. This was in line with Germany's designs as well. With Carranza's approval, President Wilson's sent a punitive expedition led by General "Black Jack" Pershing in what amounted to a fruitless effort to capture the guerilla leader. The maneuvers of the American army as it moved south concerned Caranza and led to clashes with the Mexican army, which inflicted some ignominious defeats on Pershing's forces almost bringing the United States and Mexico to the brink of war. It would have diverted American resources from Europe, the same rationale used by the Germans for support of the Easter Rebellion in Ireland.[243] Villa's raid occurred about five weeks prior to the Easter Rising. Pershing's forces were withdrawn by February 1917, two months before the United States entered the war. Interestingly, there was a debate on the issue in the United States Congress spear-headed by Representative Atkins J. McLemore of Texas, an anti-war Democrat, urging troops remain in Mexico in order to maintain peace along the border. It failed to pass. According to Viereck, the resolution was written by Shaemus O'Sheele, an Irish Nationalist, and like McGuire, an employee of the German Information Service.[244]

The upshot of all this was it revealed the the multinational efforts of McGuire and others in a variety of schemes designed to win independence for Ireland. It is impossible to prove the extent of German involvement in these efforts. Interestingly, the role of Sommerfeld was investigated by a senate investigation committee similar to that which also probed the activities of James K. McGuire.[245] Nonetheless, Germany's goal was almost achieved. Over 150,000 National Guard members were deployed along the Mexican border. Since the Guard constituted forty percent of troops sent to Europe, a significant number were diverted from Europe. And despite the fact the San Diego Plan was a failure, there were elements of it resurrected by Germany in a vain effort to make Mexico America's Ireland. This was revealed in the Zimmerman Telegram.

Despite American recognition, Carranza was suspicious of America's intentions and he needed a counter-weight to its power. Hence, he tilted towards Germany. Playing on those sentiments, Foreign Minister Zimmerman urged a Mexican-German alliance, promising it the same territories named in the San Diego Plan[246]. The United States President was pursuing peace proposals at the time. As a gesture of good faith, he allowed the German government access to its State Department cable to send coded messages to America. The cable passed through British territory whose Naval Intelligence had cracked the German code. The message arrived January of 1917 and was translated by February, the same time Pershing was withdrawing from Mexico. The British gave the Anglophile American ambassador Walter Hines Page the message who forwarded it to the State Department. Wilson was outraged and made it public. Pro-German elements pronounced a fake and a forgery, but by March its authenticity was confirmed. Zimmerman's admission as to its accuracy destroyed what was left of pro-German sentiment in America.[247] Within a month, Germany and the United States were at war, forcing McGuire to change directions and become a "pragmatic patriot".

Despite increased tensions with Germany, Britain did not enamor itself to the United States during this period. For example, in July 1916, it arbitrarily increased its contraband list, interfered with United States shipping and searched mail going to Germany. Its blacklist of June 1916 forbade British businessmen from trading with American firms with German contracts, heightened tensions between the United States and Britain.[248] Thus from the German-Irish perspective, America, Ireland and Germany should forge an alliance to protect freedom of the seas, a point noted previously by both Sir Roger Casement and James K. McGuire. It was not to be. Yet despite the acrimonious debates, the diplomatic maneuvers, and increasing evidence of German subversion, the peace was maintained. In the interim, German-and-Irish-Americans increased their agitation for American neutrality and fought a losing battle to win public opinion to their cause. In addition, American prosperity increased as result of its overseas trade with the Allies, and because Wilson embraced the idea that such trade was a logical extension of neutral rights on the sea, made any attempt to obtain an arms embargo fruitless. This policy had two results–it increased German subversive efforts to disrupt the manufacture and trade in arms in the United States, and it pushed Germany towards the resumption of unrestricted submarine warfare and ultimately American intervention on the Allied side. Perhaps sensing the growing disenchantment with the Irish, von Bernstorff, then in Germany, responded favorably to a request from the Clan-na-Gael in December 1916 to send arms to support another rebellion. The offer was rejected since the Irish felt no rebellion could be effective without German troops.[249] The Germany-Ireland connection was apparently frayed beyond repair.

Waning confidence in President Wilson's leadership gave German-and-Irish-Americans justification for opposing his re-election in 1916. Since they could not change his policies, they would work to change leaders. They almost won, but events and individuals upset their plans. Intimately involved in these efforts, was James K. McGuire and his associates.. The failure of the Wilson administration to take a strong stand against the execution of the Irish rebels was deeply resented by most Irish in America. Many took out their hostility by working against his re-election. The President became his own worst enemy when he injected the hyphenate issue into the campaign. In addition, the German- Irish alliance in America, on the surface apparently strong, had numerous fissures that failed to upset Wilson's re-election in November 1916.

Notes

1 Feilitzsch, Heribert. The Secret War Council: The German Fight Against the Entente in America in 1914. Ammissvile, Va.: Henselstone Verlag, 2015, 11-30

2 aan de Weil, Jerome. The Irish Factor, 1899-1919:Ireland's Strategic and Diplomatic Importance for Foreign Powers. Dublin: Irish Academic Press, 2011, 184.

3 Ganachari, Aravind Guraro. "An Early Contributor to India's Struggle For Freedom: Myron Phelps(1856-1916)" in Ganachari, Aravind Guraro (ed.) Nationalism and Social Reform in a Colonial Situation. Delhi, India: Gyan Books Ltd. 2005, 150.

4 Ibid., 151-153.

5 Ibid., 154.

6 Fischer-Tine, Harald. "Indian Nationalism and World Forces: Transnational and Diasporic Dimensions of the Indian Freedom Movement on the Eve of the First World War". Journal of Global History, 2007 (2), 325-344.

7 Aan de Weil, op. cit., 49; 127-125.

8 Independent Hindustan, December 1920. Https://janoed.com/primary-source/primary-source-2. Retrieved 27 June 2028.

9 Das was an anti-British Bengali revolutionary. He studied at Berkeley, moving to Vancouver in 1908 where he established the India Independence League and began publishing the Free Hindustan. Das moved to New York City forming a close association with George Freeman, John Devoy's editor of the Gaelic American. Ker, James. Political Trouble in India: A Confidential Report, 1917; 247;251.

10 "Who was Swami Abhedananda?" Quora. https:// www.quora.com/who-was-swami-Abhedananda?

11 "Lala Har Dayal" (1884- 1939). http://biography.vasra- Shasna-org./2015/10/10/lal-har –dayal.html..

12 Fischer-Tine, op.cit., 335.

13 Hoover, Karl. "The Hindu Conspiracy In California, 1913-1918". German Studies Review. 8 (2) May, 1985,251.

14 Brown, Giles. "The Hindu Conspiracy, 1914-1917". Pacific Historical Review. August 1917 (3) 301.

15 Ker, op. cit.,247.

16 De Rosa, Peter. Irish Rebels: The Rising of 1916. New York: Fawcett-Columbine, 1990, 21-24.

17 Plowman, Matthew Erin. "The British Intelligence Station in San Francisco During the First World War." Journal of Intelligence History 12 (1) 7.

18 Hoover, op. cit., 252; Brown, op. cit., 303.

19 Plowman, 81-105., op. cit.,.
20 Von Papen, Franz. Memoirs. London: Andrew Deutsch, 1952, 35.
21 Plowman, 2003, op. cit., 87.
22 Ibid., 98.
23 Ibid.,88.
24 On the last day of the trial, Ram Singh, who believed Ram Chandra betrayed the Ghadar Party, smuggled a gun into the courtroom and shot him dead. He was immediately shot dead by a federal marshal. Plowman, op.cit., 2013,
25 "Laws Prevent Adequate Punishment, Court Declares Prisoners Termed 'Tools of Inhuman Country', Plotters Warned Against More Activity After Release". L A Times, May 19https://newsikhpioneers.org/hindu-spies-sent-jail.
26 Plowman, op. cit.,2013,
27 Wittke, Carl. German-Americans And The World War (Columbus, Ohio: Ohio State Archaeological and Historical Society, 1936), 9; Link, Arthur S. The Struggle For Neutrality, 1914-19(Princeton: Princeton University Press, 1960), Heribert Freilitzsch. "Men of the Secret War Council: Bernard Dernburg" http://felix Sommerfeld.com/news/mexican-revolution-blog/2015/12/6/men-of -the-secret- war-council.
28 Jones, John Price, and Hollister, Paul H. The German Secret Service In America. (Boston: Small, Maynard and Co., 1918), 181-Feilitzch, Heribert. The Secret War Council: The German Fight Against the Entente in America in 1914. Amissville, Va. Henselstonr Verlag, 2015; 14.
29 Jones, op. cit., 246.
30 Bernstorff, Count Johann von. My Three Years In America. (New York: Scribners, 1920), Child, Clifton. The German-Americans In Politics, 1914-(Madison: University of Wisconsin Press, 1939), 36, fn 26.
31 Jones and Hollister, op.cit., 238-39; Bernstorff, op.cit. 48; Brewing And Liquor Interests And German and Bolshevik Propaganda: Report And Hearing of the Subcommittee On The Judiciary Untied States Senate (Washington: Government Printing Office, 1919), Vol I, xv.
32 van Dopperen Ron and Graham, Cooper C. Shooting the Great War: Albert Dawson and the American Correspondent Film Company, 1914-1919. Charleston, South Carolina: Creatspace, 34.
33 Ibid., 42
34 Ibid., 61.
35 van Dopperen and Graham, op.cit., 82.
36 Ibid.; Fulwider, Chad. "Film Propaganda and Culture: The German Dilemma, 1914-1917" Film and History: An Inter-Disciplinary Journal, 45, No. 2 Winter 2015, 4-12.
37 van Dopperen and Graham, op. cit., 138-138.
38 Ibid., 34.

CONFLICTS AND CRISES   399

39 Ibid., 137.
40 Ibid., 138-140.
41 Link, Neutrality...op.cit 31; 555; Jones and Hollister, op cit 230-31. Brewing and Liquor Interests, vol I op.cit., xv.
42 Feilitzsch, Heribert. "William Bayard Hale: Icon or Traitor?" http://felixsummerfeld.com/news/mexican-revolution-blog/2013/11/3william-bayard-hale.
43 Link, Neutrality op.cit...31; Viereck, George Sylvester. Spreading Germs of Hate (New York: Horace and Liveright, 1930), 52-54. Brewing and Liquor Interests, op.cit, xvi; 1392-94.
44 Jones and Hollister, op.cit., 194.
45 Bernstorff, op.cit., 65.
46 Thomas R. Marshall (1854-1925) was Wilson's two-term vice-President. A prosperous lawyer and Progressive Democratic Governor of Indiana, he helped win the state for Wilson in 1912. His political views varied from those of Wilson during his first term. His second was marred by advisors close to Wilson who did not want Marshall to assume the Presidency during Wilson's recovery from a stroke. For a full treatment, see Bennett, Davis J. He Almost Changed The World: The Life And Times of Thomas Riley Marshall (Freeman and Costello, 2007).
William J. Stone (1848-1918) was a lawyer, a Progressive Democrat and former Governor of Missouri. He presided over the Senate Foreign Relations Committee and was at odds with Wilson over foreign policy. He was one of the six Senators to vote against US entry into the war. See "Stone William Joel". Biographical Directory of the United States Congress http://bioguide.congress.gov/scripts/biodisplay.pl? index=s0000968.
Gilbert M. Hitchcock (1859-1934) was a successful Omaha lawyer newspaper editor and Democratic Congressman. Some of his formal education was in Germany. As Senator, he served on the Foreign Relations Committee and subsequently supported Wilson on the Versailles Treaty. "Hitchcock, Gilbert Monell". Biographical Directory of the US Congress. http://bioguide.congress.gov/scripts/biodisplay.pl?index=H000645.
William E. Borah (1865-1940) was a successful Idaho lawyer and Republican who was isolationist in his foreign policy later opposing Wilson on ratification of the Versailles Treaty. "Borah, William Edgar". Biographical Directory of the US Congress. http://bioguide.congress.gov/scripts/biodisplay.pl?index=B000634.
Alexander M. Palmer (1872-1936) was a Quaker and progressive Democratic from Pennsylvania. He was Attorney-General in the last years of the Wilson administration supporting the President's position on the League of Nations. He is possibly best-known for the "Red Raids" of 1919 against suspected

radicals. "Palmer, Alexander Mitchell". http://bioguide.congress.gov/scripts/biodisplay.pl?index=P000035.

47 "Hale, William Bayard". In Johnson, Allen and Malone, Dumas (eds.) Dictionary of American Biography, IV (New York: Charles Scribner's and Sons, 1931-32), 112-113. Hale suffered from his German connections. When cables from Ambassador Bernstorff exposing his involvement were intercepted in 1918, he became a virtual pariah. Social clubs shunned him, publishers refused his manuscripts, books expunged his name and he was forced to live in virtual seclusion, ending his years in Munich, Germany in 1924, one year after his GIS colleague McGuire passed away. Hale's final effort, The Story of Style (1920) ridiculed Woodrow Wilson's literary ability.

48 Bernstorff, op.cit., 66-67; Link, Neutrality, op.cit., 317-19

49 "Edward Rumely: Maker of a World of Difference "http://whatsnewlaporte.com/2013/12/27 edward-a-rumely-maker-of-a-world-of-difference.

50 "Former Mayor Asks To Be Judged…" Post Standard 15 December 1918. McGuire File. Onondaga County Public Library; Wittke, Carl. The Irish In America (Baton Rouge: Louisiana State University Press, 1956), 277. Dorries, Reinhard. Imperial Challenge: Ambassador Count Bernstorff and German-American Relations, 1908-1917. Chapel Hill: Universityof North Carolina Press, 1989, 74.

51 Brewing and Liquor Interests And German And Boshevik Propaganda. Report and Hearings Of The Subcommittee On The Judiciary. United States Senate, vol. I, Report, XVI; (Washington, D.C.: Government Printing Office), 1396-97. For his efforts, McGuire was paid between $14,800 - $22,000 for his books, for his operation of the Irish Press and News Service and for the expenses of his agents sent to Ireland to gather information. Ibid., 1397. Park, Robert. The Immigrant Press And Its Control (New York, 1922), 427-8.

52 Bernstorff, op.cit., 54; Dorries, op.cit., 74.

53 Wittke, Carl. The German-Americans. op.cit., Viereck, op.cit., 24-5; Brewing and Liquor Interests II, op.cit, 1307; 1504.

54 "Mr. McGuire In London". Catholic Sun 28 August 1914-15. The article noted that McGuire arrived shortly after the war began. He was hoping to board ship for Ireland "in a day or two". "Mrs. Day Writes She And Doctor Are In London, Have Plenty Of Funds". Syracuse Herald 18 August 1914: 3; "James K. McGuire's Great Book". Syracuse Herald 16 March 1916:6.

55 McGuire, James K. The King, The Kaiser And Irish Freedom (New York: Devon-Adair, 1915), 9.

56 Ibid. 5.

57 Ibid., 18, 119-22; 139; 156-59.

58 For a complete list of Irish heroes, see Ibid., 177-78.

59 Ibid., 234; 210; 214.

60 Ibid., 21.
61 Ibid., 34-41.
62 Ibid., 46-49.
63 Ibid., 51.
64 Ibid., 147-49.
65 Ibid., 69; 70; 80; 84-87.
66 Ibid., 95.
67 Ibid., 99-102; 152.
68 Ibid., 162-63; 168-69; 285.
69 "McGuire Says Book Is Made Necessary By Studied Violations Of Neutrality". Syracuse Herald. 15 March 1915:3.
70 Thomas Addis Emmet (1828-1919) was the grand-nephew of Robert Emmett, the subject of numerous articles in McGuire's Catholic Sun. Thomas Addis Emmett graduated from medical school in 1850. He was recognized as an outstanding surgeon and author of medical texts. Emmet endorsed Home Rule, especially after an 1871 visit to Ireland. Emmet authored a condemnation of Britain in Ireland Under English Rule (2 volumes, 1903). He served as President of the Irish National Federation, an anti-Parnell support group, for over a decade. In Johnson, Allen and Malone, Dumas (eds.), Dictionary of American Biography VI (New York: Charles Scribner's Sons, 1931), 145-146.
71 John Mitchel (1815-1875) was a Presbyterian lawyer, Irish nationalist and political journalist for the Nation, edited by Charles Gavan Duffy. Mitchel later established his own paper, The United Irishman. His criticism of British mismanagement of the famine crisis brought his imprisonment in the penal colony of Tasmania, where he wrote his Jail Journal (1854). His vehement hatred of England was at the time inconsistent with the moderate policies of O'Connell and Parnell. Mitchel escaped to New York, began an anti-British paper, The Irish-American, which became controversial because of his advocacy of slavery and his criticism of Lincoln, for which he was again imprisoned. He returned to Ireland and was elected to Parliament. The results were invalidated because he was a convicted felon. He died before the issue of his contested seat was resolved. "Mitchel, John". In Malone, Dumas (ed.), Dictionary of American Biography vol. 13 (New York: Charles Scribner's Sons, 1934), 35-36.
72 McGuire, James K. What Could Germany Do For Ireland? (New York: Wolfe Tone Company, 1916).
73 Ibid.
74 Ibid., 61-63; 280-305.
75 Ibid., 70; 81.
76 Ibid., 255.

77 Ibid., 307. McGuire was probably correct in this regard. For example, Arthur S. Link in Woodrow Wilson And The Progressive Era, 1910 – 1917 (New York: Harper Brothers, 1953) in his "Essay on Sources: German Atrocities" stated the accusations against Germany were untrue since American reporters with the German armies in Belgium and France repudiated the British charges in numerous articles in the American press. Hence, their impact on American public opinion was minimal. For a list of the articles and authors, see Ibid., 307.

78 Ibid., 59-60; 82; 285.

79 Ibid., 284-85.

80 The Syracuse Herald advertisement headlined with the phrase "Fair Play For Germany", January 1916. The New York Times noted McGuire's first book was banned in both Ireland and England. "What Could Germany Do For Ireland?" New York Times 29 January 1916:5. Apparently McGuire also wrote another book for the G.I.S. entitled, "What Germany Could Do For America. Liquor Interests, vol. II, 1504.

81 McGuire, What Could Germany..,op. cit., 115.

82 Ibid., 119; 121-123.

83 Ibid., 126.

84 Ads for The King, The Kaiser, and Irish Freedom appeared in The Catholic Sun on 12, 19, 26 November 1915, pp. 6, 9, 10 respectively, and on 3 December 1915: 6. "The King, The Kaiser and Irish Freedom". James K. McGuire. Illustrated. Devon-Adair Co., $1.35 New York Times 16 May 1915.

85 Ads for McGuire's, What Could Germany Do For Ireland? were in the Catholic Sun 21 January 1916: 9; and on 11 February 1916:2. The book review from Irish World appeared in the Catholic Sun in an article entitled, "Ireland's Case Clearly Stated" 18 February 1916:2; 12 May 1916: 7; 15 September 1916:8.

86 "Former Mayor Asks.... McGuire File, vol. 15, (Ma-Mc Onondaga Public Library). This endorsement probably contributed to his books being banned after the United States entered the war.

87 Casement, Roger. The Crime Against Ireland And How The War May Right It" (New York, 1914); "Casement's Alliance Idea". New York Times 31 December 1914.

88 Casement, The Crime... op.cit.,1; 24; 61; 62; 64.

89 Ibid., 26; 27; 29; 30.

90 Ibid., 17; 77; 79; 83.Ironically, these same troops would be actively recruited by Casement during his stay in Gdermany. His efforts to raise an Irish Brigade were a dismal failure.

91 Ibid., 14; 24; 27-28; 33; 59.

92 Ibid., 24; 84; 85.

93 Ibid., 8; 13; 47.

94 Ibid., 1; 34; 81; 96
95 Aan de Weil, op. cit., 48; 49; 53.
96 Cuddy, Edward. "Irish-American Propagandists And American Neutrality, 1914-1917". Mid-America vol. xlix, 1967, 252-75.
97 Hirst, David. "German Propaganda in The United States, 1914-1917". Unpublished Ph. D., Northwestern University, 1962, 46.
98 Landau, Henry. The Enemy Within: The Inside Story of German Sabotage In America (New York: Putnam and Sons, 1937), 276.
99 Peterson, H. C., Propaganda For War: The Campaign Against American Neutrality, 1914-1917 (Norman: University of Oklahoma Press, 1939), 138.
100 Link, Arthur S. "Essay On Sources: Irish-Americans And The War". Woodrow Wilson and the Progressive Era, 1910-1917. (New York: Harper Brothers; 1953), 310.
101 Leslie, Shane. The Irish Issue In Its American Aspect (New York: Scribner's and Sons, 1917), 180. John Randolph Leslie (1888-1971) was a member of the Protestant Anglo-Irish land-owning establishment. A cousin to Sir Winston Churchill, Leslie converted to Catholicism, adopted Home Rule Nationalism and changed his given name to appear more Irish. He served in the British Ambulance Corps during World War I, was invalided out and later sent to the United States to work for American intervention on the Allied side after the failed Rising in 1916. His book revealed his knowledge of Irish and American history. His political career was aborted by the success of Sinn Fein in 1918.
http://www.pgil-eirdata.org/html/pgil_datasets/authors/l/Leslie,S/life.htm.
Leslie worked closely with the British Embassy, later endorsing its claim the Easter Rising was primarily a German plot. Because of is support for Home Rule, his efforts were regarded with suspicion by some high-ranking British officials. Hartley, Stephen. The Irish Question as a Problem in British Foreign Policy. New York: St. Martin's Press, 54-55; 154-155.
102 Ibid., 180; New York Times Book Review 16 May 1915. That a critical review of McGuire's book was published in the New York Times in May 1916 should not have surprised him. At the time, the paper was owned by Adolph Simon Ochs, a second-generation German-American, one of the newspapers many Irish Nationalists believed was under the influence of Britain. The Times sided with Wilson on preparedness, its general manager, Julius Ochs Adler, attending military camp at Plattsburgh, New York in 1914. "The New York Times Company". http://www.funduniverse.com/company-histories/The-New-York-Times-Company-Co.. Kington, Donald M. "The Plattsburg Movement And Its Legacy". Relevance: The Quarterly Journal of The Great War Society, 1-6 http://www.worldwar1.com/tgws/reloll.htm.
103 "Works of Syracuse Two Score Writers On Exhibition At Library". Syracuse

Herald 11 November 1917; Syracuse Library Bulletin, vol. XI, no. 2 December 1917; "Syracuse An Unusually Good Place To Reside". Post-Standard 10 March 1917.

104 For different views, see "Too Proud To Fight". http://ushistorysite.blogspot.com/2007/04/too-proud-to-fight-vs-involvement-in.html; "Wilson and The Lusitania" New York Times 15 November 1921.

105 Bernstorff, op. cit., 145-6.

106 Liquor Interests, vol. I, 1381-85; vol. II, 1484-1502; According to the German military attaché, he was authorized as early as 26 January 1915 to use sabotage on American territory. Von Papen, Franz. Memoirs (London: Andre Deutsch, 1952), 46.

107 "Dernburg Takes Up Peace Principles". New York Times 9 May 1915; "Would Silence Dernburg". New York Times 12 May 1915.

108 "Meyer, Kuno". http://celt.ucc.ie/meyerext.html.

109 Broecker, Galen. "Germany And The Irish Revolutionary Movement, 1914-1918". (M.A. Thesis. University of Oregon, 1951), 10-11; 14; 22. This was later proven untrue. Richard Meyer was one of a few Jews working in the Foreign Office of the Berlin government. He volunteered to work with Casement in Germany. Years later, in gratitude for his years of service, the Nazi government allowed him to emigrate to Sweden. Doerries, Reinhard R. Prelude To The Easter Rising: Sir Roger Casement In Imperial Germany (London: Frank Cass, 2000), 26-27; fn 27.

110 Plowman, 2003,op.cit.,91

111 O'Luing, Sean. Kuno Meyer: A Biography. Dublin: Geographic Publications, 1991, 89.

112 Plowman, 2003, op.cit., 93-94.

113 "Former Mayor Asks".... op. cit..

114 "M'Guire Praises Germany's Role". Syracuse Herald 15 July 1916:6. It was later shown the Lusitania carried munitions destined for the Allies. See "Too Proud To Fight". http://ushistorysite...

115 Golway, op. cit., 187; 197; 223; Liquor Interests, vol. II. op. cit., 3699.

116 Documents Relative To Sinn Fein, 16 – 17. One of those "Irish" was apparently James K. McGuire, whose Washington connections have already been noted. The evidence is in a letter by Von Skal to Devoy, requesting assistance from him to obtain a passport to enable him leave the United States. Van Skal states: "I have since learned that the hitch is in the Department of Justice which intervened at the last moment. I want to ask you whether you could help by finding out, through Mr. Maguire [sic] perhaps or somebody else, who must be seen in the Department of Justice in regard to this matter".

There is no response to the letter, but it's references to someone high up in the Democratic Party being able to get the request forwarded as far as the State Department and then falling through at the behest of the Department of Justice, reveals again the importance of James K. McGuire in the higher circles of German subversion in America("The Von Igel Raid Recalled". Letter George von Skal to John Devoy 22 March 1920, in William O'Brien and Desmond Ryan (eds). Devoy's Post Bag, vol II, 1880-1928 Dublin: C.J. Fallon Ltd., 1984, 540.

The date of the letter indicated McGuire was still on good terms with his colleagues in FOIF, a situation that would change in the near future, earning him the ire of Devoy. See "Fenian Chief's Estimate of James K. McGuire", Catholic Sun 19 July 1923.

117 Broecker, op. cit., 35-36; Golway, op.cit., 9; Documents Relative To Sinn Fein, 8; "Mayor Accuses Hylan As A Member Of The German Propaganda Here: Associate of O'Leary and Cohalan" New York Times 31 October 1917; "Mitchel Quotes German Praise of Hylan's Aid". New York Times 2 November 1917.

118 Jones and Hollister, op.cit., 248; Wittke, German-Americans... op.cit., 62.

119 Liquor Interests, vol. II, op.cit., 1540-44; 2696.

120 Ward, op.cit., 93; 130-131.

121 Liquor Interests, vol. II, op.cit., 2697-99.

122 (122) Tuchman, Barbara. The Zimmerman Telegram., 71. "David Lamar: The Original Wolf of Wall Street" https://unrememberedhistory.com/tag/david-lamar/.

123 Gompers, Samuel. Seventy Years Of Life And Labor: An Autobiography (New York: E. P. Dutton, 1925), vol. II, 31 – 32.

124 O'Connor, Richard. The German-American In America: An Informal History (Boston: Little, Brown and Company, 1968), 402-403.

125 Butler, Richard J. and Driscoll, Joseph. Dock Walloper: The Story of "Big Dick" Butler. (New York: G. P. Putnam's Sons, 1933), 193- 204. Edward von Mach (1870 – 1929) was a German-born Harvard-educated writer and art historian. During World War I he sought to encourage pro-German sentiment in What Germany Wants. His ties to Harvard were questioned by then President A. Lawrence Lowell. He, with George S. Viereck, endorsed Harding's candidacy in 1920. "Von Mach's Position At Harvard" New York Times 3 March 1916; "Dr. Von Mach Heads German Vote Drive". New York Times 6 September 1920.

Paolo Vaccarelli 1876-1936 was a Sicilian-born gangster who adopted an Irish name upon coming to America after becoming a prize fighter. He founded the Five Points Gang and used its many members in service of Tammany Hall politician "Big Tim" Sullivan. Vaccarelli obeyed Tammany orders to clean up the Bowery because of the negative publicity he had drawn to it–gang fights, murder plots, and bordellos frequented by New York's social elites. www.laendb.com/php/Info.php?name=Paul%20Kelly. "Foiled German Plot To Tie Up Docks". New York Times 14 September 1915.

126 Gompers, op.cit., vol. II, 334-40; John Brisben Walker (1847-1931) was the Pennsylvania-born publisher of Cosmopolitan Magazine which he sold to William Randolph Hearst in 1905. Walker was active in the Friends of Peace, acting as Chairman of its national convention in 1915. "Walker, John Brisben". Dictionary of American Biography, vol. 19 (New York: Charles Scribner's Sons, 1936), 347-48. Henry Weisman was a German immigrant, labor leader, President of the New York Chapter of the National German-American Alliance and National Chairman of The Friends of Peace. See "Gompers Denounces Friends of Peace". New York Times 3 September 1915. The national conference adopted a resolution calling for a ban on the shipment and sale of munitions to belligerents. For its full text, see Viereck, George S. Spreading Germs of Hate, New York: Horace Liveright, 1930), 99. According to Gompers, a third activist of Labor's Peace Council was Alexander P. Moore (1867-1930), publisher of the Pittsburgh Leader who was head of publicity for the Chicago convention. He is possibly best known as the fourth husband of actress Lillian Russell. After her death, Moore was a diplomat to Spain and later Peru. Gomper's, Seventy Years… 342; "Plan For Peace Meeting" New York Times 20 August 1915; "Lillian Russell A Bride". New York Times 13 June 1912.

127 Dorries, Reinhard. The Imperial Challenge: Ambassador Count Bernstorff And German-American Relations, 1908-1917 (Chapel Hill: University of North Carolina Press, 1989), 184.

128 Gompers, op.cit., 349; Dorries, op.cit., fn 266, 340; "The Providence Journal Company: Information From Answers.Com http://www.answers.com/topic/the-providence-journal-company.

129 "Friends of Peace Already In Clash". New York Times 5 September 1915; Child, 81; Jones and Hollister, 172-182; Link, Neutrality.. 562-63; Liquor Interests, vol. II, 1404; 1571-74; 1582-85. The full text of the goals of the Labor's National Peace Council can be found In Ibid., 1573; "Quits Labor's Peace Council In Disgust". New York Times 11 August 1915; "Asks US To Stop War Supply Ships". New York Times 9 July 1915. The official American government investigation of the war credits Gompers for the failure of Labor's National Peace Council. See Liquor Interests, Report vol I., XII.

130 "Labor's National Peace Council". Information Quarterly vol. I, No. 1, April 1915. Princeton University Elizabeth Foundation (New York: R. R. Bouker Company, 1915).

131 "Shipping Munitions: Lusitania On-Line" http://lusitania.net/munitions.htm.

132 Carroll, F. M. American Opinion And The Irish Question, 1910 – 1923

(New York, St. Martin's Press, 1978), 49; Larkin, Emmet. James Larkin, 1876-1947: Irish Labour Leader (London: Routledge and Kegan Paul, 1965), 188; Dorries, op.cit., 183; 331, note 196; O'Connor, Richard: The German-Americans...op.cit., 403. Benjamin Gitlow refers to Larkin as the founder of the American Communist Movement. The Whole of Their Lives (New York: Scribners and Sons, 1948), 42.

133 Larkin, Emmet. James Larkin 1876-1947: Irish Labor Leader. London: Routledge and Kegan Paul,1965, 190-193.

134 Larkin, op. cit.,.,349, fn 266; Schwab, op.cit., 367;384

135 Golway, op.cit., 209; Carroll, op.cit., 49. Larkin, Emmett, op.cit., 193-94; 205-208, Doerries, op.cit., 183; 340 fn 264 lists his contacts as high-ranking members of the the German diplomatic corps and members of the Clan-na-Gael. They included Franz von Bopp, Roger Casement, Franz von Papen, Bernard Dernburg, Karl Boy-Ed Wolf von Igel, Kuno Meyer and Lothar Witzke, and James K. McGuire, all tied to German sabotage and subversion. Emmett Larkin(no relation) contends that Larkin was especially attached to the cause of revolutionary Irish nationalism. This brought him the support of Thomas J. Clarke of the IRB. Clarke wrote a note introducing Larkin to John Devoy, editor of The Gaelic American and leader of the Clan-na-Gael. Emmett Larkin cites extensively from a document published years later revolving around monetary claims against the German government for alleged sabotage by German agents in America and Mexico, 1914-17, including James K. McGuire. Emmett Larkin, 190-93, fn. 2. Affidavit of Mr. James Larkin, no. 990-A, Record of the Boundary and Claims Commission and Arbitrations, National Archives, Department of State, Washington, D. C. 22 January 1934.

136 Gitlow, Benjamin, The Whole of Their Lives (New York: Scribners and Sons, 1948), 39.

137 Schwab, op.cit., 381.

138 Landau, Henry. The Enemy Within: The Inside Story of German Sabotage In America (New York: G. P. Putnam's Sons, 1937), 276-277.

139 Dorries, op. cit., 340.

140 Gitlow, op.cit., 39

141 Schwab, op.cit., 382.

142 Liquor Interests, vol. II, 1397-98.

143 Landau, op.cit., 8-9; Jones, J. R. and Hollister, Paul M. The German Secret Service in America (Boston: Small, Maynard, 1918), 171-172; Documents Relative To Sinn Fein, 8.

144 O'Dea, John. History of the Ancient Order of Hibernians and Ladies Auxiliary, (Philadelphia: Keystone Printing Co., 1923), vol. III, 1500-1501.

145 Larkin, Emmett, op.cit., 214; Thomas J. Mooney (1892-1942) was the son of

an Irish labor leader and Socialist, a career path he soon followed. Mooney and an aide were tried and convicted and sentenced for their alleged involvement in the bombing of a Preparedness Day Parade in San Francisco in July 1916 in which ten people were killed and 40 injured. After serving 23 years in prison, he was pardoned when an investigation revealed perjured testimony resulted in his conviction. Georgakas, Dan. "About Tom Mooney". http://www.english.illinois.edu/maps/poets/m_r/ridge/mooney.htm. Franz von Bopp was later convicted for violating America's neutrality laws and served five years in prison, being released in 1920. "Free German Consuls From Prison Today". New York Times 5 October 1920. Lore continued his ties to Germans and Irish revolutionaries for at least a year following the conclusion of hostilities. In Gitlow, op.cit., 41.

146 Larkin, Emmett, op.cit., 214. Black Tom was a major munitions depot in New Jersey. The German government authorized sabotage of the facilities to prevent the supplies from reaching the Allies. The losses were estimated at $20 million and seven people were killed. "The Forgotten Attack On New York Harbor". http://www.oldsaltblog.com/2009/07/30/the-black-tom-explosion-theforgotten-attack-on-new-york-harbor.

147 Ibid. 217-218, fn 4; Gitlow, op.cit., 43-44.

148 Larkin, op. cit., 218. Given their close association, the Clan member who aided Larkin was probably McGuire.

149 O'Dea, op.cit., vol. III, 1491. Cronin, Sean. The McGarrity Papers (Tralee, County Kerry, Ireland, 1972), 50-51.

150 "German Filibusterer Caught Off Irish Shore". Catholic Sun April 1916: 1,2; "Roger Casement, Gentlemen and Patriot" Catholic Sun 5 May 1916:2.

151 "Sinn Fein Revolutionaries Wage War In Dublin". Catholic Sun 28 April 1916:2. This plan is very close to that mentioned in the message sent by Daniel Cohalan to German Ambassador von Bernstorff on 17 April 1916.

152 "Uprising In Ireland". Catholic Sun 5 May 1916: 1,2.

153 Golway, op.cit., 213.

154 Documents Relative To Sinn Fein, 1; Broecker, 15.

155 Devoy, Recollections of An Irish Rebel, 397-98; Wittke, op.cit., 280; Golway, op.cit., 203.

156 Golway, op.cit., 203-204.

157 Cronin, Sean. The McGarrity Papers: Revelations of the Irish Revolutionary Movement In Ireland and America, 1900-1940 (New York: Anvil Books) 53.

158 Spense, Richard. "Englishmen in New York: The SIS – The American Station, 1915 – 1921". Intelligence and National Security. 19 (3), Autumn, 2004, 511-537.

159 Devoy, Recollections...; Golway, 204. They had legitimate grounds for their

suspicion of Quinn, a second-generation Irish-American, wealthy corporate lawyer and prominent patron and collector of modern art. While associated with Devoy and Cohalan, he also worked for British Intelligence, prior to, during and subsequent to World War I. He was supposedly the case officer for a British agent whose mission was to infiltrate Irish and German anti-British groups in the United States. During the war he acted as custodian of alien property seized under the Trading With The Enemy Act. For details, see "Quinn, John." National Cyclopedia of American Biography vol. XVIII (Ann Arbor, Michigan: University Microfilm, 1967), 39; Spence, Richard B. Secret Agent 666: Aleister Crowley, (Port Townsend: Feral House 2000), 54-57; 60-61. Spence's work is considered speculative and lacks documentation.

160 Dudgeon, Jeffrey. "He Could Tell You Things". http://www.drb.ie/more_details/08-09-28/he_could_tell_you_things.aspx 12pp. See also Reinhard Dorries, Prelude to the Easter Rising, London: Frank Cass, 2000, 18-19. There were rumors McGoey had been detained in Germany or executed by the British. Dorries suggests such was his fate. Dudgeon contends McGoey survived the war, but his movements after he left Germany for Ireland in 1916 remain a mystery.

McGuire belatedly reached similar conclusions. The Catholic Sun published a letter from the sister of Countess Markiewicz who fought with the rebels in the Rising for which she received a life sentence. The letter was to Mr. Gavan Duffy, one of Casement's defense attorneys. In it, the author quotes Casement as believing the Rising was a "fatal mistake". See "Roger Casement Landed From Germany Submarine At Tralee To Prevent Irish Revolution". Catholic Sun 8 December 1916:8.

161 Devoy, John. Recollections of an Irish Rebel. Shannon, Ireland: Irish University Press, 1969, 442-

162 Ibid.,

163 Ibid.,

164 Bureau of Military History, 1913-1921: Statement by Witness Document No. W.S. Witness:1,108 Jeremiah O'Leary. File No.,S.2431, 6.

165 Capt. Hans Walther Luigi Boehm (1873-1959) worked in the department of the German General Staff responsible for Intelligence, Press and Propaganda. His nominal responsibility was to assist Roger Casement's recruitment efforts of Irish POW's in Germany from March to September 1He was a key contact with Anthony Brogan and John Kenny, a Clan member and courier in the United States. Boehm was surveilled by the BOI in the United States since his activities included being a spy and a saboteur. On his return to Germany in January 1917, his ship was stopped by British authorities. He was interrogated and imprisoned. "Hans W L Boehm" http://irishbrigade.eu/other-men/germans/boehm.html, 1-10.

166 Ibid., 1.
167 Chinn, Carl. "Voices of War and Peace/Kitchener's New Army". http://voicesofwarandpeace.org/portfolio/kitcheners-new-army/
168 Bureau of Military History, 1913-1912, File no.5-2431, op. cit.,7.
169 Dorries, Reinhard. Prelude to the Easter Rising: Sir Roger Casement in Imperial Germany. London: Routledge, 2Sir Roger Casement to Joseph McGarrity, 1 March 1915 #41, 83.
170 Ibid. Lieuteneant Ret. H.W. Boehm on Casement and Ireland. 2 March 1915 #54, 98.
171 Ibid. Chief of the Admiralty to Secretary of State of the Foreign Office Gottlieb von Jagow 17 March 1915, #54, 98
172 Ibid. Foreign Office to Deputy Chief of Staff of the Army, Dept. IIIb Pol.29. 29 March 1915, #62, 106-107.
173 Richard Meyer worked in the German Foreign Office. All Casement's mail, from Novemeber 1914 to April 1916 went through him. John Devoy to Joseph McGarrity, 23 April 1915 He worked for the German government until Hitler took control and revoked the citizenship rights of Jews. "Richard Meyer" http://irishbrigade.eu/other-men.germans/meyer/meyer.html.
174 Dorries, Prelude... op.cit., Draft of letter from German Foreign Office to the Deputy Chief of the Admiralty. 8 March 1915, #46, 90.
175 Ibid. Sir Roger Casement to Count Georg von Wedel 13 March 1915, #49, 93. Wedel (1862-1943) was Chief of the English Department of the Foreign Ministry, serving as Casement's day-to-day contact with the Foreign Office. http://www.irishbrigade.eu/other-men/germans/von-wedel/von-wedel.html.
176 Ibid. Sir Roger Casement to Richard Meyer 15 March 1915, #51, 95. John Devoy to Joseph McGarrity 23 April 1915 #70.
177 Bureau of Military History, 1913-1921, File No.S-2437, op. cit.,7.
178 Ibid., 7-8.
179 Dorries, Prelude..op cit., Memorandum by Ret. H. W. Boehm 24 June 1915, # 82, 131.
180 "Boehm, Irish Brigade, op. cit., 3. Fenian Graves: John Kenny (1847-1924). http://feniangraves.net/Kenny/%20 John/Bio. Htm.; Christ, Francis. "My great-grandfather, Ireland's forgotten Fenian, led secret missions for 1916" http://www.irishcentral.com/roots/history/my-great-grandfather-irelands-forgottenfenian, 6pp.
181 George Gavan Duffy (1882 – 1951) was a London-born Irishman and lawyer who served as Casement's lawyer. Following Casement's death, he moved to Dublin and became active in Sinn Fein. With Sean O' Kelly, he was Irish Republic representative to the Paris peace Conference where his protests earned him expulsion. Duffy later served briefly in the Free State government. https://www.charledgavanduffysociety.com/george-gavan.duffy.html. 3 pp.

182 "Boehm" irishbrigade, op. cit.
183 "Fenian Chief's Estimate of James McGuire". Catholic Sun. 19 July, 1923.
184 One of Lamar's most notorious events in the Rockefeller case was the hiring of members of the notorious Monk Eastman gang who savagely beat his driver, James McMahon he was unable to testify against him. Asbury, Herbert. Gangs of New York: An Informal History of the Underworld. New York: Thunder's Mouth Press,1990, 263-264.
185 "Roger Casement Letters Sent From Germany To J. K. McGuire". Catholic Sun 8 December 1916:19. McGuire indicated all proceeds from his German edition of The King, The Kaiser and Irish Freedom be given to the German Red Cross Fund. Note this was Dernburg's front for his propaganda ring in the United States.
186 "Roger Casement, Gentlemen and Patriot". Catholic Sun 5 May 1916:2; "Sir Roger Casement, Patriot". Catholic Sun 11 August 1916:2. "Says Execution of Casement Will Aid Irish Revolution". Syracuse Herald 25 April 1916:16.
187 "Sir Roger Casement's Speech From The Dock". Catholic Sun 7 July 1916:1,4. It also appeared in "Casement's Speech Recalls Emmett Farewell". Syracuse Herald 20 August 1915:5.
188 "Sir Roger Casement Executed". Catholic Sun 4 August 1916:1,4. The fact that Casement converted to Catholicism prior to his execution was duly noted.
189 "Casement Knew His Exploits Were Dangerous". Syracuse Herald 28 April 1916:12. The article cites both Jeremiah O'Leary and John Devoy as sources. O'Leary's comments justify "physical force" as the only vehicle whereby Ireland could be free. His remarks, not surprisingly, were echoed by John D. Moore, National Secretary of The Friends of Irish Freedom, who referred to similar efforts by Wolfe Tone and Robert Emmett. See also, "Who Betrayed The Irish People". Catholic Sun 12 May 1916:7. "British Planned A Pogrom". Catholic Sun 19 May 1916. Tansill, Charles Callan. America And The Fight For Irish Freedom, 1866-1922 (New York: Devon-Adair, 1957), 193. The seized papers revealed the depths to which Daniel F. Cohalan and the Clan-na-Gael and its leaders, including James K. McGuire, were involved in planning the Rising.
190 Spense, op.cit., 511-537.
191 Hartley, op.cit., 51-53;56.
192 "U.S. Government Did Not Inform England of Irish Plot, Says Lansing". Syracuse Herald 28 April 1916:12.See also Hartley, op. cit., 51-53.
193 Doyle, a Democrat still loyal to Wilson despite his role in the Casement trial, thought the clumsy handling of the Casement affair gave aid and comfort to Republicans in the election of 1916. In Cuddy, op.cit., 34. For Doyle's role and the complete wording of Senator Martin's resolution, see "President Wilson Interceding For Casement". Catholic Sun 28 June 1916:2. It was

Doyle who allegedly found out Eamon DeValera was born in New York City and had never renounced his American citizenship. He presented this through Tumulty to Wilson, who forwarded it to the British government, possibly saving DeValera's life. In "Letters, Ap. 15, 1940" Time Magazine. http://www.time.com/time/magazine/article/0.9171.789720-200.htmls. Probably it was this which led to Doyle representing DeValera and other Irish leaders when tried by Britain in the 1920's. Doyle also served as advisor to the Irish Free State Commission, 1922. For his life, see "Doyle, Michael Francis". The National Cyclopedia of American Biography, vol. XLVI. (Ann Arbor, Michigan, 1967), 454-455. As to De Valera's citizenship, he was born in New York City in 1882 of a Spanish father and an Irish mother. At the age of two he was sent back to Ireland to be raised by relatives and changed his name several times. For years he kept the story alive that it was his American citizenship which saved him from execution after the failure of the Rising 1916. DeValera fully expected to be shot. However, by the time of his trial there was widespread revulsion at the executions of the rebellion's leaders. DeValera was not then considered by British authorities as important. Only in 1922 did he admit it was more likely the lateness of his court martial which saved him. For details, see Robert Schmuhl, "Eamon De Valera: Man of Mystery" Irish AmericaFeb/Mar 2015 Http:// irishamerica.com/2016/02/eamon-de-valera-man-of-mystery/ Also Robert Schmuhl, "What Saved Dev From the Firing Squad?" Http://www.independent.ie/irish-news/1916/the- rising-explained/what-saved-devalera-from-the-firing -squad? As to Wilson's rejection of clemency, see Tansill, op.cit., 204. According to Ward, Doyle was wary of the close ties between the Clan and the German Imperial Government, an issue that would grow in the coming months. In Ward, op.cit., 107.

194 Tansill, op.cit., 207-212; Doorley, Michael. Irish-American Diaspora Nationalism: The Friends of Irish Freedom, 1916-1935 (London: Four Courts Press, 2005) p. 50.

A Catholic Sun article implied that American betrayal was the cause of both Casement's capture and the insurrection's failure. "It was impossible to listen to the day's depositions without gaining the strongest impressions that the authorities were warned and that they expected the arrival of Sir Roger Casement in Ireland. The farmers and constables apparently went out of their way at unusual hours to find themselves in the path of Sir Roger". "Sir Roger Casement Sentenced to Death". Catholic Sun 30 June 1916:2. Other evidence suggests the execution would have proceeded regardless. See Blum, Joseph Tumulty, op.cit., 107-109; Doorley, fn 40, 50. Cuddy, quoting Frank P. Polk, counselor for the State Department, in October 1916, that the resolution was transmitted to the British government before the execution, but it was rejected by them. Secretary of State Lansing however, indicated the White House wanted it sent on the day before the execution. On the day of the execution, an American official presented the petition, with both sides showing "only casual interest in it". Cuddy, 114, fn. 34. The Polk interpretation suggests Wilson was trying to curry support among the hyphenates on the eve of the election of 1916. The Lansing assessment reveals Wilson's long-term, if latent, Anglophilism.

195 "Roger Casement, Patriot". Catholic Sun 11 August 1916:2. "Determined To Learn Reason For Delay On Casement Message". Syracuse Herald 8 August 1916:4. Interestingly, the Senate resolution requesting clemency for Sir Roger Casement was introduced by Joseph D. Phelan, author of the Report condemning James K. Sullivan, McGuire's ally in the Santo Domingo asphalt scandals. To his credit, a telegram from Senator Phelan was printed in The Catholic Sun in response to McGuire's request for an inquiry. Addressed to McGuire, Phelan said the message was sent and received on a timely basis. See "Casement Senate Resolution". Catholic Sun 8 September 1916:8.

196 "Press Denounces Killing of Sir Roger Casement". Catholic Sun 18 August 1916:7.

197 "Sir Roger Casement Executed". Catholic Sun 4 August 1916:2. Above the article was a large photograph of Sir Roger Casement described as an "Irish Rebel, Victim of British Vengeance, Executed on Thursday, August 3 1916; Became A Catholic Some Weeks Ago. He Died For Ireland. May He Rest In Peace". Sir Arthur Conan Doyle denounced British repression in "A Most Unlovely Spectacle – Sir. A. Conan Doyle's Scathing Criticism". Catholic Sun 1 December 1916:2.

198 "Irish Uphold Revolt In Dublin". New York Times 1 May 1916:1.

199 "Call Executed Men Martyrs To Cause". New York Times 4 May 1916:2.

200 "Crowd Theater At Memorial To Irish Patriots!" Syracuse Herald 5 June 1916: 11; Goff and O'Leary To Address Irish of Syracuse". Catholic Sun 2 June 1916: 5;" Irish Martyrs Acclaimed At Great Meeting" Catholic Sun 9 June 1916:8. See, Devoy's Post-Bag vol I, 517 (Dublin, 1953). On the submarine issue, an article extolling the efforts of John Holland is found in "An Irish Inventor of The Modern Submarine." Catholic Sun 2 June 1916:9. The author states Holland was not a Fenian, although he longed for Irish freedom.

201 "Egan Denounces Devoy". New York Times 4 May 1916:2. "Warns Against Irish Made In Germany". New York Times 9 June 1915:5.

202 W. Bourke Cochran speech at Carnegie Hall, New York 14 May 1916. Cochran papers, New York Public Library. Cited in Cuddy, 109. By the end of the year, Cochran was advocating intervention by the Papacy to bring the hostilities to an end. See, "Bourke Cochran's Pleas For The Pope As World's Peace Power." Catholic Sun 8 December 1916:3.

203 "Uprising In Ireland." Catholic Sun 5 May 1916:2; "Home Rule A Sham." Catholic Sun 9 June 1916:8.
204 "Seven Leaders of Irish Rebellion Executed." Catholic Sun 12 May 1916:7; "Reign of Terror In Ireland". Catholic Sun 12 May 1916:2;8; "England's Greatest Blunder." Catholic Sun 12 May 1916:2;8; "Eighth Plunkett To Die A Martyr". Catholic Sun 19 May 1916:2. On the theory the British instigated the revolt on order to disarm the Volunteers, see "British Planned A Pogrom". Catholic Sun 19 May 1916:2.
205 "Death Speech of Thomas MacDonough, the Young Irish Poet." Catholic Sun 14 June 1916:2; "No Apology," Thomas MacDonough's Last Letter, A Tragic Document." Catholic Sun 22 September 1916:2. "Irish Martyrs of 1916", Catholic Sun 26 May 1916; "Dead Who Died For Ireland" Catholic Sun 2 June 1916:7. American Poets Memorial To Executed Irish Poets". Catholic Sun 7 July 1916:2. This last article noted poems by executed rebels Patrick H. Pearse, Thomas MacDonough and Joseph Plunkett were read. Contributors included Joyce Kilmer, Saemus O'Sheele, William Dean Howells and Peter Golden, among others. Resolutions were adopted by those present to the families of the deceased declaring respect and sympathy for the cause for which they died. Subsequent poems embracing the theme of Irish freedom were published in "The Irish Country Side: The Men Who Kept Alive The Insurrectionary Feeling In It." Catholic Sun 8 September 1916: 1,4.
206 Carroll, op.cit, 85-86.
207 "A Pathetic Figure" (Interview With Mrs. O'Hanrahan, The Aged Mother of Michael O'Hanrahan, Executed, May 4 in The Irish Revolution, and of Henry, His Brother, Sentenced To Twenty Years Imprisonment As A Rebel). Catholic Sun December 1916:2. The article was accompanied with a poem by L. M. McCraith, entitled the "Poor Old Woman". A note at the conclusion indicated the phrase "Poor Old Woman" had long been a symbolic name for Ireland. Michael O'Hanrahan was a member of the Gaelic League, Sinn Fein, the IRB and the Irish Volunteers. He was instrumental in planning the rebellion. O'Hanrahan authored two books dealing with Irish problems. "Michael O'Hanrahan" http://www.Carlowcountrymuseum.com/personalities/Michael-o-harralan/index.html.
208 "Will Gaunt Famine Destroy Ireland?" Catholic Sun 1 December 1916:2.
209 "Is Ireland Facing A Famine" Catholic Sun 9 February 1917:5.
210 James Connolly (1868-1916) was a Scottish-born, Irish Nationalist and Socialist, who spent several years in the United States organizing for the radical I.W.W. He was one of the founders of the Irish Citizen Army and a confidante of Tom Clarke and the IRB. He was executed following the 1916 rebellion. http://1916rising.com/bioConnolly.htm. For the interview,

see "Mrs. James Connolly-Interview With The Wife of The Iron Man of The Dublin Rebellion". Catholic Sun 20 October 1916:2.

211 Edward Thomas Kent (1881-1916) changed his name to the Gaelic version, Eamonn Ceannt after joining the Gaelic League. He joined the I.R.B., helped found the Irish Volunteers and was involved in planning the Easter Rebellion. He was one of the signatories of the Irish Declaration of Independence. Kent was executed by the British soon after the rebellion was crushed. "The Seven Signatories - Eamonn Ceannt"- http://unitedirelander.blogspot.com/2006/04/seven-signatories-eamonn-ceannt-html. "Interview With The Widow of Edward Kent". Catholic Sun 19 January 1917:8.

212 "The Killing of Skeffington, The Dublin Pacifist". Catholic Sun 14 June 1916:2. The circumstances of his death resulted in a government cover-up. The informer was dishonorably discharged from the army; the perpetrator spent some time in a mental asylum and was later sent to Canada on a full pension. The widow refused any government compensation. Sean MacAodh, "Irelands Own-Francis Sheehy-Skeffington Feminist and Socialist Patriot (1878-1916)." http://irelandsown.net/sheehy.html., "Hannah Sheehy-Skeffington". http://multitext.uccc.ie/d/Hanna-Sheehy-Skeffington. In another article for the Irish Press and News Service, Mrs Skeffington described conditions in Ireland, summed up by its subtitle, "Famine, Conscriptions or Revolution: Ireland's Choice In The New Year". Catholic Sun 5 January 1917:7. Mrs. Sheehy-Skeffington even appeared in Oswego, New York making an address, "British Militarism As I Have Known It". Mrs. Sheehy-Skeffington speaks in Oswego". Catholic Sun 9 March 1917:2. Apparently, this was the standard talk she gave in the lecture circuit, having delivered a similar one to a packed house at Carnegie Hall three months earlier. See "Unique Demonstration". Catholic Sun 19 January 1917:8.

213 Leslie, Irish Issue op.cit., 184.

214 "Padraic Colum, http://www.answers.com/topic/padriaccolum, "The Irish Countryside: The Men Who Kept Alive the Insurrectionary Feeling In It." Catholic Sun 8 September 1916:1;4.

215 "Seamas' McManus Coming To Syracuse To Lecture". Catholic Sun 17 November 1916:7, "Seamas McManus To Lecture In Syracuse On December 7; Catholic Sun 1 December 1916:5. For his second lecture, tickets were sold to at the office of the Catholic Sun, among other places.

216 On McGuire, see Catholic Sun 15 September 1916:8. On Casement, see Catholic Sun 8 December 1916:10.

217 "Irish Republican Flags". Catholic Sun 25 August 1916:2. These latter two were printed by Wolfe Tone Publishing Company, the same house which published McGuire's first pro-German book. McGuire was apparently not

above profiting from these tragedies. The ad for his book appeared in the <u>Catholic Sun</u> 15 September 1916:8.
218 Ward, op.cit., 112; Carroll, op.cit., 78; Doorley, op.cit., 52.
219 "Living Condition In Dublin". <u>Catholic Sun</u> 1 July 1916:2.
220 Carroll, op.cit., 79.
221 "Irish Relief Fund:" <u>Catholic Sun</u> 8 September 1916:8.
222 Lady Aberdeen, Ishbel Maria Majoribanks (1857-1939) was the wife of a Liberal politician who was Lord Lieutenant of Ireland in the 1860's and again from 1906-1915. She worked tirelessly to improve Irish industry, especially arts and crafts. Her husband was later Governor-General of Canada. She was interested in Women's health issues and founded several organization's to improve their condition. McGuire's <u>Catholic Sun</u> article may have been a response to Lady Aberdeen's appeal for funds to assist the women and children in those districts of Dublin damaged in the Rising. It did not specify, as did the Irish Relief Fund, the dependents of the martyrs executed or imprisoned as a result of the Rebellion. In addition, her work in Ireland received mixed reviews, where she was described as being "loved, loathed, respected and ridiculed." In 7Biogaphies. http://www..scoilnet.ie/women in history/content/unit4/biog/html. For a brief biography, see "Ishbel; Marchioness of Aberdeen and Temair http://www.geocities.com/darniella/geo/ishbel.html? 20095. For her letter, consult" Ireland's Soul Needs." <u>New York Times</u> 6 June 1916. Apparently numerous "relief" funds were established following the Easter Rebellion, and monies designated for relief of the dependents and executed martyrs was mistakenly sent to the wrong organization. The groups differed, not only by specifying for whom the funds were to assist, but philosophically, claiming the money was not sent as charity, but as a tribute to the valor and patriotism of their beloved dead. The government is well able to help the wives and families of other sufferers of the revolution. See "Mix Up In Relief Fund." <u>Catholic Sun</u> 7 July 1916:2.
223 <u>Documents Relative To Sinn Fein</u>. 16-17; Carroll, 78
224 Ward, op.cit., 128-29; Carroll, op.cit., 80-81.
225 "England Bans Out Two New York Irishmen." <u>New York Times</u> 26 July 1916:35.
226 Hartley, op.cit., 109; 110.
227 Carroll, 81, "John A. Murphy Returns From Dublin". <u>Catholic Sun</u> 15 September 1916:10.
228 Doorley suggests that Cohalan's comparison of Irish suffering to that of Belgium and America in the wake of The Rebellion was an exaggeration. Peasants were prosperous as a result of the war, and such destition as did exist was due primarily to social and economic conditions, not the aborted revolution. Doorley, op.cit., 52.

229 Documents Relative To Sinn Fein, 27-28; Ward, op.cit., 128.
230 Documents Relative To Sinn Fein, 25-6; Ward, op.cit., 130.
231 Goff, cited in Doorley, op.cit., 54. John J. Curley was the brother of Boston Democratic politician, James M. Curley. Apparently this revealed a growing opposition to the Irish-German political alliance by the Irish political establishment.
232 Hohlt to Perl. German Foreign Archives Office 15 January 1915.
233 Benbow, Dr. Mark. "The Spies Among Us In World War I" http://mapado.com/en/arlington-2/spies-among-us-in- world-war-I 13 October 2016.
234 Sherburne Hopkins (1867 – 1932) was a prominent Washington, D. C. lawyer and lobbyist who traced his roots back to America's earliest settlers. He was a Navy veteran, served in the Spanish – American war and was a member of the Naval reserve. His clients were among America's wealthiest industrialists. He also served the interests of businessmen and politicians in Central America which linked him to arms smuggling and the Mexican Revolution. When his affairs became public knowledge after a break – in of his office his interest in Mexican affairs waned but he continued to work through surrogates such as Felix A. Sommerfeld. His activities were investigated by Congress in 1920.
235 Freilitzsch, Heribert von. In Plain Sight: Felix A. Sommerfeld, Spymaster In Mexico, 1908 – 1Henselstone verlag, 2012, 115.
236 "Captain Hopkins Charges Letters Were Stolen As Part of a Conspiracy". Washington Times. 28 June 1914.
237 "Great War Blog." http://ww1blog.osburneink.com/? P =6889
238 "Bridgeport Projectile Company" http://connecticutmills.org/find/details/bridgeport - projectile- co.
239 Ibid.
240 "Western Cartridge Company ".Into the 21st Century" http:// Winchester.com/company.info/history/pages/into -the – 21st – century.aspx.
241 Katz, Friedrich. The Secret War In Mexico: Europe, The United States and the Mexican Revolution. Chicago: University of Chicago press, 1981, 253-511.
242 Tuck, Jim. Pancho Villa As German Agent". http:// www.mexconnect.com/articles/1853-pancho-villa-as-german-agent,6pp p.3-4
243 Katz, Secret War…, op. cit., 253 – 526.
244 Viereck, George S. Spreading Germs of Hate. New York: Horace, Liveright, 1930, 105.
245 Investigation into Mexican Affairs. Hearing Before a Subcommitteee of the Committee on Foreign Relations. United States Senate, sixty-sixth Congress, pursuant to S. Res. 106, (1920) 2536 – 2537;2564 – 2567.
246 Katz, Secret War…op. cit., 354.
247 Ibid., 350-383.

248 Heckscher, August. Woodrow Wilson (New York: Scribner's and Sons, 1991) These policies produced a series of bitter diplomatic protests between Britain and the United States. In addition, a strong public posture towards Britain might put Wilson in better standing with the alienated hyphenates. Arthur S. Link, in Wilson: Confusion and Crises, 1915-1916 (Princeton: Princeton University Press, 1964) devotes two chapters to the issue. See pages, 222-280.

249 Documents Relative To Sinn Fein 25-61; Ward, op.cit., 130; "Irelands German Ally." New York Times 21 December 1916, 11;.

Chapter III - E

Shamrocks, Subversion, Sedition, and Sabotage–The Piratical Cruise of the Good Ship Gladstone, or; Raiders of the Lost Shark

Germany had a late start in obtaining bases in both the Pacific and Atlantic oceans during the 19th century. It's maneuvers to obtain them were certain to cause consternation to both Britain and the United States. Its first attempts came in Samoa and the Philippines.

Samoa was strategically located so as to control the naval approaches to the British possession of Australia and New Zealand. British, German and American rivalries emerged over Samoa in the 1870's, resulting in a tripartite division of the islands in 1889.[1] Within a decade, the United States had annexed Hawaii. En route to the Philippine Islands during the Spanish American War, US troops occupied Wake and Guam, the US government formally annexing them by the turn of the century. After Admiral Dewey destroyed the Spanish fleet at Manila, a flotilla of foreign gunboats arrived to protect the interests of rivals England and Germany. German diplomatic correspondence suggests a growing concern over the increasing power of the United States, both in the Pacific and the Caribbean.[2] The presence of its fleet in Manila was to make sure the Philippines did not go to another power without Germany obtaining territorial compensation elsewhere.[3] Germany signed a secret agreement with Spain for several islands in the Carolines and the Ladrones,[4] holding them until World War I. In addition, Germany's attempt to obtain European support to mediate events in Cuba were fruitless. Germany continued to probe into the Caribbean, but there too, it would fail to achieve the coaling stations so essential for a trans-oceanic navy, but it was not for want of trying. It was these maneuvers in an area made sensitive by the successful completion of the Panama Canal in August 1914 which undoubtedly played a role in the demise of the diplomatic career of James K. McGuire's associate, James M. Sullivan.

American involvement in the Caribbean became more important after the United States wrested from a decaying Spanish empire, almost all of its last vestiges of power in the Caribbean and in the Pacific. Cuba became a virtual protectorate and Puerto Rico, the Philippines and Guam came under direct control. Other areas were brought under American domination to protect the strategic Panama Canal and to eliminate any potential rival to American hegemony in the area. Hispaniola, incorporating both Haiti and Santo Domingo, occupied a key area with its two main access channels to the Panama Canal. Their chronic indebtedness, their political instability and the machinations of Imperial Germany to obtain a naval base in the area, gave these territories a significant potential for sabotage and subversion. Given the technology of the time, many ships were powered by coal which meant periodic refueling at friendly or neutral ports.

Dating back to the Grant administration, there were persistent rumors of the desire for possessions in the Caribbean by either France or Germany. The latter was interested in the Antilles, the Galapagos Islands, or bases in Costa Rica, Colombia or Venezuela. German intrigues in the Virgin Islands were stopped by US purchase of them for $25 million in 1917, after an initial failure in 1902.[5] German designs along the South American coast made the Venezuelan situation potentially more explosive, but US President Theodore Roosevelt resuscitated the Monroe Doctrine and backed his threats with the presence of Admiral Dewey's naval squadron. A similar problem over debt collection led to American involvement both Santo Domingo and Haiti. Again, America's interests in these possessions date back to the expansionism of the Grant administration and the diplomacy of William Seward in 1867. But, in the wake of the purchase of Alaska, US expansionism was for the time being satiated, and the treaty for annexation of Santo Domingo and Haiti was defeated.[6] Years later, with the construction of the Panama Canal in progress, the strategic location of Hispaniola became even more important. The Dominican government was threatening to default on its foreign loans. President Roosevelt, fearing Germany would provoke a crisis similar to that in Venezuela, evoked a policy of "preventive intervention" whereby the US took over the customs revenues of the territory, but guaranteed payment to all foreign creditors. It was this sensitive political crisis into which James Mark Sullivan and James K. McGuire were drawn.

Germany had always been envious of America's exclusive control of the Panama Canal. In fact as early as 1903, German agents were busy in Bogota, Colombia and its businessmen were interested in buying out the French interest in Panama.[7] That same year, Germany was also attempting to acquire Haiti, as well as the Dominican Republic, by trying to purchase from Spain a debt of $12 million owed to it by the Dominican Republic and thereby realize the German imperial ambition of obtaining an important base in the Caribbean. Hence, Theodore Roosevelt's intervention in Dominican affairs in 1905. A decade later, the opening of the Panama Canal placed Haiti in a strategic location for world traffic. In July 1914, Germany insisted on obtaining a coaling station at Mole St. Nicholas in Haiti as partial payment for an old debt and a new loan. In addition, the Imperial German government sought to obtain control over customs in Haitian ports. In fact, Germany was about to land marines there when the Great War broke out.[8] In response to vehement protest from the US State Department, America denied Germany's attempt to control Haiti and aroused much suspicion as to its intentions. Germany also renewed its demand for debt payment, as well as threatening to seize the Dominican customs house if its demands were unmet.[9] The opening of the Great War diverted Germany's attention to Europe. However, given the prevailing philosophy of geopolitics, the Caribbean was to figure in Germany's – and America's –foreign policy and draw James Mark Sullivan and James K. McGuire into controversy, scandal and allegations of subversion. The failure by Germany to obtain coaling stations for its naval squadron would reveal how deeply involved James K. McGuire was in subversive activities for the Imperial German Government.

A defensive move initiated by the German Government was commerce raiding, a strategy used by naval powers to destroy their rivals overseas trade. This prescription suited Germany, but belligerents on both sides were involved in the practice on the Atlantic and Pacific coasts. However, as will be shown, there was little the United States could do as it had few laws prohibitng such practice until 1917. Both British and American operatives were nonetheless active in monitoring the movements of German agents. Heinrich Albert and Captain Karl Boy-Ed, German naval attaché in Washington, were intimately involved in these operations as were other diplomats.[10]

Given the success of the British blockade, German ships could not return home for refueling and refitting. In addition, much of its high seas fleet was locked in home ports after its defeat by the British navy. Its merchant marine was rusting away in neutral harbors. The German government had two key concerns as a result: how could German reservists return to the Fatherland to assist in the war effort, and ; how could Germany supply raiders still at large in both the Atlantic and Pacific Oceans?

The answer to the first question was a scheme to issue fraudulent passports from Germans living in the States, a plan which involved diplomats at the highest level. When discovered, it led to their expulsion in 1915. The second meant German raiders had to be supplied by ships from neutral ports. The same personnel were involved in both operations. According to Schmalenbach, Germany had been pursuing the use of auxiliary cruisers by a variety of means for at least a half century preceding the Great War.[11]

There were at least 37 German auxiliary vessels in the South Atlantic during the first months of the war. Bisher notes German ships in both North and South America were equipped as auxiliary vessels for the German fleet, complete with armaments. Their role was to transfer supplies, especially coal and food and ammunition to German warships at sea. If caught violating the laws of their host country, the ships were interned.[12] Some supply ships were apparently successful. There was a rendezvous of several in the Easter Islands in November 1914. One, the Sacramento, had cleared a United States port with a large cargo destined for Valparaiso, Chile. Mysteriously, it arrived empty, the Captain insisting his cargo was commandeered by the German navy. The use of false manifests to mask their ulterior goals and destination was commonplace for both sides. German shipping and trading companies played leading roles in supplying the Imperial German Navy evoking vigorous diplomatic protests from the British. Major German shipping companies included the Hamburg

– America Shipping Company (HAPAG), the North German Lloyd Company and the smaller American-owned Gans Company. HAPAG was the first German company to convert an express liner into an auxiliary cruiser in 1895.[13] Given that shipping supplies by sea was the only means available for Germany to obtain supplies, it was natural that HAPAG and other lines became extensions of the German Imperial Navy. By 1914, under the astute management of Albert Ballin, the company had 73 shipping routes, a fleet of 175 steamships, including the three largest ocean liners in the world, and 20,000 employees. This property was lost as part of post-war reparations, a factor which probably contributed to Ballin's suicide.[14]

Captain Karl Boy-Ed
(1872-1930)
German Naval Attache
Library of Congress /Harris and Ewing
No Known copyright restrictions

Norman R. Hamilton
Collector of Customs of Virginia
(1877-1964)
Public Domain
(Source: Library of Congress)

Charles Evans Hughes
(1862-1948)
Lawyer, Governor of New York Republican Candidate for President, 1916
Public Domain

Ironically, neither of HAPAG's major ocean liners saw any service as auxiliary cruisers. The <u>Vaterland</u> was immobilized in Hoboken, New Jersey at the start of the was and was later used as a troopship by the United States after US entry into the war. The <u>Imperator</u> never left its home harbor in Hamburg, but was used after hostilities ceased to bring American soldiers home.[15]

The North German Lloyd line built several liners which became auxiliary cruisers for the German navy, two of which had notable success. The <u>Prinz Eitel Friedrich</u> destroyed eleven Allied ships including one American vessel during its short career. In the South Atlantic and Pacific Oceans. With supplies running low, the ship entered Newport News, Virginia in 1915 and was interned. The <u>Kronprinz Wilhelm</u> also began its career as an ocean liner, converting to an auxiliary cruiser in the beginning of the war. It focused on shipping in the South Atlantic, destroying 16 Allied merchant vessels. It too ran short of supplies and rather than risk being sunk by the British navy, it sailed into Newport News, Virginia and was interned from 1915-1917. Similar to the <u>Prinz Eitel Friedrich</u>, it became a troopship, transporting United States military to and from Europe.[16]

Telegrams intercepted by the United States State Department reveal communications between Captain Karl Boy-Ed, Ambassador Bernstorff and the German Admiralty, informing it of merchant ship movements.[17] As Bisher notes, the large colonies of German immigrants in Latin America were a source of supply, sentiment and support for its commerce raiders.[18] Similar comments were appropriate to some members of the German-American community and their Irish-American sympathizers in the United States as well.

One of the main ports of call for German commerce raiders and supply ships was Norfolk, Virginia.[19] An important shipyard almost from its founding in the mid-18th century, it officially became the Norfolk Naval Shipyard during the Civil War As noted above, many foreign vessels were interned there -or resupplied- during the war. Norfolk would be the scene of significant incident in the life of James K. McGuire.

Germany responded to British mastery of the seas in three ways:

first, it used its most formidable weapon, the submarine, but it had relatively few of them during the early stages of the war. Secondly, it used commerce raiders, referred to as Hilfskreuzer (auxiliary cruisers). There were initially built as freighters or passenger ships, but were armed and went to sea and fought as warships, manned and led by German seamen. They were lightly- armed, had no armor but were extremely fast which gave them an advantage in evading Allied naval vessels. Their purpose was to harass British and French sea lanes. The German raiders were able to paralyze and delay Allied shipping by the mere threat of their presence, as well as by inflicting damage through their sinkings and capture.[20] Given their size, the consumption of coal for these vessels was enormous which limited use by the German Navy.[21] The ships had a coal consumption of up to 240 tons daily making them vulnerable and limiting their scope of operations. That made them reliant on their own or captured colliers. During refueling, they were tied tied to them, making them helpless if spotted by Allied vessels. It was often the lack of coal, rather than Allied countermeasures which ended their careers. When supplies ran out, they could only run to a neutral port to be interned. The Imperial German Navy decided to use small, oil-fueled freighters, well-armed and capable of remaining at sea for several months. They would provision themselves by capturing enemy ships, but they needed additional logistical support. This was the third weapon in the German naval arsenal, the Etappendienst - the Secret Naval Supply Department. It was initially begun in 1911 to obtain intelligence on the commercial activities of potential enemies and to service its marine vessels spread throughout the globe. Through the Etappendienst, commerce raiders could stay at sea for years. It was effective for a time as a successful counter – measure to the British blockade. [22] It not only supplied commerce raiders, but also auxiliary cruisers (Hilfskreuzer), blockade-runners and submarines.[23]

By 1914, James K. McGuire, was intimately involved in various activities and organizations which tied him to Germany. By then, he had visited Ireland, ostensibly to do research for his two books that were funded by the German Information Service. And the Clan was engaged in planning the Easter Rising in collaboration with the Imperial German government.

President Woodrow Wilson issued a proclamation of neutrality at the outbreak of hostilities in August, 1914, urging Americans to do the impossible - "be impartial in thought as well as in action".[24] As was shown, most Americans sympathized with the Allies. Despite a century of Anglophobia and diplomatic incidents, most could not forget their Anglo-Saxon cultural heritage. In addition, relations between the two powers had warmed in the wake of the Venezuela incidents of 1895, 1902 and the resolution of the Panama Canal tolls exemption.[25]

Relations with the Imperial German Government were, at best, chilly. It's saber-rattling behavior in attempting to acquire coaling stations, its rampant militarism, and the notorious "rape of Belgium"[26] moved American public opinion to sympathize with the Allies, but few were willing to enter the fray on either side at this point. Every member of Wilson's cabinet, save Bryan, was pro-Ally. Wilson, of British ancestry, admired its culture and political institutions. Wilson earnestly sought peace, but America had not only cultural, but economic ties to the Allies. In addition to our language and government, Jay P. Morgan was the designated purchasing agent for England and France obtaining $3 billion worth of materials for them and earning $30 million for himself. Economics trumped Wilson's efforts a meaningful neutrality. Later, as German efforts to undermine America's role in assistance to the Allies, Wilson backed the Entente. But it took 33 months during which time America was rocked by German efforts at espionage, subversion and sabotage. McGuire was part of those efforts. During America's period of neutrality, the United States loaned $1,900,000,000 to the Allies, compared to $27 million for Germany. The German Ambassador, Von Bernstorff, noted Wilson's proclivity for peace.[27] Dr. Karl Buenz, former German consul in New York, and most recently, a director of the Hamburg-America Line,[28] conspired with German Naval attaché, Captain Karl Boy-Ed, to obtain the necessary Etappendienst vessels. Boy – Ed leased a fleet of merchant ships. False manifests and destinations allowed these ships to resupply German ships on the high seas. Freilitzsch lists 27 such vessels as part of Boy – Ed's armada. One of them, the Gladstone, was among those which made several successful forays[29]. It was this ship which involved James K McGuire.

Boy - Ed spent $750,000 of Dr. Heinrich Albert's money to acquire a fleet in various ports throughout the United States. Their mission - to rendezvous with German naval vessels and provide them with supplies and fuel. Dr. Karl Buenz had been a highly respected diplomat during his decade long tenure in New York. His departure for a new post in Mexico occasioned a grand reception hosted by German-Americans. The chief speaker in that occasion was Nicholas Murray Butler, President of Columbia University who toasted to the "esteem and good will" that New York held him.[30] That would soon change. After a brief tenure in Mexico, Buenz was made Managing Director of the Hamburg-American Line in 1912, the only non-diplomatic post he ever occupied. That, and his close friendship with the Kaiser, may have provoked his being surveilled by the United States Secret Service,[31] despite his previous popularity in New York City. According to a post-war investigation, "the Hamburg-America Line [was] practically the German government in shipping matters".[32] According to The New York Times, Buenz had little to do with the Company's daily operations. His primary function was the handling of the German naval supply service. In other words, Buenz was co-ordinator of the Ettappendienst. The article stated further, the Hamburg-America Line had perfected details for aiding the German fleet in time of war. The Hamburg -America Line was aided and abetted by the North German Lloyd and a number of other subsidiaries.[33] Communication between ships was done in the German Admiralty's secret code. Twelve ships were chartered or purchased to set forth from Atlantic ports, carrying food and fuel to German raiders. Many were successful. Others achieved notoriety because of the conditions under which their secret missions were discovered. One such vessel was the Gladstone.

James K. McGuire fits into this story through what became

known as the Gladstone Incident. The Gladstone was a vessel built in England in 1909 for a Norwegian firm.³⁴ The vessel had transported goods between Canada and Australia. Shortly after the outbreak of the war in 1914, The Gladstone put in at Norfolk, Virginia. German Captain Hans Suhren later appeared in New York, met with Captain Boy-Ed and later showed up in Norfolk, buying The Gladstone for $280,000. Suhren maintained communications with Boy-Ed, installed a wireless radio, and hired an operator. Boy-Ed gave him a German naval code book and a map designating locations in the South Seas where he was to await German cruisers. The Gladstone was an Ettappendienst. It's cargo of coal, food and two cases of revolvers was purchased and loaded by agents of the North German Lloyd Line. This information was communicated to Captain Karl Boy-Ed, the German naval attaché. Apparently, there was a problem in allowing the ship to clear the port. Captain Suhren insisted he owned the ship, but a New York corporation, Browne Willis, lay claim to it and had provisionally registered it with Costa Rica. In order to obtain permanent registration, the Gladstone, now rechristened the Marina Quesada, had to go to Costa Rica. Suhren hauled down the Norwegian flag, and ran up the Costa Rican flag.³⁵

McGuire had a family connection to Norman Hamilton, the collector of customs in the port of Norfolk. Hamilton had been a successful journalist, businessman and supporter of Woodrow Wilson. He obtained his position through the same patronage that won a diplomatic post for James M. Sullivan to Santo Domingo.³⁶ The Marina Quesada captain, Hans Suhren, applied for clearance and was approved on the same day by the Collector of Customs. It's stated destination was Valparaiso, Chile. Hamilton may have had prior knowledge the ship was an Ettappendienst and its coal was destined for German warships. Hamilton supposedly investigated the circumstances, found the ship with its (false) manifest not in violation of United States neutrality and granted the vessel clearance. Along with the application for clearance was a certificate from the Costa Rican minister in Washington, Roberto Brenes Mesen,³⁷ showing the vessel had provisional Costa Rican registry. Its status was to be made permanent when it stopped at Limond, Costa Rica. The Marina Quesada was the first vessel to fly the Costa Rican flag in the United States. The new owners, Browne-Willis, indicated the vessel would be used for trade between New York and San Francisco, sailing for the United States and Central American Steamship Company. According to Norman Hamilton, he gave the Marina Quesada clearance after Browne-Willis swore it was the owner of the cargo and George W. Atkinson was the shipper of the coal, even though Hamilton had no authority to administer the oath. Hamilton later claimed he would have not have cleared the ship if he knew its manifest was false.[38] When war was declared, President Woodrow Wilson placed the enforcement of United States neutrality under the Treasury Department. Collectors of Customs at designated ports were the principal Treasury agents whose duty it was to enforce the Neutrality Act. Among his many duties, the Collector of Customs was in control of vessels and their captains, a mission that included the examination of all outbound foreign vessels for armaments.[39] Given his duties noted above, did a simple affirmation by the ship's captain fulfill the obligation of the Collector of Customs? Unfortunately, this occurred only after the United States entered the war, too late for Hamilton to do anything more punitive.

The problem was that the Collector of Customs had limited powers. Privately-owned foreign vessels could restrict access below decks to government officials,[40] hence only a limited inspection could have been possible. Still, the probability of collusion with James K. McGuire is apparent, especially given the fact that McGuire was working with the German Information Service at the time, had a family connection in Hamilton and at the time was on good terms with president Wilson. This was subsequently revealed in a post-war Senate investigation.

After departure, the ship was re-named the Gladstone and flew the Norwegian flag, the captain telling his chief engineer their goal was to contact German ships. The captain gave him a book containing the German cipher code. Costa Rica declined to give Suhren permanent papers and he was thus unable to legally leave port. He slipped out during a storm under the Norwegian flag. No contacts were made with German ships and the Gladstone landed at Pernambuco, Brazil. The port officer boarded the vessel and when Captain Suhren was handing over the ship's papers, they "fell" into the water. The papers were later retrieved from the belly of a dead shark.[41] His supplies never reached German ships. Suhren was later reported to have been taken prisoner to Canada.

According to Jones, the Gladstone and other Ettappendienst ships failed in their mission at great cost to the German government. However, Feilitzsch reports the opposite. The operation was a success" with many ships making numerous successful runs, including the Gladstone.[42] The discrepancy may be due to the fact Jones was writing during the war and had no access the German documents. His text may have been more propaganda than fact given the 1917 date of its publication. James K. McGuire's comments were more in sympathy with those of Feilitzsch. He wrote to Dr. Heinich Albert: "I have reason to believe our friends will have no trouble hereafter, of a like nature, at this port (Norfolk) etc. There should be a special agent or consul stationed there."[43] That optimism would be overcome by subsequent events, but it speaks loud and clear as to McGuire's ties to Imperial Germany's subversive activities.

German raiders were supplied on the West Coast through the efforts of Frederick Jebsen, a San Francico – based shipping magnate. His company was allegedly the front for the Annie Larsen affair. A Danish immigrant and veteran of the German navy, Jebsen was was a successful merchant and an extremely popular socialite. His business affairs included shipping arms to Mexican revolutionaries, which landed him in a Mexican prison. Only the timely intervention of the German consul in San Francisco, Franz von Bopp, whose connections to the German consul in Mexico, von Hintze, were able to effect his release. As a German reservist, he was under command of Karl Boy – Ed, thus putting his entire fleet at the disposal of the German Navy. He was discovered supplying German raiders and arrested. But as noted previously, there was no law preventing such activity at the time. Jebsen allegedly made a fortune in his dealings with Boy – Ed, who was subsequently expelled with other diplomats in December 1915.[44]

Despite Wilson's pious efforts to remain "neutral", British ships continued to be supplied from ports in the United States.[45] One McGuire ally, James M. Sullivan, then ambassador to Santo Domingo, refused to allow British ships to resupply on the island. This may have been an additional reason for his ouster by Wilson.

One reason for America's action could have been what Jones alleged - that Boy-Ed violated the Hague Conference Treaty of 1907 which stated: "Belligerents are forbidden to use neutral ports and waters as a base of naval operations against their adversaries".[46] Despite Jones' words to the contrary, Secretary of State Lansing who had replaced Bryan, was very careful in distancing himself from the statements later made at Boy-Ed's trial in November 1915. "Furnishing funds for sending out vessels from neutral ports to provision warships does not per se involve violation of law…unless the same supplying vessel had repeatedly used an American port as a base for taking supplies" This was based on a State Department memo issued in September 1914,[47] months before the Gladstone incident. Wilson was still working hard at maintaining the appearance of a neutral stance, but some Americans were becoming more pro-active. Many of them were "hyphenates" especially German-and Irish-Americans. Among the leaders of those who were becoming stridently more pro-German was James K. McGuire. His books, activities and articles while in the employ of the German Information Service, pushed him and his Irish nationalist colleagues deeper into domestic and international intrigue and subversion. And they could do so with relative impunity. Until the passage of the Espionage Act in 1917, foreign agents did not even have to register with American authorities. Their clandestine operations into finance, commerce and manufacturing were all legal. Like McGuire, they were surveilled by U.S. government agents, but their activities were seldom interfered with.[48]

Notes

1 Robert Louis Stevenson, a resident in Samoa during this controversy, wrote about it in his 1889 Footnote To History: Eight Years of Trouble In Samoa. http://authors directory. am/c/fnhst 10.htm.
2 Bailey, Thomas. "Dewey and the Germans At Manila Bay". American History Review XLV 1939, 59-81. Shippee, Lester Burrell." Germany and The Spanish-American War." American Historical Review XXX (July 1925), 759, fn 16; 763.
3 Shippee, op. cit.,765.
4 Bemis, Samuel Flagg. A Diplomatic History of the United States. (New York: Henry Holt and Company), 521.
5 Ibid., 521.The US tried to acquire the Virgin Islands in 1867 and again in 1902, but failed due to the internal politics of both countries. Their acquisition became especially important to the USA after the building of the Panama Canal and the sinking of the Lusitania.. The US feared Germany would annex Denmark and thus secure the Virgin Islands as a submarine base and/or a refueling station. Secretary of State Lansing threatened to occupy the islands to preent their seizure by Germany. Denmark relented and a treaty was signed in 1916. Formal transfer occurred one month before the US entered the war in 1917.of the Lusitania. "Purchase of the US Virgin Islands, 1917" US Department of State Archives https://2001-2009.stategov/r/pa/ho/time/wwi/107293.htm.
6 Ibid., 402-04. There was a second potentially explosive confrontation over Venezuela involving the United States, Great Britain and Germany in 1902. Despite Germany's disavowing of any territorial ambitions, President Theodore Roosevelt was suspicious of the Kaiser's intentions, sending a naval squadron under Admiral Dewey to monitor the situation. After intense diplomatic maneuvering, both Germany and Britain agreed to arbitration. See Edmund Morris, "A Matter of Extreme Urgency: Theodore Roosevelt, Wilhelm II and the Venezuela Crisis of 1902". Naval War College Review. Spring 2002 Vol. LV, No. 2, 73-85. Interestingly, Dr. Karl Buenz, German consul at the time, was instrumental in bringing a peaceful resolution to the issue noting the determination of Roosevelt to prevent a German acquisition of territory close to the proposed site of his Isthmian canal.
7 Scheiber, Clara. The Transformation of American Opinion Towards Germany (New York: Russell and Russell, 1923), 182.
8 Bemis, op. cit., A Diplomatic History..., 529.
9 Scheiber, op. cit, The Transformation...140; 193.
10 Captain Boy-Ed figures prominently in McGuire's machinations as Irish Nationalist.

11 Schmalenbach, Paul. German Raiders: A History of German Auxiliary Cruisers of the German Navy, 1895-1945. Annapolis: Naval Institute Press, 1979, 17.
12 Bisher, Jamie. "German Raiders in Latin America Waters." http://www.military history on line.comww1/german commerce raiders. aspe.1 This type of deception was not limited to the Germans. Britain had 60 such vessels registered as armed merchant cruisers (AMC), one of which was the Lusitania. Its construction was subsidized by the British government on condition is be registered as such. The vessel was fitted for deck guns in 1913 but it was unarmed at the time of its sinking. Its manifest, published prior to its sailing in the New York Times, listed it as carrying ammunition and artillery shells. Hence Dernburg's rationale for its sinking. For details see Beesly, Patrick. Room 40: British Naval Intelligence, 1914-1918. London: Harmish-Hamilton, 1982.
13 "Albert Ballin, the HAPAG Shipping Company and Immiigrants to America". http://web.nli.il/sites/NLT/English/collections/personalities/israel-germany/world-war-1/pages/Albert-Ballin.aspx;
14 "The German Way and More: Albert Ballin" https://german-way.com/notable-people/featured-bios/albert-ballin/.
15 SS Leviathan (American Passenger Liner1914. OriginallyGerman SS Vaterland. http://www.ibiblio.org/hyperwar/OnlineLibrary/photos/sh-civil/civsh-1/leviathan.htm. SS Imperator(German passenger liner 1913. Served as USS Imperator (ID # 4080 in 1919. Later British Berengia. https:illibiblio.org/hyperwar/Online/Library/photos/sh-civil/sh-civil/civsh-1/impereator.htm.
16 Halpern, Paul G. Naval History of World War 1. London: UCLP, 1994, 72,82.
17 Schmalenbach, op. cit., 48.,48.
18 Bisher, Jamie, op. cit., 2-3; Most German commerce raiding in the South Atlantic ended by March, 1915 There were large expriate German communities in various South American countries. At the time, the German population of various countries varied from two to eight percent of their total population. See Tock, David. German Immigration and Adaptation to Latin America. Senor Thesis, Liberty University, Spring 1974, 72pp..
19 Bisher, Jamie, op. cit., 3.
20 (20).Schmalenbach, Paul, 11; 14. Get citation.
21 "Hilfskreuzer" http://www.scharnhorst-class.dk/hilfskreuzer/hilfskereuzer_introduction...Schmalenbach, op. cit., 45.
22 Ibid.
23 Ibid. The use of these ships was considered so successful, their use was implemented by Admiral Canaris beginning in 1927. The Etappendienst was reactivated a dozen years later. The methods of the Hilfskreuzer was simple – a prize was sighted, the distance closed under a different flag. If it

surrendered, a prize crew boarded it, and if neutral, was allowed to continue its journey. If not, the cargo was seized, the crew taken on board and the vessel was either sunk or sent under a prize crew to a port to be converted into a Hilfskreuzer or Ettappendienst ship. With its ports effectively blockaded by the end of 1914, and with only 46 submarines in service, a multi-ocean submarine warfare was impossible. The German navy in 1915 decided to arm freighters as Hilfskreuzer. They were faster than the Allied merchant fleets, had greater range and were armed with hidden guns, torpedoes and mine-laying equipment. For details on several of these successful German raiders, see "German WWI Naval Raiders".
http://www.forumeersteweeldoorlog.ml/viewtopic.php?t=14916&sid... "US Merchant Ships, Sailing Vessels and Fishing Craft, lost, captured, ..." lists 150 American vessels sink or damaged by German raiders and submarines, 1915-1918.
http://www.usmm.org/ww1merchant.html. A detailed account of each German raider can be found at "German Armed Merchant Raiders During World War I"
http://www.ahoy.tk-jk.net/MaraudersWWI/Moewe.html.

24 Bailey, Thomas. A Diplomat History of the American People. 6th ed. (New York: Appleton-Century Crofts, Inc., 1958), 564.

25 The Venezuela issues revolved around the conflicting boundary claims of Venezuela and British Guiana. In the wake of the American public and Venezuelans diplomatic demands to do something, President Cleveland had his Secretary of State issue a stern warning to Britain urging arbitration of the dispute using the guise of the Monroe Doctrine. The British refused the American offer and war fever gripped the United States. Saner minds prevailed and Britain, preoccupied by the Boers in South Africa, agreed to arbitration. For details, see Bailey, Thomas, A Diplomatic..; 438-49. The crisis revolved around German desires to acquire bases near the projected Panama Canal. Attempts to buy the Danish West Indies by the United States were thwarted amid rumors German diplomacy had a hand in its undoing. The Venezuelan dictator owed a number of European contractors. Germany, Italy and Britain blockaded Venezuela to force payment. President Theodore Roosevelt sought a peaceful resolution to the crisis. The claims were peacefully adjudicated by international commissions. Bemis, Samuel Flagg. A Diplomatic History of the United States (New York: Henry Holt and Company), 1942,524. The Panama tolls issue concerned American exemptions from tolls in the Panama Canal a violation of the Hay-Pauncefote Treaty of 1901. The British considered it an act of bad faith. The recently-elected Woodrow Wilson urged repeal of this provision in March, 1914. In Bailey, Thomas, A Diplomatic... 549-551. As noted, these events outraged

German-and Irish-Americans who saw in these events the United States capitulating to British interests.

26 The term refers to Belgium's heroic but futile resistance to German invasion, the wanton destruction of the Louvain library, the brutal suppression of civilian resistance and the German diplomatic blunder of referring to Belgium's declaration of neutrality as a "scrap of paper."

27 Bemis, A Diplomatic History... 591-92.

28 The Hamburg-Amerika Line (HAPAG) was one of the oldest German transatlantic steamship line. Founded by wealthy Germans in 1847, it was the largest German, and at times, the world's largest shipping company. It was established to transport German and other immigrants and cargo to the United States, later expanding its operations to other continents. By 1896, it had a fleet of 102 ships, maintaining 19 separate services. "The Hamburg-America Line" http://norwayheritage.com/p_shiplist.asp?co=haaml

29 Feilitzsch, Heribert. The Secret War Council: The German Fight Against the Entente in America in 1914. Virginia: Henselstone Verlag, 2015., 73.

30 "Honor Karl Buenz". New York Times 13 January 1909:6.

31 "Karl Buenz Dies In Atlanta Prison." New York Times 16 September 1918:11. The Secret Service, initially established in the Treasury Department to investigate counterfeiting during the Civil War, had become the government's main intelligence agency during the Spanish-American War. After the assassination of McKinley, it assumed the function of protecting the President. In 1915, Secretary of State William Jennings Bryan decided the German diplomats should be investigated for possible espionage and had the Secret Service assigned to the task." American Intelligence Services: Pre/Post World War I, vol. I, ch. 3, "Post-Civil War To World War I." pp. 108 http://www.fas.org/irp/ops/ci/docs/cil/on3a.htm.

32 Brewing and Liquor Interests and German and Bolshevik Propaganda. Report and Hearings of the Subcommittee on the Judiciary. United States Senate. In three volumes. Vol. 2 (Washington: Government Printing Office, 1919), 1467. "Boy-Ed Managed Ship Plot Details". New York Times 25 November 1915. This article referred to the Hamburg-America Line as a "virtual branch of the German Navy".

33 "Boy-Ed Managed Ship Plot Details". New York Times 25 November 1915; "Try to Bar Evidence of Quesada's Cruise". New York Times 27 November 1915. The two other firms were the Inter-American Steamship Company and the Ganz Steamship Line. A similar supply service was established on the West Coast at the German consulate in San Francisco. It's front was the Northern and Southern Steamship Company. In John Price Jones, America Entangled (New York: A. C. Lant, 1917), 104. The "Introduction" was

written by Roger B. Wood, United States Attorney who prosecuted Dr. Karl Buenz and other German conspirators in 1915.

34 S. S. Severance (American Freighter 1909) previously named Gladstone and Marina Quesada. Served as USS Severance (ID#2063) 1918-1919. In "Civilian Ships Beginning With The Letter S". Department of the Navy, Navy History and Heritage Command http://www.history.navy.mil/photos/sh-civil/civsh-s/seveancehtm. The article contains a picture and a brief description: "She was a bulk cargo carrier of the trunk deck type, with distinctive continuous hatch openings atop long coamings about a deck level high that were inset from the hull sides."

35 Jones, John Price. America Entangled (New York: A. C. Laut, 1917), 113-115.

36 Norman Hamilton, (1877-1964), as Collector of the Port of Norfolk from 1914-22. Similar to James M. Sullivan, he was on the fringes of the Democratic party, serving as a Congressional page, and as secretary of the local school board. He acquired his "special fitness for his duties through his familiarity with the shipping of that section, during his long years as a newspaperman". The Gladstone affair was over-shadowed by two subsequent incidents, the Prinz Eitel Friedrich and Kronprinz Wilhelm and the S. S. Aparn docked in Norfolk. He apparently negotiated with the commanders of the ships interning them. Hamilton was commended by President Wilson for enforcing our neutrality. He later served as a one-term Congressman, 1937-39.. "Hamilton, Norman". Who Was Who In America, vol. IV, 1961-68 (Chicago: Marquis Who's Who, Inc.), 399; "Norman R. Hamilton". Encyclopedia of Virginia Biography vol. IV (New York: Lewis Historical Publishing Company, 1915), 376-77. "Praise For Hamilton As Collector of Port." The Suffolk Herald, 14 May 1915:1.

37 Roberto Brenes Mesen (1874 – 1947) was a Costa Rican politician, journalist, educator and author of over a dozen books. He served as acting minister for Costa Rica in Washington, D.C. He stayed in the USA and had a successful career as a university professor. Returning to Costa Rica in 1939, he waged a constant struggle to imrove the rights of workers against the depredations of the United Fruit Company and the powers of the Catholic church.

38 Untitled typescript. "Norman R. Hamilton Files, 1914-1915"; "Boy-Ed Managed Ship Plot Details". New York Times 25 November 1915. This comment is probably a stretch given that false manifests were the rule rather than the exception. They were often amended after the ships left port and were in international waters.

39 Saba, Ann. "True Heroes In The Customs Tradition: The Port of New York and The Customs Intelligence Bureau During World War I". http://www.cbp.gov/xp/CustomsToday/2001/February/custoday_tradition.xml

40 "Happenings Below Decks of Interned Teuton Ships Still Remain A Mystery". Syracuse Herald 3 February 1917:1.
41 Hence the Chapter sub-title. "Try To Bar Evidence of Quesada's Cruise". New York Times 27 November 1915; also noted, in "Boy-Ed Managed Ship Plot Details". New York Times 25 November 1915. The total cost of the operation was $1,420,000. For a list of the ships, see Jones, America Entangled, 110. This may be unreliable given the date of its publication.
42 Feilitzsch, op. cit., 73.
43 Brewing and Liquor Interests and German and Bolshevik Propaganda, 1397-1398.
44 Feilitzsch, op. cit., 77 – 78.
45 Ibid., 81.
46 Brewing and Liquor Interests and German and Bolshevik and Propaganda, 1398.
47 "The Case of Boy-Ed". New York Times 25 November 1915.
48 Feilitzsch, op. cit., 72.

Chapter III - F

They Voted Their Illusions:
The Contested Election of 1916

Both the hyphenate alliance and Woodrow Wilson did their best to discredit each other prior to the election of 1916. Hyphenates believed Wilson was not playing fairly to both Allied and Central Powers. As previously noted, Wilson's alleged bias with reference to the British blockade of Germany, the opening of mails, the sale of munitions, his failure to protest the hasty execution of Irish rebels in the Easter Rebellion of 1916 and of the substantial loans made by the American financiers to the Allies, had made Wilson a defacto ally of Britain. Wilson's protest, that American markets were open to any buyer, had a hollow ring, especially since England controlled the seas. Hence the demands by German-and Irish-Americans for an embargo on munitions sales and the demand for legislation forbidding Americans from traveling on belligerent's vessels.

The "hyphen" issue was first raised by President Woodrow Wilson in May 1914 in a speech dedicating a monument to John Barry, the Irish-American naval hero of both the American Revolution and the undeclared naval war with France. In his speech, Wilson stated that Barry's heart crossed the ocean with him, and "when the whole man had come over the hyphen drops of its own weight out of his name". "The man was not an Irish-American, he was an Irishman who became an American."[1] The speech, picked up in the Irish press, including the Catholic Sun, was interpreted by many Irish-Americans as a veiled attack on their politics, possibly dating to their resistance to Wilson on the Panama Canal tolls controversy two years previous. The incident raised the issue of ethnic politics, despite the fact Irish politicians such as William Gibbs McAdoo, Joseph Tumulty, James Burke, James M. Sullivan, and James K. McGuire were part of his political entourage at the time. However, John O' Dea, author of History of The Ancient Order of Hibernians and Ladies Auxiliary, condemned Wilson's remarks.[2] Adding to the animus were remarks of former President Theodore Roosevelt, which contributed not only to a bitter campaign in 1916, but to increased hostility against hyphenates by Nativist Americans during the war years.

In hyphenate eyes Wilson's pro-Allied stance was best revealed in his treatment of American diplomats, Thomas St. John Gaffney, consul to Munich, Walter Hines Pages, Ambassador to England and James W. Gerard. Page was an unrepentant Anglophile from his early childhood. A journalist, ambassador to England, editor, friend and supporter of fellow Southerner Woodrow Wilson, he was rewarded with the post of ambassador. At the outset of war, Page and Wilson differed in policy, the former seeing the conflict as a struggle against Prussian militarism and the latter proclaiming neutrality. Page's dispatches to America were often regarded as Anglophile propaganda. During the presidential campaign of 1916, Ambassador Page returned to the United States for consultations. Secretary of State Lansing devoted several pages in his <u>Memoirs</u> as to "how extraordinary" it was for an American ambassador to press British concerns rather than those of his own country, indicating it was impossible for either himself or President Wilson to get behind "the pro-British wall with which he had enclosed his mind".[3] Nonetheless, Page was retained which simply reinforced Wilson's pro-British bias in the eyes of the hyphenates. In fact, by March 1917, Page notified Wilson the Allies would collapse without American aid. One month later, The United States declared war on Germany. Despite his strident pro-British views, Wilson kept Page at his post insisting he remain, obtaining the financial means from private sources to keep him in his position.

Wilson even tolerated the Ambassador to Germany, James W. Gerard. A wealthy lawyer, his wife was the daughter of a millionaire. Gerard was tied to Tammany Hall. Through its intervention he became a judge on the new York State Supreme Court. His wealth allowed him to contribute substantial sums to the Democratic campaign of 1912, for which he was rewarded with the ambassadorship. He was ineffective as diplomat and Wilson regarded him as incompetent.

Wilson's tolerance of bias and incompetence, noted previously in his treatment of James M. Sullivan in Santo Domingo, was apparently limited only to those who shared his views. Thomas St. John Gaffney, the Irish-born Republican, was appointed Consul to Munich by President Theodore Roosevelt for his services in the election of 1904. He was recalled and asked to resign by Wilson allegedly because of his Irish birth, his daughters marriage to a German aristocrat, and his pro-German, pro-Irish Nationalist activities.⁴ Gaffney's dismissal received widespread coverage in the Irish press, including <u>The Catholic Sun</u>. An article, sub-titled, "Former American Consul Treated In English Port and Mis-represented In New York", summarized the hyphenate press' attitude as to Wilson's bias in foreign policy. The article noted how Gaffney's luggage was searched, private papers and books taken and how he was personally searched by British agents. The rationale for their actions was that "no printed matter giving Germany's point of view was allowed to reach the United States...."⁵

Wilson did not endear himself to the hyphenates with his verbal assaults on their loyalty. One particularly galling speech was made 7 December 1915 in which he denounced citizens of foreign birth who "poured the poison of disloyalty into the very arteries of our National life, sought to destroy our industries and were involved in foreign intrigues. Such creatures of passion, disloyalty and anarchy should be crushed out".⁶ Along with these comments, the pro-Allied <u>New York Times</u> published reports of the intrigues of German agent Franz Rintelen. The result was nativism became synonymous with patriotism and the hyphenates, particularly German-Americans, came under increasing attack.

Probably the best example of Wilson's anti-hyphen attitude was his publicized clash with McGuire associate Jeremiah O'Leary. Wilson personally refused to cater to the hyphenate vote. The Irish press continued to lambaste Wilson as supporting British interests. Especially obnoxious to Wilson were pamphlets of Jeremiah O'Leary, which hammered the President for his munitions sales to the Allies, for adhering to the gamblers and newspapers of Wall Street. O'Leary parlayed the standard Nationalist line, used by McGuire and others, that Britain was America's traditional enemy.⁷ In October, 1916, O'Leary, piqued at a Democratic candidate for not supporting his views, stumped for the Republican who won. He telegrammed the President informing him of the Republican's victory in an overwhelming Democratic district, considering it a significant protest against Wilson's pro-English policies.⁸ Wilson upped the ante when he responded, "I seek neither favor nor fear the displeasure of that small alien element amongst us which puts loyalty to any foreign power before loyalty to the United States".[9] O'Leary escalated the conflict, once again noting the primary electoral triumph of an anti-Wilson Democrat, Senator James Martine of New Jersey, echoing his comments as to it being a repudiation of Wilson's foreign policy. According to the New York Times the Wilson response was:

> Your telegram received. I would feel deeply mortified to have you or anyone like you vote for me. Since you have access to many disloyal Americans and I have not, I will ask you to convey this message to them.[10]

This reply not only gained support for Wilson, but weakened Hughes, who had been publicized as seeking a the hyphenates' vote. And it reinforced the rising Nativist sentiment in the country.This was undoubtedly the turning point in the election.

Wilson won by a narrow margin. It was through a fortuitous set of circumstances. Wilson had no opposition to his candidacy once he declared himself in February 1916, but party unity was enfeebled by political considerations based on mutual need. For example, Tammany Boss Charles F. Murphy and his chief political advisors, Daniel F. Cohalan and John Quinn, preferred "Champ" Clark for the party's nomination in 1912.[11] Wilson, in the early years of his first term as President, retaliated by eliminating key patronage positions both in New York City and upstate. First he denied it access to federal patronage jobs, choosing as his Collector for the Port of New York, Dudley Field Malone, an anti-Tammany Democrat. Malone used his position against "Boss" Murphy with Wilson's blessing. Wilson later asked Malone to back off, fearing a split in the party.[12] The "reformist" versus Tammany schism was reflected in upstate politics as well and involved James K. McGuire.

Despite the increasingly radical rhetoric, McGuire had not openly broken with the first Wilson administration. In fact, McGuire had worked with it to secure Roman Catholics for cabinet positions. In addition, Irish Nationalists had initially supported Wilson's statement regarding strict American neutrality. McGuire had been a factor in Wilson's 1912 Presidential victory. For example, responding to an article in the <u>Gaelic American</u> noting Woodrow Wilson's desire to appoint an Irish Catholic to his cabinet, McGuire stated the reasons he thought Wilson was open to such a proposal. He noted many Catholics were moving into Republican ranks. McGuire said Wilson had received few votes from the centers of Roman Catholicism in the country suggesting the President's textbook, <u>The History of the American People</u> with its negative terminology of Catholic as "Romanists" and "Papists" and his opposition to Catholic Senator James Smith of New Jersey, caused resentment among Irish Catholic voters. Accordingly, James G. McAdoo, James A. O'Gorman and James K. McGuire were placed in command of a bureau to encourage Irish Catholic involvement and support during Wilson's first bid for the Presidency. McGuire was purportedly chosen because he was already known nationally, had been involved in six previous presidential campaigns, had traveled widely due to his business connections and was owner of several Irish Catholic publications which would be used for proselytizing. McGuire actively supported Wilson, circulating thousands of pamphlets and sending out over 280,000 letters to members of the Ancient Order of Hibernians. Among the Irish possibilities for selection were not only three listed above, but also Mayors James D. Phelan of San Francisco and John J. Fitz Gerald of Boston and Justices Daniel F. Cohalan and John W. Goff.[13] Many of these people were with whom McGuire was familiar from his Tammany and Irish Nationalist connections.

McGuire followed up these activities, praising the selection for Joseph W. Tumulty as the President's Secretary and John Burke as United States Treasurer.[14] Hence, it was no surprise when McGuire testified in favor of James M. Sullivan as ambassador to Santo Domingo that his counsel was taken seriously. Initially friendly to the Wilson regime, McGuire and many of the notables listed above, would became its bitter enemies. Those same organizations and papers that he used to support Wilson's presidential bid, would be turned against the President as America moved towards increased involvement in The Great War.

McGuire continued to meddle in Onondaga County and Syracuse city politics for over a decade mixing it with his economic interests in asphalt paving and national politics.

During the height of the Whitman John Doe proceedings in 1914 the split between McGuire and Onondaga County Boss William H. Kelley was aired over the appointment for an internal revenue collector, each seeking to seat his own candidate. McGuire's intervention, according to his critics, was holding up approval of Kelley's candidate. McGuire denied those charges in addition to reports alleging he was about to re-enter local politics. McGuire also criticized his brother George for attacking Kelley, complimenting Kelley for his support during his "recent troubles". With the passage of the Sixteenth Amendment mandating a federal income tax, it made this an important fight for control of federal patronage. McGuire's choice for the position, Neal Brewster, was chosen over the objections of both Kelley, a power in Onondaga County politics with strong ties to Tammany Hall, and John R. Clancy, a local businessman and Democratic Congressman. It indicates McGuire was still a force to be reckoned with given his connections to the Wilson administration. Or, having been virtually abandoned during the asphalt scandals, McGuire may have sought revenge on Tammany by allying with Wilson and the reformers.

Despite his protestations of friendship to Kelley, McGuire intervened once more a year later in Onondaga County politics, again challenging Kelley's candidate for Deputy United States Marshal for the Northern District of New York.[15] The appointment of an anti-Kelley candidate as Assistant United States District Attorney for Northern New York in January 1915 reignited the simmering feud with McGuire. Kelley had assurances from several Congressmen and the United States District Attorney for Albany that his candidate would be chosen. Kelley believed McGuire was behind the move as part of a strategy to replace him as Democratic State Committeeman. For McGuire that was a forlorn hope.[16] By then McGuire had become deeply enmeshed in the intrigues associated with Irish nationalism and German subversion and propaganda. In addition, by late 1916 not only had Wilson patched up his relations with Tammany due to the upcoming elections, McGuire had also been "outed" as a prominent member of the Irish Nationalist coalition to defeat Wilson as president.

Possibly to show sibling political solidarity and to distance themselves from Tammany which gave only tepid support to Wilson in the election of 1912, George H. McGuire paid public homage to the President as a "masterful politician", a statesmen and a "patriot", believing Wilson's policies of peace, preparedness, and tariff reform would keep the American people on his side in the election of 1916. He noted his brother James' popularity among German-Americans as a result of his two pro-German works, <u>The King, The Kaiser and Irish Freedom</u> and <u>What Could Germany Do For Ireland</u>?[17] This may also have been a not-so-subtle hint a hyphenate alliance might work to oust the President in the election of 1916 should there be any radical departure from current policies.

When it became public that James K. McGuire was a member of Jeremiah O'Leary's American Truth Society in October 1916, it came as a surprise to many since it had been noted McGuire "had been one of President Wilson's strongest supporters and admirers". McGuire's pro-German stance was regarded as his reason for joining the American Truth Society. What was considered a shock was the society had as its goal the defeat of Wilson in the election of 1916. It was alleged James K. McGuire backed O'Leary because he felt Wilson had moved too close to the Allies and hence hindered German prospects for success. Local politicians feared a negative impact on federal patronage jobs as a result of the disclosures given that McGuire had played a prominent role in securing several key positions for men who did not have the backing of the local machine. It was ruefully admitted that such influence was now gone.[18] In response to the allegations, McGuire vehemently denied being an enemy of President Wilson, claiming he was not a signatory to a petition published by the American Truth Society which condemned not only the President's policies, but those of Charles F. Murphy and others. In his statement, McGuire declared his continued allegiance to the Democratic party, its principals and its candidates.[19] However, machinations on both sides encouraged suspicion and doubt as to their respective intentions and loyalties. To Wilson, it appeared as German-and-Irish Americans were involved in a conspiracy against what he perceived as in the best interests of the country.[20] The great watershed with reference to Wilson and for most Irish-Americans, was the Easter Rebellion. However, even prior to that, McGuire was extremely active and vociferous in his actions favoring both Irish freedom and the need for a German victory.

Similar to Daniel F. Cohalan, the demands of Irish freedom drew McGuire away from local and state politics and into the dark side of international politics and subversion. As with other Nationalists, the cause of Irish Independence superceded all others. If Wilson had an Anglophile bias with little understanding of the depth of Irish-and German-American concern for their homelands, the hyphenates also has a distorted perception of their political power. A brief article in the Syracuse Herald lampooned the alleged hyphenate solidarity castigating in particular "Messrs [Herman] Ridder and [James K.] McGuire who believe they have an army of several million who could whip puny Britain to a standstill".[21] Perhaps the anonymous author linked them given McGuire's position as publicist for the German cause and Ridder's efforts to advocate "fair play" in the press for the Central Powers.

The Republicans chose Charles Evans Hughes as their standard-bearer, after an unsuccessful bid by Theodore Roosevelt. Hughes was a Supreme Court Justice, a two-time reform Governor of New York and an independent progressive Republican who defied his party's political bosses. The party by-passed Roosevelt because of his strong anti-hyphenate rhetoric. Roosevelt, having learned from his experience in 1912, barnstormed for the Republican party and was linked in the public mind to Hughes. His speeches created problems for the latter since Roosevelt, like Wilson, was for preparedness, intervention on the Allied side, and had made disparaging remarks about hyphenates. This was the despite the official Republican platform calling for strict neutrality, protection of American rights and studiously avoiding any mention of hypenism.[22] It also signified the end of the Progressive Party. A minority held a convention and decided to support Wilson. Its leaders, John H. Parker, Matthew Hale and Bainbridge Colby brought many former Progressives with them, a significant factor in Wilson's victory. Many prominent Irish-Americans who also endorsed Wilson included Bourke Cockran, Frank P. Walsh, Edward Dunne, the Governor of Illinois, New York Supreme Court Justice Victor Dowling and California lawyer, activist and future attorney for defendants in the Hindu-German onspiracy trial Daniel O'Connell.[23] In addition to Irish moderates, virtually all Progressive reformers and intellectuals moved solidly into the Wilson camp.[24]

The keynote speaker at the Democratic Convention was the first Catholic Governor of New York, Martin H. Glynn, whose historical references to cases where American refused to go to war, gave the Democrats what would be their winning slogan: "He kept us out of war!"[25] His comments were echoed by other convention speakers including William Jennings Bryan. The Democrats had become the defacto peace party. Despite the fact that Wilson as early as October 1916 believed that war with Germany was inevitable, he continued to play the peace card.[26] Wilson drove the issue home starting with a speech on 30 September 1916 in the East and carrying that theme throughout his campaign trips to the Midwest, sharing his dream of a peaceful community of nations acting together to prevent future wars.[27]

Hughes' botched efforts to win the German vote were castigated in the press. For example, a cartoon in the <u>New York World</u> showed the Kaiser holding an electoral poster supporting Hughes for President. It was titled "Berlin's Candidate".[28] In addition, the Democrats were aided by the fact that timely legislation in the face of a national railroad strike won them the endorsement of organized labor.[29]

The National German-American Alliance and Friends of Irish Freedom officially supported Republican candidate Charles Evans

Hughes. He suffered from some serious handicaps. The man who handled his advertising in the foreign language press was Louis Hammerling, noted earlier for his questionable activities on behalf of the German government. Hughes worked to obtain hyphenate support, yet he had Theodore Roosevelt's bitter condemnations of them to contend with. There was the divided political allegiances of the hyphenates, many of whom remained in the Democratic fold. In addition, William J. Bryan and Bainbridge Colby, both of whom had endorsed Irish freedom, supported Wilson. Hughes was haunted by Democratic Committee reports leaked to the New York Times late in the campaign, that he had met with the American Independence Conference, a German-financed front group, promising to attack British embargo policies and embrace true neutrality. Among those present at the meeting were Jeremiah O'Leary, Thomas St. John Gaffney and Daniel F. Cohalan.[30] Hughes would later modify his view saying foreign intrigues and divided loyalties would not be tolerated by his administration. Hughes promised to stand four square to all nations. He reiterated the message in Philadelphia that he would not tolerate interference with American mail or commerce and that no American business exercising its legitimate commercial rights should be blacklisted.[31]

Apparently there were questions about Hughes' position since his most vociferous campaigner, Theodore Roosevelt, had made defamatory remarks concerning hyphenates during a speech in Maine. In addition, as noted previously, the militant Irish Nationalists had been disappointed by the minimal support received from Germany in the Easter rebellion and in their appeals for aid for a subsequent rising. They obviously wanted to be sure of Hughes position to eliminate any further embarrassment. The composition of the National Committee of the American Independence Conference included many Irish extremists - Jeremiah O'Leary, Thomas St. John Gaffney, Daniel Cohalan, John D. Moore, John A. McGerry, Hugh O' Neill, Robert F. Ford, J.P. Mooney, Charles Noonan, Joseph A. O'Donnell, J.P. O'Mahony suggesting an agenda which sought more than to secure genuine American neutrality.

St. John Gaffney was particularly suspect. It was rumored he had brought money from Germany to support the Hughes campaign, a charge he vigorously denied in the <u>New York Times</u>. Others involved in the Conference raised additional doubts as to the organization's intent. For example, Gustav H. Jacobson subsequently indicted by the federal government for pro-German war plots, was described as the principal field agent for the American Embargo Conference. In addition, the issue was further clouded by the fact that William R. MacDonald was also the General Manager of the American Embargo Conference, a group whose primary purpose was to prevent the shipment of munitions to belligerents. Jaspar T. Darling was the organization's president. Hughes denied any quid pro quo with the American Independence Conference. The Democrats said no more anti-Hughes hyphenate charges would be forthcoming since their case had been proved.[31] The entire incident was an embarrassment to the Republican campaign, especially so close to the election. William R. Wilcox, Republican National Committee Chairman, was quick to disassociate himself from the American Independence Conference following a disastrous meeting with German Catholic priests in Wisconsin set up by Gustav H. Jacobson. Not only was he heckled by his audience, it passed a resolution declaring it would take no political action.[32]

Irish-American opinion was slow to back Hughes until it had a clear understanding of his position. However, despite his approval by German and Irish representatives, an endorsement was held up by militant Clan member Daniel F. Cohalan who considered Hughes' remarks "inadequate". It was only after Hughes made a more emphatic declaration in Philadelphia that the headquarters of the "German-Irish Entente" sent out literature in his support.[33]

After the exposure of Hughes' flirtation for the hyphenate vote, the Republican campaign appeared to flounder and become desperate. The slogan, "He kept us out of war" was immensely popular throughout the country as was his espousal of self-determination. The tactic was both idealistic and pragmatic. It would garner support from German and Irish voters and position him as a leader in peace negotiations. It indicated sympathy for Ireland, but as a then neutral power' hr could not guarantee it a place at the peace table. That policy would continue in his post -war politics as well. The Republicans apparently could offer no meaningful alternative program or policy, all the while having to deal with Theodore Roosevelt's bellicose speeches broadening the gap between the two candidates.

In addition to the spectacle created by the publicity surrounding the flirtation with the hyphenate vote, there was the gaff with Governor Hiram Johnson of California which sealed the fate of Hughes' beleaguered campaign. Hughes apparently allowed himself to be linked to the Republican Old Guard against Johnson, a reformer. He failed to meet with Johnson when the two were at the same hotel at the same time.[34] Nonetheless, the Irish irreconcilables-the Clan-na-Gael, The Ancient Order of Hibernians, the American Truth Society and their respective organs, the Gaelic American and The Irish World-were strong for Hughes.

However, there is evidence which suggests Wilson's aides were counting on the hyphen vote as well. For example, Wilson may have had an agenda in choosing Martin H. Glynn as a keynote speaker. Glynn claimed to be independent of Tammany Hall, insisting like Sulzer, that he would allow no man to dictate to him. Glynn accordingly, joined the "Get Murphy" movement, but failed to obtain Wilson's support, possibly because he was lukewarm in his backing of Wilson in 1912. As noted, the "Get Murphy" movement failed and Wilson patched up his relationship with Tammany for the election of 1916. Wilson may have chosen Glynn as keynote speaker as an apology for his curt dismissal of him two years earlier and as vehicle to attract the moderate Irish vote. A factor in Glynn's gubernatorial loss was the anti-Catholic religious bigotry which at the time flooded the state and the nation. Glynn's nemesis was not Murphy, but former Governor William Sulzer, who ran against him on both the Prohibition and American Party lines. The latter was nativist, anti-Catholic and anti-immigrant. "Boss" Murphy was no asset, failing to get out the party vote for Glynn. An additional reason for Wilson choosing Glynn was because he was a friend of William

Jennings Bryan, leader of the "peace" wing of the Democratic Party. Glynn was also strongly identified with Irish Nationalists. Bryan, as noted, had become the poster-boy for the Irish Nationalists after endorsing Irish freedom.[35] So while Wilson publicly deprecated the hyphen vote, his supporters were actively courting it.

An interesting perspective on the hyphenate issue can be gleaned by a careful reading of the series of articles in The New York Times in late October 1916 on the Hughes-O'Leary meetings. They implicate James K. McGuire. Since many of the hyphenates were lukewarm in their enthusiasm for Hughes, there were efforts on the part of Democratic politicians to obtain the ethnic vote. For example, The Times reported Martin Glynn conferred with Jeremiah O'Leary, promising if O'Leary could deliver the 3.5 million hyphenate votes of his organization for Wilson, the administration would respond with some strong action against England, possibly refusing clearance papers for Allied munitions ships unless the tampering with U.S. mails by Britain ceased. The telegram reporting this episode was sent by William R. MacDonald, Secretary of the American Independence Conference. Glynn allegedly arranged a meeting between O'Leary and Vance McCormick, the Democratic National Committee Chairman, who reportedly was anxious to meet with O'Leary. George Sylvester Viereck reported the National Committee of the Democratic Party offered to purchase a million copies of The Fatherland if it would publish an article authored by James K. McGuire which posed embarrassing questions to the Republican candidate as to the assertion of American rights against both belligerents. Viereck refused to do so noting a speech by Hughes answered all of McGuire's questions.[36] Hughes' biographer, Merlo Pusey, denied Hughes' was "trucking" to the German vote given his statement that "we are one country" and he "would not tolerate any native division of allegiance". Further, Pusey quotes Hughes as stating in a New York Times article of 25 October 1916, that he did not want the votes of anyone who did not champion the USA over any other country. Hughes, at the time of the meeting did not know any of the individuals.[37] In addition, despite Theodore Roosevelt's public hyphenate-baiting, he was apparently sought by some of them as a better alternative to Hughes. According to Viereck, Professor Hugo Munsterberg distrusted both party nominees, believing Roosevelt the man who could bring peace. Munsterberg arranged a meeting between Viereck and Roosevelt, who had been friends prior to the outbreak of war. The former President told Viereck of his confirmed belief that Germany planned to planned to invade the United States. Roosevelt was so convinced of this it destroyed any chance of Munsterberg obtaining unified German-American sentiment for his candidacy.[38]

The election returns yielded Hughes a virtual sweep of the East, but the West and South had not been decided. Gradually, as the returns came in, the latter states moved into the Wilson camp. The reasons for Wilson's ultimate success were, as noted, that many German-Americans and Irish-Americans largely sided with Wilson, as did labor and women who could vote in the Western states, and former Progressives and Socialists. The unifying themes for these disparate groups were peace, progressivism and prosperity, suggesting they voted primarily on their domestic concerns with little regard to foreign affairs.[39] Despite the disappointment of the Irish irreconcilables in the election of 1916, the obvious fact that many Irish supported Wilson was a harbinger of things to come. They would also endorse the President when America entered the war because it marked the end of their policy of dependence on a German victory to achieve Irish freedom. In addition, Wilson's espousal of self-determination breathed hope into their dream of independence for Ireland. But between November 1916 and April 1917, the professional Irish spared no effort to keep America out of the conflict.

Notes

1 "Wilson Condemns Foreign Alliances". <u>New York Times</u> 17 May 1914, "Commodore John Barry". <u>Catholic Sun</u> 8 May 1914:1; "Father of the American Navy". <u>Catholic Sun</u> 22 May 1914:1.

2 O'Dea, John. <u>History of the Ancient Order of Hibernians and Ladies Auxiliary</u> (Philadelphia: 1923), vol. III, 1481-86; Ward, Alan J. <u>Ireland and Anglo-American Relations, 1899-1921</u> (Toronto: University of Toronto Press, 1909), 81-82.

3 Lansing, Robert. <u>The War Memoirs of Robert Lansing, Secretary of State</u> (New York: Bobbs-Merrill, 1935), 166-73.

4 Ward, op. cit, 86-87 and John P. Buckley, <u>The New York Irish: Their View on American Foreign Policy, 1914-21</u> (New York: Arno Press, 1976), 69. Walter Hines Page". <u>http://sss.knowsouthernhistory.net/biographies/WHPage/</u>. For Gerard, see "Gerard, James Watson". Johnson, Allan, Malone, Dumas. <u>Dictionary of American Biography</u> vol. IV (New York: Charles Scribner's Sons, 1959), 241-242. Based on his experience, Gerard wrote several books, the first of which, <u>My Four Years In Germany</u> became a pro-Allied propaganda play. For St. John Gaffney, see "Gaffney, T(homas) St. John", <u>Who Was Who In America, vol. 2</u> (Chicago: A.N. Marquis Company, 1953), 202. His memoirs were printed years later in <u>Breaking the Silence: England, Ireland, Wilson and the War</u> (New York: Horace Liveright, 1930).

5 "Thomas St. John Gaffney Arrives From Germany". <u>Catholic Sun</u> 8 September 1916:8. Gaffney's resignation was in November 1915 and he was by then in Germany carrying out Irish Nationalist activities. Gaffney's note of protest to the American ambassador in London, Walter H. Page, probably received little sympathy given Page's pro-British attitude.

6 Cited in Link, Arthur S., <u>Wilson: Confessions and Crises, 1915-1916</u> (Princeton, N.J.: Princeton University Press, 1964), 36-7.

7 Buckley, John Patrick. <u>op.cit</u>., 68. The pamphlets authored by O'Leary were, <u>Are Americans Industries In Peril?</u> (1915), <u>Who Wants War?</u> (1916), <u>The Fable of John Bull and Uncle Sam</u> (1916).

8 Buckley, <u>op.cit</u>., 90.

9 Link, Arthur. <u>Woodrow Wilson: Campaigns For Progressivism And Peace</u> (Princeton: University Press, 1965), 95.

10 O'Leary's Letter and Wilson's response are printed verbatim in Kelly, Michael, "Biographical Sketch of the Author", Part I in O'Reilly, Jeremiah, <u>My Political Trials and Experiences</u> (New York: Jefferson Publishing Co., 1919), 1-96. See "The O'Leary-Wilson Telegrams", 45-51. Also <u>New York Times</u> 30 September 1916.

11 Buckley, <u>op.cit</u>., 86.

12 "Malone, Dudley Field", DAB, 542.
13 "Wilson to Appoint Irish Catholic to Cabinet". Catholic Sun 24 January 1913:1,4.
14 "The Catholic Chosen". Catholic Sun 21 February 1913:2. McGuire's article contained a brief biography of Tumulty. A full treatment can be found in Blum, John M. Joe Tumulty and the Wilson Era (New York: Houghton-Mifflin, 1951). John Burke (1859-1937) is less well-known. After receiving his law degree from the University of Iowa, Burke moved to Dakota territory, becoming a lawyer and newspaper owner. After serving in the state legislature, he was elected Governor (1907-1913). Known as "Honest John", Burke was noted for ousting a corrupt political machine, endorsing primary elections and various other reforms. He served as United States Treasurer, 1913-21. Returning to North Dakota, Burke served on its Supreme Court until his death. "John Burke". State Historical Society of North Dakota. http://history.nd.gov/exhibits/governors/governors10.html. McGuire reports on Burke's Roman Catholic background and his membership in both the Knights of Columbus and The Ancient Order of Hibernians. "John Burke". Catholic Sun 4 April 1913:6.
15 "McGuire Denies He's Holding Spillane's Job". Syracuse Herald. 14 April 1914:3; "Brewster Or Dillon Will Get Place, Says M'Guire". Syracuse Herald. 24 July 1914:12; "Clancy Insists Upon Spillane Being Appointed". Syracuse Herald. 11 April 1914:6. 108-109.
16 "Kelly Machine Shattered, Claim of Insurgents". Syracuse Herald. 28 January 1915:2.
17 "McGuire Says Wilson Is Masterful Politician". Syracuse Herald. 20 February 1916:24. Tammany preferred "Champ" Clark and Wilson lost New York State because of Murphy's political indifference. Recall also, the McGuires were virtually abandoned by Tammany in the recently concluded asphalt investigations.
18 "McGuire Member of Truth Society and Wilson Foe". Syracuse Herald 7 October 1916:6. Despite some nominal cooperation on Nationalist issues, the rivalry between William Kelley and James K. McGuire was still strong at this point. There was the lingering bitterness of the asphalt scandals. In addition, McGuire had obtained key federal patronage jobs in Onondaga County against those sponsored by Kelley.
19 "McGuire Denies He Is Against Wilson". Syracuse Herald 14 October 1916:3.
20 Viereck suggests otherwise, believing Wilson in mid-1916 was livid at British interference with neutral trade and opening US mails. "His Irish blood, of which he was keenly conscious, revolted against the treatment meted out by the British government to the Irish rebels." Viereck, George S. The Strangest

Friendship in History: Woodrow Wilson and Colonel House (New York: Liveright, Inc., 1932), 140.

21 "Lights and Shadows". Syracuse Herald 12 February 1915:8. Ridder (1851-1915) was a German-American Catholic journalist and later manager of the New-Yorker Staats-Zeitung, the foremost German-American paper in the United States. He was prominent in Democratic party circles. Hyphenations (New York: Max Schmetterling, 1915) an anthology of articles written by Ridder and his son entitled "The War Situation Day By Day" was designed to "correct the false impressions of Germany and Austria-Hungary sown by a "hostile press" in the interests of truth and justice. See "Herman Ridder, Editor, Is Dead" New York Times 2 November 1915.

22 Republican Campaign Textbook (New York, 1916), Democratic Textbook, 1916 (New York, 1916), cited in Link, Arthur S. Woodrow Wilson And The Progressive Era, 1910-1917 (New York: Harper Brothers, 1954), 232; 233.

23 Matthew Hale of Massachusetts was Acting Chairman of the National Progressive Party in 1912. He met with Democratic National Committee Chairman Vance McCormick, successor to William F. McCombs. Hale worked for the Wilson campaign. In "Local Bull Moose Bolt Hughes Movement". New York Times 7 July 1916; "Matthew Hale Out As Wilson Worker" New York Times 9 August 1916.

John M. Parker was a Louisiana Democratic, friend of Theodore Roosevelt and Progressive candidate for Governor in 1912. See Mike Miller, "Biography of Hon. John Milliken Parker, Bethel Church, MS". http://files.usgwarchives.org/la/or6oms/bios/p-000007.txt; "Parker Wants New Moose Convention". New York Times 13 July 1916; "Parker Assails TR Praises President". New York Times 15 October 1916.

Bainbridge Colby was a New York lawyer, member of the State Assembly and a founder of the Progressive Party. For his pro-Wilson efforts in 1916, he was appointed to the U.S. Shipping Board and was a special Assistant to the Attorney-General. Colby was Wilson's last Secretary of State and his law partner after they left public office in 1920. "Washington Astonished By Nomination of Bainbridge Colby To Succeed Lansing; Appointment Criticized On Many Grounds". New York Times 26 February 1920; On the prominent Irish Catholics who supported Wilson, see Ward, op.cit., 139.

Daniel O'Connell, was an active California Nationalist and Democrat who could not desert the party during the election of 1916. He sought to get Bryan the nomination before yielding to the party's choice - Wilson. He was a lawyer prominent for the defence of the Indo-German conspirators.

24 See Link, Arthur S. Woodrow Wilson And The Progressive Era, 1910-1917, op.cit., 239-40; 241 for a list of many of the Progressives who supported Wilson.

25 Lizzi, Dominick. Martin H. Glynn: Forgotten Hero. (New York: Valatine Press, 2007), 67. The slogan was strictly a function of the convention. As late as February 1916 the party slogan was to be "Wilson In 1916". See "Wilson In 1916". New York Times 16 February 1914. Glynn had the manuscript of his speech proofed in advance by Secretary of State Robert Lansing. War Memories of Robert Lansing (New York: Bobbs-Merrill Publishers, 1935), 159. According to Lizzi, Glynn had talked over his speech with William Jennings Bryan. Lizzi, op.cit., 67.
26 Pusey, Merlo J. Charles Evans Hughes vol. I (New York: MacMillan Co., 1923), 356.
27 Link, Woodrow Wilson And The Progressive Era, 1910-1917, op.cit. 241-42.
28 O'Leary Hoped to Curb Government". New York Times 25 October 1916. Also in Esslinger, Dean. "American German And Irish Attitudes Toward Neutrality, 1914-1917: A Study of Catholic Minorities". Catholic Historical Review, vol. 53, 1967, 194-216. New York World 24 October 1916, cited in Link, Woodrow Wilson And The Progressive Era, op.cit., 246.
29 Pusey, op.cit., 352; Link, Arthur. Woodrow Wilson And The Progressive Era, op.cit., 238.
30 "Says Glynn Sought Aid of O'Leary". New York Times 25 October 1916. There may be reasons to question William R. MacDonald's veracity – he was Secretary of the American Independence Conference; his report was issued after the Democratic National Committee had publicized Hughes meeting with key members of the Conference, and; O'Leary had recently filed a second libel lawsuit against Vance McCormick, suggesting a meeting with O'Leary was the last thing the Democratic National Committee Chairman wanted. "O'Leary Sues McCormick". New York Times 25 October 1916. Others reportedly attending the conference included Carl F. Schmidt, William R. MacDonald, Frank Sieberlich, G. H. Jacobsen, Jaspar R. Darling, Joseph Frey and Victor Ridder. Link, Woodrow Wilson And The Progressive Era, op.cit., fn57.
31 Viereck, George Sylvester. The Strangest Friendship In History: Woodrow Wilson and Colonel House. (New York: Liveright, Inc., 1932), 161; Ward, op.cit., 137. "Says O'Leary Hoped To Curb Government". New York Times 25 October 1916; "Says Hughes Made Deal With O'Leary". New York Times 23 October 1916; "McCormick Case Proved". New York Times 26 October 1916; "Duped By Germans Darling Declares". New York Times 23 September 1917.
32 "Wisconsin Priests Shun Propaganda". New York Times 26 October 1916.
33 Viereck, Spreading Germs…252. Hughes specifically declared he would tolerate no improper interference in American mails, commerce or property,

and any American exercising his legitimate rights should be blacklisted by belligerents.

34 Link, Woodrow Wilson And The Progressive Era, op.cit., 245; Pusey devotes an entire chapter to the incident, blaming Hiram Johnson's ego and Wilcox's ineptitude as campaign manager. See Pusey, vol. I, chapter 32, "The California Incident", 335-349; 362-63.

35 Lizzi, op.cit., 65; 67.

36 Child, Clifton James, The German-Americans In Politics, 1914-1917 (Madison: University of Wisconsin Press, 1939), 147 citing Viereck, George Sylvester. The Strangest Friendship In History, op.cit., 159. In Spreading Germs of Hate (New York, Horace Liveright, 1930, 243-4), Viereck gives a slightly different version – implicating a "trusted henchman" of William Jennings Bryan who was employed as correspondent by Viereck's newspaper and by Dr. Karl A. Feuhr's Trans-Oceanic News Service. His cover name was Josiah Wingate. In reality he was a former Captain in the United States Army named J. J. Dickinson whose testimony was cited in a post-war investigation.

37 Pusey, op.cit., 354-55.

38 Viereck, The Strangest Friendship…, op.cit., 162. Leary, William.

39 Buckley, John Patrick. op.cit., 102-103; Link, Wilson And Progressive Era, op.cit., 249-50; L

Chapter III - C

Accommodation to Intervention: Protests, Surveillance, Pragmatic Patriotism

Within five months of his election, President Wilson and the United States were at war with the Central Powers, despite his campaign slogan, "He kept us out of war". The Irish-and German-Americans fought a long and ultimately losing campaign to prevent America from being dragged into the conflict. Since the war was being fought in the name of American interests, their ethnic loyalties to the United States came into question. This complicated the allegiance of Irish – Americans to Irish freedom and their association with German-Americans. An Irish-American who exemplified this dilemma was Frank P. Walsh.[1]

Frank P. Walsh, like many Irish-Americans, was initially opposed to American entry into the conflict, but he endorsed it once Congress declared war. For his efforts he was made co-chairman of the War Labor Board with ex-President William Howard Taft. In an address given in his hometown of Kansas City, Missouri in 1917, he referred to his previous pacifist convictions, noting now that we were in it, all Americans should be of one mind to prosecute the war vigorously until victory was achieved. Briefly reviewing America's new allies, he praised France as a long-time friend and ally of Ireland and a sanctuary for Irish rebels. Russia's suffering millions are "democrats at heart," he declared. Passing lightly over the German-Irish connections, Walsh echoed sentiments similar to McGuire holding out an olive branch to German – Americans stating he could not speak of the German race as the enemy, given the patriotic sacrifice of many Germans in the wars of the United States. Walsh regretted the "exigencies of the modern advance towards world-wide liberty and democracy" which put America at war with this "noble and beloved people". And despite the fact that England was now our ally, the past was not easily forgotten. "The Celt… looks back on the bloody history of his own stricken land, for from time immemorial the laws of England might make a man a criminal in Ireland…". He continued by saying:

> Perhaps we ought not to be critical of our friendly ally at this time, yet should we not be excused from not enthusing over the presence of Mr. Balfour, known to

us of Irish blood as "Bloody Balfour," who in exercise of his autocracy over Ireland, put to death more Irish patriots than any man of his time.

Walsh went on to urge that small nations be given their freedom at the conclusion of hostilities, especially that nation

> ...which has furnished statesmen, warriors and teachers to the entire World from time immemorial, a nation that has never surrendered its own ideals, its religion, its language, its customs and for more than Seven hundred years in every generation has shed the blood of its Best manhood to repeal the armed invaders from its shores – Ireland, The imperishable, the dauntless small nation that has never surrendered.[2]

James K. McGuire showed a similar ambivalence. Visiting Syracuse following an extended trip through the West and South after American entry into the war, McGuire, like Ryan, said discussion as to the merits of the war was over now that the United States was on the Allied side. Similar to Ryan, McGuire predicted German-Americans, like Irish-Americans would remain loyal to their adopted country. "Our people of German blood are showing on all sides manifestations of patriotism, forbearance and devotion to our common country. Disloyalty will be unknown among them during the war". McGuire predicted huge food surpluses produced by farmers using new technologies to replace the manpower lost to urban migration. Women, especially black women, were also moving into cities to take advantage of higher-paying war industries. Still betraying his sympathy to Germany, McGuire warned of the impact of the submarine menace on supplies to the Allies, believing it only a matter of time before they would be stopped. Taking a swipe at Wilson's plan for armed merchant vessels, McGuire believed it fruitless as since the submarine was invisible. Waving the flag of Irish nationalism, McGuire assailed British policy in Ireland for turning arable land into pasture, making starvation in Ireland a distinct possibility. Echoing Wilson's remarks as to the destiny of small nations, he urged Ireland be considered a candidate for independence along with Serbia and Poland.[3] Symbolic of the diversity of Irish American opinion was the attitude of former Tammany Boss, and McGuire rival, Richard Croker. Diverging from McGuire, he urged Ireland remain loyal to England for the duration of the war, believing a German victory would dash all hopes for an Irish republic. Croker condemned Casement as a traitor, and praised Redmond's efforts who he referred to as a "true Irish patriot". He denounced British oppression as retarding Ireland's development, but believed Irish statesmen could make the needed adjustments to guide the country to independence. Endorsing Home Rule as a stepping stone to independence, Croker urged Ireland aid the Allies in the defeat of Germany.[4]

The speeches and articles reveal the diversity of opinion of many American Irish towards the Wilson administration. And despite the fact that many leaders of the "professional" Irish were subsequently harassed by the Wilson administration, most, like Walsh and McGuire, pinned their hopes on a post-war settlement that would grant Ireland its independence. It also created problems for President Wilson and American foreign policy in that few Irish friends of moderation remained in positions of power. The President was vulnerable to criticism from hyphenate militants because of his denunciation of them, his failure to make a public statement about the Easter Rebellion and, in Irish eyes, the mismanagement of the appeal for clemency for Sir Roger Casement. In order to mollify Irish opinion in American, Wilson sought to mediate the conflict, a move which received significant support from the hyphenate press. According to Buckley, they supported the President's efforts since a negotiated peace would place England at a military disadvantage if a settlement could be arrived at by early 1917.[5] Germany initiated the process in December 1916. President Wilson asked both parties to submit their conditions. Neither side was conciliatory, exacting either huge territorial concessions, fiscal reparations or demanding total military emasculation.[6] Irish-Americans demanded independence for Ireland as a precondition for peace, a point noted both by the British government and Ambassador von Bernstorff.[7] In view of British foot-dragging on the issue, militant Irish were discussing with Germany the possibility of a subsequent rebellion. For example, Patrick McCartan, appointed ambassador of the Provisional Irish government in mid-1917, and Liam Mellows, were planning to leave for Europe on forged passports.[8] Both were arrested. In addition, St. John Gaffney and George Chatterton-Hill[9] had organized a German-Irish Society in Berlin and put the case for an independent Ireland at the International Socialist Peace Conference in June 1917.[10]

Many Irish-Americans continued to maintain their pro-German bias, interpreting events in Europe from an anti-British perspective. Buckley, for example, discounted reports of deporting Belgian laborers to Germany as a war-time necessity to keep them from harm's way. This "hypocrisy" was reinforced with appeals for equitable treatment for those Irish rebels still in prison months after the Rising.[11] In late January 1917 President Wilson made his famous "Peace Without Victory" speech which held both good and bad news for Ireland and Irish-Americans. Some, such as Jeremiah O'Leary, hailed it as a great message. Even Daniel F. Cohalan lauded it, using it to call for independence for Poland, Belgium and Ireland.[12] Others, such as John Devoy, saw Wilson's plan for a "League for Peace" as a tool to preserve the decadent British Empire.[13] This opposition would not only defeat the Treaty of Versailles, but would also split Irish-Americans and impair progress towards Irish independence. One of the key players in these events was James K. McGuire.

Its peaceful overtures rebuffed, its efforts at subversion and sabotage stymied, its merchant raiders and high seas fleet impotent and with an increase its submarine fleet, Germany announced the resumption of unrestricted submarine warfare after 1 February 1917. The United States responded by severing diplomatic relations two days later. Assuming its unilateral policy would lead to American intervention on the Allied side, the German military believed it could defeat the Allies before the United States could mobilize and enter the war. Irish-and German-Americans exerted themselves to prevent American involvement from February through March of 1917. The militant Irish, especially the Friends of Irish Freedom, continued to push the theme that intervention by the United States on the Allied side was tantamount to endorsing the continued subjection of colonized peoples throughout the world.[14] The Catholic Sun gave full coverage of a speech by William Jennings Bryan who proclaimed the American people did not want war. Some of his proposals were those announced by Irish nationalists, including keeping Americans off belligerents' ships, refusing clearance for American ships carrying contraband and keeping American ships out of the war zone.[15]

Bruce Bielaski
(1883-1964)
Chief Of The Bureau of investigation, 1912-1919

Walter Hines Page
(1855-1918)
Ambassador to Great Britain, 1913-1918
Public Domain

Frank P Walsh
(1864-1939)
Lawyer, Social reformer, Irish nationalist
Public Domain

Jeremiah A. O'Leary
Source Jeremiah A. O'Leary My Political Trials and Experiences. New York Jefferson Publishing Co, 1919 No Known Copyright Restrictions

During the first week of January 1917, The Friends of Irish Freedom unanimously adopted a resolution including Ireland along with Belgium and Poland as free nations. Smarting from the slight that German peace overtures made no mention of Ireland, they demanded Ireland be classified a belligerent since it was allied with Germany in the Irish Uprising, and further requested Germany clarify its policies as to Ireland.[16] The resolution was also endorsed by the Cuman na m'Bainn. Further mass meetings were planned.

In addition, on 18 January 1917, FOIF launched an American Sinn Fein organization with a slate of officers from the entire spectrum of Irish Nationalism-the O'Leary brothers from the American Truth Society, along with Peter Golden, Stephen W. Johnson, John D. Moore, Dennis Spellissy, Robert Monteith and James Larkin. The following month, two days after the severing of diplomatic ties between the United States and Germany, the new organization under the chairmanship of Daniel Cohalan held a conference in New York City. The 1200 delegates passed a resolution condemning American intervention in the war on the Allied side as supportive of colonialism in general and of British rule in Ireland in particular. Over $100,000 was pledged for the support of "the complete national independence of Ireland,"[17] words that would come back to haunt Cohalan in his subsequent conflict with Eamon de Valera for control of Irish support in America.

Subsequently, a meeting on 10 February 1917 of the Friends of Irish Freedom prepared an address expressing its opinion as to why America should stay out of the European war. The message also expressed concern over pending legislations for the suppression of revolutionary conspiracies against friendly governments. James K. McGuire was part of a delegation which presented the FOIF resolution. McGuire's participation was a logical choice. He was still a ranking member of the Clan and FOIF, had been an outspoken advocate of the Irish cause and had numerous contacts in Washington, including members of Congress and Joseph Tumulty. McGuire had communicated with Tumulty on the Wilson administration with reference to the Catholic Church in Mexico in 1915.[18] Other members included Victor Herbert in his capacity as President of FOIF, Joseph J. Lawless, a prominent judge from Virginia, John Jerome Rooney, Dr. John F. Kelly, the engineer and author and Robert E. Ford, editor of The Irish World. The petition was accepted on behalf of the President by Joseph Tumulty, Wilson's Secretary.[19]

McGuire also continued his pro-German, Irish Nationalist efforts. For example, shortly before American entry into the war, in January 1917, FOIF members protested the showing of the film, "Whom the Gods Would Destroy". Loosely based on the life of Roger Casement and the Easter Rising, the plot revolved around two friends, one an English naval officer, the other an Irish patriot, both in love with the same Irish woman. The Irish patriot had recently returned from Germany to lead insurgents against England. The Englishman, blinded in a naval engagement, was recuperating at the women's home, where the Irish patriot was hiding. Irish rebels came to claim their leader. The blinded officer signaled an English warship and in a bloody encounter, the insurgents are killed and scattered. The Irish leader is captured, and sentenced to be hanged. He is pardoned by the king through the timely intervention of a friend.[20] The Vitagraph Film Company charged FOIF members with encouraging disorders over the film. The historical distortions objected to were the depictions of the Irish rebels as a disorganized mob armed only with sticks and stones, and a pardoning of Roger Casement by a benevolent King, rather than his hasty execution. Among those indicted were James K. McGuire, Thomas Addis Emmet and John Goff. FOIF sent letters to theater owners throughout New York City protesting the film's contents. "It portrays Sir Roger Casement and the Irish patriots as traitors and applauds their execution by a government which would have hanged George Washington, John Hancock and Benjamin Franklin, just as it hanged Sir Roger Casement and shot down like dogs Padriac Pearse, James Connolly and their followers in their brave fight for freedom." Several protestors were defended by John O'Leary, brother of Jeremiah O'Leary, the "anti-British Irishman who was rebuked by President Wilson." The defendants were found not guilty by

Police Court Justice Walsh after they admitted making an "orderly protest" of the film.[21] Ironically, while pro-Irish groups thought it pro-British, it was considered too pro-Irish by British authorities which banned the American-made film.

Daniel F Cohalan
(1867 1946)
Tammary Politician New
York Supreme Court Justice Leader of the
Friends of Irish Freedom,1916-1934
L1brary of Congress ID cph 3b 15359
No Copyright Restrictions

George Creel
11876-1953)
Journalist, Head of the Committee
on Public Information, 1917-1918
Public Domain

The Friends of Irish Freedom continued to hold public demonstrations despite increasing pressure from "patriotic" groups which sought to curtail their activities. For example, Cleveland Moffett,[22] Chairman of the American Defense Society declared the goal of his group was to fight pro-German sedition in New York. His group monitored FOIF street corners orators for anti-British comments, believing FOIF was funded by German money. FOIF spokesperson Stephen Johnson denounced Moffett as a meddling Anglomaniac, defending Roget Casement from the charge of "traitor". Moffett previously interrupted a speaker and had been arrested. He subsequently wrote a letter to the President asking to have treason clearly defined. Theodore Roosevelt, a member of the Advisory Council of the society, endorsed the group's call for an anti-sedition bill.[23] All the while, McGuire continued his propaganda efforts. In a <u>Catholic Sun</u> article of November 1916, McGuire referred to the wasted lives of Irish lads who were sacrificed in the trenches for the conquerors and rulers of Ireland. He criticized the British blockade of the Irish coast, the censorship depriving Ireland of the news of British defeats and the "harried and frightened Irish Parliamentary Party clinging to British coat tails". McGuire reviled I.P.P. members as benefitting from British rule through jobs, and war-related businesses. Prophetically McGuire stated, "they must take a stand for Ireland or they are doomed at home." The native Irish clergy had repudiated them, its cash flow from America had dried up, and Home Rule was a failed policy. To resuscitate its program, McGuire stated the I.P.P. had made six demands to the British government: 1. No conscription in Ireland; 2. Immunity for prisoners interred during the Rising; 3. Reduction of life sentences for internees; 4. End martial law; 5. Abolish rule from Dublin Castle; 6. Home Rule. All, save the first, said McGuire, had been defeated.[24]

Shortly before America entered the war, as McGuire and FOIF continued to lobby frantically against that possibility, McGuire gave a speech in his hometown of New Rochelle, New York. His co-speaker was Nellie Gifford, a dispatch bearer for the rebels in the Rising, who was later confined to Kilmainham jail for her efforts.

Gifford voicing a position FOIF would later openly endorse, urged the meeting adopt a resolution demanding the recognition of an independent Ireland at the peace conference after the war.

McGuire followed. Using President Wilson's words as to the liberation of small nations, McGuire questioned why Ireland was not among those listed. He asked the United States to join with the Friends of Irish Freedom in recognizing the just claims of Irish independence. Again reiterating the sacrifices of Irish-Americans in past wars, he questioned why the paramount concern over Belgium by the United States, when it had never assisted America in its struggles. He echoed Nellie Gifford's call for a resolution including Irish representation at the post-war peace conference.[25]

Writing in early February, McGuire noted the British Imperial War Conference was about to recommend an Irish Home Rule Act. Stating the war was going badly for England, McGuire believed Germany would have the upper hand in negotiations and should demand freedom for Ireland as a condition for peace. "It is to either Germany or the United States that the friends of Irish freedom must look if Ireland is to represented in the peace conference."[26] Interestingly, on the same page was an advertisement for Poems of the Irish Revolutionary Brotherhood and an article by Dr. William Bayard Hale. It was the same Hale who had been a confidante and biographer of President Wilson. He was also employed with McGuire as a propagandist for the German Information Service. Currently, Hale was the European correspondent for the anti-British Hearst newspapers. German Colonial Secretary Dr. Wilhelm Solf, interpreted President Wilson's 22 January 1917 statement, "government's deriving their just powers from the consent of the governed" as having applicability to the Irish situation.[27] Such public utterances revealed that Germany and Irish Nationalists' policies despite the strains between them, were still in tandem.[28]

A fortnight later, McGuire saw in the German notice of unrestricted submarine warfare the hint of aid to Ireland. The U-boats would end the exporting of food from Ireland and thereby prevent starvation. Freedom of the seas for Germany will never occur, he said, until England is conquered. Ireland will be unaffected by the blockade since it will retain its food supply. McGuire ended his article taking a swipe at the idea of conscription: "the truth is the only way to save the remnants of the Irish race is to conserve their own food supply and keep out of the army."[29]

McGuire continued to use The Catholic Sun to agitate for the Irish independence, publishing long letters of Mrs. Francis Sheehy-Skeffington's condemnation of conscription.[30] She predicted dire consequences for Ireland in the coming year - conscription, famine and revolution.

McGuire also reviewed several books dealing with the Irish uprising. McGuire's critique of George Chatterton-Hill's, The Significance of Ireland In This War, was favorable because it was from the "patriotic point of view" and possibly because he wrote the introduction to the American edition. Three others, published in Britain, were critical of Ireland stabbing Britain in the back during its hour of need, its leaders condemned by McGuire as sincere but men of bad judgment. He generously said they are not unfairly written from a British stand point.[31] Obviously, his bias was toward Chatterton-Hill, an outspoken supporter and activist of the cause of Irish nationalism, but his attempt to achieve balance in his book reviews may reflect the shifting attitude of Irish Nationalists towards Germany and the increasing pro-Allied position of American public opinion.

Despite the increasing drift of America towards intervention on the Allied side, McGuire still clung to the idea of a tripartite alliance between Germany, Ireland and the United States. Speaking at a meeting of the Friends of Irish Freedom in early February 1917, McGuire stated Ireland's claims for freedom must be presented by either Germany or the United States at any peace conference following the close of hostilities. Cognizant of the fact that Britain was in dire straits because of its manpower losses and the failure of its policy of voluntary recruitment, McGuire stated a second revolution was needed in Ireland in order that it achieve independence.[32] According to official British documents this was still an item of concern at the time.[33]

In a subsequent article in The Syracuse Herald, during the first week of February 1917, James K. McGuire, in his capacity as Chairman of the Executive Committee of the Friends of Irish Freedom, called a meeting of the organization's Executive Committee "to deal with the present situation affecting world peace and the attitude of Irish-Americans in the present crisis." The object of the meeting was to demand President Wilson observe strict neutrality, insist England cease interfering in American mail and commerce, and that her "spies" be driven from the country. The article stated the current policy in Washington was biased towards Britain.[34] FOIF National Secretary, John D. Moore, appeared before a Congressional committee as one of several witnesses urging continued American neutrality.[35] Believing the inevitable was about to occur, President Wilson requested from Congress permission to arm American merchant vessels. His efforts were blocked by a "little group of willful men" who filibustered against it.[36] According to Villard, they were called "traitors, Iscariots and worse", but this crusading editor of the Evening Post instead referred to them as a "true roll of honor.[37] The President, acting as Commander-In-Chief, ordered the arming of merchant vessels. The Irish press responded by reiterating the theme that an unholy conspiracy of plutocrats, munitions' makers, major newspapers and British propaganda were pushing America towards an unwanted war.[38] The idea also received support from several Congressmen.

By 1 March 1917, the public acknowledgment by its author as to the authenticity of the Zimmerman note and the sinking of three American vessels with a large loss of life on 18 March 1917, moved American public opinion towards the Allied cause. Wilson realized the Irish issue was an obstacle to effective collaboration with the Allies. After America entered the war, in April 1917, he asked both Secretary of State Lansing and Ambassador Walter H. Page have Britain's Prime Minister David L. George settle the Irish question. The British sent Foreign Secretary Arthur Balfour to the United States to assess how the issue could be resolved. Balfour met with "moderate" Irish-Americans.[39] The Clan-na-Gael and Friends of Irish Freedom, of which James K. McGuire was a ranking member, were not included. Nonetheless, despite the biased representation of the commission, Balfour came away with the impression that a peaceful resolution of the Irish issue was essential.[40] This was followed by a petition from the American Congress, requesting its speedy resolution. The effort, headed by "Champ" Clark, suggested a peaceful solution to the Irish crisis would greatly encourage American enthusiasm towards the war. Letters from prominent Americans such as Theodore Roosevelt, Charles W. Eliot, William Howard Taft, Cardinal Gibbons, Mayors John P. Mitchel of New York City and John F. Fitzgerald of Boston, applied additional pressure to the beleaguered British government.[41] Nonetheless, Wilson continued to resist the pressure, preferring instead to take the British offer of an Irish convention as the most effective solution to the problem at face value.

Wilson encouraged a peaceful resolution to the Home Rule crisis, in part to mollify his Irish critics. As a result of his pressure, Lloyd George and John Redmond introduced a plan for Home Rule, excluding Ulster. The proposal met with a scathing condemnation by Irish militants. Daniel F. Cohalan and John Goff were especially contemptuous of this half measure, insisting the Irish people demanded complete independence. The Catholic press, including James K. McGuire's Catholic Sun, was adamant. In banner headlines, McGuire's paper denounced the idea of a convention in an article co-authored by stalwarts of the Friends of Irish Freedom- including Victor Herbert, Thomas Addis Emmet and James K. McGuire. The article condemned the convention in concept, principle and execution because it denied the adult population of Ireland any input into the process; its delegates were a majority hand-picked by the British government; its alleged inclusion of Sinn Fein was "specious" since its most important leaders were in prison, and the chairman was a British government appointee who could control the secret proceedings. The FOIF leaders declared the proposal as impractical, insidious and foredoomed to failure. The proposals were criticized at length in a pamphlet distributed by the Friends of Irish Freedom, entitled, <u>Criticism of the Irish Convention As Proposed By Premier David Lloyd George: The Opinions of Prominent Americans of Irish Blood</u>. It was the effort of Captain W. J. M. A. Maloney, M.D., wounded survivor of several British campaigns during the war. The slaughter of the war, the executions in the wake of the Easter Rebellion and the hanging of Casement turned him into an Irish Nationalist. Maloney was linked to Oswald Garrison Villard, liberal editor and owner of the <u>Evening Post</u>. The FOIF pamphlet, states the <u>Post</u> was "scholarly and intensely pro-Allied". McGuire's contribution, along with Judge John Goff, Victor Herbert, and Thomas Addis Emmett, was in their capacity as officers of FOIF. McGuire's comments focused on the economic, and cultural decline of (Southern) Ireland under British rule, ending his article with a demand for a free Constitution and an independent Irish Parliament. FOIF President John D. Moore kept up the pressure on President Wilson. In a letter to Joseph Tumulty, he denounced Home Rule as a "pitiful travesty".[42]

Because of these and other pressures, the British Irish Convention effort was a dismal failure. Redmond endorsed the convention concept, but Sinn Fein refused to participate despite the fact its imprisoned leaders were freed by Britain as a show of good faith. The Irish Nationalists sought to use this to score a public relations coup. Dr. Patrick McCartan[43] the new envoy of the Irish Republic to the United States, met with the prisoners to draft a statement of their views on the conditions on Ireland. Prominent Irish Nationalist, Dr. Eoin MacNeill[44] wrote it. Among the twenty-six signatories was Eamon de Valera, Diarmuid Lynch and John McGarry.[45] Given war-time censorship, the statement was smuggled into the United States on a starched linen handkerchief stitched into the clothing of McCartan. The petition was copied in John Devoy's office and edited by Judge Cohalan and McCartan, who accompanied by James K. McGuire and John D. Moore presented the petition to Joseph Tumulty.[46] They petitioned Wilson using his own words, that he address the sovereignty of small nation of which Ireland was one. Wilson could not meet with delegation since McCartan represented a government the United States did not recognize, but he was willing to give them a hearing given the contentious nature of the Irish vote in America. It was presented to the President's Secretary, Joseph Tumulty. Despite their efforts, it had little impact. The document was quietly shelved and given no response. While in Washington, McGuire introduced the delegation to several Congressmen sympathetic to the Irish cause.[47]

The Unionists were adamant in support of partition with the inevitable result the Irish convention collapsed. The Syracuse Herald, noted the election of "Edward (sic) deValera, the Sinn Fein candidate", to a seat vacated by the death of William Redmond, brother of the Irish Parliamentary Party leader, John Redmond. It was perceived as a repudiation by the Irish public of I.P.P. policies.[48] James K. McGuire, not surprisingly, given his key leadership positions in the Clan and FOIF, was extremely outspoken against the proposal made by Lloyd George. This was not his first denunciation of the concept. A year earlier, shortly after the Rising of 1916, he condemned British repression and the idea of partition as "a gerrymander designed to concentrate poor Catholics in a skeleton state which was destined to fail". Possibly referring back to his Tammany feuds with Bosses Croker and Murphy, he called the U.I.L. a "Tammany machine" distributing patronage jobs via the British government". Since militants, including Sinn Fein, and the Citizens' Army were excluded, McGuire derided the scheme as a burlesque".[49] His official public statement on the plan condemned the British economic exploitation of Ireland and castigated Ulster's attitude of superiority towards its impoverished Southern neighbors. Using prominent Catholic Irish-Americans, such as William Farrell, head of United States Steel Corporation, Thomas Fortune Ryan, the transit, tobacco, insurance magnate and William Grace, the shipping tycoon and others to prove the point that when given the opportunity, southern Irish could overcome the obstacles of poverty and prejudice. The only logical solution was a "true Constitution and an Irish Parliament created by, and responsible to, the people of Ireland.[50] The efforts of Irish Nationalist in America did have some impact. For example, a planned visit by I.P.P. leader,

T. P. O'Connor in June 1917 resulted in a storm of protest organized by FOIF and the Clan-na-Gael. O'Connor was amazed at the lack of response by moderate Irishmen to his visit.[51]

Despite his professing an interest in the peaceful resolution of the Irish issue, Wilson continued his harassment of "professional" Irish. The public activities of McGuire and other Nationalists were engaged brought them under the scrutiny of of government agencies given greater powers by wartime legislation. Chief among them was the Bureau of Investigation, created in 1908 by Attorney – General Charles Bonaparte within the Department of Justice during the presidency of Theodore Roosevelt. Both men embraced the Progressive philosophy of efficiency and expertise in government. That led to the creation of a corps of agents from the Secret Service. Starting with a staff of 34, it increased almost ten – fold during the Great War. Within a year, Bonaparte's successor, George Wickersham, named it the Bureau of Investigation. Field offices were established in major cities and along the Mexican border, "where they concentrated on smuggling, neutrality violations and intelligence collection, often in connection with the Mexican Revolution."[52] With American entry into the war in April 1917, the Bureau now under the leadership of lawyer Bruce Bielaski, took up the role of policing war – related violations of the law, including draft evasion and sabotage. The agents were assisted with the passage of three laws: the Espionage Act of June, 1917 and its supplements – the Trading With the Enemies Act of October 1917 and the Sedition Act of May 1918.

The Espionage Act prohibited interference in military operations, recruitment and support for enemies of the United States during wartime. Wilson had asked for such legislation as early as December, 1915 but action was delayed due to prolonged debate over the issue of press censorship. Once that was removed, it became law. Enforcement was left to local U. S. Attorneys who were not that numerous. Through the influence of Postmaster – General Albert S. Burleson, the Department of Justice could depend on a nation – wide system of postal inspectors to ban any materials they deemed "subversive". Newsapers banned were John Devoy's <u>Gaelic American</u> and The <u>Bull</u>

of Irish nationalist Jeremiah O'Leary- despite McGuire's efforts to prevent it, and the <u>The Watchtower</u>, journal of Jehovah's Witnesses, which had been critical of the war and recruitment. Included as well were the works of radicals such as Emma Goldman and Max Eastman.[53]

The Trading With the Enemies Act of 6 October 1917 was designed to restrict trade with those countries hostile to the United States. It also provided for censorship as well. Wilson used it to create the Office of Alien Property Custodian whose powers included the confiscation of property of persons whose actions posed a threat to the war effort. The man in charge was A. Mitchell Palmer who confiscated the property of interned German immigrants and German – owned businesses. This enabled the United States to not only seize their firms, but use their patents as well. Chemicals were especially noted as a result of the destruction of ships carrying supplies to the Allies and the efforts of German agents to use chemical warfare. Not only was trade targeted, but communications as well. No publication of news critical of the war effort, of United States conduct of the war effort or conscription was allowed. Foreign publications had to submit their copy to the Post office for review. If censored, they lost their second – class mailing privileges, a death knell to their survival. McGuire and his associates would find themselves targeted under these war-time prohibitions.[54]

The Sedition Act, largely a series of amendments to the Espionage Act, included a broad range of offenses which put the war effort in a poor light, or for interfering with the sale of government bonds. Because it applied to wartime conditions, it was repealed in December 1920 after hostilities ceased. About 1500 cases were tried resulting in about 1000 prosecutions.[55]

In addition, there was the creation of Committee on Public Information,(CPI) established by Executive Order of President Wilson the same month as the United States entered the war, April 1917. Also known as the Creel Committee after its head, muck – raking journalist George Creel. Its goal was "positive" propaganda to encourage popular opinion to support the war. It had no enforcement provisions, instead encouraging conformity to "voluntary guidelines". Like the laws noted previously, it was an effort to limit dissent. A variety of divisions were responsible for publicizing war aims in newsprint, posters and movies. Apparently its efforts were a success as there were few demonstrations of disloyalty. But it begs the question--was it the positive message of the Committee or the threat of vigilante justice which induced conformity? Not only were movies made, but between reels "Four Minute Men" would deliver talks supportive of the American war effort.[56]

The government efforts were supplemented by the creation of the American Protective League begun in March 1917. Believing the Department of Justice was understaffed as to counter – intelligence and with the threat of American intervention in the war imminent, Chicago businessman A.M. Briggs established a volunteer auxiliary to identify alleged German sympathizers and to counteract activities of anti-war activists and radicals. While not a government agency, with no enforcement authority, the APL had the imprimatur of the Attorney – General Thomas W. Gregory, primary architect of the Espionage and Sedition Acts. At its height the APL had over 250,000 members in 600 cities who reported alleged violators. Despite President Wilson's misgivings as to its activities, he deferred to his Attorney – General and took no action to suppress its vigilante activities.[57]

Given the repressive social and political climate, McGuire's move to a pragmatic patriot was appropriate and significant. It was undoubtedly an important reason why he was not prosecuted for his actions. Nonetheless, McGuire came under surveillance by the Department of Justice from June 1916 with a brief hiatus until December 1917 and then again through December 1918.

Under this new legal umbrella, the Bureau of Investigation became the government's primary agency for suppression of anti – war sentiment. Collectively it limited free speech, used investigations to intimidate and harass opponents and skeptics of the war, in addition to pursuing allegations of subversion from concerned citizens. James K. McGuire became a person of interest given his high profile with individuals and organizations whose activities were perceived as disloyal.

The BOI documents McGuire's association with both German and Austrian consuls in New York City.⁵⁸ Initial reports also noted his pro – German books, his spreading of German propaganda and his many speeches in favor of Irish independence.⁵⁹ Then almost 18 months later, in December of 1917, there was a follow – up report revealing McGuire's ties to Daniel Cohalan, his close associate in the Clan – na- Gael and FOIF. Was this an effort to tarnish his reputation and link him to the subversive actions of Cohalan reported in the just released von Igel papers? The investigation concluded McGuire had connections to German Ambassador Bernstorff, had access to "all (American) government departments" and that he was a "very dangerous man to be at large".⁶⁰ A January 1918 account revealed his efforts to rally German and Irish residents in Syracuse to support an arms embargo were derailed by Mayor "Hill."⁶¹. By February, under orders from Bielaski's BOI, postal authorities were investigating the contents of his books. The BOI had its Syracuse agent investigate McGuire. His report turned out quite favorable, calling him a "man of higher character", and despite his books "absolutely loyal to the United States".⁶² A follow – up investigation of his first book, <u>The King</u>, <u>The Kaiser</u> and <u>Irish Freedom</u>, was labeled "seditious". However, given its publication date of 1915, the agent concluded its contents were presumed not malicious in intent, and although it did support dissent, it was intensely pro – German and anti- -British. Yet the report stated McGuire was "pro – American".⁶³ His second book, <u>What Could Germany Do For Ireland?</u> was found to be more provocative and possibly in violation of the Trading With the Enemies Act. This was a serious accusation, as well over 1000 Americans were imprisoned under its provisions. Yet the only consequence McGuire suffered was having his book banned from military libraries in September 1918 by Director of Naval Intelligence Hugo Johnstone.⁶⁴ A month later a BOI report labeled McGuire "a rank Sinn Feiner" and recipient of $26,000 from Dr. Heinrich Albert for his propaganda efforts. These and other facts were brought out in a subsequent Senate investigation of his activities.⁶⁵ Despite all this McGuire was never prosecuted. Letters testifying as to his good character and professed loyalty to the United States, his sale of war bonds, the fact his son was to enroll in the military, his patriotic articles in his newspapers were all undoubtedly factors contributing to that. And perhaps BOI investigations were incomplete. There was no mention of his involvement in the efforts to smuggle Casement into Germany or of his deep involvement in the Clan – na -Gael. One might wonder what his fate might have been had these other facts been uncovered. But could his lack of indictment been a function of timing? McGuire associates Jeremiah O'Leary and James Larkin were prosecuted after the war, but that may have been because they refused to recant their views. The armistice was signed in November and his book <u>What Could Germany Do for Ireland</u> was banned only a month previously. Was Wilson still maneuvering to obtain support for his League of Nations, especially given the opposition to it by many in the Irish – American community?

The Irish leaders' protestations of loyalty following American entry into the war, of necessity meant further collaboration with German-Americans came to an end. By summer 1917, the Friends of Irish Freedom widely circulated a petition calling for Irish independence, enrolling several hundred thousand signatures. Wilson's response to their opposition was to have Secret Service agents investigate the finances of the Friends of Irish Freedom, assuming German money was behind their efforts. Wilson pressured its leadership even more, publishing the contents of the von Igel papers in September 1917.⁶⁶ Seized in a Secret Service raid in April 1916, the papers revealed the subversive activities of German agents in America, including revolutionary plots in Ireland and India. Despite State Department denials, the "professional Irish" believed the release of the details of the Irish involvement led to the arrest and execution of Sir Roger Casement. Of particular importance were the revelations surrounding the subversive activities of John Devoy, Daniel F. Cohalan and John T. Ryan. In them was an unsigned note to the German Foreign office from Cohalan recommending German fleet and submarine action in the North Sea to coincide with the Easter Rising. Cohalan thought his public career was over, but he fought back, declaring it was part of a British plot to destroy him.[67] Cohalan denounced it as a forgery, citing a meeting with pro-British Irish (Shane Leslie and Dr. William Maloney) in which they sought evidence to silence Cohalan by destroying his reputation. Devoy asserted the note was planted in the Von Igel papers in an effort to silence Cohalan. However, there is no evidence in the official archives to support the allegation. Devoy likewise denounced the publication as an attempt to injure the "cause of real Irish nationalism in the minds of the American people".Rather than disgrace Cohalan, it had the opposite effect as many Irish-Americans resented the late release of the documents, 17 months after the Von Igel raid.[68] The Syracuse Herald was especially critical of Cohalan in light of the new evidence, declaring his claim of a frame-up as a "ridiculous assertion". Once again, the timely intervention of Tammany Hall saved Cohalan's career.[69] This was a major factor leading to the cancellation of a second Irish Race Convention scheduled for late 1917 by James K. McGuire, despite complaints from fellow militant Jeremiah O'Leary.

The FOIF Executive scheduled a convention for mid-November 1917, but official notification was never sent out to delegates. America was already at war and many Irish Nationalist leaders were hesitant to confront Wilson. Jeremiah O'Leary was adamant an Irish Race convention be held. He outlined his position in a long letter to McGuire, condemning Cohalan's temerity and praising McGuire for his heroic bravery and devotion to the Irish cause. O'Leary believed a convention was timely and necessary to clarify the position of Irish-Americans as to Wilson, the war and the Irish question. Inaction, O'Leary pleaded, not only gave support to Wilson, but cast aspersions on the courage of the "fighting Irish" race. O'Leary reiterated McGuire's proposals noted in a letter to the Irish World, the advantages such a convention would have. It would achieve consensus as to the program Irish Americans should pursue, protest Wilson's polices jeopardizing free speech and naval policies that could interfere with any outside support of subsequent Irish rebellion, and demand freedom for Ireland as a prerequisite for American involvement.⁷⁰ McGuire was silent which suggests he was sympathetic Cohalan at the time. There were other concerns as well. Dooley states there was more to Cohalan's cancellation of the Irish Race Convention, citing the increased repression and harassment by the Wilson administration, the public condemnation of Irish-American leaders by former President Theodore Roosevelt in his capacity and honorary president of the American Defense Society, and the barring from the mails of both the <u>Gaelic American</u> and <u>The Irish World</u>.⁷¹ And while it did not silence them, Cohalan and his militant Irish allies were put on the defensive. Devoy responded by claiming any such charges against the extreme Irish nationalists were committed prior to American entry into the war. Wilson responded by publishing correspondence from Ambassador Bernstorff from January 1916 in October 1917 implicating Joseph McGarrity, John T. Keating, and Jeremiah O'Leary in sabotage efforts in the United States.⁷² Wilson was obviously escalating pressure against his Irish critics, attempting to taint their leaders with the charge of disloyalty, despite their public comments to the contrary.

The ultimate showdown over British policy towards Ireland was the attempt to introduce conscription in April 1918. With America now in the war, there was increasing resentment of Ireland's exemption. Rumors of conscription in Ireland were rife for a year preceding its enactment. Even John Redmond was opposed although the <u>Catholic Sun</u> did not expect him to make a determined stand.⁷³ The British government persisted, despite warnings of its dire consequences from highly-placed British sources, including Sir Edward Carson, Lord Winborne, Lord Reading and the new British ambassador to the United States. Even in America, Colonel House warned such a policy would exacerbate the Irish issue in America. The only person who might have been able to dissuade Lloyd George, John Redmond, passed away 6 March 1917. T. P. O'Connor, Redmond's lieutenant, also condemned the conscription concept as did Sir Horace Plunkett.⁷⁴ Moderate Irish opinion in America, including Shane Leslie, said conscription was justified as an essential war-time necessity given

German pressure on the exhausted manpower of Britain and the fact that American troops would not arrive before Summer. Militant Irish opinion was vocal in opposition, even including the hierarchy of the Catholic Church given the many broken promises of Britain relative to Home Rule. The British government struck back hard, arresting over 150 Irish nationalists, including Eamon DeValera and Arthur Griffith on flimsy charges that such resistance was evidence of a continued Sinn Fein-German conspiracy ultimately sentencing a number of Sinn Fein leaders to prison in September 1918.[75] It was this same charge of conspiracy which Wilson leveled at Irish leaders in America when he decided to publish the von Igel papers and the Bernstorff communications. Similar efforts were made to impugn the character of other militant nationalists, such as Jeremiah O'Leary. For example, at his trial it was intimated that he was seen with the beautiful German spy, Maria de Victorica, at the Waldorf-Astoria, a story O'Leary absolutely denied.[76]

The fact is that O'Leary had several meetings with her which he admitted. A German agent, Herman Wessels, an associate of Victorica, was anxious to meet with Irish revolutionaries. A meeting in January 1917 included O'Leary, John Devoy and retired businessman Emil Kipper, the German agent tried to interest O'Leary in sabotaging ships loaded with supplies going to the Allies. O'Leary, like Larkin, was not interested. A subsequent meeting, including Victorica, discussed the situation in Ireland. Additional meetings included John T. Ryan, Buffalo attorney and like McGuire and O'Leary, a member of both the Clan and FOIF. Ryan supplied Victorica with payments of $1000 month. The conduit was Margaret Sullivan who was recommended by O'Leary as a maid for Victorica in early 1917. She later acted as her confidante and courier.

O'Leary met with Victorica on several occasions, seeking to ascertain the whether Germany would support another Irish rebellion, only this time with troops. Given that Germany's electronic communications were compromised, they decided to send a courier to Germany to obtain a reply. He was Willard J. Robinson, O'Leary's private secretary and himself an ardent Nationalist. He left for

Europe in March 1917 returning in June. By then the United States and Germany were at war and O'Leary broke off communications with Victorica. The reply was that Germany would support total independence for Ireland in a post war conference. A disagreement occurred between O'Leary and Ryan, possibly over the German unwillingness to supply troops without which, a rebellion would be foredoomed to failure, a point noted byMcGuire as well. O'Leary had nothing more to do with negotiations. By then Victorica was being intensely surveilled and receiving messages from a "Frank Richards' who was alleged to be a cousin of John T. Ryan. Ryan had difficulties supplying Victorica with funds. As with other German conspirators, she looked to agents in Mexico for assistance and Ryan agreed to help her escape. This forced the hand of American intelligence. She and her accomplices- O'Leary, Ryan, Kipper, Robinson, Wessels - were indicted and arrested. When arrested, Victorica played down her role in both sabotage and espionage, saying it was simply to encourage pacifist activities, Irish unrest and Catholic resentment against Italy for restricting the activities of the Pope. In fact, she was involved in a plot to import the explosive Theta used to bomb ships; for pursuing actions to damage the Panama Canal, and investigating locations of American submarine bases.[77]

The revelations by Secretary of State Lansing that O'Leary was part of a conspiracy to create a "reign of terror on the Canadian border" were greeted with both dismay and denial. O'Leary's supporters agreed that prior to American entrance into the war he was extremely critical of Wilson's policies, but since then, he has been "one of the most loyal supporters of the government"[78], a position also taken by James K. McGuire.

In June 1918, a broad spectrum of Irish Nationalists organized an appeal to President Wilson opposing the introduction of conscription. The Unionists under Sir Edward Carson also appealed to Wilson supporting the recent imprisonment of Nationalists opposed to conscription charged with conspiracy with the enemy. The vehement opposition of both the Irish Parliamentary Party and the Sinn Fein towards conscription was duly reported in the Catholic Sun.[79]

An article was printed containing a full text of the resolutions of both parties condemning conscription and the imprisonment of its opponents. The Sinn Fein resolution was introduced by Dr. Eoin MacNeil, Celtic scholar, historian and founder of the Irish Volunteers in 1913.

The whole issue of conscription in Ireland, while exacerbating tensions on both sides of the Atlantic, proved to be a non-issue. By then, American troops were turning the tide of the war in Europe and the issue became increasingly irrelevant. The real issue, independence for Ireland, in the post-war settlement, was becoming the main focus of Irish and Irish-American attention. Whereas some Nationalists fled for cover under the guise of patriotism, others, such as John T. Ryan literally fled the country, finding refuge in Mexico. On the other hand, those FOIF members not intimidated by the efforts of the Wilson administration, formed the Irish Progressive League on 13 October 1917, maintaining its position of vocal opposition to American participation in the war. Among its more active members, was Hannah Sheehy-Skeffington who was subsequently invited to speak with President Wilson in January 1918. She handed him a petition requesting his consideration of Irish claims to self-determination.[80] Wilson may have been simply being gracious, but he also may have been exploiting the rift in Irish-American ranks. Her efforts, however, like those previously, brought no changes to Wilson's policies. Events in Europe and America spurred FOIF to call another convention in 1918. For example, the collapse of the Russian army allowed Germany to transfer personnel from the Eastern to the Western Front. The massed forces faced by depleted British manpower pressed Britain to implement conscription. There was also the need for a uniform policy in the face of the newly-formed Irish Progressive League. The League was more aggressive and more critical of President Wilson's leadership. It was outspoken in its criticism of conscription, inundating Congress with letters condemning it. As noted, the IPL led a delegation to the White House, handing President Wilson a petition to consider its demands for Irish independence.[81] In addition, the day before the proposed Irish Race Convention, Britain arrested a number of leading Irish nationalists including Eamon DeValera announcing they were involved in "a German Plot".[82] The term was a strategic move by intelligence officers. It undoubtedly conjured up memories of the Hindu-German conspiracy trials of 1917-1918 which lead to the incarceration and fining of high-ranking German officials, Indian revolutionaries and Irish Nationalists. In America, the trial of two German agents, Sanders and Malitz, employees of the American Correspondence Film Company who allegedly sought to smuggle rubber goods to Germany, received wide-spread publicity. In addition, FOIF was under pressure from Dr. John Forrest Kelly, prominent President of the Massachusetts Council of the Friends of Irish Freedom. Kelly demanded, given the issues noted above, from James K. McGuire, Chairman of the FOIF Executive Committee, that a second Irish Irish Race Convention be held in order to maintain the unity of the movement.[83] There was some question as to where the meeting would be held. Because protests from patriotic organizations that Madison Square Garden not be rented to radical Sinn Feiners, the site was moved to the Central Opera House.[84] The second Convention endorsed a resolution initiated by Judge Goff calling for self-determination for Ireland based on President Wilson's stated principles. The assembled Irishmen pledged their loyalty to the United States and unity with Ireland in its struggle for independence. Allegations of Sinn Fein leaders being involved in a German plot were vehemently denounced.[85] Ward suggests the second convention was a victory for moderation[86] and to some degree it was. Cohalan took the lead in defeating more radical resolutions and supporting those reiterating Irish loyalty to America and advocating self-determination for Ireland. A bitter McGarrity said Cohalan wrapped himself in the American flag, having called Wilson "our greatest President."[87] Nonetheless, the 2500 delegates represented a panorama of Irish organizations - the Clan na Gael, the Friends of Irish Freedom, the Ancient Order of Hibernians, the Irish Progressive League and members of Irish literary societies. James Larkin, McGuire's associate in fomenting labor unrest, was scheduled to speak as was Liam Mellows. Diarmuid Lynch, a recent refugee from the Irish rebellion, was elected National Secretary. Father Peter E. Magennis was elected President of the Friends of Irish Freedom. Magennis was Provincial of the Carmelite Fathers whose priory "was a home for every Irish exile". Magennis had presided at an Irish protest meeting at Madison Square Garden two weeks prior to the second Irish Race Convention, for which he was censured by the local bishop.[88]

Ostensibly called to show unity among various groups in the cause of Irish freedom, the second Race convention instead showed fissures within the movement. The "pro-Irish independence faction" - Liam Mellows, Peter Golden, W. J. Maloney and Joseph McGarrity found themselves at odds with the Daniel Cohalan, John Devoy, Diarmuid Lynch "America-first" faction.[89] It would be a schism which would divide Irish-American in the post-war era. James K. McGuire would find himself enmeshed in this struggle as he tried to moderate between the two. The Convention decided to send a petition to President Wilson urging him apply the principles of self-determination to Ireland. A committee consisting of Goff, Magennis and Reverend Thomas J. Hurton, a vice-President of FOIF, was commissioned to present the petition to President Wilson. The delegation was not allowed to see the President. As on two previous tries, the Irish petitions were shuttled through Joseph Tumulty who simply accepted the petition without comment. Tansill was extremely critical of Tumulty's role in these events noting Tumulty regarded the speeches of the Second Irish Race Convention as "seditious".[90]

Some Irish Nationalist organizations were quick to support Wilson as the threat of war loomed closer. President Joseph McLaughlin of the Ancient Order of Hibernians pledged the loyalty of his 250,000 member society should a war break out receiving a warm response from the President. After war was declared, the organization pledged $1 million to benefit families of Hibernians in the American armed services. John O'Dea, Pennsylvania State Secretary of the Order, in a speech soon after American entered the war, reminded his audience of the valorous military service of Irishmen in the wars of America.[91] McGuire was in a tenuous position. Having been closely identified with Wilson during his first term, he was later "outed" as a member of the German Information Service as one who had sold himself to our now declared enemy. In addition, McGuire, as a ranking member of the Clan-na-Gael and the Friends of Irish Freedom, had been intimately tied to subversion and the Irish Rebellion of 1916. McGuire, under the circumstances, had little option but to reinvent himself as, what I have called a "pragmatic" patriot. For example, soon after American entry into the war, poems proclaiming liberty and loyalty were prominently displayed in The Catholic Sun, as were articles reminding America of the contributions of the Irish to America.[92]

The Catholic hierarchy in America urged all to rally around the flag during the crisis. Cardinals Farley, Gibbons, O'Connell and Glennon made calls to patriotism all featured in McGuire's Catholic Sun. Similar support was continued as noted in the Catholic Sun through 1918.[93] Glennon was particularly critical of Germany, indicating dissociation of the Catholic hierarchy from Germany, possibly in response to increasing hostility towards German-Americans in the United States. "Myths of Anglo-Saxon or Teutonic supremacy, he stated, should receive the immediate attention of our vigilantes".

Simultaneous with articles expounding Irish loyalty to their adopted country, were those extolling Ireland's long struggle for freedom. In some cases printed side-by-side, the articles implored a quid-pro-quo: in return for sacrificing its sons in America's wars' the United State was obligated to stand firm in demanding Irish freedom as a condition of a post-war peace accord.[94]

The turnabout towards pragmatic patriotism was possibly best seen in advertisements in the Catholic Sun denouncing the Republican peace candidate, Walter W. Magee and endorsing instead Republican rival Giles H. Stilwell, regional director of the National War Industries Board. Placing Magee's non-interventionist views adjacent to President Wilson's war message to Congress, the article castigated Magee for his lack of vision and his ignorance as to the "great principles involved in the war". Noting that winning the war was a "man-sized job, this was no time for the weak wabblings of the professional politician". It declared Stilwell as the "leader of public sentiment" and "an ideal citizen of integrity and ability". Ironically Magee's views were those of the professional Irishmen who Wilson was harassing. Magee was re-elected after a bitter primary contest within a Republican party divided over prohibition, local party boss control and accusations of pro-Germanism. Magee was one of several Congressmen endorsed by the National Security League, a militaristic, patriotic organization, noted for its anti-German hysteria during World War I.[95] The endorsement of Stilwell is puzzling except for two facts: the internal dynamics of the Onondaga County Republican party at the time and the climate of unjust repression and prosecution of dissenters in the wake of the passage of the Espionage Act in June 1917 and the Sedition Act of May 1918. As noted in preceding chapters, McGuire had been at odds with the Republican machine dating back to his mayoralty years. McGuire may have been trying to embarrass Onondaga Republicans as well as distance himself and other Irish nationalists from any taint of disloyalty during these political witch hunts.[96]

The Catholic Sun was loud in proclaiming its loyalty after America entered the war. Ads for bond drives proliferated as the war years progressed. For example, an advertisement for Liberty Loan Bonds proclaimed such investments a "patriotic privilege". A subsequent advertisement called buying bonds as "the Supreme Test of Onondaga's Patriotism".[97] Cartoons consigning the Kaiser to the rubbish bin under the weight of Liberty Bond Loans were also featured.[98] An additional source of government revenue was the sale of war savings stamps. The Catholic Sun urged it subscribers to "Be A Pershing Patriot: Buy as many war stamps as possible, even though the armistice had been signed ten days earlier.[99] In addition, the Catholic Sun published numerous advertisements sponsored by private corporations encouraging enlistment in the United States Marines.[100] Indicative of this pragmatic patriotism were several small advertisements in the Syracuse Herald. In June 1918, a notice was published indicating Mrs. George H. McGuire, wife of James' brother and business partner in insurance and asphalt scandals noted previously, was Chairman of the Ward 18 War Chest Committee.[101] George H. McGuire was listed an outstanding contributor to the war savings Stamp Club, having bought $1000 worth. Not to be outdone by simply donating money to the war effort, George H. McGuire was congratulated by the War Savings Bureau of the United States Treasury for a poem, "Might Will Be Right" he wrote which would be used in the Bureau's advertising efforts.[102] Buried also was a miniscule notice in the Catholic Sun that Philip McGuire, son of the former mayor of Syracuse, was appointed midshipman and reported for training at Annapolis.[103]

On the surface then, it would appear that McGuire and his family were in line with the mass appeal to patriotism and repression of dissent then current in America. This in no way curtailed his advocacy for Irish freedom. Possibly this was the reason for his book, What Could Germany Could Do For Ireland?), being removed from army camp libraries and destroyed by order of Secretary of War Newton D. Baker. The reason apparently was that the book had given aid and comfort to the Sein Fein movement and obstructed the work of England which was now an American ally. McGuire was not alone. Other authors and works banned included those by Alexander Berkman, John W. Burgess, Frank Harris, Hugo Munsterberg, George S. Viereck, Seamus MacMannus, and Scott Nearing and many others.[104] The authors were famous for their radical social views, their pacifism and/or their pro-German sentiments.

Throughout the years of American involvement, articles authored by McGuire or printed in the Catholic Sun reflect his continued adherence to Irish independence. For example, in August 1918, the Catholic Sun printed an appeal from Ireland's Nationalist leaders. Once again reiterating America's overthrow of British colonial domination, the leaders demanded the same right of self-determination. The appeal denounced the new conscription act as a violation of past practice since all military aid granted from Ireland to Britain was voluntary. It outlined past rebellion, famines and emigrations. Further, the appeal noted the participation of Irish exiles in the wars of America. Leaders praised in the current struggle included Eamon de Valera, Eoin MacNeil, Arthur Griffith, John Dillon and others. Interestingly, the petition was transmitted through Ambassador Page whose antipathy to the Irish cause has already been noted.[105] Articles similar in content would be front page news in the Catholic Sun throughout the year. For example, in a full-page advertisement of 29 November 1918, the Catholic Sun demanded self-determination for Ireland, urging all Irish-Americans of Syracuse to sign a petition to that effect. There was concern once again the British would betray Ireland's dream of independence. Using President Wilson's advocacy of "self-determination", the Catholic Sun praised him as "the terror of autocracy and the savior of democracy", noting it was American intervention that saved the Allied cause. The advertisement condemned partition, urging all Irish-Americans and their kindred societies demand "Self Determination For Ireland At The Coming Peace Conference". In line with its consistent policy of Irish independence, the Friends of Irish Freedom declared 8-16 December 1918 as "Ireland's Self-Determination Week". The Catholic Sun urged all liberty-loving Irish-Americans in Syracuse to petition the President to demand self-determination for Ireland. The policies of Lloyd George noted above were condemned. The courage of Wilson to win this concession for an "ancient, indestructible, unconquerable race" was praised, his name being idolized in Ireland. In addition, the public was urged to inundate the President's secretary, Joseph Tumulty, with letters requesting parity for Ireland with such other small nations as Poland, Czechoslovakia, Finland, Serbia and Belgium. Prominent Syracuse clergy, including Bishop Grimes, endorsed the petition. Alongside the advertisement was a "Petition To The President" endorsing Irish independence. It was to be cut out, signed by as many as possible and sent to the Office of The Catholic Sun.[106]

Despite his continued bickering over Irish policy with the leadership of the professional Irish, Wilson was politically astute enough to publicly acknowledge their new-found support for his war efforts. For example, an article in the Catholic Sun praised the efforts of the Knights of Columbus "in prosecution of the war against the dominance of militarism and the protection of our homes". An unselfish America, Wilson noted, will not hesitate to make the supreme sacrifice to liberate Europe "without regard to race or creed or nationality". Wilson was careful to balance his praise by noting the efforts of other groups – the Young Men's Christian Association and the Young Men's Hebrew Association – given the constant reiteration of the theme of Irish Catholics who gave their lives in America's wars. The <u>Catholic Sun</u> noted President Wilson's daughter's visit to Camp Kelly, Texas where her singing was heartily applauded. The Knights of Columbus appealed for thousands of civilians to enlist for military service. Promising to pay travel expenses and fair compensation, the article urged men "sacrifice something for the boys who are already sacrificing their all".[107]

As the war moved toward closure, the Catholic papers pressed Wilson to push his agenda for self-determination of small nations, praising the President for ennobling the barbaric war as a struggle for democracy and self-determination as the basis for American entry into the war. The real test to Wilson's ideals was Ireland's freedom. "Great as has been the career of President Wilson, his greatest achievement lies still before him – liberty and justice for all alike…". The test case upon which Wilson's ideas rested – Ireland.[108]

After the armistice, the pressure on Wilson to argue for self-determination became intense. Aware of the behind-the-scenes diplomatic maneuverings, the Irish Nationalists pressed their case. It would be a long and ultimately fateful struggle. A hint of British attitudes can be gleaned from a brief article in The <u>Catholic Sun</u>. By a vote of 196-115, the House of Commons defeated a motion made by John Dillon that the Irish question should be settled without delay on the basis of President Wilson's principle of self-determination.[109] A second bad omen for the Irish was Lloyd George's dual proposals to partition Ireland and postpone Home Rule. Lloyd George refused to coerce Ulster, reiterating the recent failure of the Irish convention to resolve the issues forced him to pursue these two policies.[110] Wilsonian ideals would clash with revanchist politicians and both Wilson and Ireland were the main casualties.[111]

Irish nationalists nonetheless pressed their case to the public. The <u>Catholic Sun</u> restated a theme of years past, recounted the 800-year struggle for Irish freedom, its ancient culture, its ruined industries, depopulated areas and high taxes. The article insisted 80 percent of the Irish people want independence. The article noted the large members of Irishmen in the United States Armed Services during the recent war – 33 percent of the Army, 40 percent of the Navy – who fought for the principle of self-determination espoused by President Wilson. The British government efforts to suppress meetings and articles in favor of independence were criticized in hopes of a favorable post war election in Britain. Interestingly, the article's last paragraph states: "Until the adult population of Ireland is granted self-determination in the freest and fullest manner, and the desires of her people guaranteed by a League of Nations, there can be no peace in the world".[112]

The signing of the Armistice on 11 November 1918 was greeted by Irish America with fervent hope that Wilsonian idealism on behalf of suppressed nationalities would prevail in the post-war settlement. Had he been successful, the President would have garnered enthusiastic support for his League of Nations. The hopes of both parties were both dashed on the shoals of vengeful politics by the victorious Allies, by British intransigence on the Irish problem, and by schism from Wilson by Irish-Americans.

Notes

1 Frank P. Walsh (1864-1939) was a self-taught liberal lawyer from Missouri who embraced the cause of Irish nationalism. He served under President Wilson on the Commission on Industrial Relations and with William H. Taft on the National War Labor Board. Walsh was a member of the American Commission On Irish Independence. "England Accused of War On Ireland". New York Times. 15 September 1919.

2 The speech was delivered 24 April 1917 and was carried in its entirety under the title, "Our Hopes and Aims In the Present World Conflict" in the Catholic Sun 4 May 1917:1,4. The article subtitle noted "Frank P. Walsh Pays Tribute To Germans of America".

3 "Food Supply of Nation Will Be Greater Than Ever". Syracuse Herald 8 May 1917:3.

4 "Croker Says Ireland Must Help Allies". Syracuse Herald 13 August 1917:2. Croker's career as corrupt leader of Tammany has already been noted elsewhere. At the time he retired as Boss, was resident in Ireland raising and racing thoroughbred horses. He had married a much younger woman. Croker would periodically visit America, often make comments about domestic politics or foreign affairs that were eagerly seized on by the press.

5 Buckley, John Patrick. The New York Irish: Their Views of American Foreign Policy, 1914-1921. New York: Arno Press, 1974, 104.

6 Cuddy, Joseph Edward. Irish-America and National Isolation, 1914-1920. New York: Arno Press, 1976, 130; Link, Arthur S. Woodrow Wilson and the Progressive Era: 1910-1917 (New York: Harper, 1954), 259.

7 Documents Relative To The Sinn Fein Movement; London: His Majesty's Stationery Office, 1921, 26. Bernstorff. My Three Years In America (New York: Scribners' and Sons, 1920), 372-373.

8 Documents Relative To Sinn Fein, op.cit., 27-28; Patrick McCartan. With DeValera In America, New York: Brentano, 1932, 16; 27.

9 Dr. George Chatterton – Hill was a writer, philosopher and Irish nationalist born in Madras, India, educated in Geneva, Switzerland who spend World War I in Germany. With Kuno Meyer and St. John Gaffney, he organized the German-Irish Society in February 1917. He was an associate of Roger Casement. Chatterton-Hill authored the "Introduction" to Count Reventlow's indictment of British policy, Vampire of the Continent (NY: Jackson Press, 1916). His Sinn Fein ties were later investigated by the British government. "Viereck Got $100,000 From The Germans". New York Times 26 July 1918; "Says Irish Plotted Here After 1917". New York Times 11 January 1921.

10 Documents Relative To Sinn Fein op.cit., 9, 29, 38, 56-58; Gaffney, St. John.

Breaking The Silence: England, Ireland, Wilson And The War (New York: H. Liveright, 1930).
11 Buckley, op.cit., 105-106.
12 "The President Has Made History". Catholic Sun 26 January 1917:5.
13 Cuddy, op.cit., 131.
14 Documents Relative To Sinn Fein, op.cit., 28-28.
15 "Americans Should Protest Against Entering This War". Catholic Sun 9 February 1917:2.
16 "Want Irish Included With Poland And Belgium As Free Nations". Catholic Sun 5 January 1917:1. The article contains a full text of the resolution.
17 Documents Relative To Sinn Fein, op.cit., 27-28. At the time, Irish Nationalists were conspiring with Germany for another insurrection against Britain. They also planned, in anticipation of a German victory, to present their case for independence in a post-war peace conference. Some leaders of the Irish Progressive League (I.P.L). included: Jeremiah A. O'Leary and John J. O'Leary, Irish-American lawyers with a long history of involvement in Irish affairs. Jeremiah was the active head of the American Truth Society. Both he and his brother were indicted for their activities by the federal government in June 1918.
Peter Golden was an actor, singer and journalist who migrated to America around the term of the century. He was among the more militant members of FOIF, organizing Sinn Fein in America with James Larkin and Robert Monteith. He was later a founder and Secretary of the IPL in 1917 and the AARIR in 1920.
John D. Moore was the first President of the Friends of Irish Freedom. With Dr. Patrick McCartan and James K. McGuire, he presented a petition to Wilson on behalf of Irish Freedom.
Dennis Spellissy was a New York lawyer with a long association to Tammany Hall. He was national treasurer of a fund to arm the Irish volunteers for the 1916 Rising.
Robert Monteith was an associate of Sir Roger Casement in Germany and in the aborted attempt to get assistance to the Irish rebels in 1916.
James Larkin, alluded to earlier, was a Socialist, labor activist, Irish Nationalist, who the Germans sought unsuccessfully to recruit as an agent, and a founder of the American Communist Party.
Stephen W. Johnson was President of the 1776 Branch of FOIF in New York City. He was one of the outspoken "soap box orators" denounced by Cleveland Moffett and the American Defense Society. After Jeremiah O'Leary was acquitted, Johnson's article in Nationality, an Irish journal edited by Arthur Griffith, was read to an appreciative audience, claiming

his trial was a "political frame-up" instigated by American hirelings of the British government.

18 "Friends of Irish Freedom Deliver Appeal to President". Catholic Sun 23 February 1917:2. The full text of the appeal is included in the article. See also Tansill, Charles Callan. America And The Fight For Irish Freedom, 1866-1922 (New York: Devon-Adair, 1957), 220. Mexico was then embroiled in a bloody revolution and despite urging from Roman Catholic clergy and the Catholic press including McGuire's Catholic Sun, Wilson urged patience and understanding, except when American lives and property were endangered. See Blum, John M. Joseph Tummulty and The Wilson Era (Boston: Houghton-Mifflin, 1951), 91-94.

19 Victor Herbert (1850-1924) was a Dublin-born Protestant, German-raised composer. He married a German opera singer and moved to America in 1886. He was a member of the Clan-na-Gael and the first President of FOIF. His Protestant background and his German connections made him useful as a frontman for the organization and its Pro-Irish, pro-German propaganda efforts.
Joseph T. Lawless was a judge from Virginia, who later sided with Cohalan in his dispute with DeValera.
John J. Rooney was an Irish Nationalist, judge and active supporter of the Irish Rebellion of 1916. He was temporary Chairman of The Second Irish Race Convention of May 1918. After America entered the war, he, John Goff and Edward Gavegan sent a telegram to President Wilson supporting the war effort, requesting the President use it as a vehicle to seek justice for Ireland.
Dr. John Forrest Kelly was a successful electrical engineer and inventor and a prolific contributor of articles to the Irish World. He was later critical of Cohalan for his failure to support DeValera. His attempt to organize an American boycott of British goods in 1920-21 as a means of pressuring Britain to alter its policies towards Ireland was a failure.
Robert E. Ford was the son and successor of Patrick Ford, founder of the Irish World. The son repudiated his father's moderate support of the I.P.P. and John Redmond, editorially complimenting John Devoy's Gaelic American. Robert E. Ford was a founding member of the Friends of Irish Freedom, serving until his death in 1919. The same editorial policies continued under his brother, Ashton J. Ford, who supported deValera in his struggle with Cohalan.

20 http://www.stanford.edu/~gdegroat/AJ/reviews/wtgd.htm;l-.3http://www.ted.ie/irishfilm/show.php/?fid+58178 Unfortunately the film is presumed lost. Critics from Variety, New York Dramatic Mirror and Moving Picture World believed treatment of the subject to be evenhanded. The producer, J. Stuart Blackton, was considered on a par with contemporary D.

W. Griffith. In 1897, he formed American Vitagraph, making propaganda films based on contemporary events up through World War I. ("J. Stuart Blackton Biography" http://fandango.com/j.stuartblackton/biographies/p185011).

21 "Say Irish Friends Start Movie Rows". New York Times 25 January 1917:7.

22 Cleveland Moffett (1863-1926), was a successful journalist, playwrite and poet. During World War I, Moffett advocated American preparedness becoming a trustee of the American Defense Society in 1915, a splinter group of Republicans unhappy with the National Security League's unwavering support of President Wilson. During the highpoint of ADS power, 1915-1918, Moffett made numerous patriotic addresses, often challenging soap box orators whose comments he considered seditious. "Moffett, Cleveland". National Cyclopedia of American Biography vol. XXIV. Ann Arbor, Michigan: University Microfilms, 67, 43-44; "Moffett, Cleveland". Dictionary of American Biography vol. 13, New York: Charles Scribner's Sons, 1934, 76-77. See also "Guide To Records of American Defense Society, 1915-1942" http://dlib.nyu.edu/eadapp/transform?source=nyhs/americandefsoc.xml.

23 "Soap Box Orators Denounce England". New York Times 19 August 1917; "Asks President To Define Treason". New York Times 17 August 1917; "Disloyal Preaching Under The Law". New York Times 22 August 1917:4.

24 "Ireland At Bay". Catholic Sun 24 November 1916; 1,4.

25 "Ireland A Belligerent Says Miss Gifford". Catholic Sun 26 January 1917:5.

26 "Ireland Must Look To U.S. And Germany For Freedom". Catholic Sun 2 February 1917:2.

27 "Germany Wants Ireland Free". Catholic Sun 2 February 1917:2.

28 For example, see the Inaugural Address of the German-Irish Society, in Documents Relative to Sinn Fein, op.cit., 29.

29 "Effect Of War Zone Blockage On Ireland". Catholic Sun 16 February 1917:2.

30 "Ireland's Choice In The New Year". Catholic Sun 5 January 1917:7.

31 "British Books on the Irish Rebellion". Catholic Sun 19 January 1917:8.

32 "Freedom Of Ireland Up To U.S. Or Germany". Syracuse Herald 9 February 1917.26.

33 Documents Relative to Sinn Fein, op.cit., 28.

34 "Irishmen To Urge Neutral Attitude". Syracuse Herald 8 February 1917:6.

35 Tansill, Charles C. America And The Fight For Irish Freedom, 1866-1922. (New York: Devon-Adair Co., 1957), 220.

36 "Sharp Words By Wilson". New York Times 5 March 1917. The "little group of willful men included Senator Robert M. LaFollette of Wisconsin. (1855-1925), Progressive Republican and reformer, whose opposition to American entry into the war earned him the enmity of Theodore Roosevelt. Wilson's opponents included other Republicans as well as Democrats and represented

a geographical cross-section of the country. For example, there was Senator James K. Vardaman, a one-term Democratic Senator from Mississippi (1861-1930), a former Governor and self-proclaimed champion of the poor whites. James A. O'Gorman (1860-1943) was a Tammany Democrat, lawyer, judge and one-term senator from New York. Asle J. Gronna (1858-1922) a successful businessman and farmer, was a Progressive Republican from North Dakota who consistently opposed Wilson's policies. Another Progressive Republican opponent was Senator Albert B. Cummins (1859-1926) of Iowa. A successful lawyer and reform governor, Cummins was a two-time aspirant for his party's nomination for President. Also on the roster of Republican opponents was Senator George W. Norris (1861-1943) from Nebraska. A progressive Republican, Norris endorsed some of Wilson's programs but turned vehement isolationist, fearing Wall Street was maneuvering American into war. He was outspoken in his condemnation of the Versailles Treaty.

William J. Stone (1848-1918) was a lawyer and former Governor of Missouri, later serving both in the House and in the Senate. He was a ranking member of the Senate Foreign Relations Committee. Stone was one of the six Senators who voted against the declaration against Germany.

John D. Works (1847-1928) was an Indiana native, a lawyer, and after moving to California, State Supreme Court Justice. He was elected as a Republican to the Senate, serving from 1911-1917.

William F. Kirby (1867-1934) was a lawyer, a former judge, a state attorney general, serving as Democratic Senator from 1916-1921. Kirby served on the Military Affairs Committee. In that capacity he was a strong advocate for American neutrality.

William S. Kenyon (1869-1933) was a Progressive Republican attorney, Assistant Attorney-General of the United States. He served as Senator from 1911-1922. Opposed to arming U.S. merchant vessels, he supported Wilson's declaration of war against Germany.

Harry Lane (1855-1917) was a medical doctor, Democratic reform Mayor of Portland, serving as Senator from 1913 until his death in 1917.

37 Villard, Oswald Garrison. Fighting Years: Memoirs of A Liberal Editor (New York: Harcourt Brace and Company, Inc., 1930, 322.

38 Buckley, op.cit., 111.

39 This was an especially difficult situation for the British. A month earlier, the Home Rule issue was abandoned given government support for the exclusion of Ulster. ("Home Rule Shelved By Lloyd George" Catholic Sun 10 March 1917:5). Partition and limited Home Rule were considered insulting by most Irish. Even Redmond claimed he was betrayed ("Irish Parliamentary Party Bolts House of Commons" Catholic Sun 16 March 1917:2). A month later, the Home Rule Act of 1914 was suspended for the duration of the war

("Home Rule Act" Catholic Sun 20 April 1917). Doorley noted the biased membership of the American-Irish with whom Balfour met, including pro-British Irishmen, John Quinn and Shane Leslie. FOIF was purposely excluded because it demanded complete independence, a position Britain was not yet ready to accept. Doorley, Michael. Irish-American Diaspora Nationalism: The Friends of Irish Freedom, 1916-1935. Dublin: Four Courts Press, 2005, 63-64.

The "Moderate" Irish-Americans included:

John Quinn was a prominent New York City lawyer and Irish Nationalist and collector of modern art. He may have been in the pay of British Intelligence.

Fr. John J. Wynne, S. J. was the founding editor of America in 1909-1910, the primary purpose of which was to defend the Catholic Church from anti-Catholic prejudice.

Fr. Sigourney Fay was a convert to Roman Catholicism who, despite his faith, was a pro-English propagandist and associate of Shane Leslie. He allegedly influenced F. Scott Fitzgerald who was his student 1911-12. Fay was later personal representative of Cardinal James Gibbons to Rome.

Lawrence Godkin was the journalist son of the founder of the Nation, Irish-born Edwin Lawrence Godkin, a lawyer, journalist, advocate of social reform and author of numerous books and articles.

Colonel Robert T. Emmett, a West Point graduate, commanded a unit of Buffalo soldiers in an encounter with Apache Indians in 1879 for which he later received the Medal of Honor. He was the Great-Grandson of Thomas Addis Emmet, brother of Irish nationalist martyr, Robert Emmet.

Morgan J. O'Brien was a New York City Democrat and former New York Supreme Court Justice who had served on the Democratic National Committee of 1912. He reported favorably on conditions in Ireland immediately prior to the start of World War I. He was later associated with the American Committee For The Relief of Ireland during the Anglo-Irish War.

John F. Fitzgerald was a Democratic politician, state legislator, Congressman and Mayor of Boston. His political rival, Patrick Kennedy, later became his ally when Fitzgerald's daughter married Kennedy's son initiating the most famous family in American Democratic politics.

40 Ward, Allan J. Ireland and Anglo-American Relations, 1889-1921. Toronto: University of Toronto Press, 1969, 149; Carroll, F. M. American Opinion and the Irish Question, 1910-23; A Study In Opinion And Policy. New York: St. Martin's Press, 1978, 90-91; Doorley, op.cit., 63.

41 "Ask England To Settle Irish Question". Syracuse Herald 29 April 1917:2. The article contains the full text of Clark's message. "American Pressure For Irish Home Rule" Syracuse Herald 27 April 1917:6. The Herald cites Roosevelt's letter in full regarding it as "typical" of the rest.

42 "Irish Convention Scheme Illusory and Deceptive". Catholic Sun 1 June 1917:1. Doorley, op.cit., 64 states Sinn Fein refused to participate. See, Criticism of The Irish Convention As Proposed By Premier David Lloyd George: By Prominent Americans of Irish Blood: New York: Friends of Irish Freedom, 1917. McGuire's comments are noted on pp. 58-60. See also, McCartan, op.cit., 15-16. Tansill, is extremely critical of Maloney's role in the struggle for Irish freedom, referring to him as an ambitious, "adroit schemer", possibly because of Maloney's criticism of Cohalan and his past as an officer in the British Army. See Tansill, op.cit., 228, 237-38, 278-9 fn. 58.

43 Dr. Patrick McCartan (1878-1966), Irish nationalist, journalist, politician, medical doctor. Arrested and interred in England during the 1916 Rising, he escaped to Ireland, being elected to the Dáil in 1918. He was appointed Sinn Fein representative to the United States, later working with Joseph McGarrity and Eamon DeValera against Cohalan and Devoy.

44 Eoin Mac Neill (1867-1945), Irish scholar, nationalist and revolutionary. He was a co-founder of the Gaelic League, and organizer of the Irish Volunteers. He refused to send them into action during the Rising of 1916 after learning of the Casement debacle. Nonetheless, he was arrested, imprisoned and later released. Elected to Parliament as a Sinn Fein member, he sat instead in the Dáil. He was a supporter of the pro-Treaty forces in 1921.

45 John McGarry of Chicago was an original member of the FOIF Executive Committee. He was later a member of the American Committee For Relief in Ireland. McGarry reportedly leaked information to McGarrity as to FOIF plans to oust deValera.

46 Tansill, op.cit., 228-30; O'Doherty claims to have been the one who starched and inserted the handkerchief into McCartan's clothes for the trip to America. Her account carried the petition in full with all the signatories. In Doherty, op.cit., 5-6.

47 Documents Relative To Sinn Fein op.cit., 30-33; "Redmond Reject Home Rule". New York Times 18 May 1917; McCartan, Patrick. With DeValera In America New York: Brentano, 1932, 14; Tansill, op.cit., 229-30; Doorley, op.cit., 66-67.

48 "The Sinn Fein In The Saddle". Syracuse Herald 19 July 1917:8. Many saw the death of William Redmond as a vehicle to bring the contending parties of Irish Nationalism together. The British press was unsparing in its praise of a man who gave his life for the country that was its bitterest political enemy" ("Redmond's Death May Heal Irish Feuds Of Years". Syracuse Herald 12 June 1917:1).

49 "Home Rule A Sham: Puts Burden On Poor". Catholic Sun 9 June 1916:8.

50 "Former Mayor McGuire Writes On Irish Rule". Syracuse Herald 22 June 1917. This was a reprise of his comments in the FOIF pamphlet of May, 1917.

51 Carroll, op.cit., 101; Doorley, op.cit., 66. T. (Thomas) P (Power) O'Connor was an Irish member of the Irish Parliamentary Party from Liverpool who came to America on several occasions to raise money for Home Rule. As Sinn Fein support increased in the United States after the brutal repression of The Rising of 1916, he found his efforts less successful. The I.P.P. was initially non-existence after the Parliamentary elections of December 1918.

52 "History of the Federal Bureau of Investigation." http://fas.org/irp/agency/doj/fbi/fbi.hist.htm, 1-2; "Bureau of Investigation." International Encyclopedia of the First World War (WW 1) http://encyclopedia. 1914-1918-online.net. article/bureau_of-investigation.

53 Primary Documents-United States Espionage Act 15 June 19http://www.firstworldwar.com/source/espionageact.htm.

54 "Trading With the Enemies Act, 1917" http://criminalgovernment.com/docs/enemy.html

55 "U.S. Congress Passes Sedition Act" https://www.history.com/this-day-in-history/u-s- congress-passessedition-act.

56 "Committee on Public Information (CPI)https://sourcewatch.org/index.php/Committee-On-Public-Information, War propaganda > World War I: "The Committee on Public Information htttp://www, propagandacritic.com/articles/ww1.cpi.htm.

57 Hagedorn, Ann. Savage Peace: Hope and Fear In America, 1919. New York: Simon and Schuster, 2007, 27 – 28.

58 Bielaski to Ford. 12 June19United States Department of Justice, Bureau of Investig ation, file # 18National Archives and Records Administration, Washington, D.C.Hereafter referred to as USDOJ/BOI/#1898.

59 Ford to Bielaski 19 June 1918 USDOJ/BOI #1898; Bielaski to Harrison 24 June 1918 USDOJ/BOI #1898

60 H. G. Pratt to Harry A. Taylor.26 December 19USDOJ/BOI #1898

61 F.T. Walters to Harry A. Taylor. Confidential memorandum. 19 January 1918USDOJ/BOI #18The report recorded the name of the mayor as Hill. The agent may have confused it with Mayor Louis Will 1914-1916, a Progressive mayor from 1914-19The date of the memo suggest the Mayor was Walter R. Stone 1916-1919, a Republican, who served from 1916-19See "List of Mayors for Syracuse, New York" http://www.syracuse.ny.us/Mayors-Syracuse-.aspx.

62 R. H. Van Daman(sic) to Bielaski. 4 February 1918 USDOJ/BOI #18Ralph H. Van Deman (1865-1952) was a Harvard graduate and an MD who began his career in military intelligence just prior to the Spanish-American War he served in the Philippines where his job was to suppress the Filipino Nationalist movement. Much of his information was obtained through the use of torture. He retained many of the prejudices typical of WASP male elites of the time, distrusting blacks, "new" immigrants, political activists, labor organizers

and Jews. On the eve of World War I, the MID was resuscitated and its mission expanded from collecting foreign intelligence to spying on American citizens. He used the vigilante group, American Protective League to assist his efforts. Van Deman was head of the War Department's Military Intelligence Division which was formally established in May 19Under his direction the MID expanded and like the BOI, established field offices in major cities. He is regarded as "the father of military intelligence". Kruss, Peter. "Famous Miliitary Spies: Ralph Van Deman http//warfarehistorynetrwork.com/daily/military-history/famous-military-spies-ralph-vandeman, 4 pp. Hochschild, Adam. "How a Young Army Officer Built an American Empire of Paranoia From 85,000 Index Cards: The Amazing Story of Ralph Van Deman, Commie Hunter" https://motherjones.com/politics/2018/01/how-a-young-army-officer-built—americas-empire-from-85000-index-cards, 17 pp. See Michael E. Bigelow ".A Short History of Military Intelligence", July – September, 2012, 11 – 19 (59 pp.) This suggests that McGuire was a high profile suspect at the onset of his surveillance. And, given the hysteria of the times, lucky to escape incarceration.

63 Bielaski to Tormey 18 February 19USDOJ/BOI #1Tormey to Bielaski 26 February 1918 USDOJ/BOI #1898.

64 Johnstone to Bielaski 28 September 19USDOJ/BOI #1898.

65 DeWoody to Bielaski, 14 October19USDOJ/BOI #1898

66 Tansill, op.cit., 234; Ward, op.cit., 152.

67 Ward, op.cit., 157; Carroll, op.cit., 103; Tansill, op.cit., 237. The Syracuse Herald was especially critical of Senator LaFollette's role, condemning his remarks as to American foreign policy as "disloyal", coming from a champion of Germany's cause and urged his expulsion. Ironically, it published an article relative to the publication of the von Igel papers and Justice Cohalan, urging no precipitous action until there was strong evidence of his involvement in subversive activities. "The Rising Wrath Against LaFollette". Syracuse Herald 29 September 1917:8; "A Friend Set Right". Syracuse Herald 29 September 1917:8.

68 French Strother, in Fighting Germany' s Spies (New York: Doubleday, 1918, pp154-155 has both the coded and translated versions of the letter. It reads:" No. 335-16 Very Secret. New York, 17 April, 1916. Judge Cohalan requests the transmission of the following remarks: "The Revolution in Ireland can only be successful if supported from Germany. Otherwise England will be able to suppress it, even thought only be after hard struggles. Therefore help is necessary. This should consisit of aerial attacks in England and a diversion of the fleet simultaneous with Irish revolution. Then if possible, a landing of troops, arms and ammunition in Ireland and possibly some ofcers from Zeppelins. This would enable the Irish ports to be closed against England and the establishment of stations for submarines on the Irish coast, and the

cutting off of the supply of food for England. The success of the revolution may therefore decide the war. He asks that a telegram to this effect be sent to Berlin 51328170230 to His Excellency Count Bernstorff, Imperial Ambassador, Washington, D.C. Also in Hartley, op. cit., 157-159.

69 "The Case of Judge Cohalan". Syracuse Herald 26 September 1917:3; "Cohalan Inquiry Likely At Albany". New York Times. 25 September 1917; Documents Relative To Sinn Fein, op.cit., 12-13.

70 O'Leary, Jeremiah, My Political Trials And Experiences. New York: Jefferson Publishing Co., 1919, 40; Doorley, op.cit., 67, 75. McCartan, op.cit., 18-19. "Irish Vote Used As Club By Devoy". New York Times 16 November 1917.

71 Tansill, op.cit., 238.

72 "Conscription In Ireland". Catholic Sun 5 January 1917.

73 Ward, op.cit., 157; 159; Tansill, op.cit., 244;253. Ward emphasizes how delicate the conscription issue was even affecting American units. Given the realities of submarine warfare, it was feared only small detachments of American troops could be sent to Europe, and hence would be deployed under British command. Pershing wanted autonomous American units because he feared the effectiveness of American troops under British officers could be compromised unless the issue of Ireland was addressed. In addition, Pershing believed British manpower would be sent to Ireland to enforce conscription (Ward, op.cit., 162-163).

74 Tansill, op.cit., 246-48; 269; Ward, op.cit., 160-161.

75 O'Leary, op.cit., 419; For details on Maria deVictorica see Yardley, Herbert. The American Black Chamber. Indianapolis: Bobbs-Merrill Co., Chapter V, 90-119.

76 The historical Maria Victorica was a beautiful women of noble German birth and a master of several languages. She moved in elite circles in both Europe and the Unted States She was introduced to the head of the German Intelligence service and was hired as an agent in 1910. She married an Argentine German agent and was being surveilled by British agents as early as 1914. Some considered her the directing genius of German espionage in America, whereas others thought she was harmless. She arrived in America iin January 1917. She was later found in possession of documents involving plots of sabotage and espionage. One such plan involved smuggling explosives inside religious statues. Victorica was arrested in April 1918 and indicted for conspiracy to commit espionage. A confirmed drug addict, she died in 1920 before facing trial. Also see Yardley, Herbert O. "How They Captured the German Spy Maria Victorica, Told At Last". Ames Daily Tribune. Ames, Iowa, 31 July 1931.;Dooley, John. Codes, Ciphers, Spies: Tales of Military Intelligence in World War I. NewYork: Copernicus Books, pp. 2016, 207-210;214; 241-249, 251-254;313; Weyl, Nathaniel. Treason: The Story of

Disloyalty and Betrayal in American History. Washington, D.C. Public Affairs Press, 1950, 313.
77 "O'Leary Friends Say He Is Loyal". Syracuse Herald 13 October 1917:3; "Witness Upholds O'Leary". New York Times 25 February 1919.
78 "Coercion and Conscription Threats In Ireland". Catholic Sun 4 October 1918:1.
79 McCartan, op.cit., 11-14; Doorley, op.cit., 71, fn. 49. Carroll, op.cit., 105. This was in direct contrast to pressure put on her by the Wilson administration. She was on a speaking tour under contract by FOIF. Her remarks were bitterly denounced in many newspapers and there was allegedly a plot to kidnap her and bring her to Canada. Tansill, op.cit., 234.
80 "Irish Progressive League". Funchion, Michael F. (ed). Irish American Voluntary Organizations. (Westport, Connecticut: 1983), 2006-210; Tansill, op.cit., 270-274.
81 Doorley, op.cit., 76.
82 "Sinn Fein Meeting May Likely Be Stopped". New York Times 3 May 1918.
83 Doorley, op.cit., 75.
84 Tansill, op.cit., 271.
85 Ward, op.cit., 143.
86 McCartan, op.cit., 71.
87 Doorley, op.cit., 76; Cronin, op.cit., 70; Tansill, op.cit., 271; Buckley, op.cit., 159; McCartan, op. cit., 40.
88 Doorley, op.cit., 76-80.
89 Tansill, op.cit., 271-273; 274, fn. 51.
90 "President Wilson Thanks The Ancient Order of Hibernians". Catholic Sun 23 February 1917:1; "National Board of AOH To Raise $1,000,000". Catholic Sun 25 May 1917:12; "Irish In Wars Of The United States". Catholic Sun 13 April 1917:1,4.
91 "Our Flag" Catholic Sun 4 May 1917:7; "The Irish Race In American History". Catholic Sun 8 June 1917:4; "The Irish In The United States". Catholic Sun 27 April 1917:1.
92 "Archbishop Ireland Sounds Patriotic Keynote". Catholic Sun 23 February 1917:1; "American Cardinals Appeal To Patriotism". Catholic Sun 20 April 1917:1; "A Struggle For Principles, Not of Race". Catholic Sun 23 August 1918:1. McCartan was effusive in his praise of the endorsement of the Catholic clergy of the Irish cause. See, McCartan, op.cit., Chapter VIII, "The Hosting Of The Clergy", 49-62.
93 "Ireland's Struggle For Freedom". Catholic Sun 13 April 1917:3; "Evil In Store For Emerald Isle". Catholic Sun 26 January 1917:1.
94 "See How Far Mr. Magee's Views Fall Short of President Wilson's" Catholic Sun 30 August 1918:13. Giles H. Stilwell (1854-1936) was a lawyer, and law

professor at Syracuse University. He served for a time as corporate counsel (1914-1916) for the City of Syracuse and was a lawyer to several Syracuse banks and businesses. Stilwell was involved in public service including the Board of Education and various charities. A life-long Republican, he temporarily left the party to run unsuccessfully as a Progressive candidate for Congress. http://boards.ancestry.com.au/localities.northam.usa.states.newyork; "Stilwell, Giles Heath". National Cyclopedia of American Biography vol. XXVII. New York: James T. White and Co., 1939, 277-278. Walter W. Magee (1861-1927), a Harvard graduate, lawyer and corporate counsel for the City of Syracuse (1904-1914), Magee served in Congress from 1915-1927. For details, see "Syracuse Split Widens". New York Times 1 September 1918; "Naval Bill Seen As 'Pork' Measure". New York Times 14 August, 1916; Robert D. Ward, "The Origin And Activities of The National Security League". Mississippi Valley Historical Review, vol. 47, no. 1 (June, 1960), 51-65.

95 The scandals and political smearing reached the office Republican Governor Charles Whitman, who won the office as a result of his crusades against corruption in asphalt paving scandals and the Becker-Rosenthal murder case, both involving McGuire and/or his associates. Whitman's Lieutenant-Governor, Edward Schoeneck, had defended a German employee accused of "disloyal utterances". The timely intervention of former President Theodore Roosevelt, who had been lavishly entertained by Onondaga Republicans during the Barnes trial of 1915, ended the legal turmoil. For details, see "Ray B. Smith Sues Hearst Paper For $50,000 Because of Tolishus Case Article". Syracuse Herald 1 September 1918:1; "Schoeneck Faces Charge of Aiding A Foe of Nation". New York Times 14 July 1918; "New Jury Will Hear Case of Tolishus". New York Times 16 July 1918; "Tolishus Is Indicted On Sedition Charges". New York Times 24 July 1918; "Tolishus Case Taken Up". New York Times 23 July 1918.

96 "Buy A Liberty Loan 3 ½ % Bond". Catholic Sun 25 May 1917:7; "The Supreme Test of Onondaga's Patriotism". Catholic Sun 4 October 1918: "Lend Uncle Sam Your Money". Catholic Sun 27 September 1918:8. Apparently public displays of patriotism by purchasing war bonds was encouraged by public servants as well. Police in New York City, for example, were knocking on doors and stopping pedestrians and motorists encouraging them to financially demonstrate their loyalty ("Police Push Liberty Loan" New York Times, 2 May 1918).

97 "Buy Bonds To Your Utmost". Catholic Sun 4 October 1918:7.

98 "Be A Pershing Patriot". Catholic Sun 29 November 1918:8.

99 "You'll Go In Good Company – U.S. Marines". Catholic Sun 19 July 1918:2; "Go Get'em With U.S. Marines". Catholic Sun 2 August 1918:8;

100 "Obtain War Chest Window Stars From Ward Majors Today". Syracuse Herald 19 June 1918.

101 "One Last Chance". <u>Syracuse Herald</u> 2 December 1918; "Government To Use Poem Of Geo. H. McGuire". <u>Syracuse Herald</u> 28 April 1918:12. The poem is printed below.
"Might Will Be Right"
"Wars waged with the strength and blood of the bold
Off to the field to turn back the Hun;
The toil and brain and by the gold
Of the others that stick 'till the struggle is won.
Out of the new world's crucible springs
Out of the land of the free and the brave
A giant, full-armed, borne on Liberty's wing
To crush blind force and Democracy save.
Celt, Saxon, Slav, black, white and all
Came forth, reborn from a freeman's strife
Ready to answer the old world's call
With work or wealth or life."

102 "Philip McGuire Appointed Midshipman". <u>Catholic Sun</u> 18 October 1918:5.

103 "War Department Orders James K. McGuire's Book Removed From Libraries". <u>Syracuse Herald</u> 1 September 1918:1. The entire list of authors and their banned works is included in the article.

104 "Ireland's Message To The American People". <u>Catholic Sun</u> 2 August 1918:1.

105 "Call Issued For Irish Cause". <u>Catholic Sun</u> 29 November 1918:5; "Urgent!" <u>Catholic Sun</u> 29 November 5; "Let Us Be Up And Doing For Ireland". <u>Catholic Sun</u> 29 November 1918:5.

106 "President Wilson Praises K of C Work". <u>Catholic Sun</u> 2 August 1918:1.

107 "President Wilson and Ireland". <u>Catholic Sun</u> 8 November 1918:2.

108 "House of Commons Rejects Dillon's Motion". <u>Catholic Sun</u> 15 November 1918:1. John Dillon (1851-1927), Irish Home Rule politician, land reformer and last leader of the Irish Parliamentary Party. His timely intervention saved many rebels from execution in the wake of the failed Easter Rising of 1916. Dillon succeeded as I.P.P. leader after the death of John Redmond. He opposed government conscription in 1918. That same year his effort to achieve Home Rule through Parliament failed. He was defeated for re-election in 1918 by Sinn Fein leader, Edmon deValera.

109 "To Be Sure, And Of Course, Ulster Wins". <u>Catholic Sun</u> 22 November 1918:1.

110 See "President Wilson's Address To Congress". <u>Catholic Sun</u> 15 November 1918:1; "Thanksgiving 1918 By The President of The United States: A Proclamation". <u>Catholic Sun</u> 22 November 1918:1.

111 "Why America Should Insist On Self-Determination For Ireland". <u>Catholic Sun</u> 6 December 1918:1.

Chapter IV - A
Post-War Irish Nationalist Politics 1918-1923

The pressure of the Wilson administration on the leaders of Irish Nationalists had the result of silencing its most outspoken leaders, especially Devoy and Cohalan. This quiescence presaged a schism within their ranks that would grow into an open break pitting Devoy, Cohalan and Diarmuid Lynch against DeValera, McGarrity, Maloney, and McCartan. This break had a history dating back to the Fall, 1917. James K. McGuire initially sought to heal the breach between the more militant Irish leaders both at home and abroad, and the "America First" wing led by Cohalan. As the struggle to win control of Irish policy in America evolved, McGuire's politics moved left, endorsing DeValera and earning the enmity of long-time ally John Devoy.

The break began with the arrest of Liam Mellows on charges of conspiracy after he unsuccessfully tried to return to Ireland. Neither Devoy nor Cohalan assisted Mellows in raising the bail necessary to procure his freedom. This fissure was papered over as the funds for Mellows' release were secured by Dr. William Maloney, but suspicions remained.[1] In the void of FOIF leadership, the vacuum was filled by the formation of the Irish Progressive League in October 1917, under the auspices of Peter Golden, Nora Connolly, the daughter of the martyred James Connolly and Mrs. Hannah Sheehy-Skeffington. Its goal was to insure an Irish presence at the post-war conference. Mrs. Skeffington officered the IPL propaganda arm in Washington, D.C. and began lobbying for the cause of Irish independence. Through the efforts of Dr. Patrick McCartan and members of the IPL, an unofficial embassy was opened for which the IPL was congratulated by Eamon deValera.[2] It was the IPL which organized demonstrations in America protesting conscription in Ireland. And, it was IPL pressure which coerced FOIF to call a second Irish Race Convention in May 1918. James K. McGuire, chairman of the FOIF Executive Committee, was compelled to call a convention in order to preserve the unity of the Irish cause in America. McGuire was pushed by Dr. John Forrest Kelly, head of the Massachusetts Branch of the Friends of Irish Freedom. Born in Ireland, Kelly became a wealthy electrical engineer who lavishly supported the cause of Irish Nationalism both with cash and by authoring articles in various periodicals in the name of Irish freedom. Given the internal crisis of FOIF with its leadership under attack, the militancy of the IPL, the conscription crisis of 1918, with the subsequent arrest of Sinn Fein leaders, McGuire was in no position to refuse.

The second Irish Race Convention attracted 2100 delegates and inaugurated a new slate of officers-Reverend Peter E. Magennis as National President and James O'Sullivan as Treasurer, who was soon replaced by Michael B. McGreal. Diarmuid Lynch was made National Secretary. A commission appointed by the Convention to present a resolution on Irish independence to President Wilson, had to settle for leaving it with his Secretary, Joseph Tumulty.

The Second Convention revealed the potential for schism in the ranks of Irish-Americans since it represented organizations from a broad spectrum of political sentiment-the FOIF, the Clan, the AOH, the IPL, and literary and cultural societies. Essentially it split the Irish into those advocating an Ireland first position and an America first position.[3] The majority favored the latter course, although it would embitter advocates on both sides. The schism between militants and moderates was revealed in the choice of chairman for the convention. Moderates led by John Devoy, wanted Father Thomas J. Hurton.[4] James Larkin and Mrs. Hannah Sheehy-Skeffington wanted John Forrest Kelly. After strenuous debate, Father Hurton was chosen as Permanent Chairman. Judge John Goff made a conciliatory address to President Wilson urging him to take such measures as best calculated to bring about the independence of Ireland. Cohalan closed the session by urging patience, referring to Wilson as "our greatest President".[5]

The second Irish Race Convention, then, was a "timid affair", pledging loyalty to the war effort and revealing Cohalan and Devoy in control of FOIF. The election of Magennis presaged a more active and more prominent role for the Catholic clergy in the years to come, especially after the war was concluded. Joseph McGarrity's response was condemnation of the Clan's slavish submission to Cohalan. Liam Mellows and Mrs. Hannah Sheehy-Skeffington were likewise shocked by its reluctance to become involved in any activities which could be considered "unpatriotic".[6]

FOIF increased rapidly after the war and flexed its muscle sponsoring a Third Irish Race Convention in Philadelphia, in February 1919. Some evidence suggests the convention sought to capitalize on the grassroots wave of support which occurred following the proclamation of an Irish Republic and the appearance of Dr. Patrick McCartan as its official envoy to the United States.[7] For example, in Syracuse local groups of Irish supporters held rallies, made speeches and passed resolutions urging self-determination for Ireland. The New York State Ancient Order of Hibernians also passed a resolution endorsing Irish freedom based on Wilson's principles of self-determination.[8] In the wake of the November 1918 armistice and the Sinn Féin victory in the Irish elections for December 1918, The Catholic Sun even went so far as to publish a campaign poster from the December election.[9] FOIF leadership basked in the publicity of the convention yet unlike the previous two, the third was held in Philadelphia. This was largely due to the efforts of Joseph McGarrity, a successful Philadelphia businessmen and active member of the Clan-na-Gael who would later come down for DeValera in his struggle against Cohalan. Since Cohalan's strength was located primarily in New York, this was the precursor of what was to become a major schism in Irish Nationalist politics. James K. McGuire would find himself in the middle of those factions, trying to mediate between the two. The primary purpose of this convention was ostensibly to give moral and financial support to the Irish Republic in pressing its claims for recognition at Versailles.[10] At the third Irish Race Convention, the 5000 delegates urged President Wilson to support Irish participation in the Paris Peace Conference. During the third Convention, the schism between the Irish in America widened. Devoy, Cohalan, Diarmuid Lynch and the majority of FOIF were focused on an "America First" perspective, whereas Golden, Mellows, Maloney, and McGarrity favored a more militant pro-Ireland position. Continuing its increased visibility, the Third Irish Race Convention attracted numerous clergy. FOIF had previously sponsored "Self-Determination Day" for Ireland in December 1918 at Madison Square Garden. Municipal and state politicians were present, as were the FOIF triumvirs-Goff, Devoy, Cohalan.[11] Along with numerous members of the clergy-Protestant, Catholic and Jewish-were Socialists, foreign visitors from Canada and India, labor leaders and representatives of various Irish-American societies. Among those listed as "distinguished visitors" was James K. McGuire.[12] The Catholic press, including James K. McGuire's Catholic Sun, gave the convention extensive coverage, reiterating the historical debt America owed to Ireland given its adopted sons multiple sacrifices and support in the name of Liberty.[13]

Prominent among these attending the Third Irish Race Convention were major prelates of the Catholic Church in America including James Cardinal Gibbons of Baltimore who spoke in favor of a resolution endorsing self-determination for Ireland.[14] Virtually the entire edition of McGuire's Catholic Sun 28 February 1919 was dedicated to the Convention including a verbatim copy of Cardinal Gibbon's resolution endorsing self-determination for Ireland and an in-depth article on it from Seamus McManus. Two of the three men later selected as members of the American Commission on Irish Freedom were given key positions at the convention - Michael J. Ryan was made Chairman of the Resolutions Committee, ex-Governor Edward F. Dunne of Illinois was designated as Chairman of the Committee to go to Independence Hall. James K. McGuire was made Chairman of the Rules Committee.[15] The article lists many prominent attendees including clergy, politicians and leaders of Irish nationalist organizations. Cohahan, given the mutual antipathy between him and the militants, was careful not to use the term "independence" or "Irish Republic". Instead he chose "self-determination" in order to avoid the past label of being called "un-American."[16] The Rev. Peter Magennis, FOIF President, also picked his words carefully, using "self-determination" at the Friends convention in February 1919.[17] The tensions between him and the militants who steadfastly advocated an Irish Republic pushed the two sides even further apart. The overwhelming victory of Sinn Féin on the election of

December 1918 exacerbated tensions even more. The consistent references to "self-determination", not "independence", indicated how effectively Cohalan was in control of FOIF. The net result of the Third Convention was a victory for the pro-America agenda. And whereas the Third Irish Race Convention revealed the growing division in the ranks of those advocating the cause of Ireland, it was successful in two areas both of which would cause further schism in the ranks of Irish-Americans. The first was the creation of the American Commission on Irish Independence headed by Frank P. Walsh, Ex-Governor Edward F. Dunne and Michael J. Ryan.[18] The second issue, was the establishment of the Irish Victory Fund.

Cohalan and Lynch sought a strong centralized organization which widened the gulf between FOIF and the IPL. The three issues which brought the schism into the open was the battle over the League of Nations and control over the FOIF and funding. Had Wilson been able to use his influence to win concessions for Ireland, Irish-America might have rallied behind his vision of an international security plan. What was initially a wave of support for the President by Irish-Americans became an almost solid mass of implacable opposition.

The anti-treaty forces gained support from three key people, all denouncing the proposed Covenant for a variety of reasons: Senator William Borah of Idaho, an extreme isolationist; Senator Henry Cabot Lodge of Massachusetts, a "reservationist", who would accept the treaty with extensive modifications designed to maintain American sovereignty in world affairs, and Eamon deValera, who initially endorsed the League with modifications but whose later speeches condemned British imperialism.[19] Other ethnic Americans including Poles, Jews, Italians, Germans, Russians-also were against the Treaty, believing their homelands were badly treated in the final document. But it was the Irish who felt most betrayed by Wilson. And they were the best organized-through FOIF, the Clan-na-Gael, the AOH and Society of Friendly Sons of St. Patrick.[20] Wilson possibly made three incorrect strategic assumptions: that he could ignore the Irish vote, having successfully done so in 1916 and that he could get the treaty through Congress without alteration.[21] He also underestimated the power of the leadership of the Catholic Church in America, which rallied to the banner of Irish freedom, leaders of which had been loathe to criticize Wilson during the war years. In addition, possibly to further undermine Irish opposition to treaty ratification, the government began public hearings on German propaganda during the war under the auspices of Bruce Bielaski.[22] Irish-American nationalists' activities were investigated. Prominent among them were Jeremiah O'Leary, Shaemus O'Sheel, James K. McGuire[23] and others. Revealing the divisions within the Irish-American community, only the IPL sought to raise money for O'Leary's defense.[24] O'Leary abandoned by FOIF, became an open and angry supporter of DeValera, calling Cohalan an "altar-whacking Judge" who believed himself to be the only spokesperson for the Irish in America.[25] Data suggest the divisions had not become permanent as late as of June 1919. The Catholic Sun printed an official copy the Irish Republic's case to be presented at the Paris Peace Conference as received by FOIF President Diarmuid Lynch.[26] Ironically, immediately adjacent to the article was a brief article about Pancho Villa indicating his physiology suggested the bandit leader was "born bad". DeValera's opponents in America would later call him "Pancho Villa"[27] when the breach had become a permanent schism, each with its own rival organizations, spokesmen, and newspapers.

Local organizations of FOIF passed resolutions demanding the application of Wilson's principles of self-determination for Ireland. For example, the Syracuse branch adopted a resolution demanding the American government recognize the Irish Republic and apply the President's ideas of self-determination for small nations.[28] The Irish harbored a lingering resentment of President Wilson given his pro-British foreign policy bias, his anti-hyphenate speeches and his harassment of Irish leaders. The chasm grew wider between the two as it became clear the new world order was to be an Anglo-Saxon partnership. Wilsonian idealistic statements about self-determination were sacrificed on the altar of political expediency to save his League. A meeting between Wilson and an Irish-American delegation encouraging the President endorse the claims of Irish independence was devoid of results.²⁹ The meeting was a tactical necessity as some leaders of Irish opinion in America, were supportive of Wilson's efforts. McGuire, trying to solidify Irish support against ratification of the treaty, found many Irish politicians rallying to President Wilson, especially Senators Thomas J. Walsh of Montana and Joseph D. Phelan of California. For example, Senator Phelan, with whom McGuire had prior contact in the wake of the asphalt scandals in Santo Domingo, and Senator Walsh justified their support for the treaty believing it would avert war, peacefully resolve international disputes and encourage Ireland's peaceful admission to the League of Nations.³⁰ Within a year, McGuire would bemoan the fact to Cohalan that Ireland was initially absent from the consciousness of most Congressmen. Machine politicians such as Charles F. Murphy, largely focused on local issues. McGuire said the divisions among the Irish movement in America had made the issue of Irish independence a matter of "contemptuous indifference" to them.³¹

Wilson had indicated a willingness to meet with representatives of Irish America during one of his return visits to the United States. Following the Third Irish Race Convention, pressure was put on Wilson to meet with Irish representatives and the President relented. The two parties met on 4 March 1919 at the Metropolitan Opera House following a scheduled address by the President. Wilson, regarding his nemesis Cohalan as "disloyal" because of his previous support for "Champ" Clark and because of the revelations concerning his subversive activities, made Cohalan withdraw before he would meet with them. The delegates pressed Wilson to use his influence to pressure for Ireland's independence. The President did not rule out consideration of Ireland, but he refused to present its case in person.³²

In addition to the negative impact of Wilson's dismissal of Cohalan, according to Judge Goff, there was a major misunderstanding between the two parties. The President allegedly would meet with the delegation, accept their resolution and hear any arguments they wished to make. Goff, however, insisted the President was to make his position on Ireland clear. Instead, Wilson declared the problem to be a domestic issue of Great Britain and hence would make no commitment on the question. The Irish delegation came away with no assurance from the President. Meanwhile, pressure on Wilson increased when the House of Representatives overwhelmingly passed the amended Gallagher resolution endorsing the cause of self-determination for Ireland.[33] An American Commission on Irish Independence consisted of three distinguished Irish-Americans was designated by the Irish Race Convention to go to Paris to appeal to Wilson to put the Irish cause before the Peace Conference. Consisting of Frank J. Ryan, Wilson's former Labor Conference Board member, Edward F. Dunne, a liberal Democrat and former governor of Illinois, and Michael J. Ryan, Philadelphia lawyer and former head of the UIL, its agenda also included obtaining consent to have an Irish delegation selected by the Dail appear at the conference to advance the cause of the Irish Republic.[34] Their departure was preceded by a banquet replete with speeches, toasts, poems and prophecies of success. Interestingly, among those listed as hosts and speakers for this momentous occasion, James K. McGuire was not noted. Subsequent issues of <u>The Catholic Sun</u> gave biographies of the three American delegates complete with their pictures and their contributions to the cause of Irish freedom.[35] In anticipation of a favorable result of their efforts, the Friends of Irish Freedom displayed the tricolor of the new Irish republic. To put the religious fears of Protestant America at rest, the Irish National Bureau, recently taken over by FOIF from the I.P.L., issued a statement which indicates the colors-"orange and green with a white stripe of justice between are the nation's new national colors." It also announced the Republic's new envoy, Patrick McCartan.[36] Perhaps a combination of idealism and pragmatism, the Irish and Irish-Americans put their faith in President Wilson given the political reality that France and Italy did not rank Ireland as a major concern. Neither they would belatedly realize, did Wilson.[37] The President was apparently willing to sacrifice Ireland for British support for his League of Nations. In Paris, both sides believed an accommodation had been reached. In the interim, the Americans were permitted to visit Ireland and were warmly greeted.[38] However, their statements in support of the Irish cause created a backlash in Britain. Frank J. Ryan was the spokesperson whose remarks may have engendered the reaction. For example, in a speech in Dublin, Ryan said he believed America was sincere in its pledge to honor the concept of "self-determination". Further, he noted, the suffering of the Irish under British rule, predicting success for Ireland within six months to a year as their cause was "unconquerable and bound to be victorious". In addition, they had visited Sinn Fein captives at Mountjoy Prison. And although the delegates went to Belfast and met with Unionist leaders, the mission left a bitter taste with both British and American representatives in Paris.[39] The net result was the cancellation of any plans to have representatives of an independent Ireland visit Paris. One of the Commission's acts was to publish a polemical description of conditions in Ireland. Wilson used the statements of the Americans as an excuse to defer action on the Irish question[40]. Despite its ostensible failure, the Commissioners' efforts were lauded by FOIF leader Daniel Cohalan and Sinn Fein Representative John O'Kelly,[41] the Provisional Irish government's envoy to the Paris Peace Conference. This, however, was not the final act of the Commission. It would become intimately involved in the Bond Certificate Campaign, aligning its members with DeValera and the pro-Ireland faction against Cohalan and the pro-America group.[42] McGuire, caught in the middle, sought with others to bring the factions together.

The Friends of Irish Freedom initiated a public relations campaign, urging President Wilson use the Peace Conference to push for Ireland's claims for independence using his own words of "self-determination" to hold him to his pledge.[43] Then the Irish-American war against Wilson began in earnest. Both sides dug in their heels. The Irish-American anti-covenant forces allied with the isolationists led by Senator William E. Borah. The brewing discontent over Wilson spilled into Irish-American politics and contributed to the growing division in its ranks. Cohalan, et al, sought to denounce the League, yet others – his rivals within the Irish community, McGarrity, Maloney, McCartan held out hope the embattled Wilson would belatedly support the cause of Irish freedom.[44] This hope was given strength by Eamon deValera's initial endorsement of the League which strained the relationships with the Devoy/Cohalan camp. FOIF, dominated as it was by Cohalan, was determined to hold Wilson true to his promises. The focus of their attention revolved around two key issues in the proposed treaty – freedom of the seas and Article X of the Covenant. Many Irish-Americans perceived these two as simply vehicles to extend and protect the British Empire. Article X was a particular stumbling block, because Irish leaders saw it as an instrument for either using American troops to suppress an Irish rebellion or to prevent Ireland from obtaining external aid for another attempt at winning freedom from British rule.[45]

Sinn Féin leaders in Ireland visiting the United States to drum up support for Irish independence raised other issues. John O'Kelly, representing the Provisional Government of Ireland, noted the problem with Article VII which restricted admission to the League to "self-governing countries", including dominions and colonies. He also intimated continued war was possible should Ireland's claims go unrecognized.[46] Addressing a local meeting of FOIF, Liam Mellows visited Syracuse, New York in February 1919. Following the standard Irish line, he noted American participation in the Great War was the means by which it repaid France for its assistance during the Revolution. America, he proclaimed, owed a similar debt to Ireland, given the sacrifices of its sons in their adopted country's wars. It should be repaid by United States support for Irish independence.[47] Not to be outdone, Judge Cohalan visited Syracuse and the local FOIF organization the following month, delivered a similar address, although the text of his message focused more on the threat Britain and Japan posed in the post-war world.[48] Interestingly, given the rancor which would grow in the ensuing years, over "self-determination" or "independence, Cohalan's "Plea For Irish Liberty" was published in full in the Syracuse Herald under the headline "Ireland Demands Independence and Recognition of the Irish Republic". A resolution calling for such action was adopted "unanimously and enthusiastically".[49] Both DeValera and Cohalan shared the dais at a monster rally at Madison Square Garden in June 1919, prior to the former's departure on a nation-wide speaking tour.

The breach was not yet public. In fact, as late as February 1920, FOIF was still actively soliciting funds for the Irish bond drive.[50] Another issue between contending factions was the control of the $5 million Irish Victory Fund. Initially endorsed at the Third Irish Race Convention in January 1919, the goals of the fund were vague - financing political agitation in the USA and Ireland.[51] James K. McGuire was heavily involved in FOIF's initial support for DeValera, entertaining him at his home in August 1919, enthusiastically supporting the Bond Drive and predicting its fiscal success.[52] McGuire backed up his words with action. He ran a half-page advertisement encouraging "every reader of the Catholic Sun who loves liberty and justice" to contribute. In block letters it proclaimed "American Dollars Will Win Ireland's Independence". The Catholic Sun reported that James K. McGuire initially donated $2000 when the fund was started.[53] An article in McGuire's Catholic Sun reiterated FOIF policy: America entered the war to guarantee the self-determination of small nations; the issue of Irish independence was non-sectarian, and; the goal of the Irish Victory Fund was a propaganda effort in America. To that effort, the Syracuse Branch of FOIF had raised over $2200. Individual subscriptions ranged from $1 to $200, with "Jas. K. McGuire" contributing $100 to the cause. His brother, George H. McGuire, gave half that amount.[54]

McGuire was never totally enamored with DeValera. He realized DeValera could be a difficult personality, a mix of romantic idealism and egotistical materialism. "McGuire interpreted DeValera's clumsiness as the mask of a gentle, brave, kindly, noble-souled, determined idealist like Desmoulins, St. Just and the guillotined Girondists who died to make a new world and succeeded, but a most difficult man to fit into the most selfish, self-centered, materialist great[est] country in the world". McGuire urged Cohalan to deal with DeValera cautiously: "Do not raise DeValera's hand high and hurt it when you shake hands with him or any other underfed man and speak to him, not at him". Cohalan, Devoy and other American Irish leaders saw only the unpleasant side of deValera, a factor which did not bode well for future relations between the "President of the Irish Republic" and his hosts[55] in line with the FOIF policy of dealing effectively with DeValera. The Catholic Sun published a long article in late April 1919 praising DeValera's character and political and military skill, affirming their unity in the cause of Irish freedom: "The Irish in America agree with deValera and follow his bold and wise leadership, and deValera, in the plainest and clearest terms, expresses approval of their words and actions. Let us hold resolutely and loyally to this most hopeful unanimity of aims, purposes and declarations of policy perfect our organization, gather in the great resources of the race and victory will come to the Irish cause as surely as tomorrow's sun will rise".[56] The pro-Ireland faction led by McGarrity wanted to use the Irish Victory Fund money for providing support for Irish revolutionary nationalists, whereas Cohalan sought to use it to defeat the League Covenant. In order to access the cash Sinn Fein sent over Harry Boland and Eamon deValera.[57] Eventually $250,000 was sent to Ireland after a protracted debate with Cohalan. The struggle only embittered the two sides. A surface harmony was maintained between the two factions through mid-1920. An article in The Catholic Sun of 25 June 1920 quoted Daniel F. Cohalan:

> I regret greatly the efforts being made in certain quarters to spread the impression that there are divisions and dissension in the ranks of those who are interested in the independence of Ireland.

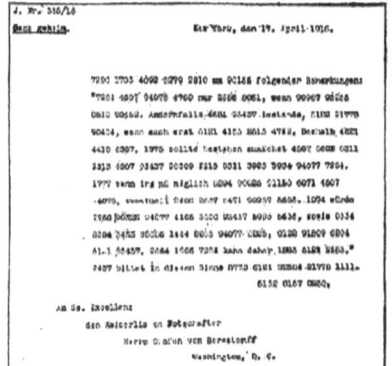

Source: French Strother. Fighting Germany's Spies. Doubleday, 1918, pp. 154-155. Not in copyright.

General John T. Thompson
(1860-1940)
Inventor of the Thomson Submachine Gun
Creative Commons Attribution
(Source: Tommy Gun)

Harry Boland
(1887-1922)
Irish Revolutionary
Public Domain
(Source: https://Getty Imagaesile:iedetail/news-photo/irish-repeublican-and-sinn-fein-politicians-harry-boland-in-new-photo-3350714)

Eugene Kinkhead
(1876-1960)
Irish Nationalist
Library of Congress, Harris and Ewing No Known Copyright Restrictions

Michael Collins
(1890 1922)
Irish nationalist
Public Domain
(Source: Encyclopedia Britannica Ina)

Eamon DeValera
(1887-1975)
Irish revolutionary, President and Prime Minister of Ireland
Library of Congress ID cph 3b51291
No Known Copyright Restrictions

Liam Mellows
(1892·1922)
Irish Revolutionary
Public Domain

Terence MacSwiney
(1879-1920)
Martyr to Irish Independence
Public Domain
(Source: http://tiocfaiharlaa.blogspot.com/2008-10-01archive.html)

There is no division in the ranks on any question of principle and I am confident there will be none...

Nonetheless, the article went on to hint of a split in Irish America, with Cohalan emphasizing his role in the debate as an American:

> On questions of procedure, there are bound to be occasions where millions of men are engaged in a cause when all may not agree in the manner of presenting the proposition...
>
> I am in this work as an American whose first and only loyalty is to my country...I shall continue to work as I have done in the past with all who strive to bring about the independence of Ireland.[58]

A temporary truce was broken when James O'Mara, DeValera's financial agent in the fundraising drive, demanded an accounting of the monies disbursed from the Irish Victory Fund from Diarmuid Lynch.[59] Not only were there demands by DeValera to obtain control of the Victory Fund, but his actions were increasingly denounced by FOIF. New President Michael J. Gallagher castigated DeValera for his actions, blaming him for the increased violence in Ireland. Cohalan also issued a report condemning DeValera's divisive actions. In addition, the IPL continued its public demonstrations and its open support of DeValera, despite the repressive atmosphere generated by Attorney General A. Mitchell Palmer's Red Raids.[60] Because of these actions, FOIF ultimately expelled the IPL from its ranks. Bitterness increased when DeValera in his effort to reorganize FOIF in a confrontational meeting in September 1920, was referred to by Cohalan supporters as a "foreign potentate".[61] The divisions widened as both Cohalan and DeValera appeared at the Republican Convention in 1920 urging the adoption of different resolutions as to the fate of Ireland. DeValera's attempt to obtain a resolution in favor of an Irish Republic was defeated. Because of the divisiveness of the Irish, the Republicans abandoned Cohalan's more moderate proposal. Because of his appearance at the convention, and the general hoopla it engendered, FOIF condemned DeValera's dictatorial methods and his refusal to follow the guidance of the American leadership.⁶² Control over finances caused an open rupture. John Splain suggests the fiscal struggle was initiated by DeValera, who shortly after his arrival sought a plan for a Irish loan underwritten by American banks and sold by them. He was advised that such a plan was inconsistent with American banking laws. By June 1919, DeValera conceded the point and decided to issue Bond Certificates. FOIF accommodated itself to DeValera's wishes to the point of suspending fund raising for its Irish Victory Fund in August 1919, making its headquarters the center of arrangements for DeValera's tours, and extending him $20,000 for expenses.⁶³ At this point, both segments of Irish opinion appeared to come together to present a united front on the resolution by Republican William F. Mason of Illinois in December 1919. The bill provided for funds to establish a diplomatic mission for Ireland in the United States. Among the many speakers in favor of the resolution was James K. McGuire. Despite their best efforts, the bill languished in committee. Outrage in America over the atrocities in Ireland committed by the Black and Tans produced a watered-down resolution advocating sympathy for the Irish cause, but it never came to the floor.⁶⁴ During the Mason Bill hearings, DeValera, in response to a query whether Irish independence would jeopardize the security of America's ally Great Britain, committed a faux pas which plagued him during the remainder of his visit in America. DeValera allowed that Britain should do what America did to Cuba – create a Platt Amendment. The verbal slip brought outrage from FOIF who saw in it a betrayal of the ideal of independence.⁶⁵ Despite DeValera's subsequent explanation, it only served to further divide the two groups, each side blaming the other for disunity. A bitter exchange of letters between Cohalan and DeValera followed but they maintained a façade of unity as late as March 1920, appearing jointly at a parade and a banquet. Boland relates how the incident put DeValera on edge. Prominent Irish-Americans met at the home of James K. McGuire and promised to stand by "The Chief" during this crisis in Nationalist ranks. Also present were Major Eugene F. Kinkead, Frank P. Walsh and W. Bourke Cockrane. Five days later,

Boland again met with McGuire discussing the pros and cons of the situation and deciding on a plan of action. Boland, in his diary, referred to Cohalan as "an evil for Ireland". McGuire was trying to conciliate both sides and avoid an irrevocable split.[66] Throughout much of the ensuing factional strife, Boland remained on friendly terms with McGuire going to church, the opera and even obtaining a birthday present of a handmade necktie from McGuire's wife, Frances.[67]

The split in ranks became permanent with Boland establishing the Reorganized Clan-na-Gael for which he got him into trouble with Nationalist leaders in Ireland. Boland asked McGuire to write Michael Collins to endorse his efforts to bring the two sides together without sacrificing his nationalist principles or convictions. Beneath the surface amity, however, the dissention continued. In January 1920, DeValera had requested and obtained weekly meetings with ranking FOIF and Clan members – John DeVoy, Daniel Cohalan, Joseph McGarrity, James K. McGuire, Diarmuid Lynch and Richard F. Dalton. Inexplicably and suddenly the meetings ended with Splain blaming the machinations of Dr. William J. Maloney as the chief cause.[68] Cohalan decided to hold a meeting to debate DeValera's conduct. Despite being uninvited, McGarrity, DeValera and Harry Boland showed up. Each side berated the other for eight hours with the compromise being that each promised not to interfere in the affairs of the other.[69] The truce was soon broken once more over money, personalities, and policies. It was access to cash which exacerbated tensions between the two camps. Devoy reopened the wound by accusing DeValera of using $50,000 of bond money to send a "nondescript" aggregation of individuals which presented a "deplorable spectacle" to the Republican Convention as rival of FOIF to undo the work of Justice Cohalan in obtaining an endorsement for the Irish issue. Such a plank had been narrowly supported by the Platform Committee, but DeValera rejected it, insisting on full recognition for Irish independence, not simply self-determination. Devoy rejected the idea that Irish in America accept leadership from Ireland.[70] The divergence in attitude was revealed in Irish ranks by

Andrew J. Gallagher a member of the American Commission On Irish Independence, and a close friend of DeValera at the Democratic Convention in San Francisco, who called for recognition of the Irish Republic.[71] The net result of the division in Irish ranks was they got commitment from neither major party. Ward documents how, despite his comments to the contrary based on his voting record, Republican candidate Warren G. Harding had hardly been sympathetic to the Irish cause. James M. Cox also of Ohio, who was the Democratic candidate, made more forceful statements and was reportedly willing to compromise on Article X but garnered little support from the Irish faithful.[72]

Other factors may have been at work as well. Irish-America was caught up in the "return to normalcy", its politicians focusing on election results and its resultant patronage positions, their concern for Ireland seemed limited to making cash contributions and ending Prohibition. James K. McGuire warned that politicians could ignore Ireland as the various hyphenate groups in America, Irish included, were more focused on the liquor issue.[73] By summer, the situation had not significantly changed with McGuire again writing to Cohalan about the lack of concern by the American Congress for Ireland's future.[74] Almost despairingly, McGuire followed up his previous letters to Cohalan, noting that Democratic politicians were predicting a victory for Cox and given the divisions within the Irish camp in America, they had little concern for the Irish vote.[75] McGuire was obviously disturbed by the factionalism within the Irish nationalist community, to the extent the aging patriarch of Irish independence, John Devoy, remarked to Cohalan, "This, I think, was one of the things that James [K.] McGuire objected to. He calls it "fighting".[76]

The split between Cohalan and DeValera over control of the Irish movement in America widened even more, despite efforts by some to reach an accommodation. Meanwhile DeValera established a rival to FOIF, The American Association For the Recognition of the Irish Republic (AARIR) which soon garnered strength from deserting members of the rank and file of FOIF, yet its leadership remained loyal to Cohalan. FOIF members fell from over 100,000 to about 1/5 of that by mid 1921 and the AARIR rose to an estimated 500,000. Thus deserted by its more militant pro-Irish element, FOIF became even more American in outlook.[77] This was made easier by the departure of DeValera to Ireland in December 1920. The Republican victory initiated a policy of American isolationism which virtually excluded Ireland as an issue for the United States government. It gradually subsided from the consciousness of most Americans, with the exception of the so-called "professional Irishmen" whose infighting kept the issue alive.

The most contentious issue was the existence of two rival organizations – FOIF and AARIR – with divergent philosophies. DeValera needed an organization that he could control with its sympathies linked directly to Ireland. He was successful in attracting new blood into his organization, especially Edward L. Doheny,[78] the oil magnate, previously not connected to the Irish cause. DeValera was also successful at recruiting former FOIF members, including Judge John Goff and Father Peter F. Yorke, the Irish-born radical priest and California labor activist, and Rossa Downing, President of the Padraic Pearce branch of FOIF. Peter Golden of IPL fame was also an active member. The AARIR claimed 700,000 members at its height in 1921, but members decreased to one-tenth of that in the wake of the bitter struggle over treaty ratification. By then McGuire became an active supporter of DeValera and the AARIR, although he never quite divorced himself from Devoy given their long association in the Clan-na-Gael. According to Devoy, relations between the two camps became extremely bitter to the extent that DeValera sent out an assassination squad targeting Devoy "for betraying the Republic". It was McGuire, privy to actions in both camps, who warned Devoy of the murder plot as they were going to lunch together. Devoy told McGuire to relay a message to DeValera stating in the event such a plan transpired it "will be taken out of DeValera's hide". The threat stopped, but apparently was reopened later with the additional target of Daniel F. Cohalan.[79]

Not only was there the bitter quarrel between Cohalan and DeValera, the following month saw the creation the Clan-na-Gael

Reorganized, a DeValera dominated group to rival Devoy which it was hoped would cut off some of Cohalan's support. The split was due both to the rivalries within the Irish community in America and a reaction to them by Nationalists in Ireland itself. In Ireland, it was the result of Michael Collins' resentment of Devoy's constant criticism of DeValera. Harry Boland was responsible for causing the break, the I.R.B. severing all connections with the American Clan-na-Gael recognizing instead the reorganized Clan as its American affiliate under the leadership of Luke Dillon.[80] McCartan says he heard about the plans of the I.R.B. to sever its relationship to the American Clan-na-Gael from James K. McGuire. Believing it unwise to have the schism made public, McCartan tried but failed to prevent it.[81] McGuire was working behind the scenes to keep the movement together, but it was already too late.

The AARIR attracted some people of note and much of the FOIF rank and file, but made little progress in obtaining recognition for Irish independence. The ratification of Anglo-Irish Treaty of December 1921, brought division to Ireland and to Irish Americans. AARIR also split into pro-and- anti-treaty factions with Doheny being replaced by James "Red" Murray, a Montana labor lawyer, who was subsequently replaced by John F. Finerty who kept the rump organization firmly behind De Valera during the Civil War.[82]

Meanwhile events in Ireland had taken a turn for the worse. The victory of Sinn Féin in December 1918 destroyed the last vestiges of the Irish Parliamentary Party. Sinn Féin withdrew from Parliament and created a shadow government, complete with courts, taxes and an army. The British response, in March 1920 was brutal repression, best known for its introduction of the infamous Black and Tans and the Auxiliaries. The Irish Republican Army under Michael Collins responded in kind.[83] A bloody reign of terror began. The bickering of two Irish factions in America made it difficult for them to cooperate in exploiting the publicity of the hunger strike death of Terence MacSwiney, Lord Mayor of Cork, in October 1920.

Through all this confusion, James K. McGuire was active. His membership in both FOIF and the Clan-na-Gael, apparently was no barrier to his joining Irish Nationalists from rival factions in America to pursue the cause of Irish independence. For example, in September 1920 McGuire, along with Frank P. Walsh, a member of the American Commission on Irish Independence and Daniel C. O'Flaherty, Under Secretary of State, had tried to get the State Department to intervene on McSwiney's behalf. O'Flaherty had told Cardinal O'Connell there was no legal precedent for American intervention. Bainbridge Colby, who had replaced Lansing as Secretary of State, after listening to the arguments of the three Irish-Americans, was willing to entertain an unofficial appeal to the British Embassy on behalf of McSwiney. Given Colby's previous statements in favor of the Rising in Ireland in 1916, it was assumed they would get a favorable hearing. Wilson, however, would have none of it. Responding to their telegram requesting intervention, Wilson curtly told his Secretary, Joseph Tumulty, "This is more than futile; it is grossly impertinent".[84] A month later, McGuire was part of a delegation which pressed for Irish independence that was officially received by Colby at the State Department. Among others present were John Goff, Joseph McGarrity, Eugene Kinkead, Frank P. Walsh.[85] The incidents above are noteworthy for several reasons. Frank P. Walsh, as ranking member of the American Commission on Irish Independence, had been delegated as the chief fund-raising agency for DeValera's Bond Certificate campaign. Hence, Walsh was strongly identified with the DeValera wing of Irish support in America. McGuire, as noted, was active in the Clan and served on the FOIF executive committee. He had previously petitioned President Wilson to intervene in the Casement affair and had been associated with German propaganda agencies during the war. This suggests that despite the acrimony between the warring factions of Irish America, some segments, at least, still cooperated in areas of mutual concern. Also, Wilson, who felt betrayed by Irish American leaders in the fight over the League, and who was also sick and tired, probably recalled the negative public reaction to his handling of the Casement issue, and was not about to be moved. Judge Goff had moved away from Cohalan and was prominent in the AARIR.

Major Eugene Kinkead was an Irish-born retired military intelligence officer and a Congressman from New Jersey who was involved in smuggling arms to Republican forces in Ireland. Joseph McGarrity, was a prosperous Philadelphia businessman, Clan member and avid supporter of DeValera both in America and Ireland during the Civil War. McGuire's presence at these and other meetings with those who were so strongly identified with DeValera begs the question as to his motives. Disgusted as he was by the factional infighting, was he trying to maintain a façade of unity? Was he a liaison between both segments? The data suggest it was probably the latter. Harry Boland had been encouraged by the Supreme Council of the IRB to maintain contact between it and Devoy's faction. McGuire, with his positions both in FOIF and the Clan, was a perfect conduit. McGuire, disgusted with the constant bickering and the rumors of a "reorganized" Clan in process, announced his intent to resign as Chairman of the Executive Committee. In a final effort to prevent the birth of a second Clan, Boland met with McGuire and laid out the proposal for a Reorganized Clan-na-Gael, controlled and directed from Ireland. McGuire passed on the plans to Devoy warning if the American Clan did not concur with such a program, it would be severed from its Irish roots. McGuire worked hard to obtain a settlement. His remarks to Cohalan reveal his fears of schism, noting a divided Clan was breaking Devoy's heart, an organization he had helped establish, brought together after a break at the turn of the century and in whose name he had selfishly dedicated his life. McGuire also praised Boland's efforts, who, "working under great difficulties, made a lasting and most favorable impression on all present, who exemplified the real fighting man that enkindles the spirit of our people".[86] McGuire had temporarily replaced Captain John T. Ryan as Chairman since the latter was a political refugee in Mexico and would not return until early 1922. McGuire was in turn, to be replaced by Devoy's choice, John Archdeacon Murphy of the Buffalo Clan. Murphy had gone to Ireland with John Gill to distribute relief money in the wake of the 1916 rebellion. He and John Trigg replaced Walsh, Dunne and Ryan in 1919 as representatives of the

American Commission on Irish Independence in Paris.[87] Strategically, it gave Devoy a strong ally in place of the disenchanted McGuire. As noted previously, Devoy had a suspicious nature, possibly as a result of his long association with a maligned and persecuted secret society, distrusting DeValera, especially in the wake of the recent murder plot. He especially disliked Maloney, and given his flirtation with the AARIR, he had reason to suspect the loyalty of the wavering James K. McGuire.

By November 1920, McGuire had withdrawn from the factional fighting. In a letter to Harry Boland, McGuire revealed his intimate knowledge of Irish history yet leveled criticism of DeValera's power-grabbing tactics:

> I have a horror of all Irish organizations as a result of thirty years experience with them and would not join another one. The rivalries of individuals for leadership for control are the curse and the bane of the movement. In the old days of the Clan-na-Gael, the Ancient Order Of Hibernians, the Land League, the Irish National League, etc., three-fourths of the efforts put forth were fighting fellow members instead of fighting England. In every case there has been a boss or a clique dominating and the struggle of the caucus and the dictatorship has resulted in paralysis of the hopes and aims of pacific and earnest men.

Still further, McGuire noted any new organization would be factional and barren of good results. Praising DeValera's unexcelled devotion to principle, McGuire criticized him as a leader: he was a lamentable failure as a negotiator, lacking in decision, changeable, unsteady.[88] McGuire having been unsuccessful in healing the rift, apparently felt he could criticize both sides.

Having split the Irish movement in America and realizing little more could be done by him here and motivated by the turn of events in Ireland, DeValera left his lieutenant in charge and returned home.

The situation in Ireland was rapidly deteriorating. A massacre of British Army officers by the IRA was followed by reprisals at a Gaelic football match, best known as "Bloody Sunday". The British responded by imposing martial law. The vicious cycle of murder and reprisal began once again.

In order to mask his departure, DeValera used the good offices of James K. McGuire. "The Chief" had left America in mid-December and was smuggled into Ireland by Christmas. There were persistent rumors that DeValera, worn out by his labors on behalf of Ireland, had retired to the country outside of New York, allegedly at the home of James K. McGuire who had hosted him when he first arrived. As late as 30 December 1920, The <u>New York Times</u> stated an Irish newspaper in Albany reported that DeValera was "recuperating at the home of his friend, James K. McGuire", a statement disavowed by McGuire's wife. Her denial was plausible. The McGuires had recently sold their home and moved to an apartment in New York City. In addition, DeValera was by then in Ireland. The article may have served as a smokescreen to confuse British and American authorities who refused to believe, despite Harry Boland's statement to the contrary, that DeValera was in Ireland[89]. It also reveals the close relationship McGuire maintained with DeValera and his associates, despite the rift among Irish-Americans.

McGuire let go of one of his long-time business interests. In September 1920 he sold his share in the Syracuse Printing and Publishing Company to James E. Doyle, a Syracuse native and former editor of the <u>Syracuse Herald</u>, and previously a deputy superintendent of public works[90] in New York State. That gave new leadership to not only his Syracuse paper but to those in Albany, New York and Scranton, Pennsylvania. And while significant space continued to be given to events in Ireland, especially the depredations of the Black and Tans, and the martyrdom of Terrence Mac Swiney,[91] there seemed to be a shift in coverage with reference to domestic Irish politics. After the sale of his papers, there were more articles covering DeValera's endeavors and those of the AARIR than were dedicated to FOIF activities. For example, the 3 December 1920 edition of the Catholic Sun carried an article about the formation of the New York chapter of the AARIR which featured an address by President Eamon DeValera.[92] In February 1921, the Catholic Sun reported on the state convention of 500 AARIR delegates in Syracuse, estimating its total national membership at 500,000. Its featured speaker was Lord Mayor Donal Callaghan of Cork. A brief addendum to the article simply noted the local John Barry branch of FOIF held a meeting with its many new members subscribing to the bond certificate drive.[93] A subsequent Catholic Sun article carried a detailed report to the state AARIR convention in Syracuse. Guests included Mrs. Catherine Wheeler of Rochester, DeValera's mother. Featured speakers included Padraic Fleming, an Irish Republican escapee from Mountjoy Prison, Harry Boland, head of the Irish mission to America and Sailendra Nath Ghose, head of Indian delegation who also demanded freedom from Great Britain. Ghose was national organizer for The Friends of Freedom for India and head of the unofficial American Commission to Promote Self-Government for India. He was also an indicted co-conspirator in the Indo-German Conspiracy trials.[94] The convention passed a series of anti-British resolutions, urging dissolution of the British Empire as essential to the safety of America.[95] A week later the Catholic Sun published a full page article with the names of the national and state directors of the AARIR and the full text of the resolutions passed by the Convention.[96] Interestingly, about a month later an article commemorating the founding of the Irish Republic by the Syracuse branch of the AARIR was published. The featured speaker was J.L. Fawcitt, whose description of the "glory and tragedy of the Ireland of today" was considered by those present as "the most finished exposition on the subject yet presented in Syracuse.[97]

The Catholic Sun also carried a large article detailing events for the national AARIR Convention in Chicago in March 1921. It was described as "the greatest convention ever held by supporters of independence for Ireland." The leaders of AARIR were introduced-John Goff, Edward L. Doheny, Rossa Downing, Rev. Peter C. Yorke, Mary MacWhorter, Eugene Kinkead and Peter Golden.

The cheering continued for Irish envoys Harry Boland and T.D.E. McEnvoy. Numerous resolutions endorsing independence were passed and forwarded to members of Congress and President Harding.[98] Two weeks later, the paper followed up with an article featuring the pictures and brief biographies of the AARIR national leaders.[99] The following week, the Catholic Sun published a brief article with pictures of the leaders of the AARIR membership campaign, the goal of which was to increase enrollment to over one million.[100]

In addition to the small article of FOIF fund raising activities, the only other article with reference to it was the brief notation of a speech made in Chicago by Daniel F. Cohalan calling for the dissolution of the British Empire.[101]

Coverage of AARIR activities in the Catholic Sun continued through 1923 with virtually none for FOIF. The Syracuse branch of the AARIR featured Mrs. Muriel MacSwiney, widow of the martyred mayor of Cork in October 1922, who openly addressed the schism within the ranks of supporters of Irish freedom urging financial support for the AARIR.[102] A brief article in February noted the election of new officers for the local organization and plans to celebrate Robert Emmet's birthday.[103] All this suggests the new owner's endorsement of AARIR policies.

McGuire's continued collaboration with DeValera's associates previously linked to the Hindu-German gun-running conspiracy were repeated in the East Side incident, another intriguing episode in the struggle for Irish freedom. This is pertinent in so far as he maintained connections to both factions in America, which they in turn held in Ireland. There had been attempts on both sides to bring at least the severed segments of the Clan-na-Gael together in the wake of Harry Boland's high-handed expulsion of the American Clan from the IRB. Boland was undermined by the IRB claim he had received no authorization for such action, although it supported him in the end. Possibly to shore up his credibility, Boland pressed hard to obtain arms and ammunition for Irish rebels in 1920. Boland faced an uphill struggle, given the checkered success of previous gun – running episodes. Bell summarized it best: "The history of the

IRA arms supply has been one of repeated failure, short falls, aborted transport, wasted funds and futile arrangements, brightened from time to time by a special success."[104] The Catholic Sun reported that Boland had recently returned from Ireland "to report on matters in America to the Irish Republican cabinet". According to the article, Boland boasted of the success of the guerilla struggle, but noted they were not as well-armed as they would like, although some weapons were obtained from defeated regiments of the British army.[105]

Boland's focus of attention was the Thompson submachine gun. The weapon had its origins in the efforts of Col. Marcellus Thompson, whose experience in the Spanish – American War convinced of the need for better armaments for the US military. After retiring from the Ordnance Department in 1914, he was employed by Remington Arms to resesearch the feasibility of an automatic rifle.[106] Further development was impeded by the Great War after which Thompson could once again devote himself to the weapon, obtaining multiple patents. Working models were produced by 1919.[107] Interestingly, Thompson saw the weapon most useful as a riot control weapon for urban police departments engaged in efforts to control labor unrest and ethnic violence then plaguing the country. There was a need to market the product to the largest number of buyers in order to recoup the losses incurred in research and development[108]

By the end of the war with the defeat of Germany the best source of weapons for the IRA was the United States which had a large pro-active Irish diaspora community and the industrial capacity to produce them. Both came together in the East Side episode in which McGuire played an important role. According to Bell, "the IRA did not simply import the Thompson submachine gun, but remnants of the Clan – na - Gael in the United States had underwritten the weapon's development, made the first great purchase, arranged shipment and oversaw subsequent supplies ....The IRA funded the research and development for one of the world's great infantry weapons..."[109].

Since Collins was interested in submachine guns, Boland's efforts to have a shipment of Thompson submachine guns smuggled into

Ireland included his friend James K. McGuire. Fitzpatrick says it was arranged through George Gordon Rorke, a Georgetown University graduate, a member of the Protestant Friends of Ireland, an acquaintance of Boland[110] and a member of the AARIR. With the weapons and ammunition obtained, he now had to get them shipped. The bulk of the guns were loaded by an Irish crew as few sailors were available due to a seamen strike. They were eventually hidden on the East Side, a steamship owned by the United States Shipping Board, operated by the Cosmopolitan Shipping Company and chartered by the Irish White Cross to bring supplies to Ireland. Fitzpatrick says it was Liam Pedlar, an employee of Joseph McGarrity, who obtained the weapons. Pedlar was "Military Attache" of the IRA in the United States until 1925. He had previously been involved in the Aud gun-running incident. Pedlar was imprisoned following the Easter Rising with Michael Collins at Frongoch in Wales. Allegedly, the captain of the ship was curious about the activity on board and simply investigated. That story strains credibility given intensive surveillance by the FBI weeks before the seizure of the guns. As with the Hindu-German Conspiracy trial, the British Secret Service was behind the confiscation, having followed the development of the weapon's manufacture, sale and its links to Sinn Fein. The guns were seized by U.S. Customs agents in June 1921 and removed to New Jersey. Boland tried to have Major Eugene Kinkead use his political connections to smuggle the weapons out of police custody before they could be properly secured by the authorities all to no avail, although 105 of the 600 submachine guns were never accounted for.[111] The guns were impounded until 1925 when, according to Luke Dillon, Joseph McGarrity and John T. Ryan obtained them through the intervention of Senator Wordsworth of New York, with the Clan paying the legal fees and costs of maintenance.[112] The McGuire link to the incident is the fact that he had connections to the United States Shipping Board, organized in 1916 to revitalize the American merchant marine, building its own ships and using those commandeered from Germany after America declared war.[113] After World War I, McGuire was a sales representative for the McIntosh-Seymour Company of Auburn,

New York, a manufacturer of turbines and diesel engines for ships and mills with clients in Central and South America and Europe. In his sales capacity, McGuire traveled frequently between Washington, D.C., and Norfolk, Virginia dealing with foreign corporations, their representatives and the U.S. Shipping Board.[114] In addition, Boland's diary notes during the time the arms transaction was taking place, McGarrity, McGuire, Pedlar, Boland and Kinkead were in constant contact with one another.[115] Devoy minces no words in his reaction to McGuire's involvement.

McGuire was at the time, on very intimate terms with DeValera and him [sic] and Harry Boland met frequently at his house in New Rochelle. He was obsessed with the delusion that he could bring about harmony by yielding to DeValera on every point in the controversy. That is a foolish course at all times, but with DeValera it is utterly absurd. Every concession made to him only encourages him to demand more and makes the situation worse. McGuire was with Harry Boland night and day during the purchase of the only large consignment of arms and munitions sent to Ireland during the Black and Tan warfare, and gained the impression that Boland would drop the fight if he was allowed.

In the article quoted above, Devoy notes how anxious McGuire was for peace between the two factions.

He [McGuire] was haunted all the time by memories of the "Triangle" split and was constantly reminding his colleagues of the murder incitements, but this is always a wrong argument to use with Irishmen. No Irishmen worth his salt would change sides through fear for his life. Yet McGuire thought the information about the gunmen would force DeVoy to submit to DeValera's intolerable pretensions. When the split actually came, McGuire dropped out, but his activities after that, such as they were, were all on the DeValera side.[116]

Having noted previously McGuire's connections to subversive activities during World War I, his involvement in the East Side incident is especially telling. McGuire's previous connections to the Gladstone incident due to his connections at Norfolk, Virginia reinforces the point, since the ship containing the contraband was to sail from Hoboken to Norfolk, from whence it would move to Ireland.[117] In addition, McGuire's assistance in smuggling Roger Casement into Germany, the American Clan's funding of the Easter Rebellion and McGuire's ties to the various Irish Nationalist organizations, his friendship with Boland and Devoy's statement cited above, it is logical to assume that James K. McGuire was involved with Boland in the arms smuggling operation. In addition, there was the fact that the New York Clan made arrangents to demonstrate the weapon at the 69th Street armory. As to Bell's assertion of Clan involvement, there was Boland, who transferred the funds from the Dail Eirean to de Lacey. Liam Pedlar was in charge of transport. The Irish American financier, Thomas Fortune Ryan, was a major backer of the Auto Ordnance Company, developer of the Thompson submachine gun, which he helped establish in 1916.[118] Ryan, of famine Irish parents, was penniless and orphaned. At 14 he began his business career as a Wall Street runner and clawed his way to the top in transportation, tobacco, banking and overseas investments, earning a personal fortune estimated at $200 million. His interest in Thompson, however, was more than pecuniary. John Thompson's son, Marcellus, married the daughter of Colonel George B. M. Harvey, Ryan's friend and business associate. Harvey was a conservative Democrat and an early supporter of Wilson, who later broke with him over domestic and foreign policy differences, particularly his opposition to the League of Nations, a position endorsed by many Irish nationalists. Harvey made his acquaintance with Ryan as a journalist, allegedly using his journalist ties to whitewash Ryan's spotty business reputation. Harvey was reputedly one of the several men in the "smoke-filled room" who won the Republican nomination for Warren G. Harding in 1920. Harvey's reward was appointment as U.S. Ambassador to Great Britain, serving until Harding's death in 1923. This might explain Harding's support for the Commission on Conditions in Ireland, much to the chagrin of British authorities. It was through Harvey that Ryan heard of the investment opportunities in the Thompson submachine gun. In exchange for a controlling interest, Ryan supplied the development and operating funds. Ryan, according to Helmer, had a long interest and involvement in pro-Irish activities.[119] There were rumors Ryan was one of the key figures in the gun-smuggling plot with at least one shipment arriving to assist the rebels. The stories are given credence by the fact of Ryan's strong Irish Republican sympathies, his friendship with DeValera and his substantial contributions to the Irish cause. In addition, in the wake of a Justice Department investigation of the gun-running plot, it was discovered that the corporation's sales force was well-staffed with "Sinn Féiners". Marcellus Thompson allegedly told his sales staff to, "See what the Irish crowd thinks of the guns "in December 1920. The first order from Irish interests came in February 1921. In April, there was additional interest in the guns. A special envoy demonstrated the guns to Michael Collins and his agents in Dublin. More orders were placed by Rorke and others with ties to Ryan, AARIR and the Auto-Ordinance Company. By June, the guns were in a warehouse operated by "Frank Williams", a.k.a. Laurence DeLacey, a militant Irish Republican in the USA on the run for his involvement in a dynamite plot. He spent time in a US prison for his attempt to free German consular officials Franz Bopp and E. von Schack from military authorities. DeLacey was also active in the Clan as was McGuire. Delacey had a history of activism dating back to his 1907 involvement with the IRB. As noted previously, he was tied to the Indo-German Conspiracy to send guns to the Ghadarite revolutionaries. It was his attempt to smuggle indicted conspirators into Mexico which lead to his early trial and imprisonment.[120] On 12 June, the guns were loaded on the East Side. When the guns were discovered, DeLacey returned to Ireland after a failed effort to have his property returned. Interestingly, the US Attorney handling the case was fired for "incompetence" and replaced. He told the press it was because prominent Americans – Marcellus Thompson, Thomas F. Ryan and Ambassador Harvey were involved.[121] Later indictments were drawn up by a federal grand jury for several of the lower-ranking conspirators, but they were not pursued because Britain had entered into delicate peace negotiations with the Republicans in Ireland, and;

the law under which they were indicted was a war-time measure and no longer in effect. The guns were reclaimed in 1925 by Joseph McGarrity, authorized agent for "Frank Williams" and, according to Helmer, McGarrity probably "continued smuggling them to the illegal IRA in subsequent years.[122] Despite their best efforts, the gun had limited use given the scarcity of weapons, ammunition and trained personnel. Nonetheless, the gun took on a life of its own becoming part of Irish Nationalist myth and legend.[123]

Meanwhile, other Nationalists were working hard to keep the issue of Ireland in the public mind. The controversial Dr. W. J. M. A. Maloney obtained support from DeValera to publicize the atrocities in Ireland. Using his family connection to Oswald Garrison Villard, publisher of the liberal journal The Nation, a panel of 150 distinguished Americans was convened calling itself the American Commission on Conditions In Ireland. Most of the panelists had no prior identification with the Irish causes. The Commission held hearings from November 1920 to January 1921, interviewing almost forty witnesses and obtaining testimony in a transcript of over 1000 pages. The Commission's Interim Report of March 1921 was published by the Benjamin Franklin Bureau, the publicity arm of the American Association for the Recognition of the Irish Republic.[124] The Final Report published in July of that year was almost anticlimactic in that peace talks had been initiated between Ireland and Britain. The two Reports condemned the depredations of the IRA, but reserved its harshest criticism for the conduct of the British forces in Ireland. The Commission's work was controversial, since neither British nor Ulster representatives chose to participate, but it was successful in two key areas: it kept alive the issue of Irish independence in the wake of the Versailles Treaty, and; it was done by a panel of prominent Americans.[125] At the same time as the American Commission On Conditions In Ireland was meeting, Dr. W. J. A. Maloney also established the American Commission For Relief In Ireland, obtaining the financial backing of Edward L. Doheny, and winning the endorsement of President Warren G. Harding. It raised over $5 million. An American delegation which toured Ireland noted the widespread devastations and suffering, a fact denied by the British government. Nonetheless, the Commission's observations, reinforced the statements of the Reports of the Commission on Conditions In Ireland and may have been instrumental in pushing the government into negotiations with DeValera.[126]

As the AARIR was involved in a more activist program for Ireland, FOIF focused on Britain's wartime debts to the United States, championed American isolation, kept up its attacks on the AARIR, and worked at counteracting nativist prejudices.[127] McGuire showed his continued links to both segments in Irish American politics by advocating the FOIF program. He encouraged the Irish Free State's share of the British war debt, estimated at $100 million, be paid to the United States. The brief Times article indicated his proposal had support from Irish leaders on both sides. Even more telling, given his attempted fence-mending, was his downplaying of the split among Dail leaders, "saying it was not personal, but on principle." The article also noted Collins and Boland rescued DeValera from prison, McGuire calling them, "the three guardsmen".[128]

Irish-Americans had successfully embarrassed the British through the American Committee For Relief In Ireland. In Ireland, the rebels were running out of cash to continue the struggle. DeValera was willing to negotiate. A truce was arranged in July 1921 and a treaty signed in December. In America, FOIF supported the treaty, John Splain echoing the comments of FOIF leadership calling it a step on the road to a Republic.[129]

Initially, the AARIR endorsed the Treaty, then reversed itself, supporting DeValera and his adherence to an Irish Republic. The AARIR established an Irish Republic Defence Fund. Ironically embodying the dictatorial methods of Cohalan they had so rancorously condemned, all members who failed to contribute to it were expelled. The result was a turnover in leadership and a large loss of membership. By March 1922 Frank P. Walsh told Stephen O'Mara, the AARIR was "shot to pieces".[130] As with the I. P. P. and the revolutionary Nationalists in the prewar period, both pro – and anti-treaty factions sent delegations to the United States, each denouncing the other, opening offices, raising funds. Elections in Ireland revealed widespread support for the treaty, but DeValera and his allies, now called Republicans, rejected it. The intransigence on both sides precipitated a bloody civil war. One of the important persons appealed to by both sides was James K. McGuire who warned Republican envoy Harry Boland of America's increasing indifference to Ireland. "The American public views with mingled feelings of disgust, perplexity, amazement and misunderstanding of events in Ireland. Most American friends of Ireland, as most Irish, believe that the majority had spoken."[131] Apparently Harry Boland agreed with McGuire's sentiments. Boland, like McGuire, worked to achieve a compromise between three parties: DeValera, Collins and the British government. Boland was able to draft a compromise document he thought acceptable to all parties for which he was complimented by James K. McGuire. Unfortunately, the British government refused any changes. DeValera thought the treaty gave too little. Nonetheless, the Irish people, like the American Irish, were tired of bloodshed. The Dail, by a narrow margin of 64-57, ratified the Anglo-Irish Treaty on 7 December 1922. DeValera resigned his seat, urged his followers to fight on and thus initiated the Irish Civil War, June 1922 – May 1923. Both sides lost key figures who had played prominent roles in the struggle for Irish freedom. The provisional government lost Collins, Griffith; the Republicans lost Brugha, Boland, Mellows, Rory O'Connor, Joe McKelvey, Dick Barrett and Liam Lynch. In the wake of the bloodshed, DeValera ordered his men to lay down their arms. In the subsequent elections of August 1923, the pro-Treaty forces elected a plurality and formed the Irish Free State despite the efforts of John McGarnty who raised $100,000 for Republican candidates.[132] Ireland was at last free to go its own way. James K. McGuire did not live to see a peaceful Ireland come into existence. He passed away three months previously, in June 1923.

Notes

1 Doorley, Michael. Irish-American Diaspora Nationalism: The Friends of Irish Freedom, 1916-1935. (Dublin: Four Courts Press, 2005), 71. Maloney was a controversial figure in Irish Nationalist politics, in part because of his prior service in the British Army, but also because of his maneuvering for power. Through his connections to Oswald G. Villard, he had access to the influential New York Post which publicized his efforts. Maloney would later side with DeValera in his struggle with Cohalan. There were also some wo believed he was a British agent. For more insight, see Maxwell, Kenneth. "Irish-Americans And The Fight For Treaty Ratification". Public Opinion Quarterly 31: No. 4, 1967, 620-641.

2 Doorley, op.cit., 72-72; Funchion, Michael (ed.) Irish American Voluntary Organizations (Greenwood Press: Westport, Connecticut, 1983), 208.

3 Doorley, op.cit., 75-77; Splain, John. "The Irish Movement In The United States Since 1911". In William G. Fitzgerald (ed.). The Voice of Ireland (Dublin: John Heywood, Ltd., 1923), 230-231. John Splain was National Vice-President of The Friends of Irish Freedom. He sided with Cohalan in the feud with DeValera.

4 Fr. Thomas J. Hurton was Chairman of the Irish Race Convention of 1918. He was a member of a delegation sent to petition President Wilson which was received by Wilson's Secretary, Joseph Tumulty. Fr. Hurton, among others, testified in Congress in December 1918, in favor of Irish independence. He supported Cohalan in his struggle with DeValera.

5 "Irish Here Address Appeal To Wilson", New York Times 19 May 1918:1; Doorley, op.cit., 76-77; Cronin, Sean. The McGarrity Papers: Revelations of The Irish Revolutionary Movement In Ireland and America, 1900-1940 (County Kerry, Ireland: Anvil Books, 1972), 71; Carroll, E. M. American Opinion And The Irish Question, 1910-1923: A Study In Opinion And Policy, (New York: St. Martin's Press, 19788), 113.

6 "Friends of Irish Freedom: A Case Study of Irish American Nationalism, 1916- 1921". http://www.historyireland.com/volumes/volume16/issue2/features/?id....;Doorley, op.cit., 75-76.

7 "Sinn Féin Party Scores Extraordinary Victory". Catholic Sun 3 January 1919;1; "Greet Irish In U.S. As Envoy". Catholic Sun 3 January 1919:2.

8 "Magnificent Irish Meeting At Weitung Sunday Night". Catholic Sun 17 January 1919:1:5, "State Hibernians Appeal To Wilson That The Principle Of Self Determination Be Applied To Ireland". Catholic Sun 24 January 1919:1,5.

9 "Can Ireland Stand Alone". Catholic Sun 17 January 1919:8.
Many Irish assumed the election was a referendum on Irish independence. The Catholic Sun published a photograph of the Irish Parliament with

biographical sketches of its members in its 14 March 1919 issue ("The Members of Ireland's Constituent Assembly". Catholic Sun 14 March 1919:9).

10 O'Doherty, Katherine. Assignment: America; DeValera's Mission To The United States (New York: DeTanko Publishers, Inc., 1957), 34.

11 Buckley, John Patrick. The New York Irish: Their View of American Foreign Policy, 1914-1921. (New York: Arno Press, 1976), 209.

12 O'Doherty, op.cit., 34. The Indo – Irish alliance would persist through the 1920's.

13 See "Ireland's Trade With England And America". Catholic Sun 14 March 1919:15; "The Psychological Reason For America To Repay Its Debt To Ireland". Catholic Sun 14 March 1919.

14 "Cardinals" To Attend Irish Race Convention". Catholic Sun 7 February 1919:1; "Venerable Cardinal Pleads For A Free Ireland". Catholic Sun 7 March 1919, 1,7.

15 "Catholic Sun 28 February 1919:1;8. For additional participants, see Splain, "The Irish Movement…" op.cit, 233.

16 Doorley, op.cit., 85; Ward, Alan J. Ireland And Anglo-American Relations, 1899-1921. (Toronto: University of Toronto Press, 1969), 215.

17 "Freedom of Ireland Is Demanded In Convention". Syracuse Herald 23 February 1919:2.

18 Frank P. Walsh was a successful Kansas City lawyer, a member of Wilson's War Labor Conference Board, who was appointed Chairman of the American Commission on Irish independence. Upon his return he testified before Congress as to conditions in Ireland. Later, with other Commission members, he was used to obtain support for DeValera's AARIR bond drive.
Edward F. Dunne was a lawyer, judge, ex-mayor of Chicago and a former Governor of Illinois.
Michael J. Ryan, a prominent lawyer from Philadelphia and former head of the United Irish League of America. His open advocacy of a German victory during the was alienated him from moderates within the Irish American community and those abroad.

19 Doorley, op.cit., 96; Cuddy, op.cit., 202.

20 Doorley, op.cit., 103; Ward, op.cit., 193; Maxwell, op.cit., 622.

21 O'Grady, James. How The Irish Became Americans (New York: Twain Publishers, 1973), 136; Cuddy, Joseph Edward. Irish America and National Isolationism: 1914-1920 (New York: Arno Press, 1967, 207-208.

22 Bruce Bielaski, a Maryland lawyer and member of the Justice Department, rose through the ranks to become head of the Bureau of Investigation. He was largely responsible for the voluminous government report, Brewing and Liquor Interests and Bolshevik Propaganda in 1919.

23 Brewing and Liquor Interests and Bolshevik Propaganda: Report and Hearings

of the Subcommittee of the Judiciary. United States Senate. (Washington, D.C. Government Printing Office, 1919), 1392; 1396-97; 1543.
24 Carroll, op.cit., 130, n. 22; 233.
25 Wittke, Carl. The Irish In America (Baton Rouge: Louisiana State University Press, 1956), 290. Jeremiah O'Leary impugns Cohalan's character in his My Political Trials And Experiences (New York: Jefferson Publishing Co., 1919), 173, and in his letter to James K. McGuire, op.cit., 494.
26 "Irish Claims To Freedom Score British". Syracuse Herald 22 June 1919:4.
27 "Boy Photo of Villa Shows Bandit Chief Born Bad". Syracuse Herald 22 June 1919:4. An interesting article, given the activity of German agents in Mexico and their efforts to use Villa to create a war between the United States and its southern neighbor which almost succeeded.
28 "Recognition of Irish Republic Urged In Speech and Resolution". Catholic Sun 2 May 1919:11.
29 The efforts of the delegation to meet Wilson and present its petition are noted at length in "President To Hear Claims of Irish Delegation". Syracuse Herald 2 March 1919:1, 3. See also Blum, John M., Joe Tumulty and The Wilson Era (Boston: Houghton-Mifflin, 1951), 176-77. Among those present was James K. McGuire, Frank P. Walsh, Judge John Goff, Daniel Cohalan, Matthew Cummings, John P. Grace and other prominent Irish Americans.
30 Letter, J. Phelan to J. K. McGuire 29 July 1919 New York. American Irish Historical Society, Daniel F. Cohalan papers. Cited in Buckley, op.cit., 317.
31 Letters, J. McGuire to D. Cohalan, 11 March 1920; 5 June 1920, 4 August 1920, 12 August 1920. New York American Irish Historical Society, Daniel F. Cohalan Papers. Cited in Buckley, op.cit., 346-347; 348. Thomas J. Walsh, (1859-1933) a Democrat from Montana was extremely sympathetic to the Irish cause, but not active in Nationalist organizations.
32 Tansill, Charles C. America And The Fight For Irish Freedom, 1866-1922 (New York: Devon Adair, 1957), 302; Ward, op.cit., 173-176; Splain, op.cit., 234. "The Irish Movement...", has a complete list of the Committee members. They are representative of Irish politicians, clergy, and the professions from the Northeast and Midwest. James K. McGuire is not mentioned.
33 "Conference Between Irish Race Convention and President Fails of Result". Catholic Sun 7 March 1919:2.
34 Carroll, op.cit., 131; Splain, op.cit., "The Irish Movement...," 235.
35 "Irish Race Committee Sails". Catholic Sun 4 April 1919:1,2; "The Irish Delegation In France". Catholic Sun 18 April 1919:2.
36 "Irish Flag Displayed At National Capital". Catholic Sun 6 June 1919:1.
37 "Wilson To Be Urged to Ask To Free Ireland". Catholic Sun 18 April 1919:2; "DeValera Sees New Hope In Envoy's Visit". Catholic Sun 16 May 1919:1.
38 "Envoys For Ireland At Paris Going To Dublin". Catholic Sun 2 May: 11.

39 "Dunne And Ryan Leave Dublin For Belfast". Catholic Sun 9 May 1919:1; "Freedom In A Year, Ireland's Hope". Catholic Sun 16 May 1919:1; "Ireland Presents Her Claim For Freedom". Catholic Sun 16 May 1919;1,4. "Interesting Experiences of Irish American Envoys". Catholic Sun 30 May 1919:1; "Ryan Finds Irish United For Freedom". Catholic Sun 6 June 1919:1.

40 Funchion, op.cit., Carroll, op.cit., 136; 254, fn. 29,30,31; O'Doherty, op.cit.,40-41. "American Commission On Irish Independence". Catholic Sun 4 July 1919: 1,2; "New Atrocities In Erin Reported To Paris". Catholic Sun 4 July 1919:9; "England Is At War With Ireland; Army of 100,000 Backs Tyranny Says Dunne." Catholic Sun July 1919:1. As to its claims for success, see "Irish Envoys Greeted As Victors". Catholic Sun 11 June 1919:5.

41 John O'Kelly/Sean O'Ceallaigh (1882-1996) was a long-term supporter of Irish nationalism and a founder of Sinn Féin. He was arrested and interned during the Easter Rebellion. Two years later he was elected to the first Dail Éireann. As noted previously, he toured America, agitating for Irish independence. He was a close associate of Eamon DeValera and as such rejected the Anglo-Irish Treaty of 1921. "Biography of Sean Tomas O'Ceallaign" http://www.archontology.org/nations/eire/eire_rep2/oreily.php). Additional details on the Commission can be found in "Irish Question And The Peace Conference". New York Times 14 September 1919, and Francis M. Carroll, "The American Commission on Irish Independence And The Paris Peace Conference of 1919" Irish Studies In International Affairs vol. 2 no. 1 (1985), pp. 102-118). O'Ceallaigh's statement relative to Irish freedom is given at length in "Ireland Presents Her Claims For Freedom". Catholic Sun 16 May 1919:1.

42 Funchion, op.cit., 21.

43 For a sample, see "Hope For Peace Can't Come Until Ireland Is Free, Says Rev. Howard". Syracuse Herald 18 March 1919.

44 McCartan, Patrick. With DeValera In America (New York: Brentano, 1932), 82-85.

45 Cuddy, Joseph Edward. Irish-America And National Isolation, 1914-1920 (New York: Arno Press, 1976), 194; 195.

46 "Terrorism Is Real Threat of Irish Says Sinn Féin Leader In Interview". Syracuse Herald 17 April 1919.

47 "200 Friends of Irish Freedom Hear Liam Mellowes". Syracuse Herald 1 February 1919:3.

48 "World Peace Without Irish Freedom Fails". Syracuse Herald 26 May 1919:13.

49 For the full text, see "Ireland Demands Independence And Recognition Republic". Syracuse Herald 28 May 1919.

50 "Ireland Will Never Give Up The Fight To Be Free". Syracuse Herald. 10 February 1920:14.

51 Carroll, op.cit., 128; Splain, "The Irish Movement..." op.cit., 233, noted $1.5

million was pledged for a campaign of education which had shown such splendid results in turning American sympathies towards Ireland". Among its goals were insistence upon the recognition of a "Republican form of government in Ireland and refrain from entry into the League of Nations".

52 Letter, F. Walsh to G. Duffy, 18 August 1919. New York Public Library, Frank Walsh Papers. Cited in Buckley, op.cit., 298; Letter, J. McGuire to D. Cohalan, 8 February 1920. New York. American Irish Historical Society, Daniel F. Cohalan Papers. Cited in Buckley, 299.

53 "Sinn Féin Movement And The American Revolution". Catholic Sun 4 July 1919:8; "Eamon DeValera To Speak In Syracuse". Catholic Sun 11 July 1919:5.

54 "Irish Victory Fund Growing Fast". Catholic Sun 6 June 1919:5. "The Irish Victory Fund and Its Object". Catholic Sun 27 June 1919:5; The goals were specified in a follow-up article in the Catholic Sun noting an increase in donations. The monies were to be used to educate and direct public opinion to: a) urge the object for which America entered the war by fully attained; b) urge the recognition of the Republican form of government; c) urge America not enter the League of Nations; d) maintain American ideals of government and oppose British propaganda; e) maintain a publicity campaign for the following purposes and; f) defray the expenses of Irish American delegates to the Paris Peace conference. "Irish Victory Fund Now At $2580". Catholic Sun 13 June 1919:2. The American agenda of Cohalan is obvious in the six articles, but item B would become problematic as later developments would reveal.

55 Letter, McGuire to Cohalan 22, 31 August 1919. AIHS, Cohalan papers. Cited in Fitzpatrick, David. Harry Boland's Irish Revolution (Cork, Ireland: Cork University Press, 2003), 125. Fitzpatrick refers to McGuire as the Treasurer of the Friends of Irish Freedom.

56 "Edward DeValera and Irish America". Catholic Sun 25 April 1919:3. In the article, DeValera's "mixed" racial background was noted and praised – "His father was a Spaniard and there is no more tenacious race in Europe than the Iberians". This praise would turn to rancor as the schism between the two factions of Irish in America became an open split. According to Carroll, deValera's father was Cuban (op.cit, 196-197).

57 Doorley, op.cit., 97. Harry Boland (1887-1922) was a Dublin-born member of the Irish volunteers who was active in the Easter Rising of 1916. He was an elected member of the Dail. Boland arrived in America with deValera to raise awareness and support for the Irish cause, succeeding Patrick McCartan as envoy to the United States. Returning to Ireland, he opposed the Anglo-Irish Treaty and was killed in a skirmish with Free State soldiers. For details on the controversy as to the goals of the Funds, see McCartan, op. cit., 91-92;133-134.

58 "Irish Independence". Catholic Sun 25 June 1920.
59 Ward. op.cit., 218,220. James O'Mara, a prosperous Irish businessman and former I.P.P. member, later elected as a Sinn Fein member to the Dail in 1918. He was sent to America to take control of the bond certificate drive, later resigning his position over policy differences with DeValera. He was the brother – in – law of McGuire associate James Mark Sullivan, now a disgraced diplomat and occasional representative of the Provisional government. The O'Mara family would split into warring factions, one side following Collins, the other De Valera.
60 The Red Raids occurred from 1919-1920 under the direction of Attorney-General A. Mitchel Palmer. They resulted in the deportation of over 500 "radicals" and were a response to the Bolshevik Revolution, labor union agitation and the hyphenate scares of World War I.
61 Doorley, op.,cit 131-132; Funchion, op.,cit 123.
62 "Friends of Irish Freedom" http:Wittke, The Irish op., cit. 289 states that Devoy suspected DeValera was a compromiser, a comment no doubt inspired over DeValera's controversial remarks about Cuba.
63 Splain, John "Under Which King?" in Fitzgerald, William G. (ed) The Voice of Ireland (Dublin: John Heywood Ltd., 1923), 244.
64 Tansill, op.,cit, 353-358; Splain, op.cit., "Under Which ..." 244-245.
65 Doorley, op.,cit., 116-117. There were eight articles to the Platt Amendment. Article I, disallowing Cuba to make a treaty that would impair its independence, and Article III, allowing for American intervention were provisions particularly troubling to the American Irish. For details see "Platt Amendment". Andrews, Wayne (ed.). Concise Dictionary of American History (New York: Charles Scribner's Sons, 1962), 738-739. Tansill, op.,cit., 361 notes DeValera's remarks got him into trouble at home, although they rallied to his defense.
66 Harry Boland's Diary 16-22 February 1920. Cited in Fitzpatrick, op.cit., 154. Boland's reference to "cleaning the Augean stables of this evil" refers to the enormity of the task entrusted to McGuire, as well as his attitude towards Cohalan.
67 Harry Boland's Diary 19 January 1919; Letter, Frances G. McGuire to Harry Boland, 26 April 1921; Letter MC (Field to HB (Woods) 7 February 1921, Cited in Fitzpatrick, op.,cit 162; 161; 220; 210.
68 All have been noted previously, except Richard F. Dalton, a New York native, and head of the United Irish-American Societies influential enough in American-Irish circles to have been consulted on the First Irish Race Convention, and, like McGuire, condemning the Irish Home Rule Convention of 1917. Dalton testified at Congressional hearings on behalf of Ireland, and served on Villard's American Commission on Conditions In Ireland. He also was

among the many consultants who advised DeValera against his original bond drive in 1919. The motivation behind Maloney's alleged maneuvers was his desire to become a key adviser to DeValera in America.

69 Splain, op.cit., "Under Which"... 247. Splain implies it was to be an orderly meeting of those associated with Cohalan. Dooley, op.cit., 121 refers to it as a "trial" of DeValera from which the FOIF leadership would demand he leave the country.

70 "Valera Spent Irish Funds In Chicago, Claim". Syracuse Herald 18 June 1920:1; "Charge $50,000 In Irish Bonds Wrongly Used". Syracuse Herald 22 June 1920: 22; Doorley, op.cit., 129; 131; Splain; "Under Which"... 248.

71 "Irish Demand Recognition In Platform Plank." Syracuse Herald 27 June 1920:8.

72 Ward, op.,cit 221-222; Cuddy, op.cit, 222.

73 Letter, McGuire To Cohalan, 11 March 1920 American Irish Historical Society. Cohalan Papers. Cited in Buckley, op.cit. 346.

74 Letter, McGuire To Cohalan. 5 June 1920, American Irish Historical Society. Cohalan Papers. Cited in Buckley, op.cit., 347.

75 Letter, McGuire To Cohalan. 4 August 1920. American Irish Historical Society. Cohalan Papers. Cited in Buckley, 347; Letter, McGuire to Cohalan 12 August 1920. American Irish Historical Society, cited in Buckley, 347.

76 Letter, Devoy to Cohalan, 31 August 1920. Cited in Tansill, op.cit., 391.

77 Doorley op.cit., 134-136.

78 Edward L. Doheny was a descendant of famine Irish immigrants. He worked for the U.S. Geological Survey, later becoming a prospector of limited success until he discovered oil in Los Angeles. Doheny multiplied his holdings and was reputedly the richest man in America by 1920. Doheny had little interest in Irish affairs, but contributed to Catholic churches, colleges and the American Committee For Relief In Ireland. His reputation diminished in the wake of the Teapot Dome Scandal of 1924. Doheny was a logical choice. He had contributed to Wilson's campaign in 1916, assisting his winning of California and hence, Wilson's re-election. Doheny had also worked hard to win a pro-Ireland resolution at the Democratic Convention in 1920. Several sources reported his generous contributions to the Irish cause in the past (Carroll, op.cit.,) as well as his support for DeValera's mission to America. (Ansell, Martin R. Oil Baron of the Southwest: Edward L. Doheny and The Development of the Petroleum Industing in California and Mexico (Columbus, Ohio State University Press, 1998,) 180-186. Dr. Peter C. Yorke, (1864-1925) was an Irish-born priest, who became head of the San Francisco California diocese. He was active in establishing parochial schools, protesting anti-Catholic bigotry, a labor activist, temperance advocate and Irish Nationalist. He was California state president of the A.A.R.I.R.

"Yorke, Peter Christopher". Dictionary of American Biography, vol. 20. (New York: Charles Scribner's Sons, 1936), 614-615. Rossa Downing was President of the Padrias-Pearce branch of the Friends of Irish Freedom who with DeValera toured historic sites in Washington, D.C. in 1920. "DeValera In Washington". New York Times 8 August 1920.

79 "Fenian Chiefs Estimate of James K. McGuire". Catholic Sun 19 July 1923.

80 Funchion, op.cit., "Clan Na-Gael," [74-93] 90-91; "Harry Boland Dies; Sought Arms Here." New York Times 2 August 1922; McCartan, op. cit, 209.
Luke Dillon was the son of famine Irish parents who migrated first to England and later to the United States. After military service, he joined the Clan na Gael and took an active part in the bombing campaigns in England during the 1880's. He worked with Devoy to reunite the Clans in the wake of the Cronin murder. His attempt to blow up the Welland Canal locks earned his a long prison sentence in Canada. Upon his release, Dillon was tied closely to John McGarrity hence his ties to the AARIR.

81 McCartan, op.cit., 209.

82 Funchion, op.,cit, "American Association For The Recognition of The Dependent Irish Republic", 9-12.
James E. Murray (1876-1961) son of Irish immigrants, was a Canadian-born, naturalized American citizen. With financial help from a wealthy uncle, he became a labor lawyer and banker in Butte, Montana and later a federal senator, serving from 1934-61. He was briefly head of the A.A.R.I.R. "Murray, James Edward". Dictionary of American Biography, Supplement Seven, 1961-1965. (New York: Charles Scribner's Sons, 1981), 861-563.
John Finerty was a lawyer and member of the United States Railroad Administration. He was a leader of the AARIR after the Civil War broke out in Ireland and was an ardent supported of the Republican cause. McCartan, op.cit., devoted a chapter to this relief effort. See, Chapter XXV, 220-231. McCartan also states it was James O'Mara who provided the money for its publication. See p. 230.

83 O'Grady, op.cit., 135. For details on the Black and Tans, see Edgar Holt, Protest In Arms: The Irish Troubles, 1916-1923. London: Putnam and Sons, 1960 W. Allison, Phillips, in The Revolution In Ireland, 1906-1923. (NY 1923) 186-89 suggests the depredations of the Black and Tans were exaggerated, but their bloody image conjured up much sympathy for the Irish cause in America.

84 Carroll, op.,cit.,161.

85 "J. K. M'Guire In Irish Delegation Seeing Colby." Syracuse Herald 27 October 1920:1.

86 Letters, McGuire To Devoy 16 July 1920; Boland To Devoy 17 July 1920;

Devoy To Cohalan 20 July 1920,; McGuire To Cohalan 19 August 1920. Cited in Fitzpatrick, op.cit. 184; 185.

87 John T. Ryan, a prominent Clan leader from Buffalo, was under indictment for treason by the Wilson administration in the wake of America's declaration of war against Germany. Ryan was a prominent lawyer and a member of The Revolutionary Directory and was a veteran of the Philippine Insurrection. Ryan was active in obtaining arms from Germany for the Republican side in the Irish Civil War. See also, "British Goading Irish To Revolt, Murphy Says" Catholic Sun 11 July 1919:5.

88 Letter, McGuire to Boland 16 November 1920. Cited in Fitzpatrick, op.cit., 189.

89 "Denies Being Hostess To Eamon DeValera". New York Times 30 December 1920; "Says DeValera Is Back in Ireland; British Deny It". New York Times 1 January 1921.

90 "James E. Doyle Purchases McGuire Interest In Syracuse Printing and Publishing Company," Catholic Sun 10 September 1920: 5, "Syracuse Editor Gets State Post." New York Times 18 June 1919.

91 "MacSwiney Sacrifices Life For Ireland." Catholic Sun 29 October 1920; 1, 3. For a representative sample of articles on the depredations of the Black and Tans, see Murder and Pillage Rule Ireland". Catholic Sun 19 November 1920: 1, 5, "England Employs Large Army of Spies To Create Disturbances In Ireland." Catholic Sun 3 December 1920:1, 3; "British Rule of Force In Ireland Not Justified." Catholic Sun 24 December 1920: 1, 2.

92 "DeValera At Meeting In Albany." Catholic Sun 3 December 1920.

93 "Callaghan Expected At Convention." Catholic Sun 18 February 1921.

94 94 S. N. Ghose was referred to as a "native agitator" by the New York Times. See" S.N. Ghose Predicts Revolution In India", New York Times 29 November. He urged a widespread revolution against the British Empire in such widespread areas as India, Ireland, Egypt, and Mesopotamia with support from the Soviet Union and Germany in alliance with the Friends of Freedom for India, which he claimed was Sinn Fein of India. For details see, Norwich Bulletin 19 March 1918.https://wwwbing.com/search?q=Sailendra+Nath+Ghose+Ameri can+ Communist+to+Promote+Self+Government+ in+India&qs=n&inform; "Hindu Rebels Sound Their Protest". Butte Daily Bulletin 13 December 1920, p.3 https://chronicling America.giv.lccn/sn83045085/1920-12-13.ed-1/ seg-3/. At a St. Patrick's Day parade in California, Gopal Singh, a member of the Indo-German Conspiracy, presented a tricolor flag and a sword to Eamon DeValera whose remarks compared the histories of both countries under British rule. Note the current flag of both countries has the same colors – orange(saffron to Indians), white, green-to symbolize the countries' two great religious traditions (Catholic-Protestant, Hindu- Muslim) the

white band urging peace, truth, unity. The Irish flag flew over the GPO during the Easter Rebellion. It was adopted during the War of Independence in 1919 and made official in 1937. India adopted its flag in 1947, the same year Ireland became a republic. After the death of Devoy in 1929 and the prejudice against people of color in the United States at the time (Hindus were declared ineligible for citizenship)and the emergence of DeValera as a force in Irish politics, the center of Indian resistance to British rule moved to Dublin. All of which suggests the alliance between Indians and Irish in the cause of freedom was moore than simply a pragmatic response to a common enemy, but rather a philosophical commitment to independence for both countries. See Plowman, 1997, 100-103.

95 "Recognition of Irish Republic Demanded at Convention In Syracuse," Catholic Sun 25 February 1921:5.

96 "Officers And Directors Elected At The Convention of The American Association For the Recognition of The Irish Republic." Catholic Sun 4 March 1921. Interestingly the article listed Judge John Goff and Austin Ford as National Directors, from New York, Jeremiah J. O'Leary as a State Director, and former Governor Martin H. Glynn as Albany regional director.

97 "Five Years of The Republic of Ireland." Catholic Sun 28 April 1921:5.

98 "The First Convention of The A.A.R.I.R. is Triumph for Cause." Catholic Sun 21 April 1921:3.

99 "New Leaders In Movement To Secure Recognition of Republic of Ireland From American Government." Catholic Sun 12 May 1921.

100 "They're Directing Membership Campaign For The A.A.R. of I.R." Catholic Sun 19 May 1921:3.

101 "Our Peace Endangered By England." Catholic Sun 25 March 1919: 19.

102 "Irish Women To Speak For The Republic." Catholic Sun 19 October 1922:5; "Irish Meeting Is Largely Attended Catholic Sun 26 October 1922:5.

103 "McCarthy Is Re-elected By Irish Council." Catholic Sun 22 February 1923:5.

104 Bell, J. Bower. The Gun In Poliitics: An Analysis of Irish Political Conflict, 1916 – 1986. New Brunswick: Transaction Publishers, 1991, 39.

105 "DeValera Aid Back Eluding English." Catholic Sun 30 July 1920

106 Ibid., 35.

107 Ibid., 35; 36 – 37.

108 Ibid., 39 – 40.

109 Ibid.,38.

110 Fitzgerald, op.cit., 212; Helmer, op.cit., 57.

111 "Seized Guns Ready For Use On Ships." New York Times 19 June 1921.

112 Fitzgerald, op.cit., 212-215; Cronin, op.cit., 98-99.

113 "US Shipping Board http://flagspot.net.flags/us_ussb.html/; Higgs, Robert. "How the Federal Government Got Into The shipping Business

http://www.independent.org/publications/articles.asp? Id=1233.
114 Gabak, Jason. "Auburnian Stoked Engine Business" Auburn Industry Scrapbook, vol. iv. Local History Collection. Cayuga Community College, n.p.,n.d.;"James McGuire", July 12, 1868-June 29, 1923 Post Standard Obituaries 247 James K. McGuire File Onondaga County Historical Association, n.d.,n.p. The McIntosh-Seymour Connection was also noted in "City Stirred By Sudden Death of Former Mayor James K. McGuire." Catholic Sun 5 July 1923: 5., 7.
115 Fitzgerald, op.cit., 214.
116 "Fenian Chief's Estimate of James K. McGuire". Catholic Sun 19 July 1923.
117 "Seized Guns Ready For Use On Ship." New York Times 19 June 1921; "Seized Irish Guns Provided Mysteries Within Mysteries." New York Times 17 June 1921.
118 Smith, Charles H. "History of The Thompson Sub Machine Gun." http://www.auto-ordnance.com/AO-1.html.
119 Helmer, William J. The Gun That Made the Twenties Roar. (New York: McMillian, 1969), 16-19.
120 Ibid., 59. DeLacey was deeply committed to both Indian and Irish freedom. His direct ties connected him to Ghadarite leader Ram Chandra who kept his papers in DeLacey's vault which was located in the Rincon Building owned by Father Peter Yorke, a radical priest, who had resigned from FOIF and was the leader of the California AARIR. Yorke was the funnel through which DeLacey received funds for the operation. DeLacey also served as editor for Yorke's paper, The Leader. DeLacey, like McGuire, sided with DeValera in the FOIF-AARIR split (Plowman, 1997, 97-98). In the dispute, it was DeLacey, who with Tommy O'Connor broke into Devoy's office to obtain his mailing list of Clan members. O'Connor, when employed as a sailor on the Cunard line, served as a courier between the Clan-na- Gael and the IRB. He served time in a US prison for violation of the Trading With the Enemy's Act. Mulvaney, Francis. "Man Who Carried Thousands of Dollars Across the Atlantic to Fund 1916" 4pp. https:// www.irishcentral.com/roots/history/the-man-who-carried-thousands-of-dollars-across… Also "Stories From 1916: The O'Connor Brothers" 9pp. http:// www.stories from 1916.com/1916-easter-rising/tommy -and-johnny. His brother Johnny took part in the Rising and was imprisoned. He later fought in the Dublin Brigade in the War of Independence. Despite Tommy O'Connor's break-in of his office, Devoy praised his work as a courier for the Clan-na-Gael. Devoy, Recollections, op. cit., 393.
121 Ibid.,62; Bell, op. cit., 48.
122 Ibid. 64;65. McGarrity's involvement should come as no surprise. As shown, he was involved in the Annie Larson affair of 1915, a dismal failure and the

East Side incident was almost as bad. Of the 653 Thompson submachine guns only 158 were sent. The rest went on regular merchant ships sailing from New York to Liverpool in small lots ranging from as few as three to 49. The use of the gun was praised but limited by a shortage of ammunition and trained personnel. Irish-American ex-military men volunteered to train IRA gunmen in its use. By 1936 the original supply of Thompsons had been sent. "Arms Smuggling Routes http:// thompsongunireland.com/Arms%20 Smuggling%20Routes.files_Arms%20Smuggling %Routes_htm.

123 Possibly the most famous of the folk songs was "The Merry Ploughboy". Authorship is in doubt, but most likely it was the work of Dominick Behan (1928 – 1989) in the early part of the 20th century. Behan was a socialist, an Irish republican, a songwriter and a member of the IRA during the "Time of Troubles of the 1970's. For the lyrics see, "The Merry Ploughboy" https:// genius.com/The -wolf-tonesthe-merry-ploughboy-lyrics.

124 Doorley, op.cit., 135. Cuddy, op.cit Funchion, op.cit. "American Commission on Conditions In Ireland", 12-17. Funchion notes among the most sympathetically received witnesses were the widow and sister of Terence McSwiney.

125 Funchion, op.cit., 12-17. McCartan claims he and Maloney were for the formation of the Commission. At a meeting with DeValera, Dudly Field Malone, McGarrity, Maloney and McCartan, all agreed on the panel being established. McCartan also claims Villard was reluctant to endorse the commision, but relented when prominent Americans signed on to serve. In McCartan, op.cit., 210-14;221-24. McCartan's account refers to it as "The Commission on British Atrocities."

126 Carroll, Francis. "American Commission for Relief In Ireland". In Funchion, op.cit., 224-30.

127 Doorley, op.cit., 138-40; Funchion, op.cit., "Friends of Irish Freedom" 125.

128 "Wants Irish Debts Paid To US" New York Times 13 January 1922.

129 Splain, op.cit., "Under Which…?", 253; Carroll, op.cit., 129.

130 Carroll, op.cit., 181.

131 Letter, "McGuire to Harry Boland 7 April 1922. Cited in Fitzpatrick, op.cit., 274.

132 Cronin, op.cit., 137.

Chapter IV - B

Epilogue, 1923: "Such a Marvelous and Phenomenal Boy"

James K. McGuire died of heart failure in Washington, D.C. on 29 June 1923 while on business representing companies which had dealings in the nation's capital. Obituaries noted his past successes, his rise from humble beginnings, his business interests, and his youthful accomplishments based on his oratorical and organizational abilities which helped him become a successful three-term mayor of Syracuse, New York. It was in Syracuse where McGuire gained his first political laurels, making friends and enemies within his party and without. His first two terms as mayor were victories for efficiency and municipal improvement. In his third term, he may have yielded to the temptations of power and patronage, in part due to the passage of the White Charter, and possibly because of his awakened political ambitions. Also noted were his links to the Asphalt Trust, and his work for the Imperial German government prior to American entry into World War I. Despite the controversies which enveloped him in life, in death he was surrounded by friends, admirers and supporters. The police honor guard, for example, had many officers on it who were appointed during his successive administrations as mayor. The Syracuse Herald was extremely charitable to McGuire in that regard, excusing his pro-German writings as "an error of judgment and sympathy, which now may be pardoned"[1]. A former classmate of his at Christian Brothers Academy,[2] Monsignor Albert Hayes celebrated High Mass in his honor. Father Dougherty delivered the eulogy to the packed crowd at St. John the Evangelist Church. Father Dougherty noted "the collective sorrow at the premature death of the boy mayor, "a man of the state and the nation, of whom the community may be proud". Perhaps carried away by his own rhetoric, the good Father extolled the virtues of "Jimmy McGuire", who "carried out all the injunctions of the Master", "the ideals of the true America to the marrow of his bones, to his country, his state, his city. Though young in years, he was old in experience by the many things that crowded into his life". Father Dougherty went on, "such a marvelous and phenomenal boy has not risen here in thirty years, and there has not been a man who deserves the respect and honor of this community more than James K. McGuire."[3] Also at his funeral mass were several huge floral pieces. Two floral harps were on display-one from the Irish Free State and the other from the Old Board of Syracuse, a group which advocated Home Rule for Ireland.[4]

Interestingly, even though Representatives of Congress, the mayor, notables and old friends of McGuire were present, no representatives from either the Clan na Gael, The Friends of Irish Freedom or the AARIR were listed as present at his funeral.[5] Neither Daniel F. Cohalan, John Devoy, nor Diarmuid Lynch were noted among the mourners. No public references as to these men and their expressions of sympathy were recorded. Only later were there articles in the Catholic Sun detailing his death. On 19 July 1923, the Catholic Sun published an article by John Devoy that was critical of McGuire as to his activities on behalf of Irish nationalism.[6] All this reinforces the notion that McGuire, in resigning from FOIF and being linked with activities of the AARIR, was written out of official FOIF historiography. McGuire was buried in Syracuse, even though he had not lived in the city for over twenty years. This may have been due to his diminished circumstances. An editorial in the Catholic Sun of 6 July 1923, reported McGuire was "a big earner, he left Syracuse in debt and died poor".[7] This suggests that McGuire, like Joseph McGarrity,[8] gave generously of his time, talents and resources to friends and causes.

It is ironic that in his final years, McGuire saw his beloved Ireland sundered by partition and a cruel civil war, dying six months before the Irish Free State came into its own, although not as a Republic, but as a Dominion of the hated British Empire. Probably it is not an overstatement to say that McGuire, like many Irish-Americans, was completely disillusioned with events in Ireland. Only a small segment of them were still willing to risk all for Ireland. By mid-1922, as the Republicans were facing military defeat, DeValera issued an urgent appeal for Irish-American volunteers to save it from the Free State Forces. The response was zero-no men, no mass demonstrations, no propaganda, no effective nation-wide organization.[9]

There was, however, Joseph McGarrity, who, like McGuire, found himself with friends on both sides of the treaty issue. McGarrity would come down later on the side of deValera and the Republicans against Collins and the Free State as would McGuire. McGarrity was able to rally Luke Dillon and one other unidentified member of the eleven member Clan na Gael executive committee to the anti-Treaty faction and win its support.[10] The identity of the other committee member is unknown. McGuire had been a high-ranking Clan member, but was he a part of the IRB –sanctioned Clan, or the rump organization of Devoy? Given his multiple friends on both sides of the issues in America, it gives cause for speculation.[11]

A month prior to McGuire's death, the Free State had applied for admission to the League of Nations, a position which earned condemnation from the declining ranks of the Friends of Irish Freedom.[12] It also marked the end of the bloody civil war.

In addition, 1923 also saw the end of Justice Cohalan's judicial career, but he continued to warn against British imperialism and in favor of American isolationism.[13]

In 1923, William G. Fitzgerald edited <u>The Voice of Ireland</u>, an anthology of writings by Irish and Irish-American authors. With the exceptions of Rossa F. Downing, and Edward F. Dunne, the Irish-American writers were firm supporters of the Free State and the policies of Daniel Cohalan and John Devoy. Among its Irish-American authors were not only Daniel Cohalan, but John J. Splain, national vice-president of FOIF, and Daniel T. O'Connell, Director of the FOIF National Bureau in Washington, D. C. With DeValera out of power given the triumph of the Free State forces, the writers were free to criticize his policies. Splain was particularly vindictive. Referring to DeValera, he subtitled his article, "Under Which King", the Tragi-Comedy of President DeValera's Errors in the United States", essentially rationalizing FOIF's policies and condemning DeValera's. Interestingly, McGuire, a prolific writer, was not represented in the anthology. His name is mentioned only once, in the Splain article noted above when McGuire appeared in Congress to speak in favor of the Mason Bill.[14] So, why was this prominent Irish-American omitted? He had serious intervals of illness while as Mayor. His obituary noted he had problems recovering from a recent bout of pneumonia and heart problems. Perhaps he was too ill to write. Or too busy, since the obituary noted his involvement in numerous business activities, but that was not unusual for him.[15] Was he disinterested, given his disgust at the schism between DeValera and Cohalan and his frustrated attempts to mediate the conflict and his resignation from the Executive Committee of The Friends of Irish Freedom? Or was he politically out of favor?

The evidence suggests the latter. In the gubernatorial election of 1922, the colorful upstate Democratic leader from Buffalo, William "Fingy" Conners, was maneuvering to unseat Tammany incumbent Al Smith. Conners was attempting to revitalize an upstate Democratic team by endorsing William Randolph Hearst. This brought him into conflict with Tammany-backed Onondaga County Democratic Boss, William H. Kelley. The man who was organizing the pro-Hearst campaign was not, however, the periodic foe of Tammany, James K. McGuire. Instead, it was his brother, George H. McGuire. George H. McGuire's political ally in this anti-Tammany effort was Melvin Z. Haven, a supporter and later rival of James K. McGuire.[16] James K. McGuire had made peace with William H. Kelley in supporting Al Smith's initial bid for Governor in 1918, overthrowing Republican incumbent, Charles Whitman, the man responsible for McGuire's indictment in the asphalt scandals almost a decade previously. Note that James K. McGuire had a history of meddling in Onondaga County politics even after he had moved downstate to attend to his various business interests. Nonetheless, having advised Hearst not to run against Al Smith in 1918, it appeared he had distanced himself from state politics. Locally, the political void was being filled by his brother George who not only was active in the World War I bond drives, but had recently become involved in promoting civic activities in the City of Syracuse.[17]

James K. McGuire may also have had an agenda. His second indictment for bribery dating back to the asphalt scandals was filed on 22 January 1923. The paper work must have been initiated during the waning days of conservative Republican Governor Nathan Miller, who, like his Republican predecessor, Charles S. Whitman, enjoyed the reputation of a fighter against corruption. Allowing the McGuire indictment to move forward would have tainted Al Smith, "Boss" Charles Murphy and the Tammany machine and perhaps derailed their plans to re-elect Smith as Governor. Despite the efforts of George H. McGuire, "Fingy" Conners, William Randolph Hearst and Governor Miller, Al Smith was re-elected. James K. McGuire, similar to his pragmatic stance after America entered the Great War, may have chosen quiescence since he had made public statements in favor of Prohibition contrary to the official "wet" line of Tammany Hall "Boss" Murphy and Al Smith. Slayton suggests there was more to the issue. The Volstead Act required that various states enforce the law and provide a mechanism for doing so. Under conservative Republican Governor Nathan Miller, New York passed the Mullin-Gage Act on 4 March 1921 to do just that. Two years after his re-election, the state legislature repealed the Mullin-Gage Act, creating a political crisis for Al Smith who was eyeing a run for the Presidency. Under pressure by the Anti-Saloon League to veto the bill, Smith was also squeezed by his Tammany Hall mentor, Boss Charles Murphy to sign the bill. He would also be castigated as a hypocrite, since he had publicly criticized the Volstead law. Smith rejected a compromise suggested by Franklin D. Roosevelt and on the last possible day, signed the repeal bill, thus eliminating any mechanism for state enforcement. The action was condemned by teetotaler William Jennings Bryan but it put Al Smith in the limelight as the leading "wet" candidate in the nation.[18] Given that Smith and Murphy were now on record favoring repeal of prohibition, it is possible that James K. McGuire's remarks in favor of it enraged them. McGuire had a reputation as a teetotaler. The Syracuse Herald in fact, remarked he "lived clean, seldom took even a social glass in the days when drinking was the rule [and he] abstained for years" according to his associates.[19] McGuire, weeks before his death, was touring the South to assess its views on Prohibition for the Democratic campaign of 1924, justified Smith's repeal of the Mullin-Gage Bill, yet hedged his remarks by stating the noble experiment was a great blessing to the Nation and would not be repealed.[20]

Miller had his own agenda as well. The article in the <u>Catholic Sun</u> warmly endorsing the re-election of Al Smith in October 1920, was harshly critical of Nathan Miller, referring to him as an "unwilling candidate". Miller had repeatedly stated he would not accept the initial nomination because of the financial sacrifice it entailed. Miller had resigned his position as a judge on the Court of Appeals and was counsel for Solvay Process in Syracuse and several other large corporations. The <u>Sun</u> article stated only when encouraged by Horace Wilkinson, President of Crucible Steel in Syracuse, did Miller consent to become the Republican candidate. While asserting Miller's good character, the article stated Miller was "out of touch" with the great mass of the people of the State and out of sympathy with the humane measures which most concern the greatest number of our inhabitants. "He will follow the path of least resistance and will not be the progressive, hard-working governor that the position demands".[21] As a resident of Syracuse, Miller was extremely aware of its politics and personalities. Perhaps he was taking vengeance on McGuire, or using McGuire's past to leverage victory from Al Smith.

Possibly this added stress to a man with a history of illness, who had faced investigations before as mayor, as Barber Asphalt lobbyist, as agent and propagandist for the German Imperial government and as active member of various secret Irish Nationalist societies. Collectively, these may have contributed to his early demise.

McGuire was not only excluded from the Fitzgerald anthology, he was not mentioned as being present at the 29 July 1921 banquet honoring John Devoy's sixty years of devotion to the cause of Irish Freedom. This was not unusual given McGuire's dropping out of FOIF and Clan activities and his close identification with the AARIR. According to John Devoy, McGuire had acted similarly during the Devoy-Sullivan schism within the Clan na Gael in 1890's. Apparently disgusted with the murder of Cronin, McGuire dropped out of the Clan, rejoining it only at the outbreak of World War I. Later, during the dispute between Cohalan and DeValera, Devoy noted it was James K. McGuire who had a key role in thwarting a death threat against Devoy. In addition, Devoy credits McGuire with using his connections with Post-Master General Burleson to try to have the <u>Gaelic American</u> removed from its ban in using the public mails.[22] There was also McGuire's outspoken support in the Casement Affair, and his pro-German writings prior to American entry into the Great War. Given his past services, surely an invitation would not have been implausible. McGuire was also absent from the 2800 delegates attending the fourth FOIF national convention at the Hotel Astor in New York City on 11-12 December 1921. And what, if any, was his role in the activities of the All-American National Council, an organization designed to promote and safeguard American national interests and sovereignty.[23] It's goals reflect the isolationist, pro-American agenda of Daniel F. Cohalan, McGuire's long-time collaborator in FOIF and Clan activities, yet McGuire is not mentioned. McGuire's silence may also have been occasioned by the rising tide of nativism in contemporary America, an issue he had fought against since its re-emergence on the American scene in the 1890's.[24] In part, the new nativism was unleashed by the spectacle of rival Irish factions – those pro – and anti-treaty ending the Anglo-Irish War on 6 December 1921 – each castigating the other and each attempting to raise funds and rally support among Irish-Americans. Nativist sentiment was fueled further by the unsuccessful efforts of Dr. John F. Kelly to affect a boycott of British goods, Boland's role in fomenting a dockworkers' strike, allegations that Irish relief funds were being used for arming revolutionaries, as noted in the <u>East Side</u> debacle and the publicity surrounding Irish collusion with German and Soviet agents. It produced a groundswell of opposition, primarily advocating the maintenance of our traditional friendship with Great Britain.[25] Chief among them was novelist Owen Wister whose <u>A Straight Deal or The Ancient Grudge</u> assaulted the "loyalty" of Catholic Irish in American history, contradicting the claims of McGuire, Cohalan, Goff and others that such actions constituted a moral claims for Irish independence.[26] These allegations were repeated in the publicity following the controversial "jackass" speech by American Rear-Admiral William S. Sims in June 1921.[27]

The atrocities committed on both sides during the bitter civil war and the outbreak of religious conflict in Northern Ireland undermined any confidence that nativist America may have had in Ireland's ability for self-government. By 1923, the AARIR was in disarray, having experienced multiple changes in leadership over treaty ratification. FOIF was also in decline. From 725 branches registering over 100,000 members, in less than a decade, FOIF had slipped to only 13 branches with less than 700 members.[28] Not only was 1923 significant in that it saw the death of James K. McGuire, but obviously the Irish Nationalist organizations were at the twilight of their respective careers as well. In addition, the Irish Civil War ended. DeValera was arrested in August, having emerged from hiding to campaign in the elections of 1923.[29] And as noted previously, the Irish Free State applied for entry into the League of Nations, much to the dismay of The Friends of Irish Freedom. Yet, its two most prominent leaders, Daniel F. Cohalan and Diarmuid Lynch made a triumphal tour of the Irish Free State, obtaining warm praise for their efforts on behalf of Irish freedom. Soon after, in October 1923, the Free State government of William Cosgrave, Griffith's successor, introduced a constitutional amendment aimed at the IRA, abolishing terrorist organizations. Physical force nationalism was, for the time being, over.[30]

The following year, the United States extended diplomatic recognition to the Free State and, in the swansong of his career, John Devoy visited Ireland, receiving a warm welcome for his life-long efforts on behalf of Irish freedom.[31] The bitter animosities which divided Ireland and Irish America began to fade. Reconciliation between AARIR leader Major Kinkead and FOIF leaders Daniel F. Cohalan and John Devoy occurred in 1927. Diarmuid Lynch had returned to Ireland, having failed to resuscitate FOIF. The only thing keeping the moribund FOIF alive was a lawsuit over control of the Irish Victory Fund, finally resolved in 1931. Four years later FOIF disbanded.[32] Joseph McGarrity, in alliance with Harry Boland and James K. McGuire, held out working for a Republic and advocating violence to that end. McGarrity's policies were later repudiated even by long-time friend and ally Eamon DeValera.

So, where does James K. McGuire fit? The man was, in many ways typical of Irish immigrant success stories, rising from poverty as the son of a shoemaker in Syracuse, New York, to move in the higher circles of American society and politics. As with other Irish and Irish-Americans of his generation, McGuire's social mobility was a reflection of that groups upward mobility, from despised minority to prominence in business, politics and diplomacy.

McGuire knew and worked for the two Democratic Presidents who held office during his lifetime – Grover Cleveland and Woodrow Wilson. With both men, he had his differences as he did with two Democratic presidential contenders – William Jennings Bryan and David B. Hill. McGuire associated with many members of Wilson's cabinet including William McAdoo, Wilson's son-in-law and Treasury Secretary, Josephus Daniels, the Secretary of the Navy and Albert Burleson, Postmaster-General. He openly supported Republicans during his tenure as mayor of Syracuse and flirted with endorsing Charles Evans Hughes in 1916 because he made remarks favorable to the Irish cause, yet he remained a loyal Democrat, endorsing Al Smith for Governor of New York two years later. Grover Cleveland thought so much of his efforts, he offered McGuire a diplomatic post, a position the latter refused. His influence in Democratic circles was such that his advice was sought by the Wilson administration in obtaining Catholic Democrats to serve in cabinet and diplomatic posts. He maintained an on-going love/hate relationship with Tammany Hall leaders Richard Croker and Charles Murphy, both of whom abandoned him for political gain. Croker would later remark he should have backed McGuire for governor in 1898 and perhaps it would have aborted Theodore Roosevelt's political career.[33] The two rivals apparently mended fences. McGuire visited Croker at his estate in Ireland in 1922.[34] During his multiple careers, McGuire was embroiled in controversy, not only as three-time mayor of Syracuse, but in the issues surrounding Progressivism in America – machine politics, trusts, civil service reform, free silver, immigration and world peace. By far, the issue which most identified the man was Irish Nationalism. It had been an issue which permeated American politics since the Civil War, increasing in intensity in the two decades of the 20th century. McGuire had links to the Clan na Gael and had been a close associate and confidante of John Devoy, a relationship which soured when McGuire dropped away from the FOIF/Cohalan/Devoy faction and supported DeValera and the AARIR. McGuire personified the many shifts in Irish-American Nationalism, espousing then repudiating Home Rule in favor of Sinn Fein. His involvement in clandestine organizations such as FOIF, the Clan na Gael and his activities as an agent of the German Imperial government, indicate how close he was to the cause of Irish independence. The efforts of McGuire and his fellow Irish Nationalists were successful in that they were able to influence and alter both American domestic and foreign policy prior to and after World War I. The concerns of Irish-Americans were often carefully considered by the government before policies were carried out. When they were not, the organized wrath of Irish-America was a force to be reckoned with. Their successes possibly gave them an exaggerated sense of power, but once the goal of Irish freedom was close to reality, they strove to emphasize the "American" aspect of their identity, a point McGuire never lost sight of.[35] It is probably fitting that McGuire passed away in 1923. He saw the fulfillment of his dream of Irish independence, although not as a republic. He witnessed and participated in the key events and organizations that made it possible. It is no small tribute to the man he was honored by the Free State, which he helped establish which gave testimony to his efforts in the floral tributes at his funeral. Ironically, the flag which he refused to lower to half-staff in memory of the death of Queen Victoria in 1901, was lowered in his honor.

1923 may be significant in another way. Ireland was about to set its own course. Most of his friends and colleagues of earlier days had predeceased him or would follow soon after. A symbol of his pre-war links to Geman subversion and sabotage, Lothar Witzke was released from prison. Originally sentenced to death for his activities, he was saved by the armistice of November 1918. His sentence was commuted to life in 1920. Three years later he was pardoned and deported to Germany.[36] In addition, former political enemy Richard Croker died in April 1922; fellow Irish Nationalist W. Bourke Cockran passed away in March 1923. The following year saw the demise of Woodrow Wilson, Charles F. Murphy and McGuire's associate in the German Information Service, William Bayard Hale. Joseph McGarrity and Daniel F. Cohalan survived until the 1940's, their organizations and influence a fleeting memory. McGuire labored for over thirty years to see his dream of a free Ireland come to fruition. To that end he gave generously of his time, his wealth, and his talents from his multiple careers, jeopardizing his own financial future in the process. He represented a microcosm of America in transition, with its manifold problems and prejudices. McGuire was a man of intense passions. He knew the prejudices faced by Catholic Irish in America, but he also had his biases which his comments about Mormons, Ulster Protestants, Jews and blacks attest. He used his ambition and abilities in various endeavors which brought him both notoriety and acclaim in his own lifetime. Perhaps the best summary of McGuire's life is found in the words of James E. Doyle, his successor as editor of the Catholic Sun: "From most humble beginnings James K. McGuire rose to eminence in his native land. He worked hard and he meant well. May God have mercy on his soul".[37]

Notes

1 Obituary: "James K. McGuire" Syracuse Herald 30 June 1923 James K. McGuire File, Onondaga County Historical Association.
2 A second source says he was educated at public schools and St. John's Academy. "James K. McGuire". Herald American 29 August 1900.
3 "Obituary, James K. McGuire, 12 July, 1868-29 June 1923" James K. McGuire File, Onondaga County Historical Society; "Tribute To Former Leader, His Deeds Praised, Fr. Dougherty Eulogizes Remarkable Career of 'Boy Mayor'" James K. McGuire File. Onondaga County Historical Association; Hundreds Pay Last Tribute To James K. McGuire". Syracuse Herald 2 July 1923:2.
4 "Tribute To Former Leader..." op.cit.
5 "Hundreds Pay Last Tribute To James K. McGuire". Syracuse Herald 2 July 1923:6.
6 "City Stirred By Sudden Death of Former Mayor, James K. McGuire." The Catholic Sun 5 July 1923. For Devoy's comments see, "Fenian Chief's Estimate of James K. McGuire." Catholic Sun 19 July 1923. The New York Times, which had covered much of McGuire's career, gave only brief mention of his passing. See "J.K. McGuire Found Dead". New York Times 30 June 1923:11.
7 "James K. McGuire": Catholic Sun 5 July 1923.
  Devoy's article, cited above, suggests that during the war, McGuire lost numerous contracts on President Wilson's orders, "the President never missing a chance of punish(ing) him when he got the opportunity."
8 For McGarrity, see Tarpey, M.V. "Joseph McGarrity Fighter For Irish Freedom." Studia Hibernica, No 11, (1971), 164-180. The extent of McGuire's fortune is open to debate. His wife continued to live in their West side apartment in New York City and until her death. She was involved in charity galas for the benefit of the Knights of Columbus. When he passed away, there was no public record as to the monetary value of his estate. See "Opera For K of C." New York Times. 7 December 1930: 138; "Opera Benefit Tomorrow" New York Times 19 December 1930:29. An article in the Syracuse Herald carried the news of a sale from the estate of James K. McGuire from his summer home in Cleveland, New York. Items included bronzes, oriental rugs early American glass and antiques. See "Auction Syracuse Herald. 7 June 1938.
9 "The Green Flag In America". http://www.americanheritage.com/articles/magazines/ah/1979/4/1979; Doorley, Michael. Irish-American Diaspora Nationalism: The Friends of Irish Freedom, 1916-1935 (Dublin: Four Courts Press, 2005), 152. The spectacle of Irishmen killing one another was such that Diarmuid Lynch considered resigning his post as National Secretary of the Friends of Irish

Freedom in 1923. The national executive persuaded him to remain. Lynch resigned in 1932. In Doorley, op.cit.,153-165.

10 Tarpey, Marie V. op.cit, 173.

11 This other co-conspirator of McGarrity may have been Hugh Montague, key leader of the New York Clan who was involved with McGarrity, Boland and McGuire in the East Side affair. But Fitzpatrick refers to James K. McGuire as a member of the Virginia Clan. McGuire had both business associates and family in Virginia. See David Fitzpatrick, Harry Boland's Irish Revolution (Cork, Ireland: Cork University Press, 2003), 443. However, in the writers' personal communications to Fitzpatrick, the latter could not clarify McGuire's Virginia Clan affiliation. Fitzpatrick to Schultz email 8 February 2013.

12 Doorley, op.cit., 154; "Asks Place In League Of Nations For Ireland." Catholic Sun 26 April 1923:1.

13 Doorley, op.cit., 155; Cohalan, Daniel F., "America's Advice To Ireland" in Fitzgerald, William G. The Voice of Ireland (Dublin: John Heywood, Ltd), 212-214; "Our Peace Endangered By England, Says Cohalan". Catholic Sun 25 March 1921:19.

14 Splain, John J. "Under Which King?" in Fitzgerald, op.cit., 242-254; especially 245.

15 Reports of McGuire's precarious health are noted from the outset of his first term as Mayor. See "McGuire's First Day". Syracuse Post 2 January 1896. The article reported the new mayor was suffering from "neuralgia". See also Mayor McGuire "Coming Home" Syracuse Journal 6 December 1899:6; "Mayor McGuire's Condition" Syracuse Journal 15 December 1899:5; "Mayor M'Guire's Ocean Trip". Syracuse Journal 13 November 1899:5; "McGuire Taken Ill While Speaking". Syracuse Herald 7 October 1900:1. Obituary, "James K. McGuire, 12 July 1868 – 29 June 1923", op.cit. A subsequent obituary mentioned McGuire's heart had been weakened by a recent bout of pneumonia and had not responded to treatment. See "City Stirred by Sudden Death of Former Mayor James K. McGuire". Catholic Sun 5 July 1923,: 5,7

16 "Seeks Legislature Pledged To Hearst". New York Times 21 June 1922: 14; "Hearst To Get Delegates In Every District". Syracuse Herald 18 June 1922:19. "J. K. McGuire Out of Local Politics". Syracuse Herald 18 August 1913:6; "Kelley Machine Shattered, Claim of Insurgents". Syracuse Herald 28 January 1915:2; "News of Politicians". Syracuse Herald 11 August 1918:17; "3rd District Fight Most Bitter Yet". Syracuse Herald 28 August 1918:6; "News of Politicians". Syracuse Herald 31 July 1918:26; "In The Wake of the Convention". Syracuse Herald 26 July 1919:6.

And although he no longer owned the Catholic Sun in 1922, having sold it to James E. Doyle in September 1920, it's interesting to note Al Smith's re-nomination for Governor was mentioned only in a two sentence article with an accompanying photograph ("Smith Nominated". Catholic Sun 5 October 1922:2), contrasting it with full page ads and endorsements for Al Smith in 1920. The same ads condemned the Republican candidate, Nathan Miller. See "Vote For Alfred E. Smith And Endorse His Welfare And Reconstruction Measures" Catholic Sun 22 October 1920. See also "James E. Doyle Purchases McGuire Interest In Syracuse Printing and Publishing Company". Catholic Sun 10 September 1920:5.

17 "Dyer Appoints Committee For League Opening". Syracuse Herald 12 April 1922:11.

18 Slayton, Robert. Empire Statesman: The Rise and Redemption of Al Smith (New York: Free Press 2001), 196-201.

19 "Body of JK McGuire On Train Arriving Today; City Will Bow In Tribute". Syracuse Herald. 1 July 1923:24.

20 "South Already Dry, Asserts J. K. M'Guire". Syracuse Herald 9 June 1923. For his concern about the liquor issue and its impact on Irish politics, see McGuire's letter to Daniel F. Cohalan 11 March 1920. American Irish Historical Society, Daniel F. Cohalan Papers. Cited in John P. Buckley. The New York Irish: Their View of American Foreign Policy, 1914-1921 (New York: Arno Press, 1976), 346.

21 "Vote For Gov. Alfred E. Smith And Endorse His Welfare And Reconstruction Measures". Catholic Sun 22 October 1920.

22 "Fenian Chief's Estimate of James K. McGuire," Catholic Sun 19 July 1923.

23 Splain, op.cit., 253-254.

24 "James K. McGuire". Catholic Sun. 5 July 1923:4.

25 Carroll, F. M. American Opinion And The Irish Question, 1910-1923: A Study In Opinion And Policy (New York: St. Martin's Press, 1978), 162-171.

26 Wister was the author of The Virginian. For his impact, see Carroll, op.cit., 173.

27 Carroll, op.cit., Sims' remarked that Irish Americans were jackasses with their votes. This wasn't the first time Sims was criticized. In February 1921, Sims complained that Sinn Fein was responsible for American deaths by its interference with ships and troop movements. ("Sims Irish Attack to Be Investigated". Catholic Sun 4 February 1921, p.1.)

28 Doorley, op.cit., 150; 151; 154; Cronin, Sean. The McGarrity Papers: Revelations of the Irish Revolutionary Movement In Ireland and America, 1900-1940). (Tralele, Ireland: Anvil Books, 1972), 144.

29 Carroll, op.cit., 186.

30 Cronin, op.cit., 150; 170.

31 Carroll, op.cit., 186.

32 Doorley, op.cit., 157.

33 "Fenian Chief's Estimate of James K. McGuire." Catholic Sun 19 July 1923.

34 "Croker Won Big Syracuse Fight to Unseat Hill." <u>Syracuse Herald</u> 30 April 1922:1.
35 "James K. McGuire". <u>Catholic Sun</u> 5 July 1923:435.
36 Witcover, Jules. Sabotage at Black Tom: Imperial Germany's Secret War in America, 1914-1917. Chapel Hill: Algonquin Books, 1989, 323.
37 <u>JamesK. McGuire Catholic Sun 5 July 1923.</u>

WORKS CITED

A

Ann de Wiel, Jerome. "Imperial Germany and Irish-American Contacts, 1900-1917. http://history.com/20th century-contemporary-historyireland.com/20th century-contemporary-history/imperial-germany-and irish-american contacts-1900-1917. 11pp. 1982

. The Irish Factor,1899-1919: Ireland's Strategic and Diplomatic Importance for Foreign Powers. Dublin: Irish Academic Press, 201

Abernathy, Tom 'Remembering a Courageous American Voice For Irish Freedom Norman Thomas'. http://1916 societies.com/2016/05/ /courageous american-voice. Retrieved 22 April 2017.

"Analysis of Serial Numbers".http://http//wwwthompsonguninireland. com/serial%numbers/Serial%20 Numbers.htm. 4 pp.

"ArmsRoutes" https:??thompsonguninireland.com?Arms%20 smuggling%20routes_files/Arms%smuggling......

B

Bannon, Theresa. Pioneer Irish In Onondaga County, 1776-1847. New York: Putman, 1911.

'Baldwin Roger, Dies At 91, Crusader For Civil Rights Founded ACLU" https //www nytimes com/1981/08/27/obituaries/roger-baldwin does at 91-was-crusader-for civil rights founded the html New York Times 27 August 1981 Retrieved 27 August 2017.

Bailey, Thomas, A Diplomatic History of The American People New York: Appleton, 1964.

Barry, Tom. Guerilla Days In Cork. 1955.

Bass, Herbert. I Am A Democrat: The Political Careers of David B. Hill. New York: Syracuse University Press, 1961.

Beesly, Patrick. Room 40: British Naval Intelligence, 1914-1917. London: Harmish-Mailton, 1982.

Bell, J. Bower. The Gun In Politics: An Analysis of Irish Political Conflict, 1916-1986. New Brunswick: Transaction Publishers, 1991.

Bemis, Samuel Flagg. A Diplomatic History of the United States. New York: Henry Holt and Co.,

Bernard, Rudolph. From Minyan To Community: A History of The Jews of Syracuse. New York: Syracuse University Press, 1970.

Bernstorff, Count Johann.. My Three Years In America New York: Scribner's, 1920.

Bisher, Jamie. "German Raiders In Latin American Waters" http://www.militaryhistoryonline.comwww1/german commerce raiders. aspei.

Blum, Joseph. Joe Tumulty And The Wilson Era. Massachusetts: Houghton-Mifflin, 1931.

Brewing and Liquor Interest and German and Bolshevik Propaganda: Report and Hearings of the Subcommittee of the Judiciary. United States Senate. Vol. II: Washington, D.C. Government Printing Office, 1919.

Brewster, Arthur Judson, Life Was Never Dull: Memories of Clinton Square and Other Tales of Syracuse. Syracuse University Press, 1953.

"British Espionage in the United States: A Secret Memorandum Prepared by the United States Department of Justice, February 15, 1921. MID document 9944-A-178,17pp.

Brown, Giles. "The Hindu Conspiracy, 1914-1917". Pacific Historical Review 17 (3), 299-310

Bruce, Dwight. (ed.) Onondaga Centennial. Boston: History Company 1896, vol. I.

Buckley, John P. The New York Irish: Their Views on Foreign Policy, 1914-1921. New York Arno Press, 1976.

"Bureau of Investigation" International Encyclopedia of the First World War (W W I) http://encyclopedia. 1914-1918-on-line-net/article/bureau-of-investigation.

Bureau of Military History, 1913 – 1921: Statement by Witness Document No. W.S. 1,108. Witness:Jeremiah O'Leary File No.S2431, 6pp.

Buskupski, M.B.B. The Most Dangerous German Agent In America: The Many Lives of Louis N. Hammerling. Northern Illinois University Press, 2015

Butler, Richard J and Driscoll, Joseph. Dock Walloper: The Story of "Big Dick" Butler. New York: Putman, 1933.

C

"Captain Hans W. L. Boehm" http://irishbrigade.eu/other-men/germans/boehm/boehm.html, 10 pp.

Carnes, Mark; Garraty, John. American Destiny: History of A Nation 3rd ed. New York: Pearson-Longman, 2008.

Carrol Francis. American Opinion and The Irish Question, 1910-1923. New York: St Martin's Press, 1978.

Casement, Roger. The Crime Against Ireland And How the War May Right It. New York, 1914.

Child, Clifton. German-Americans In Politics, 1914-1917. New York: Arno Press, 1970.

Chinn, Carl. "Voices of War and Peace: Kitchener's New Army" http://voicesofwarandpeace.org/portfolio/kitchener - new- army/

Christ, Francis. "My Great-Grandfather, Ireland's Forgotten Fenian, led secret Missions For 1916" https://www.irishcentral.com/roots/my-great-grandfather-ireland's-forgotten -fenian, 6 pp.

Coleman, Barry. The Catholic Church and German-Americans. Milwaukee, 1953.

Connable, Alfred and Silberfarb, Edward. Tigers of Tammany: Nine Men Who Ran New York. New York: Holt, Rhinehart, Winston, 1967.

Connors, Dennis. Crossroads in Time; An illustrated History of Syracuse. Syracuse, N.Y. Onondaga County Historical Associates, 2006.

Criticisms of The Irish Convention as Proposed By Premier David. Lloyd George By Prominent Americans of Irish Blood. New York: Friends of Irish Freedom, 1917.

Cronin, Sean. The McGarrity Papers: Revelations of The Irish Revolutionary Movement in Ireland And America, 1900-1940. New York Anvil Books, 1972.

Cuddy Joseph. Irish-Americans And National Isolation, 1914-1920. New York: Arno Press, 1976.

Curry, Sir Charles. Roger Casement's Diaries: His Mission to Germany and the Findley Affair. Munich:Archie Oress, 1922.

Cyclopedia of National Biography. Ann Arbor: University of Michigan, vol. A.

D

Das, Tarak Nath.Dictionary of American Biorgraphy. 1972 Vol. I, pp. 364-365.

DeAlva, Alexander Stanwood. Four Famous New Yorkers: The Political Careers of Cleveland, Platt, Hill and Roosevelt, Political History of The State of New York, 1882-1905, vol. IV. New York: Holt, Rhinehart, Winston, 1923.

Deming, Arthur. Corporate Promotions and Reorganization Massachusetts: Harvard University Press, 1914.

Devoy, John. Recollections of An Irish Rebel. Dublin: Irish University Press, 1969.

Dictionary of American Biography. New York: Charles Scribner and Son, 1935.

Dignan, Don. "The Hindu Conspiracy in Anglo-American Relations During World War I". Pacific Historical Review, 40, (1), 57-76.

Documents Relative To Sinn Fein. London: H. M. Stationary Office, 1921.

Doerries, Rheinhard, Prelude to The Easter Rising: Sir Roger Casement In Imperial Germany. London: Frank Cass, 2000.

, Imperial Challenge: Ambassador Bernstorff and German-American

Relations, 1908-1917. Chapel Hill; University of North Carolina Press, 1989.

Donal. Come Here to Me:The Appearance of a General and Extreme Poverty Among the Local People Is Amazing" https://comeheretome.2014/06/11-the-appearance—of-a-general-and-extreme-poverty-among-the -lower-people-is-amazing

Doorley, Michael. Irish-American Diaspora Nationalism: The Friends of Irish Freedom, 1916-1935 Four Courts Press, 2005.

DuBois, W. E. B.https:wwwtheatlantic.com/past doc/unbound/flashbks/black/mcgillbh/html. Retrieved 7 July 2016.

Duff, John. The Irish In the United States. California Wadsworth Publishing Company, 1971

E

Encyclopedia of Religion And Ethnics, vol. III New York: Charles Scribners and Sons, 571-573.

Encyclopedia of Virginia Biography, vol. VI New York: Lewis Historical Publishing Company. 1915.

Epstein, Jonathan A. "German and English Propaganda in World War 1". Paper presented at NYMAS (New York Military Affairs Symposium, CUNY Graduate Center, 1 December 2000. 30 pp. http://bobrowen.com /nymas/propagandapaper.html.

F

Fagg, John. Cuba, Haiti And the Dominican Republic. New Jersey: Prentice-Hall, 1965.

Farragher, John N., Mary Jo Czitron, Susan Armitage. Out of Many: A History of The American People 4th ed. New Jersey: Prentice-Hall, 2003

'FBI records-SS Eastside case 52-505" http://www.thompsongunireland.com/FBI%20/US%20 RECORDS% 20 1921htm

Felgenbaum Willoam M "Socialist Profiles No 10-"Isaac Hourwich" 'The New Leader' vol 15, No 8 (25 February 19320 pp 8-9).

Feilitzsch, Heribert. "Men of the Secret War Council: Bernard Dernburg" http://felixsommerfeld.com/news/mexican-revolution-blog/2015/12/6/men-of-the-secret-war-council

_____ "William Bayard Hale-Icon or Traitor?" https[://felixsommerfeld.com.news/Mexican-revolution—blog/2013/11/43william-bayard-hale.

_____ The Secret War Council: The German Fight Against the Entente in America in 1914. Virginia: Henselstone Verlag, 2015.

"Fenian Graves: John Kenny (1827 – 1924)" http://feniangraves.net/Kenny/%20/John/Bio.htm

Finn, J. Michael. "Illuminations: Ben Franklin and Ireland http://songgsandhistories.net/myblog/ohio-irish-american-news-a-story-from-this-months-issue. 18 December,2012

Fischer-Tine, Harald. "Indian Nationalism and the 'World Forces': Transnational and Diasporic Dimensions of the Indian Freedom Movement on the Eve of the First World War" Journal of Global History, 007 (2), 325-344.

Field, Sara Bard (1882-1947) http//www oregon Encyclopedia org/articles/field-sara bard_1882 1974/ Retrieved 7 March 2016.

Fitzgerald, William G. (ed). The Voice of Ireland. Dublin: John Heywood, Ltd., 1924.

Fitzpatrick, David. Harry Boland's Irish Revolution. Ireland: Cork University Press, 2003.

Flagg, Samuel B. A Diplomatic History of The United States. New York: Henry Holt and Company, 1942.

Foner, Philip. The History of the Labor Movement in the nited States. From the Founding Fathers of the AFL to the Emergence of American Imperialism. New York: International Publishers, 1975.

Ford, Nancy Gentile, Americans All. Texas: Texas A and M Press, 2001.

"Friends of Irish Freedom: A Case Study in Irish-American Nationalism, 1916-1921: History Ireland http:// www.history.ireland.com/1916-21/20th-century-contemorasry history/the-friends-of-irish-freedom-a-case-study-in-Irish-American-nationalism-1916-1921

Fulwider, Chad R. "Film Propaganda and Culture: The German Dilemma, 1914-1917". Film and History: An Interdisciplinary Approach, 45, no.2, Winter, 2015, 4-12.

Funchion, Michael (ed). Irish-American Voluntary Organizations. Connecticut: Greenwood Press, 1983.

Chicago's Irish Nationalists, 1881-1890. New York: Arno Press, 1976.

G

Gaffney, T. St. John. Breaking The Silence. New York, 1930.

Galway, Terry. Irish Rebel: John Devoy and America's Fight For Ireland's Freedom. New York: St. Martin's Press, 1998.

Ganachari, Aravind Guraro. "An Early American Contributor to India's Struggle for Freedom: Myron H. Phelps (1856-1916, 149-160 in Ganachari, Aravind Guraro(ed.) Nationalism and Social Reform in a Colonial Situation. Delhi, India: Gyan Books, 2005.

"German Way and More: Albert Ballin" http://www.german-way.com/notable-people/featured-bios/albert-ballin.

Gibbon, Florence E. The Attitude of The New York Irish Towards State And National Affairs, 1848-1902. New York, 1951.

Gitlow, Benjamin. The Whole of Their Lives. New York: Scribners, 1948.

Golway, Terry. Irish Rebel: John Devoy and America's Fight For Irish Freedom. New York: St. Martin's press, 1999.

Gompers, Samuel. Seventy Years of Life And Labor: An Autobiography. New York: Dutton, 1925.

Greaves, Desmond. Liam Mellows and The Irish Revolution. Belfast: Foileachin and Ghlior Gafa, 2004.

Gwynn, Denis. The Life of John Redmond, London, 1932.

H

Hagedorn, Ann. Savage Peace: Hope and Fear In America, 1919. New York: Simon and Schuster, 2007.

Halpern, Paul G. Naval History of World War I. London: UCLP, 1994.

Hartley, Stephen. The Irish Question as a Problem in British Foreign Policy, 1914-1919. New York: St. martin's Press, 1987.

Hayes, Richard. Ireland And Irishmen In the French Revolution. London, 1932.

Hennessy, John A. What's The Matter With New York? A Story of The Waste of Millions. New York: O'Connell Press, 1916.

Heckscher, August, Woodrow Wilson. New York: Scribners, 1991.

Helmer, William. The Gun That Made the Twenties Roar. New York: Macmillan, 1969.

'Herrick, Robert, 70, Aide of Ickes Dies' New York Times 24 December 1938, p.15.

Higham, John. Strangers in The Land: Patterns of American Nativism, 1860-1925. New Jersey: Rutgers University Press, 1955.

"Hilfkreuzer" http:// www.scharnhorst-class.dk/hilfkreuzer introduction.

"History of the Federal Bureau of Investigation"http://fas.org/lirp/agency/doj/fbi/fbi/hist.htm.

Hogan, Gerard. " George Gavan Duffy(1882-1951)http;?/treaty. national archivesie./wp/content/uploads/2011/11/Duffy.pdf. 6pp.

Hoover, Karl. "The Hindu Conspiracy In California, 1913-1918" German Studies Review. 8 (2) 1985, 245-261.

Howe, Frederick. Confessions of a Reformer. Kent Ohio. Kent State University Press. 1988.

Hudson, Berkely and Boyajy, Karen. "The Rise and Fall of an Ethnic

Advocate and American Huckster" <u>Media History</u>, 15, no.3, 2009, 287-302.

I

<u>In Common: Council Manual of The City of Syracuse, 1896</u>. Syracuse N.Y. E.N. Grover Company, 1896, 49-51.

J

Jensen, J.M. "The Hindu Conspiracy: A Reassessment'. <u>Pacific Historical Review</u> 48, (1), February 1979, 65-83.

Johnson, Charles T. <u>Culture At Twilight: The National German American Alliance, 1901-1918</u>. New York: Peter Lang, 1999.

Jones, John P. and Hollister, Paul H. <u>The German Secret Service In America</u>. Boston Small, Maynard and Company, 1918.

Jones, John P. <u>America Entangled</u>. New York: A.C. Laut, 1917.

K

Katz, Frederick. <u>The Secret War In Mexico: The United States and the Mexican Revolution</u>. Chicago: University of Chicago Press, 1981.

Kingsley, J., Knauler, J. C., Neville, C C.., Buckenleger, A.C.(eds). <u>Political Blue Book Of Central New York</u>. E. H. Gover, 1902.

Knight, Melvin. <u>Americans In Santo Domingo</u>. New York: Vanguard 1928.

L

Landau, Henry. The Enemy Within The Inside Story of German Sabotage In America. New York: Putnam, 1937.

Lansing, Robert. The War Memoirs of Robert Lansing, Secretary of State. New York: Bobbs-Merrill, 1935.

Larkin, Emmet. James Larkin, 1876-1947: Irish Labor Leader. London: Routledge And Keagan Paul, 1965.

Lavelle, Patricia. James O'Mara: Staunch Sinn Feiner, 1873-1948. Dublin: Claymore and Reynolds, 1961.

"Laws Prevent Adequate Punishment, Court Declares Prisoners Termed Tools of Inhuman Country, Plotters Warned Against More Activity After Release". Los Angeles Times, May 1918.

Lay, N. G. Ways of The World: A History of The World's Roads and The Vehicles That Made Them. New Jersey. Rutgers University Press, 1992.

Lefkowitz, Abraham. https//reuther wayne edu node/ 3475 Wayne State University. Retrieved 27 October 2017.

Leslie, Shane. The Irish Issue In Its American Aspect. New York: Scribners, 1917.

LeSeuer, Meridel Crusaders. The Radical Legacy of Marian and Arthur LeSeuer St. Paul Minnesota. Minnesota Historical Society Press,1984.

Link, Arthur. The Struggle For Neutrality, 1914-1915. New Jersey: Princeton University Press, 1960.

Woodrow, Wilson And the Progressive Era, 1910-1917. New York Harper Brothers, 1953.

Confusion and Crises, 1915-1916. New Jersey Princeton University Press, 1964.

. Campaigns for Progressivism And Peace. New Jersey: Princeton University Press, 1965.

Lizzi, Dominick. Martin Glynn: Forgotten Hero. New York: Valatine Press, 2007.

'Lochner Louis (1887-1950)' http//traces org/ Louis Iochner/html. Retrieved 17 July 2017.

Logan, Rayford. Haiti And the Dominican Republic. New York: Oxford University Press, 1968.

Logan, Andy. Against The Evidence: The Becker-Rosenthal Affair. New York: McCall, 1970.

Lowie, Robert H 'Franz Boas, 1858-1942' National Academy of Sciences Biographical Memoirs 24 pp 303-322.

M

'Malone, Dudley Field' http//www.imdb.com/name/nm0540418/ retrieved 17 August 2017.

Maurer, James H. 79. A Socialist Leader, Vice-President Candidate, Union Official. New York Times 3 March 1944.

May, Ernest. The World War and American Isolation, 1914-1917. Cambridge: Harvard University Press, 1959.

McBeth, Brian S. Gunboats, Corruption and Claims: Foreign Intervention In Venezuela, 1899-1908. Connecticut: Greenwood Press, 2001.

McCartan, Patrick. With DeValera in America. New York: Brentano, 1932.

McDonncha, Michael. Sinn Fein: A Century of Struggle. Dublin: 2005.

McGuire, James K. (ed). The Democratic Party of The State of New York. History Book Company, New York; 1905.

The King, The Kaiser and Irish Freedom. New York: Devin-Adair, 1915.

What Could Germany Do For Ireland? New York: Wolf Tone Company, 1916.

McGurrin, James. Bourke Cochran: A Free Lance In American Politics. New York: Scribners and Sons, 1948.

McMaster, John B. United States In The World War, 1914-1918. New York: Appleton and Company, 1918.

McNichol, Dan Paving The Way: Asphalt in America. Maryland: National Asphalt Paving Association, 2005.

Men of Affairs In New York: A Historical Work. New York: Hammersly and Co. 1906.

"Merry Plowboy" Complete Lyrics. http://www.irish-folk-somgs.com/the-merry-plowboy-lyrics-and-chords.html.

"Meyer, Richard" htttp://irishbrigade.eu/other-men/germans/meyer/meyer.html.

Miller, John. Triumph of Freedom, 1775-1783. Boston, 1948.

Moody, John. The Truth About Trusts. New York: Moody Publishing Company. 1904.

Murphy, Richard and Marmion, Lawrence. History of The Society of the Friendly Sons of St. Patrick of The City of New York, 1784-1955. New York, 1962.

Morton Richard A "Edward Dunne Illinois Most Progressive Governor" ISHS Winter, 1990. pp 218- 234. https// web archive.org/web/29100803150042//http//dig lib nin edu/ISHS/ishs-1990-winter/218pdf. Retrieved 21 August 2018

Myers, Gustavus. History of Tammany Hall. New York; Boni and Liveright

N

National Cyclopedia of American Biography, vol. XXI New York: James T. White and Company, 1921.

"Norman Hamilton" Who Was Who In America, vol IV, 1961-1968. Chicago: Maquis Who's Who, Inc. 1968, 399.

"Norman Hamilton" Encyclopedia of Virginia Biography, vol. IV. Lewis Historical Publishing Company, 1915, 376-377.

O

O'Brien, William and Ryan, Desmond. Devoy's Post Bag, 1871-1918. Dublin: C. J. Fallon, 1948.

O'Broin, Leon. Dublin Castle and The 1916 Uprising. London, Sedgewick and Johnson, 1970.

O'Coisdnenilha, Tomas 'Dr Gertrude Kelly'. http//fenian graves net/Kelly%20Dr%20Gertrude/Dr/%20/Kelly%20biohtml. Retrieved 17 March 2016

O'Connor, Richard. The German-Americans: An Informal History. Boston: Little, Brown and Company, 1968.

O'Dea, John. History of The Ancient Order of Hibernians And Ladies Auxiliary, vol. III Philadelphia: Keystone Printing, 1923.

O'Doherty, Katherine. Assignment America: DeValera's Mission To The United States. New York; DeTanko Publishers, 1957.

O'Leary, Jeremiah. My Political Trials and Experiences. New York: Jefferson Publishing, 1919.

O'Luing, Sean. Kuno Meyer, 1858-1919: A Biography. Dublin: Geographic Publications, 1991.

P

Papen, Franz von. Memoirs. London: Andrew Deutsch, 1952.

Park, Robert. The Immigrant Press and Its Control. New York: Harper, 1922.

Peterson, H. C. Propaganda For War: The Campaign Against American Neutrality, 1914-1917. Norman: University of Oklahoma Press, 1939.

Plowman, Mattew Erin. "Irish Republicans and the Indo-German

Conspiracy of World war I". New Hibernia Review. 7 (3), 2003, 81-105.

"The British Intellligence Station In San Francisco During the First World war". Journal of Intelligence History 12 (1),1-20. http://www.tandfonline.com/doi/full/10.1080/16161262.2013.755016.

Phelan, James. Santo Domingo Investigation: Copy of The Report Findings and Opinions. Washington, D.C. Gibson Brothers, 1916.

Poppelwell, Richard. Intelligence and Imperial Defense: British Intelligence and the Defense of the Indian Empire, 1904-1924. London: Frank Cass, 1995.

"The Surveillance of Indian 'Seditionists' in North America, 1905-1915". Intelligence and International Relations, 1987, 49-75.

Pusey, Merlo. Charles Evans Hughes, vol. I. New York MacMillan, 1923.

R

Rippy, J. Fred. The Caribbean Danger Zone. New York: G.P. Putman, 1940.

Roberts, Edward. Ireland In America. New York, 1931.

Roe Gilbert Attorney Cites 15 Ways the Laws of New York Discriminate Against Women. American Journalism Org retrieved 27 May 2018

Rodman, Seldon. Quisqueya: A History of The Dominican Republic. Seattle: University of Washington Press, 1964.

Roseboom, William and Schraum, Harry. They Built A City: Stories and Legends of Syracuse and Onondaga County. Fayetteville, N.Y Manlius Publishing Company. 1976.

. Syracuse From Salt to Satellite. Syracuse Chamber of Commerce, 1979.

S

Saba, Ann. "True Heroes of the Customs Tradition: The Port of New York and the Customs Intelligence Bureau During World War I" http:// www.cbp.gov/xp/CustomsToday/2001/february/custoday_tradition.xml.

Sanyasi, "The Madness of Jodh Singh:Patriotism and Paranoia in the U.S., 1913 and 2013".http://chapatti.mystery.com/archivists/imperial_watch/the_madness_of_jodh_singh_paranoia_and_patriotism

in_the_us_in_1913_and_2013.html.

Scheiber, Clara. The Transformation of American Political Opinion Towards Germany. New York; Russell and Russell, 1923.

Schlossberg Joseph Dies at 97 Co Founder of Clothing Union. NYT 01/16/1971

Schmalenbach, Paul. German Raiders: A History of German Auxiliary Cruisers of the German Navy, 1895-1940. Annapolis: Naval Insitutue Press, 1919

Schmuhl, Robert. "Eamon De Valera: Man of Mystery. Irish America. Feb/Mar 2016. http://irishamerica.com/2016/02/eamon-de-valera-man-of-mystery.

. "What Saved Dev From the Firing Squad?" http://www.idependent ie/irish-news/1916/the-rising-explained/what-saved-dev-

from-firing-squad?

Schwab, Stephen Irving Max. "Sabotage at Bl -Intellligence 25 (2) 367-391. https:// doi.org/10.1080/08850607.2012.623012.

Schonreich, Otto. Santo Domingo: A Country With A Future. New York: MacMillan, 1918.

Shannon, William V. The American Irish. New York: MacMillan, 1963.

Shippee, Lester Burrell. "Germany and the Spanish-American War". American Historical Review XXX, July 1925, 754-777.

"Shipping Munitions: Lusitania Online" http://www.lusitania.net/munitions.html.

Spence, Richard. "Englishmen in New York: The SIS-the American Station, 1915-1921" Intelligence and National Security. 19(3) Autumn 2004, 511-537.

Slayton, Robert. Empire Statesman: The Rise and Redemption of Al Smith. New York: Free Press, 2001.

'Smedley, Agnes' http// www.asu.edu/lib/archives/smedley/html. Retrieved 28 August 2017

Smith, Ray B. and Brown, Roscoe. History of The State of New York: Political and Governmental, 1922, vol. III, 316-317.

"S.S. Severance" http:// www.history.navy.mil/photos/sh-civil/civsh-s/severance.htm.

Stevenson, Robert Louis. Footnote to History: Eight Years in Samoa, 1888.

Stoddard, Dwight. Notable Men of Central New York of the XIX and XX Centuries, 1903.

Strother, French. Fighting America's Spies. New York,: Doubleday, 1919..

Sutherland, N. The City of Syracuse And Its Resources. Syracuse, N. Y. Syracuse News Publishing Company, 1893.

Syracuse And Onondaga County, New York: Pictorial and Biographical. New York: S. J. Clarke, 1908.

T

Tansill, Charles C. America and The Fight For Irish Freedom, 1866-1922. New York: Devon-Adair, 1957.

Thomas, Samuel Bell, The Boss or The Governor. New York: Truth Publishing Company, 1914.

Tock, David. German Immigration and Adaptation to Latin America. Senor thesis, Libert University. Spring 1974. 72pp.

V

Viereck, George S. Spreading Germs of Hate. New York: Horace Liveright, 1930.

The Strangest Friendship In History: Woodrow Wilson And Colonel House. New York: Liveright, 1932.

Villard, Oswald Garrison. <u>Fighting Years: Memoir of A Liberal Editor.</u> New York: Harcourt Brace, 1930.

W

Walsh, Frank P. https//openlibrary.org/books/OL2213985/Frank_P_Walsh

And_The_Irish_Question. Retrieved 19 August 2017

Ward, Alan S. <u>Ireland And Anglo-American Relations, 1899-1921</u>. Toronto: University of Toronto Press, 1969.

"Wedell, Georg von (1862-1943)". http://www.irishbrigade.eu/other-men/germans/von -wedel/von-wedel.html.

Wells, Sumner. <u>Naboth's Vineyard: The Dominican Republic, 1844-1924</u>. Savile Books, 1966.

Werner, N.R. <u>Tammany Hall</u>. New York: Garden City Publishing Company, 1928.

Whitford, Noble E. <u>A History of The Barge Canal of New York State</u>. New York: J.B. Lyon Company, 1922.

<u>Who Was Who in America?</u> Vol. I,1887-1942. Chicago:Maquis Who's Who,1942

Willits, Bryan. "How Germany Courted the Irish Americans and Supported the Rising of 1916" https://irishcentral.com/roots/history/how-germany-courted-the-irish-americans-and-suported-the-rising -of 1916.

"Witness Statements-Military Archives-Defence Forces Ireland".

http://thompsongunireland.com/witness%statements/witness%20 statements%20Bureau of Military History.

Wittke, Carl. The Irish in America. Louisiana: Louisiana State University Press, 1956.

German-American And the World War. Ohio State Archeological And Historical Society, 1936.

INDEX

Symbols

(The) Crime Against Ireland and How The War May Right It 346
(The) King, the Kaiser and Irish Freedom 270, 328, 343, 345, 348, 402, 411, 448, 483, 589

A

Abhedananda, Swami 326, 332, 397
Albert, Heinrich xi, 280, 300, 302, 303, 322, 336, 339, 340, 341, 351, 354, 362, 365, 392, 393, 423, 429, 483
Albert Sander 338, 351
Altgeld, Gov. John 86
American Association For the Recognition of the Irish Republic (AARIR) 530
American Commission on Irish Independence 331, 516, 519, 533, 535, 550
American Correspondence Film Company 490
American Defense Society 473, 486, 499, 501
American Embargo Conference 349, 452
American Protective League 482, 506
American Sinn Fein 386, 469
American Truth Society 280, 290, 298, 306, 307, 308, 309, 351, 352, 369, 448, 453, 469, 499
Amos, Mayor Jacob 6, 32, 89, 112, 150, 161
Ancient Order of Hibernians (AOH) 245, 253, 254, 256, 266, 267, 278, 283, 289, 296, 304, 312, 318, 366, 367, 407, 442, 446, 453, 456, 457, 490, 491, 508, 514, 591
Andrews, Judge W. S. 35
Anglo-Irish Treaty 285, 287, 532, 546, 550, 551
Anglophobia 241, 244, 294, 428

Annie Larsen affair 432
Anti-Imperialist League 306, 324
Anti-Saloon League 18, 21, 22, 42, 214, 564
Armistice, 1918 320, 484, 493, 496, 497, 514, 569
armistice of November 1918 569
Article X Versailles Treaty 399, 502, 544
Asphalt Association 232, 233
Asphalt Trust x, xi, xiv, 36, 37, 39, 46, 68, 90, 105, 122, 132, 139, 148, 150, 151, 155, 156, 157, 161, 217, 232, 284, 560
Auto-Ordnance Co. 543
Auxiliary Cruisers 423, 426, 427

B

Baldwin, Charles 50
Balfour, Arthur 476
Ballin, Albert 424, 435, 584
Barakatullah, Mohammad Abdul 334
Barber, Amzi 149, 151, 156, 159, 161
Barber Asphalt 37, 124, 128, 148, 149, 152, 154, 155, 156, 157, 160, 180, 181, 182, 183, 188, 214, 215, 217, 220, 224, 303, 565
Barnes, William 167, 223, 229, 238
Bartholdt, Richard 306, 307, 320
Baseball 5, 6, 14, 15, 16, 17, 18, 20, 22, 40, 123, 140
Battle, George 222
Becker, Charles 194, 199
Becker-Rosenthal Murder Case 164, 165, 176, 187, 193, 194, 196, 197, 260, 509
Beecher, Henry W. 252, 261
Beer, William C. 201
Belden, James x, 35, 89, 90, 94, 117, 119, 178
Belmont, August 117, 164
Benjamin Franklin Bureau 544
Bensel, John 169, 204, 220, 223, 224, 228, 229

CONFLICTS AND CRISES 601

Benton, Joab 231
Bielaski, Alexander Bruce 467, 480, 517, 548
Bitulithic Asphalt 157
Black and Tans 528, 532, 536, 554, 555
Black, Gov. Frank 95
Black Tom Explosion 334, 363, 364, 365
Boehm, Hans 372
Boers 244, 245, 246, 247, 258, 259, 296, 312, 351, 436
Boland, Harry x, xv, 523, 525, 529, 532, 534, 535, 536, 537, 538, 541, 546, 551, 552, 554, 558, 567, 572, 583
Bonaparte, Charles 480
Bond Certificate Drive (Irish) 537, 552
Bopp, Franz 316, 333, 543
Borah, William 340, 516
"Bossism" 89, 90, 135
Boy-Ed, Karl 307, 322, 363, 364, 392, 407, 423, 425, 426, 428, 430
Brady, Anthony 97, 99, 100, 180, 188
Brewster, Arthur J. 8, 11, 12, 116, 262, 577
Bridgeport Projectile Company 392, 393, 417
Brogan Affair xiv, 371
Brogan, Anthony 372, 409
Bryan, Willian Jennings 63, 85, 86, 94, 102, 107, 108, 115, 122, 126, 164, 192, 193, 196, 202, 203, 228, 229, 306, 324, 335, 348, 360, 370, 377, 437, 450, 451, 453, 459, 460, 466, 564, 568
Buchanan, Frank 352
Buenz, Dr. Karl 428, 429, 434, 438
Bureau of Investigation (BOI) 467, 480, 482, 505, 548, 578, 585
Burgess, Rev. A. P. 20
Burke, John 446, 457
Burleson, Albert 568
Butler, Dick 353

Butternut Street Riot 30, 71

C

Callaghan, Mary Rose 192, 280
Carlisle, John N. 154, 167, 177, 179, 180, 183, 217, 218
Carmody, Thomas 177, 236
Carnegie, Andrew x, 8, 294, 303, 307
Carranza, Venustiano 389, 391, 392
Carson, Sir Edward 267, 271, 279, 346, 486, 488
Casement, Sir Roger 131, 313, 320, 325, 329, 332, 334, 338, 342, 347, 365, 367, 368, 369, 375, 384, 395, 404, 410, 411, 412, 413, 464, 470, 484, 499, 580
Chatterton-Hill, George 297, 313, 314, 475
Christian Endeavors 22
Christian Endeavors' Conference 22, 42
Clan na Gael x, 245, 259, 286, 307, 347, 490, 554, 561, 562, 565, 569
Clapp, Edwin J 302, 315
Clark and O'Brien Company 80
Clark, "Champ" 164, 197, 445, 457, 477, 518
Clarke, Tom E. 363, 370, 414
Clark, John K. 223
Claussen, Matthew 322
Cleveland, Grover 9, 78, 83, 84, 86, 89, 108, 122, 139, 245, 257, 568
Cochran, Bourke 82, 120, 128, 246, 275, 413, 589
Cohalan, Daniel F. x, xi, 170, 194, 265, 363, 369, 386, 408, 451, 469, 483, 491, 520, 529, 549, 562
Colby, Bainbridge 450, 451, 458, 533
Coler, Bird 103, 105, 124, 127
Collins, Michael 373, 525, 529, 532, 540, 543
Colum, Padraic 381, 383, 415

Committee on Public Information (CPI) 338, 481, 505
Condit, Filmore 156, 214, 215, 234, 235
Connolly, Dick 374
Connolly, James 363, 365, 381, 382, 414, 415, 470, 512
Connolly, John 170
Connolly, Nora 381, 512
Connors, William "Fingy" x, 126, 141, 180, 563, 564
Cooperstown Meeting 181, 183, 190, 214, 217
Cosgrave, William 567
Cox, James 530
Creel, George 338, 472, 481
Croker, Richard x, 30, 60, 63, 78, 80, 85, 96, 98, 100, 101, 102, 108, 122, 125, 140, 318, 464, 568, 569
Cronin, Dr. Patrick 264, 286
Cummings, Homer 197, 209
Cummings, Matthew 312, 353, 549
Cummins, John 9, 295
Curran, Joseph 225

D

Daly, Jidge 53, 101, 116
Das, Tarak Nath 331, 333, 334, 580
Davies, Judge John C. 61
Davitt, Michael 244, 245, 247, 256, 260, 353
Dawson, Albert (American Correspondent Film Company) 337, 398
Dayal, Lala Har 333, 397
DeGraw, Charles 58
DeLacey, Larry 334
DeLaney, JOhn H. 168, 169, 222, 224, 225, 238
Democratic Party of the State of New York 78, 111
Depression of 1893 22, 23

Dernburg, Dr. Bernard 322, 349, 353, 364, 388
Deutschland (submarine) 320, 355, 375
DeValera, Eamon x, 233, 264, 332, 412, 487, 490, 504, 512, 516, 521, 523, 526, 537, 550, 551, 555, 567
Devery, William 123
Devoy, John x, xi, xiv, xv, 244, 256, 257, 264, 265, 268, 270, 283, 285, 286, 288, 290, 298, 302, 304, 306, 307, 313, 323, 332, 334, 347, 351, 352, 356, 358, 363, 364, 365, 369, 371, 376, 377, 379, 380, 397, 405, 407, 410, 411, 465, 478, 480, 484, 487, 491, 500, 512, 513, 530, 561, 562, 565, 567, 569, 584
Dillon, Luke 246, 259, 286, 287, 381, 532, 540, 554, 562
Dix, John 126, 195
Doerries, Reinhard 358
Doheny, Edward 531, 537, 544, 553
Doyle, James 536, 555, 570, 572, 573
Doyle, Michael 377
Driscoll, George W. 66
Driscoll, Michael 65, 66
Duffy, Gavan 401, 409, 410, 585
Dumba, Dr. Constantine 280, 301, 307
Dunfee, Sim x, 21, 30, 33, 34, 37, 52, 53, 94, 95, 114, 124, 127, 148
Dunn, Bart 225, 228
Dunne, Edward 331

E

East Side Incident 332, 538, 541, 558
Egan, Patrick 296, 379
Emmet, Thomas Addis 269, 275, 401, 470, 477, 503
Engler, Gustav 338
Erzburger, Matthias 337
Espionage Act (1917) 433, 480, 493

Etappensdienst (German Secret Naval Supply Department) 427

F

Facett, J. Sloan 80
Federal Bureau of Investigation 505, 585
Fenians 208, 243, 246, 264, 275
Feuhr, Dr. Karl A. 322, 460
Fighting 69th 251, 253
Film Company of Ireland (FCOI) 281, 289
Finerty, John 259, 264, 284, 554
Fitzpatrick, William 168, 174, 230
Flower, Governor Roswell 23, 79, 89, 99, 109, 110, 125
Flynn, William 354
Foley, Charles 220, 223, 224, 228
Ford, Patrick 244, 252, 256, 260, 269, 296, 353, 500
Ford, Robert 287, 307, 352, 379
"Four Minute Men" 482
Fowler, Everett 182, 183, 189, 217, 221, 236, 237
Fowler, Robert 352
Frawley Committee 174, 175, 186, 216, 229
Freeman, George 313, 323, 324, 333, 397
Friends of Freedom For India (FFI) 242, 537, 555
Friends of Irish Freedom (FOIF) x, 242, 264, 275, 276, 278, 282, 285, 288, 307, 317, 356, 378, 379, 383, 384, 411, 412, 450, 466, 469, 472, 473, 474, 475, 476, 477, 478, 484, 490, 491, 492, 495, 499, 500, 503, 504, 512, 519, 520, 547, 550, 551, 552, 554, 558, 561, 562, 563, 567, 571, 579, 581, 583
Friends of Peace 290, 306, 307, 351, 352, 379, 406

G

Gaelic renaissance 252
Gaffney, James E. 166, 169, 219, 223
Gaffney, T. St. John 269, 276, 281
Gallagher, Andrew 530
Gallagher, Michael 527
Gallagher Resolution 519
Galligher, Rev. Guy B. 16, 17, 20
Gavan, Joseph 282, 379
Gaynor, John F. 87, 103
Gaynor, William 168, 176
George, Lloyd 276, 477, 478, 479, 486, 495, 496, 502, 504, 579
Gerard, James W. 300, 303, 443, 456, 585
German-American Literary Defense Committee 351
German Imperial Government 267, 370, 412
German Information Service x, xiv, 136, 282, 297, 319, 339, 345, 366, 380, 394, 427, 431, 433, 474, 492, 570
German-Irish Committee 302
German Publication Society of New York 293
German Red Cross 319, 322, 336, 341, 411
Ghadarite Movement 297
Ghose, Salendra Nath 331, 537
Gibbons, James Cardinal 503
Gifford, Nellie 473, 474
Gill, John 385, 534
Gladstone Incident xiv, 430
Glynn, Martin 166, 173, 174, 177, 187, 196, 201, 218, 220, 221, 225, 228, 229, 239, 240, 450, 453, 454, 459, 556, 588
Goff, Judge John 193, 194, 195, 270, 274, 275, 387, 470, 477, 478, 500, 513, 531, 533, 537, 549, 556
Golden, Peter 331, 332, 385, 386, 414, 469, 491, 499, 512, 531, 537

Gompers, Samuel 352, 358
Gonne, Maude 247, 250, 251, 260, 261
Gore-McLemore Resolution 275, 349
Grady, Thomas F. 83, 122, 139
Gray, Judge George 197, 209
Gray, Samuel M 35
Greene, General Francis V. 149, 151, 152, 159, 303
Grimes, Fr. John 19

H

Haeckel, Erenst 303
Haiti 206, 210, 211, 280, 388, 421, 422, 581, 588
Hale, William B 322, 328, 339, 340, 389, 399, 474, 570, 582
Hamburg-America Line 246
Hamill, James 197, 201, 209
Hamilton, John 204
Hammerling, Louis 299, 302, 451
Hancock, Theodore 101
Hansen, Ferdinand 281
Harding, Warren G. 318, 530, 542, 544
Harvey, Colonel George 542
Hassett, Thomas 201, 204, 211, 224
Hatzfeldt, Prince 322, 341
Haven, Melvin 9, 36, 62, 64, 72, 99, 106, 116, 124, 127, 295, 563
Hayes, Monsignor Albert 560
Hearst, William R. 126, 140, 406, 563, 564
Hendricks, Francis x, 32, 61, 62, 89, 90, 108, 112
Hennessy, John x, 168, 173, 217, 223, 224
Herbert, Victor 269, 470, 477, 478, 500
Herrick, Cady 97
Herrick, Robert 331
Hexamer, Charles 295, 312, 336
Heynen, Karl 393
Hindu-German-Irish Conspiracy 335

Hirst, David 347
Hiscock, Frank x, 32, 46, 61, 63, 90, 151, 208
Hitchcock, Gilbert 306, 340, 399
Hobson, Bulmer 304, 316
Hoefer, Herman 169, 225
Holland, John 243, 272, 275, 379, 413
Home Rule 131, 139, 247, 256, 264, 265, 266, 267, 268, 269, 270, 277, 278, 284, 285, 286, 287, 289, 304, 305, 306, 312, 316, 318, 323, 344, 346, 348, 353, 363, 366, 370, 379, 382, 401, 403, 414, 464, 473, 474, 477, 478, 487, 496, 502, 503, 504, 505, 510, 552, 561, 569
Hopkins, Sherburne 417
Horgan, Matthew 174
Huerta, Victoriano 391, 392
Hughes, Charles Evans 127, 176, 425, 449, 450, 459, 568, 592
Hughes, Eugene x, 28, 33, 52, 99, 106, 107
Huntington, Rev. Frederic Dan 15, 27
Hurton, Fr. Thomas 491, 513, 547
Hylan, Judge John H. 230, 231
Hyphenates 291, 442

I

Indian Independence Committee(Berlin Committee) 333
Indian National Congress 332
Indian Nationalists 242
Indian Sociologist 324
Ingersoll, Robert 15, 27, 40
International Longshoreman's Association 353
International Mercantile Marine 362
International Socialist Peace Conference 281, 465
Irish Brigade (WW1) 247, 259, 281, 348, 368, 372, 374, 386, 402, 410

CONFLICTS AND CRISES 605

Irish Land League 207, 324
Irish Parliamentary Party (IPP) 257
Irish Press and News Service 340,
  347, 381, 400, 415
Irish Progressive League 489,
  490, 499, 508, 512
Irish Race Convention 269, 275,
  277, 287, 304, 345, 346, 348,
  485, 486, 489, 490, 491, 500,
  512, 513, 514, 515, 516, 518,
  519, 522, 547, 548, 549, 552
Irish Relief Committee 384
Irish Republican Army (IRA) 532
Irish Republican Brotherhood
  (IRB) 256, 285, 317
Irish Victory Fund 516, 522,
  523, 527, 528, 551, 567

J

Jacobson, Gustav 452
Jebsen, Frederick 432
Jennings, J.J. 251
Johnston, James 374

K

Keating, John P. 366
Kelley, William H. 124, 125, 127,
  136, 137, 168, 182, 183,
  186, 189, 215, 230, 231,
  266, 369, 447, 457, 563
Kelly, Dr. John Forrest 332,
  490, 500, 512
Kelly, "Honest John" 122, 135, 139
Kelly, Thomas H. 385
Kennedy, John J. 178, 228
Kennedy, Judge Samuel S. 4
Kennedy, Michael 251
Kenny, John 374, 409, 410, 582
Kenyon, Rev. J.B. 20
Kiely, Commissioner 57
Kings County Democracy 78, 79, 96
Kinkhead, Maj. Eugene 525
Kipper, Emil 487
Kirk, William B. 9, 52

Kitchener, Horatio 372
Kline, Jay 20, 38, 62, 65, 69, 119
Knights of Columbus 457,
  495, 496, 571
Koelbe, Alphonse 309
Koenig, Paul 319, 355
Koester, Frank 302, 315

L

Labor's National Peace Council
  349, 352, 353, 406
Lake Side Railroad 28
Lamar, David 352, 356, 375, 405
Landau, Henry xvi, 347, 403, 407, 587
Landy, James 370
Lansing, Robert 377, 456, 459, 587
Larkin, James x, xiv, xv, 336, 347,
  363, 381, 386, 407, 469,
  484, 490, 499, 513, 587
League of Nations 399, 484, 497, 516,
  518, 519, 542, 551, 562, 567
Lee, Edward E. 87
LeSeuer, Arthur 587
Leslie, Shane xvi, 348, 383, 403,
  485, 486, 503, 587
"Letters to the Indian People" 324
Levy, Aaron 174, 195
Lewis, Ceylon 62, 72
"Long Talk, The" 136
Lore, Ludwig 364, 365
Ludden, Rev. Patrick 15
Lusitania 239, 303, 306, 308, 318,
  339, 340, 348, 350, 353, 362,
  404, 406, 434, 435, 594
Lusk Committee 231
Lynch, Diarmud 381, 478, 490,
  491, 512, 513, 514, 517,
  527, 529, 561, 567, 571
Lynch, Maj. Thomas 251
Lynn, Gordon 168

M

MacBride, Maj. John 250
MacBride, Maude Gonne 260

Mack, Eugene 137
Mack, Norman 102, 126, 142, 237
MacManus, Seamas 278
MacNeil, Eoin 489, 495
MacSwiney, Muriel 538
MacSwiney, Terence 526, 532
Madero, Francesco 389, 390, 392
Magee, Walter 492, 509
Magennis, Fr. Peter 491, 513
Mahan, Admiral T. 345
Maher, Edward 193
Main, Rev. W. H. 19
Malitz, Felix 338
Malone, Dudley F. 229, 239,
　　355, 362, 445
Maloney, Dr. J. M. A. 544
Mann, John 201
Manoil, James 393
Manton, Martin 196
Manz, Adolph 62, 64, 65, 125
Mason Bill 528, 562
Mason, William 246
Matty, Frank x, 10, 18, 20, 21, 28,
　　29, 33, 34, 35, 36, 39, 41, 51,
　　53, 59, 61, 63, 64, 88, 92, 93,
　　94, 95, 96, 105, 106, 107,
　　108, 113, 118, 148, 295
Maurer, James 331
May, Mitchell 217, 236
Maynard, Isaac 82, 109
Mazet Committee 126, 134, 141
McBride, John 247, 251
McCabe, Patrick 174
McCall, Edward 167, 174, 176
McCarren, Patrick 99, 127, 140, 168
McCarthy, John 254
McClellan, George 126
McCormick, Vance 454, 458, 459
McDermott, Sean 373
McGarrity, Joseph 285, 287, 347,
　　370, 373, 410, 486, 491, 504,
　　513, 514, 529, 533, 534, 540,
　　544, 561, 567, 570, 571
McGoey, John 371
McGowan, George 335

McGuire, Charles 56, 70
McGuire, Edward 265
McGuire, Frances 552
McGuire, George 32, 137, 179,
　　180, 181, 182, 183, 188, 190,
　　202, 214, 215, 216, 222,
　　224, 225, 232, 236, 448,
　　493, 494, 522, 563, 564
McGuire, James K. iii, x, xi, xiv, xvi,
　　2, 3, 6, 7, 8, 9, 12, 15, 20, 33,
　　34, 39, 50, 60, 65, 70, 72, 76,
　　79, 82, 83, 85, 86, 89, 90, 91,
　　92, 93, 99, 104, 105, 108, 109,
　　111, 112, 113, 114, 116, 117,
　　118, 122, 123, 124, 126, 128,
　　132, 137, 138, 139, 140, 142,
　　143, 144, 149, 151, 154, 155,
　　157, 159, 164, 165, 166, 167,
　　170, 175, 177, 178, 180, 181,
　　182, 183, 184, 188, 192, 193,
　　194, 196, 197, 198, 201, 202,
　　203, 205, 208, 210, 211, 214,
　　215, 216, 217, 219, 220, 222,
　　224, 225, 229, 230, 231, 232,
　　233, 234, 235, 236, 239, 240,
　　242, 243, 245, 246, 248, 254,
　　256, 258, 260, 261, 264, 265,
　　267, 270, 275, 276, 277, 279,
　　280, 281, 282, 283, 284, 287,
　　288, 289, 290, 294, 297, 302,
　　305, 307, 310, 313, 322, 325,
　　332, 333, 334, 335, 336, 339,
　　340, 341, 344, 347, 350, 351,
　　352, 358, 366, 367, 370, 371,
　　372, 375, 376, 384, 385, 394,
　　395, 396, 400, 402, 404, 405,
　　407, 411, 420, 421, 422, 426,
　　427, 429, 431, 432, 433, 442,
　　445, 446, 448, 454, 457, 463,
　　465, 469, 470, 476, 477, 478,
　　479, 482, 485, 488, 490, 491,
　　499, 510, 512, 514, 515, 519,
　　522, 528, 529, 530, 532, 535,
　　536, 540, 542, 546, 549, 554,

557, 560, 563, 564, 565, 567, 568, 570, 571, 572, 573, 574
McGuire, Philip 113, 494, 510
McIntyre, John C. 194, 195, 208
McKinley League 93, 95, 115
McLaughlin, Hugh 99, 103, 119, 126
McLean, Arthur 183, 219, 221, 237
McMahon, James 352, 411
McWharter, Mary 307
Meagher, James 125
Mellows, Liam 269, 287, 332, 381, 465, 490, 491, 512, 513, 521, 526, 584
Mesen, Roberto Brenes 430, 438
Meyer, Kuno 253, 261, 298, 313, 314, 330, 349, 350, 363, 369, 404, 407, 498, 591
Meyer, Richard 373, 404, 410
Miller, Nathan 231, 563, 564, 565, 573
Mitchel, John P. 176, 187, 229
Moffett, Cleveland 473, 499, 501
Mooney, Tom 366, 408
Moore, John D. 282, 290, 331, 379, 384, 385, 386, 411, 451, 469, 476, 478, 499
Morgan, J.P. 164
Mormons 131, 570
Mowry, Henry 9, 91
"M" Telegram 182, 183
Mullen-Gage Act 564
Munsterberg, Hugo 322, 455, 494
Murphy, "Boss" Charles x, 105, 123, 125, 126, 130, 132, 135, 139, 142, 150, 164, 166, 167, 168, 169, 171, 177, 178, 179, 180, 186, 195, 196, 215, 216, 218, 220, 221, 228, 229, 230, 231, 232, 238, 239, 445, 449, 518, 564, 568, 570
Murphy, Charles Jr. 215
Murray, James "Red" 532
Myers, Gustavus 135
Mylod, John 81

N

Nast, Thomas 7
Nathan, Sir Matthew 240
National German-American Alliance (NGAA) 293, 295, 296, 304, 305, 307, 309, 312, 316, 318, 336, 351, 406, 450
National Security League 493, 501, 509
Newell, James 9
New York and Bermudez Company 150, 151, 152, 154
New York Contracting and Trucking Company 166, 169
New York, New Haven and Hartford railroad 166
Norfolk, Va. 243, 367, 426, 430, 541
North German Lloyd Company 424
North Side Association 31
Norton, John 168

O

O'Connell, Daniel 256, 335, 450, 458
O'Connor, T.P. 266, 273, 284, 353
O'Connor, T. V. 353, 354
O'Dea, John 287, 312, 407, 456, 491, 591
O'Donnell, Frank Hugh 323, 327
O'Flaherty, Daniel 533
O'Gorman, James A. 164, 186, 222, 239, 251, 296, 314, 362, 446, 502
O'Grady, Thomas 128
Ohlinger, Gustavus 298, 316
O'Kelly, John 520, 521, 550
O'Leary, Jeremiah A. 468, 499
O'Leary, Jeremiah J. 556
O'Leary, John J. 308, 499
Olin, Franklin 393
O'Mara, James 289, 527, 552, 554, 587
O'Mara, Stephen 545
Onondaga Supreme Court 60
Orders-In-Council 310
O'Reilly, John Boyle 207, 244, 256

Osborne, James W. 177, 178, 202, 218, 220, 222, 223, 228
O'Shea, Kitty 264
O'Sheel, Seamus 302, 314

P

Page, Walter Hines 395, 456, 467
Palmer, A. Mitchell 340, 481, 527
Panama Canal 156, 388, 420, 421, 422, 428, 434, 436, 442, 488
Pan-Aryan Association 324
Paradise of Graft 170
Parker, Harold 181
Parkhurst, Rev. Charles 14
Parnell, Charles S. 244
Pass-Seymour Company 2
Patronage 19, 33, 35, 50, 51, 52, 54, 56, 60, 69, 75, 87, 92, 93, 97, 104, 106, 107, 110, 136, 164, 167, 187, 197, 203, 209, 229, 240, 369, 430, 445, 447, 448, 457, 479, 530, 560
Pearce, Patrick 304, 383
Peck, Duncan 16, 20, 21, 90, 125, 175, 228
Pedlar, Liam 540, 542
"Perfidious Albion" 270
Perl, Dr. Fritz 206
Pershing, Gen. "Black Jack" 390, 394
Phelan, Joseph D. 200, 279, 280, 446
Phelan Report 194, 197, 201, 202, 203, 207, 209, 211, 279
Phelps, Myron 323, 334, 397
Phillips, Wendell 252, 261
Piedmont Pictures Corporation 338
Pitch Lake Trinidad 149, 150, 160
Planck, Max 303
Platt, Thomas 61, 80
"Playboy of the Western World" 279
Polk, Frank 378
Preston, John W. 335

Q

Quinlan, Patrick 28

Quinn, John 370, 445, 503

R

Raines Law 16, 18, 19, 41
Raines, Sen. John 18
Rapid transit Company 29, 32
Rathom, John 362
Redmond, John E. 251, 258, 264, 265, 270, 273, 276, 278, 284, 289, 304, 316, 317, 366, 367, 382, 477, 479, 486, 500, 510, 584
Red Scare 231
Reel, Gordon 169, 179, 182, 183, 186, 220, 223, 228
Reventlow, Ernst zu 297, 313
Richardson, Clifford 149, 161
Ridder, Bernhard 290
"Robbers Row" 6
Robinson, Gov. Lucius 129
Robinson, Willard J. 487
Rockefeller, John D. 8, 303, 352
Roosevelt, Franklin 164
Roosevelt, Theodore 31, 61, 62, 88, 89, 96, 99, 102, 126, 144, 152, 164, 165, 198, 238, 247, 303, 316, 319, 324, 421, 422, 434, 436, 442, 443, 449, 451, 453, 454, 458, 473, 477, 480, 486, 501, 509, 568
Rose, "Bald Jack" 193, 195, 200
Rosenthal, Herman 195
Rossa, O'Donovan 244, 353
Royal Irish Constabulary (RIC) 247
Rubino, Henry 178, 181, 218, 224
Rumely, Edward 302, 340, 357, 372, 400
Russell, Helen 381
Russell, Rev. Howard 22
Rutherford, Reginald 351
Ryan, Edward 254, 277, 287, 379
Ryan, Frank 519, 520
Ryan, John T. 265, 287, 288, 341, 347, 484, 487, 488, 489, 534, 540, 555

Ryan, Michael J. 266, 305, 307, 515, 516, 519, 548
Ryan, Thomas F. 543

S

Samoa 420, 434, 595
San Diego Plan 393, 395
Sanitation (Syracuse) 32, 33, 65, 71
Santo Domingo 111, 164, 165, 184, 187, 191, 192, 194, 196, 197, 198, 201, 202, 203, 204, 205, 206, 207, 209, 210, 211, 217, 279, 280, 289, 388, 413, 421, 430, 433, 443, 446, 518, 586, 592, 594
Saul, Charles 91
Schiemann, Dr. Theodor 313, 323, 325, 329, 347, 375
Seabury, Samuel 196
Secret War Council 322, 341, 389, 397, 398, 437, 582
Sedition Act 480, 481, 493, 505
Sehl, Jacob 60, 61, 71
Seward, William 243, 421
Sheehan, William 79, 83, 89, 125, 142, 143, 164, 165
Sheehy-Skeffington, Hannah 382, 415, 489, 512, 513
Sinclair, Upton 331
Sinn Fein 139, 193, 265, 269, 284, 285, 349, 368, 372, 375, 385, 386, 403, 404, 405, 407, 408, 410, 414, 416, 417, 418, 469, 477, 478, 479, 487, 488, 489, 490, 498, 499, 501, 504, 505, 507, 508, 510, 513, 520, 523, 540, 552, 555, 569, 573, 580, 589
Sisson, W. Lee 201, 202, 203
Slocum, Henry 79, 109
Smith, Alfred E. 226
Smith, Carroll E. 90
Smith, Joseph 385
Smith, Judge Wilmot 61, 62

Snap Convention 82
Society of the Friendly Sons of St. Patrick (SOFSOSP) 251, 269, 289, 590
Solf, Dr. Wilhelm 474
Sommerfeld, Felix 322, 388, 393
Spanish - American War 88, 111, 151, 152, 160, 247, 251, 342, 434, 437, 505, 594
Spellisy, Denis 290
Splain, John 528, 545, 547
"Stage Irishman" 253, 254
Stanchfield, John 78, 96, 99, 115
"Steal of the Senate" 81
Stillwell, Giles 492, 508
Stillwell, Stephen 228
Sturtevant, James 169
Suhren, Hans 430
Sullivan, Alexander 264, 284, 286
Sullivan, "Big Tim" 123, 126, 176, 194, 195, 196, 405
Sullivan, James Mark x, xiv, 150, 164, 165, 184, 192, 193, 194, 195, 197, 199, 201, 202, 207, 210, 211, 265, 279, 289, 290, 388, 420, 421, 422, 430, 433, 438, 442, 443, 446, 552
Sullivan, Margaret 487
Sullivan, Timothy 201, 202, 203
Sulzer, Governor William x, 138, 180, 190, 196, 222, 223, 238, 453
Sussex Pledge 387
Syracuse Printing and Publishing Co. 128, 230, 384, 536, 555, 573

T

Tamanend 133, 134, 144
Tammany Hall xiv, 7, 50, 60, 67, 73, 78, 81, 104, 105, 116, 119, 127, 128, 132, 133, 134, 135, 138, 139, 140, 141, 142, 143, 144, 145, 150, 164, 165, 185, 186, 193, 194, 195, 196, 208, 209, 217, 218, 219, 220,

222, 223, 228, 231, 236, 238,
   239, 405, 443, 447, 453, 485,
   499, 564, 568, 590, 596
Tauscher, Hans 322
Thaw, Harry 193, 194
Thomas, Norman 332, 576
Thompson, Col. Marcellus 539
Tilden, Samuel 78, 129
Tone, Wolfe 256, 279, 283, 368,
   375, 384, 401, 411, 415
Trading With The Enemy Act 409
Trainor, Patrick 61, 71, 103
"Tramps" 22, 24, 76
Trinidad Asphalt 36, 38, 46,
   150, 151, 154, 155, 161
Tuchman, Barbara 316, 352, 405
Tumulty, Joseph 197, 209, 230, 378,
   412, 442, 469, 470, 478, 479,
   491, 495, 513, 533, 547
Tweed, William Marcy 7

U

Ulster 143, 266, 267, 278,
   285, 305, 477, 479, 496,
   502, 510, 544, 570
Ulster Covenant 267
Ulster Volunteers 305
Union Oil Co. 156, 214, 215, 232, 235
United "Colored" Democracy 87
United Irish League 251,
   256, 259, 266, 284, 285,
   304, 305, 307, 548
United Irishmen 383
United States Fidelity and Guarantee
   Co. 178, 190, 205, 237
United States Marines 493
United States Secret Service 376, 429
Unrestricted Submarine Warfare
   387, 396, 465, 474

V

Vaccarelli, Paolo (Paul Kelly) 354, 405
Van Buren, Martin 129
Van Wyck, Robert 97, 99, 144

Venezuela Boundary Dispute 244
Victoria, Queen 208, 244, 247, 248,
   249, 251, 258, 260, 569
Victorica, Maria D. 487
Viereck, George 294, 299, 309, 311,
   314, 339, 349, 352, 454
Villa, Pancho 389, 390, 392,
   393, 417, 517
Vollmer, Henry 306
Von Bernhardi, Friedrich 296
Von Bernstorff, Count Johann x, 322
Von Bopp, Franz 363, 366,
   407, 408, 432
Von Brincken, Wilhelm 333, 335, 350
Von Halle, Ernest 295
Von Hintze, Paul 392
Von Igel, Wolf 276, 360, 363, 365, 407
Von Mach, Dr. Edmund 306, 354, 405
Von Papen, Franz 276, 280,
   307, 322, 335, 351, 356,
   363, 365, 393, 407
Von Rintelen, Franz 330
Von Skal, George 351, 352
Von Wedel 281, 410

W

Wagner, Robert 128, 167,
   169, 218, 225
Walker, John B. 358
Walsh, Frank 287, 331, 450,
   462, 498, 516, 528, 533,
   545, 548, 549, 551
Walsh, John 246
Warner-Quinlan Asphalt Co.
   151, 161, 181, 214
Warren, Fred 156
Weisman, Henry 304
Welland Canal 246, 259, 286, 554
Wessels, Herman 487
"What Could Germany Do
   For Ireland" 283, 341,
   343, 344, 345, 346, 401,
   402, 448, 483, 589
White Charter 29, 62, 63, 65, 71, 560

White, Horace 61, 64, 65
White Wings 33
Whitman, Charles x, 137, 170,
    171, 176, 177, 180, 195,
    196, 197, 202, 205, 219,
    220, 221, 228, 230, 231,
    232, 236, 238, 509, 563
"Whom The Gods Would
    Destroy" 470
Wickersham, George 480
Wilson, Henry Lane 391, 392
Wilson, Woodrow 138, 157, 158,
    164, 166, 187, 194, 196, 206,
    228, 229, 305, 322, 344, 357,
    362, 368, 389, 400, 402, 403,
    418, 428, 430, 431, 436, 442,
    443, 446, 456, 458, 459, 460,
    498, 568, 570, 585, 595
Wise, Henry 182
Wiseman, Sir William 376
Wister, Owen 566
Witzke, Lothar 363, 407, 569
Wood, Eugene 176, 180, 188

Y

Yorke, Fr. Peter 332, 557

Z

Zfa (General Cental Purchasing
    Agency for Service
    Abroad) 337
Zimmerman, Arthur 300, 303

www.ingramcontent.com/pod-product-compliance
Lightning Source LLC
Chambersburg PA
CBHW021421070526
44577CB00001B/3